STATE POLITICS

Wadsworth Publishing Company, Inc.   **Belmont, California**

STATE
POLITICS

readings on political behavior

edited by *Robert E. Crew, Jr.*
University of Minnesota

L. C. Cat. Card No.: 67-25822
Printed in the United States of America

PREFACE

This is a collection of articles on politics in the American states. Unlike the "readings" utilized in many other books of this sort — which stress case studies or "fundamental issues" — the selections presented here are based on empirical research into what *is* happening in politics at the state level, not what ought to be happening. These articles go beyond a description of the formal structure of government to an analysis of the effect of variations in this structure upon political activity. They were selected in an effort to gather knowledge of a general nature rather than to provide anecdotes of ephemeral value.

Two assumptions underlie this collection. The first is that an analysis of state politics such as is provided in these articles will yield insights into those features of the political process which are common to political phenomena in general. The research reported in these articles, while using the states as laboratories, leads to an understanding of those factors which affect all political institutions and the behavior of all public officials. Secondly, the articles reflect the belief that the techniques and theories being used in other areas of political science can be fruitfully applied to the study of state politics. Until very recently, "State Government" has been several years behind the rest of the discipline of political science with regard to methods of investigation and object of inquiry. Many authors in the field have been content to describe and enumerate — at a very low level of generalization — the formal, constitutional and legal aspects of state government and have done this, in the great majority of cases, without any conceptual framework whatsoever. In contrast, the authors presented here have focused upon the behavioral characteristics of state politics and have examined them through the use of the most recent techniques available to political science. The result, I think, is a volume in which conceptual refinement and sophisticated methodology are combined with objects of inquiry that will show the beginning student that the study of state politics involves more than detailed descriptions of legal relationships and organs of government.

The organization of the book itself is based upon one of the more recent and most significant conceptual frameworks in the discipline, the political system. State politics is viewed here as a system of activities; the selections are intended to illustrate the four elements of this system: (1) the environment in which the system operates; (2) inputs into the system (demands and supports); (3) authoritative "decision-making" agencies and activities; and (4) system outputs (rewards and deprivations). Every effort was made to select articles that examine these four features in comparative fashion, but the primary emphasis is on showing the characteristics of the features and variations in them among the states. The use of the "systems approach" reflects the author's concern with introducing conceptual rigor into the study of politics at the state level.

I am indebted to several people for their help during the preparation of this volume. Chief among them are Donald J. McCrone and Herbert Jacob of the University of Wisconsin, both of whom offered suggestions and encouragement at various stages of the project. I would like to acknowledge my gratitude to Charles Mayo of the University of Southern California for his helpful and encouraging comments. I would also like to acknowledge my obligation to the authors and publishers who have given their permission to reprint their original works. Finally, thanks must go to Maureen Eachus for secretarial assistance and to Sara Nash for her help in the final stages of the manuscript's preparation.

Robert E. Crew, Jr.

CONTENTS

STATE POLITICS

Introduction

American State Political Systems

Shortly after the publication in 1953 of David Easton's *The Political System,* the concept of politics as a system of activity became the dominant analytical framework used by political scientists. The "systems approach" has been applied to such diverse objects of inquiry as a congressional committee,[1]* a national government,[2] and the American legislative process.[3]

The popularity of this framework for analysis stems from the advantages which it offers those trying to understand the complexities of political life. In the first place, if we use the political system as an organizing framework, we can analytically separate political life from the rest of social activity and examine it "as though for the moment it were a self-contained entity surrounded by, but clearly distinguishable from, the environment or setting in which it operates."[4] As political scientists we are not interested in all kinds of social activity. We are interested only in those activities which involve the "authoritative allocation of values for the society" as a whole. Consequently, we need some device which will make it possible for us to focus on these activities to the exclusion of others. Viewing politics as a system of activities which have unique characteristics allows us to do this in a parsimonious fashion. It is not, to be sure, the only way to view political life. It is, however, one that is not entirely foreign to us. The concept of a political system has many parallels in other disciplines and in endeavors outside of academia. Consequently, when we speak of "demands" and "supports," of "feedback" and "outputs," we are using not altogether unfamiliar terms. Thus, we have a framework which allows us to sharpen our focus of attention in an economical fashion and which is already somewhat familiar to us — an advantage, I think, which no other conceptual device offers to such an extent.

The author is much indebted to two of his colleagues at the University of North Carolina, Charles F. Cnudde and Lawrence G. Flood, for their comments on early drafts of this essay.
*Notes are listed at the end of each article.

1

Secondly, use of the political system offers an insight into the relationships among the various aspects of politics. Use of the political system permits us to see that "each part of the political canvas does not stand alone but is related to each other part."[5] Consequently, we avoid looking at the political process in piecemeal fashion; we also avoid a common pitfall of political analysts: overemphasis of the particular phase of political life that they are examining.

Finally, in viewing politics as a system of activities, we are led to the understanding that the environment within which the system functions is vitally important to the operation of the system. Political scientists have long understood that factors other than the generally recognized political institutions and behavior of a political system are important to the operation of that system. The socioeconomic characteristics of the individuals who reside within the boundaries of a system, the physical features of the system's territory, and the values of the system's citizens are all important factors which shape activity within a particular system. These things have not, however, been treated in a very systematic fashion; a major reason for this has been the absence of satisfactory conceptual tools. By viewing these aspects of the system as part of the environment, we are able to include them in the analysis in a systematic fashion, while, at the same time, we recognize that they impinge upon the system in different ways and with different degrees of intensity over time.

Despite the advantages accruing to the users of systems analysis and despite the popularity of the approach, it has been used relatively little in the study of state politics. With the exception of the recent volume edited by Herbert Jacob and Kenneth Vines,[6] the concept has not been applied systematically in a study in this area.

The present essay is an attempt to ameliorate this situation. It reflects the author's belief that viewing state politics as a system of activities is a useful way in which to organize the great variety of institutional arrangements, formal and informal norms, and political behaviors existent in the American states and to introduce systemization into the study of these phenomena. By applying the concept of the political system to politics at the state level, the essay attempts to describe similarities and differences among the states and to evaluate the effect of these similarities and differences on political behavior in the states.

POLITICAL SYSTEMS: THEIR DISTINCTIVE FEATURES

At the most general level, state political systems, like all political systems are made up of several distinctive features: inputs, authoritative decision-making agencies and activities, outputs, and an environment.

The term "inputs" refers to those activities which make a system possible. They are "the disturbances or influences" that arise from behavior in the environment and that cross the boundaries of the political system.[7] Taking the form of "demands" and "supports," inputs are responses of individuals and groups within a society to the scarcity of that society's resources. As groups and individuals vie for the things which their society has to offer, conflict arises. This conflict engenders demands, "directed toward the authorities, . . . that some kind of authoritative allocation ought to be undertaken."[8] It also brings out varying degrees of supports — actions promoting the making of these decisions and the whole decision-making structure. Inputs, then, are the reason a political system exists.

The second major feature of the political system is the "authoritative decision-making agencies or activities." These activities are performed by identifiable political structures. In "modern" societies such structures as parliaments, presidents, and governors make up this feature, and it is characterized by some division of labor or differentiation in function. That is, certain types of structures, such as legislatures, perform functions which differentiate them from other structures, such as courts. In less modern societies, on the other hand, all these functions can be performed by a single person or group of persons — the most skilled hunter or a group of elders. Whatever its composition, however, this feature of the system actually "processes" the inputs and transforms them into the next feature of the system, "outputs."

Outputs are the decisions about the conflict expressed in the inputs; they are the translation of demands and supports into public policy. In modern societies outputs are most often expressed in statutes, laws, or other written decisions; in less developed societies they are likely to be expressed in less formal terms. However, the consequence of outputs is similar for all systems. Some individuals or groups in the system are "rewarded" in that their demands are given the weight of formal approval by the authoritative decision-making agencies. Others are "deprived" in that they do not receive this recognition.

The final feature of a political system is the environment within which it operates. This environment is composed of many parts: the formal rules and laws that govern the system; the culture of the society; the beliefs that citizens hold about a wide range of things; and the legal and religious heritages. The environment of a system is vitally important to the activities of the system, for it is in response to the various aspects of this environment that inputs are generated. Therefore, systems with different environments will induce different demands and supports. For example, a society that has a relatively fluid class structure generates demands that are quite different from those of a system with rigid class or caste differences. Thus an understanding of a system's environment goes a long way toward providing an explanation of the activities within that system.

With this brief look at the general features of political systems, we now turn to a more specific examination of the features of the political systems of the American states.

THE ENVIRONMENT OF STATE
POLITICAL SYSTEMS

Since all political systems respond to the environment within which they operate, we begin our discussion of state political systems by considering their environment. This environment has many aspects; we limit our discussion to those which research has indicated are most important in understanding why state political systems operate as they do.

Formal Framework

All political systems are structured to some degree by the formal rules which distribute power, authority, and responsibility among the several levels of government and, at a single level, among the various agencies of government. Recent findings in political science have led some to argue that these formal arrangements deserve no attention and that informal organization "really" governs political activity within a nation or state. Indeed, empirical observation has shown that political practices do not invariably follow formal prescriptions. On the other hand, the contention that formal arrangements are without effect on behavior patterns is also inaccurate. There is strong evidence, for example, that different constitutional prescriptions raise or lower the likelihood of particular political patterns.[9] Thus, in the United States, political behavior is particularly affected by the nation's commitment to the idea that government should be of "laws and not of men." Two features of this formal, institutional environment are particularly pertinent in structuring the activities of the American states. The first of these features is the federal system of government; the second is a state's constitution.

Federalism   "When considering the problem of state politics, one fact of fundamental importance must be kept firmly in mind: The American states operate not as independent and autonomous political entities, but as units of the nation."[10] Several consequences for state politics follow from this structural arrangement. In the first place, public attention cannot be focused sharply on state affairs since national, and even local, affairs often overshadow the issues being discussed at the state level. People are more interested in what the President of the United States is doing than they are in what the governor of their state has to say. The same is true of the national Congress and the state legislatures. As a result, politicians at the state level are often unable to develop the support they need to carry out their programs. And, on the other hand, their lack of public visibility provides opportunities for self-serving state politicians to use public facilities to achieve their private goals.

A second consequence stemming from the place of the states in the federal union is the rarity of a state political issue that is discussed on its own merits and that engenders partisan divisions. Instead, national issues, national campaigns, and national parties project themselves into virtually every aspect of state politics, making it difficult for politicians and the electorate generally to deal with state issues alone. Indeed, it often appears that there are no purely state issues.

Finally, the structure of federalism provides extra points of access for those persons or groups in society who are attempting to influence governmental decisions. Thus an interest denied access or "defeated" at the state level may recoup its losses through appeal to national or local government. The same is true in reverse; that is, groups defeated at the national level may be victorious at the state level.

The major point being made here is that the American states are units of a larger political system which is somewhat independent of their control. Therefore the range of political activities in the states is, to a large degree, fixed; whereas, if the states were part of a confederation or unitary form of government, these limitations would not exist.

State Constitutions   The second feature of the formal framework of state political systems is what Duane Lockard calls "constitutionalism."[11] People in the United States are particularly addicted to the belief that the laws under which they live shall not be arbitrarily set or administered and to the idea that certain freedoms are guaranteed to all members of the society. Although commitment to the latter point breaks down somewhat in application, there is virtual consensus on the ideal.[12]

Concurrent with these ideas about the nature of government in the U. S. is the belief that the ideals should be expressed in a written document, a constitution. The constitution, therefore, becomes part of the environment within which governments operate. It limits or expands the types of things that governments can do. In the U. S., at the national level, these limits are expressed in relatively short, general, and somewhat vague terms. The constitutions of the American states are longer, more specific, and somewhat less opaque — though, perhaps, not so flexible. Constitutions, then, serve to structure the political activities of the government concerned. They do this in several ways.[13]

In the first place, constitutions establish the basic structure of the governments concerned and distribute power among the agencies of these governments. State constitutions go to an extreme in performing this function. The average state constitutional provision relating to the distribution of power within the state goes far beyond the essentials set forth in the national constitution. Not only is the general structural framework described, but intricate details of administrative structure are also set forth. By thus stating very specifically the duties of and the interrelationships among the major agencies of state governments, state constitutions set up a tight framework within which state governments must function. This framework "inhibits a high degree of concentration of all opposition groups, encourages diffusion, and helps prevent clear identifiability."[14]

A second way that constitutions structure the politics of the American states is by limiting the powers of their governments. The major limitations upon state governments are expressed in bills or declarations of rights. Although similar to the Bill of Rights of the United States, state bills of rights often go beyond the provisions covering freedom of speech, press, assembly, etc., to include protection from imprisonment for debt and the rights to organize labor unions and to alter or change the government. These provisions thus influence the conduct of politics within the states by legitimizing certain activities and prohibiting others.

Finally, state constitutions provide a framework for state politics by developing support for the system through "pious proclamations, unenforceable provisions, and other high ideals of the society that may be unattainable but that are to be hopefully sought."[15] Proclamations stating that the purpose of the state government is to preserve "our civil, political, and religious liberties" and to establish "better government" are examples of such statements. These ideals are embodied in state constitutions in the hope that they will be accepted by the residents of the state and by the public officials. To the extent that they are accepted, they affect the activities of state political systems.

The Physical Environment

All political systems are affected to some degree by their place in the world. Such factors as size, availability and accessibility of natural resources, and proximity to transportation are extremely important to the politics of a system since the presence or absence of these factors leads to varying demands and supports that must be dealt with by the system.

Even though the American states exhibit greater similarities than differences, there is fairly wide variation among them with regard to geographic features. These variations have important consequences for politics within the states. Duane Lockard has pointed out that the presence of abundant supplies of forests and waterpower in Maine has had a significant influence upon that state's legislative politics. Interest groups seeking to exploit these resources have dominated the politics of this state with an openness rarely seen in American politics.[16] In other states also, features of the geography have become central political issues. For example, the distribution of water in many of the Southwestern states is an issue that creates a high degree of emotion in these water-shy areas.

Finally, the vagaries of geographic location have provided some states with natural resources and climatic conditions that produce great amounts of revenue for their treasuries. Oil in Texas and Oklahoma, coal in Pennsylvania, and sunshine and water in Florida and California are examples of such features.

For the most part, geography has been kind to the American states. There are, however, variations in the degree of this "kindness," and these variations are important factors in structuring political activities within the states.

The Socioeconomic Environment

Just as variation in the physical environment creates different demands on political systems, so differences in demographic and economic features exert differential influences. Some systems have large populations, high levels of education and income, and high degrees of urbanization. Others are characterized by rural-based populations, small in number and widely dispersed, and low levels of education and income. Seymour Martin Lipset argues persuasively that the presence or absence of these features bears heavily upon the nature of government within the system involved. Comparing European, English-speaking, and Latin American countries, he finds that "in each case, the average wealth, degree of industrialization and urbanization, and level of education is much higher for the more democratic countries."[17]

The political systems of the American states are sufficiently similar that all can be classified as democracies. Nonetheless, there are demographic and economic differences among these state systems, and these differences have a definite bearing upon their politics.

First of all, there are great differences among the states with regard to population. Sheer numbers produce increased demands — for education, for housing, for police protection, and for other amenities and necessities of the modern society.

Secondly, the composition of a state's population is important. For example, composition has an important bearing on the nature and level of political participation within a state. Recent research has shown that in many states having a sizable proportion of ethnic or minority groups living within their borders there is likely to be little political activity among the minority groups, whereas the dominant segment of the population expends a considerable amount of political energy toward the subjugation — and, in some cases, the eradication — of the minorities. Thus Matthews and Prothro, in an examination of thirteen Southern states, found the *percentage* of Negroes within a state to be the single most important variable in explaining the political activity of the Negro. As the proportion of Negroes in a state increased, the political activity of Negroes decreased.[18]

Other research suggests that once ethnic or minority group participation in political activity is accepted — or tolerated — the presence of such groups can alter radically the structure of political activity within a state. Thus, Duane Lockard attributes the historically recent respectability of the Democratic party in New England to the settlement of new ethnic elements in that region. He points out that the early willingness of the Democratic party in that region to accept — even encourage — the Irish, the Italians, and the French-Canadians increased the political participation of these ethnic groups and cemented a bond which, in some cases, has upset the traditional Yankee-Republican dominance in that area.[19]

The voluminous literature on the correlates of political participation[20] shows that participation rises as the levels of education, income, and other socioeconomic variables increase. This conclusion does not mean to imply that social characteristics determine political participation. It serves simply to point out that these characteristics are important variables in understanding the political activities within a state.

A final point on the effect of socioeconomic factors upon state political systems is that their relative importance varies from issue to issue. In two separate studies, Matthews and Prothro found that thirty-one demographic variables showed a significant correlation with Negro voter registration in the Southern states but increased by only one fifth the explanatory value of eight political variables in the area of school desegregation in the same states.[21] Therefore, if we are to understand the implications of socioeconomic factors for political activity in the states, we must examine the specific issue involved as well as the characteristics of a state's population.

The Cultural Environment

A nation's *culture* is "a historically derived system of explicit and implicit designs for living, which tends to be shared by all or specially designated members of a group at a specified point in time."[22] A national culture includes knowledge, belief, art, morals, law, custom, and other capabilities and habits acquired by man as a member of a society.

Sociologists and anthropologists have long recognized the differential effects of various cultural backgrounds upon individual behavior. Bronislav Malinowski, an anthropologist writing in the 1930s, said that "man varies in two respects: in physical form and in social heritage, or culture."[23] Malinowski went on to assess the impact, for individuals, of variations in culture:

> A pure blooded Negro infant, transported to France and brought up there, would differ profoundly from what he would have been if reared in the jungle of his native land. He would have been given a different social heritage: a different language, different habits, ideas and beliefs; he would have been incorporated into a different social organization and cultural setting.[24]

Political attitudes and beliefs make up a major part of a nation's culture. Therefore, an understanding of this culture will assist us in understanding the politics within that country. Three aspects of the American culture appear to have particular bearing upon the politics of the United States: ideological factors, religious heritages, and political factors. These factors are common to all Americans; they vary only in degree among the several states. Thus, Mississippians and Californians have more in common than do Mississippians and the residents of any region outside the United States. However, the differences in degree among the states with regard to these three factors are important to an understanding of political differences within the states.

Ideological Factors

Societies everywhere in the world have evolved sets of ideas by which life is made understandable for their members. These ideas tell people about the nature of their society and about its place in the world. They give people a framework for relating themselves to others, and to life in general. They tell people about the approved goals and values of the society. Such sets of ideas are referred to as "ideologies."

As political scientists, we are interested in a particular kind of ideology, political ideology, a system of interrelated ideas about the polity. A political ideology includes: (1) a conception of the community, (2) preferences as to "who shall rule," (3) a sense of socioeconomic class, (4) a sense of cultural class or caste, and (5) "attitudes toward the legitimate method of allocating values."[25] Although very few Americans consciously hold a particular ideological position with regard to politics — the authors of *The American Voter* were able to classify only 2 1/2 percent of their national sample as "ideologues"[26] — several studies show that at least one ideology has implications for politics within the American states. This ideology is white supremacy. Its most overt expression is found in the Southern states.

V. O. Key's monumental study *Southern Politics* discusses the implications of this ideology for politics in the eleven states of the Confederacy. Key sees two results stemming from this ideology: First, "in all southern states bipartisanism is stifled by racism in the sense that attachment to the Democratic party nationally has been dictated by a common determination to resist the rest of the nation on the Negro question."[27] This unity on the part of the Southern states with regard to the Negro question has great effect on the practice of state politics. Since to support a Republican candidate (given the national position of the Republicans toward the Negro in the 1860s) was to give aid and comfort to the enemy, the Southern Republicans were reduced to a position of ineffectiveness and the party system of the South became oriented toward the fulfillment of sectional purpose in national affairs.

Secondly, "the Negro question hampers the maintenance within the Democratic party of factions that amount to political parties."[28] Whenever a natural cleavage develops within the Democratic party, the Negro question arises to suppress the tendency. Thus, in South Carolina just after Reconstruction, "Pitchfork Ben" Tillman, by appealing to white supremacy, succeeded in smothering a Democratic party conflict that had all the markings of an emerging two-party system.

There is a second ideology that is becoming significant for American politics but that has been little studied for its effect on state politics. This ideology is variously known as "conservatism," the "new American Right," and the "Radical Right." Several propositions are implicit in this ideology: (1) political leaders should be recruited from among the more affluent citizens, (2) the community is made up of individuals and not conflicting interest groups, (3) the middle class is the class most deserving of respect, (4) they (the "Radical Right") are "culturally deprived" because they are categorized by the community leadership as part of a "lunatic fringe," (5) oligarchy is the most desirable kind of regime, and (6) the ideal community is a "natural product of governmental noninterference with private allocation of social, economic, or other resources according to the individual's ability to compete for them."[29]

While the greatest successes of the right-wing movements have been at the local level — particularly with regard to school boards, libraries, and fluoridation of city water supplies — their activities have implications for state politics simply because the demands made upon local political systems become inputs for state systems. Although relatively little has been done in systematic fashion to assess the impact of right-wing groups upon state politics, it is generally agreed that these movements influence the course of events in the states by distracting and limiting political discussion.[30]

Religious Heritages

Although there are systematic political differences among the major religious groups in America, most of these differences are based more on class status than on religion. That is, the ranking of the various denominational groups on political issues is identical with their class rank. Thus, poor, uneducated laborers are similar politically whether they are Presbyterians or members of the Church of Christ.[31]

Nevertheless, religious affiliation does sometimes become independently important for politics in America. This is especially true for state politics since the concentrations of particular religious groups in states or regions gives those groups a high degree of political power in their states — power which, of course, they do not have in national politics. Thus, Louisiana, which has a large number of Catholics, is peculiarly susceptible to the influence of this group; and political activity within the state is definitely affected by the group's presence. John Fenton and Kenneth Vines, for example, found that "Negro voter registration, in percentages of potential eligibles, was almost twice as great in the state's French-Catholic parishes as in its non-Catholic parishes."[32] Catholicism has similar implications for politics in the New England states. In Connecticut (until very recently) and Massachusetts, for example, the purveyance of birth-control information has been forbidden by law. Although, according to Duane Lockard, "the laws themselves date from Victorian times and were not passed in response to Catholic political pressure, no one would deny that the only reason they remain on the statute book is the support of the Catholic community."[33]

The point is that in those areas where the law and public morals become interrelated, the religious differences in the American states become extremely important and can foster or alleviate many political problems for the states.

Political Culture

Political scientists have long tried to explain political variations among countries or states with references to differences in "political cultures." Often referred to as "political style" or "the rules of the game," this feature of political systems has become a major independent variable in political analyses. Despite the popularity of the concept, there is little agreement among its users with regard to its measurement. Efforts to deal with the problem have been based on impressions and inferences from history, on inferences from the precepts of various political ideologies, on certain kinds of sociological analysis, and on psychological insights into the political attitudes of the members of various societies.[34] All of these analyses, however, accept political culture as an important datum in understanding the activities in political systems because, by setting the culturally defined goals for the political process, the concept plays a major role in determining the operation of that process.

Although political cultures of the American states do no vary greatly — primarily because they all contain certain elements of a common "American culture" — there is more diversity among them than is commonly supposed. A major study illustrating this diversity is the Almond and Verba five-nation study. Utilizing individual attitudes toward the political system and its various parts as their definition of political culture, the authors conducted extensive interviews in Great Britain, Germany, Mexico, Italy, and the United States in an effort to understand "the political culture of democracy and the social structures and processes that sustain it."[35] Their findings within the United States reveal that the residents of the Southern states are more alienated from public life, more distrustful of government, and less likely to participate in governmental affairs than residents of other states.[36]

Other studies, using different measures of the concept, are more self-consciously concerned with the effect of variation in the political culture upon political activities within the states. Matthews and Prothro demonstrate that differences in the political environment of the Southern states are extremely relevant to the responses of the citizens of those states toward such things as Negro voter registration and school desegregation. Certain Southern states are more moderate in their responses to these activities than are others, and the difference is in some degree dependent upon the nature of each state's political environment.[37] In another study Edgar Litt suggests that the uses made of political institutions are to some degree dependent upon the nature of the political culture. In Massachusetts, for example, the uses of the governorship varied quite considerably with changes in that state's political culture.

> Before 1928, the governor symbolized a Republican hegemony in which private and public power was effectively blended. . . . During the Democratic wave of the early thirties, the governorship became the key instrument for the dispensing of patronage and the formation of economic power. . . . Finally, the 'patrician-managerial strata,' which presently seeks integrated centers of political powers within the state to which they can link national politics and economic developments, find that the governorship and the party systems are vital instruments for bringing about rational, managerial change.[38]

The foregoing comments have been directed toward describing the nature of the environment within which state political systems operate and toward assessing the implications of variations in this environment for political activity in the states. The discussion has pointed out that the environment both sets limits and provides opportunities for groups and individuals within the system and therefore affects the frequency, intensity, and quality of the demands made upon the system. For this reason, an understanding of that environment is important to an understanding of the political process within the states. Variations in these environments help us explain the properties and performances of the several state political systems.

INPUTS OF STATE POLITICAL SYSTEMS

Inputs are those activities and institutions by and through which individuals express their views about the polity. Like the environments of state political systems, input activity varies throughout the United States; and this variation accounts, to a great extent, for political differences among the states. The following discussion examines the similarities and differences in inputs among the American states.

Public Opinion in the States

All political systems must perform the basic function of identifying the interests existing within the system. In the United States, this is accomplished as citizens express their opinions about the nature of their society, through letters to their representatives, by marches on the state capitol, and by direct contact with public officials. In turn, public officials concern themselves to some degree with the opinions of their constituents. By examining the structure of opinions in the various states we can tell a great deal about the interests present and, thus, about the type of demands that are being made upon the governmental machinery.

A distinguishing characteristic of public opinion in the United States is that "on most broad issues for which the data are available, the mass of the people of all sections divide in approximately the same manner."[39] Only rarely does opinion differ widely between any two states. Even on the most emotional issues, the similarities rather than the differences in the distribution of opinions from state to state attract attention. The Southern states, for example, are often assumed to be the home of opinions far different from those in other states in the Union. However, apart from its attitude on the Negro question, "the South takes positions in mass opinion on broad questions of policy remarkably similar to those of the nation."[40] Even with respect to the Negro, the unity of the South varies from one area to another. Southerners tend to take a fairly extreme position on school desegregation, for example, but on such questions as the protection of the economic rights of Negroes, the South is divided in about the same way as is the rest of the nation.

The Midwestern states have also been cited as an example of a group of states with at least one unique opinion characteristic since, for many years, this section of the country was regarded as the stronghold of isolationism in the United States. Supposedly, the Midwest held American foreign policy in check between

World Wars I and II. The "conventional wisdom" about these states was that their physical insularity led their citizens to be less sensitive than coastal residents to events abroad and to feel that the United States could live alone with impunity. Recent research dispels this notion[41] and shows that "the hard core of isolationism in the United States has been ethnic and emotional, not geographical."[42]

This lack of sharp sectional differences does not imply that public opinion in the states is uniform. Various states and regions differ on specific issues, and often these differences are sufficient to give the politics of those states and regions a distinctive style. The Far West, for example, exhibits a more marked concern for civil liberties than other sections, takes a more permissive attitude toward government participation in power projects than does the rest of the nation, and is more "hard-headed" on taxation than other states.[43] The South is relatively antagonistic toward the use of lotteries as a means of raising public funds, relatively favorable toward prohibition, and relatively unfavorable toward the possibility of a Catholic President.[44] Finally, the Midwest appears overwhelmingly more prudish on matters of sex than the rest of the United States.[45] Such differences set limits within which state officials and governments must act and, at the same time, help us understand differences in official actions.

State Political Parties

The mere presence of political opinions within a political system does not ensure their recognition by public officials. Some method must be devised to link these two factors if citizen opinions are to be translated into public policy. In democratic systems, this linkage is made largely through political parties. Political parties are one of the basic institutions through which mass preferences are made known to governmental officials and through which leaders are selected to transform these preferences into law. Thus, they perform the "interest articulation" and "leadership selection" functions for the political system.[46]

Although the political parties in the American states perform similar functions for their systems, these are not party systems uniformly alike throughout the country. Even though all fifty states have two-party systems in the sense that both Republicans and Democrats have organizations in all states, the nature of competition between these parties varies throughout the nation. Thus, in some states there is little competition, and one of the two parties wins virtually all public positions for long periods of time. In other states a fierce rivalry between the parties results in almost constant alternation of majority status and closely contested general elections. The nature of interparty competition is the primary criterion by which political scientists have differentiated the party systems of the states. Measurement of the extent of this competition occupies a good deal of the time of some political scientists, and several classificatory schemes have been developed.[47] Virtually all of these measurement schemes use some combination of the proportion of a party's success, the duration of that success, and the frequency of divided control over the government. Based on computations concerning the extent of these three variables, state party systems are placed on a continuum ranging from one-party Democratic to modified one-party Republican. Table 1 shows the breakdown of the states in these categories.

Table 1 The fifty states classified according to degree of interparty competition

One-party Democratic	Modified one-party Democratic	Two-party	Modified one-party Republican
South Carolina	Virginia	Alaska	Pennsylvania	Wisconsin
Georgia	North Carolina	Missouri	California	New Hampshire
Louisiana	Tennessee	Rhode Island	Nebraska	Iowa
Mississippi	Oklahoma	Washington	Illinois	Kansas
Texas	Kentucky	Delaware	Idaho	Maine
Alabama	Arizona	Nevada	Michigan	South Dakota
Arkansas	West Virginia	Massachusetts	New Jersey	North Dakota
Florida	Maryland	Hawaii	Indiana	Vermont
	New Mexico	Colorado	Oregon	
		Montana	Ohio	
		Minnesota	Wyoming	
		Utah	New York	
		Connecticut		

Source: Austin Ranney, "Parties in State Politics," in Jacobs and Vines, eds., *Politics in the American States*, p. 65.

Additional studies relate these differences in party competition to other characteristics of the states and show that, in comparison with the other categories, the two-party states are more urbanized, more industrialized, have higher levels of income, higher proportions of "foreign stock," and smaller percentages of citizens engaged in agriculture.[48]

Experts on political parties have long debated the effect that various types of party systems have upon political activity within a particular political system. The merit of two-party systems as opposed to one-party systems is hotly discussed. Many of the arguments advanced in these discussions have become part of the literature that analyzes the effect of variations in party competition upon policy outputs in the states. At least three lines of thought have developed here.

On the one hand, Key and Lockard argued that the nature of a state's party system "determines" the content of its public policy. Key felt that "more liberal policies" were adopted in those Southern states that exhibited a degree of regular factional competition than in those where party competition was less structured;[49] Lockard found, in New England, a distinct difference in the types of policies initiated by the two-party states and those initiated by the one-party states.[50]

Subsequent research questioned these findings; several authors argued that the demographic characteristics of a state are most important for the level of state expenditures and that party competition has no independent effect upon this level. Richard E. Dawson and James A. Robinson tested this hypothesis with regard to welfare policies in the states and found, when they controlled for the effect of party competition, that "the level of public social-welfare programs in the American states seems to be more a function of socioeconomic factors, especially of per capita income" and that "interparty competition appears to be related to the extent of public social-welfare policies through their joint relationship with per capita income."[51]

Thomas R. Dye improved the Dawson-Robinson technique and applied it to an analysis of the variations within the states with regard to *three* areas of outputs in the states: education, welfare, and taxation. Again, he found that "economic development in the American states is related to party competition and to many policy outcomes, but party competition appears to have little independent effect on policy outcomes. . . . differences in the policy choices of competitive and non-competitive states turn out to be a product of differences in economic levels rather than a direct product of party competition."[52]

Finally, David Koenig suggested that Dye and Dawson and Robinson erred in assuming spuriousness between party competition and the level of expenditures within a state. In reanalyzing their data, he used one of the most sophisticated techniques available to political scientists in their search for causal relationships. His findings support both of the above arguments to some degree. On the one hand, "environmental factors" seem to be more important than party competition for such measures of public policy as aid to the blind, old-age assistance, per-pupil expenditures for education, and average annual salaries of public school teachers. On the other hand, party competition *is* important for other measures of this output — specifically, unemployment insurance and aid to dependent children.[53]

Thus two classes of policy output can be posited: those partially dependent for enactment upon party competition and those generally favored policies whose extensive application is limited chiefly by a state's finanacial capabilities within the context of competing demands on scarce resources.[54]

There remains, then, solid support for the idea that competitive parties influence the nature of decisions within a political system. As parties vie for the support of the electorate, they are induced to take positions and offer "rewards" that they would not have to offer in the absence of competition. Consequently, the type of party system existent in a state has great import for the nature of politics in that state.

Pressure Groups in the States

Pressure groups also may be regarded as links that connect the individual and his government. Although they are different from political parties in both composition and function, pressure groups are an integral part of the politics of all democratic systems.

The nature of pressure group activity and influence, no less than that of political party activity and influence, varies throughout the American states. Some states — Maine, Michigan, Montana — are characterized by strong pressure systems, while others have moderate or weak systems.[55] Furthermore, the configuration of interests within these categories may vary.[56] Although Zeller puts Maine, Michigan, and Montana in the same category, there are obvious differences in the pressure politics of these states. Maine, for example, is dominated by an alliance of three interests; timber, power, and manufacturing. In the words of Duane Lockard, "these groups . . . have done more than merely 'influence' Maine politics; 'control' is probably a more accurate term."[57] Michigan politics, on the other hand, is structured largely by the demands made by *two* powerful, competing groups: automotive labor and automotive management. Although other pressure groups operate in the state, "no major issue of policy . . . is likely to be decided in Michigan without the intervention, within their respective parties and before agencies of government, of automotive labor and automotive managers."[58] Finally, Montana pressure politics is characterized by dominance of a single mining interest, the Anaconda company. In a state in which the mining of minerals is the major source of personal income outside of farming, "the company," as it is known in Montana, is the state's largest employer. Thus, "its strength rests not only in its wealth and resources but also in its elaborate network of relationships with key citizens, banks, legal firms, and business organizations throughout the state."[59]

Although the nature of the pressure system in the states varies somewhat according to the characteristics of the groups themselves — that is, the nature of their leadership, their cohesion, etc.[60] — it is also dependent upon the socioeconomic conditions of the state and upon other components of the political system. The authors of *The Legislative System* suggest that in Tennessee "the comparatively less developed character of pluralistic group life," which stems from Tennessee's position as an agricultural state with a homogeneous population, contributes to the weak pressure system which they found in that state.[61] In addition, Zeller found strong support for the hypothesis that the influence of pressure groups in the states is weakened by the existence of strong party systems. Over 85 percent of the states that exhibited weak pressure systems were characterized by strong party cohesion in the legislature, whereas 75 percent of the states in the strong pressure system category had weak party cohesion.[62]

The significance of interest groups in the states, then, varies with the influence of other factors in the political process and with the nature of the environment in which the interest groups are set. That these groups structure state politics is unquestioned. The degree to which they are effective, however, can be understood only in light of other long-term and immediate factors within the state.

State Electoral Systems

Elections have often been ignored as *official* agencies of government which perform specific functions for the political system. Because of their sporadic nature and because the Constitution is relatively vague about the structure of the electoral system, the agencies of government concerned with the output functions — legislatures, executives, judiciaries — have received the primary emphasis in political science. Nevertheless, electoral systems are official agencies of governments which, in democracies at least, perform two vital input functions for the political system: interest articulation and leadership selection. That is, they serve as conduits for the transmission of policy preferences to governments[63] and as devices by which persons are selected to wield the official power of government. Thus, the electoral systems of the states deserve attention at this point.

In their broad outlines state electoral systems are very similar. With regard to the nominating process, the direct primary is now used or is available in some form in all fifty states. Although the convention is the principal method of nominating candidates in Connecticut, Indiana, and New York, the primary remains the almost universally used nominating procedure. Similarly, the states have the same general requirements governing the qualifications of those who may participate in the electoral process. Thus all states have election laws concerning citizenship, residence, and age requirements. Finally, all states have similar regulations regarding the election process itself. Laws regulating conduct in campaigns and regarding the administration of the election — choosing polling places, printing ballots, choosing precinct officials and counting ballots — are in evidence in every state.

These similarities, however, hide notable differences which have important implications for the politics of a state. Despite the prevalence of the direct primary, for example, this method of nomination does not perform the same function in all the states which utilize it. Thus, in most of the Southern states, the primary of the Democratic party has performed the electoral rather than the nominating function because the Republicans have been too weak to mount any challenge in the general election. The nominating process, therefore, is pushed back one step and, depending on the nature of intraparty competition, takes place in a "first primary" or within the confines of a particular "machine." The general election in these states serves only to ratify the selection made in the Democratic primary.[64]

Differences among the states with regard to the rules regarding who shall vote also have important bearing on the politics within the states. *The American Voter* pointed out that the "legal limits on political participation and the rules governing the conduct of partisan politics" as embodied in state electoral regulations had significant impact on the level of participation in the voting act and on the development of partisan loyalties within the various states. In those states outside the South,

> Voters governed by rules most likely to promote partisanship are most likely to be strong party identifiers and least likely to classify themselves as Independents.

Conversely the voters in states that provide minimal encouragement of partisanship are significantly more often self-classified Independents and less often strongly identified with a party.[65]

Partisanship in the South does not appear to be related to the nature of electoral laws for two reasons: (1) There is so little variation in the electoral laws of the Southern states that differences on the measure of partisan facilitation are slight, and (2) "the unique monopoly enjoyed by the Democratic party throughout the South alters the impact of many factors that might otherwise be associated with independence in the partisan competition for allegiance."[66] However, the *voting behavior* of party identifiers in the South *is* related to the differences noted above. In those Southern states characterized as having "high facilitation of partisanship," a visibly higher proportion of votes were cast which were consistent with party identification than in those states having electoral laws characterized as "low" in facilitation of partisanship.[67] Further, "in the South, the proportion of citizens who have never voted is clearly associated with state-imposed restrictions on voting."[68] The inescapable conclusion is that "election laws are significant elements of our political system and not merely the esoteric interests of election officials and manipulative politicians."[69]

THE AUTHORITATIVE DECISION-MAKING AGENCIES OF STATE GOVERNMENT

Certain agencies in all political systems perform the function of translating the demands made by its citizens into public policy. In the American states, as in the United States, this function is performed by four readily identifiable political agencies, the legislature, the executive, the courts, and — to a lesser extent — the bureaucracy. Despite their outward similarity, these agencies exhibit a wide range of difference in structure and in process. Such differences have important consequences for politics within the states.

The State Legislature

On the surface, the legislatures of the American states are very similar. With the exception of Nebraska, all are bicameral. With the exception of Nebraska and Minnesota, all are elected on a partisan basis. Finally, all are organized internally in the same general fashion, i.e., they have committee systems, legislative leaders, formal rules, and "informal norms" — all of which serve to structure the activities of the members of the body.

Behind this surface similarity lie myriad structural and procedural differences. To begin with, there are wide variations in the manner in which state legislatures represent their citizens. In some states there is a relatively close relationship between population distribution and legislative representation. In others, certain segments of the population are vastly overrepresented. The manner in which state legislatures are apportioned has been one of the most emotional and most studied issues in all of state politics. "Malapportionment" has been singled out as *the* cause of much of the weakness of state government by political scientists and journalists alike.[70] It has been deemed largely responsible for unfair distribution of funds, lack of party competition, unprogressive legislation, and divided government.

While the nature of legislative apportionment is certainly a major factor affecting the state legislative process — because it provides the framework within which the legislators are selected — recent research has questioned whether it is the only, or even the major, determinant of that process. At least one author has argued that the "relationships that appear between malapportionment and public policy are so slight that reapportionment is not likely to bring about any significant policy changes."[71] Others have been less assertive and have argued merely that "malapportionment in and of itself is not associated with some of the major ailments of state politics."[72]

The possibility of resolving this controversy and of examing the problem of the effect of legislative apportionment on the state political process will be greatly improved once the present stream of reapportionment suits has run its course. Until then, malapportionment will remain a major issue in American state legislatures.

A second difference among state legislatures which bears upon their performance as authoritative decision-making agencies is the degree of party influence existing within those bodies. This influence is by no means uniform throughout the states. Obviously, parties in one-party legislatures do not exercise the degree of party discipline over the actions of legislators that parties in more competitive states bring to bear. For example, Wahlke, Eulau, Buchanan, and Ferguson found that few Democratic legislators in Tennessee felt that their party had significant influence over their actions.[73] This does not mean that party influence is uniform throughout the competitive states. As Jewell points out, "party voting does not vary proportionately with party competition in the state."[74] It appears that three general factors affect the degree of influence exerted by parties within the state legislatures. First among these factors are the socioeconomic characteristics of the states. Party cohesion is greatest in the legislatures of the large, urbanized, industrialized states. A second factor is the nature of the constituencies represented by the two parties. "A legislator is more likely to vote with his party if his district is typical of most others represented by his party."[75] Although this statement has to be modified to some degree, the constituency-pressure theory still has, in the works of one author, "substantial merit."[76] Finally, legislative cohesion is related to the issues involved at the time of voting. Party influence is greatest on the major social and economic issues which divide the two parties. Therefore, we find the greatest party cohesion on votes regarding taxation and appropriation, welfare, education, and regulation of business and labor.[77]

These two factors, legislative apportionment and cohesion, are but two of many ways in which American state legislatures differ. There are also variations in the political organizations of the chambers, in the characteristics of the individual legislators, and in the degree to which legislative actions are affected by such "external" factors as pressure groups and the governor. All of these factors must be considered if we are to understand the role of the state legislatures as agencies which formulate policies and work out compromises among opposing interests.

The State Executive Office

In the past twenty-five years the position of governor has become the center of public attention at the state level, and the governors themselves have become the most important figures in state politics. The rise of this office to its position of prominence has corresponded with the rise of the United States as a large, industrial, urban, and complex society. As the problems faced by state governments in the twentieth century become more complex, state legislatures proved unable to furnish the leadership necessary to solve them, even when they were given substantial authority. Moreover, "independently elected administrative officers felt no obligation to support any common program, and state politics turned into a melange of unrelated and often competing or contradictory activities."[78] In response to this situation, the governor's office acquired new powers and won a new reputation as the only governmental agency able to bring order out of the chaos of state politics in the eighteenth century and early nineteenth century.

Despite the general preeminence of the office, no two governors exert equal amounts of influence in their states. There are significant differences in their formal powers and in their informal positions in the political tradition of their states. While these differences certainly affect the role played by the governor in state politics, our knowledge about the extent to which these differences are important is very limited.

Much has been written about the variation in the formal powers and duties of the American governors. Indeed, the description of these differences and of the historical development of the office has constituted the major portion of the literature on the subject. Practically every work on the state chief executive has described that office in terms of its formal features. Generally, such works have stopped at this point. Consequently, we have an enormous amount of data concerning differences among the governors with regard to such factors as salaries, selection and removal procedures, formal qualifications for office, and legal powers, but very little data concerning the correlates of these differences or their consequences for state politics.[79] We know, for example, that the governors in some states — New York and California — are well paid, while others — in Arkansas and Maine — receive comparatively little remuneration for their work. We know that some state chief executives — those in Illinois and Pennsylvania — possess a considerable number of formal powers, while others — those in Texas and North Dakota — have relatively few. We know that some governors have relatively long terms in office, with a chance to succeed themselves, while others are limited to short terms, with no succession possibilities. We do not know what effect these variations have upon the governor's ability to pursue his objectives in the state political system.

We are at approximately the same point in our understanding of the role played by the various governors within their particular political systems. Coleman Ransone has done some preliminary work in this area and has found that "the modern American governor is primarily concerned with three broad areas of operations — policy formation, public relations, and management."[80] He has also pointed out regional differences in gubernatorial commitment to these functions.

In the South, legislative leadership probably would be ranked first in a listing of the governor's functions. In the rest of the nation, the governor's role in administrative policy formation probably would receive equal emphasis.[81]

However, Ransone was unable to systematically assess the impact of these variations on the ability of the governors to perform their constitutionally prescribed duties. Consequently, our information about the "informal" aspects of the governor's office is limited to a somewhat incomplete description of differences among governors' perceptions of the function of their office in the system.

Our understanding of American governors, then, is almost exclusively limited to (1) an encyclopedic knowledge of their formal powers and (2) a description of variations in the way individual incumbents perceive their roles. Although differences in formal powers and role-perception surely affect the role played by the executive office in state political systems, we are unable presently to state the nature of this effect.

State Judicial Systems

No feature of the state political system exhibits more variety than the judiciary. Tremendous diversity is evident among the states with regard to structural arrangements of the courts, methods of selecting judges, and judical tenure. Many of these differences have important consequences for the course of justice in the state political system since they affect the selection of judges, the nature of the decisions made, and the length of time involved in litigating a case.

There is an almost incredible number and variety of state courts, ranging from justices of the peace through chancery courts to supreme courts. Generally, these varieties can be classified into three, sometimes four, major groupings: (1) courts of limited jurisdiction, (2) courts of general criminal and civil jurisdiction, and (3) courts of last resort. In some states, primarily large ones, a fourth type of court has been interposed between the second and third levels mentioned above. Such courts are empowered to serve as tribunals of final determination in a wide variety of cases so as to relieve the courts of last resort from their heavy appeal work. The functions of these various types of courts range from relatively routine administration of cases that have little significance beyond the personal concern of the litigants; through deciding civil and criminal cases arising out of the major statutes, common law, and constitutions of the states; to settling major controversies involving social and political conflicts where precedents are not clear.

There is also wide diversity among the states in the way people are selected to fill these positions. Five different methods of selection are used: (1) partisan election, in which judges run for office on party tickets in the same manner as other public officials; (2) non-partisan election, in which judges are popularly elected, but without official party assistance; (3) election by the legislature; (4) appointment, normally by the governor; and (5) the "Missouri Plan," in which the governor selects individuals from among those recommended by a special commission; the judges so chosen must run against their record when so "ordered" by a referendum.

Structural variations such as these have direct bearing upon judicial activity in the states. Different selection systems, for example, tent to sort out judges with different social and political backgrounds. These differences in background, in turn, result in varying decisions on the same or similar issues. Herbert Jacob has shown that judges who have been selected under the "Missouri Plan," for example, tended to be born outside the district in which they served, almost always attended law schools in their state, were more likely than judges selected under any other system to have attained honors in law school, and were the least likely of all "types" of judges to have held prior public or party office.[82] From what we know about the association between socioeconomic factors and political behavior, we can be certain that these judges would react differently to the issues which came before them than would, say, partisanly elected state judges. Jacob found that the latter were likely to serve in the district in which they were born, practically never achieved law school honors, and very often had no prior college degree.[83]

We should not, however, limit our analysis of those factors which affect judicial activity in the states to the formal features of state judicial systems. The making of judicial decisions, like the making of all political decisions, is influenced by the personal experiences of the individuals involved. State judges are not robots, responding mechanically to legal reasoning and precedent. They are complicated human beings. They are influenced by their own sets of individual interests, biases, and predispositions, as Stuart Nagel has illustrated nicely in several studies.

Basing his analysis on divided decisions of state supreme courts, Nagel found significant differences between the decisions made by Catholic and non Catholic judges and between those made by judges with non-Anglo-Saxon backgrounds and those with Anglo-Saxon backgrounds. Judges with non-Anglo-Saxon backgrounds were more likely to decide for the defense in criminal cases and for the wife in divorce cases. Catholic judges tended to decide for the employee in employee injury cases and for the debtor in creditor-debtor cases.[84]

Nagel also found evidence that the partisan affiliation of state judges influences their decisions. Using an analysis identical to the one mentioned above, he found Democratic state judges differing significantly from Republicans in that the Democrats decided more frequently for the claimant in unemployment cases, for the defense in criminal cases, and for the tenant in landlord-tenant cases.[85]

The conclusion to be drawn from these studies is that the state judiciary, no less than the state legislature and executive, is subject to the "vagaries and varieties" of political winds. The structural forms evident in the various states must be taken into consideration in assessing the impact of the judiciary in the state system, for form and structure distribute advantages and disadvantages among the participants in the process. However, these various formal arrangements must be considered as conditioning factors rather than determining ones. Variation in state judicial behavior is also affected by the characteristics of the judges themselves, the nature of the litigants, and the prevailing sentiment within the state.

OUTPUTS OF STATE POLITICAL
SYSTEMS

Outputs are the actions taken by the political system in response to inputs. In the American states these outputs normally take the form of laws, administrative regulations, or judicial decisions. As such, they both provide services and regulate the behavior of individuals and groups. [86]

Generally speaking, the outputs of the state political systems can be characterized more as services and less as regulation of behavior. The states sponsor programs which range from management of state-owned forest land for recreational purposes to the establishment and maintenance of educational systems which often stretch from preschool training to postgraduate work. In monetary terms, a far greater proportion of state funds are expended for such services than for police and other regulatory functions. Education, welfare, and highway expenditures alone accounted for 73.4 percent of the total state expenditures in 1965. [87]

This is not to say that *all* state funds go to provide services for the residents of the states. Every state has a highway patrol; every state licenses individuals to perform certain tasks; and every state sets standards for the performance of various duties. For example, the state governments in 1965 spent 352 millions of dollars for police protection. [88] Overall, however, states are "providers of services" as opposed to "regulators."

Despite their similarity in emphasis on service, the American states diverge in the variety and the quality of the services which they offer their citizens. Some states have excellent highway systems, others do not; some have internationally recognized universities, others go about the business of educating their citizens as though we were still in the Middle Ages. Similarly, some states offer a veritable plethora of services to their citizens, while others perform only minimal functions. New York, for example, provides many functions that Mississippi is unable or unwilling to offer.

Such variations among the states have recently come under close scrutiny by political scientists; some of the most significant research in the field of state politics has sought to explain them. [89] This body of research shows several factors to be associated with high or low rates of expenditures on various functions.

To begin with, certain socioeconomic characteristics appear to have an impact upon the level of expenditures for specific services. Dawson and Robinson and Dye found a state's wealth, its degree of urbanization, and its level of industrialization positively associated with expenditures for welfare programs; Dye and Salisbury found the same associations between wealth and education expenditures; Friedman found the degree of urbanization significantly but negatively associated with expenditures for state highway systems, i.e., "the smaller the percentage of people living in metropolitan areas within a state, the more likely that state is to spend its money on highways." [90]

Another factor which has often been designated as the "cause" of variations in state expenditures for various programs is the nature of the state's political system, as measured by the level of interparty competition. Both Key and Lockard argued that the "competitive" states adopted "liberal" policies with regard to social-welfare programs because the existence of an alternative ruling group made it necessary for those who held public office to appeal to the "have-nots" with programs designed with their benefit in mind.[91] Although none of the other authors cited above have found party competition to be a significant, independent factor in determining the total level of expenditure for welfare, education, or highways, recent research has shown party competition to be relevant for individual measures of these concepts. Koenig, for example, found party competition to have a significant impact upon the level of state expenditures for unemployment insurance and aid to dependent children.[92] Consequently, we must add an additional level of complexity to the Matthews and Prothro finding that the relative and absolute importance of political factors and demographic factors varies with different political issues [93] — we must say that "different political factors affect different issues differently. . . ."[94]

A final factor which has relevance for at least one area of outputs in the American states is the traditional posture of the state toward particular programs. Robert Salisbury has discussed the effect of the states' traditions with regard to support of public schools and has shown that the value placed on good schools "provides a context within which legislators operate, and that context has much to do with the level of expenditures."[95]

We now know more than we have ever known about those factors which "determine" the output of the American states. We have not, by any means, exhausted the range of things which might have such an impact. For example, the strength of the state executive office and the nature of state pressure systems surely are important for the determination of the level of expenditure for specific policies by the states and for the nature of state ouputs generally. However, no research has sought to assess the impact of variations in these things. Obviously, if we are to fully understand state policy outputs and the way in which decisions about them are made, additional research is needed.

CONCLUSIONS

This introductory essay has described, in very general terms, the major features of the political systems of the American states and has assessed the impact of variations in these systems on political behavior in the states. There are major gaps in the analysis. Virtually no attempt was made to assess the relationship of the major features of the systems to each other. That such relationships exist is certain. Indeed, to some extent each major feature is a complete subsystem whose outputs become inputs for other subsystems, and whose inputs are outputs from those subsystems. An analysis of the extent of these linkages must await the development of more knowledge about them. Nevertheless, this discussion should point out that such interdependencies exist; moreover, it may provide a framework within which such relationships can be analyzed.

NOTES

1. See Richard Fenno, "The House Appropriations Committee as a Political System: The Problem of Integration," *American Political Science Review,* 56 (June 1962), 310-324.

2. See Marion D. Irish and James W. Prothro, *The Politics of American Democracy*, 3rd edition (Englewood Cliffs, N. J.: Prentice-Hall, 1965).

3. See Malcolm E. Jewell and Samuel C. Patterson, *The Legislative Process in the United States* (New York: Random House, 1966).

4. David Easton, "An Approach to the Analysis of Political Systems," *World Politics*, 9 (1955–57), 384.

5. Easton, 383.

6. *Politics in the American States: A Comparative Analysis* (Boston: Little, Brown and Co., 1965).

7. David Easton, *A Framework for Political Analysis* (Englewood Cliffs, N. J.: Prentice-Hall, 1965), 108–118.

8. Easton, 120.

9. See Robert A. Dahl, ed., *Political Oppositions in Western Democracies* (New Haven: Yale University Press, 1966), 349–352.

10. V. O. Key, Jr., *American State Politics: An Introduction* (New York: Alfred A. Knopf, 1956), 18. The following paragraphs are also based on Key's analysis.

11. See Duane Lockard, *The Politics of State and Local Government* (New York: Macmillan Co., 1963), 59–66.

12. See James W. Prothro and Charles M. Grigg, "Fundamental Principles of Democracy: Bases of Agreement and Disagreement," *Journal of Politics*, XXII (May 1960), 276–294.

13. The following paragraphs are based on Lockard's work, cited above.

14. Dahl, *Political Oppositions*, 349.

15. Lockard, *Politics of State and Local Government*, 64.

16. See *New England State Politics* (Princeton, N. J.: Princeton University Press, 1959), chap. IV.

17. Seymour Martin Lipset, *Political Man* (New York: Doubleday & Co., 1960), 33.

18. Donald R. Matthews and James W. Prothro, *Negroes and the New Southern Politics* (New York: Harcourt, Brace & World, 1966).

19. Lockard, *New England State Politics*, chap. XI.

20. For a good summary of this literature, see Lester Milbrath, *Political Participation: How and Why Do People Get Involved in Politics* (Chicago: Rand McNally & Co., 1965).

21. See Donald R. Matthews and James W. Prothro, "Social and Economic Factors and Negro Voter Registration in the South," *American Political Science Review,* 57 (March 1963), 24-44; and "Stateways versus Folkways: Critical Factors in Southern Reactions to *Brown vs. Board of Education,"* in Gottfried Dietze, ed., *Essays on the American Constitution* (Englewood Cliffs, N. J.: Prentice-Hall, 1964), 139-156.

22. C. Kluckholm and W. H. Kelly, "The Concept of Culture," in Ralph Linton, ed., *The Science of Man in the World Crises* (New York: Columbia University Press, 1945), 98.

23. *Encyclopedia of the Social Sciences,* IV (New York: Macmillan Co., 1930), 621.

24. Ibid.

25. Robert E. Agger, Daniel Goldrich, and Bert E. Swanson, *The Rulers and the Ruled* (New York: John Wiley, 1964), 19.

26. See Angus Campbell, Philip E. Converse, Warren E. Miller, and Donald E. Stokes, *The American Voter* (New York: John Wiley, 1960), 229.

27. V. O. Key, Jr., *Southern Politics* (New York: Vintage Books, 1949), 142.

28. Key, 142.

29. Agger, Goldrich, and Swanson, *The Rulers and the Ruled,* 19-28.

30. See Raymond E. Wolfinger et al., "America's Radical Right: Politics and Ideology," in David Apter, ed., *Ideology and Discontent* (New York: The Free Press, 1964), 262-293, for a discussion of the sources of right-wing extremism and the characteristics of the people who are attracted to it.

31. Wesley and Beverly Allinsmith, "Religious Affiliation and Politico-Economic Attitude, A Study of Eight Major U.S. Religious Groups," *Public Opinion Quarterly,* 12 (Fall 1948), 377-389.

32. See John H. Fenton and Kenneth N. Vines, "Negro Registration in Louisiana," *American Political Science Review,* 51 (1957), 704-713.

33. Lockard, *New England State Politics,* 307-308.

34. See Robert Dahl, *Who Governs?* (New Haven: Yale University Press, 1961), Book I; Alexis de Tocqueville, *Democracy in America* (New York: Vintage Books, 1954); Seymour Martin Lipset, *Political Man* (New York: Doubleday & Co., 1960); Harold

Lasswell, *Power and Personality* (New York: The Free Press, 1946); and Gabriel A. Almond and Sidney Verba, *The Civic Culture* (Princeton, N. J.: Princeton University Press, 1963).

35. Almond and Verba, *The Civic Culture,* 3.

36. Data supporting this assertion are taken from the Almond and Verba study. Given the nature of the sampling procedure in this study, the assertion here could be made only if consistent and strong differences between the South and the rest of the nation were noted in the study. Although such differences were found, the authors of that study did not make this assertion and are not responsible for my interpretation of their data.

37. See Matthews and Prothro studies, cited in footnote 21.

38. Edgar Litt, *The Political Cultures of Massachusetts* (Cambridge, Mass.: M. I. T. Press, 1965), 204-205.

39. V. O. Key, Jr., *Public Opinion and American Democracy* (New York: Alfred A. Knopf, 1961), 109.

40. Key, 104.

41. See Gabriel Almond, *The American People and Foreign Policy* (New York: Harcourt, Brace & World, 1950), 131-135.

42. Samuel Lubell, *The Future of American Politics* (New York: Doubleday Anchor Books, 1956), 140.

43. See Alfred de Grazia, *The Western Public* (Stanford: Stanford University Press, 1954).

44. American Institute of Public Opinion, "The Public Pulse," May 1959 and November 1959.

45. "The Public Pulse," November 1959.

46. See Gabriel A. Almond and James S. Coleman, eds., *The Politics of the Developing Areas* (Princeton: Princeton University Press, 1960), 3-64, for a discussion of the functions performed by the political system.

47. See Austin Ranney and Willmoore Kendall, "The American Party Systems," *American Political Science Review,* 48 (1954), 477-485; Joseph A. Schlesinger, "A Two-Dimensional Scheme for Classifying the States According to Degree of Inter-Party Competition," *American Political Science Review,* 49 (1955), 1120-1128; and Richard I. Hofferbert, "Classifications of American State Party Systems," *Journal of Politics,* 26 (1964), 550-567.

48. See Key, *American State Politics: An Introduction,* chap. VIII; Leon D. Epstein, *Politics in Wisconsin* (Madison: University of Wisconsin Press, 1959), chap. IV; and

Heinz Eulau, "The Ecological Basis of Party Systems: The Case of Ohio," *Midwest Journal of Political Science,* I (1957), 125-135.

49. Key, *Southern Politics,* 298-314.

50. Lockard, *New England State Politics,* 320-340.

51. Richard E. Dawson and James A. Robinson, "Inter-Party Competition, Economic Variables and Welfare Policies in the American States," *Journal of Politics,* 25, 289.

52. Thomas R. Dye, "The Independent Effect of Party Competition on Policy Outcomes in the American States," in a paper presented to the 1965 Annual Meeting of the American Political Science Association (September 8-11), 15.

53. David J. Koenig, "Public Policy, Background Variables and Political Variables: A Reappraisal," in an unpublished MS. (Department of Political Science, University of North Carolina at Chapel Hill, 1966).

54. Koenig, 47.

55. For the complete typology upon which this statement is based see Belle Zeller, ed., *American State Legislatures* (New York: Thomas Y. Crowell Co., 1954), 190-191.

56. See Harmon Zeigler, "Interest Groups in the States," in Jacob and Vines, eds., *Politics in the American States,* 101-147.

57. Lockard, *New England State Politics,* 79.

58. Joseph LaPalombara, *Guide to Michigan Politics* (East Lansing: Michigan State University, Bureau of Social and Political Research, 1960), p. 104. Quoted in Zeigler, "Interest Groups in the States," 123.

59. Thomas Paine, "Under the Copper Dome: Politics in Montana," in Frank H. Jonas, ed., *Western Politics* (Salt Lake City: University of Utah Press, 1961), 197-198. Quoted in Zeigler, 119.

60. See David Truman, *The Governmental Process* (New York: Alfred A. Knopf, 1951).

61. John C. Wahlke, Heinz Eulau, William Buchanan, and LeRoy C. Ferguson, *The Legislative System* (New York: John Wiley, 1962), 322-323.

62. Zeller, *American State Legislatures,* 191-192.

63. See V.O. Key, Jr., *Public Opinion and American Democracy,* chap. XVIII.

64. See Key, *Southern Politics,* chap. XIX, for a discussion of the nominating procedure in the South.

65. Campbell, Converse, Miller, and Stokes, *The American Voter,* 269-270.

66. Campbell et al, 269-270.

67. Campbell et al, 273.

68. Campbell et al, 276-277.

69. Campbell et al, 272.

70. See, particularly, Key, *American State Politics,* 76; Charles R. Adrian, State and *Local Governments* (New York: McGraw-Hill Book Co. , 1960), 306-307; and Malcolm E. Jewell, *The State Legislature, Politics and Practices* (New York: Random House, 1962), 30-33.

71. Thomas R. Dye, "Malapportionment and Public Policy in the States," *Journal of Politics,* 27 (1965), 599. See also, Richard I. Hofferbert, "The Relation between Public Policy and Some Structural and Environmental Variables in the American States," American Political Science Review, 60 (March 1966), 73-82.

72. Herbert Jacob, "The Consequences of Malapportionment: A Note of Caution," *Social Forces,* 43 (Winter 1964), 260.

73. See Wahlke, Eulau, Buchanan, and Ferguson, *The Legislative System,* 356.

74. Jewell, *The State Legislature,* 51.

75. Jewell, 68.

76. See Thomas A. Flinn, "Party Responsibility in the States: Some Causal Factors," *American Political Science Review,* 58 (1964), 60-71.

77. Jewell, *The State Legislature,* 59-60.

78. Herbert Kaufman, *Politics and Policies in State and Local Governments* (Englewood Cliffs, N.J.: Prentice-Hall, 1963), 40-41.

79. One exception to this method of analysis is Joseph A. Schlesinger, "The Politics of the Executive," in Jacob and Vines, *Politics in the American States,* 207-236.

80. Coleman E. Ransone, Jr., *The Office of Governor in the United States* (University, Alabama: The University of Alabama Press, 1958), 115.

81. Ransone, 149.

82. Herbert Jacob, "The Effect of Institutional Differences in the Recruitment Process: The Case of State Judges," *Journal of Public Law,* 12 (1963), 275-290.

83. Jacob, 275-290.

84. Stuart Nagel, "Ethnic Affiliation and Judicial Propensities," *Journal of Politics,* 24 (1962), 92-110.

85. Stuart Nagel, "Political Party Affiliation and Judges' Decisions," *American Political Science Review,* 55 (1961), 843-851.

86. See Theodore J. Lowi, "American Business, Public Policy, Case Studies, and Political Theory," *World Politics,* 16 (July 1964), 677-715, for an effort to conceptualize outputs in a different fashion.

87. U. S. Bureau of the Census, *Summary of State Government Finances in 1965,* 2-3.

88. Ibid. , 7.

89. See Dawson and Robinson, "Inter-Party Competition, Economic Variables and Welfare Policies in the American States"; Dye, "The Independent Effect of Party Competition on Policy Outcomes in the American States"; Hofferbert, "The Relation Between Public Policy and Some Structural and Environmental Variables in the American States"; and the chapters by Robert Salisbury, Dawson, and Robinson and Robert Friedman in Jacob and Vines, eds. , *Politics in the American States.*

90. Robert Friedman, "State Politics and Highways," in Jacob and Vines, eds. , *Politics in the American States,* 441.

91. See Key, *Southern Politics;* and Lockard, *New England State Politics.*

92. See Koenig, "Public Policy, Background Variables and Political Variables: A Reappraisal," and McCone and Cnudde, "State Political Systems and Social Welfare: Some Causal Models."

93. See Matthews and Prothro, "Stateways versus Folkways: Critical Factors in Southern Reactions to *Brown v. Board of Education. "*

94. Koenig, "Public Policy," 39.

95. Salisbury, "State Politics and Education," in Jacob and Vines, eds. , *Politics in the American States,* 364.

Part One

THE
ENVIRONMENT
OF
STATE POLITICS

Part One

Political activity in the American states is, to a large extent, shaped by the nature of the environment within which it is set. Responses by individuals and groups to this environment make up the inputs which are necessary to the maintenance of the state political system. Many observers have noted the significance of various parts of this environment for state politics. The importance of the federal form of government, state constitutions, and the underlying social character of individual states has been examined extensively. Less noted but also important are such factors as religious heritages, political culture, and physical characteristics.

The articles reprinted in Part One were chosen to illustrate certain features of the environment of state political systems and to point out the linkage between these features and political behavior within the states.

THE FORMAL
FRAMEWORK

An Autonomous State Politics?

V. O. Key, Jr.

When considering the problem of organization for the conduct of state politics one fact of fundamental importance must be kept firmly in mind: the American states operate, not as independent and autonomous political entities, but as
units of the nation. Within the states public attention cannot be focussed sharply
on state affairs undistracted by extraneous factors; political divisions cannot occur
freely on state questions alone: national issues, national campaigns, and national
parties project themselves into the affairs of states. Political parties within the
states become at times but the shadow of their national counterparts, and always
the states' position in the federal system profoundly affects the form and character of their politics.[1]

Given the nature of the interconnections between national and state politics,
the state candidates of a party at times become the undeserving beneficiaries of
the exploits of their fellow partisans on the national scene. By the same token,
either party, no matter how commendable its state record may be, is, from time
to time, booted from office for the shortcomings of its national allies.

Both governmental reformers and professional politicians take note of the
lack of autonomy of state politics and conduct themselves accordingly. Reformers,
clergymen, editors, and good citizens in general, commonly urge that the tariff,
farm policy, military problems, and other such national matters should have no
bearing on the choice of governors and of state legislators. The admonition is to
the effect that state questions should be considered separately, "on their merits,"

rather than handled in terms of party by straight-ticket voting. Professional politicians, perhaps more concerned with survival than with principle, contrive ways and means of offsetting or of capitalizing upon the relations between state and federal politics.

The practical yearning for a state politics uninfluenced by external forces does not diverge markedly from the theoretical presupposition about how a federal governmental arrangement ought to operate. Federal theory, at least tacitly, assumes the feasibility of a more or less autonomous politics within each unit of the system. Moreover, when the doctrine of popular government is superimposed over federal theory, the notion becomes implicit that each state of the federal system has the capacity to generate a party system adequate to perform the functions of recruitment of candidates, of competition for power, of conduct of the government, of criticism of public administration and public policy. In a word, federal theory, by its inner logic, must presuppose a political capacity congruent with the constitutional competence of each federated unit. Otherwise, political means do not exist for the exercise of the autonomous sphere of constitutional power held by the units of the system.

Yet the American states differ greatly in the degree to which they fit this pattern. In the organization and spirit of their politics the states vary markedly. Their oddities and variations may be accounted for in part by the fact that they are members of a federal system. The impact of national policies and parties powerfully influences the form and behavior of state political systems. The manner in which that impact strikes different states, differently constituted and situated, contributes to the variations in organization and conduct of state politics.

The narrow question to be examined here is the relationship of position in the federal system to the form, structure, and broad conduct of state politics. Such a focus of attention excludes, of course, many other ways in which state and federal politics are interwoven. In the polling booth one usually votes simultaneously for candidates for state and for national office. The bonds of party unite in common cause candidates for Congress and for state legislatures. Politicians often move from a governorship to the United States Senate, and occasionally the reverse occurs. States depend, in varying degrees, upon the actions of Congress for their revenues. Though these and many similar relationships have their relevance to the broad question of the interplay of state and federal politics, they are excluded from the present discussion by the choice of the narrower problem for analysis.

FEDERALISM, SECTIONALISM, AND ONE-PARTYISM

From the conditions associated with the formation of federations, a federal constitution by its nature obstructs to some extent in some states of the union the development of a full-blown party politics around state issues. The pursuit in national politics of ends of peculiar and overriding importance to a state or region demands a solidarity whose maintenance influences the workings of state politics. When the advancement of national objective requires that people within a state or region unite, that unity must affect the way in which they fight among themselves on state questions.

Although these propositions seem more or less self-evident, they need to be spelled out. The creation of a federal system implies the existence of territorial differences among the people of a nation. To some degree these geographical political cleavages solve themselves by the division of powers between national and state governments. So long as a sphere of action remains solely in the hands of the states, the people of New York cannot, through the national government, impose their views about a matter within that sphere upon the people of Texas or vice versa. Not all issues that set section off against section can be so nicely handled, or avoided, by the leaving of their settlement to the states. Some sectional questions fall to the jurisdiction of the central government. On such matters sectional differences will be projected into Congress and into the national political arena generally.

Political conflict on state issues may tend to be blurred or smothered to the extent that most of the people in a section place a high premium on a set of national policies of concern to the section. External defense of the sectional cause requires a degree of sectional unity internally. Essentially the argument is that the organizational tendencies and necessities of sectional solidarity nationally react back on state politics and induce a less complete mobilization of conflict over state questions than prevails in the absence of the conditions creative of regional unity on national questions.

The states of the South constitute, of course, the prime example of this phenomenon. Southern unity in national politics emerged from the complex of events climaxed by the Civil War. Hardened by Reconstruction, that unity persisted to defend, among other things, the view that the federal government should leave to the states the control of race relations. That defense did not, to be sure, require the maintenance of a steady fire. The issue was not continuously a live one. Yet it occasionally flared up, at least in symbolic form, which sufficed to keep sectional memories green and to maintain a posture of mobilization for defense. By the 1930's and 1940's the only type of issue on which southern Representatives and Senators held together in high degree against most Republicans and Democrats from the rest of the country were race measures, such as anti-lynching bills, anti-poll tax proposals, fair employment practices schemes, and the like.[2]

The maintenance of southern sectional unity in national affairs involved a drastic modification of the practice of politics locally. In view of the attitude of national Republican leaders toward the Negro, to support a Republican candidate for governor was in effect to give aid and comfort to the sectional enemy — the sectional enemy both in memory and in prospect. At least such was the view assiduously propagated by southern Democratic politicians. By a variety of means the Republican party was reduced locally to an innocuous position, and the party system of the region came to be oriented toward the fulfillment of sectional purpose in national affairs. So complete was Democratic control at home that during the first half of the twentieth century the rolls of governors of the 11 Confederate states were sullied by only two Republican names, both chief executives of Tennessee.

A set of special circumstances also affected the party system in the South, viz., the presence of large numbers of Negroes whose disenfranchisement was to be accomplished. The white primary came to provide a mechanism ideally designed to permit the maintenance of southern Democratic solidarity in national politics, with the simultaneous existence of quite warm political conflict among southern Democratic whites on state questions. Indeed, Democratic unity against the Negro locally perhaps was quite as important as the compulsion toward unity against the friends of the Negro elsewhere in the fixing of the form of the southern political system. For many decades the consensus on sectional interest in national affairs remained so complete that local differences could be fought out within the Democratic white primary with an extremely low probability that the local battle would spill over into the general election and become a cleavage between Republicans and Democrats threatening regional solidarity nationally.

The transfer of state politics in the southern states to the Democratic primaries was so complete that the consequence amounted more to an alteration in the form of state politics than in its substance. The fundamental change in form was from a conflict of parties to a conflict of personalities or of more or less amorphous factions within the Democratic party. While that alteration in the form was undoubtedly of significance for the substance of politics, the effects on substance remain extremely difficult of estimation and doubtless vary from time to time and from state to state within the South. In some circumstances nonparty politics may place a premium on demagogic qualities. In others it may deprive of safeguards by its lack of institutionalized opposition to criticize, to harass, and to heckle. It may hinder mass movements by the ambiguity of the choices faced by the electorate. Those choices are in terms of candidates rather than of parties with divergent traditions and contrasting leadership cores. Yet in other instances party factions develop that appear to possess a coherence, a continuity, and a habit of competition not sharply at variance with the two-party model. That development, however, may be most apt to occur as sectional solidarity is in a state of erosion, at a stage when the primary battle is on the verge of spilling over into the general election and becoming a battle between Democrats and Republicans. In Louisiana, for example, the primary battle between the Long and anti-Long factions for years divided the people along lines similar to those that separated Republicans and Democrats outside the South. In 1952 the anti-Long voters crossed the line in large numbers to support General Eisenhower.[3]

Over the entire country the primacy of sectional purpose nationally has for considerable periods projected itself back into state affairs. The party that functions as the sectional instrument becomes overwhelmingly dominant in state matters. The hopeless minority, although it may have a good cause locally, remains handicapped by the fact that it bears the name of the party that is the sectional enemy nationally. In the post-Civil War development of Republican dominance in the northeastern and midwestern states a sectional memory not unlike that of the South prevailed. Those who raised in this region the banner of the Democracy were not only serving illy the memory of the boys who fought at Bull Run but also were threatening the predominant sectional concern in national affairs. By the management of both sentiment and interest a party could gain a firm grasp of state affairs — a grasp that enabled it to resist or to minimize the effects of the great tides of national politics that wore upon its local hegemony.

Although in the older states of the Northeast and the Middle West the results for state politics were neither so spectacular nor so durable as in the South, the tendency was the same. The impact of sectionalism, in our peculiar historical and institutional setting, induced a fairly high degree of regional unity in national affairs which contributed to the entrenchment of Republicans in control of the state governments of the region. In these states Democrats made great gains in presidential politics in the 1930's yet their advances in state affairs were not proportionate. While only Vermont has a record of Republicanism in state elections that matches southern consistency in electing Democratic governors, some other states of the Northeast and of the Middle West only infrequently deviate from the straight and narrow and elect Democratic governors.[4]

The impact of national issues upon cleavages within state politics depends, to be sure, in part on the socio-economic composition of each state. State boundaries may happen to encompass a population made virtually homogeneous politically by its response to the national political alternatives. A state consisting largely of active members of the CIO would probably harbor few Republicans. Or a state made up mainly of rural dwellers, not greatly diluted by in-migration since their ancestors wore the Blue in the Civil War, would not be a hotbed of the Democracy.

These relationships between population composition and party inclinations appear neatly in the upper New England States. Vermont, the least urbanized and the least affected by immigration, maintains the most impressive Republican record. In other states urbanization and immigration are associated with a lesser degree of Republican attachment. The relationships are suggested by the following figures:

	Mean Percentage Gubernatorial Vote Republican		*Per Cent Urban 1950*	*Per Cent Foreign-Born 1930*
Vermont	(1916–52)	69.5	36.4	3.6
Maine	(1912–52)	58.2	51.7	12.6
New Hampshire	(1910–52)	55.3	57.5	17.8
Massachusetts	(1913–52)	51.8	84.4	25.2

The question may well be raised whether the character of state parties is not determined by such factors of population composition rather than by the organizing impact of our federal history upon state electorates. Would predominantly rural Vermont, for example, have a lively two-party politics in state affairs if it were not pushed towards Republicanism by its historical national affinities? Perhaps both the impact of national politics and the social structure of the state operate to depress the minority party. For the gravitation of national issues to nudge a state towards one-partyism its population must possess a certain uniformity of response to those issues. Yet the people of the state might well divide otherwise on state issues if they were unaffected by their traditional national commitments.[5]

In recent decades the issues and forces of national politics have tended to wear down sectional groupings. The new issues push people, wherever they live, toward divisions different from the traditional sectional partisan cleavages, and the states gradually become more alike in the manner of their presidential voting. In the strongly Republican states the Republican majority has become a little less overwhelming than it once was. In the states of the South a more striking deterioration of the Democratic hold over the electorate has been taking place. Yet the data on presidential voting point to the conclusion that changes in sectional political attachments on the American scene occur slowly. The nature and rate of change are suggested by Figure 1, which indicates the deviations of the Republican percentages of the presidential vote in Florida and in Vermont from the Republican percentages of the national presidential vote. The division of the vote in Florida over half a century has approached more nearly the division of the nation as a whole. The Florida curve reflects the special effects of individual elections, such as 1928, but also shows a more gradual, secular movement upward in Republican strength. The forces driving toward a political realignment, of course, strike Florida more powerfully than they do most other southern states. The Florida trend, in fact, reflects more the influx of sun-seeking northern Republicans than a realignment of the natives. Figure 1 also presents the data for Vermont, whose divisions in presidential voting manifest a slight secular tendency toward greater similarity with the divisions within the country as a whole.[6]

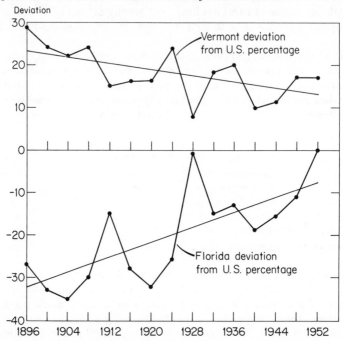

Figure 1   Erosion of sectionalism: Deviation of Republican percentages of total presidential vote in Vermont and Florida from Republican percentages of total national vote, 1896-1952.

Sectionalism in national politics may very well be undergoing a decline, yet its effects on the organization of state politics will long survive its demise. From evidence to be presented later, it becomes clear that changes in the politics of a state government may lag considerably behind alterations in the presidential voting habits of the people of the state. The politicians in command of the statehouse may confidently be expected to demonstrate a fairly impressive staying power, even though there turns out to be a long-run trend toward a more competitive presidential politics.

STATES AND THE TIDES OF NATIONAL POLITICS

The general drift of the argument to this point has been that the pursuit of particularistic regional, sectional, or state aims in national politics reacts on the organization of state politics. The imperative of unity in national affairs depresses the minority party in state affairs and profoundly affects the manner of organization of state politics in areas dominated by sectional concerns or traditions. In the extreme type of situation state politics comes to be the business of groupings and factions within the locally dominant party rather than a competition between the local arms of national parties. In any case state offices are monopolized with varying degrees of thoroughness by a single party. Vermont, thus, steadfastly clings to its Republican faith and turns back Democratic aspirants for the governorship for scores of years. And southern states maintain an equally imposing indifference to the blandishments of Republican candidates for governor. In other states the same broad influences contribute to one-party control only occasionally interrupted.

A different, and perhaps superficially contradictory, effect of national politics on the political process within the states now demands attention. Some states may be nudged toward one-partyism in local affairs by their position in the federal system, but others tend to be carried along by the great swings of political cycle which mark the alternation in dominance of Democrats and Republicans on the national scene. The capacity of the state to act independently of national issues and with a focus on state questions withers as the affairs of states are swept along by the tides of national politics.

The great tides of national politics may not affect seriously the bastions of one-partyism but they engulf most of the states of the North and West and sweep them along in the same direction. The presidential candidate who leads his party to a landslide victory carries into office with him large numbers of gubernatorial candidates of his party, who win without much regard to their role or place in the state but because they float along with the national movement of sentiment. Similarly, those state candidates allied with the losing party on the national scene are caught up by the common misfortunes of their partisan allies over the nation.

A picture of the process emerges from Figure 2, which depicts the relation between simultaneous presidential and gubernatorial voting in states outside the South in the presidential years from 1920 through 1952.[7] The great upthrusts in the presidential strength of each party, as the chart graphically reveals, are paralleled by similar gains within the states. In the Republican sweep of 1920, Harding carried all the 28 states covered by the analysis as did his fellow Republicans in the races for governor. The election of 1936, the peak of Roosevelt's strength, saw also a peak in the proportion of states carried simultaneously by Democratic presidential and gubernatorial candidates. The pendulum swung in 1952 to an opposite extreme, when Republican aspirants for governorship found the company of General Eisenhower on the ticket most congenial.

Whether in these wide fluctuations in partisan strength the presidential candidate carries governors into office or the gubernatorial candidates give the presidential candidate a boost poses an interesting question, though one that is irrelevant to the main argument. Whatever the relation of mutual re-enforcement between national and state tickets, the states do not operate independently of these broad national sweeps. Evidently in the public mind — at least in the framework of these great cycles of sentiment — no sharp differentiation between state and national affairs prevails. The electorate, on the whole, has no eye for fine distinctions but uses the only weapon it has or knows and elevates to power or relegates to oblivion according to party label — with exceptions, to be sure.[8] These exceptions are least numerous at elections that mark the greatest party triumphs on the national scene. Note in Figure 2 that the states splitting their presidential and gubernatorial vote were fewest in 1920, 1936, and 1952. In 1952, Democrats Frank J. Lausche of Ohio, G. Mennen Williams of Michigan, Phil M. Donnelly of Missouri, and Dennis J. Roberts of Rhode Island survived the Eisenhower victories in their states and accounted for the states with split results shown in Figure 2. On the other hand, as the national political cycle moves away from landslide presidential peaks the number of states with split presidential and gubernatorial results increases. Perhaps the decline in forces driving toward unanimity nationally gives room for freer play of factors and circumstances peculiar to each state.

The great swings in the fortunes of the national parties are also associated with alternations in control of lesser state offices. A cyclical swing toward the Republicans on the national scene is accompanied, for example, by a similar movement in state legislative races in those states not almost completely immune to the fluctuations of national politics. Similarly, when Democratic candidates lead

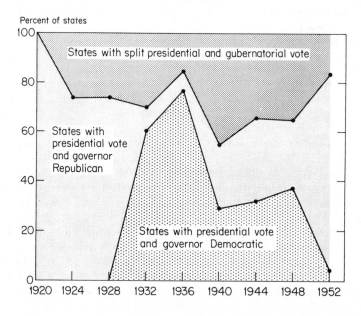

Figure 2 Presidential tides and the governorship: Relation between results of presidential and gubernatorial voting in 28 non-southern states, 1920-1952.

in the presidential sweepstakes, a considerable company of Democrats occupy seats in state legislatures that had been warmed by Republicans in the earlier stage of the cycle.

An illustration of the relation between presidential and state legislative politics appears in Figure 3, which shows the percentage of Missouri counties with popular pluralities for Democratic presidential candidates, along with the percentage of seats in the lower house of the state legislature won by Democrats over a period of a half century. While the two series do not march up and down in exact unison, their major movements manifest a remarkable similarity. It need scarcely be said that the fluctuations are not so closely aligned everywhere as in the competitive state of Missouri. A like analysis for all legislative districts and all counties over the nation as a whole would show a considerably wider fluctuation in the presidential series than in the state legislative series.[9]

The association between fluctuations in the presidential vote and in the results of legislative contests has effects that differ in consequence from state to state. In states strongly committed to one party or the other the only result is that the legislative minority, at the most minuscule, is a bit larger at some times than at others. For states not overwhelmingly Republican or Democratic — and not gerrymandered irrevocably to one party or the other — the consequence is sooner or later an overturn of the more or less normal legislative majority in harmony with shifts in presidential voting sentiment.

The association through time between national and state voting points to difficulties in the separation of state and national politics. The governmental system may be federal but the voter in the polling booth usually is not. Evidently great upsurges of sentiment are not often accompanied by widespread popular differentiation between state and federal politicians. Both tend to be the targets of the blasts of popular confidence or hope. Although this sort of behavior may not be regarded as rational, it may in truth make a good deal of sense, for, at least at times, the fulfillment of popular aspirations requires that the same crowd be thrown

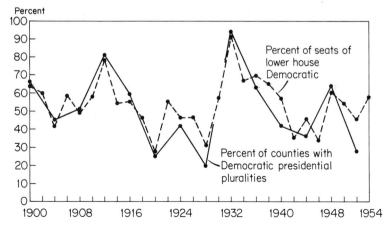

Figure 3 Interrelation of cycles of national and state politics: Proportions of Missouri counties with Democratic presidential pluralities and proportions of Missouri House seats won by Democrats, 1900-1954.

out of both Washington and the state capitals simultaneously.[10] That process may be both facilitated and made sensible by the tendency of state and national candidates of the outs to advocate similar or related lines of action. Certainly in times of deep and pervasive discontent few politicians saddled with the sins of the old order, no matter how cherubic their countenances, or whether they be state or federal officials, can expect to survive the anger of the multitude. And perhaps that is the way it should be. . . .

ISOLATION OF STATE POLITICS

Framers of state constitutions have given thought to ways and means of diking off from state elections extraneous national influences on local decision. Their most common stratagem is to schedule gubernatorial elections in years when no presidential election is held. Usually this arrangement involves a four-year term for the governor with the election falling at the middle of the presidential term, a practice prevailing in 15 states. Kentucky, Mississippi, Virginia, and New Jersey achieve a more complete separation by scheduling the gubernatorial election in odd-numbered years, while Louisiana's state elections fall in April of presidential years.[11]

Though the separation of gubernatorial and presidential elections undoubtedly produces results that differ from what would occur with simultaneous state and federal elections, only in the most limited sense does such scheduling make for a state politics independent of national influences. The unlovely truth is that the manipulation of the gubernatorial election calendar is often merely a tactic in party warfare. Adjustments in the timing of elections may be made, not to permit a freer choice, but to create circumstances that will tend to favor one party or the other.

The effects of the timing of gubernatorial elections upon party fortunes differ both from time to time and from state to state. The choice of governors only in the off years greatly handicaps the attempts of a weak minority party to build up its strength. If the governor is chosen in presidential years the minority, despite the weakness of its local forces, gains advantage from the fact that in these years the voters are aroused by the issues and events of the national campaign. The minority candidate for governor may have little chance for victory but with politics in the air and with some help from the national ticket he may make a respectable showing. On the infrequent occasion when a presidential candidate wins by a landslide, his margin may be so wide that he carries into office the most improbable gubernatorial candidates in states where his party is ordinarily in the minority. An occasional victory, rare though it may be, helps mightily in building up a minority party. On the other hand, if a gubernatorial candidate of the weak minority must make his race in an off year on the slender local means of his party and without benefit of the presidential-year surge of popular political interest, his chances of even making a strong showing decline.

The record of Oklahoma illustrates how the separation of elections may handicap the minority and snatch from it the opportunity for a state victory in the wake of a national landslide. The Sooner State commonly rates as a Democratic stronghold, yet it harbors a goodly number of Republicans who for almost fifty

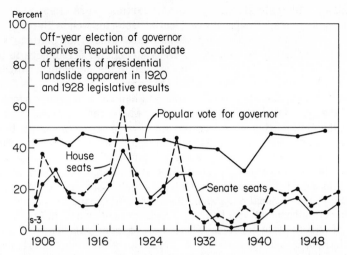

Figure 4 Insulation of governorship from national political tides: Republican percentages of two-party vote for governor and of seats in legislative houses, Oklahoma, 1920-1952.

years have not managed to elect a governor. Their vicissitudes flow partly from the off-year election of governors. The state is by no means isolated from the great currents of national politics, yet those tides run at the wrong time to benefit the Republicans of Tulsa and environs. The point is established by the graphs in Figure 4 which picture the voting performance of Oklahoma since statehood. Republican strength in the lower house of the state legislature, chosen once every two years, shot upward in the elections of 1920 and 1928, years of Republican sweeps. On the other hand, the state's Republican gubernatorial candidates, as the chart indicates, could not benefit from the great swells of the Republican national landslides as they undoubtedly would have under a different election schedule.

　　In states with a traditionally one-sided division of strength between the parties, such as Oklahoma, four-year gubernatorial terms with elections in non-presidential years clearly handicap a long-run build-up of minority strength. In other types of situations, however, other sorts of consequences follow. Where elections are normally more closely contested, the effects of the segregation of elections differ from time to time with changes in the balance of power in the national political arena. In states in which the popular followings of parties are of about the same size — in which the parties are genuinely competitive — the simultaneous election of President and governor tends to tip the balance in favor of the gubernatorial candidates of the party winning the presidency. When the Republicans are riding high nationally, their gubernatorial candidates have brighter prospects for victory in presidential-year elections than in off-year elections. When the Democrats enjoy national favor for a string of elections, their gubernatorial candidates enjoy similar advantages and disadvantages.

　　The contrasts between the results of gubernatorial elections in presidential years and in off years, in both Republican and Democratic eras, are in accord with these general propositions. In the 1920's Democratic candidates for governor, even in states with quite strong Democratic parties, were often snowed under in the presidential years. The great presidential victories won by Harding, Coolidge, and Hoover left by the wayside as incidental casualties of the political wars many Democratic candidates for governor. Even so popular a Democratic leader as Alfred E. Smith of New York fell victim in 1920 to the Republican national sweep, although in 1924 he survived the Coolidge victory.

In this era, however, the Democrats had some hope of recouping their losses of the presidential year in those states whose governors served a two-year term. At the next polling when they did not have to struggle against the national Republican appeal, local Democrats could often recapture the state. The general rule prevailed that the narrower a state's Republican presidential margin in popular vote, the greater was the probability that the Democratic gubernatorial candidate would win at the next off-year election. With his opponent deprived of the momentum of the national campaign, the Democratic candidate could turn to his advantage both discontent with national Republican policy and dissatisfaction about matters of purely state concern. The nature of these relationships between the presidential voting and the outcome of gubernatorial elections in presidential and nonpresidential years appears from Table 1.

Table 1 Two-year governors outside the South, chosen in presidential years and in off years, 1920–30, related to Republican percentage of state presidential vote.[a]

Republican Presidential Percentage	Number of States	Per Cent of Governors Republican	
		Presidential Years	Off Years [b]
45–49	2	100.0 [c]	50.0
50–59	11	63.6	36.3
60–69	22	90.9	45.5
70–79	16	87.5	68.7
80–89	6	100.0	100.0

[a] The states included in the tabulation are Arizona, Colorado, Connecticut, Idaho, Iowa, Kansas, Maine, Massachusetts, Michigan, Minnesota, Nebraska, New Mexico, New York, North Dakota, Ohio, Rhode Island, South Dakota, Wisconsin, Wyoming.

[b] The off-year elections are classified according to the Republican presidential vote in the preceding presidential election. Thus the two columns, presidential and off years, compare the outcomes of gubernatorial elections in the same states in the two types of years.

[c] The two states with Republican governors but Democratic presidential pluralities were Massachusetts and Rhode Island in 1928. These instances, deviates in this tabulation, suggest that state political shifts may lag behind presidential shifts.

When the Democrats gain the upper hand in presidential politics, their state candidates enjoy advantages in presidential years but their Republican opponents often re-assert their local strength in the nonpresidential years. In elections of the 1930's and 1940's Roosevelt carried many of his fellow Democrats into governorships which the Republicans retrieved in the off years. By the same token, governors elected in presidential years for four-year terms were more likely to be Democratic than were governors elected in the nonpresidential years for four-year terms. The state Democratic disadvantage, in an era Democratic nationally, under a scheme that schedules gubernatorial elections in the off years appears plainly from Table 2.[12]

Table 2 Four-year governors outside the South, chosen in presidential years and in off years, 1932–1950, related to Democratic percentage of state presidential vote.[a]

Democratic	Presidential Years		Off Years[b]	
Presidential	Governors	Per Cent	Governors	Per Cent
Percentage	Elected	Democratic	Elected	Democratic
45–49	5	40.0	6	33.3
50–54	10	40.0	13	23.1
55–59	15	80.0	4	50.0
60 and over	10	100.0	11	63.6

[a] The states electing governors in presidential years covered by the table were Delaware, Illinois, Indiana, Missouri, Montana, Utah, Washington, West Virginia. The off-year states were California, Idaho, Maryland, Nevada, New York, Oregon, Pennsylvania, Wyoming. Some of these states elected in the off years only for a part of the period 1932-1950.

[b] The off-year states are grouped according to their presidential vote in the preceding presidential election. The two groups of gubernatorial elections compared are thus, of course, elections in different states with similar Democratic presidential margins. Apart from the fact that few cases are involved, it should be kept in mind that doubtless factors in addition to the presidential division affect the results of the gubernatorial elections.

During the years of Democratic dominance of presidential politics, Republicans in various states contemplated the causes of their fate. In several states they initiated movements for a constitutional reform which might incidentally alleviate the sadness of their lot. In some instances they succeeded in bringing their states into that group which chooses governors for four-year terms in the off years. Thus their candidates for governor were relieved of the inconvenience of running, in effect, against Franklin D. Roosevelt; Democratic candidates would perforce be deprived of the advantages of being on the slate with him. Probably the advocates of these reforms did not weigh carefully the full consequences of their plan, for it was certain to rise up to plague them at a later date. Perhaps they worked on the assumption that Democrats would control the Presidency in perpetuity. Among the converts to the four-year term were Connecticut and New York. In the off year of 1954, Mr. Harriman in New York and Mr. Ribicoff in Connecticut eked out Democratic victories which would have doubtless been beyond their reach had they been running against a ticket with General Eisenhower at its head. In 1954 also the Democrats carried Pennsylvania, another four-year state, a feat which would have been most difficult of accomplishment had the General been on the ticket.[13]

The simple trick of election scheduling clearly affects the degree of integration of state and national politics. At one extreme the attempt at insulation of state politics apparently retards long-term shifts in relative party strength by depriving a weak minority of the fillip that comes from the association of local candidates with presidential campaigns. In states with a more competitive party politics concentration of state politics in the off years evidently deprives the state associates of a popular President of the benefit of his pulling power and by the same token aids the other party. Competitive states with off-year elections are by no means untouched by the great fluctuations in party strength nationally; they are simply less closely articulated with the national tides than are those close states whose local campaigns coincide with the commotion generated by a presidential election.[14]

Probably the preponderance of judgment among the architects and reformers of state government supports attempts to separate state and federal politics. A dissent from that view may be expressed, although the line of action promotive of the general weal in any particular state at any particular time is rarely patent. In terms of average long-run effects the case against attempts to isolate state politics hinges on the evident tendency of integration with national politics to strengthen party competition within the states on state matters. Competition may not invariably promote the public good but perhaps over the long term the maximization of competition among politicians turns out more happily than does the maximization of security for politicians.

Quite apart from the effects of separation of gubernatorial and presidential polling on the outcome of state elections, it is evident that over the past 75 years a gradual decline has occurred in the capacity of parties to carry states simultaneously for their candidates for President and for governor. In all the states with simultaneous presidential and gubernatorial elections — a group of states whose composition has changed from time to time — the proportions of elections that produced pluralities for presidential and gubernatorial candidates of the same party by groups of presidential elections have been as follows: 1880-92, 93.1 per cent; 1896-08, 89.5 per cent; 1912-24, 81.2 per cent; 1928-40, 77.8 per cent; 1944-52, 75.5 per cent. This general trend in the absence of separation of elections suggests that perhaps some of the independence apparently achieved by segregation of choice through scheduling may have been the result of a long-run increase in the disposition of voters to view state and national affairs independently.

THE STATES IN THE NATION

It becomes evident from this analysis that the balance between the confederative and nationalistic elements within our federal system conditions fundamentally the manner of conduct of politics within the states. To the extent that the confederative element has the upper hand, a state or a group of states maintains political unity in national affairs against the remainder of the country. To that extent, too, the internal politics of the state tend to be warped away from the competitive two-party pattern and find expression in forms and practices not well fitting the conventional concepts by which the instruments of popular government are described. Among the American states this phenomenon has been most marked in its connection with the heritage of the Civil War, and it has been far more severe and more persistent in the states of the South than elsewhere. In the nonsouthern states, apart from the vestiges of party loyalties with the same historical foundation as those of the South, from time to time transient sectional drives for national action have reacted back on the politics of the states concerned.

It would, to be sure, be absurd to attribute the special qualities of the politics of the American states, in all their variety, entirely to the effects of their peculiar federal institutional setting.[15] Yet the functioning of the states as legally separate units in the federal system is conditioned by the fact that they are politically inseparable units of the nation. This interconnection of state and nation, commonly regarded as an indication of the disposition of the electorate to rely on its reflexes rather than on its intellect, may be, and often is, an entirely rational politics. Certainly at moments when great issues of domestic economic policy clamor for attention generally, similar divisions in state and federal voting may make good sense. Yet the looseness of the party system compounds the complexities of the politics of a federal system; it blurs and confuses the alternatives presented to the electorate simultaneously in national and state affairs. The electorate faces a formidable task in the discernment of the realities underlying the inevitable confused particular situation on which it must act. The pursuit of even a politics of the meanest interest becomes difficult in the institutional maze, and the notion of party responsibility for state affairs often becomes almost completely irrelevant.

The long-run social trends are wearing down sectionalism. Perhaps eventually the areas of one-partyism in state affairs will lose their special characteristics, although a forecast in terms of decades rather than years would be prudent. The disappearance of the one-party areas would, of course, have most profound consequences for national politics. The states of the respective sectional cores of the major parties have contributed significantly to the form of national politics. The one-party states have sustained the minority party in the nation. Yet it should not be assumed that we must have one-party states to keep the national minority alive.

This discussion of the impact of the position of the state vis-à-vis the nation upon the internal structure of state politics should not obscure the fact that in various ways the form and pattern of state politics have their national effects. For example, the states, as substantial political entities in the federal system, develop party structures which must be founded on the cleavages peculiar to each state. Within the national party system, these peculiarities may project themselves upon the national leadership of the party. Thus, in a group of midwestern and plains states, the Democratic party, if it is to exist at all as a statewide party, must ordinarily exist as a party different from the Democratic party of an industrial state. In periods of Democratic triumph, as in the 1930's, these western state parties provided, on the whole, a relatively conservative bloc which had to be taken into account by the national leadership of the party. Other examples could readily be cited of the same general question as it applies to both of the major national parties.

NOTES

1. In turn, of course, the position of the states in the federal system bears on the form and nature of the national parties. See David B. Truman, "Federalism and the Party System," *Federalism Mature and Emergent,* Edited by A.W. Macmahon (Garden City: Doubleday, 1955).

2. The question of southern congressional solidarity is analyzed in some detail in Key, *Southern Politics* (New York: Alfred A. Knopf, 1949), chaps. 16-17.

3. See Rudolf Heberle and P.H. Howard, "An Ecological Analysis of Political Tendencies in Louisiana: The Presidential Elections of 1952," *Social Forces,* 32 (1954), pp. 344-50.

4. Illustrative of the point are data on frequency of election of Democratic governors for the period 1920-1950. Over this period, in which the following states had fifteen gubernatorial elections each, the numbers of Democratic gubernatorial victories were: Vermont, 0; New Hampshire, 1; Maine, 2; North Dakota, 3; Iowa, 3; Kansas, 3; South Dakota, 4; Michigan, 5.

5. For a suggestive discussion somewhat related to the argument of these pages, see C.B. MacPherson, *Democracy in Alberta: The Theory and Practice of a Quasi-Party System* (Toronto: University of Toronto Press, 1953).

6. The dispersion of the states according to the division of their presidential vote gives a crude measure of the tendency of states to become more alike in their presidential vote. In terms of the Republican percentage of the total state vote, the states fell within the following percentage-point ranges at the elections indicated: 1896, 73; 1920, 78; 1928, 67; 1936, 55; 1952, 41. The semi-interquartile ranges for these elections were: 1896, 13.2; 1920, 7.3; 1928, 5.2; 1936, 6.5; 1952, 4.7. The use of these years as indicators probably exaggerates both the smoothness and extent of the trend. The similarity of the states apparently is greatest in years of presidential landslides.

7. The chart covers, for most of the period 1920-52, 28 states outside the South with gubernatorial elections falling in the years of presidential elections. Excluded are Alabama, Arkansas, California, Florida, Georgia, Kentucky, Louisiana, Maryland, Mississippi, Nevada, New Jersey, North Carolina, Tennessee, Texas, Virginia, and Wyoming. In the later years of the series several states that changed the timing of their gubernatorial elections to the off years were dropped: New York, Idaho, Connecticut.

8. Instruction in American civics over the generations has had distressingly slight effect in drilling into the American voter a full comprehension of the complexities of the American governmental system. The Honorable Emanuel Celler, long a Member of Congress from Brooklyn reflects on his constituents' grasp of federalism: "The

feeling of intimacy with the national government is much greater than that which people have for their own city or state. This, too, is unfortunate. My mail is heavy with letters from constituents who inform me that the traffic light is broken on their street and would I please get it repaired? Or the policeman on the beat has been discourteous and would I have him reprimanded? Or there is no public library within walking distance from the constituent's home. Or the principal of the school is anti-Catholic, or anti-Semitic, or just 'anti'; would I please have him removed?" — *You Never Leave Brooklyn* (New York: John Day, 1953), p. 266.

9. An analysis of county presidential pluralities and of the outcomes of legislative elections for 32 nonsouthern states lumped together, on the order of that of Missouri in Figure 3, shows the Democratic presidential curve at a considerably higher level than the curve for lower-house seats in 1932 and 1936. At another stage of the cycle, 1952, the proportion of counties carried by Eisenhower was substantially higher than the proportion of legislative districts won by Republican candidates. In states with parties less evenly matched than Missouri the legislative series has a narrower amplitude of variation than does the presidential series.

10. The impression develops that the states with parties powerfully enough entrenched to resist the national tides are not so immune to national movements of sentiment as might appear. Within the intraparty affairs of such states different types of individuals probably tend to rise to positions of leadership, depending on the tenor of the predominant national sentiments. That is, in Democratic states the fortunes of progressive and conservative leaders may depend somewhat on variations in the temper of the nation as a whole which is reflected in more competitive areas in shifts between parties.

11. The broad conclusions and tabular material of this section appeared in the *New Republic,* November 23, 1953, under the title, "Now That 1954 Is Here."

12. With reference to Table 2, as elsewhere in this analysis, it needs to be kept in mind that at least a modicum of variety exists among the situations classified on the basis of the party label of the candidate. For example, one case hidden away in Table 2 is the election of Harry Nice as Republican governor of Maryland in 1934. Roosevelt had won Maryland in 1932 with 63 per cent of the two-party vote. The year 1934 probably marked the peak of Democratic strength generally. Yet Albert Ritchie in 1934 lost to Nice. Nice claimed that he would be a better New Dealer than Ritchie, a notable conservative of a states'-rights persuasion, and attacked Ritchie for his coolness toward the New Deal. The exaggerations of campaign fulminations perhaps did reflect the underlying realities. A partisan deviation by the electorate, within the limits of the alternatives available, may have been in reality an ideological consistency.

13. On occasion adjustments in ballot form are similar in motive to the tactic of election scheduling. Thus, in 1941, under Republican leadership, Delaware divided its ballot into two, one for voting for President and Vice-President and another on which candidates for other offices were listed. The supposition was that with this separation of choice Republican candidates for other offices would fare better in the immediate

circumstances of Democratic dominance in presidential politics. Similarly in Michigan during the Roosevelt era the legislature made it impossible to vote a straight ticket with one mark or with the movement of one lever on the voting machine. In 1955, however, the legislature, still Republican, viewed the problem of ballot form differently, an alteration of opinion probably not unconnected with the probability that Mr. Eisenhower would be a candidate in 1956. The legislature acted to permit a straight-ticket vote with one mark.

14. The determinism of the election calendar also influences the extent to which governors confront legislatures controlled by opposition majorities.

15. The contention could well be made that federalism, as such, has little to do with the interaction between sectionalism nationally and the form or practice of state politics. In any polity, federal or nonfederal, with fairly sharp geographic cleavages on issues of national policy a similar relationship might be expected to prevail, that is, if the nonfederal polity had subordinate political units of considerable extent. Such an argument is plausible enough and perhaps correct. Yet it would be expected that federal regimes, by virtue of the circumstances of their emergence, would be especially marked by sectional or geographical concerns in national politics, with the consequent reactions on the forms of politics in those states sectionally oriented toward national questions. Yet one should be wary of extending the argument of this chapter to all federal systems; the argument here is explicit limited to the peculiar features of the American federal system.

The Shaping of Intergovernmental Relations in the Twentieth Century

Daniel J. Elazar

One very practical manifestation of the political changes that have characterized the twentieth century has been the great increase in government activity, much of it in the form of new intergovernmental programs. Despite popular views to the contrary, intergovernmental collaboration is not a new phenomenon. Cooperative federalism — the patterned sharing of governmental activities by all levels of government — has been characteristic of the American federal system since its establishment. American governments have traditionally assumed responsibilities only in response to public demands but, where governments have acted, federal, state, and local governments usually have acted in concert. Whether this "co-operative federalism" was intended by the founders of the Union or not, it was quickly demonstrated to be necessary. Governments operating in the same territory, serving the same people, generally sharing the same goals, and faced with the same demands could not maintain a posture of "dual federalism" (the separation of functions by levels of government).[1]

THE AMERICAN PARTNERSHIP

By the mid-twentieth century, certain basic principles and mechanisms for intergovernmental collaboration have become part of the American governmental tradition, most of which came into existence a century ago and persist to color the character of American federalism today. Among the principles are: national supremacy, broad national legislative and appropriation powers, noncentralized government, and maximum local control. Among the mechanisms are: a nondisciplined, noncentralized party system; routinized legislative "interference" in administration; regular intergovernmental consultation; and a system of grants-in-aid from higher to lower levels of government.

From the very first, Congress has acquired the authority to legislate very broadly under the Constitution. Although this authority was frequently diluted by the Supreme Court and by Congress itself until the 1930's, it was nonetheless apparent in the general expansion of federal activities in the intervening years. Also demonstrated from the first was the inherent superiority of the federal government as a raiser of revenue because of the tax sources available to it and the reluctance of the people to allow equally substantial state and local tax levies. For these reasons, federal funds provided the stimulus for new programs in a majority of the states throughout the nineteenth century.[2]

Reprinted from *The Annals of The American Academy of Political and Social Science*, Vol. 359 (May 1965), pp. 10-22 by permission of the publisher.

These two trends, coupled with the great political decisions of the nineteenth century, firmly established the principle of national supremacy. Along with it, however, the equally important principle of noncentralized government was also established. If the general government was early cast in the role of stimulator and partial supporter of such major governmental functions as education, internal improvements, and public welfare, the states — either directly or through their local subdivisions — were simultaneously cast in the role of managers and administrators of these functions. Policy-making for these programs became a joint state-federal activity.

This arrangement is often mislabeled decentralization. Decentralization implies the existence of a central authority having a legitimate monopoly of governmental power which can concentrate, devolve, or reconcentrate functions more or less as it pleases. Noncentralization — on the other hand, the keystone of every true federal system — implies the constitutional coexistence of a general government and governments with more particularized authority which share governmental power. In the American case, the basic authority of the states is delineated in the Constitution and cannot be withdrawn except with their consent, thus making dynamic federal action possible without concomitant reduction of local self-government by protecting the less formal institutions that deconcentrate power.

The American commitment to noncentralization has forced federal authorities to seek ways to develop nationwide programs with minimum national requirements within the framework of the co-operative system and has enabled the states to secure federal assistance without fearing any real loss of their integrity.

Thus it has always been the prerogative of the states to decide whether or not to accept any federal aid proffered under formal grant programs. And, despite the prevalent idea that no state can resist federal subsidies, few, if any, states have ever taken advantage of every grant offered them. The strong record of state participation, particularly in the major programs in any given period, is really a reflection of the nationwide consensus as to their value and necessity. Such programs represent only a few of the over a hundred available to the states and localities today. Moreover, many states do not take advantage of all the funds available to them under grants they have accepted. In both cases, state policy-decisions rule. [3]

Even more important, noncentralization means that the states, as of right, share in the initial development of most co-operative programs before they are written into law. They share in the shaping of policies from the first and throughout the existence of each program, and develop their own patterns of program implementation within the framework of agreed-upon guidelines. [4]

The sharing process has worked both ways. The states have become involved in the fields of foreign affairs, interstate commerce, defense, and monetary policy just as the federal government has become involved in the fields of education, health and welfare, agriculture, and urban development. [5]

Moreover, local governments, public nongovernmental agencies, and private interests have acquired roles of their own as partners in the process because they have made an effort to become involved and have found ways to "pay the ante" required to sit in on the great game of government in the United States. [6]

THE FORMS OF THE PARTNERSHIP

Intergovernmental co-operation has taken on a variety of forms, all of which have histories as old as the sharing system itself.[7] Among the most common and recurring are those of *informal co-operation* through conferences, the provision of advisory and training services, the exchange of general services, the lending of equipment and personnel, and the performance of services by one government in place of another. Such collaboration is barely visible to the general public except when a conference is sponsored by the White House or when a public-health team moves into a community on the heels of an epidemic. The informal luncheon meeting, no matter how important, attracts no attention whatsoever.

Formal co-operation activities, on the other hand, are based on *contracts and compacts for co-operative action.* In the largest sense, contractual relationships are basic to a federal system which is founded upon a fundamental compact to begin with. In essence, it is the contractual relationship that makes possible large-scale intergovernmental co-operation to achieve common ends. Every formal co-operative relationship involves some form of contractual tie. The flexibility of the contract as a device enhances its usefulness and allows it to be adapted for many purposes. There are contractual relationships for co-operative research, for the division of costs to support shared activities, for provision or exchange of services, to prevent conflict or misunderstanding, for exchange of personnel, for joint enforcement of laws, for sharing revenues, and for lending agreements.

Recurring informal contracts are often formalized to the point of receiving statutory recognition and contractual ratification through *contracts for simple sharing.* These are relationships that involve nothing more than a formal agreement to share resources without formal transfers of funds or personnel from one government to another. They are often used to prevent needless duplication of time, money, and effort or to enhance the possibilities for more comprehensive execution of particular programs. State-federal crop reports, Bureau of Labor Statistics calculations, state regulation of nuclear installations, formal agreements for the exchange of tax information or co-operative inspections of public utilities are examples of this type of relationship.

Another form of co-operation involves the interchange of *personnel.* This includes the provision of "services-in-aid, " that is, arrangements by one government to lend its personnel to assist another; jointly paid agents; joint inspections by personnel of more than one government; and the deputization of personnel of one government by another for co-operative purposes. Under this type of co-operative activity, federal engineers are lent to states and localities to plan projects; county sanitarians are paid with federal, state, and local funds and have special obligations to all three governments; banks are jointly inspected by state and federal officers; and state hospital guards are deputized by the local police.

The pervasiveness of the partnership has led to the development of *interdependent activities* in which one government depends upon another (or both depend upon each other) for the enforcement of laws or the administration of programs otherwise not apparently "shared." The administration of elections is one good example of this. The election of national officials is contingent upon state implementation of the constitutional requirements. In this case, there is federal dependence upon state action. States, on the other hand, may depend upon federal authorities to exclude the transportation of prohibited goods (liquor, oleo, firecrackers) across their boundaries.

First in importance among the forms of intergovernmental co-operation are the grants-in-aid: federal transfers of funds to the states and federal or state transfers to local governments for specified purposes usually subject to a measure of supervision and review by the granting government. They are particularly distinctive because they involve the transfer of funds from one government to another in order to attain certain agreed-upon ends. The first grants-in-aid were generally transfers of land to be sold to finance specific programs. Supervision of these grants was relatively loose by today's standards but still significant; conditions attached to them governed disposition of the lands and use of the proceeds earned.

Cash grants-in-aid, like land grants, date from the nineteenth century — six were established before 1900 — but did not flower until the twentieth. Since 1911 some sixty-five new federal grant-in-aid programs have been established, fourteen of which have since been discontinued. In general, they have been more rigorously administered by all governments concerned.

Grants-in-aid are of three kinds: (1) flat grants, which provide each recipient government with an equal sum regardless of local conditions or deviations from the national means, and without requiring formal matching of funds by the recipient governments — although recipients may have to shoulder administrative costs; (2) proportionate grants, as with road-building, made to recipient governments in proportion to their own contributions to the program or project in question, and often allocated on the basis of preset formulas which take the need and capabilities of the recipient into account; and (3) percentage grants, allocated like proportionate grants but with the granter's contribution fixed as a set percentage of the cost to the grantee for maintaining a particular program. Among the best known of these are the federal public welfare grants and some state grants to local school districts. Grants-in-aid may also include grants in kind, which generally resemble flat grants and are rarely subject to extensive supervision.

Other forms of intergovernmental sharing include tax offsets (used when nationwide compliance is necessary as in the unemployment compensation program), shared revenues (such as timber and mineral royalties and shared license fees), and grants or contracts awarded on similar terms to public and private applicants (such as federal research grants to universities). These all represent variations of the grant-in-aid principle developed to meet conditions which would frustrate simpler grant mechanisms.

Supplementing the regular channels of co-operative control, the sharing system is strengthened through the maintenance of a nondisciplined, noncentralized party system which encourages elected representatives to follow the interest of their districts — from wards through states — rather than maintain party responsibility. This system encourages them to frame programs in such a way as to guarantee the maintenance of local control, thereby increasing their own power. One of the consequences of this has been the development of routinized mechanisms for continuous legislative "interference" (used in the neutral sense) in the administration of government programs, further enhancing local control over program execution as well as policy-making.[8]

THE COURSE OF THE TWENTIETH-CENTURY PARTNERSHIP

The record of the partnership since approximately 1913 has been one of maintaining and appropriately modifying the patterns established earlier, in the face of a continually increasing "velocity of government" — the amount of total government activity in relation to the total activity of society — through the formal institutionalization of the co-operative system.[9]

This has meant (1) the development of more complex and sophisticated techniques for administering co-operative programs to secure better financial control by the granting government, (2) improved sharing of policy formation by all participants, including the panoply of interest groups that contribute so much to policy-making in the United States, (3) expansion of the range and variety of shared activities so that today one is hard-pressed to find any area of public concern that does not somehow involve government and in turn, federal-state-local collaboration, and (4) the adjustment of the theories and mechanisms of federalism to meet new times, situations, and demands. This, in turn, has led to growing public recognition of the co-operative system for what it is and an increased interest on the part of public officials and scholars in understanding how American federalism really functions.

The course of intergovernmental relations in this century can be traced through four periods and into a fifth. Understandably, the trends in intergovernmental relations are closely tied to the larger political and economic movements on the American political scene.

By 1913 the era of virtually unregulated enterprise capitalism was coming to an end. During the next generation, government regulation was progressively extended over an even more complex corporate economy while an ideological battle over the legitimacy of government's new role was being fought.

The first period may be characterized as one of *progressive agrarianism*. It was actually inaugurated when the Republican party, whose national majority status had been consolidated in the critical elections of 1892 and 1896, briefly gave way to a progressive and activist Democratic administration in 1913.[10] It reflected the first concerted national response to the Populist-Progressive-Liberal agitation for positive government action to meet the problems of an industrialized society, and laid the foundations for co-operation in the subsequent periods. Growing government activism, begun in part under Theodore Roosevelt, brought with it revival of large scale co-operative activity. The magnitude of this revival is seen in the more than sixfold increase in federal grant expenditures and the near doubling of the number of formal grant programs between 1912 and 1920 (see tables)[11] and the development of "many other forms of formal and informal co-operative activities as government at all levels took on expanded roles in American life."

This period saw three important developments that were to influence the course of intergovernmental relations thereafter: (1) the beginning of clear public

Table 1 Twentieth-century patterns of American federalism.

Year	Period	Economic Era	Political Condition	State of Intergovernmental Relations
1900 1910	Transition (1895-1911)[a]	Concentrated Enterprise Capitalism (1877-1913)[a]	GOP majority party	Passing of nineteenth-century co-operative programs. New experiments in collaboration under T. Roosevelt. Widespread state experimentation has important influence on public.
1920	Progressive Agrarianism (1911-1921)[a]	Transition Era (1913-1933)[a]	(Democratic Administration, 1913-1921)[a]	Wilson's "New Freedom" lays foundation for twentieth-century co-operative federalism.
1930	Normalized Entrenchment (1921-1931)[a]		1928 Critical Elections 1932	GOP restoration starts second period. Existing co-operative programs continued and improved, but no significant new federal starts. State experimentation again significant.
1940	Crisis-oriented Centralism (1931-1945)[a]		Democrats forge majority coalition, become majority party.	New Deal "explosion" in federal-state co-operation, heading off centralization through temporary concentration of power in Washington. Expansion of federal-local and unilateral federal programs along with co-operative ones.
1950 1960	Noncentralist Restoration (1946-1961)[a]	Regulated Capitalism (1946-)[a]	(GOP Administration, 1953-1961)[a] 1956 Critical Elections 1960	Fourth period brings great expansion of small co-operative programs, great expansion of state government expenditures, and increased concern with states' role.
	Concentrated Co-operation (1961-)[a]		Democratic Majority coalition reforged	Fifth period brings new emphasis on federal stimulatory action and new threat of centralization from outside of the co-operative system.

[a] Dating of periods is approximate.

recognition of the possibilities inherent in an intergovernmental partnership to meet the nation's new governmental needs, (2) the inauguration of modernized forms of federal-state collaboration particularly through the grant-in-aid system, and (3) the first efforts to develop a more sophisticated understanding of the functioning of the American federal system. Woodrow Wilson set the tone for all three. Concerned simultaneously with expanding the federal role and with preserving the federal-state relationship, his public expressions and the programs enacted during his administration reflected the idea that the federal government was to assist the states in developing and maintaining programs already approved or requested by a substantial number of them.[12] The agricultural-extension, highway-construction, and vocational-education grant programs — the major ones inaugurated in Wilson's administration — all reflect this. In the case of the first two, and of the forest-protection program expanded under Wilson, formal co-operative relationships were actually established to replace or prevent unilateral federal action. These new grant programs betrayed the agrarian bent of Wilsonian Progressivism, being specifically designed to benefit the declining rural American majority.[13]

Table 2   Federal grants to state and local governments, 1902-1964 (selected years).[a]

Year	Total in $ '000s	Number of Grant Programs in Operation
1902	3,001	5 b
1912	5,255	7 b
1920	33,886	11
1925	113,746	12
1933	192,966	12
1937	2,663,828	26
1942	1,819,574	27
1946	894,625	28
1953	2,762,912	38
1957	3,816,404	45
1961	7,103,983	46
1964	9,864,000	51

[a]Sources: Advisory Commission on Intergovernmental Relations, Statistical Abstract of the United States, 1964.

[b]Exclusive of fifteen land grant programs.

As both federal and state governments became involved in the same general areas of activity, it became profitable for them to work out appropriate co-operative relations, even for apparently unilateral programs. This was particularly true in matters involving government regulation. Bank regulation had been a co-operative activity since 1865; regulation of railroads became increasingly co-operative as it became more meaningful. There was even some co-operation in the administration of anti-trust legislation. Law enforcement had always led to a great deal of co-operative activity which was intensified after passage of the spate of federal criminal legislation to assist in handling interstate crimes, in this period.

Perhaps the foremost "temporary" co-operative program of the period was selective service for World War I.[14] In some cases federal-state collaboration was explicitly authorized by law. In others, collaboration just grew informally because it was mutually advantageous.

The second period was one of *normalized entrenchment.* It began when the Republicans resumed power in Washington in 1921, and was characterized by a general reluctance to increase the role of government coupled with a negative attitude toward intergovernmental collaboration. Despite the hostile political climate, this period saw the expansion of existing programs and refinements in their co-operative administration. Actual expenditures for co-operative programs increased six-and-a-half times between 1920 and 1932. After an initial period of intensive federal supervisory activity to get the new programs under way, administrative arrangements began to take on a significantly noncentralized character.

At the same time, the number and scope of administrative decisions required to implement complex grant programs gave those who made the programs work substantial influence in shaping the character of intergovernmental co-operation. The professional associations of state and federal officials engaged in the same tasks, and national associations of state officials, such as the American Association of State Highway Officials and the Association of Land Grant Colleges and Universities, whose memberships cut across all levels of government and all jurisdictions, began to assume important policy-making duties. These developments further limited the potential role of the federal bureaus to set policy unilaterally.[15]

The second period was one of considerable activity in the states, activity that would later win the period designation as the "seedtime of reform." Whereas federal expenditures rose by only $503 million between 1922 and 1932, state-local expenditures rose by $2,752 million. The expansion of state activity invariably meant an increase in state involvement in previously "local" problems. The expenditure figures are revealing. State transfers of payments to localities rose from $312 million in 1922 to $801 million in 1932, exceeding the growth of all federal transfers in the same period both proportionately and absolutely. Increases in established federal-aid programs in the 1920's and new state-initiated programs in the welfare field precipitated this growth.[16]

The third period, characterized by *crisis-oriented centralism,* coincided with Democratic achievement of majority party status. Their inauguration of the New Deal as a governmental response to the massive depression problems of a society by then over 56 per cent urban, and later a global war, brought great expansion of new federal programs, co-operative and otherwise. Some of these were in response to state and local pressures; others were developed by reformers eager to stimulate state and local action. The great acceleration of the velocity of government made co-operative federalism all-pervasive. The crisis broke down much of the resistance to federal aid. As a result, existing co-operative programs were made more national in scope, and new ones were broadly oriented from the first.

The co-operative system was subtly reoriented toward Washington, as that city became the nation's unrivaled center of political excitement, if not of governmental inventiveness. "Bright young men" of all ages were brought into the federal government to plan new schemes to meet the problems of the day, many of whom had no particular attachment to the principles of federalism, *per se.* The sheer fact of state and local dependence on federal aid meant that they were willing to tolerate pressures from Washington which they might have rejected forcefully in other times.

Yet the most significant fact that stands out in all this is the way in which the application of accepted techniques and principles of co-operative federalism prevented the tremendous growth in national government activity from becoming an excuse for an equivalent centralization of power. Regardless of the growth of federal influence, the unwillingness of some New Deal planners to develop co-operative programs rather than unilateral ones, and the notions of some political theorists popular in that day that federalism was obsolete, the entrenched forces of American politics directed most new federal programs into co-operative channels. Thus, all but one of the great public welfare programs originally designed by Roosevelt's "brain trust" to be directly administered by federal officials, were reshaped by other administration leaders and by Congress into shared programs in which state and local roles were central. So it was with virtually all the other programs inaugurated in this period that did not absolutely have to be centrally administered.

Indeed, while the New Deal brought formerly unilateral state programs into the sharing system, it also brought in several initially unilateral federal programs as well.[17] Often, experienced public servants (among them FDR himself) were plucked from successful agencies in progressive states and brought to Washington to manage new programs. Their understanding of state and local needs helped maintain the sharing system. Within the states themselves, new co-operative programs were generally subject to modification to meet special local needs.[18] In many cases of erstwhile "centralization," first appearances are deceiving. Consider the Hatch Act requiring states to establish merit systems for federal-aided programs. While this law was greeted by many as a serious limitation of state autonomy, its requirement that states adopt a single merit system of their own design in lieu of federally-imposed program-by-program controls (common in earlier grants-in-aid) helped maintain their integrity as political systems.[19]

The third period featured an expansion of direct federal-local relationships. Partly through urban assistance programs, partly through emergency relief activities, and partly through expanded agricultural programs, the federal government undertook formally to assist local communities in the same spirit of partnership that had animated other forms of intergovernmental relations.[20] This, of course, exacerbated the already complex problems of the states' co-ordination of their internal affairs, even while bringing local relief in a time of crisis.

The growing institutionalization of the intergovernmental partnership was reflected in the development of new institutions to enhance the ability of the states and localities to participate in the development of policy and the improvement of administrative procedures. The Council of State Governments and the complex of "conferences" of state officials connected with it came into being. Headquartered in Chicago, they provided the states with an able instrument to use in negotiating with Washington and a means to further interstate co-operation, providing a measure of "federalism-without-Washington." Local officials, similarly organized, were also called upon to help shape the co-operative programs of the new era.[21]

By the end of the third period, the role of government in a mixed economy had been firmly established and generally accepted. With the beginning of the fourth period a new generation of regulated capitalism, in which government played a positive role in the economy, began. But the fourth and fifth periods reflect this new generation. A Republican interlude during most of the fourth period served to consolidate and assimilate the changes of the New Deal; then it gave way to a restoration of the Democratic majority coalition through the critical elections of 1956 and 1960. The Democrats' return to office in 1961 inaugurated the fifth period in a burst of renewed federal activism.

The fourth period was one of *noncentralist restoration,* marked by a resurgence of the states as spenders and policy-makers and great expansion of local government. Its public image was set by Dwight D. Eisenhower, who repeatedly called for increased reliance on state efforts in place of federal "intervention." However, its real tone was not one of federal "retrenchment" or unilateral state assumption of previously shared responsibilities, as the President and his advisors suggested, but of continued expansion of intergovernmental collaboration — some twenty-one new grant programs were established between 1946 and 1960 — with the states and localities assuming a stronger position in the federal system.

This took four forms. There was a substantial shift in the balance of government expenditures for domestic purposes, with the states and localities coming to outspend the federal government by a two-to-one margin. There was also a marked relaxation in detailed federal supervision of state handling of established grant programs, a reflection of the increased professionalization of state and local program administrators and the growing willingness of their federal counterparts to trust their judgment. The states and localities, through their representatives in Congress, were responsible for the initiation of most of the new programs, which generally involved small grants to give them greater leverage in expanding their services. Finally, the states and localities again became centers of experimentation, developing "pilot projects" of all sorts, often aided with foundation grants or small doses of federal funds.

The states also began to concern themselves with acquiring some control over the unilateral federal programs carried on within their boundaries and in some very important cases, a role in the federal-local programs. In some cases, this was a matter of informal intervention to co-ordinate programs or to render supplementary services. In others, it involved the acquisition of very real power over the implementation of programs within the state.

An added impetus to the resurgence of the states was the increased interest in studying the federal system and its functioning by government commissions for the first time in American history and by academic scholars who continued the tradition begun in the Progressive period.[22] The official studies sponsored by the President suffered somewhat from the disability of starting with the mistaken assumption that the ideal federal system demanded maximum separation of government functions by level.[23] Those sponsored by Congress, on the other hand, were directed toward understanding how the existing co-operative system worked without questioning its legitimacy.[24] The most important direct products of these studies were the relatively small but continuing efforts by the federal administration and Congress to smooth over the rough edges of intergovernmental relations, as evidenced by the establishment of the Advisory Commission on Intergovernmental Relations.[25] As the period ended, public discussion turned to consider the problems of co-ordinating diverse federal assistance programs within the state and metropolitan areas so as to allow both to better maintain their governmental and social integrity.

With the return of the Democrats to power in 1961, a fifth period of *concentrated co-operation* was inaugurated. Increased federal activities in a number of fields was coupled with an intensification of the debate over "states rights" on one hand and widespread acknowledgment of intergovernmental collaboration on the other other. While this period is not yet sufficiently advanced to be fully characterized, it seems clear that it will be one of considerable governmental expansion, particularly at the federal level, to deal with the problems of a metropolitan society. Part of this represents federal "picking up the slack" after the fourth period and part, the extension of government in new ways.

Most of the new federal domestic programs have been resurrected from New Deal days, but recently some potentially new departures have been proposed. They are of two different kinds. There is a movement underway to raise federal minimum requirements in some programs unilaterally in a way that would seriously limit state discretion to adjust them to local needs. At the same time, serious proposals have been made to provide some federal aid through block grants and shared revenues to be used as needed at the states' discretion, thus widening their policy-making powers. However, most of the new programs enacted as of this writing, including the two most revolutionary ones (the Civil Rights Act of 1964 and the anti-poverty program) are being implemented so as to continue the established traditions of intergovernmental collaboration. Both provide for substantial state and local participation and maximum possible local control. The anti-poverty program, for example, is designed to provide federal money for locally sponsored projects and gives the states veto power over most projects proposed for within their limits.

THE MAINTENANCE OF THE PARTNERSHIP

The foregoing description of the successful maintenance of the traditional system of noncentralized co-operation to date should not obscure the great centralizing pressures operating within the American political system today which may have a decisive impact before the century's end. Nor should it obscure the rough edges within the co-operative system itself that could contribute to a drastic change in the character of the American partnership. The need for managing a national economy, meeting foreign pressures, and securing the constitutional rights of all citizens, as well as the pressures toward elimination of diversity within the country — all these operate to centralize governmental power even when steps to prevent centralization are taken within specific programs. With the constitutional barriers to centralization lowered, the pressures of reformers to secure their reforms and of politicians to secure their rewards wherever it is easiest, without regard for the principles of federalism, further complicate the situation. Finally, the great growth of direct federal relations with private parties through defense and veterans' expenditures, agricultural subsidies, and loan guarantees, none of which are susceptible to organization along traditional co-operative lines, cut into the old patterns even when they are brought into the co-operative system by the back door.

Within the co-operative system, there are problems — for example, weak state and local governments unwilling or unable to uphold their share of the partnership and proliferating "red tape" required by federal administrators to meet federal requirements. There is another problem in that the public information system, as it is presently constituted, tends to focus public attention on Washington to the exclusion of the states and localities.

Logic tells us that noncentralized co-operative federalism is not an easy system to maintain, particularly in a nation that prides itself on being pragmatic — less concerned with form than with function and willing to try anything if it "works." Yet the system has been maintained despite the pressures and in the face of all logic because it has continued to satisfy most of the particular interests in this country more often than not. If not one of them gets everything he wants, each gets something, re-enforcing their attachments to a system they feel they can hope to influence.

NOTES

1. For a discussion of federal-state co-operation before 1913, see Daniel J. Elazar, *The American Partnership* (Chicago: University of Chicago Press, 1962).

2. Adequate statistical data for most of the nineteenth century is lacking, but the author's sampling based on the available data confirms this. The figures usually cited show state-local expenditures as exceeding federal expenditures by an approximately two-to-one margin until 1933. However, when the value of federal land grants to states, localities, corporations, and individuals is included in the calculations of federal expenditures and the share of state and local expenditures derived from federal endowments is eliminated, the result is quite different.

3. As of April 1964, 115 programs were available as listed in the *Catalog of Federal Aids to State and Local Governments* prepared for the Subcommittee on Intergovernmental Relations of the Senate Committee on Government Operations (Washington, D.C., 1964). The most current and comprehensive published information on the extent of state participation in federal grant programs is available from the Advisory Commission on Intergovernmental Relations.

4. For a brief, yet thorough discussion of this aspect of American federalism, see Morton Grodzins, "Centralization and Decentralization in the American Federal System," *A Nation of States,* ed. Robert A. Goldwin (Chicago: Rand McNally, 1963).

5. See, for example, Dennis J. Palumbo, "The States and American Foreign Relations" (Unpublished doctoral dissertation, Department of Political Science, University of Chicago, 1960); Morton Grodzins, "The Federal System," *Goals for Americans,* ed. President's Commission on National Goals (Englewood Cliffs, N.J.: Prentice-Hall, 1960); and Edward C. Banfield (ed.), *Urban Government* (New York: The Free Press, 1961).

6. For further elucidation of the role of local and private interests, see Daniel J. Elazar, "Local Government in Intergovernmental Perspective," *Illinois Local Government,* ed. Lois Pelakoudas (Urbana: University of Illinois, 1960), and Morton Grodzins, "Local Strength in the American Federal System: The Mobilization of Public-Private Influence," *Continuing Crisis in American Politics,* ed. Marian D. Irish (Englewood Cliffs, N.J.: Prentice-Hall, 1963).

7. The following outline was suggested in part by Jane Perry Clark's important study, *The Rise of a New Federalism* (New York: Columbia University Press, 1938), which, as the first work to attempt to catalog the entire range of federal co-operative activities, established some essential guidelines that are still quite relevant.

8. See Grodzins, in *Goals for Americans, op. cit.,* for a discussion of this, and Kenneth E. Gray, "Congressional Interference in the Executive Branch" (Paper delivered at the annual meeting of the American Political Science Association, September 1962) for a detailed analysis of its operation at the federal level.

9. While no single date for the real beginning of the "twentieth century" is precisely accurate, 1913 is chosen as the most appropriate, since it was the first year of Woodrow Wilson's "New Freedom," which represented the first great and co-ordinated nationwide response to the problems of the new century and the beginning of a five-year period of great changes in American life.

10. A "critical election" has been defined as one in which substantial shifts occur in the voting behavior of major electoral blocs, shifts which become sufficiently "permanent" to set the voting patterns for a generation. The United States has experienced critical elections at the national level in pairs every twenty-four to thirty-two years. Every two generations, they have reflected a shift of the voting majority from one political party to the other.

11. The figures cited here and subsequently — unless otherwise indicated — are from the report of the Advisory Commission on Intergovernmental Relations, "Periodic Congressional Assessment of Federal Grants-in-Aid to State and Local Government" (June 1961).

12. See John Wells Davidson (ed.), *A Crossroads of Freedom* (New Haven: Yale University Press, 1956), the most complete edition of Wilson's campaign addresses available.

13. For a comprehensive review of federal-state relations under the formal grant-in-aid programs in this period and a discussion of the sectional bases for their support, see Austin F. Macdonald, *Federal Aid* (New York: The Macmillan Company, 1928). Statutes restricting these programs to rural areas have been progressively modified since 1921, reflecting the increased urbanization of American society. These first programs were primarily supported by the representatives of the generally rural and relatively poor Southern and Western states as a means for partial redistribution of the national wealth concentrated in the Northeast.

14. The story of how the draft was made a co-operative activity is told by Hugh Johnson in his autobiography, *The Blue Eagle from Egg to Earth* (Garden City, N.Y.: Doubleday, 1935). It is a highly significant illustration of the utility of the sharing system in a time of crisis.

15. See MacDonald, *op. cit.,* V.O. Key, *The Administration of Federal Grants to States* (Chicago: University of Chicago Press, 1937), for discussions of the development of these programs in the second period.

16. See Clarke Chambers, *Seedtime of Reform* (Minneapolis: University of Minnesota Press, 1963); U.S. Census Bureau, *Historical Statistics of the United States* (Washington, D.C., 1960).

17. Morton Grodzins discusses this in "American Political Parties and the American System," *Western Political Quarterly,* Vol. XII (December 1960), pp. 974-998.

18. A study of one such case which has become classic is Paul Ylvisaker's *The Battle of Blue Earth County* (Washington, D.C., 1950).

19. See George C.S. Benson, "Federal-State Personnel Relations," *The Annals,* Vol. 207 (January 1940), pp. 38-43.

20. Raymond S. Short, "Municipalities and the Federal Government," *The Annals,* Vol. 207 (January 1940), pp. 44-53; Robert H. Connery and Richard H. Leach, *The Federal Government and Metropolitan Areas* (Cambridge, Mass.: Harvard University Press, 1960).

21. See Clark, *op. cit.;* Key, *op. cit.,* for discussion of these developments.

22. A list of even the important publications on the subject of intergovernmental relations would be prohibitively long. There are, however, several good bibliographies that may be consulted, among them: *Intergovernmental Relations in the United States: A Selected Bibliography,* prepared for the Intergovernmental Relations Subcommittee of the Senate Committee on Government Operations (Washington, D.C., 1956); Glen L. Bachelder and Paul C. Shaw, *Federalism: A Selected Bibliography,* Michigan State University Institute for Community Development and Services, Bibliographic Series No. 1 (March 1964).

23. These studies included: The [Kestnbaum] Commission on Intergovernmental Relations, *A Report to the President with attachments* (Washington, D.C., 1955) and Joint Federal-State Action Committee, *Progress Reports* (Washington, D.C., 1957,1959). An excellent critique of the first study commission can be found in William Anderson, *The Nation and the States: Rivals or Partners?* (Minneapolis: University of Minnesota Press, 1955). The second is equally well treated in Grodzins, "Centralization and Decentralization in the Americal Federal System," *op. cit.* The first [Hoover] Commission on Reorganization of the Executive Branch of the Government also sponsored a study of federal-state relations by Mr. Hoover's own decision. The study report was prepared by Grodzins for the Council of State Governments and set forth the outlines of his later work on federalism, but the Commission's recommendations ignored his conclusions and called for a restoration of dual federalism. See *Federal-State Relations by the Council of State Governments* (Washington, D.C., 1949).

24. These studies included those of the [Fountain] Intergovernmental Relations Subcommittee of the House Committee on Government Operations issued in 1956 and those of the [Muskie] Intergovernmental Relations Subcommittee of the Senate Committee on Government Operations, issued beginning in 1963.

25. The contributions of this body are just now beginning to be felt. They have issued some eighteen reports to date, on a number of phases of intergovernmental relations, available from the Washington, D.C., offices.

Notes on a Theory of State Constitutional Change: The Florida Experience

William C. Havard

The tradition of the written constitution is so pervasive in American culture that opportunities for empirical observation of particular manifestations of its development are practically inexhaustible. The profusion of material may, however, tend to produce an exaggerated concern with detail and a resultant loss of feeling for essentials. This danger is much greater as it concerns state constitutional change than in the case of the Federal Constitution, because the stable content of the latter has tended to focus attention on informal change, thus producing a vast literature on constitutional law, a good portion of which involves a discussion of basic issues. By contrast, the fluidity of the written constitutions of the states[1] has caused attention to be centered on formal change, at least in the political science literature. A perusal of the commentaries indicates that they are, on the whole, less concerned with relating the changes to general conceptions of constitutionalism than with a narration of the process of change or a criticism of particular (and sometimes far from basic) policies established in the constitution. The very fact that the constitution is *written* apparently gives rise to the tendency to regard the documentary expression of principles as tantamount to their realization, thus affording a convenient means for avoiding debate on the broader problems of the relation of the written constitution to the *practice* of constitutionalism which takes place in the political unit.[2]

Despite the differences between the national and the state constitutions,[3] the two constitutional levels in the United States form part of a single structure of constitutionalism which makes them complementary rather than antithetical. This premise is true, at least if the doctrine of divided sovereignty on which federalism depends is still relevant to the American political system. If the state and national constitutions do form a continuum, then the standards by which the respective constitutional functions must be judged are the same and any example of constitutional change, whether state or national, formal or informal, should be considered in terms of these fundamentals. If it is not, the discussion of state constitutions is pointless, and our time could better be spent in determining how to overcome the remaining legal barriers which restrict access to national remedies in spheres of autonomous state action.

Nor is there any great difficulty in the discovery of these standards. On the contrary, the real problem may be that they occupy so habitual a place in the textbooks that their common sense content is practically lost.[4] Although there exists the possibility of making adjustments in their interpretation in the subsequent discussion, it may be said that the following is widely accepted as the standard: The constitution is defined as the basic or fundamental law, popular sovereignty, bestowal of powers, separation of powers, and the bill of rights.

Reprinted from *Journal of Politics*, Vol. 21 (Feb. 1959), pp. 80-104, by permission of the publisher.

The ascription of proper meaning to these concepts is not so easy as merely setting them out, especially in view of the fact that even though they may be inviolable in their generality, corollaries drawn from them are subject to change through historical experience. The idea that the constitution is a fundamental law, whether its source be a higher law or the generalization of certain portions of the ordinary law of the land, is more than a mere distinction between superior and inferior laws according to an hierarchical classification. It is an attempt to preserve the line between *gubernaculum* and *jurisdictio,* that is, between that plenitude of power which may be exercised by government in its capacity as legal sovereign and that area of law which is beyond the bounds of government. As such, it is a distinction on which limited government has depended since the Middle Ages.[5]

The American Declaration of Independence and the production of written constitutions, together with the transfer of sovereignty from the crown to the people which these acts entailed, added a new dimension to the distinction between fundamental and ordinary law. The principles of popular sovereignty and the bestowal of powers, which were thrust into the disputatious arena of constitutionalism by the American Revolution, meant that the legal sovereignty of government was not restricted merely in terms of areas of non-intrusion, but that the governmental organs themselves were created by and subject to direct control of the people and their powers were limited to those assigned them by the people.[6]

The introduction of written constitutions based on popular sovereignty, and operating on the principle that the structure and powers of government are deliberately allocated through the constitution, involved problems of the techniques by which the populace could articulate its constitution and hold the government so created to the terms of the constitution. For the first of these purposes, there was an early tendency to rely on the ordinary representative institution, the state legislature. Very soon, however, there appeared " two momentous ideas — that of the independent constitutional convention, and that of the submission of its handiwork to the people — . . . ";[7] and these ideas evolved into a satisfactory means of keeping constitution and government separated. Writing in 1915, Dealey found that the "really fundamental trend of change[in state constitutions]has been from a dominant legislature to a dominant electorate, working through a convention. "[8] With a somewhat casual disregard for some of the deficiencies of convention practice, the same writer later adds: "In its latest form, that of a body made up of delegates elected from districts of equal population, it is one of the greatest of our political inventions. Through it popular rights may be secured in the constitution, legislative tyranny restrained and power interests subordinated to the general welfare. "[9]

The techniques for securing compliance on the part of the government with the constitutional provisions ordained by the governed was sought through the institutional arrangements established in the constitution itself. The principle of popular sovereignty played a direct role through the establishment of regular elections of the representative agents who were to exercise their power within the constitutional framework. The main internal check was provided by the separation of powers and by the checks and balances which were assigned to each of the powers against the others. Bills of rights defined the old areas of personal inviolability against governmental action.

Time has modified some of these devices and brought new ones to supplement them: The concept of the "people" who are sovereign has broadened to the point at which the most serious claim of arbitrary legal exclusion from political participation is made on behalf of those under twenty-one years of age. The arrival of the political party system has beneficially weakened a perhaps unworkable complete separation of powers, has made the chief executive a representative figure, and has (where excessive conformity or the presence of a single controlling issue like racial integration has not stultified it) translated the vague idea of popular responsibility into something approaching actuality. And the development of constitutionalism at the hands of the courts, especially through the doctrine of judicial review, need only be mentioned to recall the scope of the change that has taken place in the remote phases of constitutionalism.

But if the changes in the remote or secondary characteristics of the constitutional system have been extensive, these alterations may be said to have been worked out from the immutable principles which lay at the foundation of the constitutional system. The changes effected might further be said to be implicit in the fundamentals and unfolded through historical experience as new sociological conditions were confronted. It is difficult to deny that there are basic propositions about American constitutionalism which, if abandoned or changed fundamentally, would lead at the very least to a different constitutional order than that which has hitherto existed. The distinction between constitution and government, popular sovereignty and the opportunity for its actual influence on the construction and maintenance of the constitutional form (including changes in its detailed content), and the principle of holding the government popularly responsible for operating within the constitutional framework[10] are indispensable for the conception of the system. The manner in which these principles are affected by a constitutional change is the measure not only of the adequacy of the constitution's efficient parts, but of the degree to which the constitution itself has been preserved.

II

The state of Florida has recently attempted to rewrite its constitution. Its efforts represent yet another of those recurrent movements for change; but as has been suggested, each experience of change or attempted change is a link in the chain of American constitutional history and merits consideration for its general as well as for its particular lessons.

The present constitution of the state was drafted in 1885. It was the fifth constitution to be adopted by the state and exhibits the usual deficiencies of state constitutions drafted in the middle and late nineteenth century.[11] Before considering the details of the efforts to revise, however, it is necessary to digress briefly in order to set the revision process in the relevant framework of politics, much of which is a part of the present constitution as it reveals itself through action.

V.O. Key deftly captured the most striking aspect of Florida politics in a single phrase when he said that in Florida it's "every man for himself."[12] In the absence of party or factional organizations which might exercise some degree of control over the selection of candidates and their stand on issues, Florida's political relations are highly personalized. Office politics predominate over issues in elections, with the result that policy is worked out interpersonally among the office-holders after the election. Extreme localism is a marked characteristic of most political campaigns (even the support of statewide candidates for offices such as governor tends to cluster heavily around the various candidates' home areas, especially in the first primary). And the alignment of office-holders (and particularly legislators) on issues appears to shift from issue to issue and to offer few patterns that would lend themselves to the usual classifications of political groupings according to degree of advocacy of governmentally-induced social change. In part, however, this appearance is deceptive since the structure of political institutions and the sociological characteristics of the state impose rather severe limits on the potential success of the non-conservative; and the social and/or economic "liberal" is a rarity among contemporary Florida office-holders.

Despite the appearance of consensus on many social and economic questions, a fundamental political division is perceptible in Florida. That division is between old Florida and new Florida, and it is complicated by being a two-fold division. On the one hand there is the distinction between North and South Florida, and on the other there is a rural-urban split, which has a close relation to the North-South problem but is not entirely exhausted by it.[13] North Florida is the "old" part of the state. It partook of the antebellum experience and remains Southern in its predominant ruralism and in the unresolved tensions which permit the race issue to override incipient political divisions along economic or other lines. Even North Florida cities like Jacksonville reflect certain political traits (such as an occasionally perceptible Populist tinge) which relate more to the general characteristics of the section than to the urban patterns of the cities further South along the Coast. By contrast, South Florida is new and is urban in both physical characteristics and in the background of its tourist-oriented, Yankee-dominated population.

Lacking in the large-scale industrial development that might in other, more slowly urbanizing parts of the South combine with a tradition of hill-farm resistance to produce a restrained duopolistic politics, South Florida has become a sort of American urban-frontier dream run wild. In addition to growing faster than any other Southern state, Florida has had by far the highest urbanization rate. From 1920 to 1950, the state's population pattern reversed itself, shifting from two-thirds rural to two-thirds urban. Dade County alone now contains a population twice the size of the 1920 urban population of the entire state. By contrast with a pastoral Eden, however, an urban paradise cannot be developed by a solitary Adam; governmental services are a necessity, and the diversity of activity and the scale on which the transformation is taking place demands that these services be institutionalized, *i.e.*, organized, regular, and free from the characteristic of a capricious social co-operation based on informal personal relations. The demand for this rational bureaucratization does not mean that politics and administration should become pervasive or even very active except perhaps in relation to municipal development; what is desired is "good government" of the National Municipal League type rather than the welfare state.

In fact, the rather negative attitude toward systematic governmental interference in private economic life which has been produced by a rural, personalized and locally influenced mode of state politics might suit the demands of urban Florida quite well, except for the handicaps that it imposes on the solution to urban problems. Consumer and tourist-based taxes may be extremely desirable from the standpoint of the more articulate metropolite in Florida, but an allocation of these resources which takes no account of population factors or the needs resulting from the development of metropolitan agglomerations is hardly suited to his taste or his pocketbook. In addition, the difficulty of securing a satisfactory hearing on the need for general legislation to deal with planning and related urban problems adds to the tension felt by urban Florida in the face of continued rural political domination.

The conditions of Florida politics adumbrated above are sustained by an institutional lag in the face of enormous social change. And the political beneficiaries of that lag are engaged in a very sturdy resistance against pressure for adjusting the institutions, even where failure to do so results in the implicit denial of propositions crucial to American democratic ideology.

Much of the prevailing style of politics rests on a self-perpetuating system of inequitable apportionment, combined with practices rooted in a simpler society of the past. The apportionment of the house of representatives prescribed by the 1885 constitution is extremely inflexible; the five most populous counties are assigned three representatives each, the next 18 have two each, and the remaining 44 have one each. The disproportion in size of the counties compared to the ratio of representatives means that a majority of the house is elected by less than 20 per cent of the state's population (1950 census), while the six largest counties, which elect less than 20 per cent of the house members, contain a majority of the population. The constitutional arrangement under which no county can elect more than one senator, and the reluctance of the legislature to effect reapportionment of the upper chamber mean that a similar disproportion exists there.[14] Population projections since 1950 indicate a steady regression in the proportion of the population electing a majority to each house.

Although the urban influence in the legislature is severely limited by this malapportionment, it is now generally recognized that the selection of a governor is largely the prerogative of the large counties, and particularly those of South Florida. The office of governor in Florida is, institutionally, a weak one. The governor is prohibited from succeeding himself immediately, and the hangover of restrictions imposed during a period of suspicion of executive power further restricts the governor's capacity to exercise the broad representative function which devolves upon the office. The executive powers are dispersed among a number of other elective offices, and a group of these officers have come to exercise a collective function which is unique in American state government. The secretary of state, attorney-general, treasurer, commissioner of agriculture, superintendent of education and the comptroller (along with the governor) form a recognized collegial executive known as the Florida "cabinet." The cabinet meets weekly and serves as the administrative head of a number of important state agencies. Although not all members of the cabinet serve on all the agencies, some or all of its members comprise such bodies as the budget commission, board of education, trustees of the internal improvement fund, board of institutions, etc. The governor's vote counts for no more than any other member's in these meetings, and individual members are often regarded as "the authority" in a particular administrative area. Although the officials who make up the cabinet are elected from the state at large, their political style is more closely related to the legislature's pattern of popular responsibility than to the governor's. The cabinet members are not restricted on self-succession; their re-election for term after term is practically certain (in only four cases since 1885 has an incumbent failed to be re-elected); they operate largely on the basis of support of their respective clientele; and their ties with the county officials are often quite close. Although their relations with the governor are usually cordial, the cabinet members may tend to look on him as a parvenu, and they have their own personal ties with members of the legislature whose positions are solidly based on their "expertness" and long tenure.

Another condition of Florida politics which tends to obscure the locus of political power is the tie-in between the courthouse cliques and the legislature. This connection is not easy to pin down; it is evidenced more by an elimination of alternative possibilities than by overt manifestation. There is a strong "local boy" tradition in Florida, and over half of the legislators have held or are currently holding positions that relate them very closely to their county courthouses. Futhermore, local legislation is an extremely important political factor in Florida; about two-thirds of the acts passed in a session are local laws or general laws of local application, a situation that makes for a great deal of reciprocity between local units and their legislators. And when it is considered that the great majority of Florida counties are rural or semi-rural (by contrast with the concentration of a great majority of the population in a few urban counties) the support that this method of operation offers to the interpersonal politics of the state is reasonably clear.

With a governor limited in his power to exert forceful legislative leadership, with no effective party leadership and with the widespread acceptance of the idea that the representative should function as an agent of his district, it is hardly surprising that the exercise of effective power in Florida government depends on skill in bartering for legislative votes, is *sub rosa* and is often concerned with negative rather than positive programs. That such a system of power exists is clearly discernible on the occasions when larger issues manage to intrude on an otherwise purposely quiescent political scene. And such is the case with the recent move for constitutional reform.

III

The active movement for constitutional reform in Florida began in the early days of World War II. The Florida State Bar Association has had a special committee at work on the problem for many years,[15] the League of Women Voters has taken an intense interest in the revision question, and a few members of the legislature have long been committed to press for change. Since 1949, these and other groups have united their efforts through an organization known as the Citizens Constitution Committee of Florida. Despite the fact that this committee publicized the case for revision widely[16] and pressures for revision have resulted in the introduction of proposals for change in every session of the legislature since the war, constitutional revision did not become a major political issue until 1954, when a constitutional crisis over succession to the governorship arose out of ambiguities in the language of the constitution.

Upon the death of Governor Dan McCarty in 1953, the president of the senate became acting governor (there is no office of lieutenant governor in Florida), but his status and tenure in office were open to question because the meaning of the constitution's pronouncements on succession are unclear to the point of outright contradiction.[17] Three cases were required to determine that the president of the senate succeeded in the capacity of acting governor only, that the unexpired term of the governor should be filled by election at the general election of November, 1954, and that the acting governor was not rendered ineligible to run in the election by reason of the constitutional prohibition against self-succession.[18]

In the subsequent primary election, two of the three candidates — Brailey Odham and Leroy Collins (the winner) — irrevocably committed themselves to press for revision. Acting Governor Charley Johns, the other candidate, responded indifferently to pressures for a stand in favor of constitutional reform. The candidates themselves and the positions they took on revision, were representative of the division of interests and issues in contemporary Florida politics. Johns is identifiable with the North Florida small country bloc whose political power rests on the disintegrated and personalized structure of politics and administration now in existence. Extensive constitutional revision would represent a threat to the power arrangement arising from these conditions. Consequently, from the point of view of those committed to the system, revision had to be side-tracked if possible; and if this were not possible, its potential impact had to be nullified. Collins, on the other hand, is fairly typical of the emerging political figure of statewide proportions in Florida. His support is drawn primarily from the urban counties (especially South Florida), and his politics may loosely be described as those of the enlightened conservative. From this point of view, constitutional revision would represent an opportunity to realize "good government," *i. e.,* to further the institutionalization of political and administrative action, and for the urban areas to secure legislative representation and a role in government commensurate with their relative sociological position in the state. Odham, who lost in the first primary, shared Collins' concern for improvement in the formal organization of the government, but appeared to be more of a "liberal" (in the peculiarly American usage of the term) than Collins, with overtones of Populism — a declining force in Florida politics — in his appeals.

Collins assumed the office of governor in January, 1955, and pressed the case for revision at the legislative session of that year. The leading small county senators were opposed to the idea of revision, and the legislature flatly rejected the governor's proposal for the establishment of a constitutional commission with authority to report its draft directly to the people.[19] Despite this setback Collins continued the fight for the creation of a constitutional commission, and was backed in his effort by increasing newspaper and pressure support. After a number of compromise proposals had been introduced, a resolution creating a commission was finally passed by the legislature.[20] It subsequently became clear that the enactment was no victory for the group pushing for effective constitutional change; instead it was a strategic concession by the legislature which solidified the defensive forces of the supporters of the *status quo* and deprived the reformers of all initiative in proposing changes in the constitution.

The Florida Constitution Advisory Commission was composed of 37 members. The 18 members of the legislative council were included in this number, the governor appointed eight members, the chief justice of the supreme court appointed five members, the board of governors of the Florida bar appointed five members, and the attorney general was made a member. About three-quarters of the Commission was made up of legislators or former legislators. Additional protection against the loss of legislative control over the process of revision was provided by requiring that the recommendations of the Commission be reported back to the legislature for final disposition at the 1957 session. The Commission was also enjoined to preserve the full meaning and effect of certain parts of the old constitution, the most important being the Declaration of Rights and several fiscal provisions, including such controversial items as the $5000 homestead exemption, the prohibition of state bonded indebtedness, the formulas for distributing gasoline and parimutuel betting tax receipts to the counties, and the ban on the personal income tax. The contributions of the homestead tax exemption program and the prohibition of a tax on income to the financial problems of growing urban areas and to a regressive tax structure, respectively, require no further comment. And the distribution of the parimutuel tax receipts on the basis of an equal amount to each of the sixty-seven counties and of the Second Gas Tax (a tax of two cents of each seven cents per gallon) on the basis of a formula established in 1931[21] are even more symptomatic of the control of the state's fiscal resources by a rural minority in the legislature and of political habits which rely on the continuation of this control.

The Commission's activities were carried out with a due regard to proper form. An appropriation of $100,000 was made for its work, and a staff organization which included research personnel was set up to assist it. The Commission was divided into six committees, and the task of preparing preliminary drafts of various parts of the revision was distributed among them. Later the Commission met in a series of plenary sessions to review and coordinate the work of the committees.

A political observer with a gift for satire would have uncovered a wealth of material in following the work of the Commission. A great effort was made to ensure an atmosphere that reflected the qualities of statesman-like deliberation. A splendid touch was added by the inclusion of "consultants" from the universities in the plenary sessions, and special care was taken to keep the meetings open to the public and later to solicit opinions on the draft.[22]

The real forces behind the deliberations always moved near the surface, however, and occasionally erupted openly. There was no evidence to show that the reports assembled by the research personnel in cooperation with the universities had been read by the members of the Commission, and any suggestion of drawing upon the experience of other states was cursorily dismissed. Although invited to speak on any point, the consultants invariably faced an atmosphere of resigned patience if they attempted to make any interjection, even on a technical point and however brief. Almost every question was settled off the tops of the members' heads; but where help was needed the 1885 Constitution became a sort of Delphic Oracle for these wise men, and a heated controversy could be stayed immediately by the question, "What does the old constitution say about this?" This reluctance to move any great distance from the 1885 constitution was sustained by the omnipresent shadow of the legislature which hovered over the assemblage. Any excessive zeal for change could be quickly and effectively deflated by the suggestion that "the boys in the legislature will never stand for that."[23]

Despite these limitations debate was fulsome, even if confined to a relatively small proportion of the membership.[24] The Southern accents of the members from the rural counties of North Florida became thicker and thicker as they defended the institutional arrangements already in existence against the threats of anarchy and tyranny embedded in even the mildest of proposals for change. The ghost of Huey Long was evoked as an appropriate answer to suggestions for change in the executive powers or tenure of office, although the applicability of this example to Florida was never quite clear. The antipathy toward the urban areas of South Florida was manifested in recurrent remarks by certain members about "the free state of Dade" (Miami).

The Commission continued its pattern of deferring to the form of constitutional change by publishing its recommendations, together with a *Handbook* explaining the changes that had been effected shortly after the conclusion of its deliberations in early 1957. Although the Commission improved the draftsmanship and organization of the constitution, relatively few substantive changes were recommended. A new, and slightly more flexible system of apportionment of the house of representatives was included, under which each county would continue to have at least one seat and additional seats would be assigned on the basis of a gradually increasing population increment, with the scale leveling out at four representatives for the first 175,000 people in a county, plus an additional representative for each 150,000 persons above that figure. Under this plan the proportion of the population required to elect a majority of the house would be raised by about three per cent. The Commission also recommended increasing the number of senate seats from 38 to 42 and added a provision requiring that future apportionments of the senate include the three smallest districts. The Commission preserved the provision of the old constitution whereby the governor may convene the legislature in an extraordinary session of indefinite length if it fails to reapportion itself during the regular session at which decennial reapportionment is scheduled. But it also added a provision allowing the governor to adjourn the extraordinary reapportionment session after sixty days and certify to the state supreme court the failure of the legislature to reapportion itself; whereupon the court would reapportion.[25]

The Commission added a lieutenant governor to the list of elective officials and provided at length for the conditions of succession to the governorship, especially in cases of physical or mental incapacity of the governor.[26] A provision was added to the local government article extending to the counties the power to enact ordinances having the force of law.[27] Although the commission draft eliminated the provision of the old constitution extending authority to call a convention for revising the constitution, it added a section permitting popular initiation of constitutional amendments.[28] The terms of the constitutional initiative provision (petition by five per cent of the electors of each of at least 45 of the 67 counties) would, however, provide a considerable deterrent to the possibility of securing action on matters (like apportionment) which are so closely related to the rural-urban division.

The Commission did not really come to grips with the most serious problems confronting the state: the situation of the cities and the possibilities of home rule were discussed at length but to no avail; nothing was done about the disintegration of executive authority and the proliferation of constitutional boards and agencies; the central problem of local legislation was practically untouched; and the handling of the crucial question of equitable representation was characteristically evasive. Like Don Quixote, the Commission sallied forth in full public view to tilt with windmills and disperse harmless flocks of sheep; but unlike the intrepid Knight of the Sorrowful Figure, the Commission showed no disposition to confront and vanquish real dragons and redress old grievances.

IV

The work of the Commission may properly be characterized by suggesting that it performed the negative function of substituting the form of constitutional revision for its substance in the hope of pacifying a considerable popular demand for change. In its review of the work of the Commission, on the other hand, the legislature seized the opportunity afforded by the occasion of over-all constitutional change to take positive action designed to bolster the institutions and political practices which had developed under the old constitution and to protect these arrangements against the possibilities of popular depredation in the future.

The transition on the part of the legislature from the position of permitting the constitution to be revised (under close scrutiny and as a sort of placatory gesture) to one of utilizing revision as a means of consolidating the existing power structure was due in no small part to the concatenation of political circumstances attendant upon the 1957 session of the legislature. A debilitating struggle over reapportionment had taken place during the extraordinary reapportionment session which was called by Governor Collins after the legislature failed to reapportion in the regular session of 1955. The tension between the governor and the legislature which resulted from this impasse on reapportionment was increased by the differences between the governor and a majority of the legislature which arose during a special session of 1956 over the proper method of dealing with the problems of race relations.[29] The deterioration in executive-legislative relations resulting from those developments produced a noticeable solidarity within the ranks of the small county representatives and strengthened their determination not to yield to executive leadership and systematically to consolidate their control of the legislature. More by accident than design, certain house members from large counties who were closely identified with the governor had occupied positions of leadership in the 1955 session and had utilized the built-in advantages that these positions afford to promote the governor's program during that session. The situation was reversed in 1957; the small county representatives made a self-conscious resurgence which succeeded in sweeping away nearly all vestiges of large county control of the main offices of the house and of the committees most concerned with issues on which the urban and rural representatives were divided. Remarks to the effect that "big county boys" would never again be elected to positions of leadership were frequently heard. In addition, the two members of the house who had been identified most closely and influentially with the movement for revision were no longer in the legislature, one having resigned to run for governor in 1956 and the other having been killed in an automobile accident. Consequently, neither the psychological state of the assembly nor the general alignment of political forces yielded hope for the survival of even the mild changes proposed by the Commission, let alone those encouraging a trend toward substantial alteration of the constitution.

Nor were these unfavorable prospects belied by subsequent events. The committees on constitutional revision in the two houses were heavily weighted on the side of the small counties of North Florida, and they showed no disposition to readjust the balance of political forces. Although the governor, the chairman of the constitutional commission and others closely associated with the movement for change appeared before the committee, their reception ranged only between the extremes of barely-disguised hostility and an attitude of legislative self-sufficiency in which outside suggestions might be tolerated but were never encouraged. The legislature was unable to complete its consideration of the Commissions' draft during the regular session, largely because of an inability to decide such questions as the form to be used in refusing to do anything substantial about apportionment. A ten-day special session in October, 1957, was sufficient to settle the remaining problems and report the legislative draft of a proposed constitution.[30]

The legislative draft followed the organizational pattern set by the Commission's draft,[31] but a substantial number of changes took place in the content of the proposals. Compared to the present constitutional structure, three main categories of change are discernible in the legislative proposals: (1) certain of the new provisions are designed to weaken the powers of the governor to the advantage of the legislature and the cabinet; (2) other alterations place severe limits on the possibility of revising the constitution except under conditions which allow the legislature to determine the content of the change; and (3) some of the changes aim at fixing in the constitution certain accepted policies which either support existing political practices or reflect the contemporary legislative position on these issues.

The first category covers by far the most extensive changes. To a reader familiar with the old constitution and the practices under it, the consistency and subtlety with which the legislative draft formalizes an "executive council" check on the single executive and limits the possibilities for the exercise of executive leadership of the legislature in certain areas is striking. Under the 1885 constitution the cabinet system was extra-constitutional, although latterly the compilers have given their own constitutional sanction to the usage by heading certain sections with phrases in which the word "cabinet" is used.[32] By contrast the legislative draft is unequivocal on this score; it consistently employs the word "cabinet" to define the collective executive in Florida and names the governor as a member of this body.[33] Nor is this change one of nomenclature only; several modifications of the existing arrangements appear to aim at solidifying the position of the cabinet. In cases in which the old constitution established administrative boards composed of the governor and only part of the cabinet, for example, the legislative draft includes the entire cabinet as the agencies' administrative authority.[34] In addition, the power of the governor under the 1885 constitution to appoint the Game and Fresh Water Fish Commission, subject to senate confirmation, is transferred by the legislative draft to the cabinet.[35] Further confirmation of the intent implied by these changes is the inclusion in the legislature's proposals of a provision whereby "the legislature may authorize any board composed entirely of cabinet members to appoint a director of any department under the supervision of such board."[36]

Three changes are apparently aimed at specific features of the separation of powers which allow the governor to thwart the legislative will on certain matters. Given the malapportionment in Florida and the increasing recognition of the governor's function as statewide representative, these proposed changes raise interesting questions with regard to the so-called "group basis" of American politics, a mode of politics apparently favored by a large body of pragmatically oriented political scientists in this country who are able to indulge in the naturalistic fallacy without the hindrance of conscience, logic or the criticism of colleagues. The first of these changes would deny the governor the power to hold the legislature in extraordinary reapportionment session indefinitely by allowing the legislature to adjourn such a session by concurrent resolution at the end of 60 days.[37] Although the efficient cause of this proposal may have been Governor Collins' action in technically holding the legislature in reapportionment session from the fall of 1955 to the general election of November, 1956, its total effect is far-reaching. If it were adopted, the governor would be deprived of one of his most potent weapons as a representative figure — an effective institutional means for rallying public opinion against a clear-cut violation of constitutional responsibility on the part of the legislature. One of the few persuasive counterpoises to the capacity of a small group to deny a basic premise of representative government would thereby be removed.

Another change along the same lines would require the governor to give the legislature two days notice in writing before he could exercise his power to adjourn a session on the grounds that the two houses had not agreed upon a time for adjournment.[38] This alteration was obviously leveled at Collins' action in the 1956 special session which he adjourned during a brief recess in order to avoid the passage of an interposition resolution.[39]

A final change along these same lines is the stipulation in the legislative draft that the Supreme Court, subject to its rules of procedure, shall permit "interested persons" to be heard on questions presented by the governor for an advisory opinion and that such opinion shall not be rendered earlier than ten days from docketing unless a delay would cause public injury.[40] Although less obviously directed at the incumbent than the two preceding examples, it still may easily be inferred that this attempt to turn every gubernatorial request for an advisory opinion into a proceeding in litigation is due to Governor Collins' request for judicial advice on two occasions during the extraordinary reapportionment session of 1955-1956.[41]

Other changes serve to bring any future constitutional revision securely under the protective wing of the legislature. The first broadens the capacity of the legislature to revise by amendment by allowing the legislature to tie amendments together so that an amendment does not become effective unless popular approval is given to one or more other specified amendments at the same time.[42] Although the possibility that this change affords for legislative revision, together with the precedent of the present attempt at revision, would probably preclude the use of the convention in the future, a concession to the idea is made by including a provision for calling a convention in the legislative draft. This provision is carefully hedged about, however, to avoid the possibility that a future convention's work will escape legislative review. Although the proposals allow a convention to be called by two-thirds vote of each house, a three-fourths vote in each house is required to permit its draft to be submitted directly to the people. Otherwise, the convention's work would come back to the legislature, where a three-fifths vote in each house would be required for submission of the revision to the voters, and its amendment would require the approval of three-fourths of each house. The cumbersomeness of this procedure hardly adds to the potentiality of its utilization.[43]

In the category of provisions designed to fix certain policies that support present practices or reflect the contemporary legislative position on specific issues, the apportionment sections of the legislative draft are the most interesting. Even the modest proposals of the constitutional commission met with little favor

from the small county legislators, and the apportionment provisions which ultimately passed the legislature are remarkable in their tendency to give the appearance of compromise without yielding anything to the demand for equitable representation. In both houses the present basis of apportionment is retained, and the
appearance of adjustment is made by increasing the membership of both houses.
As was anticipated, the legislature was hostile to the Commission's plan to use
the supreme court as an apportioning agency, so the legislative draft continues
to leave apportionment in legislative hands. In the house of representatives, the
guarantee to each county of a representative is retained, as is the practice of
assigning a fixed number of representatives to the various counties according to
their population rank-order. The new plan would allot to the five most populous
counties five representatives each, the next two four each, the next seven three
each, the next 23 two each, and the remainder one each. Although this plan would
raise the house membership from the present 95 to 114, it would leave the proportion of the population required to elect a majority of the house practically un-
changed. Based on the 1950 population, the newly constituted house would contain
a majority elected by 19 per cent of the state's population; and the regressive nature of the proposal is indicated by the fact that if the 1956 estimate is used, the
proportion of the population electing a majority would decline to a little over 16
per cent. Comparison with the present situation reveals a remarkable coincidence
in the proportions based on the 1950 census and in the relative decline of the representative proportions (based on 1956 estimates) under the present plan and that
proposed by the legislature.

The senate apportionment plan offered by the legislature cannot be appraised
in terms of the change that it might produce because there is no arbitrary assignment of seats as in the house. In this case, too, the general provisions of the draft
are very similar to the old constitution, except that the number of senators is
raised from 38 to 45. The retention of the arrangement which prohibits the assignment of more than one senate seat to any county would alone be sufficient to limit
severely the possibility of apportioning senate seats on a population basis; even so,
the legislative draft takes the precaution, or arrogates to itself the impertinence,
of adding a clause which allows reapportionment to be "based upon population and
such other pertinent factors as may be determined by the legislature . . ." [44]

In another alteration the legislature indicated that it was prepared to increase rather than lessen the dependence of the local units upon the legislature,
with all that this dependence implies in the way of interpersonal political relations
between courthouse and capitol. The legislative draft accepted the Commission's
proposal for extending ordinance-making powers to the counties, but it added that
such powers should be extended by local law only and that the legislature could
amend or repeal the ordinance. [45]

In other actions of a similar vein, the power to punish for contempt was
extended to interim committees of the legislature,[46] possibly as a bulwark for the
work of certain interim committees which have been active in investigating race
relations. The policy stand of the legislature on the racial integration question is
more clearly exhibited in its retention of constitutional provisions prohibiting miscegenation and requiring segregation in the public schools.[47] Two legislative changes
in the proposed revision offer further attestation to the attempt to contravene by
state constitutional action the implications of the decision in *Brown v. Board of*

Education of Topeka.[48] The legislative draft includes a provision permitting the legislature to provide emergency assistance for nonsectarian schools,[49] and the constitutional provision authorizing support for a federally recognized national guard is made permissive rather than mandatory.[50]

The foregoing discussion should not be taken to imply that the proposed revision contains no substantive proposals other than those which seek to bolster a questionable style of politics and the policies which are nearest and dearest to the hearts of its central figures.[51] Several of the proposed changes in detail have much to commend them to the impartial observer: the establishment of the office of lieutenant governor, the authorization of a legislative auditor, the removal of some county offices from the constitution (particularly the elimination of dual administrative supervision over the county school system), the authorization for local units to enter cooperative contracts with other governmental units, and the addition of a few items to the list of local law proscriptions are changes that would appeal to most proponents of substantial reform. But these changes are the exceptions and are trivial when weighed against the general tendency of the legislative draft, which is typified by the types of change discussed at length above.

V

Florida's experience with constitutional revision is an illustration of the way in which the unfolding of constitutional practice may lead, particularly in the face of extensive sociological change, to a need for a change in many of the corollaries (or remote aspects) of the fundamental (or proximate) principles of the constitution. It also illustrates that these corollary aspects are so effectively related to the fundamentals (as means to ends) that they may implicitly deny the immutable propositions of the constitutional system even while giving verbal assent to them.

Three tendencies are discernible in the Florida experience which have serious implications for fundamental constitutional principles: (1) the tendency to depreciate the meaning of a fundamental law by blurring the distinction between constitution and government; (2) the tendency to make the constituent function exclusively a legislative one; and (3) the tendency to preserve certain details of the constitution which, under changed sociological conditions, prevent the fulfillment of the principle of popular responsibility and against which the impetus for constitutional reform was directed.

It almost goes without saying that these tendencies are only logically separable; empirically they are so closely interdependent as to form a whole. If they are applied against the description of the process of revision and the current political situation in Florida, little elaboration on them is necessary. The depreciation of the idea of a fundamental law is more than a mere failure to distinguish clearly between what is constitutional and what is statutory material, much of which may vary from time to time. Neither is there any doubt that the constitution under consideration would, if adopted, retain the status of superior, if not fundamental, law. What is more pertinent is that most of this document is compounded of legislative will rather than of long-accepted fundamentals emanating from a sovereign people. That certain traditional limitations are carried over is not enough; the fact that these and other more detailed limitations are largely self-imposed by the legislature implies a merging of government and constitution that is contrary to basic constitutional precepts. This first tendency reveals itself fully only through the second one, for the legislature was extremely careful to avoid losing control of the revision process at any point. In this case there is a reversion from the felt necessity for an independently constituted representative institution as a means of popular articulation of a constitution, and a return to the idea that a regular instrument of government — the legislature — is sufficient to represent the sovereign popular will both in the drafting of the basic law and in carrying out its provisions. And the denial of direct popular influence in the positive aspect of constitutional preparation imposes a severe limitation on the possibility of recovering the full meaning of popular sovereignty and its concomitant, the popular responsibility of government. Malapportionment, the denial of the representative character of the chief executive (together with the explicit rejection of the idea of a single responsible executive),[52] and other institutional arrangements provided by the legislative proposals tend to limit by constitutional prescription some of the most important means for holding government to popular accountability for its operation under the constitution.

Under the terms of the proposed revision, the Florida voters were to be given an opportunity to vote on the legislative draft in the November, 1958, general election. The proposals were to be submitted in the form of article-by-article piecemeal amendments, but there would have been no opportunity to accept parts of the draft while rejecting others because a "daisy-chain" arrangement was in effect whereby the defeat of a single article would have had the effect of rejecting all of them.[53] In the meantime, however, the Florida Supreme Court invalidated this method of constitutional revision on the grounds that it was an improper circumvention of the section of the constitution which requires complete revision to take place through a convention and that the "daisy-chain" technique would eliminate the right of origination of revision by the people.[54] Although the opportunity for comprehensive revision remains open in Florida as a result of this decision, the possibility of going beyond the legislative draft is still a moot one. And the mere opportunity for popular approval or rejection of this draft would appear to be of relatively little consequence for the practice of constitutionalism in Florida anyway, since so much of the practical effect of the proposed revision serves merely to strengthen the current mode of politics in the state. The legislative draft is an instrument of radical conservatism which answers a demand for change by proposing alterations which threaten the principles on which the requirements of change are based even more clearly than do the existing arrangements. The opportunity for the public to reject the revision has little meaning in the absence of an opportunity to influence the content of change. The counsel of Burke to the effect that "a state without the means of some change is without the means of its conservation" is very appropriate to the situation in Florida, as it is in many other states undergoing similar experiences. And for those who are seriously concerned for the future of American federalism the meaning is even clearer, because the conservation of the place of the states in the general system depends largely upon the capacity of the states to keep their particular systems in order. There is, after all, an adequate alternative.

NOTES

1. In his *Methods of State Constitutional Reform* (University of Michigan, Michigan Governmental Studies, 1954), No. 28, p. 15, Albert Sturm indicates that 134 constitutions have been in use during the course of development of the states and that the 48 constitutions then in use had more than 3000 amendments added to them.

2. A closely related development is the legalism of written constitutions which tends to substitute the question of the *existence* of political powers for their beneficent *use* as the basic problem involved in the attempt to control government. On this point see, Edward S. Corwin, "The Constitution as Instrument and as Symbol," *American Political Science Review*, XXX (1936), 1077.

3. Many of these differences (the greater length of state constitutions, etc.) are related in part to the impermanence of their written portions as compared with the federal basic law, but a real or presumed distinction is sometimes made on the delegated-reserved power division, the national constitution being a power-granting instrument and the state constitutions becoming of necessity power-limiting instruments. *E.g.*, Sturm, *op. cit.*, pp. 1-2.

4. One of the clearest expressions of these fundamentals (without apparent loss of meaning for the author at any rate) is in W. Brooke Graves, *American State Government*, fourth ed. (Boston, 1953), Chap. 2.

5. See the revealing analysis of Bracton's ideas on this question in Charles H. McIlwain, *Constitutionalism: Ancient and Modern* (Ithaca, 1947), p. 77 *ff.*

6. McIlwain's presentation of Thomas Paine's Analysis of the early American constitution, *Ibid.*, p. 9, is the simplest and clearest formulation known to the writer. It is also interesting to note that the constitution of Massachusetts, which is the oldest constitution still in use in the United States (1780) and was the first constitution to be drafted by a convention, is divided into two major parts — the Declaration of Rights and the Frame of Government — rather than articles, a usage which would reflect the preservation of the ancient restrictions in the area of *jurisdictio* as well as the deliberate construction in the constitution of the organs of government and a restricted definition of their powers. Others of the early state constitutions were also drafted in this style.

7. Allan Nevins, *The American States During and After the Revolution,* 1775-1789 (New York, 1924), p. 175.

8. James Quayle Dealey, *Growth of American State Constitutions* (Boston, 1915), p. 256.

9. *Ibid.*, p. 258. With due regard for the idealization of the convention which is contained in this statement of Dealey's, his remark on the same page, to the effect that "few

seem to realize the importance of the constitutional convention in American state governments, " is even more apposite today than at the time of writing.

10. One of the reasons the separation of powers has been extensively modified without basic harm to American constitutionalism is that it was an inadequate structural substitute (based, of course, on a premature interpretation of the British constitution) for more effective means of translating constitutional responsibility into actuality. Yet the very fact that this structural arrangement has been taken to be practically synonomous with the principle it sought to realize in practice has given the separation of powers a tenacious constitutional grip on the governmental institutions of this country. This experience is a good illustration of the general acceptance of the premise of immutable principles, even if there is often a failure to distinguish what they are.

11. For a survey of its defects see: Manning J. Dauer and William C. Havard, "The Florida Constitution of 1885 — A Critique," *University of Florida Law Review,* VIII (Spring, 1955), 1-92. Reprinted as *Studies in Public Administration No. 12,* Public Administration Clearing Service, University of Florida. The main weaknesses are defective draftsmanship, narrow confinement of policy, and excessive amendment.

12. V.O. Key, *Southern Politics in State and Nation* (New York, 1950), p. 82.

13. Most of the discussion in the present section derives from William C. Havard and Loren P. Beth, *Rural Politics in an Urban State: A Study of the Florida Legislature* (Unpublished Manuscript). Other sources useful for appraising political factors which can only be alluded to here are Herbert Doherty, Jr., "Liberal and Conservative Voting Patterns in Florida," *Journal of Politics,* XIV (August 1952), and H. D. Price, *The Negro and Southern Politics* (New York, 1957).

14. A comparative study of apportionment of state legislatures using the standard applied here indicates that, on a composite ranking of the two houses, Florida is at the bottom of the list. See, Manning J. Dauer and Robert G. Kelsay, "Unrepresentative States," *National Municipal Review* (December, 1955), 571-575.

15. The Bar Association Committee has published two drafts of *A Proposed Constitution for Florida* (1947, 1949).

16. The Committee published a series of pamphlets *(e. g. , The Citizens Constitution Committee of Florida,* 1950; *Three Recommendations for Constitutional Revision in Florida,* 1951; and *Florida: 1954 and the Constitution of 1885,* 1954), and its meetings have always had a good press. Since its inception its membership has been sizeable, broadly representative of various sociological groups and fairly influential politically, but not sufficiently so to overcome the combination of public inertia and direct political opposition that stood in the way of revision.

17. The Florida *Constitution,* Article IV, Section 19, provides that under the usual conditions of vacancy in the office, ". . . the powers and duties of Governor shall devolve upon the President of the Senate *for the residue of the term . . ."* The last

sentence of the section provides, however, that if there should be a general election for the legislature during such vacancy, *"an election for Governor to fill the same shall be had at the same time."* (Italics supplied).

18. *State* ex rel. *Ayres v. Gray,* 69 So. 2d 187 (Fla., 1953); *State* ex rel. *West v. Gray* 20 So. 2d 471 (Fla., 1954), and *Bryant v. Gray,* 70 So. 2d 581 (Fla., 1954).

19. See the retrospective survey of the political line-up on revision in the Jacksonville, *Florida Times-Union,* October 13, 1957.

20. H.C.R. 555, 1955.

21. The formula gives equal weight to area, population and proportionate county contribution to road construction prior to the passage of the amendment. *Constitution,* Article IX, Section 16. The formula thus bears only the slightest relation to needed road construction or to other considerations (such as ability to pay) that might validly be entertained in allocating such funds.

22. See the note on the rear cover of the *Recommended Constitution for Florida (undated),* published by the Commission.

23. The Florida experience bears out Bennett M. Rich's criticism of the tendency of constitutional commissions to work almost entirely within a narrow framework of consideration of what the legislature might or might not accept. See his "Convention or Commission?" *National Municipal Review,* XXXVII (1948), 133 *ff.*

24. The plenary sessions were not fully attended and a number of those attending did so spasmodically. A sizeable proportion of those present appeared to take at best a limited interest in what was going on.

25. *Recommended Constitution for Florida,* Art. III, Secs. 4-8.

26. *Ibid.,* Art. IV, Sec. 10.

27. *Ibid.,* Art. VII, Sec. 7.

28. *Ibid.,* Art. XII, Sec. 4.

29. Havard and Beth, *op. cit.,* chaps II and V.

30. *Revised Florida Constitution Proposed by the Legislature and Explanation of Changes* (Tallahassee: Issued by the Secretary of State, undated). Hereinafter cited as *Legislative Draft.*

31. In place of the twenty articles of the old constitution plus an unnumbered Declaration of Rights, the commission and legislative drafts consisted of fourteen articles. Although the proposed new constitution is considerably better than the 1885 document in terms of general organization, clarity, consistency and grammatical construction,

there was no extensive deletion of detail. It is estimated that the new draft still contains over 35,000 words. In addition certain anomalies persist, such as the carryover in Article XIV of all the special provisions for local government contained in the 1885 constitution.

32. *E.g.*, Art. IV, Sec. 20 in the 1957 compilation is headed "Governors Cabinet"; Art. IV, Sec. 27, "Report of Cabinet Officers"; and Art. IV, Sec. 29, "Salaries of Cabinet Officers." The body of the constitution, however, refers to the cabinet as "administrative officers" who are to assist the governor (Art. IV, Sec. 20); and even where the entire cabinet is to serve as an administrative board for a state agency, the usage is "The Governor and the administrative officers of the Executive Department. . ." (Art. IV, Sec. 17). Inclusion of the word "cabinet" dates from 1941.

33. *Legislative Draft,* Art. IV, Sec. 4. It is interesting to note that the legislative draft drops the usage "governor's cabinet" in favor of the simple term "cabinet."

34. Such is the case with the Pardon Board, *ibid.*, Art. IV, Sec. 1 (a) and the Board of Education, Art. X, Sec. 2.

35. *Ibid.*, Art. IV, Sec. 16. The same section also provides that the cabinet (rather than the commission as is now the case) shall appoint the executive director of this department, an arrangement that certainly gives rise to the question of who is the real administrative superior.

36. *Ibid.*, Art. IV, Sec. 6.

37. *Ibid.*, Art. III, Sec. 2 (d). The commission had recommended that the governor should adjourn the legislature after sixty days and certify the failure of the legislature to reapportion to the supreme court, following which the supreme court would reapportion. The legislature made very short work of this proposal.

38. *Ibid.*, Art. III, Sec. 2. (f). The present Constitution, Art. IV, Sec. 10, contains the usual general provision for executive adjournment in the absence of agreement between the two houses on a time for adjournment.

39. *House Journal* of the Special Session, 1956, pp. 173 and 177, August 1, 1956.

40. *Legislative Draft,* Art. IV, Sec. 8.

41. In one instance the Governor was advised that he had the constitutional power to veto a reapportionment bill, Fla. 81 So. 2d 782 (1956); in the other the court decided that he had the power to call a special session during a recess of the reapportionment session, Fla. 22 So. 2d 131 (1956).

42. *Legislative Draft,* Art. XII, Sec. 1. The same section, although specifically confining each amendment to one article of the constitution, allows related provisions in other articles to be included within an amendment dealing with any particular article.

43. *Ibid.*, Art. XII, Sec. 4.

44. *Ibid.*, Art. III, Sec. 4. Italics supplied. The attention of the legislature has frequent-
    ly been called to its failure to abide by the present constitution's mandate, Art. VIII,
    Sec. 3, that the senatorial districts be "as nearly equal in population as prac-
    tical, . . ."

45. *Legislative Draft,* Art. VII, Sec. 6.

46. *Ibid.*, Art. III, Sec. 7.

47. *Ibid.*, Art. II, Sec. 16 and Art. X, Sec. 8.

48. 347 U.S. 483 (1953).

49. *Ibid.*, Art. X, Sec. 1.

50. *Ibid.*, Art. XI, Sec. 5.

51. Although the proposition that the revision seeks *only* to perpetuate the prevailing
    system may not be entirely true; the negative of this proposition — that the revision
    does nothing to interfere with the main aspects of the prevailing mode of politics —
    appears to be quite correct.

52. Although the idea cannot be developed here, there is much evidence to show that some
    of the factors in the revision under consideration are consciously aimed at the pre-
    vention of the formation of factions or parties based on important divisions of interest
    and principle.

53. H.J.R. 32X of the special session of October, 1957.

54. *Rivera-Cruz v. Gray; Pope v. Gray,* 104 So. 2d 501 (Fla., 1958). In the November
    election the voters approved a separate amendment which permits the use of the
    "daisy-chain" in future votes on amendments.

THE SOCIOECONOMIC ENVIRONMENT

Social and Economic Factors and Negro Voter Registration in the South

Donald R. Matthews
James W. Prothro

The vote is widely considered the southern Negro's most important weapon in his struggle for full citizenship and social and economic equality. It is argued that "political rights pave the way to all others."[1] Once Negroes in the South vote in substantial numbers, white politicians will prove responsive to the desires of the Negro community. Also, federal action on voting will be met with less resistance from the white South — and southerners in Congress — than action involving schools, jobs, or housing.

Such, at least, seems to have been the reasoning behind the Civil Rights Acts of 1957 and 1960, both of which deal primarily with the right to vote.[2] Attorney General Robert F. Kennedy and his predecessor, Herbert Brownell, are both reported to believe that the vote provides the southern Negro with his most effective

Reprinted from *American Political Science Review*, Vol. 57 (1963), pp. 24-44, by permission of the authors and publisher.

This study has been supported by a grant from the Rockefeller Foundation to the Institute for Research in Social Science of the University of North Carolina. The first named author holds a Senior Award for Research on Governmental Affairs from the Social Science Research Council. We wish to express our gratitude to these organizations for providing the resources needed to engage in this analysis. Professors V. O. Key, Jr., Warren E. Miller, and Allan P. Sindler have commented generously upon an earlier version of this paper. Professor Daniel O. Price afforded us the benefit of his counsel on statistical problems throughout the preparation of the article. While we have learned much from these colleagues, neither they nor the organizations named above should be held responsible for the contents of this article.

means of advancing toward equality, and recent actions of the Justice Department seem to reflect this view.[3] Many Negro leaders share this belief in the over-riding importance of the vote. Hundreds of Negro registration drives have been held in southern cities and counties since 1957.[4] Martin Luther King, usually considered an advocate of non-violent direct action, recently remarked that the most significant step Negroes can take is in the "direction of the voting booths."[5] The National Association for the Advancement of Colored People, historically identified with courtroom attacks on segregation, is now enthusiastically committed to a "battle of the ballots."[6] In March, 1962, the Southern Regional Council announced receipt of foundation grants of $325,000 to initiate a major program to increase Negro voter registration in the South.[7] The Congress of Racial Equality, the NAACP, the National Urban League, the Southern Christian Leadership Conference, and the Student Nonviolent Coordinating Committee are among the organizations now participating in the actual registration drives.

While the great importance of the vote to Negroes in the South can hardly be denied, some careful observers are skeptical about the extent to which registration drives can add to the number of Negroes who are already registered. Southern Negroes overwhelmingly possess low social status, relatively small incomes, and limited education received in inferior schools. These attributes are associated with low voter turnout among all populations.[8] The low voting rates of Negroes in the South are, to perhaps a large extent, a result of these factors more than a consequence of *direct political* discrimination by the white community. Moreover, the low status, income, and education of southern whites foster racial prejudice.[9] Thus poverty and ignorance may have a double-barrelled effect on Negro political participation by decreasing the Negroes' desire and ability to participate effectively while increasing white resistance to their doing so. Negro voting in the South is not, according to this line of argument, easily increased by political or legal means. A large, active, and effective Negro electorate in the South may have to await substantial social and economic change.

Despite the current interest in the political participation of southern Negroes, the literature of political science tells us little about the factors which facilitate or impede it. A theoretical concern as old as political science — the relative importance of socio-economic and political factors in determining political behavior — is raised when one addresses this problem. Can registration drives, legal pressures on the region's voter registrars, abolition of poll taxes, revision of literacy tests, and similar legal and political reforms have a significant impact on Negro registration in the former confederate states? Or do these efforts deal merely with "super-structure," while the social and economic realities of the region will continue for generations to frustrate achievement of Negro parity at the ballot box? Social scientists owe such a heavy, if largely unacknowledged, debt to Karl Marx that most would probably assume the second alternative to be more valid. But the tradition of James Madison, recognizing the importance of social and economic factors but also emphasizing the significance of "auxiliary" governmental arrangements, offers theoretical support for the former possibility.

A single article cannot hope to answer such a broad question, but we can attack part of it. In this article we offer a detailed analysis of the relationships between variations in rates of Negro voter registration in southern counties and the social and economic characteristics of those counties. While we shall not be directly concerned with political variables, the analysis has an obvious relevance for their importance. The more successful the explanation of the problem with socio-economic variables, the less imperative the demand to examine political and legal factors. Alternatively, if we can account for only a small part of the variance with socio-economic factors, the stronger the case for abandoning socio-economic determinism and adding political and legal variables to the analysis. [10]

I. THE DATA AND THE APPROACH

While the literature offers no comprehensive effort to account for variations in Negro voter registration in the South, previous studies of southern politics suggest a number of specific influences. Drawing upon this literature, we collected data on 20 social and economic characteristics of southern counties (counting Virginia's independent cities as counties). Some of these items, such as per cent of population Negro or per cent of population urban, could be taken directly from the U.S. Census. Others, such as per cent of nonwhite labor force in white collar occupations or white and nonwhite median income, were derived from census figures but required calculations of varying degrees of complexity for each county. Still other items, such as per cent of population belonging to a church or the number of Negro colleges in each county, came from noncensus sources.[11] Since our focus is on Negro registration, 108 counties with populations containing less than one per cent Negroes were excluded from the analysis. All other counties for which 1958 registration data were available by race were included.[12] This selection procedure gave us a total of 997 counties for the analysis of Negro registration and 822 for the consideration of white registration.[13]

While this represents the most massive collection of data ever brought to bear upon the problem of political participation by southern Negroes, it is subject to several limitations.

To begin with, the measure of the dependent variable is two steps removed from a direct measure of the voting turnout of individuals. Registration rather than voting figures had to be employed because they are available by race whereas the number of Negroes actually voting is not known. This tends to exaggerate the size of the active Negro electorate since, for a number of reasons, some registered Negroes seldom if ever exercise their franchise. Moreover, voting lists in rural areas are often out of date, containing the names of many bonafide residents of New York, Detroit, and Los Angeles, to say nothing of local graveyards. In some states, the payment of a poll tax is the nearest equivalent of voter registration and numerous exemptions from the tax make lists of poll tax payers not strictly comparable to the enfranchised population. Finally, statewide statistics on voter registration (or poll tax payment) by race are collected only in Arkansas, Florida, Georgia, Louisiana, South Carolina and Virginia. In the remaining states, the number of registered Negro voters must be obtained from estimates made by county registrars, newsmen, politicians, and the like. Nonetheless, when analyzed with caution, the sometimes crude data on Negro voter registration can throw considerable light on Negro voting in the South.

The measure of the dependent variable is further removed from the actual behavior of individuals in that it consists of the percentage of all voting age Negroes who are registered to vote in each southern county. This employment of *areal* rather than *individual* analysis narrows the question we can examine. Rather than an unqualified examination of the relationship of social and economic characteristics to Negro registration, the effort must be understood to focus on the relationship of social and economic characteristics of given areas (counties) to variations in Negro registration among those areas. Accordingly, the data furnish no evidence of the sort afforded by opinion surveys directly linking political behavior to individual attributes. But they do permit conclusions linking varying registration rates to county attributes. Compensation for the loss of the former type of evidence is found in the acquisition of the latter type, which cannot be secured from surveys because they are conducted in a small number of counties. Our approach maximizes what we can say about counties, then, at the same time that it minimizes what we can say about individuals.

Another limitation stems from the fact that our measures capture an essentially static picture of both the characteristics of southern counties and of the relationship of their characteristics to variations in Negro registration. If data were available on Negro registration, at the county level, for earlier points in time, the analysis could be geared principally to rates of change. Only since the creation of the Civil Rights Commission, however, have adequate county registration data become available. We are necessarily limited, therefore, to analysis based on *areal* rather than *temporal* variation.

A final limitation lies in the statistical approach employed here, which is that of correlation and regression analysis.[14] The coefficient of correlation *(r)* is a measure of the association between different variables when each variable is expressed as a series of measures of a quantitative characteristic. The value of the measure varies from 0 (no association between independent variables) to 1.0 (one variable perfectly predicts the other). A positive correlation indicates that as one variable increases the other also increases; a negative correlation indicates an inverse relationship — as one variable increases, the other decreases. We shall first consider simple correlations, describing the association between per cent of Negroes registered and each of the social and economic characteristics of southern counties. In order to make a better estimate of the independence of these relationships, we shall also present partial correlations, which measure the remaining association between two variables when the contribution of a third variable has been taken into account. Finally, we shall employ multiple correlation *(R)* in order to determine the strength of association between all our independent variables and Negro registration.

While these measures are efficient devices for determining the strength and direction of association between the variables with which we are concerned, a caveat is in order. Correlations do not reflect the *absolute level* of the variables. Thus, a given amount and regularity of change in Negro registration will produce the same correlation whether the actual level of Negro registration is high or low. Only for the more important variables will we look beneath the correlations to examine the level of Negro registration.

In the analysis which follows, we shall first consider the development of Negro registration and compare the distribution of white and Negro registration rates. Then we shall examine the correlations between a battery of social and economic variables and Negro voter registration in order to determine the extent to which the former are predictive of the latter for the South as a whole. The same social and economic factors will be correlated with the registration rate of whites to ascertain the extent to which the factors are related to voter registration in general, rather than to Negro registration alone. Finally, the multiple correlation between all the social and economic variables and Negro voter registration will be presented, and conclusions and implications will be drawn from the analysis.

Table 1 Estimated number and per cent of voting age Negroes registered to vote in 11 Southern states, 1940-60.

Year	Estimated Number of Negro Registered Voters	% of Voting Age Negroes Registered as Voters
1940	250,000	5%
1947	595,000	12
1952	1,008,614	20
1956	1,238,038	25
1958	1,266,488	25
1960	1,414,052	28

Sources: Derived from U.S. Census data on nonwhite population and Negro registration estimates in G. Myrdal, *An American Dilemma* (New York, 1944), p. 488; M. Price, *The Negro Voter in the South* (Atlanta, Georgia: Southern Regional Council, 1957), p. 5; Southern Regional Council, "The Negro Voter in the South — 1958," *Special Report* (mimeo.), p. 3; U.S. Commission on Civil Rights, *1959 Report and 1961 Report,* Vol. I, "Voting."

II. NEGRO VOTER REGISTRATION: AN OVERVIEW

Immediately after *Smith v. Allwright* declared the white primary unconstitutional in 1944, the number and proportion of Negro adults registered to vote in the southern states increased with startling speed (Table 1). Before this historic decision, about 250,000 Negroes (5 per cent of the adult nonwhite population) were thought to be registered voters. Three years after the white primary case, both the number and proportion of Negro registered voters had doubled. By 1952, about 20 per cent of the Negro adults were registered to vote. Since then, however, the rate of increase has been less impressive. In 1956, the authoritative Southern Regional Council estimated that about 25 per cent of the Negro adults were registered. Four years, two Civil Rights Acts, and innumerable local registration drives later, the proportion of Negro adults who were registered had risen to only 28 per cent. Of course, the fact that Negroes held their own during this period is a significant accomplishment when one considers such factors as heavy outmigration, increased racial tensions stemming from the school desegregation crisis, the adoption of new voter restrictions in some states, and the stricter application of old requirements in other areas.

Figure 1 shows the 1958 distribution of southern counties according to level of voter registration for Negroes and whites. The point most dramatically demonstrated by the figure is that Negro registration is still much lower than white registration. In 38 per cent of the counties, less than 20 per cent of the adult Negroes are registered, whereas less than 1 per cent of the counties have so few whites registered. Indeed, the most common (modal) situation for Negroes is a registration below 10 per cent of the potential; the most common situation for whites is a registration in excess of 90 per cent. Nevertheless, the range of Negro registration

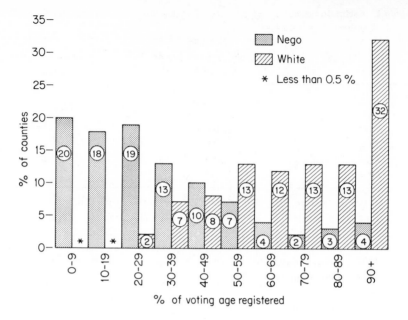

Figure 1 White and Negro registration rates in southern counties.

in the South is sizeable; in a significant minority of cases, the level of Negro registration compares favorably with that of white southerners.

III. SOCIAL AND ECONOMIC CORRELATES OF NEGRO REGISTRATION

What accounts for the wide variation in Negro voter registration rates? The simple correlations between the per cent of the voting age Negroes registered to vote and 20 social and economic characteristics of southern counties are presented in the first column of Table 2.[15]

Negro Concentration   In most political settings, the concentration of an ethnic or occupational group in a geographical area provides reinforcement of common values sufficient to produce more active political participation. But southern Negroes are in a peculiarly subordinate position. And the larger the proportion of Negroes in an area, the more intense the vague fears of Negro domination that seem to beset southern whites. Thus in virtually every study of southern politics, the proportion of Negroes in the population has emerged as a primary explanatory variable.[16]

It is not surprising, therefore, that the per cent of Negroes in the county population in 1950 is more strongly associated with the county's rate of Negro registration than any other social and economic attribute on which we have data. The

Table 2 Correlations between county social and economic characteristics and per cent of voting age Negroes registered to vote, by country, in 11 southern states.

County Characteristics	Simple Correlations (r)	Partial Correlations, Controlling for Per Cent Negro, 1950
Per cent of nonwhite labor force in white collar occupations	+.23	+.15
Nonwhite median school years completed	+.22	+.01
Nonwhite median income	+.19	+.02
Per cent of total church membership Roman Catholic	+.15	+.10
Per cent increase in population, 1940–50	+.08	.00
Per cent of labor force in manufacturing	+.08	+.09
White median income	+.08	−.03
Per cent of population urban	+.07	−.02
Percentage point difference in per cent population Negro, 1900–50	+.04	−.02
Per cent of total church membership Jewish	+.004	+.01
Difference in white-nonwhite median school years completed	−.02	−.02
Difference in white-nonwhite median income	−.02	−.05
Number of Negro colleges in county	−.05	+.01
Per cent of total church membership Baptist	−.10	−.07
Per cent of population belonging to a church	−.17	+.01
Per cent of labor force in agriculture	−.20	−.07
White median school years completed	−.26	−.15
Per cent of farms operated by tenants	−.32	−.13
Per cent of population Negro in 1900	−.41	−.01
Per cent of population Negro in 1950	−.46	—

Note: No tests of significance are reported in this paper since the correlations are based upon a complete enumeration rather than a sample.

negative value of the simple correlation (−.46) verifies the expectation that smaller proportions of Negroes register in those counties where a large percentage of the population is Negro. This does not mean, however, that the decline in Negro registration associated with increasing Negro concentration occurs at a constant rate. If the relationship between these two variables is examined over the entire range of southern counties, we see that increases in the proportion Negro from 1 per cent to about 30 per cent are not accompanied by general and substantial declines in Negro registration rates (Figure 2). As the proportion Negro increases beyond 30 per cent, however, Negro registration rates begin to decline very sharply until they approach zero at about 60 per cent Negro and above. There would seem to be a critical point, at about 30 per cent Negro, where white hostility to Negro political participation becomes severe.

One reason Negro concentration is such a powerful explanatory factor in

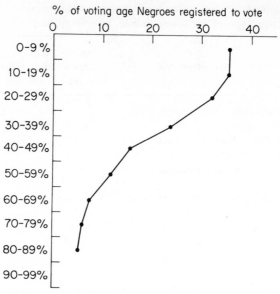

Figure 2   Median % of voting age Negroes registered to vote by % of county population
Negro in 1950: 11 Southern states

analyzing southern politics may be that it is related to so many other social and
economic characteristics of the region's counties. The simple correlation between
per cent Negro in 1950 and per cent of farms operated by tenants is +.49; the correlation with non-white median income is −.40; with non-white school years completed, −.47; with per cent of the labor force in agriculture, +.30; with per cent
of the total population belonging to a church, +.38. Such characteristics as these
are in turn related to variation in rates of Negro voter registration. It is possible
that these related factors rather than Negro concentration, viewed largely as an
index of white attitudes, account for −.46 correlation between per cent Negro and
per cent registered to vote.

The partial correlations between Negro registration and Negro concentration, controlling separately for the contribution of all other county characteristics,
reveals that this is not the case: Negro registration in southern counties goes down
as the proportion of Negroes goes up regardless of the other characteristics of
the counties. Only one county characteristic is so closely related to both Negro
registration in 1958 and Negro concentration in 1950 that the strength of their association drops when its contribution is taken into account — and this characteristic
is an earlier measurement of the same independent variable. Controlling for per
cent of Negroes in the population in 1900 reduces the correlation between 1950 Negro concentration and registration to −.21. Even with this control, the independent
tendency of Negro registration to decrease in counties currently containing more
Negroes is not eliminated, though it is reduced substantially.

Let us be clear on what a partial correlation does. It is designed to give us,
as indicated above, the strength of association between two variables that remains
after the contribution of a relevant third variable is taken into account. But when

the third variable is introduced into the equation, so are all of the additional hidden variables that are associated with it. The magnitude of the partial correlation will accordingly be reduced not only by any contribution of the third variable to the association between the two original variables, but also by any contribution of factors that are associated with the third variable. This means that, when we attempt to examine the contribution of a third variable by computing partial correlations, we can be certain about its contribution only when the results are negative. That is, if the partial correlation is not much smaller than the simple correlation, we can be sure that the third variable is not responsible for the magnitude of the simple correlation. When the partial correlation is substantially smaller, however, we cannot conclude that the third variable *alone* is responsible for the magnitude of the simple correlation. It happens in the present instance that almost all of the county characteristics are similarly associated with Negro concentration in both 1900 and 1950. As a result, virtually all of the factors that contribute slightly to the correlation of Negro registration with 1950 Negro concentration are added to the contribution that 1900 Negro concentration makes to the correlation. The result is that Negro concentration in 1900 *and the hidden factors related to it* account for about half of the magnitude of the association between 1950 Negro concentration and Negro registration.

Before we conclude that Negro concentration at the turn of the century is as important as mid-century Negro concentration for current variations in Negro registration, we need to consider both the nature of the two measures and the detailed relationships of the variables. The two measures are of the same county characteristic, differing only in the point in time from which they were taken. And the characteristic they reflect cannot reasonably be thought to act directly on Negro registration. Today's lower rates of Negro registration in counties where Negroes constitute a larger portion of the population certainly do not stem from any tendency of Negroes to crowd one another out of registration queues! Even more evident is the fact that the percentage of Negroes in a county's population over half a century ago cannot have a direct effect on current rates of Negro registration. Both measures appear to be indexes of county characteristics (most importantly, white practices and attitudes on racial questions) that are of direct consequence for Negro registration.

The 1900 measure was included in the analysis on the assumption that practices and attitudes produced by heavy Negro population may persist long after the Negroes have died or left for more attractive environs. Earlier research has suggested that Negro concentration around the turn of the century — when southern political practice was crystallizing in its strongly anti-Negro pattern — may be as important as current Negro concentration for rates of Negro political participation.[17] Since the proportions of Negroes in different southern counties have not decreased at uniform rates (and have even increased in some counties), the measures at the two points in time afford an opportunity to test this hypothesis. And it seems to be supported by the fact that Negro concentration in 1900 is almost as highly (and negatively) correlated with Negro registration (-.41) as is Negro concentration a half century later. This large simple correlation, added to the decrease in the correlation between 1950 Negro concentration and registration when 1900 Negro concentration is controlled, is impressive evidence of the stability of southern racial practices. The virtual absence of correlation (+.04) between Negro

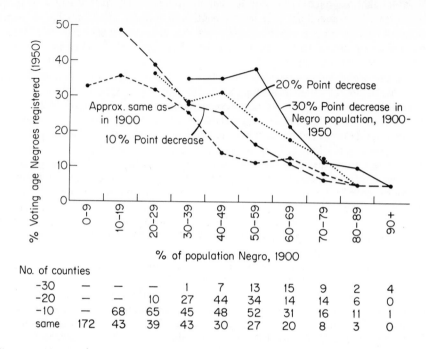

No. of counties

	0-9	10-19	20-29	30-39	40-49	50-59	60-69	70-79	80-89	90+
-30	—	—	—	1	7	13	15	9	2	4
-20	—	—	10	27	44	34	14	14	6	0
-10	—	68	65	45	48	52	31	16	11	1
same	172	43	39	43	30	27	20	8	3	0

Figure 3 Median % of voting age Negroes registered to vote, by county Negro concentration in 1900 and % point change since 1900.

registration and the percentage point difference in the proportion of population Negro between 1900 and 1950 seems to point to the same conclusion.[18]

It would be a mistake, however, to conclude either that 1900 Negro concentration is as important as 1950 Negro concentration for Negro registration, or that decreases in Negro concentration are not associated with increasing Negro voter registration. When we reverse the partialling process, and control for Negro concentration in 1950, the correlation between current Negro registration and 1900 Negro concentration disappears (it becomes -.01). The 1900 simple correlation accordingly seems to come from stable racial practices that in turn reflect a large measure of stability in Negro concentration and related county characteristics. The 1900 Negro concentration in itself has no autonomous relationship to present rates of Negro registration.

Moreover, decreases in Negro concentration are not as inconsequential as they would appear from the small simple correlation obtained from percentage point decreases. The lack of correlation seems to be an artifact of our crude measure. The largest percentage *point* decreases in Negro population have occurred in counties with very high Negro proportions in 1900, and most of these counties still have heavy concentrations of Negro population. When one looks at the relationship between registration and decreases in Negro concentration, holding constant the proportion of the population Negro in 1900, several heretofore hidden relationships emerge (Figure 3). (1) In counties with heavy (over 70 per cent) Negro concentrations in 1900, decreases in the proportion Negro seem to make little difference — their Negro concentration was still relatively high in 1950 and the proportion of Negroes registered is negligible. (2) In counties with relatively few (less than 30 per cent) Negroes in 1900, rates of Negro registration tend to be high whether a decline in the proportion Negro was experienced or not. A decline in Negro concentration in these counties, however, is associated with a somewhat higher rate of Negro registration than in those counties where the division of the two races remained approximately the same between 1900 and 1950. (3) In counties with moderate (30 to 70 per cent) Negro concentrations in 1900, a decline in Negro concentration is clearly related to higher Negro voter registration. Moreover, the larger the decrease in the Negro population percentage, the higher the registration. The average county in this moderate group with a 30 percentage point decrease in Negro proportions has a voter registration rate double or triple that of the average county which did not experience significant change in the numerical balance between colored and white inhabitants.

The proportion of the county population which is Negro is the single most important social and economic factor for explaining its rate of Negro voter registration. The -.46 correlation accounts for about 20 per cent (r^2) of the variation in Negro registration rates, an unusually high explanatory power for any variable in the complex world of political and social relationships. But it leaves room for considerable fluctuation in registration rates unrelated to the per cent of Negroes in the population. This "unexplained" fluctuation may be the result of random and idiosyncratic factors, of political variables[19] which have been excluded from this analysis, or the result of the operation of other social and economic factors. In the remainder of this paper we shall examine this last possibility.

Negro Attributes   The higher the educational level, occupation, or income of a person, the more likely he is to participate actively in politics: these are among the more strongly supported generalizations in contemporary research on political participation.[20] Moreover, these three factors are probably a pretty good index of the size of the county's Negro middle class. It is widely believed by students of Negro politics that the low rate of voter registration by southern Negroes is partly the result of a lack of leadership.[21] Only when there is a pool of educated and skillful leaders whose means of livelihood is not controlled by whites can sufficient leadership and political organization develop to ensure a relatively high rate of Negro registration in the South.

Our data support both lines of argument. The three largest positive correlations with Negro voter registration are per cent of the nonwhite labor force in white collar occupations (+.23), the median number of school years completed by nonwhites (+.22), and the median income of nonwhites (+.19). These are simple correlations, however, and fairly small ones at that. It is quite possible that they are largely, if not entirely, the result of some third factor associated both with Negro registration rates and with Negro education, occupation, and income. The large negative correlation of Negro concentration with Negro registration suggests that the percentage of the population Negro in 1950 is the most likely prospect as a key third variable. This expectation is heightened by the fact that it is also substantially correlated with Negro school years completed (-.47), income (-.40), and white collar workers (-.23). When controls are introduced for per cent of Negroes in the population (see the second column of Table II), the positive association of Negro registration with both income and education is reduced almost to the vanishing point. Thus Negro income and education levels are intervening variables, which help to explain why more Negroes are registered in counties with fewer Negroes in their population. But in themselves, they have no independent association with Negro registration; in the few counties with large Negro concentrations but high Negro income and education, no more Negroes are registered than in similar counties with lower Negro income and education.

The explanatory power of our occupational measure — the per cent of the nonwhite labor force in white collar occupations — is also reduced when per cent of Negroes is taken into account, but to a much lesser degree. It becomes +.15. While this is a small partial correlation, it is one of the higher partials obtained in this study while controlling for the important factor of Negro concentration. The proportion of the employed Negroes in white collar jobs does, therefore, have a small but discernible independent association with Negro voter registration.

Moreover, small increases in the proportion of Negro white collar workers are associated with large increases in Negro voter registration (Figure 4), and these higher rates cannot be amply attributed to the registration of the white collar workers themselves. A very small increase in the size of the Negro middle class seems to result in a substantial increase in the pool of qualified potential leaders. Middle class Negroes are far more likely to register, and they in turn appear to stimulate working class Negroes to follow their example. The average southern county with 1 per cent of its nonwhite labor force in white collar jobs has only 4 per cent of its voting age Negroes registered to vote; at 5 per cent white collar, 15 per cent of the Negroes are registered, and so on, each percentage point increase in white collar occupation being associated with a 3 to 4 percentage point increase in voter registration. This trend continues until 12 per cent of the nonwhites are in white collar jobs and 42 per cent of the potential Negro electorate is registered. After this point, additional increases in the proportion of Negroes in white collar jobs are no longer associated with increases in voter registration; indeed, voter registration actually declines as per cent white collar increases. Perhaps when the Negro middle class becomes fairly large, it tends to become more isolated from other Negroes, more preoccupied with the middle class round of life, less identified with the black masses.[22] A sharpening of class cleavages within the Negro community may lead to some loss of political effectiveness. Even so, this decline in effectiveness is not enough to wipe out the added increment from jobs to registered votes; it merely declines from 3 or 4 votes for every white collar job to about 2.

Despite the independent association of Negro white collar employment with voter registration, the correlations between Negro registration and Negro education, income, and occupation are far smaller than many of the correlations between Negro registration and the characteristics of the white-dominated community. The level of Negro voter registration in southern counties is far less a matter of the attributes of the Negro population than of the characteristics of the white population and of the total community. The rest of our correlations, therefore, are with community and white characteristics rather than with Negro attributes.

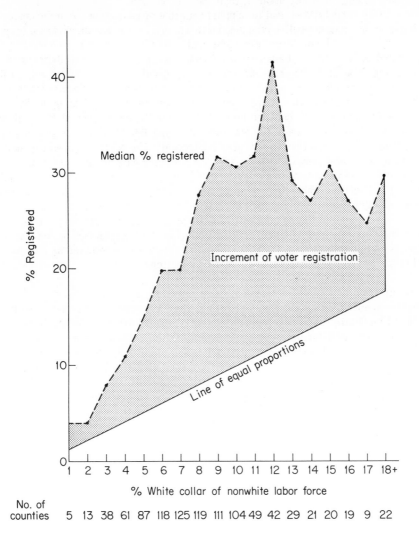

Figure 4 Median % of voting age Negroes registered to vote, by % of nonwhite labor
  force in white collar occupations.

The Agrarian Economy   It is widely believed that the South's relatively poor
agricultural economy contributes to the low levels of Negro political participation
in the region.[23] People living in poverty are unlikely candidates for active citizenship anywhere. The Negroes' economic dependence upon local whites in the rural

South serves as a potent inhibition to those few who are not otherwise discouraged from voting. Rural whites are both more hostile to Negro voting and in a better position to do something about it than their urban kin.

Our correlations tend to support this line of reasoning. Two measures included in the analysis reflect the degree to which a county has an agrarian economy — the per cent of labor force in agricultural employment and the per cent of farms operated by tenants.[24] The negative relationship of both these attributes to Negro voter registration (-.20 and -.32, respectively) indicates that Negro registration is lower in the old-style agrarian counties. But the region's Negro population is still primarily rural: the simple correlation between per cent in agriculture and per cent Negro is +.30; between farm tenancy and Negro concentration, +.49. Are these two characteristics of the counties still associated with low Negro voter registration when Negro concentration is controlled? The partial correlation between farm tenancy and Negro registration is -.13 when Negro concentration is controlled; between per cent in agriculture and registration it is reduced even further to -.07. There is, therefore, some tendency for Negro voter registration to decline as agricultural employment and farm tenancy increase which holds true even when differences in Negro concentration from one county to the next are taken into account. Nonetheless, it is a far less important factor than Negro concentration and is no more important than the size of the Negro middle class as a factor explaining Negro participation and non-participation.

Urbanization and Industrialization   If the South's agrarian economy tends to discourage Negro registration and voting, then industrialization and urbanization should facilitate them. The urban-industrial life is more rational, impersonal, and less tradition-bound; both Negroes and whites enjoy more wealth and education; the Negroes benefit from a concentration of potential leaders and politically relevant organizations in the cities. The urban ghetto may provide social reinforcement to individual motivations for political action. Many other equally plausible reasons might be suggested why urbanization and industrialization should foster Negro registration.[25] Our southwide correlations, however, cast serious doubt upon the entire line of reasoning.

The simple correlations between the per cent of the county population living in urban areas and Negro registration is a mere +.07; between per cent of the labor force in manufacturing and Negro registration the correlation is +.08. When partial correlations are figured, controlling for Negro concentration, the association between urbanization and Negro registration completely disappears, a fact which suggests that the initial +.07 simple correlation may be largely the result of the low proportion of the urban population which is Negro and associated factors. The partial correlation between per cent in manufacturing and Negro registration goes up slightly to +.09 when controls for Negro concentration are added. Partial correlations figured after controlling for many other social and economic variables do not significantly increase either correlation.

What accounts for these surprising findings? One possible explanation is the imperfections of the statistical measures we have employed. The 1950 census definition of "urban," for example, includes all places of 2,500 plus the densely settled fringe around cities of 50,000 or more. Many "urban" places in the South are therefore exceedingly small. From the potential Negro voter's point of view,

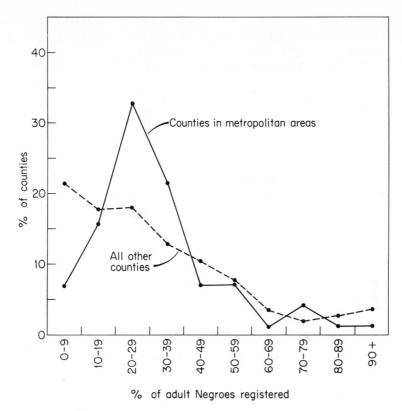

Figure 5 Median % of voting age Negroes registered to vote in metropolitan and other areas.

it may make little difference whether he lives in a town of 5,000 or in the open country, but one place is classified as "urban" and the other as "rural." Moreover a county with a relatively small population concentrated in two or three small towns may possess a higher "urban" percentage than a very large county with a medium-sized city in it. A more meaningful classification of counties along an urban-rural dimension might possibly lead to different results.

It seems plausible to assume, however, that if urbanization does facilitate Negro voter registration, the effect should be particularly clear in the region's largest urban complexes. If the Negro registration rates of the 70 counties contained in the South's Standard Metropolitan Areas [26] are compared with registration rates for the non-metropolitan counties (Figure 5), we note that the "metropolitan" counties are far more likely to have from 20 to 40 per cent of their voting age Negroes registered than the other counties. Moreover, there is a tendency for counties in larger metropolitan areas to have slightly higher registration rates than counties in less populous SMAs. However, the metropolitan counties have smaller concentrations of Negroes than the rural and small town counties. Do these relationships hold true when comparisons are made between metropolitan and non-metropolitan counties with approximately the same proportion of Negroes

Table 3 Median percent of voting age Negroes registered to vote in counties within standard metropolitan areas and all other counties, by level of Negro concentration.

% Negro in pop. 1950	Counties in SMAs of over 200, 000 pop.	Counties in SMAs of less than 200, 000 pop.	Counties not in SMAs
%	%	%	%
0-9	25. 0(6)	28. 8(11)	37. 7(236)
10-19	45. 0(11)	30. 0(12)	35. 7(133)
20-29	30. 0(6)	35. 0(6)	32. 2(153)
30-39	24. 0(6)	23. 8(7)	23. 8(142)
40-49	—	15. 0(5)	15. 9(110)
50-59	—	—	12. 0(78)
60-69	—	—	8. 1(50)
70-79	—	—	5. 8(22)
80-89	—	—	5. 0(4)
Total Counties	(29)	(41)	(928)

within their boundaries? Table 3 indicates that the answer is no: there is no meaningful difference in the rate of Negro registration between metropolitan and non-metropolitan counties when Negro concentration is controlled. Thus, neither "urbanism" nor "metropolitanism," as crudely defined by the census categories, appears to be independently related to high Negro voter registration.

The very low correlation between per cent of the labor force in manufacturing employment and Negro voter registration appears to be the result of other considerations. The word "manufacturing" conjures up images of the "New South" — with belching smokestacks, booming cities, and bulging payrolls. For the South as a whole, this is a quite misleading picture. While manufacturing in 1950 was associated with somewhat higher income for both Negroes and whites (the correlation between per cent in manufacturing and median income was +.19 for both races), it was not primarily an urban phenomenon (the correlation between per cent in manufacturing and per cent urban was +.08), nor was it associated with rapid population growth (the correlation with population increase between 1940 and 1950 is +.05). Manufacturing was negatively correlated with school years completed by both whites and Negroes (-.14 and -.05, respectively). This kind of low-wage manufacturing centered in relatively stable, small towns is not very strongly associated with growing Negro voter registration. It is possible that the recent industrialization of the region — electronics as opposed to home production of chenille bedspreads, for example — may be quite differently related to Negro participation. So few counties have this new type of industry that they tend to be hidden by the bedspreads in a county-by-county correlation.

While our analysis should not be taken as the last word on the subject, it does strongly suggest that urbanization and industrialization are vastly overrated as facilitators of Negro voter registration. Urbanization and industrialization may provide necessary conditions for high levels of Negro political participation but, by themselves, they are not sufficient to insure them.

White Educational Levels   If, as we have argued, Negro registration rates in the South respond far more to the characteristics of the white community than to the attributes of the Negroes themselves, then it seems reasonable to expect Negro voter registration to be positively correlated with white educational levels. Numerous studies have shown that racial prejudice and discrimination tend to be related to low levels of formal education.[27] Where the whites are relatively well educated, there should be less resistance to Negro political participation and, therefore, more Negro voter registration.

    Just the opposite is the case for the South as a whole. The correlation between median school years completed by whites and Negro voter registration is -.26, one of the largest negative correlations obtained in this study. When the education of whites in a county increases, Negro voter registration in the county tends to decrease.

    How can we account for this unexpected finding? In view of the surprising nature of the relationship, the first expectation would be that it is merely a reflection of some third variable which happens to be related both to Negro registration and to white education. If so, it should disappear when other factors are held constant. But the correlation holds up surprisingly well when other variables are controlled: only one of the other social and economic characteristics of southern counties reduces the correlation at all. The third variable is, once again, Negro concentration in the population. With Negro concentration in 1950 controlled, the partial correlation between white educational level and Negro registration is -.15; controlling for Negro concentration in 1900 produces a partial correlation of -.16. While these are substantial reductions, the partial correlations are among the largest obtained after controlling for the extraordinarily important factor of Negro concentration. The strong correlation (+.30) between Negro concentration and median school years completed by whites is almost as unexpected as the correlation between Negro registration and white education. The whites in the black belt counties tend to be better educated — at least quantitatively — than other white southerners. And regardless of the percentage of Negroes in the population, fewer Negroes are registered in counties where whites have more education.

    A second explanation for the negative relationship between white education and Negro registration might be that their relationship is curvilinear: at the lower educational levels, increases in white median school years might be associated with declining rates of Negro registration but, at higher educational levels, the relationship might be reversed. If this were the case, then the overall negative relationship would be a result of the generally low educational levels of the South, concealing the fact that the few counties with high white educational levels had the highest rates of Negro registration. Figure 6 suggests only a moderate tendency in this direction. As the number of school years completed by whites goes up through the primary and secondary grades, the proportion of voting age Negroes registered declines.[28] In the very few counties in which the average white adult has completed high school or received some higher education, the trend reverses

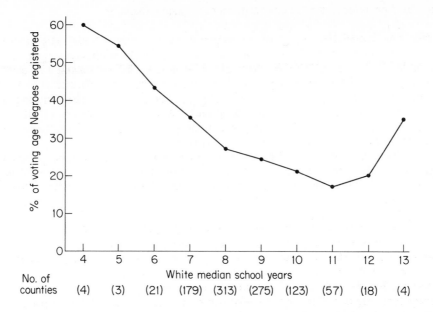

Figure 6 Median % of voting age Negroes registered to vote, by median school years
completed by whites in county.

and Negro registration rates begin to increase. But the reversal is not sharp
enough for the counties with the highest white education to reach as great a Negro
registration as the counties with the lowest white education. Southern counties
with extremely high white educational levels have only about average rates of Negro registration. The impressive fact revealed by Figure 6 is the near uniformity
with which an increase in white school years is associated with a decrease in Negro registration.

Being unable to "explain away" our finding entirely, either by examining
the correlation for hidden third variables or by examining the regularity of the
association, we must conclude that white education in southern counties is independently and negatively associated with Negro registration. Short of the highest
levels, the more educated the whites the more actively and effectively they seem
to enforce the traditional mores of the region against Negro participation in elections. The usual effect of an increase in average schooling for whites in the South
as a whole appears to be to give the white people more of the skills that are needed
to express effectively their anti-Negro sentiment. For example, the correlation
between median school years completed by whites and the presence or absence of
a White Citizens Council or similar organization is +.32. It seems to take considerably more formal education than the average southern white receives to *alter*
his attitude toward the Negro's place in southern politics.

White Religious Affiliation   A variety of studies suggest that religion plays some role — either as independent or intervening variable — in the racial politics of the South. Church-goers have been found to be less tolerant than non-attenders,[29] and the South is a church-going region. Studies of Louisiana politics have found substantial political differences between the Catholic and Protestant sections of the state.[30] It seemed worthwhile, therefore, to examine the correlation between white religious affiliation and Negro registration rates for the South as a whole.

We find that Negro registration rates are depressed as church membership among whites [31] increases (-.17), despite the fact that white membership in different churches has different functions — Baptist membership is negatively related to Negro registration (-.10) while Catholic membership is positively related (+.15). On a southwide basis, the percentage of Jews in the county's total church membership is not significantly associated with Negro registration.

Granted that Catholicism is positively related to Negro registration, we can partial out the influence of Catholicism in order to determine the correlation between non-Catholic white church membership and Negro registration. This partial correlation is, as expected, slightly greater (-.23) than the simple correlation. But the negative correlation between white church membership and Negro registration disappears when Negro concentration is held constant. (The partial correlation is +.01). Greater church membership among whites accordingly appears to be a reflection of other county attributes rather than an independent factor in relation to Negro registration. When we examine the correlations between church membership and all of our other measures of county attributes, we find very low correlations with all other variables except Negro concentration (+.38) and Catholicism (+.31). Apparently, then, white church membership *per se* is unimportant for Negro registration. White people in the kinds of counties with more Negroes and in predominantly Catholic counties are more often members of churches. In the former kinds of counties, fewer Negroes will vote regardless of non-Catholic church membership. Most non-Catholic churches presumably take on the racial attitudes of their localities; or, if they do not, they have little effect on those attitudes in so far as the attitudes are reflected in rates of Negro registration.

Per cent of Roman Catholics in the white church population appears to be by far the most important of our religious attributes of southern counties. And the relationship between Catholicism and Negro voter registration does not disappear when Negro concentration is controlled. (The partial correlation is +.10.) The presence of Roman Catholics, then, does seem to facilitate Negro voter registration on a southwide basis. Roman Catholic churches and priests presumably react less directly to other county attributes than most Protestant churches and their ministers; in any case, Catholicism is independently and positively related to Negro voter registration.

However, the concentration of Catholic population in Louisiana and the small number of Catholics in most other parts of the South dictate caution in accepting this explanation. For one thing, the distribution of Catholic percentages deviates so far from the assumption of normal distribution underlying correlation analysis that our southwide correlations may have been curiously and unpredictably affected. In the second place, the atypical political patterns of Louisiana —

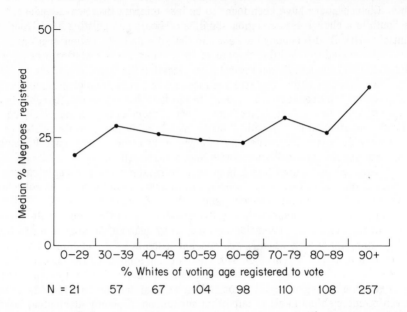

Figure 7 Median % of voting age Negroes registered to vote, by % of whites registered in same county.

rather than Catholicism *per se* — may account for a large part of the correlation obtained. Only state-by-state analysis of the correlations can indicate if Catholicism is a genuinely independent and significant factor facilitating Negro registration throughout the entire South.

IV. NEGRO VERSUS WHITE
REGISTRATION RATES

We have assumed that our analysis is of *Negro* voter registration rather than of voter registration *in general*. But this assumption might be incorrect: while Negroes register to vote in the South at a much lower rate than whites (Figure 1), the registration rates of the two races could be highly correlated with one another, both responding to the same social and economic characteristics of southern counties. The data permit two tests of this possibility: (1) an examination of the relationship between Negro and white registration; (2) a comparison of the relationships between county attributes and white registration with the relationships found between the same attributes and Negro registration.

The Relationship between Negro and White Registration   To a limited extent, Negro registration does increase as white registration increases; their simple correlation is +. 24. Figure 7 presents the relationship of Negro to white registration for every level of white registration. The detailed relationships depicted

Table 4 Correlations between county social and economic characteristics and per cent of voting age whites registered to vote, by county, in 11 Southern states.

County Characteristics	Simple Correlations (r)	Partial Correlations, Controlling for:	
		% Negro, 1950	% Urban, 1950
Per cent of nonwhite labor force in white collar occupations	−.26	−.24	−.15
Nonwhite median school years completed	−.34	−.34	−.28
Nonwhite median income	−.19	−.17	−.08
Per cent of total church membership Roman Catholic	−.09	−.08	−.03
Per cent increase in population, 1940-50	−.06	−.04	+.08
Per cent of labor force in manufacturing	+.05	+.05	+.07
White median income	−.19	−.19	−.05
Per cent of population urban	−.25	−.24	
Percentage point difference in per cent population Negro, 1900-50	+.10	+.11	+.05
Per cent of total church membership Jewish	−.03	−.03	+.04
Difference in white-nonwhite median school years completed	+.11	+.07	+.14
Difference in white-nonwhite median income	−.12	−.13	−.03
Number of Negro colleges in county	−.10	−.11	−.04
Per cent of total church membership Baptist	+.20	+.19	+.15
Per cent of population belonging to a church	+.06	+.02	+.07
Per cent of labor force in agriculture	+.21	+.19	+.06
White median school years completed	−.08	−.11	+.03
Per cent of farms operated by tenants	+.09	+.05	+.05
Per cent of population Negro, 1900	+.03	−.12	+.02
Per cent of population Negro, 1950	+.10		+.06

Note: County characteristics are listed above in the same order as in Table 2 in order to facilitate comparison of Negro and white correlations.

by the graph reveal that the lowest and the highest levels of white registration contribute most of the small correlation between the registration rates of the two races; if both of the extreme points were eliminated, the curve would be virtually horizontal, indicating that Negro registration had no relationship at all to white registration. Only when white registration is extremely high or extremely low, then, is it associated with the rate of Negro registration. For the broad middle range of counties with from 30 to 89 per cent of the whites registered — a group which contains over 70 per cent of all southern counties — Negro registration appears to be independent of white registration.

The Relationships between Socio-Economic Factors and Negro and White Registration   Table 4 presents the correlations between the per cent of eligible whites registered to vote and the same 20 social and economic factors utilized in our effort to explain Negro registration. While these factors were chosen for their presumed relevance for Negro registration, the magnitude of the simple correlations in the first column of the table suggest that they are as strongly related to white as to Negro registration. When these simple correlations for whites are compared with those for Negroes in Table II, however, we see that the direction of the correlation is reversed for 15 of the 20 social and economic factors. Not one of the 20 variables is substantially and consistently related to both Negro and white rates of voter registration.

The reversal of relationships is so regular that social and economic attributes might appear to have opposite meanings for Negro and white registration.[32] Closer inspection reveals, however, that the relationships are disparate rather than opposite.

The crucial variable for Negro registration is Negro concentration in the population, which not only furnishes the strongest simple correlation but is also the variable that most consistently accounts for other apparent "influences" on Negro registration. Indeed, Negro concentration has generally been cited as the critical factor in all dimensions of southern political behavior. Hence, one immediately suspects that all of the variables which facilitate white registration must be positively correlated with concentration of Negro population, which would thereby stand as the dominant third factor for both Negro and white registration. While this familiar interpretation would conveniently account for the striking discrepancy between correlates of white and Negro registration, it is not supported by our findings. On the contrary, *Negro concentration has a negligible relationship to white voter registration.* Moreover, the small simple correlation of Negro concentration and white registration (+. 10) drops to the vanishing point (+. 06) when urbanism is controlled.

No single variable is as important for white registration as Negro concentration is for Negro registration, but urbanism emerges as particularly significant. Per cent of population urban — which proved inconsequential in the analysis of Negro registration — furnishes one of the strongest negative correlations with white voter registration, a correlation that is not affected when Negro concentration is controlled. And the same relationship is found if, instead of per cent of population urban, we use Standard Metropolitan Areas as our index of urban-rural difference; white registration is consistently higher in rural than in urban counties. Other county characteristics associated with urbanization — such as high income and education levels for whites and Negroes — are similarly related to low white registration. Perhaps the rural white resident finds politics more meaningful in a one-party region, where personality plays such an important role in elections.[33] In any event, urban-rural differences are a key factor in variations in white voter registration.

Similar variations are found in the relationships of white and Negro registration rates to the other social and economic characteristics of southern counties. Average white education, for example, manifested a strong negative association with Negro registration — an association that held up under various controls so well that it led to novel conclusions. White education is also negatively related to white registration, but the correlation is extremely small and it is reversed when per cent of population urban is controlled.

Without an extended consideration of white registration, then, we can conclude that our analysis does apply to Negro voter registration in particular rather than to voter registration in general. The social and economic characteristics of southern counties have widely different meanings for Negro and white registration.

V. CONCLUSIONS

The proportion of voting age Negroes registered to vote in the former confederate states has increased more than 500 per cent since *Smith v. Allwright* was decided in 1944. Today, 28 per cent of the voting age Negroes are registered voters, a rate which is about half that of white adults in the South. In this article we have examined the statistical associations between selected social and economic characteristics of southern counties and Negro registration in an effort to ascertain the extent to which variations in Negro registration can be explained by the social and economic realities of the region.

The personal attributes of Negroes — their occupations, income, and education as reflected in county figures — were found to have relatively little to do with Negro registration rates. The size of the Negro middle class does appear to have an independent and positive correlation with Negro registration, but this correlation is small compared to those between Negro registration and the characteristics of the whites and of the total community.

The largest single correlation (−.46) was between the per cent of the population Negro in 1950 and Negro registration. Differences in the proportion of the population Negro up to about 30 per cent are not associated with drastic reductions in the per cent of Negroes registered, but increasing Negro concentration above this figure seems to lead to very rapid decreases. Negro concentration in the past seems almost as important as Negro concentration today until one discovers that the close association of past with present Negro concentration accounts for the finding. Indeed, declines in Negro proportions in counties with populations from 30 to 70 per cent Negro in 1900 are associated with substantial registration increases over similar counties which have not experienced such change.

The presence of an agricultural economy and farm tenancy were found to have a small, independent, and depressing effect on Negro registration rates. Neither urbanization nor industrialization, on the other hand, seems to be associated with Negro registration increases when other factors are controlled.

White educational levels were of about equal importance to the size of the Negro middle class and the existence of an agrarian economy. The more highly educated the whites in a county, the lower the rate of Negro registration — until the average white adult was a high school graduate or possessed some higher education. In these few counties, the rate of Negro registration was moderate. Up to the highest levels, increases in white educational levels apparently lead to more effective enforcement of the region's traditional mores against Negro participation in elections.

Another factor of about equal importance to all the others save Negro concentration is Roman Catholicism. The larger the proportion of Roman Catholics in a county, the higher the rate of Negro registration regardless of what other factors are controlled.

When the same social and economic characteristics of southern counties are analyzed for their relationships to white voter registration, a radically different pattern is discovered. The direction of the relationship is reversed for most of the attributes with the shift from Negro to white registration, but more than a simple reversal is involved. The magnitudes of the correlations with white registration (disregarding direction of correlation) are quite different, and a different variable emerges as the most consistent independent correlate. Whereas Negro registration tends to increase in the counties — rural or urban — that have smaller portions of Negroes in their populations, white registration tends to increase in the more rural counties — regardless of the portions of Negroes in their populations. We can accordingly have some confidence that we are dealing with an autonomous set of relationships in our analysis of Negro registration in the South.

In all of the preceding analysis, we have examined the association between selected social and economic factors and Negro registration one at a time. While controls for the impact of one social and economic factor on another have been introduced, we have not yet attempted to estimate the extent of the association between all the social and economic factors taken together and Negro registration. In order to do this, we have computed the multiple correlation coefficient between all 20 social and economic factors (plus the size of the Standard Metropolitan Area, if any, within which the county is contained — a qualitative variable for which simple correlations could not be obtained) and Negro voter registration. The correlation between all of the social and economic variables and county registration rates of Negroes is .53, which explains about 28 per cent (R^2) of the variation in Negro registration.

A multiple correlation of this magnitude demonstrates the great importance of social and economic characteristics for Negro registration.[34] To explain over one-fourth of the variance in Negro registration — or any other significant political phenomenon — is no mean achievement in the current state of political science. But almost three-fourths of the variance remains to be accounted for. This leaves room for significant variation independent of social and economic forces that have been considered here. If political variables were added to the analysis, could still more of the variance in Negro registration be explained? If political variables do emerge as having an autonomous set of relationships to Negro registration, what is the comparative importance of political and demographic variables? Finally, if variations in state systems (social, economic, and political) were taken into account, could still more explanatory power be gained? A social and economic analysis has taken us a long way in our effort to understand Negro registration rates, but we still have a lot further to go. The massive bulk and complexity of our data require that an analysis of political and legal factors, of the relative importance of demographic versus political variables, and of variations in state systems be reported separately. Our expectation is that, by an analysis of these additional factors, we can reduce the range of unexplained variation still further.

The application of our findings to the contemporary policy problem of how best to increase Negro voting in the South must be approached with the utmost caution. Our analysis deals with registration, not voting, and these are not identical forms of political participation. Our data deal with the characteristics of counties, not individuals, and the leap from the areal to the individual level is hazardous. Third, the analysis has been of variations in rates of registration and

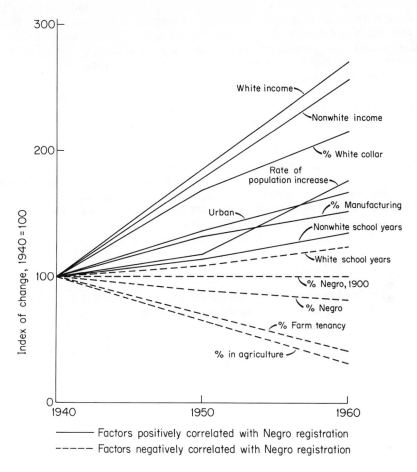

Figure 8 Rates of social and economic change in the South, 1940–1960.

not of factors which determine its absolute level. To find that an independent variable accounts for some of the variation in the dependent variable gives us no direct information on the size of the dependent variable. Fourth, correlations are not "causes" but merely associations; attributing causal relationships to variables which are correlated with one another is to engage in the drawing of inferences, which sometimes are spectacularly wrong. Finally, the bulk of our analysis has been restricted to one point in time so that it does not directly produce predictions in which time is a key factor.

    If these caveats are not forgotten but merely set aside, our correlations suggest that reformers should not expect miracles [35] in their efforts, through political and legal means, to increase the size and effectiveness of the Negro vote in the South. The Negro registration rate is low, in rather large part, because of the social and economic characteristics of southerners — both Negro and white. These facts are not easily and quickly changed by law or political action. One cannot help but be impressed by the massive indications of stability in the situation — the extremely high negative correlation between per cent Negro in 1900 and Negro registration in 1958, the apparent failure of urbanization and industrialization to provide sufficiently favorable conditions for Negro political participation, the negative correlation between white educational levels and Negro registration, and so on.

At the same time, Negro registration has increased rapidly since 1944 and the social and economic factors we have considered account for only about 28 per cent of its 1958 variation. Changes in the southern society and economy strongly argue that Negro registration will continue to increase. In Figure 8, the trend since 1940 is presented for the variables we found to be most strongly related to Negro voter registration.[36] *Every one of the variables positively associated with Negro registration is on the increase* — some have doubled in 20 years and all but one have increased by at least 50 per cent. Only one of the factors associated with low Negro registration — white school years completed — is also increasing, and there is reason to believe that a good many southern counties will soon reach the stage where this factor may tend to facilitate rather than hinder Negro political participation.[37] All the other factors negatively correlated with Negro registration (except, of course, per cent Negro in 1900) are declining rapidly.

The South's social and economic structure may be the reformer's major barrier — but it may also be a long-run cause for hope.

NOTES

1.   *New York Times,* January 7, 1962. See also H. L. Moon, *Balance of Power: the Negro Vote* (Garden City, N.Y., Doubleday, 1949), p. 7 and *passim.*

2.   71 Stat. 635; 74 Stat. 86. *Cf.* U. S. Commission on Civil Rights, *1959 Report* (Washington, 1959); *1961 Report,* Vol. I, "Voting" (Washington, 1961).

3.   *New York Times,* January 7, 1962; Louis E. Lomax, "The Kennedys Move in on Dixie," *Harper's Magazine,* May 1962, pp. 27–33.

4.   *Wall Street Journal,* November 6, 1961; *New York Times,* July 10, 1961.

5.   Baltimore *Afro-American,* October 7, 1961; *New York Times,* August 7, 1961.

6.   The 1962 Atlanta, Georgia, national convention of the NAACP had the "Battle of the Ballots" as its theme. Raleigh (N.C.) *News and Observer,* June 24, 1962.

7.   *New York Times,* March 29, 1962. Louis E. Lomax, *op. cit.*

8.   For useful summaries of the literature see Robert E. Lane, *Political Life* (New York: The Free Press, 1959), ch. 16; and Seymour M. Lipset et al., "The Psychology of Voting," in G. Lindzey (ed.), *Handbook of Social Psychology* (Reading, Mass.: Addision-Wesley Publishing Company, 1954), Vol. II, pp. 1126-1134.

9.   Herbert H. Hyman and Paul B. Sheatsley, "Attitudes Toward Desegregation, " *Scientific American,* Vol. 195 (1956), pp. 35-39; B. Bettelheim and M. Janowitz, *The Dynamics of Prejudice* (New York, 1950); Melvin M. Tumin, *Desegregation: Resistance and Readiness* (Princeton University Press, 1958), p. 195 and *passim.* James W. Vander Zanden, "Voting on Segregationist Referenda, " *Public Opinion Quarterly,* Vol. 25 (1961), pp. 92-105, finds the evidence in support of the relationship in voting on segregationist referenda in the South "inconsistent and even contradictory... this study seems to suggest that the socio-economic factor may not play as simple or as critical a role as some of us doing research in this field have been prone to assign it" (p. 105).

10. In addition to the problem of the relative importance of political variables, we are postponing consideration of still another possibility — that variations in state systems (social, economic, and political) account for a significant proportion of the variation in Negro registration among southern counties.

11. A complete list of sources used to obtain county frequencies for the independent variables used in this analysis would be too lengthy to reproduce here. A mimeographed list will be supplied by the authors upon request.

     We are indebted to the following research assistants for their help in collecting these data: Lawton Bennett, Lewis Bowman, Barbara Bright, Jack Fleer, Donald Freeman, Douglas Gatlin, and Richard Sutton. All told, the collection and coding of these data took one man-year of work.

12. Voter registration rates, by race, are presented in U. S. Commission on Civil Rights, *1959 Report and 1961 Report,* Vol. I, "Voting. " The 1958 registration data, contained in the *1959 Report,* are more complete and were used for all states except Tennessee. The 1960 figures, printed in the *1961 Report,* are the only ones available for Tennessee.

13. There are 1136 counties in the 11 southern states, 1028 of which have populations containing at least 1 per cent Negroes.

14. For a good discussion of correlation analysis see M. J. Hagood and D. O. Price, *Statistics for Sociologists* (New York, 1952), chs. 23 and 25.

15. All computations were made on the University of North Carolina's UNIVAC 1105 high-speed digital computer. The inaccuracy of some of the registration figures tends to reduce the magnitude of all correlations obtained by this analysis. The assumption of linearity underlying the computation of r also reduces the size of the correlations where the relationship between dependent and independent variables is, in fact, a curvilinear one. It is therefore safe to assume that the r's reported in this article err in the conservative direction.

16. V. O. Key, Jr. , *Southern Politics* (New York, 1949) gives little attention to Negro voting since it was of little importance at the time he wrote (see, however, p. 518). His stress upon the overriding importance of Negro concentration for all aspects of southern politics makes his study highly relevant, nonetheless. Other works

specifically on Negro voting which stress the importance of Negro concentration include: James F. Barnes, *Negro Voting in Mississippi,* M.A. thesis, University of Mississippi, 1955; Margaret Price, *The Negro and the Ballot in the South* (Atlanta, Georgia: Southern Regional Council, 1959); H. D. Price, *The Negro and Southern Politics: A Chapter of Florida History* (New York: New York University Press, 1957); Donald Strong, "The Future of the Negro Voter in the South," *Journal of Negro Education,* Vol. 26 (Summer, 1957), pp. 400-407; United States Commission on Civil Rights, *1961 Report,* Vol. I, "Voting."

17. On this point see H. D. Price, *op. cit.,* p 41ff.

18. See H. D. Price, *op. cit.*

19. In view of the relatively high associations between Negro concentration and a wide variety of political phenomena (including Negro registration rates), it might be argued that Negro concentration is, in fact, a "political" rather than a "demographic" variable. But Negro concentration is as strongly associated with many social and economic characteristics of southern counties as it is with their political peculiarities. And while the correlations of Negro concentration with political characteristics are relatively large, they fall far short of a 1.0 correlation. As we shall demonstrate in a subsequent article, a number of political variables have an association with Negro registration that is independent of Negro concentration. Under these circumstances, to call Negro concentration a "political" variable would be distinctly misleading.

20. See Lane, *op. cit.;* Lipset *et al., op. cit.;* Angus Campbell, Philip E. Converse, Warren E. Miller, and Donald E. Stokes, *The American Voter* (New York, 1960), ch. 13; V.O. Key, Jr., *Public Opinion and American Democracy* (New York, 1961), ch. 6. For a study of these variables and political participation among southern Negroes, see Bradbury Seasholes, "Negro Political Participation in Two North Carolina Cities," Ph.D. dissertation, University of North Carolina, 1962.

21. For an extreme statement of this position, see E. Franklin Frazier, *Black Bourgeoisie: The Rise of a New Middle Class in the United States* (New York: The Free Press, 1957). Less exaggerated statements to the same effect may be found in the literature cited in *n.* 16, above.

22. This is the basic argument of Frazier, *op. cit.* A more mundane explanation would be called for if counties from particular states were clustered at particular points on the curve in Figure 4, but examination of the same relationships for each state reveals no such state-by-state clustering.

23. See especially, U.S. Commission on Civil Rights, *1961 Report,* Vol. I, "Voting," pp. 143-199.

24. This and other measures of county-wide characteristics might better be considered separately for Negroes and whites, but they are not separately reported in the census.

25. On Negro voting in urban settings see Charles D. Farris, "Effects of Negro Voting Upon the Politics of a Southern City: An Intensive Study, 1946-48," Ph.D. dissertation, University of Chicago, 1953; George A. Hillery, "The Presence of Community

Among Urban Negroes: A Case Study of a Selected Area in New Orleans, " M.A. thesis, Louisiana State University, 1951; Leonard Reissman *et al.,* "The New Orleans Voter: A Handbook of Political Description,"' *Tulane Studies in Political Science,* Vol. II (1955), pp. 1-88; Cleo Roberts, "Some Correlates of Registration and Voting Among Negroes in the 1953 Municipal Election of Atlanta, " M.A. thesis, Atlanta University, 1954; Harry J. Walker, "Changes in Race Accommodation in a Southern Community, " Ph.D. dissertation, University of Chicago, 1945.

26. The Bureau of the Census defines Standard Metropolitan Areas as a county or group of contiguous counties which contains at least one city of 50,000 inhabitants or more. The contiguous counties must be socially and economically integrated with the central city to be included in the SMA.

27. See the literature cited in *n.* 9, above.

28. Eleven of the 28 counties in which the average white adult has completed less than seven years of schooling are French-Catholic parishes in Louisiana. Even if those parishes are eliminated, the trend shown in Figure 6 remains the same. The partial correlation between white school years and Negro registration, controlling for per cent Roman Catholic, is $-.25$.

29. Samuel A. Stouffer, *Communism, Conformity, and Civil Liberties* (New York, Doubleday, 1955).

30. Allan P. Sindler, *Huey Long's Louisiana* (Baltimore: The Johns Hopkins Press, 1956); V.O. Key, Jr., *op. cit.,* ch. 8; John H. Fenton and Kenneth N. Vines, "Negro Registration in Louisiana, " *American Political Science Review,* Vol. 51 (1957), pp. 704-13.

31. The most recent attempt to compile county-by-county figures on church membership is reported in a census by the National Council of Churches of Christ, *Churches and Church Membership in the U.S.,* Series C, 1956. Negro churches are not included in this census, and the figures reported for many white churches appear to be incomplete.

32. A simple Kendall tau rank order correlation of the two distributions of correlations in Tables 2 and 4 is $-.54$.

33. Urban counties in the South undoubtedly purge their registration lists with greater regularity than the more rural ones. How much effect this may have on these correlations cannot be ascertained.

34. Indeed, it was on the basis of a roughly equal multiple correlation, based on survey data rather than aggregate county data, that an early voting behavior study concluded that "social characteristics determine political preference. " Paul F. Lazarsfeld, Bernard Berelson, and Hazel Gaudet, *The People's Choice* (New York: Columbia University Press, 1948), p. 27. This work reports a multiple correlation between voting preference and social factors of "approximately .5" (p. 25).

35. For example, Martin Luther King's statement in a speech to the 1962 NAACP annual convention about southern Negroes being "able to elect at least five Negroes to

Congress in the next few years" seems to underestimate wildly the social and economic barriers to Negro political participation. *New York Times,* July 6, 1962. See also the sanguine expectations of Lomax, *op. cit.*

36. No trend data were available on religious affiliation. Median income figures, by race, were not available for 1940. In Figure 8, it is assumed that median income for both races increased at the same rate between 1940 and 1950 as between 1950 and 1960.

37. If white school years completed continues to increase at the 1950–60 rate, the average southern white will have completed 11.4 years of schooling by 1970 and many southern counties will have average white school years completed of 12 years or more. Assuming that the relationship presented in Figure 6 continues to hold true, the effect of white education on Negro registration may gradually reverse.

THE CULTURAL ENVIRONMENT

Negro Registration in Louisiana

John H. Fenton
Kenneth N. Vines

The 1944 action of the Supreme Court voiding the white primary ended the last effective legal block to Negro voter registration in the South. After that, resort to legal steps to block Negro registration was either outlawed by the courts or else could only be a delaying device. In the state of Louisiana, however, the decision in *Smith v. Allwright* did not result in Negro registration comparable to white registration. In 1956, twelve years later, 30 percent of the potential Negro voting population was registered, compared to 73 percent of the whites. This study is an investigation of some factors in that discrepancy, and in particular, of the differences in registration between Catholic and Protestant areas.

An important characteristic of Negro registration in Louisiana is the extreme range of variation to be found among the several parishes. Table 1 shows 17 parishes with fewer than 20 percent of the eligible Negroes registered, and 11 parishes with 70 percent or more of the potential Negro vote registered, Therefore, the statewide "average" percentage of Negro registration[1] has little meaning without more detailed interpretation.

Among the factors responsible for these differences is the religio–cultural variable. Louisiana offers a unique opportunity to study the influence of this variable on the registration aspect of race relations. Catholicism is dominant in southern Louisiana and Protestantism in northern Louisiana. The two regions are very nearly separate worlds. Other variables enter, but this one is the focus of this paper.

Reprinted from *American Political Science Review,* Vol. 51 (1957), pp. 704–713, by permission of the authors and publisher.

Table 1 Louisiana parishes by percentage of Negroes 21 and over registered, 1956.

Registration Percentage	Number of Parishes
0- 9	7
10- 19	10
20- 29	9
30- 39	6
40- 49	5
50- 59	13
60- 69	3
70- 79	6
80- 89	3
90-100	2

The material for this study was gathered from Census Reports and from specialized and local sources on the cultural characteristics of Louisiana. Sixteen parishes were visited throughout the state, chosen to represent different degrees of Negro registration, different socio-economic areas, and different religio-cultural areas. Interviews were conducted with state and parish officials and local political leaders, both white and Negro.[2]

I. THE RELIGIO-CULTURAL VARIABLE

Every Louisianian is aware of the religious complications of his state's politics. It has usually been thought, though experience provides exceptions, that only Protestants can be elected to state-wide offices or as congressmen from the north Louisiana districts; and only Catholics can be elected to major offices in south Louisiana. The Catholicism of Louisiana is predominantly French, and it is said that a French name is worth 50,000 votes in south Louisiana in a statewide election.

Roughly the southern 25 parishes form French Catholic Louisiana while the remaining parishes in the north are predominantly Protestant and Anglo-Saxon. The French parishes remain French-Catholic because of their assimilation of extraneous cultural elements entering the area.

As Table 2 indicates, Negro registration, in percentages of potential eligibles, is more than twice as great in Louisiana's French-Catholic parishes as in its non-French parishes. In only two of the 25 French-Catholic parishes are less than 20 percent of the eligible Negroes registered, whereas in 13 of the 39 non-French parishes less than 20 percent of the potential Negro vote is registered. In seven of the French-Catholic parishes Negro registration is 70 percent or more, while only four of the non-French-Catholic parishes equal or exceed the 70 percent mark. Yet no significant differences exist between the two groups of parishes with respect to Negro-white population balance or to urbanism.

The reasons for the different reaction of French and non-French population groups to Negro registration seem, in large part, to be due to fundamentally different attitudes of each culture toward the Negro. Both Negro and white leaders agree that social attitudes toward the Negro differ in the two cultures.

Table 2 Negro registration by religio-cultural sections of Louisiana, 1956.

	French-Catholic Parishes [1]	Non-French Parishes [2]
Number of Negroes registered	70,488	90,922
Potential Negro vote	138,000	390,000
Percentage of Negroes registered	51	23
Mean of parishes — percentage of Negroes in total population	32	38
Mean of parishes — percentage of urbanism	30	26
Mean of parishes — percentage of Catholics among all religions [3]	83	12

[1] French parishes: Acadia, Ascension, Assumption, Avoyelles, Calcasieu, Cameron, Evangeline, Iberis, Iberville, Jefferson, Jefferson Davis, Lafayette, LaFourches, Plaquemines, Pointe Coupee, St. Bernard, St. Charles, St. James, St. John the Baptist, St. Landry, St. Martin, St. Mary, Terrebonne, Vermilion, West Baton Rouge. Definition of French parishes taken from T. Lynn Smith and Homer L. Hitt, *The People of Louisiana* (Baton Rouge, 1952), p. 143.
[2] Predominantly Anglo-Saxon Protestant.
[3] From 1926 *Census of Religious Bodies,* the most reliable source available. It is recognized that the figures contain a bias because of the difference between Catholic and Protestant practice in counting children as members of the church. However, the purpose of the figures is to show differences in degree of Catholicism.

Some objective evidence of this difference is to be found in these facts: (1) at political meetings in southern Louisiana crowds are often racially mixed, even at indoor meetings, whereas in northern Louisiana such crowds are always segregated; (2) the Citizens' Council organizations have comparatively little support in French-Catholic Louisiana, while in northern Louisiana, as a Madison Council official put it, "Here the Citizens' Councils are the prominent people"; (3) racially hybrid communities occur more frequently in south Louisiana than in north Louisiana.[3]

It should be emphasized that the people of French-Catholic Louisiana are not in favor of integration. Yet they do evidence, people and leaders alike, a permissive attitude toward Negro participation in political affairs that is generally lacking in the northern parishes.[4] These permissive attitudes seem to stem in large part from the social and religious practices of the Catholic Church. The Church looks upon segregation as a sin, and Archbishop Rummel of New Orleans has led the clergy in an all-out doctrinal attack on the practice. Catholic clergy cite the "catholic" character of the Church as the reason for its advanced stand on racial issues and emphasize the fact that the Protestant churches are national in origin and tend to be exclusive in character, whereas the Catholic Church is more universal in both its background and orientation. Many Catholics also point to the effect of the Church on the Negro as a reason for the high percent of Negro registration in Catholic parishes. According to this argument, the Catholic Negro enjoys religious and ethical training which is identical with that received by the white community, and from a well-educated priest. Therefore, the Catholic Negro's value system more nearly approaches that of the white community than does that of the Protestant-Negro, and, accordingly, he is more readily accepted by the greater community.

Since the Catholic Church attempts to build a Catholic culture wherever it exists by providing educational, recreational, and fraternal organizations for its members, the influence of the Church as a social institution is great. It appears to be the principal, in many areas the only, unsegregated social institution in Louisiana. In the French parishes where Catholicism has been the major formative factor in the culture for many years, it has been, Catholics say, important in producing the permissive attitudes of the people toward the political and social activities of the Negro.

In north Louisiana, on the other hand, one finds little or no objective evidence that the dominant Protestant religion has aided in the creation of tolerant attitudes toward Negro political activity. Negro leaders in these areas rarely cited white Protestant ministers as friends of the Negro, and seldom referred to a Protestant church as an ameliorative factor in the easing of racial tensions. Although most Protestant national organizations are opposed to racial prejudice and segregation, their position has not effected many changes in the attitudes of local congregations. Protestant churches, in contrast to the authoritative control by the Catholic hierarchy, are dominated by local congregations, and Protestant ministers, though often mindful of national pronouncements on segregation, must remain passive on such matters so as not to offend their flocks.

Although the mean percent of Negro registration is low in north Louisiana, there are parishes with large Negro registration. As Table 3 shows, this usually occurs where Negroes are not an important part of the population, that is, where there are few Negroes, little economic tenancy, and no heritage of a plantation society.

Table 3 Relation between percentage of tenancy, percentage of Negro population, and percentage of Negroes registered in French and non-French parishes of Louisiana, 1956.

Percentage of Tenancy	Number of Parishes		Mean Percentage of Negro Population		Mean Percentage of Negroes Registered	
	French	*Non-French*	*French*	*Non-French*	*French*	*Non-French*
50 and over	6	11	34	52	65	11
40–49	0	4	—	43	—	23
30–39	7	6	33	39	48	25
20–29	5	6	23	36	67	36
10–19	7	9	34	25	43	53
0–9	0	3	—	19	—	59

When the parishes of northern Louisiana are grouped into areas, this correspondence of a high rate of tenancy and concentration of Negro population to a low Negro registration becomes clearly evident and significant. In the North-Central cut-over pine section where the percentage of Negroes in the total population (mean of parishes, 24 percent) and prevalence of tenancy (17 percent) is relatively low, there is a great deal of Negro registration (55 percent). In this area, there has been little fear of the Negro as a political force, and the society tends to be pluralistic.[5]

The Mississippi Delta area, in northeast Louisiana, is the section with the highest rate of tenancy (60 percent), the greatest proportion of Negroes (51 percent), and the lowest Negro registration (11 percent) in the state. It remains a plantation society. There are plantation owners in Tensas and Madison parishes who take pride in the resemblance between the plantations of 1856 and 1956, in terms of the physical appearance of the Negro and his cabin, and of the social and economic relationships between Negro and white.

The survival of this kind of society depends upon excluding the Negro from all political and economic power. Outsiders are assured that the Negro happily accepts the existing power structure, and strenuous efforts are made to demonstrate the mutual advantages which accrue from it.

Thus in non-French Louisana, Negro registration varies with the number of Negroes present and the nature of the economy. In a plantation economy, a tight power structure exists which makes it possible to exclude Negroes from the polls. In addition the numerical strength of Negroes in such communities arouses real or imagined fears of possible Negro rule if he should obtain the ballot.

As Table 3 indicates, the economic structure of many of the French-Catholic parishes differs from that of the northern portion of the state. In French-Catholic Louisiana the Negro is not typically in a tenant-master relationship to the white community. Rather, his position is that of a free wage-earner. The reason is that much of southern Louisiana is engaged in the production of cane sugar, which does not lend itself to the tenant system of farming.

The free wage-earner is more remote from his master than is the tenant farmer, and thus (at least in prosperous times) enjoys greater social and economic freedom. Therefore, the difference in the economies of the two regions undoubtedly exercises an important conditioning effect on Negro registration.

However, even in those French-Catholic parishes where a plantation economy does exist the percent of Negro registration tends to be considerably above that of the northern plantation parishes. In three French-Catholic parishes (St. Landry, Pointe Coupee, and West Baton Rouge) both the percentage of Negro population and the percentage of tenancy is 45 or more. The percentage of Negro registration exceeds 20 in all three parishes and reaches a level of 87 in St. Landry. This highlights the importance of the French-Catholic religio-culture in producing a permissive attitude toward Negro registration.

II. THE EFFECT OF NEGRO-WHITE
POPULATION BALANCE

Perhaps the most widely accepted belief concerning Negro registration in the South is that the amount will vary inversely to the proportion of Negroes in the local population. According to this theory, areas with large Negro populations, (1) were most passionately attached to the cause of the Confederacy, and (2) because of the greater number of Negroes have more reason to fear Negro voting. The theory concludes that the centers of Negro population will be the last to extend the suffrage to the Negro.

Table 4 shows that there is certainly no uniform correlation between the proportion of parish population Negro and the proportion of Negroes registered. However, at the extreme ends of the scale, the relationship is significant. The four Louisiana parishes with no Negro registration — Tensas, Madison, West Feliciana, and East Carroll, neighboring parishes in the Mississippi Delta area — are the only parishes with over 60 percent Negro population. In the parishes with less than 29 percent Negro population there is a significant increase in the percentage of Negro registration. However, in ten parishes with a majority of Negro population (50 to 59 percent) the mean percentage of Negroes registered (37 percent) slightly exceeds that for the two intervals with fewer Negroes (40 to 49 percent and 30 to 39 percent).

Table 4 also shows that the presence or absence of large numbers of Negroes has a similar effect on Negro registration in French and non-French parishes. However, as the table indicates, the range of variation tends to be much narrower in the French than in the non-French parishes. Of course, the degree of economic tenancy is another variable present in this figure, a factor which has already been discussed.

Table 4 Relation between Negroes in total population and Negro registration in parishes of Louisiana, 1956.

Percentage of Negroes in Total Population	Number of Parishes			Mean Percentage of Negroes Registered		
	Total	French	Non-French	Total	French	Non-French
60 and over	4	—	4	0	—	0
50–59	10	4	6	37	44	33
40–49	8	3	5	33	57	19
30–39	19	6	13	32	47	25
20–29	12	6	6	52	51	53
10–19	10	5	5	62	65	59
0– 9	1	1	—	94	94	—

In conclusion, it can be definitely stated that, in Louisiana, the simple fact of the presence of a high proportion of Negores and a tradition of a plantation economy (such as in St. Landry parish) does not necessarily militate against the registration of Negroes in sizeable numbers, especially where a French-Catholic culture predominates.

III. THE EFFECT OF URBANISM

Contrary to the widely held belief that Negro registration in the South is concentrated in urban areas, Table 5 indicates that no clear relationship exists in Louisiana between the degree of urbanism and the extent of Negro registration.

Table 5 Relation between urbanism and white and Negro registration, for state and by religio-cultural sections, Louisiana, 1956.

Percentage of Urbanism	Number of Parishes			Mean Percentage Registered of Potential Vote					
				Negro			White		
	Total	Fr.	Non-Fr.	Total	Fr.	Non-Fr.	Total	Fr.	Non-Fr.
70 and over	5	2	3	29	43	20	64	70	60
50–69	4	3	1	45	48	35	75	78	69
40–49	8	2	6	27	67	13	78	79	77
30–39	10	3	7	46	54	42	84	84	84
20–29	14	8	6	49	61	33	90	91	88
10–19	6	3	3	28	43	13	88	89	87
0– 9	17	4	13	43	53	40	92	93	90

The reason, in all probability, for the stereotype about urbanism and Negro registration is that those few Negroes who were registered to vote prior to 1944 resided in the large urban centers. In addition, the first increases in Negro registration after 1944 largely occurred in urban areas. The urban areas of the state contain the largest concentration of professional and business Negroes, equipped to provide leadership toward registration; and the cities provide, one might imagine, an environment of political competition better suited to encourage Negro political participation.

As Table 5 indicates, however, Negro registration in Louisiana is, if anything, lower in the large urban centers than in the more rural portions of the state. The table also shows that an identical though more pronounced pattern obtains for white registration too. Taking the religio-cultural areas of the state separately, the same relationship between urbanism and registration exists in both regions as in the state as a whole, but with both Negro and white registration in the French parishes tending to be either equal to or higher than registration in the non-French parishes.

Negro registration tends to be lower in the urban than the rural areas for a variety of reasons. Many an urban Negro is rootless, and tends to feel little identification with his community or his fellow Negroes; his leadership often works at cross purposes, and is particular rather than general. In addition, local interest in registration and voting tends to be more intense in Louisiana's rural areas, where the election of a sheriff is an important event, than in the urban areas. All of these factors tend, also, to operate on the level of white registration.

Even though the urban centers do not provide favorable environments for securing a high proportion of Negro registration, the "pilot" role of activities in urban centers toward launching Negro registration is important. In all parishes studied the registration of Negroes was initiated by business and professional Negroes residing in the major urban center of the parish. In the event resistance to Negro registration made it necessary to resort to legal and political action, the city provided the resources and locus for suits against the registrar, for requests to the F.B.I. to investigate reluctant registrars, and for bargains which might be negotiated with court-house politicians.

IV. THE POLITICAL FACTOR

The first concern of every politician is to be elected and reelected to office. Therefore, the existence in any community of a reservoir of untapped voters tends to act as a magnet on politicians in search of votes. The Negro vote in Louisiana, however, was not exploitable until the Supreme Court declared the white primary laws unconstitutional. After 1944, Louisiana politicians could legally pursue the Negro vote.

In all the Louisiana parishes except those with the very largest cities, political power and interest center in the courthouse of the parish seat. The dominant political figure in the courthouse is the sheriff, whose election occasions the most interest and largest voter turnout in the parish. Where Negro registration has occurred in large numbers, the sheriff has almost invariably been friendly to the idea.

The process by which this political variable helps bring Negroes to the polls works generally as follows. Community attitudes must, first of all, be permissive with respect to Negro registration. If the white community is strongly and unalterably opposed to Negro voting, the sheriff or other politician will rarely venture to seek the Negro vote. Instead, as in the Mississippi parishes with no registration, the sheriff will help keep the Negroes away from the polls. This is true because the politician fears the reaction of his townspeople to Negro registration and because he, too, generally shares the dominant attitude.

Secondly, the sheriff, by the very nature of his office, is subject to manifold temptations relating to law enforcement, particularly, in Louisiana, to the classic "payoff" to permit gambling. When a sheriff permits gambling, he is charged with corruption of his office by the good government, middle-class voters of his community. In this event the sheriff is compelled to turn to lower socioeconomic groups or to marginal groups in the community for support.

After Negro leaders have initiated the movement for registration and thus demonstrated their group's potential voter strength, the sheriff or other official can then use to his own profit the power of his office to prevent interference with registration, or else later encourage registration drives and voter turnout campaigns. In many parishes the Negro vote has become a "balance of power" factor.

Finally, the reward of the Negro for his vote is respect from the politicians and attendance at Negro political meetings, cessation of police brutality, and promises made and often kept regarding such matters as street improvements and better school facilities. It is ironical that this advance may thus result from an alliance of shady white and underdog Negro elements against the more "respectable" white segment of the community.

The political factor is also important as an inhibiting influence. For example, in the two French parishes (Terrebonne and Plaquemines) with a rate of Negro registration below 20 percent, the local sheriff has been instrumental in keeping the Negroes from the polls. In these cases, the sheriff is unalterably opposed to Negro voting, primarily out of fear that it will cost him the election, and, consequently,

a different sheriff could permit Negro registration without suffering a serious reaction from the white community.

V. CONCLUSIONS

     This paper is concerned with the problem of differences in the political be-
havior of the South toward the Negro. These differences have been studied, here,
through an analysis of Negro registration for voting in Louisiana. Negro registration
is basically related to Southern politics not only because it is the fundamental step
for the Negro toward the power of the ballot box but also because it appears to be
vitally related to the willingness or unwillingness of specific societies to allow
the Negro an equal place in the community. The evidence indicates that Southern
attitudes and practices toward the Negro are in large part a function of the culture
in which the relationships occur.[6] Our inquiry here is whether religio-cultural
variables in the South, long celebrated as the "Bible-belt" of the nation, are related
to Negro-white political relationships insofar as these can be defined by practices
and attitudes toward Negro registration.

     The findings of this study emphasize the importance of religio-cultural
factors in defining white attitudes and practices toward Negro registration. In the
southern French-Catholic parishes the percentage of Negroes registered is more
than twice as great as in the northern Anglo-Saxon Protestant parishes. Socio-
economic factors, urbanism and Negro-white population balance, account for some
of the difference. Yet where non-religious cultural factors are held constant, as
in cotton plantation areas with large Negro populations, the religio-cultural variable
emerges as a clearly influential factor in Negro registration.

     First-hand observations in the parishes of Louisiana support the statistical
evidence that Negro registration is related to the type of religio-cultural area involved. Permissive attitudes toward Negro registration in French-Catholic parishes
seem expressive of the basic value that the Negro is spiritually equal in a Catholic
society. Such a view of man's relation to man, a scheme of elementary justice
implicit in a Catholic society, some Catholics maintain, is sustained by traditional
Catholic theology and actively promoted by the Church in Louisiana. There is little
evidence in the Protestant parishes of cultural values assigning the Negro a spiritually equal place in the community or of activity by the church itself toward these
values.

     Dr. Frank Tannebaum has written a brilliant exposition of the comparative
treatment of the Negro in North and South America, maintaining that differences
are in large part a function of the respective Protestant and Catholic cultures.[7]
Curiously, the religio-cultural analysis has been largely neglected in race-re-
lations analysis of the United States, even though the role of the Protestant ethic,
for instance in economic behavior and intellectual development, has been well stated.

     It is not the intention of the authors to urge religious determinism in this
paper but to maintain that, on the evidence, the politics of Negro registration in
Louisiana can be understood only by consideration of religio-cultural variables
with other relevant factors. In consequence we suggest that religio-cultural analysis may be useful in understanding the whole of Southern politics. Excepting Maryland, possibly, the type of analysis employed here would not be possible in other

Southern states due to the lack of distinctive religio-cultural areas. Some attention could be given, however, to the general problem of the Protestant ethic in the South and its involvement with political behavior.

NOTES

1. Current estimates on population figures were obtained as follows: (1) The estimated total population of each parish for 1956 was obtained from *Sales Management Annual Survey of Buying Power,* May 10, 1956. (2) It was assumed that the 1950 ratio of Negroes to the total population in each parish would remain constant. (3) It was assumed that the 1950 ratio of Negroes 21 and over to the total Negro population in each parish would remain constant. (4) Thus by taking percentages of the 1956 total population estimate as derived from the 1950 census, a 1956 estimate was obtained for the potential Negro vote in each parish.

2. The authors wish to acknowledge the aid of the Southern Regional Council in support of this project. The Louisiana project was part of a Southern-wide survey of Negro registration and voting sponsored by the Council.

3. See Alvin L. Bertrand, *The Many Louisianas,* Bulletin #46, Louisiana State University, Agricultural Experiment Station, June, 1955, p. 21.

4. The more "permissive" attitude of the French-Catholic parishes may be demonstrated additionally by comparison of its record on race relations with the northern parishes on such matters as rates of lynching, 1900-1941; and the number of racially integrated state colleges. It was also confirmed in interviews with both Negroes and whites from the two areas.

5. It should be noted, however, that resistance to Negro registration is stiffening in North-Central Louisiana. Efforts to purge Negroes from the rolls are being vigorously pressed by Citizens Council groups in the section. For a detailed statement of the procedures being used there, see the letter from Assistant Attorney General Olney to Senator Douglas, *Congressional Record,* Vol. 103 (August 1, 1957), pp. 12156-7 (daily ed.); New York *Times,* August 4, 1957, which, however, misplaced the parishes cited as in the southern part of the state.

6. See, for example, V.O. Key, Jr., *Southern Politics* (New York, 1949); and Hugh Douglas Price, *Negro and Southern Politics, A Chapter of Florida History* (New York, 1957).

7. *Slave and Citizen: The Negro in the Americas* (New York, 1947).

Faubus and Segregation: An Analysis of Arkansas Voting

Thomas F. Pettigrew
Ernest Q. Campbell

In the summer of 1954 a little-known young man from the mountains named Orval E. Faubus entered a four-man Democratic primary for Governor of Arkansas. His prospects were not bright. The incumbent, Francis Cherry, was a heavy favorite to win reelection; after all, every Arkansas Governor in a generation had been returned for a second two-year term by the electorate.

Faubus ran a distant second, receiving a third of the votes; but Cherry missed accumulating the necessary majority by 7,500 votes (2.3 per cent). In the August run-off, Faubus won with a scant 50.9 per cent of the votes cast. In 1956, Faubus won the gubernatorial nomination with a convincing 58.1 per cent of the votes cast in a five-man field. But it was his sweeping 68.9 per cent first primary victory in July of 1958 that received wide attention from a world alerted to his career by his efforts on behalf of Little Rock segregation.

The present paper analyzes this "march of Faubus" in geographic and demographic terms. Particular attention is paid to the relationship between Faubus's four primary victories[1] and prosegregation sentiment. For this purpose three special segregation issues voted on by Arkansans in November of 1956 are particularly useful. Votes in these referenda for assigning public school pupils on factors other than race, for "interposition," and for "nullification" of the Supreme Court's integration rulings were widely interpreted as supporting racial segregation; thus they provide us with a convenient county-by-county index of anti-integration attitudes of the voters with which to compare the elections of Faubus.[2]

THE RELATIONSHIPS BETWEEN THE FAUBUS AND SEGREGATION VOTES

Table 1 presents the ten product-moment correlations among the Faubus votes in four gubernatorial primaries and the 1956 segregation referenda vote.[3] Using the seventy-five Arkansas counties as the units of analysis, we note that the Faubus voting patterns in the 1954 and 1956 primaries are quite similar; these three votes correlate positively with each other and negatively with the segregation vote. In other words, the same Arkansas counties that tended to support Faubus

Reprinted from *Public Opinion Quarterly*, Vol. 24, No. 2 (Summer 1960), pp. 436-447, by permission of the publisher.

This study is part of a larger project carried out on Little Rock integration by the authors. We gratefully acknowledge the advice and assistance provided us by Mr. Thomas Dearmore, Professor Samuel Stouffer, and Miss Anne Gayle Tanner. The project was financed by a grant from the Laboratory of Social Relations at Harvard University.

Table 1 Intercorrelations[a] of the pro-Faubus and prosegregation votes.

Election	Faubus, Aug. 1954	Faubus, 1956	Faubus, 1958 b	Segregation, 1956
Faubus, July 1954	+.84	+.54	-.09(-.32)	-.50
Faubus, Aug. 1954		+.56	.00(-.17)	-.68
Faubus, 1956			+.12(+.04)	-.49
Faubus, 1958				+.35

[a] These are product-moment correlations using the seventy-five Arkansas counties as the units of analysis. Correlations above .30 are significantly higher than zero correlation at the .01 level of confidence.

[b] The correlations in parentheses apply when the adjoining mountain counties, Newton and Madison, are removed from the analysis. These two counties, of which the latter is the home county of Faubus, were the only ones to run up large majorities for Faubus in all four of his elections.

throughout his initial three primary campaigns also oppose segregation relatively more than the rest of the state.

But the smashing primary victory of 1958 offers a radically different picture. Only small, insignificant correlations exist between this fourth Faubus vote and the previous Faubus votes. Indeed, if two counties — one the home county of Faubus — are removed from the analysis, a significant negative association is found between the voting patterns of the first and fourth Faubus primaries. And, unlike his previous nominations, Faubus's 1958 primary vote relates positively and significantly with the 1956 segregation vote. Clearly, a new grouping of Arkansas counties more favorable toward segregation emerged in 1958 as the base of Faubus's political power.

THE GEOGRAPHY OF THE SHIFTING VOTING PATTERNS

Three rough divisions of Arkansas can be made on the basis of both geography and current voting patterns: the mountains, the border area, and the delta, as shown in Figure 1.[4] Arkansas political interests have frequently cut across these regions in the past,[5] but this division is helpful in highlighting the geographic shift in Faubus's political strength.

Figure 2 provides bar graphs indicating the total and regional percentages in the primaries and referenda. We observe first that Faubus's native mountain area was the backbone of his support in the early campaigns; in fact, neither the border nor the delta gave him a majority in the two 1954 primaries. In the 1956 primary all three geographic areas gave Faubus a majority, though the mountain

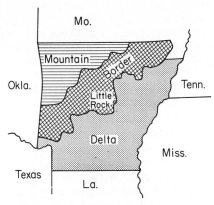

Figure 1 Three geographic areas of Arkansas.

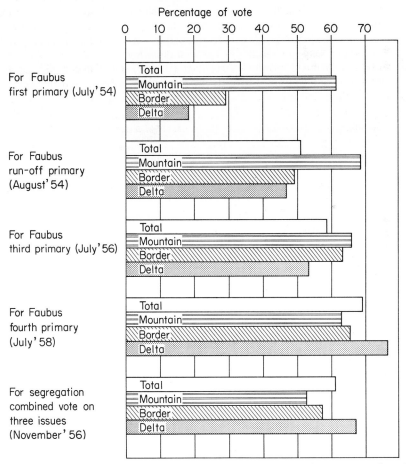

Figure 2 Comparison of four Faubus primaries for Governor of Arkansas and combined vote for segregation by region of State.

percentage remained the largest. But the areas reversed this pattern in 1958. While both the border and delta areas strikingly increased their support, the mountains actually decreased their support as compared to 1956 and became the least pro-Faubus of all — a point overlooked at the time of Faubus's overwhelming triumph.[6] This new Faubus pattern resembles the 1956 segregation vote, as shown at the bottom of Figure 2.

The principal demographic characteristics of these geographic areas are given in Table 2. The sixteen-county Ozark mountain area, bordering on southern Missouri and eastern Oklahoma, is predominately rural and has only about one-sixth of the state's population. It has the smallest percentage of people employed in manufacturing and has the smallest nonwhite ratio, 1 per 48.[7] Its Negroes are concentrated in the two cities of the region, Fort Smith and Fayetteville; they earned in 1949 the highest median family income for nonwhites of the three areas. Mountain whites, by contrast, earned the smallest white median family income in 1949. Thus, the part of Arkansas that is least in favor of racial segregation consists of the relatively nonindustrial Ozarks, populated largely by poor, rural whites.

Separating the Ozarks from the delta in a narrow, diagonal strip running from southeast Missouri to the Ouachita mountain region of Oklahoma, the twenty-four-county border area comprises about one-third of the state's population. Its voting percentages tend to be mid-way between the other areas (Figure 2), and its stands midway in terms of nonwhite percentage (1 per 8) and median family incomes of both nonwhites and whites. Little Rock, North Little Rock, and Hot Springs, three of the state's five largest cities in 1950, make this border region the most

Table 2 Demographic characteristics of three areas[a] of Arkansas.

Characteristic	Geographic Areas			Total State
	Mountain	Border	Delta	
Percentage of urban population, 1950	31.5	42.3	27.8	33.0
Percentage of rural-farm population, 1950	42.9	34.1	46.4	42.0
Percentage employed engaged in manufacturing, 1950	12.2	14.1	14.2	13.8
Percentage of white women in the labor force, 1950	20.5	21.6	17.9	19.8
Percentage of nonwhites, 1950	2.1	12.6	35.3	22.4
Median nonwhite family income, 1949	$978	$916	$683	$726
Median white family income, 1949	$1,330	$1,595	$1,709	$1,571

[a]As defined in the text.

SOURCE: *United States Census of Population, 1950,* Bureau of the Census, Vol. II, Part 4, Chap. B.

urban of the three and the least traditional as measured by the percentage of the white women in the labor force.[8]

The thirty-five county delta region of Arkansas extends from Memphis-dominated southwest Tennessee to northern Louisiana and northeast Texas; it is indistinguishable from the better-known flat, rural, and densely Negro deltaland of Mississippi. Here lies the bulwark of segregation sentiment in the state and the new center of Faubus's strength. The Arkansas delta contains approximately half the state's population and furnished from 45 to 49 per cent of the votes in the five contests under discussion. The 1860 census reveals that 7 out of every 9 slaves (78.5 per cent) in Arkansas were in this delta area. Nonwhites are today still concentrated there,[9] where they receive the lowest median family income of any part of the state. Delta whites, however, have the highest median family income. Thus, the delta has the widest disparity between white and Negro income of the Arkansas regions,[10] a situation of economic discrimination consistent with a high segregation vote. Though the most rural area, the delta had a seventh of its 1950 employed labor force in manufacturing — a good figure by the modest standards of agricultural Arkansas. Relatively few white women in the delta, however, enter the labor force, probably a result of the area's traditionalism, its relatively higher income for whites, and the availability of a large and cheap Negro labor supply.

THE DEMOGRAPHY OF THE SHIFTING VOTING PATTERNS

The varying characteristics of the mountain, border, and delta areas of Arkansas suggest that demographic factors are importantly related to the Faubus and segregation votes. Analyzing the state as a whole, the correlations of Table 3 pinpoint these demographic relationships more precisely.[11]

We have already seen that a sharp shift in the voting patterns for Faubus occurred between his first and fourth primary races (Table 1 and Figure 2); now we note in Table 3 both similarities and differences in the demography of these patterns. In both contests, significantly negative relationships exist between the amount of support for Faubus, on the one hand, and the 1950 urban population percentage and population increase from 1940 to 1950, on the other hand. But the two primaries relate differently to four other variables. In 1958, the Faubus vote by counties was at significant levels positively associated with the 1950 percentage of rural-farm residents and negatively associated with the 1950 percentage of white women in the labor force and the Negro educational level; in July 1954, these factors did not significantly relate to the Faubus vote. Moreover, the best single predictor of the first Faubus vote, nonwhite percentage, reverses sign and becomes a small and positive correlate of the fourth Faubus vote. In brief, pro-Faubus counties in both the July 1954 and 1958 primaries tended to be rural and poor;[12] yet 1958 pro-Faubus counties were likely to be more agricultural, more traditional, and more populated by poorly educated Negroes.

We noted earlier that the fourth primary victory of Faubus correlated positively with the 1956 segregation vote (Table 1) and resembled its geographic pattern (Figure 2). But Table 3 reveals that there are important demographic differences between the two votes. Though they both relate negatively to Negro education (for a restricted sample), only the segregation vote is highly associated with the 1950 nonwhite percentage.[13] And, as we have noted, the 1958 Faubus vote relates more

Table 3 · Correlations of voting and demographic factors. [a]

Variable	Faubus, July 1954	Faubus, 1958	Segregation 1956
Percentage of urban population, 1950	-.31	-.35	+.18
Percentage of rural-farm population, 1950	+.17	+.40	-.17
Percentage of population increase, 1940-1950	-.26	-.31	+.15
Percentage of white women in the labor force, 1950	-.06	-.38	+.05
Median years of education for nonwhites over 24, 1950	+.14 [b]	-.53 [b]	-.57 [b]
Percentage of nonwhites, 1950	[-.40] [c]	[+.19] [c]	[+.64] [c]

[a] Save for the nonwhite education and nonwhite percentage results, these are product-moment correlations using the seventy-five Arkansas counties as the units of analysis. These twelve product-moment correlations are significantly greater than zero at the .05 level of confidence when they are larger than .23, at the .01 level when they are larger than .30. All demographic data are taken from the *United States Census of Population, 1950,* Vol. II, Part 4, Chap. B.

[b] These nonwhite education product-moment correlations apply only for the forty-three counties in Arkansas that had enough Negroes over twenty-four years old in 1950 for the census to establish a reliable educational median. With this size of sample, correlations above .39 are significantly greater than zero at the .01 level of confidence.

[c] Since in thirty-two Arkansas counties Negroes constituted less than 5 per cent of the population, the distribution is too skewed to justify the use of product-moment correlations. The coefficients given are Kendall rank correlations. (See S. Siegel, *Nonparametric Statistics,* New York, McGraw-Hill, 1956, pp. 213-223.)

closely to the other four factors. To obtain a reasonably high relationship with this fourth primary vote, a combination of three variables is required: the segregation vote (Table 1), the rural-farm percentage, and the white women in the labor force percentage. The resulting multiple correlation is .62, with the three predictors independently accounting for approximately equal amounts of the 1958 county variance. Thus the 1958 primary triumph of Faubus was not just an expression of racial segregation sentiment; it also had an agricultural and traditional cast that was independent of segregation voting.

These data are similar to the voting for segregation in two other Southern states. Heer has offered evidence for interpreting the 1948 South Carolina vote for the "Dixiecrat" candidate for President, J. Strom Thurmond, as a direct measure of "white supremacy sentiment." [14] Like the present segregation data, Thurmond's support in South Carolina was concentrated in the counties with large Negro ratios (+.67), particularly those with poorly educated Negroes (-.59). [15] And Thurmond's strength tended to be greatest in the type of rural, agricultural county that in 1958 gave Faubus his strongest backing; the "Dixiecrat" vote in South Carolina related

related positively to the percentage of rural-farm whites (+. 37) and negatively with
the percentage of nonfarm whites in manufacturing (-. 53).[16]

The Ogburn and Grigg study of the 1956 Virginia referendum on public aid
to private education provides another segregation vote for comparison.[17] This Virginia vote was most highly associated, too, with the percentage of Negroes (+. 67)
and the median years of Negro education (-. 77).[18] It also had a poor, rural cast; it
related negatively to Negro (-. 45) and white (-. 45) income and to population increase from 1940 to 1950 (-. 47) and positively to the percentage of rural-farm
population (+. 29). Again, this poor, agricultural trend resembles the fourth Faubus primary but not the Arkansas segregation results. Indeed, from a cursory inspection of Table 3 one might conclude that segregation voting in Arkansas was
slightly stronger in the more prosperous urban counties. Actually, this is an illusion. In Arkansas, unlike South Carolina and Virginia, many counties with a large
Negro population are prosperous and urban by the meager standards of the state.
Thus, when the percentage of Negroes is controlled, the urban, rural-farm, population change, and white women in the labor force correlations with the segregation vote reverse their signs but remain statistically insignificant.[19]

The status of Negroes, then, proves to be the most reliable index of voting
on racial issues; the ratio of Negroes to whites and the level of Negro education
prove important in all three Southern states. Economic and agricultural variables
appear somewhat less important, though only in Arkansas do they fail to relate
significantly with segregation sentiment.

DISCUSSION AND CONCLUSIONS

These crude geographic and demographic analyses do not, of course, allow
us to determine the motivations and ideologies of individual voters.[20] But the findings do suggest three interesting trends.

I. The March of Faubus

The four gubernatorial primaries of Faubus have involved a drastic realignment in Arkansas politics. The "poor mountain boy" slipped into the Governor's mansion in 1954 largely on the basis of the overwhelming support he received
from the Ozark counties. Though he gained in border and delta favor in 1956, he was
still a mountain candidate. But after his role in the 1957 Little Rock school integration crisis, Faubus in 1958 had obviously become the delta favorite, and his
native mountain area began to withdraw its support of him. Faubus maintained his
"common man appeal," however; rural counties that lost residents from 1940 to
1950 tended to support him heavily in his fourth as well as his first primary.

These events are actually just the most recent reenactment of a long-time
Southern political pattern. From Bacon's Rebellion to the Farmer's Alliance, the
hill country of the South has traditionally opposed plantation interests. Though this
breach in the "solid South" has frequently been obscured by the impotence of the
upcountry in many states, a fundamental conflict of interests remains. It is not
surprising, then, that the hills have provided the South with a large share of its
deviantly liberal leaders — from Nathaniel Bacon and Thomas Jefferson of the past

to Hugo Black and Ralph McGill of the present.[21] But the hills have also produced their share of opportunists, men who began as if in opposition to the conservative planters and ended up the planters' servants. South Carolina, for instance, has had a succession of such upcountrymen: John Calhoun of the early nineteenth century, "Pitchfolk Ben" Tillman at the turn of the century, and J. Strom Thurmond of today.[22]

The march of Faubus, with differences only in detail, fits this broad outline. Faubus was the liberal alternative in the 1954 and 1956 primaries and consequently received his backing largely from the hills and his principal opposition from the delta. In 1957, by defending the segregation interests of the delta, Faubus joined the long line of opportunistic hillmen. And, like his predecessors, his political strength promptly shifted to the planter country.

2. Faubus and Segregation

The immediate press interpretation of Faubus's sweeping 1958 primary triumph was simply that the whole state had approved his prosegregation stand in Little Rock. The present results qualify this appraisal in two ways. First of all, one part of the state, the Ozarks, actually *decreased* its support of Faubus in 1958 (Figure 2).

Second, the voting patterns for Faubus in 1958 and for segregation in 1956, though moderately correlated (Table 1) and geographically similar (Figure 2), were demographically different (Table 3). The counties that ran up the largest majorities for Faubus in his fourth primary tended to be poor, traditional, and agricultural. None of these characteristics was associated with the segregation vote. Instead, only two Negro variables — nonwhite percentage and nonwhite education — predicted the segregation vote.

These differences suggest that the prosegregation areas responded differently to Faubus in 1958. More specifically, the less prosperous, more rural counties that favored segregation in 1956 responded most strongly for Faubus in 1958; other counties that favored segregation tended to increase their support of Faubus in 1958 but not as much. Two possible explanations can be offered for this finding. As mentioned previously, the "common man appeal" of Faubus demonstrated in earlier primaries probably made him more acceptable in the rustic regions. Furthermore, these poor farm counties had the least to lose from Faubus's actions in Little Rock. The damage done to the state's industrial expansion by Faubus was already apparent by the summer of 1958 and was most sharply felt by the more urban, nonagricultural counties.[23] It appears, then, that a consideration of economics as well as segregation sentiment is necessary to understand fully the voting pattern of Faubus's fourth primary.

3. Southern Voting on Segregation

Counties with a large percentage of Negroes and a low level of Negro education tend to vote heaviest for segregation in South Carolina, Virginia, and Arkansas. The importance of the Negro ratio variable is widely recognized. Not only is a large concentration of Negroes frequently seen by Southern whites as threat-of prejudice[24] and discrimination[25] — a tradition that may linger on even after the Negro percentage has been considerably reduced by out-migration.[26] And it is this entrenched tradition of discrimination that is being measured by Negro education. As an alternative explanation, Ogburn and Grigg have mentioned that whites might logically vote more in favor of school segregation when Negroes in their locality are unusually poorly educated.[27] Though this cause and effect interpretation may hold true for some white parents, it seems more likely that prosegregation voting and a long-time denial of full educational opportunities to Negroes in a county are two manifestations of the same thing: historically rooted cultural norms of racial discrimination.

NOTES

1. In Arkansas, as in other one-party states, a primary victory is tantamount to election.

2. Indication that the three referenda were seen as a single program is provided by the high correlations across counties between the three votes; each of these correlations is .90 or above. Therefore, throughout this paper we have combined the three votes into a single index of segregation sentiment for purposes of analysis.

3. From the perspective of studying *white* Arkansas voting, some systematic error is introduced by our inability to remove the Negro vote from these analyses. But this error cannot be large, for a number of reasons. Official 1957 registration data indicate that Negroes, who comprise over one-fifth of the state's population, constitute only one-ninth of the registered voters. And over half these Negro registrants are concentrated in just eight counties. (See Margaret Price, *The Negro and the Ballot,* Atlanta, Ga., Southern Regional Council, 1959, pp. 78-79.) Furthermore, unofficial calculations indicate that, save for Little Rock, a smaller percentage of Negro registrants actually vote than white registrants. Thus, later in this paper it will be shown that the segregation vote of 1956 is highly and positively related to Negro ratio — an almost impossible result had there been a large and distributed Negro vote. Ogburn and Grigg, in their analysis of Virginian voting on segregation, noted the same phenomenon; they found the white vote by counties correlated +.92 with the total vote. (See W. F. Ogburn and C.M. Grigg, "Factors Related to the Virginia Vote on Segregation," *Social Forces,* Vol. 34, 1954, pp. 301-308.)

4. The sixteen counties labeled "mountain" are: Baxter, Benton, Boone, Carroll, Crawford, Franklin, Fulton, Johnson, Logan, Madison, Marion, Newton, Scott, Searcy, Sebastian, and Washington. The twenty-four counties labeled "border" are: Clay, Cleburne, Conway, Faulkner, Garland, Greene, Howard, Independence, Izard, Jackson, Lawrence, Montgomery, Perry, Pike, Polk, Pope, Pulaski, Randolph, Saline, Sevier, Sharp, Stone, Van Buren, and Yell. And the thirty-five counties labeled "delta" are: Arkansas, Ashley, Bradley, Calhoun, Chicot, Clark, Cleveland, Columbia, Craighead, Crittenden, Cross, Dallas, Desha, Drew, Grant, Hempstead, Hot Spring, Jefferson, Lafayette, Lee, Lincoln, Little River, Lonoke, Miller, Mississippi, Monroe, Navada, Ouachita, Phillips, Poinsett, Prairie, St. Francis, Union, White, and Woodruff.

5. See V. O. Key, *Southern Politics*, New York, Knopf, 1949, Chap. 9.

6. This mountain shift cannot be accounted for in terms of Faubus's opponents. Though he faced another mountain candidate in the July primary of 1956, neither of his 1958 opponents was from the mountains; hence, they were not in a position to cut into his mountain vote as "local boys."

7. Negroes constituted 99.7 per cent of the nonwhites of Arkansas in 1950.

8. Percentage of white women in the labor force, in addition to being an economic variable, is assumed to be an index of traditionalism because of the South's traditional sanctions against white women formally working.

9. The twenty-seven counties with the largest nonwhite percentages in 1950 are all in the delta. Though these counties have been steadily losing Negroes by out-migration, the consistency of this relative pattern over time is attested to by the +.97 product-moment relationship between the 1900 and 1950 nonwhite percentages of counties.

10. Blalock has found this condition to be generally true of Southern counties with high nonwhite percentages. He noted that housing and educational, as well as income, discrimination correlated positively and highly with the nonwhite percentages of counties. (See H. M. Blalock, Jr., "Per Cent Non-white and Discrimination in the South," *American Sociological Review*, Vol. 22, 1957, pp. 677-682.)

11. Some error is introduced, particularly for the 1956 and 1958 votes, by the population changes that have occurred since 1950.

12. The poverty of these counties is indicated by their loss of population from 1940 to 1950, a factor that is related to such economic indices as family income and percentage of dwellings with refrigerators.

13. Key noted a similarly high relationship between nonwhite percentage and the Arkansas county vote pattern in 1948 for the prosegregation "Dixiecrat" ticket (Key, *op. cit.*, p. 343).

14. D. M. Heer, "The Sentiment of White Supremacy: An Ecological Study," *American Journal of Sociology*, Vol. 64, 1959, pp. 592-598.

15. The Negro education—Thurmond vote relationship was calculated from the 1950 census data by the present authors.

16. It is important to note, too, that actual school desegregation, as opposed to voting, in the border states of Missouri and Kentucky came earliest to the prosperous rural and urban counties. T. F. Pettigrew, "Demographic Correlates of Border-state Desegregation," *American Sociological Review*, Vol. 22, 1957, pp. 683-689.

17. Ogburn and Grigg, *op. cit.* Their correlations are based on restricted samples of Virginia counties, since not all the relevant data were available in the 100 Virginia counties.

18. Even after the Negro ratio factor is partialed out, the level of Negro education significantly relates to segregation voting for restricted samples in Virginia (-. 60) and Arkansas (-. 45), though not in South Carolina (-. 21).

19. These Kendall partial rank correlations (S. Siegel, *Nonparametric Statistics,* New York, McGraw-Hill, 1956, pp. 223-229) varied in magnitude from . 10 to . 01.

20. Another difficulty of such analyses is that they exaggerate the importance of the thinly populated counties by treating each county as an equal unit.

21. This is not to imply that the upcountry people are particularly tolerant of the Negro. Rather, the point is that they have not allowed concern over the Negro to shape their thinking like those in the Black Belt. Moreover, the poor uneducated hillsmen of the South have frequently noted that measures ostensibly aimed at the Negro also discriminate against them (e. g. the poll tax).

22. Tillman and Thurmond even came from the same Piedmont county, Edgefield. (See Key, *op. cit.,* Chap. 7.)

23. According to the official figures of the Arkansas Industrial Development Commission, 9, 471 new manufacturing jobs were created in Arkansas in 1956, 11, 424 in 1957, but only 5, 780 in 1958 *(Arkansas Gazette,* Sept. 27, 1959, p. 2). This is too big a drop-off to be attributed to the 1958 recession alone.

24. T. F. Pettigrew, "Desegregation and Its Chances for Success: Northern and Southern Views," *Social Forces,* Vol. 35, 1957, pp. 339-344; and "Regional Differences in Anti-Negro Prejudice," *Journal of Abnormal and Social Psychology,* Vol. 59, 1959, pp. 28-36.

25. Blalock, *op. cit.*

26. H. D. Price, *The Negro and Southern Politics,* New York, New York University Press, 1957, pp. 35-54.

27. Ogburn and Grigg, *op. cit.*

Political Factors and Negro Voter Registration in the South

Donald R. Matthews
James W. Prothro

A recent Herblock cartoon in the *Washington Post* depicts three bare-footed backwoodsmen. The oldest and most tattered of them (labeled "poll tax") lies wounded, his head propped against a boulder, his rifle abandoned near his side. As the other rifle-bearing rustics — identified as "literacy tests" and "scare tactics" — bend sorrowfully over him the older man says, "I think them Feds got me, boys, but I know you'll carry on." Perhaps it is premature to anticipate the ratification of the anti-poll tax amendment proposed by the 87th Congress as the newest addition to the federal constitution. No doubt the cartoonist is correct, however, in picturing both "literacy tests" and "scare tactics" as less vulnerable to federal government attack. These presumed barriers to equal participation by Negroes in the politics of the South may "carry on" for some time to come.

Yet at present political scientists are not able to say how much difference these and other political and legal arrangements and practices make in the rate of Negro voting in the states of the former Confederacy. About 28 per cent of the voting age Negroes in the South were registered to vote in 1958, as compared to about 60 per cent of the voting age whites.[1] It would be a gross error to attribute this substantial disparity to legal and political discrimination alone, though unquestionably official discrimination is a factor. For southern Negroes overwhelmingly possess the historical heritage of low social status, relatively small incomes, and limited educations received in inferior schools. These attributes are associated with low voter turnout among *all* populations, regardless of skin color or region. Moreover, the low status, income and education of many southern whites foster racial prejudice. Thus poverty and ignorance may have a double-barrelled effect on Negro political participation by decreasing the Negroes' motivation and ability to participate while increasing white resistance to their doing so. The low voting rates of Negroes in the South may result to a large extent from these factors, as well as from direct political or legal discrimination by the white community. So far, the methods of political science have not been successfully applied to the problem of sorting out these various factors and ascertaining their relative importance.

In an earlier paper,[2] we analyzed the relationships between a wide gamut of

Reprinted from *American Political Science Review,* Vol. 57 (1963), pp. 355-367, by permission of the authors and publisher.

Grants from the Rockefeller Foundation [to UNC's Institute for Research in Social Science], and a Senior Award for Research on Governmental Affairs from the Social Science Research Council made this research possible and are gratefully acknowledged. A portion of this paper was presented at the Duke University Conference on "The Impact of Political and Legal Changes in the Postwar South," Durham, N.C., July 12-14, 1962.

social and economic factors and the rates of Negro voter registration in the South. Twenty-one census-type demographic characteristics of southern counties were correlated with the per cent of the counties' voting age Negro populations registered to vote. A multiple-correlation coefficient of .53 was obtained, which means that these 21 variables statistically "explain" about 28 per cent (R^2) of the variation in Negro registration rates. While the magnitude of this correlation indicates that social and economic conditions have a powerful influence, it still leaves much room for significant variation independent of these forces. In this paper we shall attempt to isolate and measure the impact of political and legal factors on Negro voter registration in the 11 states of the Confederacy.

I. THE DATA AND THE APPROACH

We start with an analysis of a large number of characteristics of southern counties (counting Virginia's independent cities as counties) obtained or derived from the U.S. Census and other standard sources.[3] Since our focus is on Negro registration, 139 counties were excluded because their populations contained less than 1 per cent Negroes, or because their registration data were not available from the U.S. Commission on Civil Rights. The 997 other southern counties are included in the analysis.[4]

These data suffer from a number of limitations. While our interest is in Negro *voting,* we have had to employ *registration* figures since they are available by race as well as county, as voting totals are not. Registration figures vary in accuracy from one state to the next and in some cases are little more than informed estimates. Our unit of analysis is the county, not individuals, and it is often hazardous to transfer conclusions drawn from one level of analysis to the other. Finally, our data are for one point in time. We are therefore limited to the analysis of variations in the rate of Negro registration of southern counties in 1958.[5]

Our basic approach is that of multiple regression and residual analysis.[6] In computing the multiple correlation coefficient between the 21 demographic characteristics and Negro registration rates previously reported, we obtained an equation — called a multiple regression equation — which represents the typical relationship between these 21 variables and Negro registration rates for the South as a whole. By entering the values of these 21 social and economic attributes for each county into this equation, a "predicted" rate of Negro registration is obtained for every southern county. This is the proportion of voting age Negroes who would be registered if the relationships in that county between socio-economic structure and Negro registration corresponded exactly to those for the South as a whole. Some counties have just the level of Negro registration they "ought" to have on that basis, while others have registration rates above or below the predicted level. By examining the pattern of these deviations — called "residuals" in statistical parlance — we are able to control the effects of socio-economic structure on Negro registration, and thereby to ascertain whether political and legal factors have any independent association with Negro registration; and if so, how much. A residual of 0.0 indicates that the rate of Negro voter registration is exactly what the county's social and economic attributes would lead one to expect; the positive or negative value of other residuals indicates whether the county's actual Negro registration is above or below the level expected from its socio-economic characteristics. The larger the residual, the more likely it is that other factors are needed to explain the county's Negro registration rate.

II. STATE VARIATIONS IN NEGRO VOTER REGISTRATION RATES

Perhaps the most important political and legal fact about the South is its division into eleven states. The rates of voter registration by adult Negroes vary widely among these states.

In Table 1 the former Confederate states are ranked according to the average per cent of the voting age Negro population registered to vote in their counties. In Mississippi, the average county has only about 3 per cent of its potential Negro electorate registered to vote. The average county in South Carolina has about 12 per cent. In Tennessee, on the other hand, the typical county has 72 per cent of the voting age Negroes registered, a figure which is no doubt inflated by the state's casual approach to the niceties of electoral administration.

What accounts for these wide variations among the states? We have already shown that a part of the explanation lies in the differences in the social and economic structure of the states. Mississippi and South Carolina, for example, have a larger proportion of Negroes in their populations than the other southern states, and this has a major depressing effect on Negro registration.[7] But our ability to predict, by means of a multiple regression equation, what the rate of registration ought to be on the basis of social and economic characteristics indicates that this is only a partial explanation, not the full story.

Table 1 Mean percentage of voting age Negroes registered to vote, by county, in Southern states, compared to mean percentage predicted by 21 demographic variables (1958).

State	Actual Mean Per Cent	Predicted Mean Per Cent	Residual	Actual Mean as Percentage of Predicted Mean
Mississippi	3.4	17.7	- 14.3	19.2
South Carolina	12.5	19.4	- 6.9	64.4
Alabama	20.5	26.8	- 6.3	76.5
Virginia	24.1	34.3	- 10.2	70.3
Arkansas	27.6	32.3	- 4.7	85.4
Georgia	30.4	24.9	+ 5.5	122.1
Louisiana	31.2	31.2	0.0	100.0
North Carolina	36.0	32.8	+ 3.2	109.7
Texas	36.8	36.7	+ 0.1	100.3
Florida	39.1	32.6	+ 6.5	119.9
Tennessee	72.3	39.7	+ 32.6	182.1

The second column of Table 1 presents the predicted Negro registration percentage for the average county within each of the southern states. Mississippi not only has the lowest and Tennessee the highest actual rates of Negro registration but they also "ought" to have the lowest and highest rates on the basis of their social and economic attributes. If this were a sufficient explanation, however, the predicted and the actual rates of registration should be the same. This is very nearly the case in two states — Louisiana and Texas — but all the others have either more or less Negroes registered than the expected rate. In Mississippi, for example, about 18 per cent of the voting age Negroes ought to be registered if Mississippi counties responded to socio-economic factors as other southern counties do; but instead, only about 3 per cent are actually registered. The Negro registration rate is about 7 percentage points below the expected in South Carolina, 6 points below in Alabama, 10 points below in Virginia, and 5 points below in Arkansas. On the other hand, Tennessee (+32. 6 residual), Florida (+6. 5), Georgia (+5. 5), and North Carolina (+3. 2) have more Negroes registered to vote than expected.

These state contrasts persist, accordingly, even after we minimize the possibility of finding differences by controlling for 21 social and economic factors. Raw differences in registration rates show a wild variation — the range of differences reaching 69 percentage points between Tennessee and Mississippi (Column 1). But much of this difference clearly stems from the fact that Mississippi has so many more Negroes and is both more rural and less industrialized. When such factors are controlled the difference of 69 points between the two states is reduced to 47 (Column 3). Or, if we take less extreme cases and compare South Carolina with Florida, the raw difference of 27 points is reduced to a residual difference of 13. By the same token, residual analysis may reveal a small raw difference to be more meaningful than it appears. Georgia counties, for example, have an average Negro registration rate 3 percentage points higher than Arkansas counties. But, allowing for the social and economic attributes of these counties, one would expect the Arkansas average to be higher than Georgia's; hence, the raw difference of 3 points becomes a residual difference of 10 points.

The contrasts revealed by residual analysis demonstrate that the state political systems must be an independent influence on Negro voter registration. To say that these contrasts result from different state political systems is not to say very much. What aspects of state politics account for these differences? We turn now to this problem.

III. LEGAL REQUIREMENTS FOR VOTING

Around the turn of the century, southern Bourbons led a movement to restrict the suffrage in response to the twin threats of the Negro and of populism. In the process they developed a "variety of ingenious contrivances to inconvenience the would-be voter. "[8] Some of these contrivances survive to this day, despite the intervening rise and fall of the white primary, changing political attitudes and conditions, and the efforts of the U. S. Supreme Court. Just how effectively these electoral obstacles — today primarily the poll tax and literacy tests — serve to disenfranchise potential Negro voters is not known. In northern discussions of southern politics, these devices are often cast in "the role of chief villain. "[9] Detailed analyses by Key and Ogden suggest that their impact on the turnout of *white* voters is fairly modest. "The chances are," Key writes, "that if other things remain equal (and they rarely do), elimination of the poll tax alone would increase voting in most southern states by no more than 5 to 10 per cent of the potential number of white voters."[10] Our multiple regression analysis enables us to make a similar estimate for potential Negro voters.

Five southern states — Alabama, Arkansas, Mississippi, Texas, and Virginia — still levy poll taxes. They vary in amount from Mississippi's $2.00 to Arkansas's $1.00 and must be paid one to nine months before election day. The tax is cumulative in Mississippi, Alabama, and Virginia; new voters are required to pay the tax for the preceding two or three years before they are enrolled. Most states exempt members of the armed forces, and some also exempt veterans, the elderly, the blind, the deaf or dumb, the maimed, Indians, and other miscellaneous categories of citizens.

All the southern states save Arkansas, Florida, Tennessee, and Texas require potential voters to pass literacy tests. A recitation of the language of these requirements is scarcely necessary: "Whether a person can register to vote depends on what the man down at the courthouse says, and he usually has the final say. It is how the tests are administered that matters."[11] In one North Carolina county, for example, the registrant is regarded as literate even if he requires

Table 2 State voter requirements and Negro voter registration residuals, by county, 1958.

Voter Requirements	Mean Residual of Counties
Poll Tax and Literacy Test	
Mississippi	− 14.3
Virginia	− 10.2
Alabama	− 6.3
All counties in group	− 10.5
Poll Tax Only	
Arkansas	− 4.7
Texas	+ 0.1
All counties in group	− 1.0
Literacy Test Only	
South Carolina	− 6.9
Louisiana	0.0
North Carolina	+ 3.2
Georgia	+ 5.5
All counties in group	+ 2.3
Neither Literacy Test Nor Poll Tax	
Florida	+ 6.5
Tennessee	+ 32.6
All counties in group	+ 18.1

help in reading the following words: solemnly, affirm, support, Constitution, inconsistent, therewith, resident, township, precinct, ward, general, election, and registered. In a Mississippi county, on the other hand, the registrar of voters frankly told the authors that the literacy test was administered so that no Negro could pass.

To what extent are differences in formal voting requirements — despite variations in their administration — related to differences in registration rates, after controlling for social and economic structure? The answer is given in Table 2.

County registration rates within the three states with both the poll tax and the literacy test are, on the average, 10.5 percentage points below the predicted value. Counties in the two states with neither a poll tax nor a literacy test have registration rates 18.1 percentage points higher than expected. The pattern is not perfect. South Carolina, with only a literacy test, has a lower residual than Alabama, with both a fairly substantial poll tax and a literacy test. Texas has a small plus residual (+0.1) while Arkansas has a sizeable negative one (-4.7); both are poll tax states without a literacy requirement. Nonetheless, the tendency for the states with stringent formal voter requirements to have lower registration rates than those with more liberal requirements is impressive, even after controlling for 21 social and economic factors. If we were able to take account of the way these formal requirements are variously administered by different local officials within each state, the relationship in Table 2 would undoubtedly be even closer.

A survey of county registration officials made by the North Carolina Advisory Committee to the U.S. Commission on Civil Rights suggests the extremely wide variety of ways in which the same legal requirements are actually administered.[12] Some county registrars reported administering tests which involved the taking of oral dictation, extensive reading aloud, quizzing applicants on the meaning of words and phrases, and the like, while others settled for an ability to fill out an application form properly and to sign one's name. Several county registration officials reported that they did not enforce the constitutionally required literacy test at all. The following counties — all in the northeastern black-belt area of the state — reported literacy tests which appeared to be unusually difficult or arbitrary:

County	County Residual	Residual Adjusted for State Mean
Bertie	- 1.0	- 4.2
Camden	- 9.1	- 13.3
Currituck	- 15.1	- 18.3
Franklin	+ 3.2	0.0
Gates	- 22.1	- 25.3
Greene	- 6.1	- 9.3
Halifax	- 2.8	- 6.0
Northampton	+ 0.7	- 2.5
Warren	+ 1.8	- 1.4
Mean	- 5.6	- 8.9

Their Negro registration rate is, on the average, more than 5 percentage points below the expected and almost 9 percentage points below that expected for North Carolina counties with their social and economic characteristics.

The North Carolina counties which do not administer literacy tests are all in the mountainous west. They and their residuals are:

County	County Residual	Residual Adjusted for State Mean
Catawba	+ 23. 5	+ 20. 3
Wilkes	+ 32. 6	+ 29. 4
Yancey	+ 12. 9	+ 9. 7
Mean	+ 23. 0	+ 19. 8

On the average, these counties have 23 percentage points more Negroes registered than predicted, and almost 20 percentage points more than the state average.

Crude as these data are, they still suggest that formal voter requirements and their administration have a far larger impact on Negro voter registration than they do on white registration. Even so, other political factors are obviously at work. The structure of party and factional competition and the presence or absence of race organizations and of racial violence are less formal political variables that have been cited as offering possible explanations for Negro participation in particular localities. The remainder of this article is devoted to an examination of the importance of these variables for South-wide variations in rates of Negro voter registration.

IV. THE STRUCTURE OF COMPETITION: PARTY SYSTEMS

The South differs from the rest of the United States in so many ways that it is tempting to assume that all forms of distinctiveness are functionally linked. Thus southerners register and vote in smaller proportions than other Americans, and the South is the country's largest one-party region. Hence, the one-party politics of the South must decrease voter participation. Much can be said for this interpretation. When the results of general elections are foreordained in favor of Democracy — and despite important changes in recent years this is the most common situation for most offices in the South — general election campaigns are tepid affairs, party organizations make little if any effort to increase registration or to get out the vote, and the act of voting in general elections becomes little more than a ritual.

Furthermore, though the Democratic primaries may be hotly and regularly contested, this form of electoral competition seems less effective in stimulating political interest and activity than partisan competition. Contrary to a popular assumption, the turnout for primary elections in the South, where the primary may be the real election, is no greater than in the parts of the country where the real election comes later. [13] A sizeable group of candidates running without party labels is harder to choose between, and the likely pay-off from the election of one candidate rather than another is difficult to determine. Without the mental shorthand of party identification to structure the situation, the voter is presented with more vexing cognitive problems to solve than in a partisan contest. It is more difficult to ascertain where one's self-interest lies and the effort or "costs" of voting are correspondingly increased. While Democratic factions seek to improvise get-out-the-vote organizations in behalf of their candidates, these are transient affairs, relatively impotent even when compared to the eroded efficacy of local party organizations outside of the South. All these characteristics of one-partyism have their greatest impact on poorly educated, "have-not" groups in the southern electorate, of which the Negro is conspicuously one.

The difficulty with this explanation, as applied to voter registration or general election turnout, is the dearth of supporting data. While we do have evidence to support the argument that primaries stimulate less voter interest than more structured general elections, Robert Lane argues that it is nothing more than a "common-sense view of the causes of high or low participation" to say that "a close

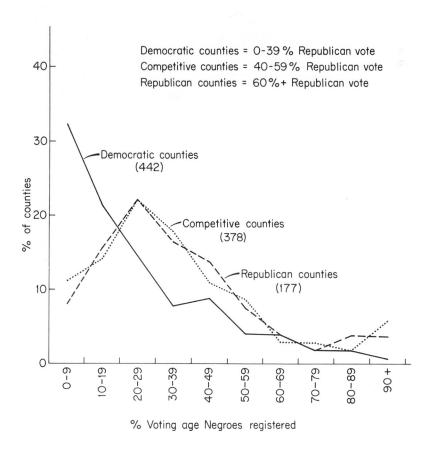

Figure 1 Party competition in presidential election of 1956 and Negro voter registration rates, by county.

election, where the issue was in doubt, would bring more people to the polls than one in which the result was determined from the beginning. "[14] As for the non-southern parts of the United States, Lane reports that, "When we eliminate regional factors by dropping the South (as a region with a special sub-culture) and examine counties instead of states, the relationship between turnout and closeness of vote disappears. . . ."[15] From this point of view, registration and voting are seen as satisfying needs of the citizen unrelated to the closeness of election contests, so that only a small correlation can be expected between one-partyism and political participation. Which line of interpretation holds up when variations within the "special sub-culture" of southern counties are examined?

Figure 1 appears to support the earlier line of reasoning: Negro voter registration increases in southern counties as party competition increases. It seems safe to assume that the counties in which Eisenhower polled less than 40 per cent of the vote for President in 1956 are Democratic in presidential as well as other electoral contests. Relatively few Negroes tend to be registered in these counties, compared to the more competitive counties (defined as those with 40-59 per cent for Eisenhower). But the rates of Negro registration seem as high in heavily Republican counties (60 per cent and over for Eisenhower) as in the competitive counties. The difficulty with these findings, as with those cited by Lane, is that we do not know whether these differences are the result of competitive elections or of the tendency for presidential Republicanism to be strongest in areas where the social and economic inhibitions against Negro voting are most attenuated.

Table 3, which shows the mean residuals for Democratic, competitive, and Republican counties, demonstrates that most of the tendency for Negro registration to increase with levels of competition in presidential voting is the result of social and economic factors. Republican counties have slightly fewer Negroes registered than would be expected on the basis of their social and economic characteristics, and Democratic counties likewise. The competitive counties, on the other hand, have 1 percentage point more Negroes registered than their social

Table 3 Party systems and Negro voter registration residuals, by county, 1958.

	Mean Residual	Number of Counties
Democratic counties	− 0. 9	442
Competitive counties	+ 1. 3	378
Republican counties	− 0. 9	177

Note: Democratic counties defined as those in which Republican presidential vote in 1956 was from 0-39% of total vote; in competitive counties the Republicans polled 40-59%; in Republican counties, 60% and over.

structure suggests. The existence or absence of partisan competition is associated with variations in Negro registration rates, then, but once we go beyond that simple co-variation we discover that the variations of both are largely accounted for by the social and economic characteristics of southern counties.

V. THE STRUCTURE OF COMPETITION:
FACTIONAL SYSTEMS

The vast bulk of all political competition in the South takes place within the Democratic party. We have already seen that this form of politics seems, in general, to have a small inhibiting effect upon Negro registration rates. But the structure of Democratic factionalism varies a good deal from one southern state to the next and this may affect the meaning of voting to southern Negroes.

Repeatedly confronted with a choice between an incumbent like Senator Eastland and a challenger attempting to outdo the senior Senator from Mississippi at his own game, thousands of potential Negro voters may never have any incentive to attempt to register. Given a choice between Frank Porter Graham and Willis Smith, they might be expected to turn out in droves — as they did. The southern Negro vote is "issue-oriented," and race is the important issue. In some southern states, all the candidates for public office are unsatisfactory from the Negro's point of view; in other states, it is usually possible for the Negro to distinguish one or more candidates as favorably disposed to Negro interests — despite the candidate's best efforts to avoid being labeled by whites as the "Negro candidate" — and these candidates have some chance of winning. Before 1958, this normally seems to have been the case in Tennessee, North Carolina, Louisiana, Florida and Texas but rarely so elsewhere.

Southern state political systems vary in other ways which may affect the nature of the choice confronting potential or actual Negro voters. In some states, two fairly clear-cut factions battle it out on rather even terms and these factions tend to persist from one election year to the next. In others, Democratic factionalism is more fluid and unstructured, the number of serious candidates tends to be larger, and there is little relationship between one electoral contest and the next. The extent to which the Democratic party divides into two party-like factions, or tends instead toward splintered factionalism, is suggested by the following figures on the percentage of the total vote polled jointly by the two highest candidates for

	Median Per Cent
Virginia	100.0
Tennessee	95.8
Georgia	94.7
South Carolina	89.8
Arkansas	81.5
North Carolina	77.9
Texas	69.3
Florida	60.5
Louisiana	58.6
Alabama	58.1
Mississippi	44.4

governor, in the initial Democratic primaries (excluding run-offs) held in each election year between 1948 and 1960. [16] In Virginia, Tennessee and Georgia, electoral battles appear to be dominated by one or two major factions which manage to attract virtually all the vote. In Mississippi, Alabama, Louisiana (of the post-Long era), Florida and Texas, state politics follows the "every man for himself" style of fluid multi-factionalism. The other states fall into an intermediate group, closer to bi-factional than multi-factional politics.

The relative strength as well as the number of factions is important. A better way to assess the competitiveness of Democratic factionalism is to look at the median per cent of the total vote polled by the leading candidate for governor in the first Democratic primary during the same span of years considered above. The percentages are:

	Median Per Cent
Virginia	65. 8
South Carolina	61. 3
Tennessee	55. 6
Georgia	49. 3
Arkansas	47. 7
North Carolina	46. 7
Texas	39. 9
Florida	34. 7
Alabama	34. 1
Louisiana	33. 1
Mississippi	28. 1

Factional struggles were unusually uneven in Virginia and South Carolina. During the fifties, these were not so much bi-factional states as states in which one faction dominated without serious challange.

From a logical point of view, the citizen should have less reason to vote where one dominant faction runs the show; there is no realistic choice to be made. It is a good deal easier for a voter of limited political interest and skill to determine where his self-interest lies in a bi-factional state than in one characterized by fluid multi-factionalism. Candidates can be identified as belonging to the Long faction, or Talmadge faction, or Kerr Scott faction, and these labels have at least some policy meaning.

We expect, therefore, that both the number and strength of Democratic factions and the extent to which candidates are identified with different racial views should be associated with different rates of voter registration among Negroes. When the 11 southern states are classified according to these criteria, and the mean county residuals of each type of state are examined, we see that this is indeed the case (Table 4). Two states, Virginia and South Carolina, have been dominated by one faction since 1948 and neither offers candidates favorable to Negroes. The mean county residual for the two states is -9.3. Alabama and Mississippi have multi-factional systems combined with white racial consensus: their mean county residual is -10.7. Arkansas and Georgia have had bi-factional Democratic politics but it has been difficult for Negroes to ascertain significant differences on racial policy between them: their mean county residual is +2.7. Louisiana, Florida, and Texas

Table 4   The structure of factional competition in southern states, 1948-60, and Negro voter registration residuals[a].

Type of Factionalism	Generally No Major Candidate Favorable to Negroes		Generally 1 or More Major Candidates Favorable to Negroes		All Counties in Group
One Dominant Faction	Virginia South Carolina All Counties in Group	- 10. 2 - 6. 9 - 9. 3			-9. 3

Two Competitive Factions	Arkansas
	Georgia
	All Counties in
	   Group
		- 4. 7
		+ 5. 5
		
		+ 2. 7
			Tennessee
			North Carolina
			All Counties in
			   Group
				+ 32. 4
				+ 3. 2
				
				+13. 7
					+7. 3

Multi-factionalism	Alabama
	Mississippi
	All Counties in
	   Group
		- 6. 3
		-14. 3
		
		-10. 7
			Louisiana
			Florida
			Texas
			All Counties in
			   Group
				0. 0
				+ 6. 5
				+ 0. 1
				
				+ 1. 4
					- 2. 4

All Counties in Group	- 4. 9		+5. 3		

[a] The numbers in the table are the mean residuals of counties in states or groups of states.

have had multi-factional politics in recent years, but they have offered candidates with discernible differences from the Negro point of view. Taken together, they have a residual of +1. 4. Finally, North Carolina and Tennessee have had both bifactional politics and perceptible differences on racial matters between the factions. The mean county residual for these two states is +13. 7. Thus the structure

Table 5   Mean Negro voter registration residuals by extent of race organization in southern counties, 1958.

Extent of Negro Organization in County	White Race Organization in County	No White Race Organization in County	All Counties
Local organization and NAACP chapter	+ 11. 4 (14)	+ 1. 0 (10)	+ 7. 0 (24)
NAACP chapter only	+ 0. 8 (74)	- 0. 3 (214)	- 0. 01 (288)
No Negro organization, no data	- 10. 5 (125)	+ 0. 4 (551)	- 1. 6 (676)
All counties	- 5. 5 (221)	+ 0. 3 (776)	

Note: Too few counties have local organizations but no NAACP chapters to permit computation of means. They have been included, however, in the means for "all counties." The number of counties upon which means are based are in parentheses.

of competition does seem to make a difference, and these differences are in the expected direction. The presence of observable differences in the racial views of candidates is associated with about 10 percentage points more Negroes registered to vote than in states where such distinctions cannot be drawn. The surplus of Negro voter registration in bi-factional states is even larger, especially when compared to states generally dominated by a single faction. Thus the structure of Democratic factionalism appears to have a major impact on Negro registration rates. [17]

VI. RACE ORGANIZATION

If neither party nor factional organizations are particularly effective in structuring electoral choice or stimulating electoral activity in the South, other kinds of organizations may seek to fill this void.

The South has seen a plethora of new racial organizations created since *Smith v. Allwright* and *Brown v. Board of Education.* Scores of Negro voters' leagues, civic leagues, community betterment organizations, ministerial alliances, etc., have been organized in local communities. The Southern Christian Leadership Conference, Student Non-Violent Coordinating Committee, and Committee on Racial Equality have entered the lists along with the National Association for the Advancement of Colored People and the Urban League as instruments of Negro protest. Local chapters have been established in the South by some of these national organizations. Among the white majority, the White Citizens Councils, sometimes by different names in different areas but all dedicated to the defense of white supremacy, have sprung up and have largely supplanted the Ku Klux Klan. Most of these racial organizations are involved in electoral politics, either quite directly and explicitly or, at a minimum, as a provider of cues in the confusing atmosphere of southern factional politics. It seems reasonable to expect these groups to have some impact on rates of Negro voter registration.

We have made strenuous efforts to ascertain — through correspondence and a systematic search of newspaper files [18] — the location of all Negro and white race organizations and their local chapters. Our list is no doubt incomplete, but we are reasonably confident that the counties we think have such organizations do have them — at least on paper.

Table 5 shows the relationships between the extent of race organization in the counties and their Negro registration residuals. Looking first at the marginal distributions at the far right and bottom of the table, we can readily see that extensive Negro organization is associated with a substantial (7 percentage points) surplus of Negro registered voters over the registration rate predicted by social and economic structure alone. Counties with white race organizations have about 5.5 percentage points fewer Negroes registed than predicted. Both types of race organizations thus seem to be related to Negro registration rates to a fairly sizeable extent.

The partial distributions in the center of the table are even more interesting. A local Negro organization, rather than an NAACP chapter, seems to have the greater impact on Negro registration. Most of these local organizations are explicitly political in orientation whereas NAACP chapters are often little more than fund-raising agencies. Forty-three per cent of the counties with such local organizations have had at least one Negro public official, either elective or appointed, in recent years; whereas only 13 per cent of the counties with only NAACP chapters have had one or more Negro public officials. Only 0.3 per cent of the counties with no known Negro organizations have had a Negro appointed or elected to public office.

Negro registration is not seriously inhibited by the existence of white race organizations, except in the areas where there are no Negro organizations at all; then the dampening effect is substantial, more than 10 percentage points. In areas where both Negroes and whites are organized, the Negro registration rate is actually higher than in counties where only the Negroes are organized along racial lines. Under these circumstances, the organization of a white counter-organization may actually have a boomerang effect, by drawing the Negroes closer together in their own organizations than they might otherwise have been. Local Negro political organizations seem to thrive on competition; white organizations upon its absence. Both, however, help account for a fair share of the variation in Negro voter registration rates in the contemporary South, even after controlling for social and economic factors.

VII. RACIAL VIOLENCE AND INTIMIDATION

The South has had a violent history. Before the Civil War, much of the region was thinly-settled frontier in which vigilantism and a "hell-of-a-fella" tradition flourished.[19] The region's "peculiar institution" — slavery — was, by definition, based upon force. A bloody civil war, fought largely on southern soil, and an anarchistic Reconstruction served to reinforce this tradition of violence. The subsequent reestablishment of white supremacy and the disfranchisement of the Negro were achieved primarily by force, threats, and intimidation. Constitutional and legal devices — such as the grandfather clause, poll tax, white primary, and legally enforced racial separation in other realms of life — followed the *de facto* realization of racial segregation and served to reinforce, maintain, and legitimize the arrangement. Most of these constitutional and legal defenses have now crumbled, a few of them voluntarily abandoned by the white South, more of them as a result of Supreme Court decisions. But even in the absence of these "legal" and "constitutional" barriers, many southern Negroes are reluctant to exercise their newly reestablished franchise and to participate fully in the political life of the region. Some of these non-voting Negroes are undoubtedly and understandably afraid of a possible violence or economic reprisal from a hostile white community.

Negroes living in areas characterized by unusual racial violence could be expected to be particularly reluctant to attempt to register and vote. Unfortunately, reliable and complete data on the incidence of racial violence in southern counties are hard to come by. Most compilations of such incidents are based upon newspaper accounts, probably adequate for the larger cities but spotty in their coverage of racial violence in rural areas. They are confined to overt acts and rarely deal with threats or the subtler forms of intimidation. Two such compilations will be used in this analysis, the Tuskegee Institute's records of lynchings in the South between 1900 and 1931 and the Southern Regional Council's listing of acts of violence occuring between 1955 and 1960 in the wake of *Brown v. Board of Education.* [20]

Racial violence in the South during these two periods was rather different. Lynching was most common ". . . in the newer and more sparsely settled portions of the South, where cultural and economic institutions [were] least stable and officers of the law [were] farthest apart, poorest paid, and most dependent upon local sentiment. "[21] Victims were almost invariably Negro and the cause of the mob action was an alleged crime by an individual Negro against a white person. In 1930, for example, the alleged reasons for that year's 21 lynchings were: murder (5), rape (8), robbery or theft (3), attempted rape (2) and bombing a house (1). No crime at all was alleged in the case of two lynchings. [22]

The new style racial violence since the *Brown* decision tends rather to occur in urban areas (Figure 2). Most recent violence has been triggered by collective efforts by Negroes to take advantage of their newly found legal rights. The targets of white violence and destruction are frequently institutions — churches, schools, temples — and include presumed white sympathizers toward the Negro cause. (Of the 29 persons reported shot and wounded in racial incidents between

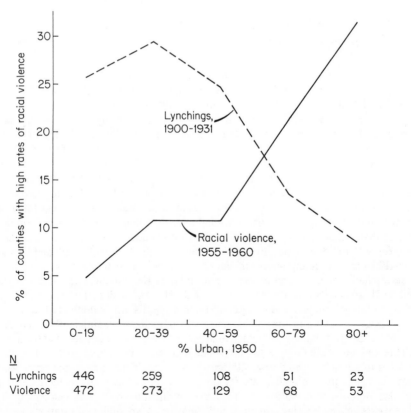

N					
Lynchings	446	259	108	51	23
Violence	472	273	129	68	53

Figure 2 Per cent of counties with high racial violence, by per cent urban, 1950.

Table 6 Relationship between lynching rate, 1900-31, and acts of racial violence, 1955-60, for Southern countries.

Lynchings Per 100,000 Total Population, 1900-31	Acts of Racial Violence, 1955-60				Number of Counties
	None	*1 or 2*	*3+*	*Total*	
	%	%	%	%	
0-9	88	9	3	100	656
10-19	90	10	0	100	144
20-29	98	2	0	100	39
30-39	95	5	0	100	19
40+	100	0	0	100	30

1955 and 1960, 11 were white. All six fatalities, however, were Negro.[23]) Counties with high rates of lynching in the early decades of this century have *not* been the areas with the most spectacular incidents of racial violence in recent years. Most of the new-style racial violence has occurred in areas with peaceful race relations in the past, at least in so far as lynchings are concerned (Table 6).

Table 7 presents the mean percentage of the voting age Negro population registered to vote in southern counties, according to their rate of lynchings from 1900 to 1931 and to the amount of racial violence reported to have occurred in them from 1955 to 1960.

The very few counties with both a history of lynching *and* recent racial violence have low rates of Negro registration, about 7 per cent. The next lowest group of southern counties are those with generally peaceful race relations, and the highest rates of Negro registration are found in counties with either heavy lynching in the past or present day racial incidents, but not both. This same rank order of counties is maintained when we control for 21 socio-economic variables by examining Negro voter registration residuals (Table 8). The counties with both high lynching and high contemporary racial violence scores have about 11 percentage points fewer Negroes registered to vote than we would expect on the basis of their social and economic characteristics. Those with either some contemporary racial violence

Table 7 Mean per cent of voting age Negroes registered to vote in Southern counties, by amount of racial violence.

Lynching Rate, 1900-31	Amount of Racial Violence, 1955-60		
	None	*Some*	*Total*
Low	14.8% (576)	29.3% (80)	16.1% (656)
High	26.6% (216)	6.9% (16)	25.3% (232)
Total	18.1% (792)	25.6% (96)	

Notes: A "low" lynching rate is less than 10 lynchings per 100,000 population in 1930. The numbers in parentheses are the total number of counties upon which the percentages have been based.

Table 8 Mean Negro voter registration residuals of Southern counties, by amount of
racial violence.

| Lynching Rate, 1900-31 | Amount of Racial Violence, 1955-60 | | |
	None	Some	Total
Low	− 0. 2 (575)	+ 2. 0 (80)	+ 0. 1 (655)
High	+ 3. 2 (216)	− 11. 3 (16)	+ 2. 2 (232)
Total	+ 0. 7 (791)	− 0. 1 (96)	

Notes: A "low" lynching rate is less than 10 lynchings per 100,000 population in 1930.
The numbers in parentheses are the total number of counties upon which the percentages
have been based. No residual figure was obtained for one county for which the percentage of voting age Negroes registered to vote was not known. Hence this table is based on
one less case than Table 7.

or a history of lynching have about 2 or 3 percentage points more registered Negroes than anticipated, while the counties with little or no violence have about the
expected rate.

   Apparently, to speculate a bit, race violence nowadays must be extremely
massive indeed in order to have a depressing effect on Negro voter registration.
Save in the most violent one or two per cent of southern counties, racial violence
seems to be more an indication of white weakness than of strength. Far lower rates
of Negro registration are found in counties with little if any racial violence. Here
Negro subordination may be so total that violence is not required to keep the Negro
"in his place" and outside of the polling booths. Racial violence, standing alone, is
overestimated as an inhibition of Negro political participation. Save in a tiny frac-
tion of southern counties, its effects, if any, seem to be to contribute to Negro mili-
tancy, solidarity, and political activity — to say nothing of Justice Department investigations.

SUMMARY AND CONCLUSIONS

   In this paper we have attempted to determine the relationships between political and legal factors and variations in the rate of Negro voter registration in the
southern states. In order to control the substantial effects of social and economic
factors on Negro registration, we employed a multiple-regression equation containing the typical relationships between 21 social and economic variables and Negro registration rates in the counties of the region. From this equation, we predicted what the Negro registration rate in each county ought to be on the basis of its
social and economic structure alone. Variations of the actual rate above and below
this predicted figure — residuals expressed in percentage points — were viewed as
largely the result of political and legal variations from county to county within the
South.[24]

   The most important political and legal fact about the South is its division
into 11 states. The counties of some states have far higher average rates of Negro
voter registration than they ought to have on the basis of their social and economic

characteristics, while others are far below the predicted levels. The range in the residuals between the highest (Tennessee) and lowest (Mississippi) states amounts almost to 50 percentage points. No other political factor examined is nearly so important. On the other hand, the meaning of these figures is not particularly clear until we probe salient features of the formal and informal political systems of the states.

Three such factors were found to have a moderate relationship with Negro voter registration rates. These were formal voter requirements (the range of residuals was 28.6 percentage points), state factional systems (24.4 percentage point range), and the amount and kind of racial organizations in the counties (21.9 percentage point range).

Two other political factors — the extent of partisan competition and of racial violence in southern counties — had very small relationships with Negro voter registration rates.

The analysis up to this point thus provides some ranking in relative importance of the various political and legal factors we have been able to consider. But it does not tell us the relative importance of these political and legal factors, taken together, in comparison with the social and economic factors considered in our earlier article.

From that study we reported, as noted, that the multiple correlation between all 21 social and economic variables and Negro registration was .53, which means that they explain about 28 per cent (R^2) of the variation in Negro registration. If we add 10 political variables [25] to the equation and calculate the multiple correlation between all 31 variables — socio-economic *plus* political — we obtain a multiple correlation of .70, which explains about 50 per cent of the southwide variation in Negro registration figures. The addition of the political variables almost doubles the explanatory power of the analysis. In so far as statistical analysis will answer such a broad and complex question, it would appear that political variables are nearly as important as socio-economic factors in explaining Negro registration in the South.

NOTES

1. U.S. Commission on Civil Rights, *Report* (Washington, G.P.O., 1959), pp. 40-41.

2. "Social and Economic Factors and Negro Voter Registration in the South," *American Political Science Review,* Vol. 57 (1963), pp. 24-44.

3. A complete list of sources used to obtain county frequencies for the independent variables used in this analysis is too lengthy to reproduce here. A mimeographed list will be supplied by the authors upon request.

    We are indebted to the following research assistants for their help in collecting these data: Lawton Bennett, Lewis Bowman, Barbara Bright, Jack Fleer, Donald Freeman, Douglas Gatlin, and Richard Sutton. All told, the collection and coding of these data took one man-year of work.

4. The 1958 registration data contained in the 1959 *Report* of the Commission on Civil Rights are more complete than the 1960 registration data contained in the

Commission's *1961 Report* (Washington, 1961), Vol. I, "Voting," and were used in all states except Tennessee, for which 1958 data were not available.

There are 1136 counties in the 11 southern states (counting Virginia's independent cities as "counties"), of which 1028 had populations containing at least 1 per cent Negroes in 1950. Negro registration figures are not available for 31 of these.

5.   For a more extended discussion see Matthews and Prothro, *op. cit.*

6.   Computations were made on the University of North Carolina's UNIVAC 1105 high-speed digital computer.

7.   See Matthews and Prothro, *op. cit.*

8.   V.O. Key, Jr., *Southern Politics in State and Nation* (New York, 1949), p. 531.

9.   *Ibid.*, p. 579.

10. *Ibid.*, p. 617. See also F.D. Ogden, *The Poll Tax in the South* (University, Ala., University of Alabama Press, 1958), ch. 5.

11. Key *op. cit.*, p. 460.

12. The returns of an Advisory Committee questionnaire mailed to county registrars are reported, in part, in "Voting and Voter Requirements in North Carolina" (mimeographed), June 4, 1961.

13. Key, *op. cit.*, ch. 23.

14. Robert E. Lane, *Political Life* (New York, 1958), p. 308.

15. *Ibid.*, Lane's conclusion is based primarily upon an analysis by Warren E. Miller, "One-Party Politics and the Voter," *American Political Science Review,* Vol. 50 (1956), pp. 707-725. Additional support may be found in James A. Robinson and William H. Standing, "Some Correlates of Voter Participation: The Case of Indiana," *Journal of Politics,* Vol. 22 (1960), pp. 96-111.

16. Primary election returns were compiled from Richard M. Scammon (ed.), *Southern Primaries '58* (Washington, Governmental Affairs Institute, 1959); from various issues of the *Congressional Quarterly Almanac, and Congressional Quarterly Weekly Report;* legislative manuals and Reports of Secretaries of State; and the New York *Times.* Contests involving incumbents in Arkansas and Texas — the only southern states in which governors may succeed themselves — and uncontested races were omitted in computing medians.

17. The above is not intended to imply a single direction of causality: a meaningful choice may lead more Negroes to register, the registration of more Negroes may lead candidates to take positions more favorable to Negroes, or both. So far as bifactional as opposed to unifactional or multifactional politics is concerned, however, one can

conceive of the pattern of factionalism as the independent variable associated with Negro registration but one can hardly imagine the registration rates of Negroes as the independent variable.

18. The New York *Times* was consulted from January, 1945, to February, 1961, and the Southern Educational Reporting Service's "Facts on Film," Rolls 1-40, first supplement Rolls 1-3, second supplement Rolls 1-11, were examined in a search of news about these organizations. Letters of inquiry were addressed to known national and statewide organizations seeking the location of their local chapters. Persons known to be knowledgeable about the racial politics of specific states and localities also were contacted.

19. W.J. Cash, *The Mind of the South* (New York, Vintage reprint , 1960), p. 52.

20. The Tuskegee data are reported, by county, in Charles S. Johnson (ed.), *Statistical Atlas of Southern Counties* (Chapel Hill, University of North Carolina Press, 1941). The reports on racial violence, 1955-59, may be found in *Intimidation, Reprisal, and Violence in the South's Racial Crisis,* published jointly by American Friends Service Committee, Southeastern Office, High Point, N.C.; National Council of Churches of Christ, Department of Racial and Cultural Relations, New York; Southern Regional Council, Atlanta, Georgia, 1960.

21. A.F. Raper, *The Tragedy of Lynching* (Chapel Hill, University of North Carolina Press, 1933), p. 1.

22. *Ibid.*, p. 4.

23. *Intimidation, Reprisal, and Violence,* p. 15.

24. These variations are, of course, also the result of chance factors and of the fact that the 21 social and economic variables do not reflect all of the complex social and economic realities of the world. Moreover, the 21 measures we did employ were not themselves perfect measures of the variables they represented.

25. These 10 political variables are (1) states; (2) per cent of presidential vote States' Rights, 1948; per cent of presidential vote Republican (3) in 1928, (4) in 1948 and (5) in 1956; (6) per cent of vote Republican in race for statewide office in year of highest Republican vote, 1950-59; (7) presence or absence of Negro race organization in county; (8) presence or absence of white race organization in county; (9) presence or absence of desegregated school in county; and (10) number of incidents of racial violence in county.

Part Two

INPUTS OF
STATE POLITICAL
SYSTEMS

The term "inputs" refers to those activities and agencies which furnish the political system with "the raw material or information that the system is called upon to process and with the energy to keep it going." Although inputs take various forms, all are the responses of individuals to situations in which they find themselves as they attempt to live in and improve upon their position in a world where scarcity prevails. The most obvious input activities are *demands* that public officials take action on particular issues.

These demands can take various forms, from innocuous letters to the governor to the burning of a cross in a state legislator's yard. Such diverse forms of activity express opinions about particular political circumstances — and are thus among a political system's demand inputs. There is also supportive input activity that promotes the political system and makes it possible for officials to bow to or reject demands. *Supports* are necessary if demands are to be satisfied, and conflict resolved. Supportive inputs may be of two kinds: (1) overt acts which promote the goals and interests of other persons (such as voting, or abiding by a legal decision); and (2) predispositions to act on behalf of individuals or other actions taken (examples of such predispositions are loyalty and patriotism).

Input activities are channeled through and performed by particular political agencies. Agencies such as political parties and pressure groups clearly are a means through which individuals make demands on authorities — in addition, such agencies, themselves, generate demands. The electoral system is less clearly an input agency. It does not, itself, seem to generate demands upon the political system. Rather, it provides the means by which supports and, to some extent, demands[1] are channeled to the "authoritative decision-making agencies." As input

---

[1] Very rarely do elections provide a mandate for a candidate or make specific demands upon him.

agencies, however, all these features of political systems perform certain functions within the system. As a result of these activities, interests in the population are identified, and leaders are selected. Both of these functions are vital to the existence of all political systems. In order to perform its authoritative decision-making function for the society, the political system must identify the interests which unite or divide it and select the leaders who will assist in making decisions.

The articles in this section of the book describe the nature of input activity and the form the input agencies take in state political systems; they analyze the impact of these actions upon political behavior in the states; they discuss the interrelationships among the input agencies and between them and other features of the system.

PUBLIC OPINION AND STATE POLITICS

Public Opinion Structures in the States

Charles F. Cnudde

Contemporary research on the role of public opinion in political systems demonstrates the efforts of modern political science at coming to grips with increasingly more theoretical concerns. On the one hand, our purely conceptual thinking gives great stress to the relationship between public opinion and public policy.[1] More specifically, traditional democratic theory implies that the institutionalization of a close articulation between citizen opinions and system outputs (to use the modern term) is basically what democracy is all about. On the other hand, much of the empirical literature on public opinion has avoided the study of this articulation. We have a wealth of information on those factors which give rise to opinions on public topics. For example, the effects on opinions of occupation, income, education, ethnicity, region, age, sex, urbanness, mass media, and partisanship have been dealt with at length.[2]

Yet only in recent times have political scientists sought the effects of opinions on public policy. The late V. O. Key, Jr., first pointed to this area as an important one for building an empirical democratic theory.[3] To the extent that our findings were relevant, in Key's terms, to the "linkage" between opinions and policy, they tended to argue against such a precise relationship even in a supposedly democratic system like the United States. The great bulk of the citizenry was found to have meager knowledge and interest in the great policy controversies which

The author is Assistant Professor of Political Science at the University of California at Irvine.

The author wishes to express his gratitude to Kenneth Sherrill and Mary Barnes for their aid in the early stages of the research project of which this analysis is a part.

divide political leaders.[4] In the absence of knowledge and interest at the citizen level it was difficult to imagine how citizen political activity could bring an opinion-output linkage in specific policy areas.

The more recent research which deals directly with this theoretical concern provides some partial answers here. In the policy areas where linkage tends to occur, the relationship tends more to be due to leadership perceptions rather than continuing citizen activity.[5] However, it seems fair to say that we have only begun to examine these relationships.

In this paper, we will attempt to further develop our knowledge in this area. But instead of examining linkage from the point of view of political leaders, we will return to research more purely at the citizen level. That is, we will attempt to specify conditions under which citizen activity can be said to provide a basis for linkage in the United States. If these conditions can be spelled out, then hopefully their presence or absence can be used as an additional explanation for the degree of linkage in democratic political systems.

In other words, we are not attempting to explain the structures of opinions in this country. Of course previous research would indicate that socio-economic background and its derivatives provide those explanations to a large extent. This paper instead addresses itself to the questions: Given existing structures of opinion, what are their effects and under what conditions are those effects maximized?

In order to narrow this research to a manageable effort we will seek only preliminary answers to these questions. We will examine only one type of citizen political activity, voting preference, and will look to party characteristics as possible specifying conditions. Thus the vote is the most widespread form of citizen activity which has been institutionalized to provide direct inputs to the political system. The vote therefore is an important first step in the chain of opinion-policy linkage from the point of view of citizen-level activity. As indicated, previous research shows little impact on the vote from opinions on public policy. Therefore, any conditions which increase this impact provide a preliminary step in the linkage chain. The literature on party reform in the United States contains hints of these possible specifying conditions. Thus adherents of the responsible party model would undoubtedly argue that the lack of linkage is due, at least in part, to the nature of the party system.[6] The absence of strongly competitive two-parties in many areas of the country plus our rather incohesive party groupings make it difficult for citizens to hold the parties responsible for their policy enactments. The result is a low articulation between public opinions on public policy and candidate selection in elections. Alternatively, greater competition and cohesion may bring a higher articulation. We will develop our primary hypothesis from the responsible party argument and, in order to test that hypothesis, will develop a contrary hypothesis from another body of thought.

The test-sites for this paper will be the states of the United States. The contention of this research is that the states provide interesting laboratories for political research. The differing political practices in our states enable researchers to gain variation on many variables that would be impossible elsewhere. If at times, as in this paper, the practices of each state can not be analyzed separately, at least convenient classification schemes allow for comparisons of groups of states which have somewhat similar characteristics. Therefore, while substantive problems are the primary concern of this paper, it is also an example of the methodological importance of the study of state politics.

In sum, then, we will examine the impact of state party characteristics on issue voting, or the relationship between opinions on public policy and voting preference in the United States. Those characteristics which limit issue voting will be seen as decreasing one of the most important citizen-level mechanisms for achieving linkage and those which increase issue voting as increasing the possibilities for linkage. The specific hypotheses to be tested and their derivation directly follow this line of thinking.

HYPOTHESES

There are two bodies of theoretical work from which we can derive hypotheses concerning the conditions under which issue voting is maximized. One of these areas of thought arises out of a normative quest on the part of many political scientists for a more responsible party system in the United States. The other is a deductive model of democratic voting behavior borrowed, in part, from the field of economics. Each of these theories will be briefly evaluated for any light they may throw on the problem of the linkage between policy opinions and policy enactments.

The responsible party model generally holds that there would be a closer articulation between the electorate's issue concerns and policy in the United States if:[7]

1. There were two political parties offering candidates for office in fairly close, competitive elections.

2. These parties presented differing programs of proposed public policy to the electorate.

3. These parties and candidates, when elected, acted as cohesive party units in implementing those policies.

4. Voters selected candidates according to the voters' policy preferences, continually holding governing parties accountable for their performance through successive elections.

Two of the ways that the American party system diverges from these prescriptions are important for our purposes. Our parties can be characterized as deviating from a competitive two-party system in many areas, and they present something less than cohesive, programatic appeals to the electorate. To the extent that party appeals are based upon grounds other than policy disputes between two cohesive alternatives, the voter would seem to have a difficult time seeing policy differences between the parties. His choice between the parties in elections would then depend less on his opinions about public policy than on other factors. Therefore, following the logic of the party responsibility model, we would predict that the relationship between policy opinions and the vote for the Democrats or Republicans would increase as party competition and party cohesion increase.

On the other hand, Anthony Downs presents an imaginative body of theoretical work about democratic politics which leads to hypotheses directly contrary to those derived from the party responsibility model.[8] That portion of his writings which is of immediate concern is his spatial model of party competition. That model rests primarily on the following presumptions:[9]

1. Political parties can be placed along a liberal-conservative scale which runs, let's say, from 0 to 100 at the extreme ends of the scale.

2.   Voters can also place themselves along this same scale.
3.   Voters will prefer scalar positions close to their own position to those which are further away.

From these assumptions, Downs concludes that in a competitive two-party situation rational parties would tend to move closer to each other and to the mode of the scale. [10] Such behavior would maximize the number of votes each party would gain from the mode. As a result, ideological distinctions between the parties would become blurred as competition forced each to sound increasingly like the other. Downs' model therefore posits that competition will not make policy differences between the parties more stark, but instead will tend to make such differences disappear. Such a situation should make voter perception of party policy differences difficult, if not impossible. Therefore, the hypothesis consistent with this model is that competitiveness would decrease voters' ability to choose between the parties on the basis of the voters' policy opinions.

Downs, of course, does not address explicitly one of the aspects of the party responsibility model, that of party cohesion. However, some minimum level of cohesion seems to be implicit in assumption 1. Thus if the members of a party do not behave in a somewhat cohesive fashion in making policy decisions, it is impossible to place the party at some point, or even in some vicinity of points, on the scale. Downs' model therefore is applicable to parties having some fairly high degree of cohesion. Therefore, both of the elements of responsible party model which are applicable to this discussion are also contained in Downs' thinking.

Thus far we have derived two alternative hypotheses concerning the effect of party competition and party cohesion on policy voting. One states that these two-party characteristics will increase the relationship between policy opinions and the vote, and the other states the converse. An empirical test of these hypotheses to find which can be rejected and therefore which can be supported essentially requires that we look for the conditions of competition and cohesion which maximize the relationship between policy opinions and the vote. The procedures that we will follow in this search therefore are important in the final test to be conducted.

METHODS

The procedures utilized to make these tests involve the relating of aggregate, state-level characteristics to individual-level opinions and behaviors gathered through sample survey interviews. The survey data is the 1964 election study conducted by the Survey Research Center. [11] As our indicator of issue voting we will take the relationship between voting preferences and opinions on specific public policies in the three policy areas of public power, federal aid in medicine, and federal aid to education. [12] These are chosen because they represent specific policies which, theoretically, at least, can be viewed as lying on the same dimension of socio-economic liberalism. These policies also represent issues related to domestic controversy which divide the parties at the national level, with the Democratic party on record as more or less favoring the extension of federal activity to these fields and the Republican party more or less opposed to that extension. Such ideological differences between the parties were more apparent than usual in the 1964 Presidential election. The Goldwater candidacy, made the minor party, in the words of the candidate's supporters, "A choice, not an echo." In this respect that election seemed to be something of a deviant case, as American elections go. We should therefore find a higher level of issue voting than in most elections.

These policy differences between the candidates in 1964 mean that we can compute the relationship between the policy opinions and the partisan vote for President with a lessened sense of arbitrary categorization than would normally be the case. Thus we would expect that those who favor the policy in question would vote Democratic while those who disfavor would vote Republican, if policy voting were to take place. Moreover, by assigning the score of 0 to those favoring the policy and to those voting Democratic and the score of 1 to those disfavoring the policy and to those voting Republican, we can very easily compute correlations between policy opinions and the vote. Such correlations then can be utilized as summary measures of issue voting. Our search for issue voting then becomes a quest for the conditions which maximize these correlations.

Our hypotheses indicate that factors in the party system might relate to differences in the magnitude of these correlations. More specifically, in order to test these hypotheses we must look for variations in party competition and party cohesion. Thus proponents of the party responsibility model might point out that one of the reasons for a comparative lack of issue voting in the United States is the low level of cohesion and competition among our parties, while the hypothesis consistent with Downs' model argues that the reason for this lack is that cohesion and competition are too high. Neither argument can be disproven by analyzing only national party characteristics in one election because the degree of cohesion and competition actually is constant. Moreover, even if a series of federal elections are used for the test, the variation in competition and cohesion might be so limited as to make the results subject to doubt.

Two alternative strategies for gaining variation on party characteristics may prove rewarding. One is to examine cross-national patterns and the other is to utilize the variety of party patterns visible in the separate states of the United States. The former strategy may prove difficult because of the necessity of controlling additional factors which may contaminate the results. One such factor is the differences in ideological distance between parties cross-nationally. However, this problem, in principle, may be overcome. The use of state party characteristics lends itself quite nicely to eliminating this problem. Thus, if there was a greater ideological distance between the parties in 1964 than in most Presidential elections, then examining the effect of state party characteristics on policy voting for President, in a sense controls for this greater distance. The same Presidential candidates are up for election in every state, so ideological distance due to the candidates in this peculiar election remains the same while other party characteristics vary in the states.

Two additional questions should be addressed in utilizing state party characteristics in our tests: (1) What kind of variation do the state parties give us? (2) Can we legitimately expect state party characteristics to be related to issue voting at the national level? Although we may never find party systems which are perfectly irresponsible or are completely competitive in Downs' ideal sense, our intuitive feelings often assume fairly important differences between state parties in these terms. For example, we think that the parties in a state like Michigan approximate one pattern in the models under discussion. In that state the parties have been closely competitive, and they have had dominant ideological differences which structured cohesive party action on public policy. The parties in many of the Southern states stand in sharp contrast to the pattern in Michigan. In the South, one party predominance is associated with a factionated pattern in state-wide candidate selection. Factional division in elections spills over to reduce the level of cohesion in policy enactments. We normally think that states like California stand somewhere between these two patterns. While California exhibits a competitive two-party system, its tradition of non-partisanship and the existence of the cross-filing primary mechanism prevented the development of party organizations. Cross-filing no longer holds sway there, but its historical effect on party organization makes contemporary efforts at increasing party cohesion more difficult than would otherwise be the case.

Supporting our unsystematic observations and intuitive feelings are studies in state politics attempting to measure party competition and party cohesion. Austin Ranney's measurements of competition are based upon:

> (1)   the average percent of the popular vote won by Democratic gubernatorial candidates; (2) the average percent of the seats in the state senate held by the Democrats; (3) the average percent of the seats in the state house of representatives held by the Democrats; and (4) the percent of all terms for governor, senate, and house in which the Democrats had control.[13]

From these scores, an index of competitiveness was created which can be folded and trichotomized into one-party states, modified one-party states, and two-party states. The amount of variation in the state party systems measured by Ranney's categorizations will be utilized in this study.

Ranney also illustrates a trichotomized measure of party cohesion in the states.[14]   Based upon the extent that party legislators vote together as party blocs states can be divided into strong, moderate, and weak cohesive states. This measure will be adopted as the indicator of party cohesion in the present study. The categories in which each state is classified by these measures generally fit our intuitive notions about what the party system is like in each state.[15]   In addition, our feelings that we can rank states like Michigan, California, and Southern states in terms of party responsibility implies that our sense of these parties' "responsibility" is uni-dimensional. If "responsibility" is uni-dimensional, then measures of factors which underly it, like those of cohesion and competition, should be highly correlated. Ranney shows that this is indeed the case.[16]

Thus these measures discriminate between state party systems in a way consistent with our intuitive notions of how responsible the state parties are, and they provide categories of states which differ in important respects in their degree of cohesion and competition. Perhaps future studies will be able to measure even more variation on these factors. However, enough variation appears to be provided by the state parties to make at least a start at testing our hypotheses.

Relating these state party characteristics to the relationship between opinions on national public policy and voting preferences in Presidential elections may over-emphasize the importance of state factors to the ordinary voter. The characteristics of the parties on the national level may be more important in policy opinion voting in Presidential elections. As was indicated earlier, in examining the impact of these state factors in one national election, in effect, we control for these other possible factors. We are then asking, given the level of policy voting in the 1964 election, to what extent can these state factors provide additional maximizing influences. Whether or not state party cohesion and competition have this effect then becomes a question answerable through empirical test.

FINDINGS

Since the 1964 election seemed to contain elements of a greater ideological contest than had been true of many other elections which have been intensively studied, we should first examine the correlation between policy opinions and candidate preference before introducing the specifying state variables. The correlations within the total sample then can be used as points of departure for the effects of our hypothesized factors. Table 1 gives the correlations for the three policy areas under study.

The correlations computed across the electorate vary somewhat with the opinion area. The highest correlation occurs among respondents having opinions on public support for medical costs. Perhaps the strength of this relationship is influenced by the relatively current debate on the Medicare bill, which could have polarized and increased the information content supporting these opinions. The rank of the two other correlations is not so easily understandable. The lowest correlation is in the area of federal aid to education. Yet the issue had become, by 1964, a perennial one in Presidential elections. The higher correlation for public power involves an area of fairly technical discussions, beyond the comprehension of much of the electorate. Perhaps, however, public power was associated in the voters' minds with Mr. Goldwater's stand on the TVA. Such a proposition more adequately explains the differences between these correlations.

Whatever reasons we can conjure up to explain these differences must be tested in later analyses. For purposes of the present study the striking character of these relationships is their overall strength. That we have found correlations between issue opinions and voting preferences which vary from .6 to almost .8 seems to fly in the face of earlier research which indicated a general lack of public policy information among the electorate. In addition to the peculiar circumstances of the 1964 election, some methodological factors account for the unexpected strength of these correlations. The nature of the SRC's issue questions in

Table 1 Correlations between opinions on public policy and voting preference by opinion area.

| | Opinion Area | | |
	Federal Aid to Education	Public Ownership of Power	Federal Aid in Medicine
Correlation	.611	.723	.795
Number of Respondents	874	698	871

Table 2 Percent of individuals responding to opinion question who favor the public policy
by state party characteristics and policy opinion areas.[a]

State Party Competition	Federal Aid to Education	Public Owner- ship of Power	Federal Aid in Medicine
One-Party	38 (207)	22 (130)	61 (195)
Modified One-Party	37 (268)	31 (210)	57 (271)
Two-Party	38 (800)	32 (571)	60 (834)
State Party Cohesion			
Weak Cohesion	39 (491)	46 (149)	57 (474)
Moderate Cohesion	34 (216)	23 (149)	50 (111)
Strong Cohesion	38 (568)	35 (396)	64 (604)

[a] Numbers in parentheses refer to totals upon which the corresponding percentages are
based.

the 1964 study tends to eliminate meaningless responses. Thus 23 percent to 38
percent of the sample indicated that these three policy areas had no meaning for
them. Those respondents are therefore not included in this analysis. Many of the
usual closed-end survey questions would have been more likely to elicit some
sort of response on these policies, even if the individuals involved had no real
opinions on the questions. Since their responses would be essentially random,
their inclusion would have the effect of depressing the correlations. Therefore,
the correlations in Table 1 should not be read as conflicting with previous findings. They are instead based upon respondents who can be estimated to have
somewhat more meaningful opinions in these areas, while they ignore large sections of the electorate who apparently have no such opinions.

The purpose of this study is to examine the effects of other possible variables, given the relationship between opinions and voting preference among these
estimated opinion-holders. As pointed out earlier, however, we are searching
for the effects of opinion structures rather than their causes. The attempt to specify those effects with state party characteristics assumes that opinion structures
are relatively independent of those characteristics. Since respectable hypotheses
may be based upon the contrary assumption, we should test our assumption by
examining the distribution of opinion structures across the state party characteristics before proceeding with the main thrust of the analysis. Table 2 illustrates
the test of our assumption.

Table 2 illustrates that the structure of opinion-holding is relatively stable across the state party variables, competition and cohesion. Party cohesion has some limited effect on medical aid opinions. In the case of opinions on public power, slight differences occur as we move down both of the party characteristics. Yet the strongest relationship of these three is a percentage point difference of eleven — occurring for public power as we move from weak cohesion to strong cohesion. Not only is this magnitude a negligible one, but the moderate cohesion states do not follow the relationship of decreasing favor for public power with increases in strength of cohesion. In the two other opinion areas, party competition has no effect on the opinions of the citizenry. The percentages favoring the public policies involved are essentially the same for one-party and two-party states. This same pattern shows up for party cohesion in the area of federal aid to education. Perhaps with larger samples and greater variation measured in party cohesion and competition, interesting differences might arise due to these state party characteristics. However, the data analyzed here show no firm bases for inferring that these structures of opinion are due to these state party characteristics.

If party cohesion and competition can not be viewed as very efficient causes of these policy opinions, can the effects of opinions be specified by these party variables? The answer to this question in terms of one possible effect, that of voting, involves a test of the alternative hypotheses set out earlier. Table 3 provides the data for that test.

Table 3 Correlations between opinions on public policy and voting preference by opinion area and state party characteristics.[a]

State Party Competition	Federal Aid to Education	Public Ownership of Power	Federal Aid in Medicine
One-Party	.909 (109)	.716 (84)	.548 (95)
Modified One-Party	.522 (200)	.591 (160)	.828 (189)
Two-Party	.577 (565)	.814 (452)	.812 (578)
State Party Cohesion			
Weak Cohesion	.754 (303)	.829 (247)	.837 (285)
Moderate Cohesion	.544 (153)	.797 (116)	.710 (146)
Strong Cohesion	.526 (418)	.616 (333)	.776 (431)

[a] Numbers in parentheses refer to totals upon which the corresponding correlations are based.

The effect of party competition on the correlations in Table 3 is mixed. Increased competition tends to reduce the correlation for opinions on federal aid to education. A reversal of this pattern takes place for the other opinion areas, with a greater increase in the correlations for medical aid than for public power. However, state party cohesion tends to decrease the magnitude of the correlations for every opinion area. This finding runs counter to our hypothesis drawn from the responsible party model, while the effect of party competition is consistent with that hypothesis in two of the three issue areas.

These results suggest that the two party variables have opposite effects on the correlations and that the mixed pattern due to party competition is the result of the positive relationship between the party characteristics. Thus party competition reduces the correlation only in the area of aid to education, the area where party cohesion has its greatest reduction in the size of the correlations. The greatest increase due to party competition takes place where cohesion brings the least reduction, the area of federal aid in medicine. Therefore we have a patterning in the rank order of the effects of the two party variables. This patterning

Table 4 Correlations between opinions on public policy and voting preference by opinion area, with simultaneous controls for party competition and cohesion. [a]

	Weak Cohesion	Moderate Cohesion	Strong Cohesion
Federal Aid to Education			
Non-Two-Party	.675 (195)	.760 (27)	.586 (87)
Two-Party	.807 (108)	.493 (126)	.511 (331)
Public Ownership of Power			
Non-Two-Party	.748 (157)	.125 (18)	.350 (69)
Two-Party	.945 (90)	.840 (98)	.666 (264)
Federal Aid in Medicine			
Non-Two-Party	.767 (183)	.600 (22)	.686 (79)
Two-Party	.942 (102)	.726 (124)	.794 (353)

[a] Numbers in parentheses refer to totals upon which the corresponding correlations are based.

could be the result of high correlation between the party variables, (which we know to be the case from previous research) if the party variables worked in opposite directions on these relationships. We can test this possibility by examining the separate effects of each of the party variables while the other is held constant. Table 4 introduces these controls for our correlations.

The use of simultaneous controls when the control variables are highly correlated often presents difficulties for empirical researchers. The general problem is that we may get conceptual cross-classification for which we have no empirical data. This problem is specifically recognized in the literature by the reduction in the size of population of controlled categories when too many control variables are introduced. Such controls often reduce the size of some categories to insignificant numbers. For example, in the present study all of the one-party states have weak cohesion party systems. In order to maintain simultaneous variation in competition and cohesion we have had to collapse the one-party and modified one-party categories. In Table 4 we therefore can only compare the two-party states to those states with something less than two-party competition. This procedure still leaves very small numbers of respondents in the non-two-party, moderate cohesion categories. As a result the correlations there are very unstable, varying from .125 to .760. Therefore, these magnitudes do not follow a pattern expected of a middle category between the weakly and strongly cohesive, non-two-party categories. Because of the small number of respondents in these categories, their corresponding correlations, for the most part, should be ignored.

Qualified by the above remarks on controlling, the pattern in Table 4 is that suggested by the results in the previous set of correlations. For the most part, party competition tends to increase the size of the correlations while party cohesion reduces them. Party competition quite consistently increases the magnitudes of the correlations by an amount greater than .1 over all three policy opinion areas. The one exception to this pattern occurs in the strong cohesion category for federal aid to education. There party competition doesn't seem to make much difference. Although the impact of cohesion is even more consistent, the size of the impact in some cases is negligible. Cohesion reduces the correlations more markedly in the two-party states than in the non-two-party states. The average reduction across the three opinion areas from weak cohesion to strong cohesion is .189 in the non-two-party states and .241 in the two-party states. Yet the greatest contributor to the reduction in the non-two-party states is the opinion area of public power. In non-two-party states cohesion doesn't seem to make much difference in the strength of the correlations for the other opinion areas. On the other hand, each opinion area contributes quite substantially to the average reduction of these correlations in the two-party states.

The overall findings thus far indicate that party competition increases the effectiveness of the translation of opinions on public policy into voting preferences while party cohesion decreases the effectiveness of that translation. Moreover, this effect of cohesion takes place to a greater degree in the two-party states than in the non-two-party states. Before turning to a discussion of these findings in terms of the hypotheses set out earlier, we will first examine the effects of a possible complicating factor which might throw the findings into question.

Previous research has shown that socio-economic factors are distributed over the American states in a systematic manner with many state-level political variables.[17] Characteristics like two-party competition and strong cohesion occur

Table 5 Average differences in correlations between opinions on public policy and voting preferences due to each state party characteristic, controlled by the other and class identification.

	Differences Due to Cohesion		Differences due to Competition	
	Non-Two-Party States	Two-Party States	Strong Cohesion States	Weak Cohesion States
Middle Class	−.250	−.195	.134	.189
Working Class	−.389	−.274	.205	.328

most often in the more industrialized, socially heterogenous states. There is a possibility therefore, that the changes in our correlations are not due to the party variables under discussion, but instead to the socio-economic characteristics of the populations in the cohesive and competitive states. This possibility means that we should control for the socio-economic status of the individuals under study. In this paper we will utilize social class identification as a control variable. This variable essentially summarizes many of the social status characteristics which could complicate our findings because it has been shown to have greater predictability for political behavior than many alternative measures of status. Table 5 introduces the control for class identification.

In Table 5 we have computed the average differences in the size of the correlations across all three policy opinion issues due to party competition and party cohesion. The average differences due to each party variable are controlled simultaneously for the other party variable and class identification. The control for class identification obviously further reduces the number of respondents in each category. For this reason we have ignored the smallest category, that of moderate cohesion. Therefore, only the extremes of the cohesion categories, strong and weak cohesion, are utilized. In addition, by computing average differences we are concerned with only the overall pattern rather than the specific correlations. The latter are not noted because they may be unstable due to the small numbers involved. Despite these safeguards, we should read the table conservatively. Thus the primary concern will be the *sign* of the differences rather than their absolute magnitudes. That is, does cohesion continue to *reduce* the size of the correlations within the categories of competition even when class identification is controlled? Similarly, does competition continue to *increase* the size of the correlations within the cohesion categories when class identification is controlled?

These questions are answered by Table 5. Even with social class identification controlled, cohesion continues to reduce the size of the correlations (indicated by negative differences) and competition continues to increase the size of the correlations. The effects of the two state party characteristics, therefore, are not due to the complicating factor of socio-economic status in the states.

In general, then, the impact of two-partyism is that postulated by the hypothesis consistent with the party responsibility model. Under conditions of two party competition, the voters appear much better able to choose between the parties according to the voters' own policy preferences. However, increased cohesion tends to reduce the correlation between policy opinions and voting preference. This suggests that when the parties behave as separate and consistent organizations in voting for policy outputs in the state legislatures, voters are less aware of differences between them. This effect of cohesion is greatest under conditions of two-party competition. Our party responsibility hypothesis runs contrary to this proposition. That is, we would expect voters to be better able to see differences between the parties when party legislative behavior is not amorphous.

Yet cohesive, two-party states are what Downs' model addresses itself to. The mere existence of two parties does not fit Downs' theory. Besides existing, these parties must operate as separate organizations. Underlying the measure of cohesion we have used is just such a dimension. When the parties are more than parties in name only, and they are in close competition, then the voters have more difficulty in transferring their policy opinions into votes. This situation is what we would expect under Downs' theory. Perhaps competitive two-party systems make it rational for the parties to obscure differences between them and to move increasingly closer to the same position in the ideological spectrum. In the American system, the result would be a weak linkage between public opinion and public policy as it is influenced by policy voting at the citizen level.

To a certain extent, then, both hypotheses find some support in these data. The correlation between policy opinions and voting preference generally increases with party competition. This finding is consistent with the notions underlying the party responsibility model. However, cohesion reduces the correlation, especially under conditions of two-party competition, a situation which we have seen is consistent with Downs' model.

On the other hand, elements of both models fail to come to grips with the complexities of the political world. The party responsibility model, since it is focused primarily at the national level, misses the relatively high degree of competition and cohesion of the parties in some of the states. As a result, it does not test its propositions under these conditions. The test conducted here indicates that hypotheses concerning the effect of cohesion on relationship between policy opinions and candidate preferences which are consistent with the model can be rejected. Downs' model, postulating as it does, an ideal state of party competition does not describe many of the empirical conditions obtaining in a political system like the United States. Thus the lack of competition in many American parties means that cohesion in those parties has less effect than the hypothesis consistent with his work would indicate.

These discontinuities seem to indicate that the two models differ merely in perspective and that with some ingenuity they can be made consistent. The party responsibility model perhaps looks to the least cohesive and competitive situation and leads to an emphasis on the difficulty of policy choice in voting in that situation. The Downs' model pictures the most competitive (and by our inference, the most cohesive) situation and predicts party movement on policies which would also limit issue voting. Thus if these models were actually consistent, we would think of party responsibility as a spectrum, and, at either extreme, issue voting should decrease. At the low responsibility pole, issue voting would be difficult following the party responsibility model, while at the high responsibility pole, issue voting would also be difficult as in our hypothesis from Downs. Therefore, as we move away from either pole, issue voting should increase in a curvilinear fashion consistent with both models.

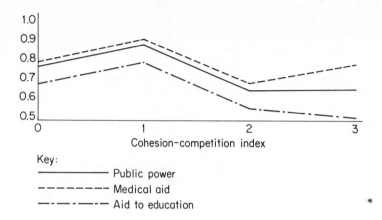

Figure 1 Correlations between policy opinions and the vote by state characteristics and
policy area.

Of course we can't directly measure party responsibility. However, we can
perhaps approximate such a measure by contructing a combined index from our
measures of competition and cohesion — two of the important elements of party responsibility.[18] The new Downs party responsibility model would then predict the curvilinear distribution of our policy voting correlations over the combined index.
Figure 1 shows the test of this hypothesis for all three policy areas.

Figure 1 describes in gross outline the curvilinear relationships predicted
by the new Downs-responsibility model. At either extreme end of the index the
correlations are lower than at the high point at score one. In the case of opinions
on medical aid the correlation at score two is somewhat lower than at the highly
cohesive competitive extreme. This may be due to additional uncontrolled variables which have an impact on this particular opinion area. However, this difference in the pattern also could be the result of utilizing such gross categories as
our measures of the two state party characteristics. If we had opinion samples
in every state, much more precise measures of the party characteristics could
be introduced. The result would be much less measurement error and perhaps a
smoother curve than that analyzed here. Yet even with these rather imprecise
measures, the curve follows our predictions quite accurately in two of the opinion
areas and is not far off in the third.

This finding suggests that our hypotheses differed only in emphasizing different poles of the same spectrum. Thus subjecting hypotheses from these seemingly conflicting theories to empirical test enables us to revise each and to infer
that they are really quite consistent. Yet each polar extreme could have the same
effect for different reasons. If this were the case our inference would be unwarranted. Therefore a further test is necessary to evaluate why the high competition
and high cohesion extreme has the same effect on the correlations as the low competition and low cohesion extreme.

An additional test of the Downs-responsibility model can be made with the survey data at hand. A cognitive dimension which helps explain the relationships between these opinions and voting preference runs throughout the discussion in this paper. Thus, implied in the hypotheses derived from the Downs' and responsibility models has been a difficulty for the voter in perceiving the policy differences between the parties. If the parties are uncompetitive and low in cohesion, voters may not see clearly any policy distinctions between the parties according to the party responsibility model. Similarly, if the parties are highly competitive and cohesive, the Downs' model would hold that policy differences would tend to disappear. Under such conditions voters would also be likely to have difficulties in connecting the parties with differing policies. According to both theoretical works then, our hypotheses of the relationships between policy opinions and voting preference depends upon the same underlying variable, voter misperception of policy differences between the candidates of each party. If our combined index really explains the curvilinear distribution of our correlations, then citizen misperception of the parties' policy stands should also demonstrate a curvilinear relationship.

The question of what is an accurate measure of citizen misperception therefore is a crucial question of these tests. Once again the 1964 election makes this an easier choice than would have been otherwise the case. Not only was the Republican candidate opposed to the broad dimension of federal activity which underlies these policies, but he was specifically on record as opposing the Tennessee Valley Authority, the Medicare bill, and proposals for federal aid to education. Therefore in order to approximate a measure of citizen misperception we have chosen the percentage of respondents who think that the Republican party is more in favor of the three public policies dealt with in this study. Figure 2 gives the distribution of these percentages over the combined Cohesion-Competition Index.

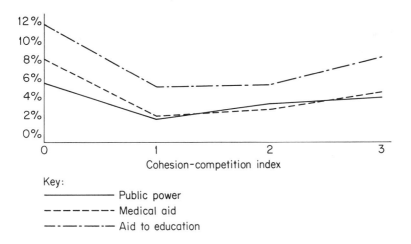

Figure 2   Percent saying Republican party more in favor of the public policy by state characteristics and policy area.

Those percentages again follow a general curvilinear distribution over the index. Of course these curves are the reverse of those for the correlations. Where the correlations are highest the percent misperceiving party policy stands are lowest. This suggests that one of the important underlying factors in the relationship between policy opinions and voting preference is citizen awareness of policy differences between the parties. Moreover, one of the reasons why the Cohesion-Competition Index isolates lower correlations at each end of the index seems to be the higher orders of misperception of party policy at the end points of the index.

The distribution of citizen misperception on these policies therefore provides further evidence for our view of the impact of cohesion and competition in the state parties on the relationship between policy opinions and voting preference. High degrees of cohesion and competition tend to hamper citizen perceptions of party policy differences. On the other hand low degrees of cohesion and competition also seem to have this effect. The result of these misperceptions under both extreme party conditions is a difficulty in translating basic policy opinions into meaningful electoral choices on the part of many citizens. Both of the hypotheses set out earlier find support in these data. This unexpected result indicates that the empirical patterns of opinion–electoral relationships are much more complex than the theoretical works from which our hypotheses were derived.

CONCLUSIONS

In this paper we began with a discussion of the problem of the linkage between public opinion structures and public policy outputs in the United States. While democratic theory would specify a fairly high degree of linkage in this more-or-less democratic political system, we have seen that few empirical analyses lend support to that proposition. In order to modify the expectations of democratic theory we have sought possible factors which exist in the American system which reduce one initial relationship in this linkage, the relationship between public opinion and voting preference. In other words, this paper has been addressed to those conditions prevalent in the United States which limit the relationship between opinions and electoral choice and which, if changed, would probably result in a greater opinion-policy articulation. Since we wished to make inferences about this type of change, we turned to the literature on party reform to guide this research. More specifically, the party responsibility argument provided the hypothesis that the low degrees of cohesion and competition in the American parties handicap the citizen's ability to see policy differences between the parties and therefore his ability to make electoral choices based upon his policy opinions.

In order to test this hypothesis we derived an alternative hypothesis and developed indicators for the variables under examination. Downs' assumptions assign to competition and cohesion the impact of reducing broad policy distinctions between the parties, which would result in weaker rather than stronger relationships between opinions and voting preference. The comparison between these alternative hypotheses depended upon measuring variation in party competition and party cohesion. To gain this variation we utilized measures of these characteristics in the American states. Within broad categories of states scored on these characteristics we computed the correlation between opinions on three public policies and voting preference. These correlations provided measures of opinion-electoral relationships only for those citizens who tended to have somewhat meaningful opinions about the policies in question.

The findings indicated that both hypotheses could be supported by the data. Thus, the less than perfect articulation between policy opinions and voting preference, even among those citizens who seem to have meaningful opinions, can be inferred to be due to the prevalence of two differing patterns of party characteristics in the United States. One is the large number of strongly cohesive, two-party states and the other is the existence of another bloc of weakly cohesive, less than two-party states. The reasons for these effects seem to be that the state party characteristics are important in the conveying of at least incremental amounts of information on party policy differences to the citizen. To the extent that the nature of the state parties helps shape the policy images of the parties, highly competitive and cohesive parties allow room for citizen misperceptions and so do weakly competitive and cohesive parties. Without clear notions of party policy differences the voter has difficulty in making electoral choices which rely on his policy opinions.

Thus it appears that a lack of competition and cohesion tends to reduce the ability of the electorate to hold parties responsible for their policy enactments in the sense that these characteristics relate to issue voting. However, wholesale increases in competition and cohesion may not result in greater party responsibility in this sense. Indeed even under the maximum conditions of cohesion and competition that we have been able to measure in the American states, there exists sufficient misperception of policy differences to weaken rather than strengthen policy voting.

What mechanisms provide these levels of misperceptions has not been under test here. Perhaps future research will indicate that Downs' thinking can be empirically supported. Possibly strongly competitive and cohesive parties so modify any disagreement on policy as to make these disagreements imperceptible to the bulk of the electorate. The heterogeneity of American society may motivate the parties in this direction (when they are cohesive and competitive) so as not to alienate any potential group of voters. When the parties are not competitive and cohesive, this motivation may not be so strongly felt.

These speculations indicate that additional tests involving measures of the motivations and policy pronouncements of party leaders should be conducted to further spell out the theoretical activity begun here. An exploration of these types of variables may pin down the more proximate mechanisms which provide low misperceptions of party policy differences under conditions of moderate competition and cohesion. Perhaps research on the national level with election campaigns over time or cross-national studies will solve the problems necessary to provide these further inferences and in addition replicate these findings.

Another line of research should be followed up. The impact of party characteristics upon the distribution of citizens who vary in having meaningful opinions on public policy needs to be examined. Of course social status, and especially educational attainment, undoubtedly is important in whether political opinions go beyond responses to candidates and parties to the more complex public policy issues. However, aspects of the political system may also provide structuring conditions for the development of policy opinion conflicts within the citizenry.

In general, the data analyzed here lead to inferences that very responsible parties in the American setting contain elements which may weaken one mechanism in the linkage between public opinions and public policy — the relationship between opinions and voting preference. These elements, strong cohesion and competitiveness, have impacts more consistent with Downs' theory than with the responsible party model. Only when the conditions specified by the Downs' theory do not obtain do patterns of opinion and policy preference follow expectations consistent with party responsibility thinking. However, basic to that thinking is the normative quest for greater two-party responsibility. The empirical effects of greater responsibility may be more complex than those envisioned by the model's adherents. To the extent that cohesion and competition would be increased by increased responsibility, citizen misinformation on party policy would tend to grow as party conditions approximate Downs' ideal. The result would be a greater, rather than lesser, difficulty for citizens to hold the parties responsible for public policy enactments and therefore a weaker rather than stronger linkage between opinions and policy.

NOTES

1. For a discussion of some aspects of this thinking see Charles F. Cnudde, "Consensus on Democratic Values, 'The Rules of the Game', and Democratic Politics: The Case of Race Politics in the South" (unpublished Ph.D. dissertation, Department of Political Science, University of North Carolina, 1967), Chap. IV.

2. Almost any text on public opinion necessarily illustrates this bias. Even Key devoted almost forty percent of his text to these topics. V. O. Key, Jr., *Public Opinion and American Democracy* (New York: Alfred A. Knopf, 1961), pp. 99-202 and 293-405.

3. *Ibid.*, pp. 441-531.

4. See Angus Campbell, Phillip E. Converse, Warren E. Miller, and Donald E. Stokes, *The American Voter* (New York: John Wiley & Sons, 1960), pp. 541-548.

5. See Charles F. Cnudde and Donald J. McCrone, "The Linkage Between Constituency Attitudes and Congressional Voting Behavior: A Causal Model," *American Political Science Review*, 60, (1966), pp. 66-72 and Warren E. Miller and Donald E. Stokes, "Constituency Influence in Congress," *American Political Science Review*, 57 (1963), pp. 45-56.

6. Although the responsible party literature is not presented precisely in linkage terms, this argument at least is consistent with that literature. See Report of the Committee on Political Parties of the American Political Science Association, *Toward a More Responsible Two-Party System* (New York: Rinehart & Co., Inc., 1950). For a related argument see James MacGregor Burns, *The Deadlock of Democracy* (Englewood Cliffs, N.J.: Prentice Hall, 1963). Additional works in this area are closely

examined in Austin Ranney, *The Doctrine of Responsible Party Government* (Urbana: University of Illinois Press, 1954).

7. See footnote 6 above.

8. Anthony Downs, *An Economic Theory of Democracy* (New York: Harper and Brothers, 1957).

9. *Ibid.*, Ch. 8.

10. Basic to this view of two-party competition is the presumption of a unimodal ideological distribution. For an evaluation of this presumption and other elements of Downs' theory see Donald E. Stokes, "Spatial Models of Party Competition," *American Political Science Review,* 57 (1963), pp. 368-377.

11. These data have been made available through the Inter-University Consortium for Political Research, Ann Arbor, Michigan.

12. The items used to measure these opinions are: "Some people think it's all right for the government to own some power plants while others think the production of electricity should be left to private business. Have you been interested enough in this to favor one side over the other? (if Yes) Which position is more like yours, having the government own power plants or leaving this to private business?"

    "Some people think the government in Washington should help towns and cities provide education for grade and high school children, others think this should be handled by the states and local communities. Have you been interested enough in this to favor one side over the other? (if Yes) Which are you in favor of, help from the government in Washington or handling it at the state and local level?"

    "Some say the government in Washington ought to help people get doctors and hospital care at low cost, others say the government should not get into this. Have you been interested enough in this to favor one side over the other? (if Yes) What is your position? Should the government in Washington help people get doctors and hospital care at low cost or should it stay out of this?"

13. Austin Ranney, "Parties in State Politics" in Herbert Jacob and Kenneth N. Vines, (eds.) *Politics in the American States* (Boston: Little, Brown & Co., 1965), p. 64.

14. *Ibid.*, p. 88.

15. *Ibid.*, Table 8.

16. *Ibid.*

17. *Ibid.*, p. 69; Richard E. Dawson and James A. Robinson, "Inter-Party Competition, Economic Variables, and Welfare Policies in the American States," *Journal of Politics,* 25 (1963), pp. 265-289; Richard E. Dawson and James A. Robinson, "The

Politics of Welfare, " in Herbert Jacob and Kenneth N. Vines, *op. cit.*, pp. 371-410; and Thomas R. Dye, "State Legislative Politics, " in Herbert Jacob and Kenneth N. Vines, *op. cit.*

18. A scoring procedure similar to that utilized in computing the issue voting correlations is used in the construction of the index.

Constituency Versus Constitutionlism: The Desegregation Issue and Tensions and Aspirations of Southern Attorneys General

Samuel Krislov

I

Some issues so cry out for immediate attention that longer-range research seems almost trivial and tends to be pushed aside. Such an issue is desegregation. It would be unfortunate if the zeal and moralistic energy which impel us toward a new solution in the field of race relations were to result in wasted opportunities. For in the desegregation process there is rich material in the field of basic social science research, for the student of politics as well as the sociologist or social psychologist.[1] In this vein, the attorney general seems a natural subject of scrutiny. The potentialities of the office are many. The struggle on desegregation has been couched primarily in legalistic terms, and the strategic importance of the post is quickly and almost intuitively grasped. Governor Coleman's youthful triumph in Mississippi, for example, was credited to public appreciation of the advantages of a legal officer in the current situation.[2] The attorney general represents the force of both national and local law within his state. He could act as a creatively legalistic interpreter of existing decisions and conditions within the state. But the southern attorney general has by and large been interesting for what he has not done as much as for his accomplishments.

The Southern School News some time ago listed 168 important developments in the desegregation process.[3] It is remarkable that such a list could be compiled without a single mention of an attorney general. Nor by and large can one quarrel with the implicit evaluation. For the attorneys general of the various states have not led in the field of desegregation. Rather they have represented a very close and sensitive evaluation of political forces within the state, following the leadership of the locality and the dominant trend of public opinion.

This conduct of the attorney general is explicable and predictable rather than haphazard or indigenous to the current situation. An analysis of the office in terms of its demands and of holders of the office in terms of their commitments suggests the patterns of behavior of the attorneys general. An examination of the actual conduct of the southern attorney general on desegregation thus becomes a useful prelude to an analysis of the motive source of that conduct. This in turn has itself broader implications. The problem is a relevant one not just for the

Reprinted from "Constituency Versus Constitutionalism: The Desegregation Issue and Tensions and Aspirations of Southern Attorneys General," *Midwest Journal of Political Science,* Vol. 3, No. 1 (Feb. 1959) by Samuel Krislov by permission of the Wayne State University Press. Copyright 1959 by Wayne State University Press.

A revision of a paper presented at the American Political Science Association Convention, New York City, September 5-7, 1957. Research was aided by a grant from the Faculty Research Fund of the University of Oklahoma. Muzafer Sherif, University of Oklahoma, and Clement Vose, Wesleyan University, were kind enough to offer detailed critiques of the original paper.

pointing of fingers or assessing praise or blame, but for deepening our understanding of the methods and operations of our democratic government. One of the great lacunae of political science is that it has not adequately explored the problem of how public opinion is conveyed to public officials and translated into public action. Dennis Brogan has aptly epitomized this by calling for more mapping of the "conduit or sluice by which the waters of social thought and discussion are brought to the wheels of political machinery and set to turn those wheels. "[4]

II

Actually it was Eugene Cook, the Attorney General of Georgia, who was the very first southern leader to challenge the Supreme Court decision on desegregation.[5] Furthermore, at that time he suggested a boycott of the later hearing which would deal with the problem of implementation.

At the same time, some border attorneys general acted with equal firmness to support the decision. John Dalton of Missouri quickly ruled that while the original Supreme Court decision did not require desegregation immediately, it made it permissive regardless of any state law.[6] West Virginia also acted decisively.

But most attorneys general sought some middle ground, and one that allowed for future flexibility of policy. Typical was the action of the Attorney General of Maryland. On the one hand, Mr. Roller ruled that nothing could be done about desegregation until after the implementing decision. At the same time, he refused to attend a conference called by Attorney General Cook of Georgia, explaining, "It seems to me that they are trying to circumvent rather than implement the will of the Supreme Court. I am not interested. "[7]

As time went on, those on the fence have generally been forced to espouse a more anti-desegregation stand. The symbol of this drift and the most dramatic example of a change of views is Attorney General Ervin of Florida. Apparently a man of great sensitivity and a keen sense of obligation, he had originally been a moderate. It was his brief before the Supreme Court that is thought to have shaped the implementation decision. But by 1956 his views began to shift palpably. Consequently Ervin and Governor Collins have in effect been in disagreement. Ervin has supported measures strengthening defiance of the state and passed by the legislature over the objections of the governor. Of the interposition resolution, for example, Collins exclaimed, "This resolution on its face is a lie. "[8]

As the southern attorney general has moved into line with public opinion, his office has tended to become a clearing house for resistance. His principal activity has been the litigation of school and recreation cases that have developed. States have had to add to their staffs.[9] Many states have authorized his office to handle all cases arising on the lower levels and absorb the costs.[10]

In contrast, and at the same time, the office has generally been used to hamper those who might turn to the courts for aid in securing compliance with the Supreme Court decision. The attorney general, on his own initiative or with a little prompting, has secured injunctions against the NAACP in barratry proceedings or on grounds of lack of registration.[11]

The power of ruling on legality and constitutionality has not been neglected. Attorney General Cook aided the forces favoring the private school referendum in

Georgia by ruling that all state provisions regarding education had been invalidated by the Supreme Court, and that if new laws were not adopted the system would not exist.

Cook has only been one of many who have tried to organize public opinion — but these all tend to be in states where there is little need for such organization. Some carry the battle abroad, where the attorney general as a legal officer can effectively utilize his prestige and standing. He is particularly valuable before Congressional committees since his combination of law and politics strikes close to the mores of Congress.[12]

With all these varied activities, the attorney general has not completely followed the dictate of the community. Some excesses have been curbed, even where the attorney general has thrown his loyalties into the battle for segregation. Attorney General Gremillion of Louisiana pursued the NAACP injunction even in the face of state and federal decisions, but he also limited to new admissions the application of a law requiring good character certificates of students at Louisiana State University. The law was later declared unconstitutional even with this modification, since educators issuing the certificate to Negroes could automatically lose their positions.[13]

Nor can we speak of any monolithic degree of opposition on the part of the attorneys general. Robert Carter, the Counsel for the NAACP, has listed the attorneys general of Missouri, West Virginia, and Oklahoma as having generally complied with the decision. He suggests that the Attorney General of Delaware has "done nothing to aid desegregation," while the Attorneys General of Maryland and Kentucky, without taking a definite stand, have been moderately unfavorable. "There is no question," he adds, "but that the attorneys general of North Carolina, South Carolina, Mississippi, Virginia, Florida, Texas, Alabama, Louisiana and Georgia are bitter opponents of the Supreme Court's decision. All of them have either condoned and sponsored legislation designed to thwart implementation of the Court's decision, or have vigorously defended against a breakdown of segregation where legal action has been brought."[14] Even among these it would be a mistake to force them into one category. Their actions have reflected the subtle interplay of individual tendencies, attitudes toward the law, and local pressures and influences. Each has reacted as a human being in the face of rival stresses. Above all, each has moved with, never against, the tide. The attorney general has, in short, been a complier in states like Oklahoma, Missouri and West Virginia. In more doubtful states like Delaware and Kentucky in the complying category, and Texas and Florida among relative non-compliers, his stand has been either ambiguous or inconsistent. Where local opinion has hardened, so too has the stand of the attorney general.

Why is it that the southern attorney general has reflected the prejudices, if you will, or the wishes, if you prefer, of his area? Of course he is a southerner, and a southern public official. Still this conduct contrasts very sharply with the conduct of others similarly situated. A specific instance seems in order. In June of 1955 a federal district court of three issued an opinion on implementation of the Supreme Court decision that Thurgood Marshall found generally satisfactory.[15] One of the judges was the father of a governor of South Carolina; as a private individual he has denounced the Supreme Court decision and helped force out his pastor for too "broad" an attitude on the race question. Another, during the course of the discussion, sneered at "a foreign Communistic anthropologist," an undoubted reference to Gunnar Myrdal, and one reflecting current southern propaganda.[16] The third judge, whose personal opinions (in all fairness) we don't know too much about, was refused confirmation to the Supreme Court in part due to objections of the NAACP; since in running for office he had once expressed views derogatory of Negroes.[17] The ability of southern judges on the federal level at least in part to set aside their personal opinions and reflect the law as interpreted by the Supreme Court is borne out most clearly by the southern opposition to the civil rights legislation without jury trial provisions and more positively, by the stand of civil rights adherents in favor of that same provision.

Why is it that on the one hand we have federal judges who can and do put aside their own opinions and ignore the immediate local pressures of public opinion, and on the other hand the southern attorney general who has reflected his own evaluations of the mores and demands of his area? What is the mechanism that compels the one to be subservient and allows the other to be independent, that makes one responsive to local opinion and the other responsive to national opinion?

It is certainly not enough to speak of the electoral process, for no southern attorney general has been defeated because of his stand on desegregation. Indeed, none has taken to the hustings in defense of either segregation or desegregation in areas where either course was unpopular. The niceties and irregularities of our democratic government, the evasions that characterize our American system of politics, have prevented the problem of desegregation from being an issue in any but the meagrest number of elections in the United States. We will have to go deeper by looking in more detail at the office of the attorney general.

The position is an historic one dating back to the British sergeant-at-arms. It is certainly a responsible and important office, and it is one that on first sight is fairly obvious in its obligations and duties. The apparent simplicity and obviousness of its responsibilities has in fact made the office largely unknown to observers because there exists virtually no body of investigation or study of what the position entails beyond simple statutory listings or descriptions of statutory requirements in the various states.

But it is a surprisingly complex office. It is curious to see how much of the annual conferences of the attorneys general is devoted to self-conscious discussion of the true nature of the position.[18]

In one sense the attorney general is subservient to federal law. Yet he is at the same time the expounder and defender of state law. Since he is called upon to give legal opinions to the various departments, the attorney general basically exercises judicial power. Yet he is not merely a judicial official. More than the independent regulatory commissions he combines the executive, legislative, and judicial functions.

The attorney general is also the chief law enforcement officer for his state, and in the words of a former president of the National Association of Attorneys General, "in many states their power literally exceed those of the governor in the law enforcement field."[19] Arthur Bromage's description of the attorney general as law enforcer as the head of a "continuous chain of irresponsibility" is no doubt accurate;[20] but his position remains more difficult precisely because of the lack of power given to him to enforce his obligations.

In addition, the attorney general is a policy-making official; as a leading elective official he is called upon and must make decisions beyond the domain of legal processes. At the same time, the attorney general is the trial lawyer — always the appellate trial lawyer and often the lower court trial attorney — for his state. He both advises and represents the administrative units and in many states rules on legal questions expounded by the legislature.

He is also, at least in theory, legal advisor to the governor. But at the same time that he is advisor he is also too often the governor's rival. Both are elective officials and both therefore have a standing with the public largely independent of each other, and often they choose or wish to compete in the future.

The conflicting pressures that are so evident and that bear so strongly upon the attorney general have been rendered particularly irreconcilable by the process of popular election. The anomalies implicit in this arrangement are already reflected in an institutional change — probably the most precise and definite measure of a contradictory governmental arrangement. In practice it is common for the governor to have a legal advisor other than the attorney general, and in many states this is a recognized position with the title of legal advisor or legal counsel to the governor.[21]

Political scientists have usually studied the process of parcelling out the executive power to a number of officials on the state level solely in terms of efficiency. It is also interesting and would be worthwhile to study these officials in terms of irreconcilable and unrealistic multiple pulls and loyalties that are imposed upon the office holder and that make successful carrying out of his office almost impossible. In this process of illogical demands and loyalties no office can hold a candle to the attorney general, for no other office is within the framework of the federal and state law, yet responsible for the enforcement of local law. No other office is elective and yet advisory, policy-making and yet administrative, legal and yet political, creating institutional rivalry with the man he is supposed to work with and advise.

The attorney general, then, is faced with a definite potential in the office. In one sense it would be theoretically possible for him to utilize his position as an important force in the advancement of a particular program or idea. Yet it is inherent in the multiple stresses and his alternative roles that the attorney general will rather seek to placate all forces and will therefore accommodate himself to these stresses and become a vector rather than a directional force. It is also inherent in the ambiguity of his position, suspended between the importance of the governor and the obscurity of the other state executive officials, that the attorney general will seek to assert some importance and yet will not move decisively and powerfully.

III

But in his choice between the various roles and in his choice between following the push and pull of particular power relationships or power formations, which will the attorney general choose? In further exploring this problem one suggestion seems appropriate. Interpretive studies have been made of office holders and political pulls and affiliations both in terms of the past and of the present. But students of politics have neglected the future.

Studies of the origins of office holders are common to many schools of thought in political science — Laswellian elite analysis, for example, or Marxist analysis for another. There has also been investigation of present pulls and present affiliations — that is, the study of pressure groups and pressure group activities as well as decision-making generally. In doing so political scientists have in part anticipated and in part followed the findings of sociology and social psychology that indicate strongly the extent to which group affiliations and group identifications influence human beings. These findings are summarized under the rubric of "reference group theory" by many sociologists and social psychologists and indicate that people conceive of themselves primarily in terms of identifications and affiliations with some group or groups. Thus faced with pencil and paper and a question, "Who am I?" individuals quickly answer in terms of some objective characteristics which identify them with some external group. Thus "I am a man, a teacher, an American, an Ohioan." All of this would indicate very sharply that individuals, particularly in our society, conceive of themselves in terms of those groups. It is only after exhausting the telling of those external groups that we come to such internal characteristics as "I am happy, I am kind," and the like.

Now in a mobile society, and this is a mobile society, there exists a special type of group which plays a part in our lives. This encompasses those groups that we are not actually members of but that we wish to belong to, not only in a sense of actually knowing and being conscious of our wish, but also in an unconscious sense. "I look up into the hills from whence cometh my promotion." For these groups an appropriate term might be "aspiration groups." [22] From the standpoint of opinion formation, their importance is that they tend to shape and form an individual's opinion often before he is conscious of the fact that he is striving for a change of his group position.

Ultimately the importance of the aspiration group from the viewpoint of the social scientist is that it could provide an additional tool for analysis. Origin analysis and group pressures tell us what is happening or what has happened, but they do not tell us to any great degree how the individual experiences or interprets either his past experiences or his present pressures. By studying the aspiration group we get in a flash an individual's interpretation of both his past and present as well as his future. Ideally the aspiration group will provide us with evidence on all of these factors; in practice it will be somewhat less useful as a tool. It is necessary to make the somewhat dangerous assumption that by studying the regular career patterns of a group of individuals we can get a clue as to what these individuals regard as a desirable future and therefore their psychic affiliations for the present. There are many difficulties involved in this approach, as with any other in social science, but perhaps the suggestions here will justify some claims and prove useful. [23]

Career patterns of a group constitute relevant evidence of current thinking in that they are overt manifestations of deeper affiliations not otherwise easily studied. There are several distinguishable patterns of influence that can be assumed to be operative.

An individual in any on-going system will find certain actions generally lead to personal enhancement while other types of activity lead to a loss of effectuality. Thus any system tends to perpetuate within limits a "modal character" (or perhaps several types of personality structures) as a by-product of its own operations. Another force tending toward perpetuation of personality structure and self-identification in any group is to be found in the recruitment pattern. Considerable evidence suggests that social systems recruit individuals who already share attitudes typical of members of the system. Above all, there is a tendency for individuals to adjust their behavior to conform with that of highly esteemed and prestigious groups and individuals.[24]

So, for example, in *The American Soldier* it was found that enlisted men with attitudes resembling those of officers had a statistically significant greater likelihood of having been promoted when restudied at a later date.[25] It is, of course, difficult to distinguish cause and effect here; the most significant aspect is the recurrence of this type of social behavior rather than the disentanglement of these forces which so often interact. An individual is shaped by what he would like to be; a system tends to recruit and reward individuals who meet important requisites from the standpoint of the system, not only in talents and equipment, but in general outlook and orientation as well.

In line with this reasoning one can consistently assemble data on the career patterns of the attorney general and derive conclusions therefrom. The general pattern that emerges from such data is that primarily the attorney general has been and is a locally oriented official. His aspiration groups are local and his affiliations are local. Those individuals who depart from this pattern tend also to depart from the pattern of politics in their states and thus help confirm the treatment given here.

The data can briefly be set off as follows. First of all, attorneys general do not generally go to Congress. The 1957 *Congressional Directory* lists only one representative and four senators with previous experience as attorneys general. This compares with two members of the House and 21 members of the Senate who have been governors. It also compares unfavorably with previous state legislator

Table 1   Previous governmental service listed by members of Congress.

List previous service as:	House	Senate
Attorney General	1	4
Governor	2	21
Lieutenant Governor	5	5
Assistant Attorney General	9	1
Highway Commissioner	2	1
State Treasurer	2	2
State Legislator	147	28

Source: *Congressional Directory*, 1957

In the compilation of this and the ensuing data I was aided by Donna Krislov and Donald Slater, now a Fellow, Department of Politics, Princeton University.

experience. Twenty-eight members of the Senate and 147 members of the House have had such state legislative experience. The attorney general's position is inferior as a stepping stone to the lieutenant governor's position — 5 members of the House and 5 members of the Senate have had such experience — and is roughly comparable to that of state treasurers or highway commissioners. We may also say, somewhat surprisingly, that the attorney general does not often move on to federal judiciary, in spite of the rather conspicuous exception at the apex of the federal judiciary. Only one Court of Appeals judge and three district court judges list previous experience as an attorney general in the only authoritative compilation of judicial office holders. Again the governorship was a more likely stepping stone to these positions, while the lieutenant governorship and such other state executive offices as those of the legal counsel to the governor and the state highway commissioner rivaled the attorney general as positions leading to the judicial chair.

Table 2 Previous governmental service listed by members of federal judiciary.

List previous service as:	Court of Appeals	District Court
Attorney General	1	3
Governor	1	6
Governor's Counsel	0	3
Lieutenant Governor	0	1
State or County Judiciary	17	60
House of Senate	4	16
Federal Judicial Experience	20	2

Source: Charles Liebman, ed., Directory of American Judges

What, then, does happen to the attorney general? The answer is that for many his is a terminal position. Particularly in the South the attorney general will often stay on for many years of service. The attorney general's position may also be terminal in the sense that it is his departure from politics. Many then return to private practice. Another resting place is the state supreme court. Here we have large numbers of former attorneys general. In one-third of the states there is at least one such individual on the bench.

Table 3 Subsequent activities of occupants of the attorneys general position.

| | Occupied office in: | |
	1927	1937
Candidate for Governor (defeated)	3	4
Served as Governor	1	3
Died in office	1	1
Remained in office ten years or more	3	4
State Supreme Court	7	6
Other State Judiciary	2	3
Private practice, corporation law, business	9	5
Federal Legislature	0	3

Source: *Who's Who in America,* various years

Table 4   Previous governmental experience listed by members of highest state tribunals.

List previous service as:	Number
Attorney General	20
Governor	3
Lieutenant Governor	3
State or County Judiciary	57
State Legislative Experience	54
U.S. House or Senate	8

Source: *As in Table 2*

Above all, many aspire to and some succeed in obtaining the gubernatorial position. And those individuals who go on either to federal legislative or judicial positions are those who have succeeded in reaching the governor's chair. This is reflected in the extraordinary attention paid to the fortunes of those who aspire to the governor's post at annual conferences of the attorneys general, and the perennial bad jokes about "demotion" to the executive mansion. [26]

Table 5   Previous governmental experience of governors, August 1957.

	Number
Attorney General	5
Lieutenant Governor	10
State Treasurer	2
U.S. House of Representatives	6
U.S. Senate	3
State Legislature	23

Sources: *Who's Who in America,* 1956-57; *Current Biography,* 1956; *New York Times,* November 8, 1956, p. 29.

In summary, then, the attorney general normally looks for promotion on the local level. He therefore identifies himself with local groups and derives his opinions from them. This is reinforced by the fact that his contact with the federal government is normally in the position of defender of the state against the national government. The Association, for example, has reflected a surprisingly local point of view. It has opposed the federal government's actions with regard to invalidation of state subversion laws and labor regulations. It has endorsed the general outline of the Bricker Amendment and was opposed to the Tidelands Oil Decision. It even formally disapproved the action of several states in suing to prevent return of the Tidelands to the states. The most revealing stand was during the war. The Association called for passage of a "Uniform Law to Oppose Federal Encroachments" authorizing the attorneys general to review federal legislation and memorialize both state and federal officials when they found legislation exceeding constitutional bounds. At least one resolution has been reactivated in the current controversy. [27]

The attorney general tends to see himself as a local popular official. This is borne out by the frequent recurrence of the term "politician" in their self-descriptions at the annual conferences. John Ben Sheppard, in his presidential address in 1956, got great applause with his observation that "an attorney general has to have the eye of an Indian scout so he can follow the trail of public opinion, avoid being ambushed along the way, and cover his tracks."[28] Supporting this, in response to a questionnaire, the small number who were willing to commit themselves espoused this view of the office. Of eleven, five thought of themselves as elected policy-making officials, three as executive policy-implementing officials, only one preferred the judicial label, and one insisted upon a combination of the elective judicial tag. On the question of federal versus local orientation, the number who committed themselves to a straight-out preference for state law when in conflict with federal law (which seems an extreme legal doctrine) was about equal to the number that were willing to espouse a balance of authority with federal predominance.[29]

Here, then, is the situation in a nutshell. The attorney general lives in a universe of local groups and local opinions. The federal judge looks to national groups and the higher judiciary for approval and promotion. It is no coincidence that those who aspire beyond their state borders are to a greater or lesser degree resistant to local opinion. Neither is it coincidence, but necessity, that forces the attorney general with his local attitudes and aspirations to follow the maxim "vox populi vox Dei." It is, in short, in the light of objective sociological data that we can predict and explain some of the social-psychological influences that lie behind overt political actions.

NOTES

1. For a digest of recent research, see Melvin Tumin, *Segregation and Desegregation* (New York: Anti-Defamation League, 1957).

2. *Current Biography,* 1956.

3. *Southern School News,* May 1957, p. 1.

4. Of course the works of Gabriel Almond, Richard Snyder, and Lewis Dexter, among others, must be recognized as important efforts to deal with precisely this problem.

5. *New York Times,* May 19, 1951, p. 1. "To officially appear . . . ," he explained, "would be like participating in the funeral ceremonies of the best friend the Negro and the white man ever had — segregation." *Southern School News,* August 1955, p. 2.

6. Opinion of Attorney General Dalton (prepared by John W. Inglish), June 30, 1954 (mimeographed).

7. *Southern School News,* September 1954, p. 6.

8. On Ervin see *Southern School News,* especially January 1956, p. 15 and February

1956, p. 10. I am also indebted to Professor Lewis Killian of Florida State University for information. Parenthetically, Ervin's Brief Amicus in the segregation cases includes an important and novel section on state leadership opinion and other psychological and sociological data, and is pathfinding in approach. On Collins see *U. S. News and World Report,* November 1, 1957, p. 20.

9. See, e. g., *New York Times,* August 4, 1955, p. 46.

10. Thus Governor Coleman offered to defend any state official indicted for denial of the right to vote. *The Reporter,* June 27, 1957, p. 10. The effects on local control, as in, say, Virginia, are significant. In an extreme case Cook has sought a court ruling that would allow withholding of school funds to any district studying the possibility of desegregation. *New York Times,* October 28, 1956, p. 15.

11. For a summary of such events see *Assault upon Freedom of Association* (New York: American Jewish Committee, 1957) and F. B. Routh and Paul Anthony, "Southern Resistance Forces," *Phylon,* XVIII (1957), 50.

12. Thus the published hearings show fully eight attorneys general of southern states testified against the Civil Rights Bill before the House Judiciary Committee, in addition to three assistants. Another attorney general testified before the Senate subcommittee hearings.

13. *Race Relations Law Reporter,* II (1957), 261.

14. Communication to writer, July 19, 1957. Indications of range of attorney general attitudes can be derived from the compilation by Cook of various opinions on interposition, "The States and Interposition," (undated, mimeographed), and the symposium in the *Journal of Negro Education,* XXIV (1955), 188.

15. *Race Relations Law Reporter,* I (1955), 73.

16. *New York Times,* July 26, 1957, p. 7; *Southern School News,* August 1955, pp. 6-9, December 1955, p. 6.

17. Some definite indications of his views, though, can be found in John J. Parker, "Chief Justice Fred M. Vinson: Meeting the Challenge to Law and Order," *American Bar Association Journal,* XLI (April, 1955), 324, especially p. 325.

18. This extends even to the title of the office. A perennial question is what the plural of "attorney general" should be and how to refer to one another. They resolve it by addressing each other as "General" and retaining the older form for the plural.

19. Louis C. Wyman, Attorney General of New Hampshire, communication to writer, May 15, 1957.

20. Bromage, *State Government and Administration in the United States* (New York: Harper & Bros., 1936), p. 255. For some treatments of the office see John A. Farlie

and Donald F. Simpson, "Law Departments and Law Officers in the States," *State Government,* XIV (1941), 237, and G.W. Keeton, "The Office of Attorney General," *Juridical Review,* LVIII (1946), 107, 217.

21. Coleman B. Ransone, Jr., *The Office of Governor in the United States* (University, of Alabama: University of Alabama Press, 1956), pp. 332-333.

22. Reference group theory is summarized in the essay by Robert Merton and Alice Kitt Rossi in *Studies in the Scope and Method of the American Soldier* (Glencoe, Illinois: The Free Press, 1954), and reprinted in the revision of Merton's *Social Theory and Social Structure* (Glencoe, Illinois: The Free Press, 1956). Muzafer Sherif has advanced the theory in a number of important statements, particularly in Sherif and Wilson, *Social Psychology at the Crossroads* (Norman, Oklahoma: University of Oklahoma Press, 1953), and Sherif and Sherif, *An Outline of Social Psychology* (New York: Harper & Bros., 1956). Other important sources include Ralph Turner, "Role Taking, Role Standpoint, and Reference-group Behavior," *American Journal of Sociology,* LXI (1956), 316, and Shibutani, "Reference Groups as Perspectives," *American Journal of Sociology,* LX (1955), 562.

    "Groups" as used here are shared-attitude groups, not concrete organizations, complex psychological manifestations rather than simple membership units. So far as I know, the use of the term "aspiration group" is a neologism, and linkage with career patterns an innovation. Turner's argument for rejecting the importance of such groups seems an over-zealous application of scientific parsimony, particularly in view of the unconscious element involved in their influence. The present suggestion would allow use of the generic term "reference group" and the sub-species "membership group" and "aspiration group." This is independent of the value versus orientation controversy.

23. Difficulties include: (1) the fact that career patterns can shift; (2) we are reduced to interpreting individual motivation in terms of mass activity, which of course is not always reliable in the individual case; (3) there may be a striking divergence between aspiration and achievement.

24. See the essay by Alex Inkeles and Daniel Levinson on modal character in Gardner Lindzey, *Handbook of Social Psychology* (Cambridge: Addison-Wesley Pub. Co., 1954) and, *inter alia,* T.M. Newcomb, *Personality and Social Change* (New York: The Dryden Press, 1957), and Elihu Katz and Paul Lazarsfeld, *Personal Influence* (Glencoe, Illinois: The Free Press, 1955). A recent study of the suburban voter seems to indicate that the change in voting behavior precedes the change in residence. This would be in accordance with the position presented here. See John Millet and David Pittman, "The New Suburban Voter: A Case Study in Electoral Behavior," *Southwestern Social Science Quarterly,* XXXIX (1958), 33.

25. Samuel Stouffer, *et al.,* *The American Soldier* (Princeton: Princeton University Press, 1949), I, 260-264.

26. Annual Conference of the National Association of Attorneys General, 1952, pp. 5-6; 1956, p. 60; 1956, p. 25. The National Association of Attorneys General, it should

be noted, was organized in 1907, and the Council of State Governments was designated in 1940 as the Secretariat for the Association. It is composed of all Attorneys General of states and territories, as well as the Attorney General of the United States. Annual meetings are held, and the proceedings published. A weekly digest of opinions of the Attorneys General is another major publication.

27. *Ibid.*, 1953, pp. 5 and esp. 34-35; 1954, p. 87; 1955, p. 22; 1956, pp. 4, 5 and 76. See also Abram P. Staples, "The Attorneys General and the Preservation of Our System of Government," *State Government,* XVI (1943), 29. *Civil Rights,* Hearings before Subcommittee No. 5 of the Committee on the Judiciary, House of Representatives, 85th Cong., 1st Sess. pp. 1170-77, contains a copy of the remarkable "uniform law." On the perennially defensive attitude of attorneys general see Walter White, *How Far the Promised Land?* (New York: Viking Press, 1955), pp. 38-40.

28. Annual Conference of the National Association of Attorneys General, 1956, p. 131.

29. The questions and the number selecting each choice were as follows: The following have been suggested as representing different views of the Attorney General's role. Which one would you choose as MOST descriptive:
   1. an elective official whose first obligation is to serve the interests of the people of his state.   (5)
   2. a judicial official whose first obligation is to carry out the general principles of law.   (1)
   3. an executive official whose first obligation is to help maintain and execute the needs of good government.   (3)
   4. requiring adherence first of all to your private conscience and conviction
                                                                               (0)
   All of the above   (2)   1 and 2 combined   (1)

   The following have been suggested as representing different views of the obligations of the Attorney General. Which one would you choose as most descriptive?
   1. a state official and in case of conflict between the national and state laws bound to obey the state law.   (3)
   2. an official of the people of his state and therefore bound in case of conflict to pick that set of laws which is most conducive to the eventual well-being of the state.   (1)
   3. bound to carry out the decisions of the federal courts in their full rigour.
                                                                               (1)
   4. bound to carry out the decisions of the federal court, but with modifications due to local conditions.   (4)
   1 and 3 combined   (1)   None   (3)

Questionnaires were sent to all 48 states, so the figures are less than conclusive. The pattern of response is of some interest, however. Of the 48, it should be noted, 13 replied to the questionnaire, and two others sent materials from which partial answers could be assumed. Eleven wrote letters indicating various reasons for non-reply. Two Attorneys General from defying states answered the questionnaire, approximately the same proportion as of the total group, but no other response was heard from the other five defying states. Of the complying states in which desegregation was a problem, the proportion of replies to the questionnaire is average — two out of eleven — but two others sent materials, and four sent letters of explanation. Thus virtually every border state Attorney General replied in one way or another.

STATE POLITICAL PARTIES

The Ecological Basis of Party Systems: The Case of Ohio

Heinz Eulau

This is an analysis of the relationship between the ecological structure of Ohio's eighty-eight counties and the structure of their party systems, as reflected in the vote for the Ohio House of Representatives over a period of six elections, from 1946 to 1956.

PROBLEM

A viable democratic political system, as any social system, has to meet certain internal-structural requisites that can be shown to be functional for achieving the goals of the system. Among the goals of a democratic political system are the continuing crystallization, institutionalization and resolution of social, economic and other conflicts. These goals are mutually interdependent. If conflicts remain uncrystallized, they are unlikely to be institutionalized; and if they are not

Reprinted from "The Ecological Basis of Party Systems: The Case of Ohio," *Midwest Journal of Political Science,* Vol. 1, No. 2 (August 1957), by Heinz Eulau by permission of the Wayne State University Press. Copyright 1957 by Wayne State University Press.

This analysis was made possible by a grant from the Political Behavior Committee of the Social Science Research Council. It is preliminary to an interview survey of the Ohio General Assembly conducted during the 1957 session. Neither the Council nor Antioch College is responsible for the analysis. The author wishes to acknowledge the aid he received in collecting the data from the members of his course, "Methods in Social Science," especially from Mr. Stanley Newman and Miss Susanne Berger.

institutionalized, they are likely to remain unsolved. The political system will be characterized by tensions making for basic political instability.

Among the structural requisites of a stable democratic system is the existence of political parties which, by competing for public support on reasonably even terms, serve as agents of conflict crystallization and institutionalization and, through bargaining and compromise, contribute to the resolution of conflicts of interest. Competitive parties are, therefore, structural requisites of the democratic political system in that they facilitate the achievement of some of its goals, notably the crystallization, institutionalization and resolution of conflicts.

But a political system is not a closed system. It functions within a series of environments which tend to condition its structure. One might mention the prevailing system of class relations, the economic system, the cultural or value system, and so on. Of such environmental systems, the ecological system, i. e., the pattern of the residential distribution of the population, has long been recognized as a major conditioning factor, but the precise relationship between the structure of the ecological system and the structure of the party system has not been widely explored. In his recent *American State Politics* (1956), V. O. Key, Jr. perceptively analyzed the effect of metropolitan and rural environments on the fortunes of the political parties in sundry states, but he was not primarily concerned with an analysis of the relationship between the structure of the ecological system as an external determinant and the structure of the party system as an internal determinant of the political system.

HYPOTHESIS

It is a most general hypothesis of this study that there is a direct relationship between the character of an area's ecological structure and the structure of its party system. In particular, the hypothesis is entertained that urban structures are conducive to the existence of competitive party systems and that there is a progressive transition to semi-competitive and non-competitive (one-party) systems as areas are located along an urban-rural ecological continuum. If this hypothesis can be supported, one may speculate that increasing urbanization, especially the expansion of metropolitan areas, is favorable to the extension of a competitive party politics as a structural requisite of the democratic political system.

THEORY

Underlying the hypothesis are some broad theoretical notions about factors in the urban environment which are conducive to a competitive party system. Without reviewing here the large and often controversial literature of urban sociology, it may be suggested that competitive attitudes, orientations and practices are functions of such major ecological variables as the size, density and heterogeneity of urban aggregates. In particular, the city, in contrast to the open country, is characterized by a greater range of individual variations, a more pervasive segmentalization of human relationships making for membership in widely divergent groups as well as for divided allegiances, a more complicated class structure and heightened social and physical mobility, a greater division of labor and more intense economic rivalry, a wider range of ideas and more secular attitudes. This kind of environment is likely to be more favorable to the development of competitive parties than small town or rural environments where social relationships are more limited and limiting, where sacred values and traditional behavior patterns are cherished, where social and ideological differences are less tolerated, where group memberships are concentric rather than tangential, and so on. In such environments semi-competitive or non-competitive party systems are more likely to predominate.

These theoretical considerations are not meant to imply that the city, as some sociologists have held, is an undifferentiated mass of people characterized by anonymity, impersonality, standardization, or disorganization, as opposed to the country with its presumed friendliness, community spirit, spontaneity of association and mutual aid. Such differentiation does violence to the continuing assimilation of city and country which has been the outstanding feature of ecological development in the United States during the past sixty years or so. "Urban" and "rural," then, are used here as convenient short-hand phrases to denote ecological differences, on the assumption that, in spite of the assimilation process, "rurbanization" has not as yet gone far enough to eliminate all distinctions between city and country. Urban and rural are not to be construed, therefore, as ideal types, but as two poles of a continuum which does not permit radically discontinuous variations as one moves from one end to the other but makes for variations nonetheless.

In order to proceed with the analysis, Ohio's eighty-eight counties had to be classified in terms of their (a) ecological structure, (b) structure of party system, and (c) party dominance. In the following we shall briefly summarize the main steps taken in the preparatory stage of the analysis.

ECOLOGICAL STRUCTURE

The nature of a person's place of residence is an easily available and tangible index of the ecological structure of a county. The United States Census divides the population into three main categories: urban, rural non-farm, and rural. For the purposes of this study the urban and rural non-farm categories were combined on the assumption that due to "rurbanization" non-farm people outside urban areas have attitudes and orientations closer to those of urban than of farm people. In order to test the reliability, if not the theoretical validity, of the combined category as an index of urban structure, it was correlated with other indices of urban and rural differentiation available in the Census. The combined urban and rural non-farm category should correlate highly and positively, for instance, with indices of size, density and heterogeneity of population, as well as with some other relevant demographic characteristics, and it should correlate highly and negatively with rural characteristics. Table 1 presents the correlation coefficients, based on 1950 Census data.

Table 1 indicates that, as expected, very high correlations were obtained between the combined index of urban and rural non-farm residence and the two measures of size and density. The coefficients for the heterogeneity factors vary — that for percent foreign-born being reasonably high, that for percent non-white only moderately high, but both are satisfactory. The high positive and negative

Table 1 Correlation coefficients for urban and rural non-farm residence, and selected
ecological and demographic characteristics of 88 Ohio counties, 1950 census data.

Factor	Census Category	Rho
Density	Population per square mile	+.95
Size	Total population	+.93
Heterogeneity	Percent foreign-born	+.68
	Percent non-white	+.49
Employment	Percent in manufacturing	+.73
	Percent in agriculture	-.96
Income	Median family income	+.76
	Percent with less than $2,000	-.77

coefficients for employment in manufacturing and agriculture, respectively, as
well as the income coefficients, further support the discriminatory reliability of
the residence criterion as an ecological index.

Table 2 Distribution of 88 Ohio counties by major ecological categories.

Category	Description	N	Percent
Metro	All counties in standard metropolitan areas	17	19
Urban	All counties with urban aggregates of 2,500+ population and a ratio of urban and rural non-farm population of more than 80%	10	11
Urban-Rurban	All counties with urban aggregates of 2,500+ population and a ratio of urban and rural non-farm population of 70-80%	31	35
Rural-Rurban	All counties with urban aggregates of 2,500+ population and a ratio of urban and rural non-farm population of less than 70%	19	22
Rural	All counties *without* an urban aggregate of 2,500+ population	11	13
	Total	88	100

However, in order to refine the urban category, a further distinction was
made between counties located in metropolitan areas, as defined by the Census,
and those not within metropolitan areas, but with urban aggregates of 2,500 population or more. Application of these criteria yielded five major ecological categories
ranging from "metro" to "rural." The description of these categories and the distribution of the eighty-eight Ohio counties by these categories are found in Table 2.

POLITICAL STRUCTURE

County election data for the Ohio House of Representatives from 1946 to 1956 were analyzed to determine the structure of the party systems in the eighty-eight Ohio counties which also serve as election districts. During this period, the Democrats organized the House only in 1948. The election of 1946 was chosen as the starting point of the series as it marked the first "normal" post-war contest.

As a number of counties are multi-member districts, i.e., more than one contest takes place in any one election, the total number of contests in the six elections since 1946 was used as an initial device to classify the counties in terms of competition between the two major parties. A competitive party system district was defined as one in which one of the two parties has won at least 25 percent, or more, of *all* the *contests* in the six elections. On this basis, only sixteen counties, or 18 percent of eighty-eight counties, could be classified as "competitive."

Inspection of the data suggested that in some counties where it had won less than 25 percent of the contests, or none at all, the second party was nevertheless able to stimulate reasonably strong opposition to the dominant party — opposition effective enough to win a contest occasionally, and to keep the dominant party on its toes. It seemed feasible, therefore, to divide the counties not classified as competitive into two categories: (1) semi-competitive, and (2) non-competitive (or one-party) systems.

A semi-competitive system was defined as one where the second party, though winning less than 25 percent of the contests, or none, had won 40 percent or more of the popular two-party vote in *at least four* of the *elections* held between 1946 and 1956. For this purpose, the vote cast in individual contests in multi-member districts was averaged, and the mean vote cast for all party candidates was used as the percentage index. On this basis, another twenty-four counties, or 28 percent of the total, could be classified as semi-competitive.

The residue of counties, forty-eight in all, are the non-competitive (one-party system) districts, where the second party has won less than 25 percent of the contests, or none, and over 40 percent of the vote in *less than four* of the elections since 1946. Table 3 summarizes the data.

Table 3 Distribution of different party systems in 88 Ohio counties, based on 1946-1956 election data for the House of Representatives.

Character of Party System	N	Percent
Competitive	16	18
Semi-competitive	24	28
Non-competitive	48	54
Total	88	100

PARTY DOMINANCE

For purposes of "control" to be applied in the analysis, it was necessary to define "party dominance" in semi-competitive and non-competitive party systems. A county or district was considered "dominated" by a party if that party had won 75 percent or more of the total number of contests in the period 1946-1956. As Table 4 indicates, the Republican party is overwhelmingly dominant through time in the non-competitive as well as in the semi-competitive counties.

Table 4 Party dominance in semi-competitive and non-competitive election districts for the Ohio House of Representatives, 1946-1956.

Party Dominance		N	Percent
Semi-competitive party systems			
Republicans dominant		21	88
Democrats dominant		3	12
	Total	24	100
Non-competitive party systems			
Republicans dominant		43	90
Democrats dominant		5	10
	Total	48	100

ANALYSIS

On the basis of the foregoing classifications, a first step in the analysis of the relationship between ecological structure and party-system structure was a complete cross-tabulation of the eighty-eight counties. Table 5 presents the results. Most evident is the marked difference between the metropolitan and the four other ecological areas with respect to party competition. Surprisingly, only one of the ten counties classifed as urban turned out to have a competitive party system. But none of the rural counties fell into the competitive system category. On the other hand, both metropolitan and urban counties differ significantly from the urban-rurban and rural-rurban counties in the semi-competitive classification. The relatively large percentage of semi-competitive party systems found in the rural counties is partly due to the absence of competitive party systems in that category, but it is also due to the fact that in some scattered counties in the southern part of the state the Democratic party has been able to maintain a certain degree of traditional electoral strength. With regard to non-competitive or one-party systems, the progression increases systematically from the metropolitan structures to the rural-rurban structures, declining slightly in the rural structures due to the relatively strong showing of semi-competitive systems in these rural counties.

Table 5 Ecological and party-system structure of Ohio counties, derived from 1950 census data and election results for the Ohio House of Representatives, 1946-1956.

Character of Party System	Metro (N = 17)	Urban (N = 10)	*In Percentages* Urban- Rurban (N = 31)	Rural- Rurban (N = 19)	Rural (N = 11)
Competitive	41	10	16	16	0
Semi-competitive	41	50	19	5	45
Non-competitive	18	40	65	79	55
Total	100	100	100	100	100

Table 5 suggests that it may be permissible, without doing violence to the data, to combine the urban-rurban and rural-rurban ecological categories into a single rurban category. Table 6 presents the re-classification. The table indicates more clearly that some kind of party competition, either of the complete or modified kind, is a quality of metropolitan and urban ecological areas, while non-competitive party systems are predominantly small town and rural phenomena. It may be interesting to note in this connection that the mean size of the largest town in the urban counties is 27,233 ± 10,800, in the urban-rurban counties only 12,081 ±6,500, and in the rural-rurban counties a mere 6,088 ± 874. In other words, these ecological areas differ not only with respect to the size of their largest urban centers, but, as the standard deviations show, the range of variation declines progressively, suggesting the greater homogeneity at the small town end of the urban-rural continuum. The table points up the small town basis of one-party systems in Ohio, while inroads into the rigidity of one-party politics are most noticeable in the large percentage of semi-competitive party systems in the urban ecological areas (a pattern disturbed only in the rural category, as explained already). If, as in Table 7, one disregards the difference between competitive and semi-competitive party systems, the relationship between ecological structure and party competition is even more evident. In fact, the table would seem to justify a recombination of the ecological categories into two single categories, a metropolitan-urban and a rurban-rural classification. Table 8 presents the data. Non-competitive or

Table 6 Revised ecological and party-system structure of Ohio counties.

Character of Party System	Metro (N = 17)	*In Percentages* Urban (N = 10)	Rurban (N = 50)	Rural (N = 11)
Competitive	41	10	16	0
Semi-competitive	41	50	14	45
Non-competitive	18	40	70	55
Total	100	100	100	100

Table 7 Further revision of ecological and party-system structures, Ohio.

Character of Party System	In Percentages			
	Metro (N = 17)	Urban (N = 10)	Rurban (N = 50)	Rural (N = 11)
Competitive & Semi-competitive	82	60	30	45
Non-competitive	18	40	70	55
Total	100	100	100	100

Table 8 Ecological and party-system structures dichotomized, Ohio.

Character of Party System	In Percentages	
	Metro- Urban (N = 27)	Rurban- Rural (N = 61)
Competitive & Semi-competitive	74	33
Non-competitive	26	67
Total	100	100

one-party systems now appear even more clearly as correlates of small town and rural ecological structures, while some form of party competition appears to predominate in the metropolitan and medium-size urban areas.

However, in spite of the clear nature of the demonstrated relationship, it might be argued that the connection between ecological structure and party system structure is spurious, particularly in the semi-competitive and non-competitive counties. Could it be, for instance, that the predominance of one-party systems in the non-metropolitan counties is a function of the overwhelming strength of the Republican party in the state as a whole? In order to deal with the party factor, it seemed advisable to control the urban and rurban areas by party dominance. Unfortunately, the number of such counties in which the Democratic party predominates is so small (four in all) that the data cannot be properly assessed, though

Table 9 Party systems in urban and rurban counties, Ohio, controlled by party dominance.

Character of Party System	In Percentages			
	Democrats Dominant		Republicans Dominant	
	Urban (N = 1)	Rurban (N = 3)	Urban (N = 8)	Rurban (N = 39)
Semi-competitive	100	0	50	18
Non-competitive	0	100	50	82
Total	100	100	100	100

they move in the expected direction. However, if the ecological categories are controlled by Republican dominance, the small town basis of non-competitive party systems in these counties is evident. As Table 9 shows, while the eight Republican-dominated urban counties are equally split between semi-competitive and non-competitive party systems, one-party systems are overwhelmingly present in the rur-ban environments where 82 percent of the Republican-dominated counties have no competitive systems of any kind.

CONCLUSION

The data presented in the analysis seem to support the hypothesis that there is a direct relationship between the ecological structure of the counties which serve as election districts for the Ohio House of Representatives and the structure of the party systems in these counties. Competitive party systems, either truly competitive or semi-competitive, seem to be functionally related to metropolitan and urban ecological structures, while non-competitive or one-party systems seem to be functionally related to small town and rural ecological structures. Increasing urbanization would seem to be conducive to the further development of a competitive party system as a structural requisite of the democratic political system.

Party Responsibility in the States: Some Causal Factors

Thomas A. Flinn

Pleas and programs for party responsibility are not new. It is remarkable, however, how little the discussion has advanced. I do not mean that I am surprised that the path of reform has been hard but that knowledge of the subject has not grown in proportion to the length of the discussion. Proponents believe party responsibility introduces desired qualities into the policy process and makes possible rational organization of the electorate in terms of policy. Not much has been done to provide adequate support for either of these propositions. In fact, it is hard to discover a serious effort to put these propositions in some form which would permit a partial but rigorous test. Opponents on the other hand conjure up visions of polarized parties, downtrodden minorities, and multipartyism as the fruits of party responsibility. They are able to make these improbable inferences by working with an exceedingly simple model, by ignoring the functions of party competition and the complex of factors which seem to shape party systems. Some observers less involved in the argument allow that the debate may have some value since it leads to notice of important realities. But, for them, proposed reforms are not to be taken seriously because they are utopian in two senses: (1) sweeping and incalculable; and (2) out of reach. This view seems to overlook the fact that party responsibility is a matter of degree and that incremental reform is, at least, possible in principle. Finally, very little attention has been paid to factors which may promote or inhibit party responsibility.

Party responsibility in some degree is a normal incident of politics in a competitive party system; in other words it is a function of party competition. Arguments might be offered to support this opinion, but let it suffice here to call it a useful theory. Given this much, then the fate of party responsibility relates to the the maintenance and spread of partisan conflict at the polls. As the margins of one-party or non-party areas retreat, party responsibility will grow. In the case of Congress, one would expect party to grow in importance as two-party competition becomes more general, and structural revision in the direction of increased concentration of power in the hands of partisan groups to grow apace. However, there is probably no one-to-one relation between party competition and party responsibility; intervening variables may encourage or inhibit the development of party responsibility. These are the factors to be explored in the present study by reference to practice in the states and by an occasional reference to Congress.[1]

But first some additional preliminary comments are necessary.

(1) Advocates of party responsibility seem to envisage a system with these identifying characteristics: (a) intra-party cohesion and interparty conflict in legislative situations; (b) communication of the facts of legislative combat; and (c) an

Reprinted from *American Political Science Review,* Vol. 58 (1964), pp. 60-71 by permission of the author and publisher.

an attentive public. At least, (a) must be present for without it the whole system falls. If only (a) is present the minimum condition is satisfied, but the values attributed to the system may well not be entirely realized. Given this understanding of party responsibility, then it is the behavior of legislative parties which must be considered and which will be considered here to the exclusion of other matters.

(2) It is taken as established that elements of party responsibility are present in many state legislative bodies[2] although a much larger collection of evidence would certainly be welcome.

(3) The conditions for theoretical advance are present in the study of state legislative parties, and this should make the subject an attractive one whether or not it is considered intrinsically interesting or important. These state parties differ from one another from time to time and from place to place, and members of one and the same state party stand in different relations to the majority of their own party. Explanation of the differences may be very difficult due to the large number of variables in the systems, but the requisite differences are present. Furthermore, they are measurable, although providing useful measures is not the least of many problems.

(4) Finally, roll call analysis is the tool to be used, and it is a good one although it has its limitations like any other technique.[3] Critics who would condemn or relegate the technique to the margins of serious inquiry are mistaken even though it must be conceded that the technique is much more difficult to apply than some practitioners seem to have realized.

I.   THE PARTY ORGANIZATION

Duane Lockard in a study of Connecticut legislative politics described the leadership "on both sides of the aisle in both houses. . .[as] highly unified and cohesive . . . [consisting usually] of the state chairman of the party, the governor, a few chosen but powerful outside party leaders . . . and intra-legislative leaders such as the speaker of the House, the president pro tempore of the Senate, the majority and minority leaders, and the chairmen of the most important committees."[4] He then reports that "the final and almost invariably binding decisions are made by the party leaders themselves. . . ."[5] Four factors contributing to the result are cited: party organizational strength; party competition; ideological agreement within each party; and potential control of legislative nominations by the party organization.[6] Considerable emphasis is placed on the impact of the external organizations; that is, party responsibility is to some extent explained by pressure from the outside party organization which is what might be called the organization pressure theory. E. E. Schattschneider[7] and Stephen K. Bailey[8] are also impressed by the importance of the outside organization in producing cohesion in legislative parties, as may be inferred by the prescriptions they have offered for increasing party responsibility.

The importance of organization pressure in generating cohesion in legislative parties in Connecticut is conceded, but it seems unimportant in other situations where high levels of party cohesion nonetheless occur. In Congress northern Democrats and Republicans are each able to close ranks on many key issues in every session. Cohesion is not perfect, but it is high. No one would suggest the result is produced by the organized pressure of the parties in the country.

The two state legislatures with which I am most familiar, Minnesota and Ohio, frequently show high levels of party cohesion,[9] but it is not due to organization pressure. In Minnesota direct action by outside party leaders to enforce party policy in the legislature would probably produce negative results.[10] In Ohio the Democratic state organization is notoriously weak, and it is split. A few sessions ago Democratic members were reported to be dissatisfied with the state party headquarters, because it showed so little interest in them.[11] The Republicans are more effectively organized at the state level, and the relation of the state chairman to the legislature is closer. However, interviews with Republican county officials in some 20 geographically scattered counties convince me that the county parties rarely make any attempt to communicate to legislators their views on policy questions. To be sure, the evidence is limited, but it does seem fair to conclude that while organization pressure may produce party responsibility, it is not a necessary condition for cohesion in legislative parties.

II.   CONSTITUENCIES

It is argued sometimes that legislators from similar constituencies will vote together and in opposition to legislators from constituencies with contrasting characteristics. To the extent that parties find their support in contrasting constituencies, party responsibility is the consequence. Aside from the fact that this statement is not operational in form, numerous objections to it arise almost at once. On some issues constituency interests are weak and on other issues only a part of all the constituencies represented have or think they have anything at stake. In addition, legislators' perceptions of their districts may be unclear or they may vary with the personality of the legislator.[12] It has been shown also that legislative roles vary, with the result that members do not respond equally to constituency interests.[13] The urban-rural factionalism thesis on state legislatures is a special version of the more general theory. Derge in particular has presented persuasive evidence which discredits the thesis.[14] His study used data from Illinois and Missouri. Studies of legislative behavior in Alabama[15] and Ohio[16] have the same effect.

Since the constituency pressure theory seems to be a tough weed, some additional evidence based on data from two sessions of the Ohio legislature is offered below. The first of the two sessions is that of 1949. Attention was restricted to the House which was organized by the Democrats. The governor was also Democratic. A roll call analysis was undertaken. Every roll call on which the minority was equal to 10 per cent or more of the majority was selected for consideration: 216 roll calls in all. The legislators were divided into four groups: urban Democrats (51); urban Republicans (12); rural Democrats (18); and rural Republicans (54). Urban members were defined as those representing counties classified by the 1950 Census as standard metropolitan areas or parts thereof. The behavior of the groups relative to each other was described by use of Rice's index of likeness.[17]

The theory requires, at least, that members from similar districts vote together more often than members from dissimilar districts. In terms of the data below, this would mean that urban members regardless of party and also rural members regardless of party would vote together more often than members of the same party representing dissimilar districts. However, inspection of Table 1 shows clearly that the predicted relationships do not occur. The data disconfirm the theory.

Table 1 Frequency distribution of indices of likeness involving designated groups, 1949 session Ohio House of Representatives.

Interval	Urban Dems Urban Reps		Rural Dems Rural Reps		Urban Dems Rural Dems		Urban Reps Rural Reps	
	N	%	N	%	N	%	N	%
0- 19	27	12	32	15	1	0	0	0
20- 39	31	14	26	12	6	3	5	2
40- 59	28	13	33	15	11	5	12	6
60- 79	40	18	56	26	40	18	46	21
80-100	90	42	69	32	158	73	153	71
Total	216	99	216	100	216	99	216	100

The second of the two meetings of the Ohio General Assembly selected for further testing of the constituency-pressure theory is that of 1959. Once again attention is restricted to the House. It was organized by the Democrats, and the governor was again Democratic. The recorded votes of the members on all roll calls between and including May 13 and July 24, 1959, were considered; and those on which the minority was equal to or greater than 10 per cent of the majority were selected for analysis.[18] The period was chosen for the reason that it was a period of sustained activity on a variety of relatively important matters but not including the first or last weeks of the session. The length of the period was determined by the need on the one hand to collect a fairly large body of data and on the other hand to limit the data to what was convenient for processing. There are 183 roll calls in the group selected for analysis, and on 113 of these a majority of the Democrats opposed a majority of the Republicans. Members were given scores which measure the percentage of their votes which were cast in support of the position taken by the majority of the Democrats on party opposition votes, with the exception that 3 Democrats and 1 Republican were dropped from the analysis altogether for failure to vote on more than 100 of the 183 selected roll calls. Then members were grouped by party and constituency characteristics, and mean scores were computed for each group. Results are shown below. It is abundantly clear that members from similar constituencies do not vote in the same way and that differences between the parties are not due to differences in the composition of the legislative parties in terms of constituencies represented. Once again the constituency-pressure theory is disconfirmed.[19]

However, use has been made of the theory in modified form; and this should be distinguished from the full-blown theory discussed above. MacRae[20] and Dye[21] have argued that variance in the degree of party loyalty shown by members of partisan legislative groups relate to differences in constituency. They maintain, in MacRae's words, that "representatives who come from districts that are most

Table 2 Mean support for positions taken by a majority of Democrats by party and constituency, selected party opposition votes, 1959 Ohio House of Representatives.

Constituency % Urban [a]	Dems		Reps	
	Mean Score	(N)	Mean Score	(N)
0- 29	83	(9)	12	(16)
30- 59	78	(18)	13	(25)
60-100	84	(48)	18	(19)

[a] 1950 Census.

typical of their parties tend to show highest 'party loyalty' on roll calls; those who come from districts atypical of their party tend to cross party lines more often."[22] Note that the statement says *variance* in party loyalty relates to constituencies, but does not offer any reason for the relatively high degree of party unity from which the analysis starts. It is not contended that members from similar districts vote together regardless of party.

Actually the constituency-pressure theory in even its severely modified form is open to question. MacRae based his Massachusetts study on a very small number of roll calls in each of three legislative sessions, and members were included in the analysis even though they may have missed as many as 50 per cent of the roll calls selected from a given session. Furthermore, MacRae offers no measure of the strength of the apparent relationship between constituency and party loyalty. It seems that his intention and accomplishment were to advance an hypothesis with enough data to make it credible.[23]

Dye on the other hand took MacRae's hypothesis, and gave it a much more rigorous test. He considered every vote in the 1957 session of the Pennsylvania legislature on which the majorities of the two parties were opposed, and computed correlation coefficients to express the relation between constituency and party loyalty. Dye's measure of roll call voting behavior is what he calls a deviation index, which is "the per cent of the votes on which party majorities were in opposition that the legislator voted with the opposition party's majority and against his own party's majority."[24] He summarized his finding in Table 3.[25]

Leaving aside electoral margin, which will be considered later, it can be seen that income and ruralism have some relationship to party loyalty in the House. As a matter of fact coefficients above .4 are remarkably good in a system as complex as the legislative system. Insofar as the Senate is concerned, constituency characteristics have virtually nothing to do with a member's behavior with reference to the majorities of the respective parties. Dye offers an interesting explanation for the contrast between House and Senate: "It appears from empirical analysis that the function of the upper chamber in Pennsylvania is to inject into legislative decision-making the influence of a body relatively more free from narrower constituency pressures than the lower chamber. Larger and more heterogeneous constituencies compel senators to align themselves with a wider variety of interests. . . . One may conjecture that the moderating of constituency influence via

Table 3 "A comparison of correlation coefficients of relationships between constituency characteristics and party cohesion for House and Senate members, 1957 session, Pennsylvania General Assembly."

	Correlation Coefficient			
Relationship	House		Senate	
	Democrats	Republicans	Democrats	Republicans
Income and Deviation				
Total Urban Legislators	.45	−.07	.08	−.29
Ruralism and Deviation				
Total Legislators	.56	−.37	.09	.00
Electoral Margin and Deviation				
Total Legislators	−.46	−.44	−.15	.12

longer terms and larger districts actually clears the way for party affiliation to exert a greater influence on voting patterns."[26] The last statement suggests an elaboration of what has been identified as the modified constituency-pressure theory; however, replication is undoubtedly required before the theory can be well accepted in any form.

An attempt to do that was made with the 1959 Ohio data already described. The procedure differed slightly from Dye's. Only 113 party opposition votes were considered, and the measure was support for the position of the Democratic majority.[27] Results are shown in Table 4.

Table 4 Product moment coefficients expressing the relation between constituency characteristics and support for positions taken by a majority of Democrats, 113 party opposition votes, 1959 Ohio House.

Constituency Characteristic (1950 Census)	Dems (N = 75)	Reps (N = 60)
% Mining & manufacturing empl.	+.246[a]	+.123
% Urban	+.170	+.257[a]
% Rural farm	−.170	−.272[a]
Median family income	+.234[a]	+.145

[a] $p = .05$.

It may be seen that support for the position taken by a majority of Democrats increases as the per cent of the labor force in mining and manufacturing increases and as urbanism and family income increase. Support for the majority Democratic position decreases as the per cent of the population classified as rural farm increases. However, the relationships are weak; and in half of the cases the coefficients are statistically insignificant.

Before accepting a negative conclusion and before counting the contrast between Ohio and Pennsylvania as a paradox it should be noted that single demographic variables are being used to order constituencies in a way which is thought to be relevant to legislative behavior. Actually they may not be able to do that. In Ohio there are some high urban areas where industry is not particularly important and also some relatively rural counties which have a large part of their population engaged in mining and manufacturing. Thus, it may be that differences in constituencies do relate significantly to legislative behavior in Ohio but that they are not properly described by any single variable. This problem may not be so acute in Pennsylvania and that might explain the contrasting findings.

To see whether there is a relation closer than yet perceived between constituency and party loyalty in Ohio, Democratic and Republican districts were each grouped on the basis of several demographic characteristics. An appropriate variance analysis procedure was employed to determine whether these classes related to variance in party loyalty.[28] Application of the procedure yields a series of equations which are forms of the equation

$$S = b_1 C_1 + b_2 C_2 + b_3 C_3 \ . \ . \ .$$

where S is the actual line of regression, b the class mean, and C_1, C_2, etc. are the classes. R-values, F-values, and probabilities are shown for each equation.

Democratic districts were divided into four classes as follows: C_1 — districts 30-55 per cent urban; C_2 — districts less than 22 per cent urban; C_3 — districts 87 per cent or more urban; and C_4 — districts more than 40 per cent industrial, i.e., more than 40 per cent of the working force engaged in mining and manufacturing. Where a district could be classified in more than one way, it was placed in the highest class. The result of the analysis of variance is shown below:

$$S = 75C_1 + 82C_2 + 85C_3 + 86C_4$$
$$R = .414 \quad F = 3.68 \quad p = .01$$

The coefficient is substantially better than that produced by the zero-order correlation (.246) between mining and manufacturing employment and party loyalty. Also, Democrats from mid-urban districts are less loyal to the party majority than Democrats from very rural counties.

Republican districts were divided into four classes as were Democratic districts, and in the following manner: C_1 — districts 25 per cent or less urban; C_2 — districts 26-68 per cent urban; C_3 — districts 71 per cent or more urban; C_4 — districts more than 40 per cent industrial. Analysis produced the following equation:

$$S = 11C_1 + 14C_2 + 15C_3 + 21C_4$$
$$R = .353 \quad F = 1.99 \quad p = .250$$

A more significant result is obtained with only a small decrease in the value of R, if classes 1 and 2 are combined.

$$S = 13C_{1-2} + 15C_3 + 21C_4$$
$$R = .327 \quad F = 2.28 \quad p = .1$$

Note that, once again, use of a combination of constituency characteristics produced a better result than that produced by the best zero-order correlation (.272) between a demographic variable and party loyalty although the improvement here is not so great as in the case of the Democrats.

Additional data [29] were collected from the Republican-controlled 1963 meeting of the Ohio House to see whether similar results could be obtained. Zero-order coefficients relating demographic variables and party loyalty are shown in Table 5.

Table 5 Product moment coefficients expressing the relation between constituency characteristics and support for positions taken by a majority of Democrats, 50 party opposition votes, 1963 Ohio House.

Constituency Characteristic	Dems (N = 46)	Reps (N = 85)
% Mining & manufacturing empl. (1950 Census)	+.350[b]	+.335[a]
% Urban (1960 Census)	+.321[b]	+.271[b]

[a] $p = .01$.
[b] $p = .05$.

Districts represented by Democrats were divided into four classes similar to but not identical with those used in analysis of the 1959 data: C_1 —districts 30-52 per cent urban; C_2 —districts less than 20 per cent urban; C_3 —districts more than 92 per cent urban; and C_4 —districts 44 per cent or more industrial. Districts qualifying for membership in more than one class were placed in the highest class. Application of the variance analysis used before produced remarkably good results.

$$S = 68C_1 + 78C_2 + 85C_3 + 72C_4$$
$$R = .687 \quad F = 9.39 \quad p = .001$$

The coefficient is dramatically better than any zero-order coefficient, which is due in part to the unexpected non-linear relationship which appears above.

Districts represented by Republicans were divided also into four classes similar to but not identical with those used in analysis of the 1959 data: C_1 —35 per cent or less urban; C_2 —37-67 per cent urban; C_3 —districts 72 per cent or more urban; C_4 —44 per cent or more industrial. Classification procedures were the same as those used before. Analysis produced the following results:

$$S = 15C_1 + 19C_2 + 18C_3 + 25C_4$$
$$R = .420 \quad F = 4.34 \quad p = .01$$

Once again a more sophisticated analysis reveals a stronger relation between constituency and party loyalty. It is fair to conclude that the modified constituency-pressure theory has substantial merit and that failures to discover the expected relations may well be due to the variables and procedures employed.

III. ELECTORAL MARGIN

A number of writers have observed that electoral margin seems to correlate positively with loyalty to party. MacRae in his previously mentioned Massachusetts study found this relationship although his findings were somewhat inconclusive.[30] Pesonen found that Democrats from safe districts were more loyal to party than Democrats from close districts but that the opposite relation seemed to exist in the Republican Party.[31] Dye in his study of roll call voting in Pennsylvania computed coefficients expressing the relation between electoral margin and party loyalty. In the House they were .46 and .44 for the Democrats and Republicans respectively, but in the Senate the comparable coefficients were only .15 and .12.[32] Patterson in a study of the Wisconsin State Assembly delineates certain legislative roles, and remarks in passing that maverick members of the Republican Party were much more likely to be from marginal districts than were the regulars. His exact finding is that 88 per cent of the Republican mavericks were from close districts while only 42 per cent of the regular were from districts so classified.[33] Democratic mavericks were either missing or rare in the session which provided the data. Becker et al., in a study of the Michigan legislature conclude that electoral competition has no relation to legislative behavior.[34]

I made a further test of the relation between plurality and party loyalty, by using the 1959 and 1963 Ohio data already discussed above. In making the analysis plurality was defined as the difference between the winner's vote and the vote of the most popular losing candidate expressed as a percentage of the winner's vote; hence, the higher the percentage the safer the election. This somewhat complex definition was made necessary by the existence of a number of multi-member districts.

From Table 6 it appears that high plurality members support their own party majority more often than low plurality members, but the relation is weak to vanishing. However, further analysis leads to a much more positive conclusion.

Table 6 Product moment coefficients expressing the relation between plurality and support for positions taken by a majority of Democrats, selected party opposition votes in two sessions of the Ohio House.

Session	Dems	Reps
1959	.228[a]	−.106
1961	.012	−.147

[a]p = .05.

Each of the four groups shown in Table 6 was divided into classes depending on plurality. Nothing was gained insofar as the 1959 Republicans and 1961 Democrats were concerned. On the other hand, the effect of plurality on the behavior of the 1959 Democrats is seen to be non-linear as shown by the following equation:

$$S = 81P_1 + 80P_2 + 85P_3 + 86P_4$$

where P_1 are members with less than 12 per cent plurality, P_2 members with 13-20 per cent plurality, P_3 members with 21-29 per cent plurality, and P_4 members with more than 29 per cent plurality. Reduction to two classes and application of the variance analysis procedure used before produces this result:

$$S = 80P_{1-2} + 85P_{3-4}$$
$$R = .272 \quad F = 2.91 \quad p = .1$$

Elimination of one member in class P_3 with a very low party support score improves the outcome significantly:

$$S = 80P_{1-2} + 86P_{3-4}$$
$$R = .369 \quad F = 4.90 \quad p = .025$$

The relation of plurality to the behavior of 1963 Republicans is also non-linear as is shown below:

$$S = 22P_1 + 18P_2 + 16P_3 + 18P_4$$

where P_1 is a class whose members have less than 11 per cent plurality, P_2 a class with members having 11-25 per cent plurality, P_3 a class with members having 26-40 per cent plurality, and P_4 a class with members having more than 40 per cent plurality. Reduction to two classes and further analysis yields the following:

$$S = 22P_1 + 18P_{2-3-4}$$
$$R = .208 \quad F = 1.88 \quad p = .250$$

Thus it may be concluded with appropriate caution that in 1959 low plurality Democrats were less loyal to party positions than high plurality Democrats and that in 1963 low plurality Republicans were more likely to support Democratic party positions than were high plurality Republicans. Further, it is important to insist that plurality does not operate continuously, that there is a threshold: when it is once passed, plurality operates no longer as a factor affecting loyalty to party. Generally, it appears that the least secure members of winning parties, *i. e.,* the least secure members of the legislature, are less loyal to party than other members. Within these limits plurality does relate significantly to legislative behavior.

Plurality has been combined with constituency in relation to party voting in another theory which runs along these lines: a comfortable plurality frees a member from constituency pressures; a close race makes him unusually sensitive to any position with constituency support. If the member with only a tenuous hold on his office comes from a district not typical of his party, he will be most likely to be deviant. On the other hand, if he represents a district typical of his party, he will be unexcelled in fidelity to party. A schematic presentation of this view is given below:

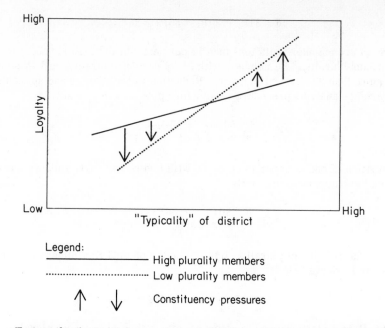

To test the theory it is necessary to hold constituency constant and to vary plurality, and this was done by use of the 1959 and 1963 Ohio data. The classification of constituencies is the same as that described earlier, and the variance analysis procedure is also the same as that employed before. In 1959 plurality related significantly to party loyalty in Democratic ranks in only the most typical Democratic districts, *i.e.*, more than 40 per cent industrial; and the relation was contrary to the hypothesis. Democrats in this class with high pluralities supported the party more than Democrats with lower pluralities as is shown by the equation for constituency class 4 Democrats:

$$S = 84P_1 + 87P_2$$
$$R = .473 \quad F = 2.55 \quad p = .1$$

where P_1 is a class composed of members with pluralities of 20 per cent or less and P_2 is a class with members having pluralities of more than 20 per cent.

Also, in 1959, plurality related significantly to party loyalty in Republican ranks in only the most typical Republican districts, *i.e.*, districts 25 per cent or less urban; and the relation is consistent with the hypothesis. Low plurality Republicans give less support to Democratic positions than do high plurality Republicans as is shown by the following equation for constituency class 1 Republicans:

$$S = 10P_1 + 13P_2$$
$$R = .558 \quad F = 2.94 \quad p = .1$$

where P_1 is a class whose members have pluralities of 10 per cent or less and P_2 is a class whose members have pluralities of more than 10 per cent. (The 10 per cent cutting point was chosen as the point most likely to yield positive results on the basis of previous analysis.)

In 1963 plurality related significantly to party loyalty among Democrats, once again in only the most industrial districts, and the relation was contrary to the hypothesis.

$$S = 62P_1 + 76P_2$$
$$R = .592 \quad F = 3.78 \quad p = .05$$

where P_1 is a class with members having less than 10.4 per cent pluralities and P_2 is a class with members having pluralities of 10.4 per cent or more. (The cutting point is at the median.)

In the same session of the Ohio House, plurality had no significant relation to party loyalty in any Republican constituency group, with 10 per cent plurality used as the cutting point. These findings from two sessions of the Ohio legislature are somewhat contradictory but generally point to disconfirmation of the hypothesis being tested; however, this negative conclusion must be accepted cautiously since an effort to relate plurality to legislative behavior in relatively small groups is almost doomed from the start when plurality itself has only a weak relation to the behavior to be explained.

IV. EXPERIENCE AND LEADERSHIP

A tendency can be seen toward a positive relation between experience in a group and conformity to its norms, a condition comforting to both the member and the group. Since loyalty to party is rather obviously the accepted thing in many state legislatures, experience should contribute to party loyalty.

This theory has, however, received little attention. One study considers somewhat tangentially the effect of experience on roll call voting. The relevant observation is that members over age 35 are more likely to vote their own social status rather than the party position if their legislative experience is limited rather than extensive.[35] The relation does not appear to be strong. A more direct test was made by use of the 1959 Ohio data. Experience measured in number of terms served was related to support for the positions of a majority of Democrats. In the case of the Democrats the coefficient is +.194, and in the case of the Republicans +.116. Neither is significant, and the finding is negative. In the absence of contradictory evidence the theory appears to be disconfirmed.

The relation of leadership to roll call behavior has received a little more attention. Analysis of voting patterns in the 1955 session of the Michigan House yielded the observation that the average House leader supported his party 89 per cent of the time he voted on partisan roll calls (party opposition votes) while the average non-leader supported his party 83 per cent of the time.[36] Leadership was defined by a panel of experts and not merely by reference to formal positions within the legislature.

Analysis of voting patterns in the 1951-1952 Massachusetts legislature produced the finding that Democratic leaders were somewhat more loyal to the party position than non-leaders, when organizational loyalty was at stake. Republicans, however, showed no such differentiation between leaders and non-leaders. With reference to votes that could be designated as liberal or conservative, it was found that an "overall association between legislative status and liberalism (for the

Democrats) or conservatism (for the Republicans) would probably not be statistically significant."[37]

The 1959 Ohio data were used for a further test with leadership defined with reference to positions of formal authority. Democrats classified as leaders were the speaker, majority leader, committee and sub-committee chairmen. Republicans classified as leaders were the minority leader, his assistant, and the legislators who had been committee or sub-committee chairmen in the Republican-controlled legislature of 1957. Twenty-seven Democrats and 18 Republicans qualified as leaders. Leaders in both parties did appear to be slightly more devoted to party positions, but chi-square tests showed the relation to be very insignificant indeed. It seems fair to conclude that in the absence of clearcut evidence to the contrary the holding or not holding of positions of leadership has little to do with voting support of party.

V. IDEOLOGY

As a guess, it is likely that voting behavior in a legislature will be influenced by the ideology of the members. The problem is to discover and measure attitude structures and to relate them to legislative behavior. For that purpose a questionnaire was sent to the members of the 1963 Ohio House of Representatives. Replies were received from 65 per cent of the Republicans and 61 of the Democrats, and insofar as it was possible to judge, respondents appeared to be a representative sample of the whole.[38] Republican responses to 10 questions concerning public policy issues constituted a Guttman scale with an index of reproducibility of 92 as did Democratic responses. Members were given a liberalism score on a scale of 100, the high positions being assigned to members more in favor of government action. The distribution of those scores is shown in the table below.

Table 7 Distribution of liberalism scores by party, 1963 Ohio House members.

Interval	Dems	Interval	Reps
100–90	3	79–70	1
89–80	2	69–60	1
79–70	3	59–50	5
69–60	9	49–40	6
59–50	6	39–30	20
49–40	2	29–20	17
39–30	3	19–10	5
29–25	2	9– 5	2
N	30	N	57
Mean	60	Mean	31
s	18	s	13

It may be noted in passing that the partisan groups of legislators differ considerably one from the other. They appear to be distinct bands of co-believers, a finding which accords with McClosky's finding concerning national party leaders.[39] This is, of course, a qualitative judgment based on quantitative data. It is made cautiously, and some may disagree.

The relation of liberalism scores to constituency characteristics is shown below, in Table 8.

Table 8 Product moment coefficients expressing the relation between designated constituency characteristics and liberalism scores, 1963 Ohio House members.

Constituency	Dems	Reps
% Industrial	+ .114	− .370 [a]
% Urban	+ .259	− .285 [b]

[a] $p = .01$.
[b] $p = .05$.

Insofar as the Democrats are concerned, the relations are in what is probably the expected direction, but they are very weak. The outcome in the case of the Republicans is totally unexpected. Republicans representing more rural and less industrial districts tend to be more liberal than other Republicans. This is even more surprising when it is recalled that the Republicans from more rural and less industrial districts gave less support than other Republicans to positions taken by the Democrats who are clearly the more liberal of the two partisan groups.

The coefficient expressing the relation between liberalism and loyalty to Democratic positions is only − .034 in the case of the Democrats, which is of no significance at all, and − .298 in the case of the Republicans ($p = .05$). Partial correlation analysis for the Republican group, using industrialization and liberalism as the independent variables and party support scores as the dependent variable, reduces the relation between liberalism and support for Democratic stands to − .199 ($p = .25$). The negative relation between liberalism and support for the Democrats remains; but the relationship itself is now so weak that it is fair to conclude that ideology has little explanatory value when the behavior to be explained is position relative to party position.

VI. CONCLUSION

Inter-party conflict and intra-party cohesion describe essentially but with varying degrees of imprecision many roll calls in state legislative bodies. Party organizations capable of imposing sanctions and discipline may raise party responsibility to very high levels, but this seems not to be a necessary condition. The view that what really happens on party opposition votes is that members vote their constituencies and that different parties represent different constituencies, is wrong. Differences in constituency do, however, relate to intra-party differences with members from districts typical of the party supporting the party position more often than other members. Constituency characteristics will not account for all the variance or even most of it, but given the complexity of the legislative system impressive results can be obtained. This is one generalization which seems now to be firmly established.

Electoral margin seems to have little to do with loyalty to party, except that the least secure members of the legislature, *i. e.,* the members of the winning party with lowest pluralities, are less loyal to party than are other members. This judgment is based on rather limited evidence, and must be taken cautiously. Experience in the legislature and the holding of positions of leadership have little or nothing to do with party loyalty. This judgment too must be taken with caution; further inquiry could lead to a revision of it, although the evidence is sufficient to indicate that is unlikely. Surprisingly, ideology seems not to have a significant relation to party voting. This observation is based only on Ohio data which show also that the Democrats and Republicans differ distinctly from one another. Within the Ohio Democratic Party attitudes do not vary with constituency but within the Ohio Republican Party the rural members are more liberal than the urban. A shift in the base of the Democratic legislative group would not produce a change in the attitude of the group, but if a more rural Republican group were to face a necessarily more urban Democratic group, there would be a closing of the gap between the legislative parties in terms of basic attitude.

To put the foregoing into the context of the theory which was outlined in the beginning: party responsibility is a consequence of party competition (an unconfirmed but a plausible and useful proposition). Various factors may intervene to inhibit or promote party responsibility, but the only important one located with substantial confidence by this inquiry is constituency. Prospects for increased party responsibility depend, therefore, on the spread of party competition and upon a sorting out of legislative constituencies so that the districts represented by the respective parties are more homogeneous. There are those who think these processes are occurring, although the application of some measures is certainly needed; and there are those who would regret the process if it is occurring, on the ground that legislative life would be much more difficult if two parties were placed on the scene representing constituencies which overlapped in characteristics very little if at all. However, this fear may be unfounded, given the distribution of attitudes within and between the parties which was noted in Ohio. Hence, it might be argued that increased party responsibility in the states is on the way and that it is desirable; but establishment of these points is a problem for further inquiry.

Assuming the theories advanced in this study are nearly correct, then it seems that there is very little chance of getting or increasing party responsibility by deliberate action. On the other hand, it is entirely possible that there are trends running which will encourage party responsibility whether it is desired or not.

NOTES

1.   This study is a revision of a paper delivered at the APSA annual meeting of 1963. I was assisted in preparation by a grant from the Ford Foundation to Oberlin College for the study of public affairs. The assistance of Robert Murphy and Virginia Woodcock is also acknowledged with deep appreciation.

2.   Malcolm E. Jewell, "Party Voting in American State Legislatures," *American Political Science Review,* Vol. 49 (Sept., 1955), pp. 773-791, and studies cited by Jewell, *The State Legislature* (New York, 1962), ch. 3.

3. A good discussion is David Truman's, *The Congressional Party* (New York, 1959), pp. 10-14.

4. W. Duane Lockard, "Legislative Politics in Connecticut," *American Political Science Review,* Vol. 48 (March, 1954), pp. 166-173, especially p. 167.

5. *Ibid.,* p. 171.

6. *Ibid.,* pp. 172-173.

7. Committee on Political Parties, APSA (E.E. Schattschneider, Chm.), "Toward a More Responsible Two-Party System," *American Political Science Review,* Vol. 44 (September, 1950), Supplement.

8. Stephen K. Bailey, *The Condition of Our National Political Parties* (Santa Barbara, Calif.: The Fund for the Republic, 1959).

9. Data on Ohio may be found in my study, "The Outline of Ohio Politics," *Western Political Quarterly,* Vol. 13 (September, 1960), pp. 702-721.

10. Some supporting evidence for this observation may be found in my case study, *Governor Freeman and the Minnesota Budget,* ICP Study 60 (University, Alabama: University of Alabama Press, 1961).

11. Wahlke, et al. *The Legislative System* (New York, 1962), p. 349.

12. Lewis Dexter, "The Representative and His District," *Human Organization,* Vol. 16 (Spring, 1957), pp. 2-13.

13. Particularly Eulau, et al., "The Role of the Representative: Some Empirical Observations on the Theory of Edmund Burke" *American Political Science Review,* Vol. 53 (September, 1959), pp. 742-756, and Charles O. Jones, "Representation in Congress: The Case of the House Agriculture Committee," *American Political Science Review,* Vol. 55 (June, 1961), pp. 358-368.

14. David R. Derge, "Metropolitan and Outstate Alignments in Illinois and Missouri Legislative Delegations," *American Political Science Review,* Vol. 52 (December, 1958), pp. 1051-1065.

15. Murray Clark Havens, *City Versus Farm?* (University, Alabama: Bureau of Public Administration, University of Alabama, 1957).

16. Flinn, "The Outline of Ohio Politics," *op. cit.*

17. Stuart Rice, "The Behavior of Legislative Groups: A Method of Measurement," *Political Science Quarterly,* Vol. 40 (March, 1925), pp. 60-72.

18. This is in effect a time sample, and it is taken to be a random sample of party opposition votes in the 1959 session. Findings are spoken of as applying to the entire session, and probabilities are given. Another time sample taken from the 1963 ses-

sion is treated in the same way. If the data analyzed do not constitute random samples, then the probabilities add nothing, of course; and certain statements must be taken to apply only to the data analyzed and not to the entire legislative sessions from which they were drawn.

19.   But see Lewis A. Froman, Jr., "Inter-Party Constituency Differences and Congressional Voting Behavior," *American Political Science Review,* Vol. 57 (March, 1963), pp. 57-62. As I understand him, he seems to argue that intra-party differences in constituency and that Democrats and Republicans tend to represent different kinds of constituencies. Therefore, differences between the parties *are* due to constituency influences. This is not necessarily true since intra-party differences may have little or nothing to do with inter-party differences, as Table 2 in this study shows. Furthermore, Froman's phi coefficients which he uses to measure the relations of constituency to intra-party differences are so weak as to suggest negative rather than positive findings.

20.   Duncan MacRae, Jr., "The Relations Between Roll Call Votes and Constituencies in the Massachusetts House of Representatives," *American Political Science Review,* Vol. 46 (December, 1952), pp. 1046-1055, reprinted in Eulau, Eldersveld, and Janowitz (eds.), *Political Behavior* (Glencoe, Ill., 1956), pp. 317-324.

21.   Thomas R. Dye, "A Comparison of Constituency Influences in the Upper and Lower Chambers of a State Legislature," *Western Political Quarterly,* Vol. 14 (June, 1961), pp. 473-481.

22.   MacRae, *op. cit.,* p. 323 in Eulau et al., *Political Behavior.* In order to understand clearly what MacRae is reporting, it should be recognized that his use of the term "typical" is somewhat unusual although convenient for lack of anything better. "Typical" may refer to central tendency, but here it means, in a sense, representative of the extreme. The finding actually summarized by reference to typical and atypical districts is that members who come from districts which have most of that characteristic which distinguishes districts represented by their party from districts represented by the opposing party are more loyal to their own party than are members who come from districts which have least of the characteristic which distinguishes districts represented by their party. Hence, use of the term "typical" in this context may be unconventional; but it is certainly convenient.

23.   Pesonen in a recent study [Pertti Pesonen, "Close and Safe State Elections in Massachusetts," *Midwest Journal of Political Science,* Vol. 7 (February, 1963), pp. 54-70] replicates MacRae's study using a more recent session of the same legislature. He uses an improved measure of party loyalty, and reaches the same conclusion as MacRae concerning the relation of constituency and party voting. However, he works with only seven roll calls; and does not measure the strength of the observed relation.

24.   Dye, *op. cit.,* pp. 476-477.

25.   *Ibid.,* p. 477.

26.   *Ibid.*, pp. 479-480.

27.   Members were also scored on 60 party agreement votes. (10 of the original 183 roll calls were dropped since one party or the other was evenly divided making it impossible to characterize the vote as a party agreement or a party opposition vote.) The scores of Democratic and Republican members on party opposition votes were each correlated with their scores on party agreement votes. The product moment coefficients were less than .1 in each case, indicating that a party opposition vote and a party agreement vote are distinctly different events in the life of the legislature.

28.   See A. M. Mood, *Introduction to the Theory of Statistics* (New York, 1950), pp. 318-326. The procedure is designed to permit comparison of variance around the overall mean with the sum of the variance around class means. It is specially useful in the present situation since it allows flexibility in the creation of classes.

29.   Fifty party opposition roll calls were selected. They are every such vote which occurred between May 15 and the July 11 recess. Members who voted on less than 35 of the 50 selected votes were dropped: 3 Republicans and 3 Democrats. Others were given scores expressing the percentage of their votes cast in support of positions taken by a majority of Democrats.

30.   MacRae, *op. cit.*, reprinted in Eulau et al., pp. 321-322.

31.   Pesonen, *op. cit.*, p. 62.

32.   Dye, *op. cit.*, p. 477.

33.   Samuel C. Patterson, "The Role of the Deviant in the State Legislative System: The Wisconsin Assembly," *The Western Political Quarterly,* Vol. 14 (June, 1961), pp. 460-472, 467.

34.   R. W. Becker et al., "Correlates of Legislative Voting: Michigan House of Representatives, 1954-1961, *"Midwest Journal of Political Science,* Vol. 6 (Nov., 1962), pp. 384-396. Actually, the number of members from districts classified by the authors as close is so small as to make the finding doubtful. What the data do show clearly, however, is that so few members of the Michigan House come from close districts that electoral insecurity could not influence the behavior of many members.

35.   Duncan MacRae, Jr. and Edith K. MacRae, "Legislators' Social Status and Their Votes," *American Journal of Sociology,* Vol. 66 (May, 1961), pp. 599-603.

36.   Margaret G. Fuller, *Leadership in the Michigan Legislature* (Master's thesis, Michigan State University: published by the author, 1957), pp. 27-28.

37.   Duncan MacRae, Jr., "Roll Call Votes and Leadership," *Public Opinion Quarterly,* Vol. 20 (Fall, 1956), pp. 543-558, at p. 552.

38.   Respondents did not differ significantly from non-respondents in terms of constitu-
      ency characteristics or in terms of party support scores; in fact, they were re-
      markably similar. Respondents were, therefore, treated as a proper sample from
      which inferences could be drawn. If there is objection, then it is only necessary to
      consider what follows as applying to about two-thirds of the members of the 1963
      Ohio House and not to the whole House.

39.   Herbert McClosky, et al., "Issue Conflict and Consensus Among Party Leaders and
      Followers," *American Political Science Review,* Vol. 53 (June, 1960), pp. 406-427.

Bifactional Rivalry as an Alternative to Two-Party Competition in Louisiana

Allan P. Sindler

As the panacea for their political ills, Southern states frequently have been counseled to develop competitive two-party systems. Presumably the very demonstration of the superiority of the bipartisan system in itself would go a long way toward achieving that desideratum. Not the least of the unhappy consequences of this uncritical approach was the accompanying tendency to lump non-two-party Southern states into the single category of "the one-party South." Fortunately, the rich diversity of Southern political processes recently has been uncovered and subjected to systematic analysis.[1] For those states of the South which lack an effective opposition party, it has been shown that Democratic politics runs the gamut from multifactional chaos to a structured and disciplined bifactionalism. Louisiana is properly classified in the latter camp, which attests to at least some beneficial by-products of charismatic demagogy. In the absence of any reasonable expectation of the imminent rejuvenation of the Republican party in Louisiana, a realistic appraisal of the state's politics must eschew exhortation and concentrate upon an empirical examination of the operation of Democratic bifactionalism.

This paper proposes to examine the extent to which Louisiana's bifactionalism has given durable structure and meaning to its state and parish (county) politics and the degree to which it approximates the workings of a two-party system. The analysis is limited, however, by the fact that no systematic investigation as yet has been undertaken which attempts to measure the extent to which the assumptions and claims made on behalf of the two-party system in the United States have been realized in the actual operation of the varieties of competitive party politics existent. It would follow that some of the general conclusions reached here on the *relative* inadequacies of Louisiana's bifactionalism are tentative and subject to re-evaluation subsequent to further analyses of the politics of two-party states.

I. THE STRUCTURE AND MEANING OF LOUISIANA'S BIFACTIONAL RIVALRY

The structure and meaning of recent factional politics in Louisiana owes much, but not all, to the commanding figure of Huey Long. At least two aspects of pre-Long politics deserve particular mention. The first is the observation that while Huey Long stamped state government with the unique brand of his genius and

Reprinted from *American Political Science Review,* Vol. 49 (1955), pp. 641-662 by permission of the author and publisher.

This paper constitutes a section from *Huey Long's Louisiana* (Baltimore: Johns Hopkins Press, 1956).

temperament, he rose to office and grasped power within the Louisiana tradition of latent class conflict. Nineteenth-century Louisiana witnessed the development of class antagonisms which, however muted by the ignorance of poorer whites, the popular acceptance of the planters' creed, and the imperative of racial unity, clearly were observable during the political crises of secession and Populism. [2] Viewed in historical perspective, Longism represented the third major attempt of the rural "have-nots" to challenge the supreme alliance of rural planters and urban business and upper-class interests.

Pre-Long politics also evidenced a considerable degree of organization as well as the development of the materials for bifactional conflict. The controlling force in state politics before the entry of the Kingfish (Huey's self-styled sobriquet) was the Democratic machine of New Orleans, more familiarly known as the "Ring," the "Choctaws," or, after a factional tiff in the early 1920's, the "Old Regulars." The prominence of Orleans in state politics was the natural product of its number of voters (about 20 per cent of Louisiana's people lived in New Orleans and usually the city's share of the total vote cast in the various statewide elections was considerably higher than that proportion) and of the size of its delegations to the General Assembly and the Democratic State Central Committee (Orleans was apportioned its fair share of seats in both of those representative bodies; the smaller urban areas of the state were discriminated against). The dominance of Orleans in state politics, however, was a consequence of the city's dependence upon and vulnerability to the actions of the governor and the state legislature. In the absence of constitutional home rule provisions, the first line of self-defense for the Choctaws lay in the election of and the maintenance of friendly relations with non-hostile state officers and legislators. However reluctantly propelled into the arena of state politics, the Ring injected elements of durable organization into the factional process and directed its efforts at both the city and the state level to the promotion of conservative interests. Businessmen were the city allies of the Ring; Delta planters and varied courthouse groupings were its state allies. Choctaw rule thus continued the pattern of upper-class control of politics. In the running battle between city and country the Ring emerged most frequently as victor, but its control of public policy helped to create the reservoir of intense dissatisfaction which Huey Long tapped in his rise to power and which ultimately brought about the humbling of the city machine itself in 1935 and again in 1950.

To Huey Long, though, must go the lion's share of the credit for the pervasiveness, durability, and substantive meaning of recent Louisiana bifactionalism. The easy characterization of Long as "just another Southern demagogue" obscures far more than it clarifies. Unlike Bilbo or Ben Tillman, Tom Watson or Talmadge, Huey Long did not indulge in "nigger-baiting," nor did he stoop to echo Tom-Tom Heflin's diatribes against the Pope. With reference to the resentments and frustrations of their class backing, all Southern demagogues performed at least — but many at most — a cathartic function. Pappy O'Daniel and Gene Talmadge posed as neo-Populist rebels only to effectuate opposite policies. Talmadge jettisoned the New Deal because it went too far; Long ostensibly because it did not go far enough. Nor did the man who dangled the lure of Share-Our-Wealth before a depression-panicked national audience change his colors, chameleon-like, when in his home state of Louisiana. The brazen political dictatorship which Huey constructed and ran should not hide his substantial accomplishment of keeping some of his promises of lower-class benefits. The Kingfish was a free-spending, heavy-taxing, direct actionist, who had little in common with the other Southern leaders with whom he is so frequently linked.

That Huey Long did more than merely bait the corporations and the urban areas, the "better elements" and the professional politicians, marked him as a legitimate heir of the suppressed dirt-farmer movements in Louisiana history. Crushed as Populists and untouched by the urban progressivism of Wilson, the rural poorer whites found themselves voiceless until the entry of Long into politics. It is a measure of Huey's undeniable genius that he was able to arouse that rural following more intensively and durably than the Populists had done.

However marred by his lust for personal power, Long did arouse the interest and participation of masses of whites, and made them aware of the relevance of state politics to the settlement of their demands.[3] Huey captured in his state the hitherto non-voting elements which the New Deal had attracted on a national scale. Such a change in the composition of the electorate by itself heralded a different content of politics than in the pre-Long days. More crucially, Longism itself set both the form and content of that later politics. The distracting appeals of localism and personality were reduced to minimal influence as the bulk of voters affiliated themselves, in a close approximation to the two-party system, with the two major factions, Long and anti-Long. Candidates for state offices and many of the candidates for Congress and for parish and local offices publicly proclaimed their loyalty to one or the other faction. Factional lines within the state legislature became firmly drawn; when combined with the customary majority support for the incumbent administration, this gave to Louisiana governors a control over legislation not equalled in most other Southern states. Huey's heavy-handed injection of realism into the content of state politics was carried forward by brother Earl (and to a far lesser extent by son Russell), so that the Long forces gained a continuity of headship normally denied to personal factions.

Longism thus was no flashing meteor of Populism, brilliant but transient. It aroused the politically quiescent have-nots and showed them unforgettably the total victory that was theirs for the balloting. It unified the fragments of politics — expectations, candidates, institutions — by means of one deeply-felt adherence, pro- or anti-Longism. It came closer to the salient issues of the day than had a raft of "good government" predecessors of Huey. The policy impact of Longism was strikingly attested to in the state office campaign of 1940, when the anti-Longs, despite the involvement of the Longites in the corruption of the "Scandals," saw fit to pledge liberal measures which, in toto, made Huey's performance eight years earlier appear conservative. After Huey was assassinated in 1935, to thousands of Louisiana voters the available political alternatives continued to be cast in the simple mold of "do-something" versus "do-nothing," "the people" versus "the interests." The persistence of the emotional loyalties and issues created by the Kingfish accounts in large part for the content and form of post-Huey politics in Louisiana.

II. BIFACTIONAL LOYALTIES
OF THE VOTERS

The sound and fury of Longite politics had sufficient substantive meaning to provide Louisiana with a well-organized politics of rational interest-voting. Huey's program and performance vitalized state politics and created a conscious, persistent bifactionalism. The voting strength of the two major factions came from distinct groups, each of which displayed a continuity of political attitudes going back to the muted class conflicts of the previous century. The basic cleavages among the voters appeared to be closely related to the antagonisms between city and rural dwellers and to those between dirt farmers and wealthier planters.

The centers of Longite and anti-Long strength may be uncovered by summarizing the results of a quartile ranking of the vote in the 64 parishes of the state in the gubernatorial primaries (where bifactionalism is sharpest and turnout greatest) from 1928 through 1952. About 50 parishes may be classified as usually pro- or anti-Long in voting behavior. The Longite sections comprised the cut-over uplands of northern and west-central Louisiana and the eastern portion of the state known as the "Florida parishes," populated by relatively few Negroes and by many poorer white farmers. In addition, sparsely settled Cameron parish in the southwestern tip of the state and the bossed parishes of Plaquemines and St. Bernard in the southeast nearly always have supported Long candidates. Several of the sugar-growing parishes in south Louisiana also have backed the Longs, although not as intensively as the upland regions. The rural class support accorded the Longs may be observed most clearly in those parishes which contained both plantation and hill-farming lands. In both the upper Mississippi and Red River deltas, pro-Longism increased as the fertility of the soil decreased. In the northeast delta parishes, the influx of white farmers from neighboring states converted East Carroll and Concordia parishes to support of Long and diluted the anti-Long performance of Madison and Tensas. The political success of Longism thus lay in its ability to capture and reinforce the allegiance of those rural groups which twice before had embarked vainly upon a politics of protest.

The core areas of persistent anti-Long sentiment encompassed the major urban parishes,[4] the plantation areas of the upper Mississippi and Red River deltas, West and East Feliciana, and most of the Sugar Bowl parishes. That even small-scale urbanism and anti-Longism went hand in hand may be shown by an examination of the voting behavior of wards containing the parish seats in 53 of the state's 64 parishes.[5] Conservative urbanites thus were the allies of planters and well-to-do farmers in common opposition to Longism, a combination of political forces which continued the pattern of nineteenth-century politics.

The general pattern of urban antipathy to Longism should not obscure the fact that two urban groups, organized labor and the Negro, have tended to be pro-Long. Labor's claims of political power, however, contained more boast than reality, while Negro voters, a new force in Louisiana politics, were loyal to the pursuit of certain group objectives rather than to the Long faction itself. The past Longite sympathies of neither group, therefore, guarantee an upsurge in Longite strength as urbanization, industrialization, and Negro voting increase.

Table 1 The persistence of anti-Longism in lesser urban areas: quartile position of support of Longism of fifty-three urban wards containing parish seats among all wards of the state, in selected primary elections, 1928-1952.

Longite Candidate and Primary Election	Quartile Position			
	Highest	2nd	3rd	Lowest
Huey Long, 1928, Gov.	1	9	27	16
Earl Long, 1940, Gov., 2nd	4	8	19	22
Earl Long, 1944, Lt. Gov., 2nd	2	7	20	24
Russell Long, 1948, Sen.	3	4	13	33
Carlos Spaht, 1952, Gov., 2nd	6	10	17	20

Source: computed from *Compilation of Primary Election Returns of the Democratic Party, State of Louisiana,* issued by the Secretary of State, for the 1928, 1940, 1944, and 1952 elections, and from unpublished election data on file at the office of the Secretary of State of Louisiana for the 1948 election.

III. PERSONAL FOLLOWINGS AND BIFACTIONALISM

Bifactional politics, to approach the organizational influence of a party system, should tend to discourage personal and localistic candidacies for governor which are unrelated to the state's political dualism. Certainly there ought not to be room in Louisiana's bipolarized factionalism to permit an alleged "personal" leader to deliver his allegedly "personal" following to the support of the gubernatorial candidate of his choice in the runoff primary. Yet experienced Louisiana politicians do compete for the backing of one or more of the lesser leaders who are eliminated in the first gubernatorial primary. And V.O. Key has concluded that " . . . some [Louisiana] leaders have a following that can, at least at times, be voted fairly solidly for another candidate."[6] The question of the existence of transferable personal followings deserves the fullest exploration because of its crucial implications for the inadequacy of the one-party bifactional system.

The runoff primary in the state campaign of 1940 affords a convenient starting point for analysis, since Key's conclusion was based upon an examination of that election. The 1940 state contest was conducted in the shadow of the Scandals, an unsavory episode in Louisiana politics which exposed many of Huey's successors as being too prone to share the people's wealth. The gubernatorial candidate of the Long organization, which was being buffeted by federal and state investigations and prosecutions, was Earl K. Long. James A. Noe, a Huey Longite on the outs with Huey's heirs since 1935, and instrumental in uncovering wholesale corruption in high places in 1939, appealed to the pro-Long elements disgusted by the Scandals. The entrant of the reform anti-Long forces was Sam H. Jones, while the fourth serious candidacy was that of James H. Morrison, a political newcomer with some localized strength in the eastern Florida parishes, who ran on an anti-Long platform. Long (226,385 votes) and Jones (154,936) made the runoff, and in the interim between primaries Noe (116,564) declared his support of and actively stumped for Jones. In the second primary Jones defeated Long, 284,437 to 265,403 votes.

The runoff primary distribution of Noe's first primary vote may be gauged

Table 2 The transferability of personal followings: the distribution of Noe's first primary vote to Long and Jones in the second primary, 1940, for selected wards.

Parish	Ward	Noe's % of First Primary Vote	Increased % of Ward Vote in Runoff over First Primary (% Vote in Runoff Minus % Vote in First Primary)	
			Earl Long	Sam Jones
Caldwell	8	59.3%	24.3%	36.4%
Catahoula	3	51.7	24.5	29.5
Jackson	5	50.5	17.2	36.0
Evangeline	5	48.0	11.0	38.1
Jefferson	6	46.2	6.3	40.7
Avoyelles	5	45.6	11.6	36.0
Winn	10	45.2	16.6	30.2
Grant	8	43.4	11.9	33.7
Webster	1	42.9	20.0	23.6
Rapides	10	40.1	8.6	34.2
West Carroll	5	39.9	12.0	30.2
Winn	8	39.4	1.6	39.4
Avoyelles	1	38.8	12.2	27.3
Bienville	7	37.7	12.5	27.5
Jackson	1	37.5	7.5	32.8
Evangeline	1	37.4	5.7	32.9
Allen	3	37.3	11.3	27.4
West Carroll	4	36.2	9.3	29.5
Beauregard	5	35.4	11.6	25.7
Avoyelles	4	34.7	10.0	25.7
West Carroll	1	34.1	8.0	27.8
Winn	9	33.9	6.8	28.4
Rapides	5	33.3	10.8	23.8
Morehouse	10	32.8	7.6	27.7
Avoyelles	7	32.3	5.1	29.0
Red River	7	30.8	11.8	21.8
Grant	3	30.7	4.4	28.4
Rapides	11	30.3	12.6	18.8
Mean		39.5%	11.2%	30.1%

Source: computed from *Compilation of Primary Election Returns of the Democratic Party, State of Louisiana,* issued by the Secretary of State, for the 1940 gubernatorial election.

by isolating those wards in which Noe received more than 30 per cent of the first primary vote and Morrison and Moseley (a fifth non-serious candidate) together received less than 3 per cent of that vote. Twenty-eight wards from 16 parishes, located largely in north Louisiana, the section of Noe's greatest support, meet the standards indicated. Nearly all the wards were strong pro-Long districts; 25 of the 28 supported Huey's bid for the United States Senate by more than 60 per cent of the ward vote back in 1930. In addition, each of the wards listed in Table 2 cast more than 200 votes in the 1940 first gubernatorial primary.

On the reasonable assumption that a minimal number of Long and Jones supporters changed their votes in the second primary, a reading of the mean figures in the foregoing table leads to the conclusion that about 73 per cent of Noe's following transferred their votes to Jones in the runoff, and the pro-Jones direction of the vote was common to each ward analyzed. Before conclusions on the existence and deliverability of personal factions may be reached, however, it must first be ascertained whether the Noe voters, most of whom were Longites in previous elections, supported Jones because of Noe's leadership or for some other reason.[7] An analysis of the runoff distribution of Morrison's first primary vote

Table 3 The transferability of personal followings: the distribution of Morrison's first primary vote to Long and Jones in the second primary, 1940, for selected wards.

Parish	Ward	Morrison's % of First Primary Vote	Increased % of Ward Vote in Runoff over First Primary (% Vote in Runoff Minus % Vote in First Primary	
			Earl Long	Sam Jones
Ascension	10	62.6%	19.4%	48.6%
St. James	8	60.2	20.8	40.8
St. James	1	60.0	14.9	49.0
Livingston	6	56.8	19.5	43.2
St. James	2	55.6	19.0	40.8
Pointe Coupee	5	50.2	1.1	53.8
Pointe Coupee	7	49.5	7.4	44.9
St. James	9	47.8	17.0	34.1
Lafourche	6	47.1	11.8	39.3
St. Charles	4	44.1	16.2	33.8
St. John	4	43.7	11.8	37.7
Terrebonne	7	43.6	9.8	37.9
St. Charles	2	43.5	13.0	36.4
Terrebonne	5	42.4	7.0	39.2
St. John	5	42.2	13.4	33.0
Mean		50.0%	13.5%	40.8%

Source: computed from *Compilation of Primary Election Returns of the Democratic Party, State of Louisiana,* issued by the Secretary of State, for the 1940 gubernatorial election.

(48, 243) throws considerable light on that problem. Table 3 includes all wards which gave Morrison more than 40 per cent and Noe and Moseley combined less than 6 per cent of the vote cast in the first primary of 1940. Of the 15 wards, located in eight parishes, all but one gave Huey Long more than 60 per cent of the ward vote cast in the senatorial campaign of 1930. In Table 3, as in the previous table, all wards chosen cast over 200 votes in the first primary.

Campaigning on an anti-Long platform, Morrison secured the support of many voters in the Florida parishes and neighboring areas who had been Longites in 1930. These presumably represented the same sort of following as Noe's. In sharp contrast to Noe, Morrison neither urged support of nor stumped for Jones, and indeed even implied a personal preference for Earl Long after the first primary. Nonetheless, as judged by the mean figures, about 75 per cent of Morrison's vote went to Jones in the runoff, a proportion roughly the same as that determined for the Noe supporters, and the Morrison vote in each of the wards studied went in the same factional direction in the runoff.

Although the analysis of the distribution of Morrison's vote does not eliminate the possibility that Noe had a transferable personal following, it does render questionable any positive conclusions on the deliverability of Noe's voters when based solely on the data on Noe. In the light of recent Louisiana politics, it seems to this writer more reasonable to conclude that Noe had no personal following to deliver. There was nothing in his brief political career as state senator and acting governor which would account for the large country parish organization of over 100, 000 votes imputed to his personal leadership. Another explanation of Noe's role in the 1940 primaries may be suggested. He was less the personal leader of a devoted following than the temporary product of transitory circumstance. His was the voice of those Longites outraged by the Long organization's betrayal of Huey and consequently hostile to Earl's candidacy. Their customary antipathy to an anti-Long candidate was muted by Jones's reiteration that his "pappy was for Huey" and by his pledge to retain and expand liberal governmental benefits. Under such conditions the majority of those who voted for Noe naturally gravitated to Jones; a better test of Noe's alleged factional headship would have occurred had he endorsed Earl Long for the runoff primary.

Another opportunity to test the proposition that some Louisiana politicians are able to control the votes of a deliverable personal following is offered by the events of the gubernatorial runoff primary of 1944, in which the reform candidate, James H. Davis, defeated Longite Lewis Morgan. Dudley LeBlanc, an opportunistic south Louisiana politico, had run unsuccessfully on an anti-Jones plank in the first primary, securing 40, 392 votes concentrated, in a "friends and neighbors" fashion, in several Cajun parishes. Before the second primary LeBlanc reversed his factional affiliation and came out for Davis. A satisfactory measurement of LeBlanc's influence may be had by noting the first and runoff primary figures for Davis and Morgan in the four parishes in which LeBlanc garnered roughly half the first primary vote. All of the first primary votes for candidates other than LeBlanc, Davis, or Morgan are credited to Morgan for the runoff, thus giving LeBlanc every chance to prove possession of a deliverable following. (For example, eight per cent of Acadia's first primary vote went to candidates other than the three indicated. That eight per cent will be subtracted from Morgan's net increase in the second primary on the arbitrary assumption that all those who voted for other candidates in the first primary subsequently voted for Morgan. This deliberate error, which credits LeBlanc for all of Davis' increased votes, has the virtue of isolating the LeBlanc vote.)

Table 4 The transferability of personal followings: the distribution of LeBlanc's first primary vote to Davis and Morgan in the second primary, 1944, for selected parishes.

Parish	LeBlanc % of First Primary Vote	Increased % of Parish Vote in Runoff over First Primary (% Vote in Runoff Minus % Vote in First Primary)	
		James Davis	Lewis Morgan
Acadia	55.7%	30.4%	25.3%
Evangeline	48.3	34.8	13.5
Lafayette	47.3	23.6	23.7
Vermilion	58.6	29.3	29.3
Mean	52.5%	29.5%	23.0%

Source: computed from *Compilation of Primary Election Returns of the Democratic Party, State of Louisiana,* issued by the Secretary of State, for the 1944 gubernatorial election.

As determined by the mean performance under the favorable statistical method here employed, Davis secured about 56 per cent of LeBlanc's votes. On a statewide basis, Davis attracted 53.6 per cent of the total vote. Although Dudley LeBlanc, reputed King of the Cajuns, performed better than Morrison had in 1940, he obviously had no deliverable following of any magnitude in 1944.

The 1948 gubernatorial campaign, in which Earl Long trounced Sam Jones, provides a third and final test of the existence of transferable personal followings. James H. Morrison and Robert Kennon were the two candidates eliminated in the first primary. Morrison, who campaigned as a Longite, urged support for the reform candidate, Jones, in the interim between primaries. The distribution of Morrison's vote in the runoff may be determined by the usual method, in this case employing all wards in which the Kennon vote was less than 5 per cent and the Morrison vote more than 30 per cent in the first primary, and in which more than 200 votes were cast. Eighteen wards from eight parishes meet those standards. It might also be noted that 13 of those wards had given Earl Long more than 50 per cent of the ward vote in his failing bid for the lieutenant governorship in the 1944 runoff primary. In spite of Morrison's open support of Jones, as judged by the mean figures in Table 5, about 82 per cent of Morrison's first primary vote went to Earl Long.[8] The Longite direction of Morrison's vote held constant for each of the wards examined.

The degree of deliverability of a personal following in recent Louisiana politics has been subjected to three tests: anti–Jones LeBlanc (1944) and Longite

Table 5 The transferability of personal followings: the distribution of Morrison's first primary vote to Long and Jones in the second primary, 1948, for selected wards.

Parish	Ward	Morrison's % of First Primary Vote	Increased % of Ward Vote in Runoff over First Primary (% Vote in Runoff Minus % Vote in First Primary)	
			Earl Long	Sam Jones
Livingston	5	82. 1%	66. 8%	16. 1%
Ascension	10	74. 0	54. 3	22. 5
Livingston	6	72. 3	61. 0	15. 3
Livingston	10	71. 4	65. 2	8. 5
Tangipahoa	6	70. 5	58. 7	15. 8
Livingston	3	70. 2	60. 8	12. 9
Livingston	4	68. 7	61. 2	11. 6
Tangipahoa	8	61. 0	54. 5	10. 0
Iberville	8	60. 7	58. 5	7. 1
Lafourche	6	58. 6	46. 1	14. 6
St. Tammany	6	58. 6	49. 6	12. 2
Livingston	8	58. 0	44. 2	18. 7
Tangipahoa	5	56. 4	51. 0	10. 1
St. John	6	54. 5	53. 6	5. 2
Iberville	5	46. 1	37. 1	13. 2
Ascension	2	31. 1	34. 7	1. 2
Ascension	1	30. 7	30. 2	3. 7
St. James	8	30. 1	30. 8	2. 8
Mean		58. 6%	51. 0%	11. 2%

Source: computed from *Compilation of Primary Election Returns of the Democratic Party, State of Louisiana,* issued by the Secretary of State, for the 1948 gubernatorial election.

Morrison (1948) could not commit their first primary supporters to anti-Longism, while defecting Longite Noe (1940) merely activated defecting Longite voters in a natural anti-Long direction. The bifactionalism bequeathed by Huey Long to the state of Louisiana is too pervading to permit the existence of many purely personal followings. While the open Democratic procedures of the first primary invite the entrance of candidates other than the leaders of the two major factions, and "native-son" voting is not uncommon in the first primary, such candidacies are offered always with reference to bifactional politics: e. g., Noe ran on an anti-Long plank, Morrison as a Longite, and LeBlanc on an anti-Jones platform. Such third candidacies are those of competing Longite and anti-Long leaders, each of whom commands some local following in support of his personal and *factional* candidacy, a candidacy which represents persistent issues and attitudes over and above the attraction of personality. Indeed the phrase "third candidacies" is quite misleading, for the purpose of the first primary is precisely to determine which of the rival factional leaders commands majority allegiance within each of the two major factions. It should not be overlooked that Louisiana's first gubernatorial Democratic primary apparently produces leaders of two opposing political groups no less regularly than do the party primaries in two-party states.

What are the comparative strengths of the competing pulls of personality and faction? In common with a two-party system, Louisiana's bifactionalism permits some play for personal loyalties, e. g., Morrison is assured of some votes on a "friends and neighbors" basis regardless of whether he supports either or neither of the dominant factions. Such a truly personal following is, however, of minimal proportions because of the greater concern with faction. Thus Morrison could not expect to attract anything like the same sources of localistic (Florida parishes) support in the same degree irrespective of whether he allied himself with or against the Longites. When Morrison is pro-Long, many pro-Long voters in the Florida parishes will go along with native-son Morrison in the first primary rather than with a rival Longite candidate from another part of the state; proportionately much fewer of the anti-Longs in the region will do so. Loyalty to the person of Morrison, far from being unconditional and blind, is conditional upon a more basic commitment to the factional system itself. Morrison's supporters, in 1940 and in 1948, consonant with their primary allegiance to faction, moved consistently in the same factional direction in the first and second primary in bland disregard of the opposite factional tack taken by their "personal leader." Noe, in 1940, by asking his supporters to vote in the second primary for the candidate most of them were going to support anyway, merely created the illusion of a following both personal and deliverable. However, LeBlanc's performance in 1944 deviated somewhat from this pattern, thereby implying that his was a more likely example of personal leadership than that of Morrison or Noe. But, in contradiction to LeBlanc's unifactional endorsement in the runoff primary, his first primary supporters split almost evenly for both factions.

The practical conclusions for state politicians are obvious: neither Noe nor Morrison had true personal followings at all, and LeBlanc had but limited influence over his Cajun supporters.[9] There would be considerably less clamor in Louisiana about the frequency and evil of second primary "sell-outs" if it were realized clearly that no leader to date had anything much to sell. The broader implication of the foregoing analyses is also clear: the fact that the runoff primary influence of the losing candidate in the first primary is overshadowed by the orientation of his followers towards the bifactional system supports Louisiana's claim to possession of something like a two-party system.

IV. THE OPERATION OF THE TICKET SYSTEM

Extensive employment by the major factions of the "ticket system," Louisiana's equivalent of party slates, together with a cohesive bifactionalism and the dominance of the governor in state politics, comprise the three distinctive traits of Louisiana's Democracy as contrasted with the rest of the one-party South. All three characteristics are interdependent, and have been interacting to create a facsimile of a smoothly operating two-party system. Louisiana governors, for example, possessed no unique formal powers, yet, unlike many other Southern governors, they usually were undisputed masters of both the bureaucracy and the legislature. The explanation lies in the Longite development of a disciplined bifactional politics and in the Longite intensification of the use of the ticket system in state and parish politics. The pervasiveness of the ticket system preserves the logical structure of bifactionalism for the voter and provides some of the cement of factional unity underlying legislative and administrative cooperation with the governor. Joint factional candidacies have been the rule in recent Louisiana state politics; every candidate is not for himself alone. At the state office level, serious contenders for the nine elective posts affiliate with one or more of several state slates, campaign together, and present their candidacies as a ticket unit to the electorate. Many of the candidates for state legislative posts and for parish offices see fit to align themselves publicly (and many more privately) with a state ticket and on occasion, state bifactionalism penetrates to the ward level of police jury contests.[10] A detailed analysis of the Louisiana ticket system, therefore, should illuminate the factional base of gubernatorial power and provide some answers to the question of how closely bifactionalism approaches the workings of a two-party system.[11]

The State Ticket System.

The practice of state office candidates campaigning jointly on public slates antedated Huey Long, and most probably originated in the early days of the Choctaws, who created the state ticket they supported and forced their opponents to adopt some sort of counter-slate. Many potential candidates for state offices sounded out the Orleans city machine before deciding whether or not to run, and the Choctaws created the equivalent of a state ticket by their endorsements of candidates for each state office. Before the Kingfish, however, ticket campaigning and ticket voting were confined largely to the Orleans area. The 1932 state primary marked the first time that a full state ticket campaigned as a unit in the country parishes, i.e., outside of New Orleans. Since 1932, all major candidates for state office have run on state tickets.

The utility of the ticket device to the parties concerned is clear. From the point of view of the gubernatorial candidate, a state ticket offers him the opportunity of broadening his appeal to all sections of the state through the skillful creation of a "balanced" slate which adequately recognizes the politically-relevant diversity within the state, e.g., the customary running mate of a north Louisiana Protestant gubernatorial candidate is a south Louisiana Catholic for lieutenant governor. From the perspective of a lesser ticket member, no matter how large he believes his personal following to be, an alliance with a major faction provides him with the statewide organization indispensable to a serious candidacy. It is not uncommon, however, for some state tickets to be "bob-tailed," i.e., not to include an affiliated candidate for every one of the nine statewide offices, and for some to include candidates for lesser state office who are also endorsed by another rival ticket. For all the participants on a ticket its core value is monetary: each candidate secures the benefit of a fully-organized campaign at cut-rate prices.

A state ticket is in reality a gubernatorial ticket, since the candidate for governor both heads and dominates it. It is an "Earl Long ticket: or a "Sam Jones ticket" that is presented to the voters. The affiliated candidates devote much of their oratory on the stump to urging support for their gubernatorial ally and for the full ticket, and often have little of substance to say on their own behalf. The latter situation is particularly true for certain of the elective posts: e. g., what can candidates for Auditor, Treasurer, and Register of the State Land Office publicly pledge by way of dramatic, winning appeal? A frequent complaint of Louisianians is that the ticket organization of candidacies at times allows the poorly qualified to secure office on the coattails of the governor, but that defect is more than counterbalanced by the heightened possibility of a rational politics through use of the ticket device.

The degree to which the state ticket system injects order into one-party politics is ultimately a function of the behavior of individual voters. In Key's informed judgment, "In Louisiana . . . the voters mark a straight ticket about as consistently as they do at a general election in a two-party state."[12] Ticket voting is, naturally, strongest in the runoff primary when the number of factional slates is reduced to two, and is considerably weaker in the more bewildering melee of the first primary.

Generally, the chances of success are slim for an "independent" candidate without a place on a major state ticket. On the other hand, affiliation with a losing ticket sometimes may be overcome, particularly by long-time incumbents of lesser state posts running for re-nomination who have personal friendships over the state, e. g., Harry Wilson as Commissioner of Agriculture, T. H. Harris as Superintendent of Education, Lucille May Grace as Register of the Land Office, L. B. Baynard as Auditor, and A. P. Tugwell as Treasurer. However, these "personal followings" provide no exception to the previous analysis of deliverable followings, for they are non-transferable and, moreover, evaporate when the veteran incumbent ambitiously seeks the highest state office. For example, Miss Grace, running for governor in 1952, polled 4, 832 votes. Continued re-election to lesser state office has not been the route to the Executive Mansion. Hence the system of state tickets dominated by gubernatorial candidates provides some basis for post-election gubernatorial control over the elective department heads.

Affiliation with a State Ticket by Local Candidates.

The issues of tremendous popular concern put forward by Longism, together with the deep penetration of state politics as practiced by the Kingfish, argued for a non-divorcement of local politics from state bifactionalism. A provision of the state primary election law encouraged state tickets and local candidates to enter some sort of working agreement to insure adequate poll-commissioner representation for each. Under that provision only candidates for local offices could submit the names of poll commissioners and watchers for the first primary; their selection for the second primary was controlled by both the gubernatorial and the local candidates participating in the runoff.[13] Affiliation with a state ticket by a local candidate satisfied the former's need for grass roots organization and enabled the latter to meet more easily the financial costs of campaigning. Such utilitarian pressures appear to be at the heart of the extension of the state ticket into parish politics.

There seems to be a sectional pattern to the practice of parish candidate alliance with a state ticket. Public affiliations are confined largely to Catholic south Louisiana, where high rates of illiteracy enhance the strategic role of poll commissioners and where politics is so highly organized that running for parish and ward offices on local tickets is traditional.[14] In north Louisiana the tie-ups between local candidates and a state faction, though not uncommon, are less frequently publicized.[15] Like the consumption of liquor, perhaps, the action is concluded behind barn doors. Factional leanings of local candidates are often known anyway, particularly in those parishes whose bifactional preferences have been quite definite. For example, in the "independent" parish of Caddo, which contains Shreveport, the majority of legislative candidates in the 1952 primaries were "known" to be anti-Long although there were no local tickets and only one local candidate publicly affiliated himself with a state ticket.[16] The situation is the same in Longite strongholds, for example, Red River parish, about which an informant related, "A majority of the local candidates are Long supporters, but with few exceptions, none have been backed by a state ticket." In most cases the factional preferences of local candidates are common knowledge, at least to the political insiders if not to the public at large, a conclusion attested to by the following replies to the writer's questionnaires with regard to the 1948 and 1952 state office primaries sent to selected parish officials.

> *East Feliciana, 1948.* "There were no public alignments of local candidates with state factions. . . . Of course, several candidates were known to have belonged to certain state factions, but they all ran for office on the public theory that they were independent of factionalism."

> *Ouachita, 1948.* "None of the candidates were publicly aligned with state tickets or other local candidates. (We do not have local tickets.) Of course there were candidates in different races who were encouraged by local leaders of state tickets to enter respective races. This was not generally known to the public."

> *Tensas, 1948.* ". . . not any of the local candidates . . . were aligned with any of the State candidates. In some instances it was generally known that several of the Parish candidates were against the administration at that time, or were for the administration at that time, but they were not aligned in any manner with respect to posters, ads, or tickets."

> *Lincoln, 1952.* "There were numerous secret alliances but for some reason the 'local ticket' practice prevailing in many Louisiana parishes has never . . . been employed in this parish."

The clearest factional guideposts to the voter obviously are provided by the non-secret alliances between state tickets and local candidates. Several examples of forthright public endorsements of state tickets by parish office seekers may be cited.

> We, the undersigned, do hereby certify that at a caucus held in the office of the Governor, Sunday, October 13, 1935, the above-named candidates for parish and district offices [in Pointe Coupee parish] did agree and pledge themselves to support all candidates on the Long-Allen state ticket, and did further agree and pledge themselves to support each other for parish and district offices. . . .[17]

In his political advertisement as candidate for coroner, East Baton Rouge parish, in the 1944 primary, Dr. F.U. Darby stated:

> My politics are not secret. I am supporting Jimmie H. Davis for Governor and am a candidate on the Parish Ticket.[18]

In his political advertisement for re-nomination as sheriff of Iberia parish in 1948, Gilbert Ozenne declared:

> I have endorsed the candidacy of Earl K. Long for Governor. My opponent lacks the political courage to acknowledge that he was supported and endorsed by the Sam Jones faction. I solicit the vote and support of all qualified voters regardless of political affiliations. [19]

Affiliation is a two-way affair, so gubernatorial tickets also spread the factional word.

In a political circular distributed by the Louisiana Democratic Association, Longite Governor Leche began:

> In order that the people of Louisiana may have correct information as to who bears the endorsement of the Louisiana Democratic Association in all second primaries, we the undersigned [the state ticket members] now make the statement that the following candidates for their respective (parish and local) offices have been endorsed. . . . [20]

Reform candidate Sam Jones urged publicly before the 1940 first primary:

> Wherever you have a Sam Jones candidate for either House or Senate be sure to vote for him. If it should happen that none of the candidates have endorsed me, vote for an anti-administration independent candidate. . . . [21]

Since the objective of the ticket system is to aid the candidacies of each of its co-participants, public endorsements between state tickets and local candidates tend to be delayed until after the first primary. Neither state nor parish politicians care to restrict their appeal to the following of one of many candidates or to gamble on who will make the runoff primary. These considerations are controlling in the case of wide-open parish and gubernatorial contests with a multiplicity of rivals. Conversely, pre-first primary alignments are common when one of the gubernatorial candidates seems likely to sweep the parish or when local incumbents are unopposed for re-nomination. Nevertheless, if as a general rule the state ticket affiliations of local candidates are not revealed until the interim between primaries, the commitments and arrangements between the two parties very often have been discussed, if not decided upon, before the first primary. [22]

Many informants suggested to the writer another uniformity in the variety of parish candidate links with state politics, namely, that the "in" parish administration tended to align with the "in" state administration, while challengers of the parish incumbents tended to affiliate with major anti-administration state tickets. The proposition appears logical in that the state administration over the course of four years establishes working relationships with the courthouse cliques and maintains some disciplinary powers over local officialdom for the three months following the gubernatorial primaries, such as the enforcement of state anti-gambling laws, the supervision of tax assessments, and the like. On the basis of evidence gathered by the writer, however, this political rule of thumb appears to be in error. Since the sheriff is usually the leader of the parish organization, under the suggested rule the majority of sheriffs who affiliated with a state ticket in their races for re-nomination would have supported Jones in 1948 (the incumbent governor, Davis, was of the reform faction) and Spaht, the Longite candidate, in 1952 (Earl Long was governor from 1948-1952). A computation of the data contained in replies to the writer's questionnaires contradicts that suggested pattern (see Table 6). In the light of the utilitarian motivations for ticket alignments, the following

Table 6 The pattern of affiliation with state tickets by sheriffs running for re-nomination, 1948 and 1952 gubernatorial first and second primaries.

	1948 Primary	1952 Primary
No. of parishes in which sheriff ran for re-nomination	55	52
No. of sheriffs neutral in state contest	20	33
No. of sheriffs aligned anti-Long	6	5
No. of sheriffs aligned pro-Long	29	14

interpretation seems most appropriate. Most sheriffs who affiliate publicly with state factions tend to align with the Longites. This may well be a passing phenomenon, since many of the sheriffs are veteran incumbents who have ties with the stable Longite leaders going back to the 1930's, and the Longs have been known for their skillful politicking in the country parishes. The general tendency noted is subject, however, to at least two major qualifications. Parish organizations are loath to endorse state tickets unpopular in the parish or unlikely to win statewide in the runoff primary. In the 1952 primaries, the sheriffs were subjected to conflicting pressures for alignment with the result that many refused to affiliate openly with either state faction. While the sheriffs' actions suggest some of the inadequacies of the ticket system which next deserve comment, it might be noted that local candidates in a two-party state also have been known to remain discreetly silent when faced with a national or state party ticket unpopular in their district.

Limitations of the Ticket System.

The penetration of local politics by the state ticket system does not carry with it an extension of the great issues of state politics: the contests for parish office are dominated by local matters. Most local candidates, even those publicly aligned with a state faction, restrict their campaigning to local issues. Of 55 contests for sheriff in 1952 on which adequate information was compiled by the writer, 48 were characterized as revolving largely around items of local concern. As a result, straight-ticket voting from governor on down through parish clerk of court occurs only in the very highly organized or bossed parishes, and it is not unusual for voters to support at the same time a parish ticket and the state ticket it opposed. One south Louisiana sheriff informed the writer:

The [parish] ticket supported Spaht [the Long candidate] in both primaries [1952] and carried Spaht in both primaries. However, a number of staunch supporters of the parish ticket just 'couldn't see' Spaht and voted Kennon [the reform candidate]. This had no effect on the local issue. Local voters are either for or against [us] politically, but when it comes to state tickets, they vote how they please, with no effect on the local issues. . . . Voters are entirely free to choose their state candidates. . . .

In another south Louisiana parish, "La Vieille Faction" has controlled public office for more than 25 years and uniformly has supported Longite candidates at state primaries, yet the parish did not place among those high in support of Longism from 1928-1952. [23] As a final point, while state legislative candidates campaign more in the mold of state bifactionalism, the difference is not one of kind. Of the

55 House races in 1952 on which adequate data were obtained, 33 were confined to local issues, with state ticket alignment adjudged as having little to no influence on the outcome. Campaign tie-ups between the governor and legislators, then, account only in part for the later cooperation of a large majority of the Assembly with the governor.

V. AN APPRAISAL OF LOUISIANA'S BIFACTIONALISM

Bifactionalism and the ticket system have served, with considerable effectiveness, as Louisiana's substitutes for a two-party system. Unlike several sister Southern states, Louisiana's politics has not been characterized by a chaotic multifactionalism, by a bewildering succession of transitory state factions without continuity in program, leadership, or voter loyalty. Localism and a "friends and neighbors" influence have been reduced to minimal proportions within a polarized politics of pro- and anti-Longism. The voter is offered a meaningful choice between factions embracing alternative leaders and programs, while the victorious faction normally is assured of a working control of the administrative and legislative branches by which to effectuate its pledges made to the voters. Huey Long thus gave Louisiana a structured and organized politics, a politics that made sense.

Although vastly superior to one-party confusion, Louisiana's bifactionalism is considerably inferior to two-party politics, or at least to the claims put forward on behalf of the two-party system in the United States. A summary review of some of the major divergences will document that conclusion.

Louisiana's ticket system together with its bifactionalism has been adjudged by Key to " . . . more closely approach the reality of a party system than do the factions of any other southern state. "[24] It is useful to an understanding of the differences between the systems to point out that bifactionalism approached the organizational thoroughness of a two-party system only in the despotic days of the Kingdom of the Kingfish. The Louisiana ticket system as analyzed is neither cohesive nor penetrating enough to provide the basis for a permanent state factional machine on a par with stable party control — resort must be had to a control of parish governments and of election machinery and to highhanded attempts to extend factional dominance for longer than a single term of office, as indulged in by the brothers Long. The state ticket device permits no governor-oriented machine at the state level because of the hard fact that the governor, alone of the elective state officers, is not eligible for immediate re-election. On the parish level, selfish political considerations, not the friendly links between local officials and Longite leaders, determine the choice of ticket alignments. The fact that a parish organization supported Earl Long in 1940 will have some but not decisive weight in its decision whether or not to support him in 1944 or 1948. In times of stress, as in the case of Longite Spaht, who was soundly beaten in the gubernatorial contest of 1952, the hollowness of what passes for a durable Longite machine stands revealed. Courthouse groupings, therefore, provide no certain permanent local organization for any state faction, much less a solid political base comparable to the ward and precinct organization of parties. Every four years there is a wild scramble *de novo* by state tickets for parish candidate and local ticket support. The popularized notion

of an Earl Long machine, therefore, does not square with the rationale and operation of the ticket system in Louisiana politics. These judgments have even greater
validity for the anti-Long faction, which suffers from inability to maintain a grass
roots organization in the period between quadrennial elections. Louisiana's experience raises the question of whether bifactionalism, in the absence of a functioning
rival party, can ever hope to attain a quasi-party system without degenerating into
factional dictatorship.

Apart from Huey's regime, the measure of the difference between bifactional and party schemes is the increasing fuzziness of the former as it extends beyond
the arena of state office politics, as in the limitations of the ticket system already
examined. No matter how lightly party attachments may be viewed, the labels in a
party system give identification and some meaning to candidacies and thereby provide clarification for the voter. By contrast, Louisiana senators and congressmen
often develop their own followings and are judged by the voters by standards independent of bifactionalism. For this reason senators often may "interfere" in state
elections even to the point of changing, as Overton and Russell Long have done,
their factional affiliation without much fear of electoral retaliation several years
later. The late Senator Overton and Senator Ellender both traced their political
lineage to close personal support of Huey Long, and yet, except for their original
primary election, neither had serious difficulty in being returned to office. The
political fortunes of Russell Long, Huey's son and Earl's nephew, illustrate the
point. When running for his first political office to fill the unexpired term of the
late Senator Overton in 1948, Russell campaigned entirely in the context of bifactionalism since he was exclusively identified with Longism. Russell barely won
office then, and the pattern of his electoral support and opposition was clearly in
the bifactional tradition of state office politics. By 1950 Russell had broader appeal
by virtue of his record in the Senate, and his bid for a full Senate term was rewarded by the support of 68.5 per cent of the votes cast and of all but one of the
state's 64 parishes. In similar fashion bifactional linkage to presidential politics
customarily has been weak, although the electoral pattern in the 1952 presidential
election bore more than a casual relationship to state bifactionalism.[25]

Notwithstanding the durability of Louisiana's two major factions, neither has
established a stable and satisfactory process of recruitment of its leaders without
reference to party primary battles. Years ago the Choctaws informally performed
that function; the Long faction in 1932 and 1936, and the anti-Longs in 1940, also
chose their standard-bearers before the first primary. But for the most part the
fairly constant Longite and anti-Long groups are wooed by competing would-be
leaders, as in 1944, 1948, and 1952. The determination of factional leadership by
open competition in the primaries presents many serious problems, not the least
of which is the frequent inability of natural allies to consolidate their forces in the
brief five or six weeks following a first primary campaign in which they were rail-
ing bitterly at each other. Bandwagon pressure, by discouraging open affiliation
between state and parish allies, also handicaps the effectiveness of the primary as
the selector of factional leaders. For example, anti-Long parish candidates were
reluctant to tie up with Jones in 1948, and many parish Longites similarly spurned
alliance with Spaht in 1952. In the absence of the regularized path to leadership usually supplied by a party system, it has become almost traditional for
Louisiana's governors and lieutenant governors to have a falling out during
their term of office.

A final grave inadequacy of Louisiana's bifactionalism is that it produces less constancy on the part of factional chieftains than of the voters. Factional defection is not limited to politicians in control of their local bailiwicks, such as Leander Perez, veteran Longite boss of Plaquemines parish, who deserted the Longs in 1948 because of their coolness to the States' Rights movement. Major political figures like Noe, James Morrison, Overton, and LeBlanc have been on all sides of the factional fence. The cross-factional support accorded the gubernatorial candidacy of Hale Boggs in the 1952 primary rarely would be duplicated in a two-party setting: reform leaders ex-Governor Jones and Mayor Morrison of New Orleans, former Longites, though not (then or now) anti-Longs, Senator Russell Long and ex-Senator William Feazel, and sometime Longite Congressman James Morrison. Here again the very lack of party labels, i.e., of identification with and responsibility to a going political organization, makes loyalty to faction less rigid and demanding than loyalty to party.[26]

A concluding word about the future of Louisiana politics may not be inappropriate. If Huey Long's class revolution of 1928 has run its course and therefore, as Boggs and Russell Long opined in 1952, "the time has come to forgive and forget old factional bitterness," then the basic task of Louisiana voters, that of identifying the Democratic rascals who should be unseated, will become increasingly difficult in the future. However defective, Louisiana's bifactionalism has injected clarity and order into the confusion of one-party politics. The gradual disappearance of that structuring influence should be looked upon with something less than optimism. For while it is certainly true that the stubborn factional cleavage within the state's Democracy could supply two different parties with their distinct core of policies and supporters, it does not follow necessarily that bifactionalism must or will develop into a two-party system.

NOTES

1. V. O. Key, Jr., *Southern Politics in State and Nation* (New York, 1949), has been of considerable methodological and substantive value to the writer in this study. Although the analysis here in part disagrees with some of Key's findings on Louisiana (and corroborates some of his findings also), this paper aims generally at extending the analysis of Louisiana bifactionalism deeper and further than Key's broader concern with many Southern states permitted him to do.

2. See R. W. Shugg, *Origins of Class Struggle in Louisiana,* 1840-1875 (Baton Rouge, 1939), for an able interpretation and documentation of this theme.

3. For statistical verification of this fact consult Key, *Southern Politics,* pp. 523-24.

4. Key, p. 178, cites Calcasieu parish, containing Lake Charles, as an apparent exception to the urban pattern of anti-Longism. An examination of the ward data, however, eliminates the exception. Ward 3 of Calcasieu, in which Lake Charles is located, fell in the third quartile (quarter) of support for Huey Long in 1928 and for Longite candidate Spaht in 1952, and in the fourth (lowest) quartile of support for Earl Long in the 1940 and 1944 runoff primaries and for Russell Long in the 1948 senatorial primary.

5. The major urban parishes of Orleans, East Baton Rouge, Caddo, and Jefferson and the bossed parishes of Plaquemines and St. Bernard have been omitted. In addition, the seats of the following parishes were not incorporated areas and therefore were omitted: St. Charles, St. James, St. John, Cameron, and Livingston.

6. Key, p. 173.

7. Using parish voting data and a somewhat different statistical technique, Key, pp. 174-75, also concluded that Jones secured the bulk of Noe's first primary vote. Key's mistaken inference from that finding came from failing to probe further in the manner undertaken in the text above.

8. Key, p. 174, footnote 34, noted James H. Morrison's inability to deliver his following, but implied that the exception of Morrison helped prove the general rule of transferable followings by resorting to the following speculation:" . . . Morrison's 1948 vote consisted in considerable measure, not of his own following, but of support from the New Orleans 'Old Regular organization, which further analysis would probably show was able in the second primary to deliver its vote against Jones, the ally of deLesseps Morrison, mayor of New Orleans and foe of the 'Old Regulars'." While the Orleans vote for Morrison behaved in the second primary as Key predicted, the fact remains that two-thirds of Morrison's vote (68,502 of 101,754 votes) came from parishes other than Orleans. It should be noted that Table 5 consists entirely of non-Orleans wards, the voting behavior of which provided the finding that Morrison's first primary vote was distributed four-to-one for Earl Long in the runoff. Because of the dominant influence of the Old Regulars in city politics, no wards from New Orleans have been included in any of the tables in this paper.

9. It would be relevant to note that reputed "personal leadership" virtually vanishes when the leader himself is not a candidate: e.g., in the 1952 first gubernatorial primary, while non-candidate James Morrison stumped for reform candidate Hale Boggs, the Florida parishes went overwhelmingly for reform candidate Robert Kennon.

10. A police jury is the governing body of a Louisiana parish (county).

11. The analysis is based, for the most part, on an extensive questionnaire, interview, and research project on the ticket aspects of the 1948 and 1952 gubernatorial primaries undertaken by the writer.

12. Key, p. 170.

13. *Revised Statutes of Louisiana,* 1950, Title 18, Chapter 2, Sections 340, 357, 358. Poll commissioners were particularly useful to candidates because they were entitled to assist illiterate voters (now forbidden by Act 309 of 1952) and physically disabled voters in the polling booth. The system forced gubernatorial candidates, in order to secure fair representation of election-day personnel in the first primary, to make overtures to local candidates who controlled the selection of such personnel. The significance of this power may be gauged by the following form letter issued under the name of Earl Long and dated January . . . , 1940: "Dear Mr. . . . . . : I am glad to note that you were drawn as an Election Commissioner, I am sure that

you realize the heavy responsibility that rests on your shoulders. Anything that you can do to see that I get a square deal in this election will be appreciated and remembered. If I can render you any assistance, do not hesitate to call on me." —Wisdom Collection of Long Materials, Howard Tilton Memorial Library, Tulane University, New Orleans.

14. Most, though not all, of the parishes in which legislative candidates aligned with a state ticket in 1952 had a firm tradition of local tickets. The sheriff usually heads a local ticket, and its rationale again lies in the practical benefits accruing to each of the participants.

15. The author's data indicate some exceptions: Union, Catahoula, Rapides, St. Helena, and Livingston parishes had both public and local tickets open local candidate alignment in either or both 1948 and 1952.

16. An informant related that in the 1952 runoff primary Kennon headquarters in Shreveport would suggest to the inquiring voter support of designated candidates for the state legislature none of whom had affiliated publicly with the Kennon ticket.

17. *Pointe Coupee Banner,* Nov. 21, 1935.

18. *Morning Advocate* (Baton Rouge), Jan. 16, 1944.

19. *Daily Iberian* (New Iberia), Feb. 23, 1948.

20. Political circular in Conway Scrapbook of Huey Long Materials, Vol. 7, p. 95, Louisiana State Library, Baton Rouge.

21. *State-Times* (Baton Rouge), Jan. 12, 1940.

22. For example, according to information received by the author in Rapides parish in the 1952 primary, Boggs, Kennon, and McLemore (all anti-Long gubernatorial candidates) jointly and secretly backed three candidates for the House. Two of them made the runoff, and then were endorsed openly by Kennon.

23. So strong was La Vieille Faction's grip upon the parish that the quadrennial appearance of a rival slate was held to be motivated by the desire to control parish patronage in the event the anti-Longs should capture the governorship. If true, here would be a Democratic factional analogy to the role of the Louisiana Republican party prior to 1952.

24. Key, p. 169. Key is correct in pointing out that Louisiana's bifactionalism fails to approximate, in absolute terms, a bipartisan scheme.

25. For a full analysis, see Rudolf Heberle and Perry H. Howard, "An Ecological Analysis of Political Tendencies in Louisiana: The Presidential Elections of 1952," *Social Forces,* Vol. 32, pp. 344-50 (May, 1954).

26. One finding from the data collected by the author bears directly on this point. In spite of the high degree of non-performance and even double-dealing engaged in by

many of the parish candidates who affiliate with a state ticket, in only one case was an affiliate termed a factional deserter. In the situation referred to, a legislative candidate from a south Louisiana parish supported Longite Spaht in the first primary in 1952, made the runoff primary, and then "flopped" (as my informant put it) to support Kennon against Spaht in the gubernatorial runoff. Both the legislative candidate and Kennon failed to carry the parish.

The Independent Effect of Party Competition on Policy Outcomes in the American System

Thomas R. Dye

While the structure and functioning of political systems has always been a central concern of political science, the content of public policy is also a dependent variable which political science must endeavor to explain. Policy outcomes express the value commitments of a political system and these commitments are important political data. The task of political science is to identify independent variables which explain differences in policy outcomes, and to ferret out intervening variables which appear related to policy outcomes but which have no effect on them.

The purpose of this paper is to explore the relationships between certain socio-economic inputs, political system variables, and policy outcomes in American state politics. These relationships are often portrayed in a fashion similar to the diagram in Figure 1; in the literature on state politics one finds these relationships sometimes made explicit but often only vaguely implied.[1] This diagram

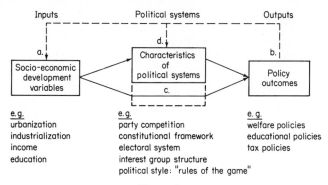

Figure 1.

assumes that the socio-economic character of a state, that is, any condition defined as external to the boundaries of its political system, determine the nature of its political system. The political system is that group of inter-related structures and processes which function to authoritatively allocate values within a state. Policy outcomes are viewed as the value commitments of the political system and as such they are the chief output of that system.

Linkages a and b suggest that socio-economic variables are inputs which shape the political system, and that the character of the political system in turn determines policy outcomes. These linkages represent the most common notions

Reprinted from a paper presented to the 1965 Annual Meeting of the American Political Science Association, Washington, D. C., Sept. 8-11, by permission of the author.

about the relationship between socio-economic inputs, political system variables, and policy outcomes. They suggest that system variables have an important effect on policy outcomes by mediating between socio-economic conditions and these outcomes. Linkage c, on the other hand, suggests that socio-economic variables affect public policy directly, without being mediated by system variables. Of course public policy is still formulated through the political system, but linkage c suggests that the character of that system does not independently influence policy outcomes. Hence the linkage between socio-economic inputs and policy outcomes is unbroken. Feedback linkage d suggests that policy outcomes have some reciprocal impact on socio-economic conditions and system characteristics.

Within this conceptual framework, the central question presented is whether or not differences in policy outcomes are independently related to system characteristics. Do system characteristics mediate between socio-economic inputs and policy outcomes (as suggested by linkages a and b), or are policy outcomes determined by socio-economic variables without regard to system characteristics (as suggested by linkage c)? To state the problem in another fashion: Assuming that socio-economic variables influence both system characteristics and policy outcomes, can system characteristics be shown to influence policy outcomes once the effects of socio-economic variables are controlled?

MEASURING ECONOMIC DEVELOPMENT, PARTY COMPETITION AND POLICY OUTCOMES

Let us now turn to the problem of making this conceptual framework operational. Among the fifty American states many of the most important system characteristics are constants. All states operate under written constitutions which divide authority between executive, legislative and judicial branches. The structure and operations of these branches are quite similar from state to state. All states function within the common framework of the American federal system. The basic institutional and legal frameworks of the fifty states may be treated as constants. However, the party systems within the fifty states have varied markedly. A number of scholars have described and classified differences in state party systems: Ranney and Kendall, Schlesinger, Key, and Golembiewski, for example.[2] The basis for these classifications is the level of competitiveness between the Democratic and Republican parties within each state, although these scholars employ different measures of party competition. In short, the American states provide an excellent laboratory to observe the impact of variations in party competition, while many other important system characteristics are held constant.

Because we are concerned here with state policy outcomes, our party competition measures center around competition for control of those institutions whose function it is to make public policy for the state — the governorship and the upper and lower chambers of the state legislature. The time span selected for measuring party competition was the decade preceding the years selected for measuring policy outcomes. Party competition is measured here by 1 minus the percentage of seats in each house held by the majority party from 1954 to 1964, and 1 minus the average margin of victory in gubernatorial elections posted by the winning candidate. Legislative competition scores range from 49 (1-51%) in the Pennsylvania and Illinois lower houses (most competitive), to 0 (1-100%) in the House and Senate of Arkansas, Alabama, Louisiana, Mississippi and South Carolina (least competitive). Gubernatorial competition scores range from 48 (1-52%) in Illinois, Iowa, Delaware, Wyoming, Massachusetts, Montana, New York, Michigan, New Jersey, Minnesota and Washington (most competitive) to under 10 (1-90%) in Louisiana, Georgia, Mississippi and South Carolina (least competitive).[3]

In comparing the fifty states, many important social and cultural conditions are also relatively constant. However, students of politics from Aristotle to Lipset have recognized that a society's economic development helps to shape its political life, and economic development is not at a constant level throughout the American states. Economic development is defined here to include urbanization, industrialization, income, and education. These four components of economic development are closely related. Industrial societies require and support concentrations of people in contrast to agricultural societies, which are more extensive users of land. An industrial economy increases worker productivity and produces a surplus of wealth. And a highly developed economy requires educated rather than uneducated workers. Students of comparative government have studied the effects of economic development on the political life of different nations.[4] But even in a highly developed society there can be marked differences in the degree of economic development from one area to another, and these differences can be related to politics in the several states. For example, in 1960 the median family income in Connecticut was two and one half times what it was in Mississippi. Over 85 percent of New Jersey residents live in urban areas, while 65 percent of North Dakota residents lived in rural areas. Only one percent of the labor force in Massachusetts was engaged in agriculture, but 33 percent of the labor force in North Dakota was in agriculture. Kentucky adults averaged only an eighth grade education while adults in seven states averaged more than 12 years of schooling. This paper will endeavor to show the relationships between these measures of economic development, party competition, and policy outcomes in the fifty states.

Policy outcomes have been operationally defined in this study to include 28 selected measures of state policy in the areas of education, welfare, and taxation. Education is the largest functional category of state spending. Ten variables reflecting important attributes of state educational systems were selected for analysis:

Public School Expenditures per Pupil in Average Daily Attendance 1960-61

Public School Expenditures per Capita 1960-61

Average Annual Salary per Member of Instructional Staff 1961-62

Percent of Secondary School Teachers with M.A. Degree 1962

Male School Teachers as a Percent of Total 1961-62

Pupil-Teacher Ratio: Enrollment per Member of Instructional Staff 1961-62

Average Size of School Districts in Pupils 1961-62

State Participation: School Revenues from State as Percent of Total School Revenue 1961-62

Federal Participation: School Revenues from Federal Sources as Percent of Total School Revenues 1961-62

Per Capita State Expenditures for Higher Education 1961

Ten welfare variables were selected for analysis:

Per Capita State and Local Expenditures for Welfare 1961

Per Capita State and Local Expenditures for Health and Hospitals 1961

Average Weekly Payment per Recipient Unemployment Compensation 1961

Average Monthly Payment Old Age Assistance 1961

Average Monthly Payment Aid to Dependent Children 1961

Average Monthly Payment Aid to Blind 1961

Average Monthly Assistance Medical Care for Aged (Kerr-Mills) 1961

Average Monthly Payment General Assistance 1961

State Participation: Percent State Expenditures of Total Expenditures for Welfare 1961

Federal Participation: Per Capita Federal Grants to the States for Health, Welfare and Related Purposes 1961

Eight measures of tax burden and revenue structure in the states were also selected:

Total State and Local Revenues per Capita 1961

State and Local Tax Revenues per Capita 1961

State Revenues as a Percent of Total State and Local Revenues 1961

Percent of Total State and Local Revenues from Federal Sources 1961

Income Tax Revenues as a Percent of State Tax Revenues 1961

Sales Tax Revenues as a Percent of State Tax Revenues 1961

Alcohol and Tobacco Tax Revenues as a Percent of State Tax Revenues 1961

Motor Fuel and Vehicle Tax Revenues as a Percent of State Tax Revenues 1961

ECONOMIC DEVELOPMENT, PARTY COMPETITION, AND POLICY OUTCOMES IN THE LITERATURE

The relationship between economic development and state party systems (linkage a in Figure 1) has already been established in the literature on American state politics. Golembiewski, in a study of the relationships between a variety of "sociological factors" and state party systems, reported statistically significant associations between urbanism, income, and industrialization, and classifications of party competition among the fifty states.[5] Ranney and Kendall, Key, and Schlesinger have also implied that one or more economic development measures correlate closely with party competition in the American states.[6] This linkage was re-confirmed in the figures gathered for the present study. Table 1 shows that three

Table 1 The relationship between economical development and party competition in the American states.

Indices of Party Competition	Indices of Economic Development			
	Urbanization	Industrialization	Income	Education
Lower Houses	.39*	.21	.71*	.66*
Upper Houses	.45*	.27	.71*	.57*
Governorships	.30*	.21	.67*	.62*

Note: Figures are simple correlation coefficients for the 48 states; an asterisk indicates a statistically significant relationship.

measures of economic development were significantly related to measures of party competition in upper and lower houses of legislatures and the governorship in 48 states. Analysis of variance tests showed all of these relationships to be statistically significant.

On the other hand, the linkage between system characteristics and policy outcomes in American state politics (linkage b in Figure 1) is *not* so well established. In the most thorough study of this linkage to date, Dawson and Robinson cite only the work of V. O. Key, Jr., and Duane Lockard as relevant research in state politics on the impact of system characteristics on policy outcomes.[7] In his *Southern Politics* Key finds that states with loose multi-factional systems with less continuity of competition tend to pursue conservative policies on behalf of upper socio-economic interests.[8] In states with cohesive and continuous factions more liberal policies are pursued on behalf of less affluent interests. Duane Lockard observed among the six New England states that the two-party states (Massachusetts, Rhode Island, and Connecticut), in contrast to the one-party states (Maine, New Hampshire and Vermont), received a larger portion of their revenue from business and death taxes, spent more on welfare services such as aid to the blind, aged, dependent children, and were better apportioned.[9] Neither of these studies, however, attempted to systematically hold constant for the impact of economic development while observing these different policy outcomes. It was Dawson and Robinson who first attempted to sort out the influences of party competition on policy outcomes from the influence of economic development. The focus·of the Dawson and Robinson study was upon welfare policy outcomes, which were defined to include percent of state revenue from death and gift taxes, per capita state revenue, per pupil expenditures, and average assistance payments to the blind, aged, and dependent children, and average unemployment compensation payments. Rank order correlation coefficients among the 46 states showed that both party competition and income, urbanization and industrialization were related to these policy outcomes. When party competition was held constant, wealth continued to correlate closely with policy outcomes. However, when wealth was held constant, party competition did *not* appear to be related to policy outcomes. The authors concluded that "interparty competition does not play as influential a role in determining the nature and scope of welfare policies as earlier studies suggested. The level of public social welfare programs in the American states seems to be more a function of socioeconomic factors, especially per capita income."[10] In short, party competition was found to have little *independent* effect on welfare policies; whatever correlations existed between welfare policies and competition was merely a product of the relationships between economic development and competition, and economic development and welfare policy.

MEASURING THE INDEPENDENT EFFECT ON PARTY COMPETI-TION ON POLICY OUTCOMES

The method chosen in this study to assess the independent effect of party competition on state education, welfare, and tax policies was that of simple and partial regression analysis. First, simple correlation coefficients (product moment) were computed for all possible relationships among the four indices of economic development, the three measures of party competition, and the 28 measures of education, welfare, and tax policies. These simple coefficients show the extent to which differences in economic development and party competition are associated with differences in party outcomes, but they do not establish whether it is economic development or party competition which is primarily responsible for differences in policy outcomes. For example, if it is shown that, in general, wealthy states have more party competition than poor states, it may be that differences in the policies of competitive and non-competitive states are really a product of the fact that the former are wealthy and the latter are poor. If this were the case, policy differences between the states might be attributable to wealth rather than to party competition. In order to isolate the effect of party competition on policy outcomes from the effect of economic development variables, it is necessary to control for these variables. This required that partial correlation coefficients be computed which show the relationship between party competition and the several measures of state policy while controlling for the effect of urbanization, industrialization, income, and education. If relationships between party competition and policy outcomes which appear in simple correlation coefficients *disappear* when these socio-economic variables are controlled, then we may conclude that there is no *independent relationship* between party competition and policy outcomes. On the other hand, if partial correlation coefficients between party competition and policy outcomes remain significant, even after the effects of socio-economic variables are controlled, then we may conclude that party competition does have an effect on public policy.

As a check on our findings, partial correlation coefficients can be computed for the relationships between economic development variables and policy outcomes while controlling for the effect of party competition. If party competition independently influences policy outcomes, the coefficients between economic development and policy outcomes should be lowered when the effect of party competition is controlled. If controlling for party competition does not lower these coefficients then we can conclude that competition has no independent effect on policy outcomes.

In interpreting correlation coefficients in this study, it was decided to dismiss as insignificant those coefficients which might easily have occurred by chance. An analysis of variance test for the significance of r is employed to identify those coefficients which can be obtained more than 5 out of 100 times in the correlation of sets of random numbers.[11]   All calculations are made on the basis of observations of 48 states; Nebraska and Minnesota were dropped because of their non-partisan character. Given a constant number of correlations, it is possible to state that only simple coefficients above .30 and partial coefficients above .35 are significant at the .05 level, and that all other coefficients can be dismissed as likely to be a product of chance.

PARTY COMPETITION AND POLICY OUTCOMES: THE RESULTS OF REGRESSION ANALYSIS

Table 2 shows the relationship between party competition and 28 separate measures of education, welfare, and tax policies in 48 states. Simple correlation coefficients are shown in the columns at the left under each measure of party competition, while partial correlation coefficients (fourth-order) — which control for the combined effect of urbanization, industrialization, income, and education — are at the right under each competition measure.

Table 2   The relationship between party competition and selected policy outcomes among the states, controlling for the effect of economic development.

	Party Competition					
	Lower Houses		Upper Houses		Governorships	
	Simple	Partial	Simple	Partial	Simple	Partial
Education						
Per Pupil Expenditures	.64*	.08	.61*	.00	.59*	.03
Per Cap. Expenditures Schools	.52*	.07	.44*	.10	.46*	.14
Average Teachers Salaries	.52*	.11	.35*	.18	.50*	.12
Teachers with M. A.	.45*	.16	.41*	.22	.39*	.05
Male Teachers	.65*	.14	.56*	.03	.58*	.22
Pupil-Teacher Ratio	-.57*	-.21	-.50*	-.15	-.64*	-.34
Size of School District	-.52*	-.34	-.34*	-.18	-.42*	-.29
State Participation	-.50*	-.31	-.39*	-.21	-.47*	-.35
Federal Participation	-.24*	-.28	-.26	-.34	-.13	-.24
Per Cap. Higher Education	.28	.22	.28	.15	.24	.11
Welfare						
Per Capita Welfare	.12	-.13	-.12	-.11	-.19	-.09
Per Capita Health	.10	.08	.20	.02	.21	.06
Unemployment Benefits	.72*	.05	.72*	.04	.52*	.11
Old Age Benefits	.64*	.01	.61*	.02	.55*	.02
ADC Benefits	.77*	.04	.71*	.03	.69*	.07
Blind Benefits	.61*	.11	.58*	.11	.53*	.02
Kerr-Mills Benefits	.15	.01	.19	.00	.05	.02
General Assistance	.70*	.16	.61*	.09	.52*	.05
State Participation	-.34*	-.20	-.26	-.12	-.36*	-.17
Federal Participation	-.43*	-.19	-.44*	-.17	-.42*	-.16
Taxation						
Total Revenue Per Capita	.50*	.19	.50*	.13	.47*	.16
Tax Revenue Per Capita	.65*	.03	.66*	.02	.59*	.07
State Percent Total Revenue	-.57*	-.40*	-.49*	-.30	-.43*	-.28
Federal Percent Total Revenue	-.29	-.21	-.31	-.14	-.26	-.24
Income Taxes	.15	.05	.12	.03	-.18	.01
Sales Taxes	-.05	-.13	-.05	-.15	-.13	.00
Alcohol and Tobacco Taxes	-.26	-.04	-.20	-.02	-.16	-.02
Motor Fuel Taxes	.05	.06	.09	.03	.09	.10

Figures are simple and partial correlation coefficients for 48 states; partial coefficients control for the effect of urbanization, industrialization, income and education; an asterisk indicates a statistically significant relationship.

In the simple coefficients, which do *not* control for the effects of economic development variables, party competition appears closely related to a number of important policy outcomes. States with a high degree of party competition tend to spend more money per pupil and per capita for public schools, per higher teachers salaries, attract better educated teachers and more male teachers, enjoy lower pupil-teacher ratios, have larger school districts, and raise more school revenue from local than from state or federal sources. These same states tend to pay more liberal benefits and tend to rely more on local welfare monies than on state or federal sources. States with competitive parties also tend to raise more total revenue per capita and more tax revenues, and they also tend to rely more on local than on state sources of revenues. In all, 18 of the 28 policy measures were significantly associated with party competition. Party competition was found to be unrelated to 10 policy measures, including expenditures for higher education, per capita health and welfare expenditures, Kerr-Mills benefits payments, and the relative reliance placed upon income, sales, alcohol and tobacco, and motor vehicle taxes as state revenue sources.

Economic development was already shown in Table 1 to be related to party competition, and a glance ahead to Table 3 will indicate that economic development is also related to those policy measures shown in Table 2 to be related to party competition. It is necessary, therefore, to sort out the influences of party competition on these policy measures from the influence of economic development. When the effects of economic development are controlled in the partial correlation coefficients shown in Table 2, almost all of the association between party competition and policy outcomes disappears. Of these 18 statistically significant correlations shown in simple coefficients, 16 of these fall below accepted significance levels once urbanization, industrialization, income, and education are controlled. In short, party competition has *no apparent independent effect* on 26 of the 28 policy outcomes investigated.

The only apparent independent effect of party competition on policy outcomes was the effect it seemingly had on state participation in the financing of public activities, particularly education. The state proportion of educational expenditures and the state proportion of total state and local government expenditures was lower in the more competitive states, indicating that the local proportion of these expenditures was higher.

In order to provide a check upon the findings that party competition has little independent effect on policy outcomes and that its association with these outcomes is merely a product of the intervening impact of economic development, the relationship between economic development and policy outcomes was observed in Table 3 while controlling for the effect of party competition. The simple coefficients in Table 3, which do *not* control for party competition, suggest many strong relationships between all four measures of economic development and a variety of policy outcomes. Twenty-one of the 28 measured policy outcomes were significantly associated with at least one of the measures of economic development. More policy outcomes were associated with wealth than with any other measure of economic development.

But the most striking comparison between Tables 2 and 3 is in the partial coefficients. The relationships between socio-economic variables and policy outcomes *do not disappear* when the effect of party competition is controlled. For the most part, the partial coefficients in Table 3, unlike those in Table 2, continue to identify statistically significant relationships even after controlling for the effect of party competition. Of the 21 policy variables for which significant simple

Table 3   The relationship between economic development and selected policy outcomes among the states, controlling for the effect of party competition

| | Economic Development | | | | | | | |
| | Urbanization | | Industrialization | | Income | | Education | |
	Simple	Partial	Simple	Partial	Simple	Partial	Simple	Partial
Education								
Per Pupil Expenditures	.52*	.44*	.36*	.36*	.84*	.73*	.60*	.35*
Per Cap. Exp. Schools	.20	.13	.05	.05	.61*	.40*	.77*	.46*
Average Teachers Salaries	.69*	.66*	.64*	.66*	.88*	.85*	.60*	.39*
Teachers with M. A.	.54*	.36*	.42*	.26*	.55*	.41*	.42*	.41*
Male Teachers	.48*	.43*	.26	.25	.64*	.42*	.67*	.39*
Pupil-Teacher Ratio	-.15	.09	-.15	-.29	-.45*	-.39*	-.48*	-.41*
Size of School District	.05	.23	.23	.25	-.19	.20	-.36*	-.08
State Participation	-.12	.06	.13	.27	-.26	.16	.35*	.01
Federal Participation	-.36*	-.32	-.10	-.09	-.02	-.14	-.08	-.28
Per Cap. Higher Education	-.21	-.11	-.22	.06	.22	.01	.28	.18
Welfare								
Per Capita Welfare	.13	.09	.01	-.01	-.13	.02	.02	.26
Per Capita Health	.14	-.01	.35*	.34*	.41*	.35*	.21	.28
Unemployment Benefits	.55*	.46*	.30*	.33*	.80*	.62*	.68*	.51*
Old Age Benefits	.51*	.38*	.20	.05	.65*	.41*	.62*	.40*
ADC Benefits	.52*	.43*	.29	.02	.75*	.60*	.56*	.49*
Blind Benefits	.62*	.44*	.36	.10	.74	.59*	.65	.48*
Kerr-Mills Benefits	.16	.15	.16	.18	.15	.17	.02	.00
General Assistance	.58*	.39*	.42*	.24	.77*	.53*	.44*	.35*
State Participation	-.11	.00	-.17	-.10	-.35*	-.14	-.18	.08
Federal Participation	-.32	-.20	-.19	-.12	-.47*	-.23	-.30*	.00
Taxation								
Total Revenue Per Cap.	.29	.21	.03	.02	.64*	.44*	.77*	.49*
Tax Revenue Per Cap.	.59*	.53*	.24	.19	.76*	.60*	.75*	.57*
State % Total Revenue	-.30*	-.18	-.13	-.10	-.40*	-.02	.23	.22
Federal % Total Revenue	-.59*	-.11	-.34*	.08	-.33*	-.04	-.07	-.20
Income Taxes	.05	.11	.02	.08	.20	.04	.19	.20
Sales Taxes	-.02	-.09	-.05	-.01	-.17	-.04	.16	-.05
Alcohol and Tobacco Taxes	-.10	-.09	-.01	-.08	-.10	-.01	-.23	-.16
Motor Fuel Taxes	-.29	-.19	-.29	-.19	-.26	-.15	-.14	-.06

Figures are simple and partial correlation coefficients for 48 states; partial coefficients control for the effect of urbanization, industrialization, income and education; an asterisk indicates a statistically significant relationship.

correlations were obtained in Table 3, 14 of these variables remain significantly related to one or more socio-economic variables even after party competition is controlled. Controlling for party competition does *not* seriously affect the relationships between economic development and educational expenditures, teacher preparation and salary levels, the proportion of male teachers, pupil-teacher ratios, welfare benefit levels, or state and local government revenues or tax receipts. Controlling for party competition had some effect on only seven policy variables, including size of school district, state and federal participation in education and welfare finance, and state and federal proportions of total revenue receipts. In short, while party competition had little independent effect on policy outcomes once economic development was controlled, economic development continues to have considerable independent effect on policy outcomes even after party competition is controlled.

These operations suggest that party competition does not play as influential a role in determining policy outcomes as the level of economic development.

CONCLUSIONS

Economic development in the American states is related to party competition and to many policy outcomes, but party competition appears to have little independent effect on policy outcomes. Differences in the policy choices of competitive and non-competitive states turn out to be a product of differences in economic development levels rather than a direct product of party competition. Economic development — urbanization, industrialization, income, and education — is a more influential independent variable determining policy outcomes than party competition. Most of the association between party competition and policy outcomes is merely a product of the relationships between economic development and party competition, and economic development and policy outcomes.

Of course these conclusions are predicated on the results obtained from analyzing 28 selected measures of state policy in three separate fields — education, welfare, and taxation. Conceivably party competition could have a more direct effect on some policy outcomes which were not investigated. However, expenditures for welfare and education, the liberality of welfare benefits, teachers, salaries, the quality of public education, and the tax and revenue structure are certainly among the most important decisions that states must make. And party competition seems to have little impact on the outcomes of these decisions.

Returning to the conceptual framework set forth at the beginning of this paper: an important system variable, party competition, has been shown to have little independent effect on a variety of policy outcomes. This suggests that the linkage between socio-economic inputs and policy outcomes is an unbroken one, and that characteristics of political systems do not independently influence policy outcomes. Political systems are, by definition, the structure and processes which function to make public policy, but these systems do not mediate between societal requirements and public policy so much as they reflect societal requirements in public policy. Political system characteristics are much less important than socio-economic inputs in determining policy outcomes.

Where does this leave the study of political system variables in the American states? It is still important to know what goes on in the little black box. Understanding the functional inter-relatedness of system variables is important regardless of the impact of these variables on policy outcomes. We want to know *how* a political system goes about transforming socio-economic inputs into policy outcomes. The way in which a society authoritatively allocates values may even be a more important question than the outcomes of these value allocations.

All that has been shown here is that party competition in the American states does not seem to have a measurable impact on certain policy outcomes, once socio-economic variables are controlled. This is not to say that party competition does not vitally affect state political systems or processes. Quantification, regardless of its degree of sophistication, necessitates a simplification of very complex processes. Perhaps the influences of party competition for policy outcomes are so subtle and diverse that they defy quantification. Certainly we need more refined analysis of the relationships between socio-economic conditions, political system characteristics, and policy outcomes. But these operations at least succeed in challenging the easy assumptions and simple generalizations about the effect of party competition on public policy.

NOTES

1. One of the more explicit formulations of the relationships between socio-economic conditions, political system characteristics, and policy outcomes is found in Richard E. Dawson and James A. Robinson, "Inter-party Competition, Economic Variables, and Welfare Policies in the American States," *Journal of Politics,* Vol. 2 (May, 1963), 265-289. See also David Easton, *A Framework for Political Analysis* (New York: Prentice Hall, 1965), pp. 59-76.

2. Austin Ranney and Willmoore Kendall, "The American Party System," *American Political Science Review,* Vol. 48 (June, 1954), 477-485; Joseph A. Schlesinger, "A Two-Dimensional Scheme for Classifying the States According to Degree of Inter-party Competition," *American Political Science Review,* Vol. 49 (December, 1955), 1120-1128; V. O. Key, Jr., *American State Politics* (New York: Knopf, 1956), 99; Robert T. Golembiewski, "A Taxonomic Approach to State Political Party Strength," *Western Political Quarterly,* Vol. 11 (June, 1958), 494-513.

3. Sources of data on party competition, socio-economic variables, and policy outcomes include *U. S. Statistical Abstract 1963* (Washington: Government Printing Office, 1963); U. S. Office of Education, *Statistics of State School Systems, 1961-62* (Washington: Government Printing Office, 1963); National Education Association, *Rankings of the States 1963* (Washington: National Education Association, 1963); U. S. Department of Health, Education, and Welfare, *Health, Education and Welfare Trends, 1963* (Washington: Government Printing Office, 1963); Council of State Governments, *The Book of the States, 1962-63* (Chicago: Council of State Governments, 1963).

4. Seymour M. Lipset, *Political Man,* (New York: Doubleday, 1960), Ch. II.

5. Robert T. Golembiewski, *op. cit.*

6.   Austin Ranney and Willmoore Kendall, *op. cit.*; V. O. Key, Jr., *op. cit.*; Joseph A. Schlesinger, *op. cit.*

7.   Richard E. Dawson and James A. Robinson, *op. cit.*

8.   V. O. Key, Jr., *Southern Politics in State and Nation* (New York: Knopf, 1951), pp. 298-314.

9.   Duane Lockard, *New England State Politics* (Princeton: Princeton University Press, 1959), pp. 320-340.

10. Richard E. Dawson and James A. Robinson, *op. cit.*, p. 289.

11. The analysis of variance test determines the possibility that any coefficient might have been obtained by chance while correlating sets of random numbers from an imaginary infinite universe of states. It does not matter that the fifty states are a universe rather than a sample. The allusion to sampling in tests of significance is a hypothetical one. It helps us to determine whether the correlations obtained might have been obtained by correlating various columns of 48 random digits. See Hubert M. Blalock, *Social Statistics* (New York: McGraw Hill, 1960). pp. 302-305.

PRESSURE GROUPS
IN STATE POLITICS

American State Legislators' Role Orientations toward
Pressure Groups

John C. Wahlke, William Buchanan,
Heinz Eulau, and LeRoy C. Ferguson

I

In modern pluralistic political systems, the legislature is a central forum where organized interest groups articulate and express their views and press for public action favorable to their concerns. Indeed, the free representation of interests crucially affects the legitimacy of modern democratic legislatures. If interest groups were removed or prevented from influencing legislative action, the authority of the legislature would be put in jeopardy and its decisions would be found unacceptable. Yet in spite of the critical importance of the relationship between interest groups and law-making institutions, research offers surprisingly little theoretical explanation and few cumulative or comparative empirical data about this phase of the representative process.[1]

Most case studies of pressure groups do little more than decide the qualities, properties or activities of some of the pressuring groups, taking for granted the persons they press upon.[2] Such studies tend to be preoccupied with assessing the relative power of the various groups active in some particular situation and to neglect other kinds of questions political science ought to be considering: What sort

Reprinted from *Journal of Politics,* Vol. 22 (1960), pp. 203-227 by permission of the publisher.

This study was made possible by grants from the Political Behavior Committee of the Social Science Research Council to each of the four authors. It has been aided also by grants and other assistance from the Institute for Research in the Social Sciences, Vanderbilt University (to Mr. Wahlke) and from the All-University Research Fund and the Bureau of Social and Political Research, Michigan State University (to Mr. Ferguson).

of *system* is it within which groups act and become represented? How do institutional structures of this sort come into being? How do they change, or why do they not change? How does the system or structure itself facilitate or hinder performance of the representative function in the governmental process?

Questions like these direct attention to the official actors in the political process — in this case, to the activities and behavior of legislators. For, after all, the legislature is describable as an institutionalized group only insofar as relevant behaviors of legislators follow certain predictable patterns. A too-simple "group approach" to the legislative process implies an unrealistic conception of legislators' behavior and of the resultant character of the legislative process. The public policy decisions of legislatures cannot realistically be visualized as simple mathematical resultants of a given number of "pressures," each of measurable direction and strength, impinging on passively reacting legislators.[3]

Role theory provides a more appropriate and useful model. While it is not possible to develop the point exhaustively here, a few observations should be made.[4] First of all, it seems obvious that legislators' *perceptions* of pressure groups — or of any other factor, for that matter — will vitally affect the part played by that factor in the legislative process.[5] More particularly, legislators' perceptions of what constitutes legitimate or desirable or harmful activity by pressure groups or other factors, as well as their perceptions of the supposedly objective "facts" about such activity, are not random or idiosyncratic opinions held independently by each legislator individually, but are opinions intimately associated with what Truman has called the "influence of office"[6] and Latham has called "officiality."[7] Membership in the legislature constitutes a *status* or *position* in society. This means that people in the society *expect* certain behaviors by incumbents of that office. Legislators have similar expectations of each other, and they all have expectations with respect to other classes of actors they encounter in doing their legislative business. The key concept to refer to these patterns of behavior associated with a given position or status in the expectations and orientations of people is *role.*

From the abstract and general principles of role theory we take the working hypothesis that legislators' conceptions of their role as legislators will be a crucial factor governing their legislative behavior and thereby affecting the access, influence or power of all groups, as well as differentiating among groups.[8] General role theory suggests that legislators' role conceptions constitute a determining factor in pressure politics at least as important as the number, size, strategy, skill or other characteristics of pressure groups themselves, the individual group affiliations and identifications of legislators, or the peculiarities of personality and personal whim of those legislators. These role conceptions can usefully be made the focal point of comparative and analytical study.

Such an approach, it should be emphasized, does not "contradict" group-focussed (or other) conceptions of pressure politics. Rather, it complements and carries them forward by linking them potentially to more general concepts and more general bodies of theory. Every hypothesis about a relation between group characteristics and group influence plainly rests upon assumptions about the behavior of the legislators supposedly reacting to the group pressures. For example, the belief that a group will have more influence if its lobbyists follow certain tactical principles rests upon assertions, sometimes quite explicit, about how legislators will react to lobbyists acting in accordance with these principles.[9] Research which tests the behavioral assumptions of group-focussed (or other) studies against the observed behavior of legislators is essential to validation of any propositions linking group power and influence to group characteristics of any sort (or to any other independent variable).

II

Among the questions asked of some 474 legislators in four states during the 1957 legislative sessions[10] were several which make it possible to explore legislators' role orientations toward pressure groups and their agents.

A Typology of Role Orientations
Toward Pressure Groups

Several cautionary remarks should be made here. We are concerned with the functioning of the legislative *institution* in general, rather than with unique historical events or outcomes in the states studied. Similarly, the concern here is not with the *particular* group affiliations and identifications of individual legislators or their relative friendship or hostility toward specific groups but rather with their orientations toward pressure groups as a *generic* class of "significant others." The typology which follows has been constructed and used to suit this ultimate theoretical concern. Furthermore, rather than attempt, at this early stage of research using the role concept to discover and describe in exhaustive detail the innumerable behaviors which add up (in the legislators' expectations) to the prevailing role conceptions relevant to pressure groups in the four state systems, attention has been restricted to what seem the most obvious areas of role orientation.

Political scientists are familiar with the doctrinal disagreement about the value of pressure politics. One view holds, as did Rousseau, that expression and promotion of conflicting private interests is inimical to discovery and promotion of the public interest; an opposing view, that of many "pluralist" theorists, holds that what is called "the public interest" is never more than the harmonization of just such partial and private interests and that organized interest groups, therefore, play an indispensable part in defining and legislating in the public interest. Legislators' views on the subject likewise differ widely. Some agree with the member who said, "Hell! We wouldn't have a government if there were no interest groups. It would be a form of anarchy if groups and parties didn't do their job." Or, as another said, when asked about the desirability of having the individual citizen participate in government directly, rather than through interest groups, "How's he going to do it 'directly'? You have to organize or go into an organization to do anything." But others agree with the legislator who said, in response to the same question, "Stop there (after the word 'directly') and you've got the whole story about our citizens and what they should do." Many legislators share the suspicion of interest groups in general expressed by the member who said, "I've heard of them all my life, but I didn't aim to fool with that, and I don't know nothing about it."

It seems obvious that a legislator's reaction to the activities of pressure groups and lobbyists will vary according to such differences in evaluation of pressure politics. Legislators' generalized attitudes of friendliness, neutrality or hostility to pressure politics were therefore measured by a four-item Likert scale utilizing replies to the questions shown in Table 1. Their attitudes were found to vary as indicated in that table.[11]

Table 1   Attitude of state legislators toward pressure politics.

| Question | Attitude [a] | | | | |
| | Friendly ◄───────► Hostile | | | | |
	1	2	3	4	5
1. Would you say that, on the whole, the legislature would work [better or worse] if there were no interest groups or lobbies trying to influence legislation? (N = 452)	41%	34%	12%	7%	6% = 100%
2. [Do you agree that] the job of the legislator is to work out compromises among conflicting interests? (N = 462)	31%	42%	2%	12%	13% = 100%
3. [Do you agree that] lobbyists and special interests have entirely too much influence in American state legislatures? (N = 464)	26%	34%	1%	22%	17% = 100%
4. [Do you agree that] under our form of government, every individual should take an interest in government directly, not through interest-group organizations? (N = 458)	19%	24%	3%	19%	35% = 100%

[a] Response categories to Question 1 were "much worse," "somewhat worse," "about the same," "somewhat better" and "much better"; to Questions 2-4, "agree," "tend to agree," "undecided," "tend to disagree" and "disagree." The most friendly responses are (1) "much worse," (2) "agree," (3) "disagree," and (4) "disagree."

It likewise seems obvious that legislators' reactions to pressure groups or lobbyists will vary with their different degrees of knowledge or awareness of group activity. The legislator who knows what the Municipal League is, what it wants, who speaks for it and when, will react differently to cues from the League than the legislator who never heard of it and doesn't identify anyone as its spokesman. Legislators' awareness of lobbying activities was therefore measured by asking them to identify a list of lobbyists more or less active in their state legislatures during the time of interviewing.[12]

It is almost universally assumed that one important factor determining the representativeness, legitimacy and authority of any given legislature is the extent and manner of its taking into account the demands of significant interest groups in its social environment. This, in turn, is no more than a reflection of the behavior of the legislators. Some members, by their behavior toward lobbyists and other group representational agents or activity, will serve to accommodate the demands of organized interest groups in the legislative process.[13]   Others will serve to resist consideration or accommodation of these demands in any form. And still others, presumably attuned to other persons or factors, will play a neutral role toward such group demands.

Assuming, then, that any given legislators' behavior in this respect will depend to a considerable extent upon his general effective orientation toward pressure politics as a mode of political activity and his awareness of such activity when it occurs around him,[14]   one can construct the following very simple typology of legislators' role orientations toward pressure groups:

Facilitators: Have a friendly attitude toward group activity *and* relatively much knowledge about it.

Resisters: Have a hostile attitude toward group activity *and* relatively much knowledge about it.

Neutrals: Either,   (1) Have no strong attitude of favor or disfavor with respect to group activity (regardless of their knowledge of it),

Or,   (2) Have very little knowledge about it (regardless of their friendliness or hostility toward it),

Or,   (3) Both (1) and (2).

By the measures of tolerance and awareness already described each of the legislators interviewed was classified under one of these three headings. They are distributed in the four states as shown in Table 2.

The reasons given by legislators for their varying opinions about groups further describe the differences among them. When legislators were asked why they thought the legislature would work better or worse in the absence of pressure-group activity, most of their responses could be coded into a comparatively few categories. These have been arranged in the order of decreasing friendliness toward group activity in Table 3. When respondents made more than one comment, only the most favorable (highest in the table) was coded. The table shows that almost two-thirds of the Facilitators think the legislature could not get along without

Table 2   Distribution of role-orientations toward pressure groups in four state legislatures.

Role Orientation	California (N = 97)	New Jersey (N = 78)	Ohio (N = 157)	Tennessee (N = 116)	Total (N = 448)
Facilitators	38%	41%	43%	23%	37%
Neutrals	42	32	35	37	37
Resisters	20	27	22	40	26
	100%	100%	100%	100%	100%

Table 3   Attitude-differences among Facilitators, Neutrals and Resisters as shown
        by their appraisals of pressure-group activity.

Most Favorable Opinion Expressed	Role Orientation[a]		
	Facilitator (N = 124)	Neutral (N = 105)	Resister (N = 76)
1. Groups are indispensable.	63%	39%	14%
2. Group activity is in general good, though certain "bad practices" of groups are undesirable.	23	41	46
3. Other less favorable opinions: *e.g.*, group activity may be objectionable but one ought not interfere with the democratic right to be heard; group influence is over-rated, it is not an important factor; group activity is a wholly disruptive force which ought to be eliminated.	14	20	40
	100%	100%	100%

[a] Total is only 305 because some legislators failed to give reasons when answering the question and others expressed appraisals not codable in these categories.

pressure-group activity, whereas a substantial number of Resisters (40%) expressed much less favorable opinions. The differences are of extreme statistical significance.[15]

In spite of these very striking and consistent differences, however, it should not be overlooked that even the Resisters express fairly tolerant appraisals of group activity, some 60% venturing opinions (numbers 1 and 2 in Table 3) which are quite favorable. We must, in other words, recognize the fact that pressure politics has become rather widely accepted among legislators in American states.

Legislators' differences in perception of groups are not simple quantitative differences of more or less, as the initial measure of lobbyist-recognition might suggest. In responding to a question asking them to name the most powerful groups in their own state, 56% of the Facilitators but only 36% of the Resisters named only or mainly *specific organizations* or lobbyists; similarly, only 36% of the Facilitators but 58% of the Resisters referred to *broad interest aggregations* ("labor," "farmers," etc.). In other words, Facilitators, significantly more than either Neutrals or Resisters, tend to see groups and group activities in concrete and specific terms.[16]   That Facilitators are more alert to perceive groups and group cues is strikingly indicated by the fact that, even though interviewers sought, by probing, to have all respondents uniformly name six groups in response to the question, Facilitators nevertheless named significantly more groups than either Neutrals or Resisters.[17]

Table 4   Facilitators think more groups worth listening to than do Neutrals or Resisters.

Number of Groups Named	Role Orientation		
	Facilitators (N = 141)	Neutrals (N = 134)	Resisters (N = 108)
0-1	11%	17%	20%
2-3	24	34	37
4 or more	29	27	23
"All are worth listening to"[a]	36	22	20
	100%	100%	100%
Mean number of groups named	4.17	3.50	3.35

[a]This response counted only if no more precise answer given (i.e., no group named).

Some of the grosser behavioral characteristics of the three types of legislator being described can also be explored. To begin with, assuming the validity of the role-orientation typology, one should expect to find Facilitators more ready than either Neutrals or Resisters to listen to the exhortations of pressure groups. This hypothesis is supported by the finding (see Table 4) that Facilitators named significantly more groups than did either Neutrals or Resisters when asked the question,

> We've been told that there are always some groups whose advice ought to be considered, whether they happen to be powerful or not. Would you name some of these groups here in [state]?[18]

Not only do Facilitators think more groups are worth listening to than do Neutrals or Resisters, they apparently tend also to give more weight to what they hear from group representatives. At least on the problem of school needs, which was selected as a typical issue, when legislators were asked to rate the influence of several factors — committee recommendations, advice of party leaders, views of constituents, etc. — on their own thinking, Facilitators attributed more importance to the "views of interest groups or lobbies" than did Neutrals or Resisters (See Table 5).[19] Finally, the data provide internal evidence that at least two of the legislative behaviors one would expect to find associated with the accommodation of group interest and demands do indeed appear more characteristic of Facilitators than of Neutrals or Resisters. Tables 6 and 7 show the former to be more ready to use, or at least to admit to using, the aid of lobbyists both in drafting bills and in lining up support for bills.[20]

There is ample justification, then, for the conclusion that there are significant differences among legislators in their role orientations toward pressure groups and group agents. It is not just that they differ in tolerance and awareness of group activity — that, indeed, was assumed in constructing the typology of Facilitators, Neutrals and Resisters. The point is, important tendencies toward different patterns of behavior are associated with these basic differences in effect and cognition. The patterns are sharper for the Facilitators and Resisters, since they are attuned,

Table 5   Facilitators rate importance of pressure groups on own views of "school needs" problem higher than do Neutrals or Resisters.

Importance attributed to views of pressure groups	Role Orientation		
	Facilitators (N= 146)	Neutrals (N = 137)	Resisters (N = 101)
Very important or important	70%	57%	40%
Not very or not at all important	30	43	60
	100%	100%	100%

Table 6   More Facilitators than Neutrals or Resisters agree lobbyists give them valuable help in drafting bills.

Answer to statement that lobbyists give valuable help in bill-drafting	Role Orientation		
	Facilitators (N = 163)	Neutrals (N = 160)	Resisters (N = 120)
Agree or tend to agree	63%	52%	52%
Tend to disagree or disagree	37	48	48
	100%	100%	100%

Table 7   More Facilitators than Neutrals or Resisters agree lobbyists give them valuable help in lining up support for the legislator's own bills.

Answer to statement that lobbyists give valuable help in lining up support	Role Orientation		
	Facilitators (N = 159)	Neutrals (N = 157)	Resisters (N = 115)
Agree or tend to agree	78%	67%	61%
Tend to disagree or disagree	22	33	39
	100%	100%	100%

favorably or unfavorably, to group behavior, and perceive, understand and react in characteristic fashion. The Neutrals, a category consisting of those who apparently fail to perceive, understand or formulate a coherent standard for judging groups-in-general, demonstrate, as one might expect, a more erratic, less distinct and consistent pattern. It is possible that each individual Neutral, at his own level of awareness or concern, behaves toward some or all group representatives in a manner that could be characterized as "role behavior," but that these patterns cancel each other out in the statistical treatment of responses. In any case, Facilitators are more likely to be aware of the nature of group demands and respond to them; Resisters to be aware of them but deliberately fail to respond; Neutrals to respond or resist, but for assorted other reasons, without caring or without knowing that a demand has been made by a group. It should be clear that these role categories do no more than classify one aspect of legislators' attitudes and behavior: They are not fixed categories of types-of-person, nor will they by any means describe all aspects of legislators' behavior. They are constructs, devised to help us explore further the working of the legislative system and, ultimately, the larger political system.

Demographic and Ecological Correlates of Role Orientation Toward Pressure Groups

"Explanation" of the differences in role orientation described above was not an objective of this study, but the data nevertheless do suggest several comments on this problem. One would naturally expect that a variable defined generally in terms of cognition and effect, as role orientation has been defined here, would be closely related to respondents' education. If, as many educators say, education liberates the mind, eliminates excessive faith in the dogmatic truth of simple ideas, and provides increased factual understanding of the social and physical world, then legislators with much education (and therefore greater knowledge and greater acceptance of group diversity) will more often by Facilitators than Resisters and those with comparatively little education will more often be Neutrals than either Facilitators or Resisters. As between the latter two types, less-educated persons will more often be Resisters than Facilitators. The data shown in Table 8 are consistent with all these hypotheses and are statistically significant.[21]

Role orientation is hardly a simple reflex function of education, however. It has already been shown (above, Table 2) that the four states studied differ significantly in the distribution of role-orientation types. Such differences among the states persist even if we compare only groups of comparable educational background. As Table 9 shows, there is, on the whole, at least as much variation from state to state *within* each educational level as there is *between educational levels* within any given state.[22] This suggests that "political culture"[23] is a significant variable differentiating the states' modes and styles of pressure politics. Quite possibly, norms and expectations peculiar to each state system are transmitted and circulated more or less generally among the population of that system.

Table 8 More-educated legislators tend more to be Facilitators and less to be either Neutrals or Resisters than do the less-educated legislators.

Role Orientation	Level of Education	
	Less than completed college (N = 201)	At least completed college (N = 247)
Facilitators	26%	45%
Neutrals	44	31
Resisters	30	24
	100%	100%

Table 9   Inter-state differences in friendliness toward pressure politics are as great
as differences between legislators of different educational backgrounds.

Legislator's Education	Mean score for friendliness toward pressure politics [a]				
	California (N = 106)	New Jersey (N = 79)	Ohio (N = 160)	Tennessee (N = 117)	Inter-state Range
Less than college	2.65	3.17	3.09	3.76	1.11
At least college	2.51	2.52	2.32	3.24	.92
Intra-state, inter-level range	.14	.65	.77	.52	

[a] Scores represent quintile groups, score 1 being the most friendly, score 5 the
least, on the scale described above, p. 264.

so that legislators, like citizens or occupants of other roles in the system, have
acquired some role orientations and potential responses appropriate to their own
specific legislature and state political system before they come actually to play
their roles.

Some very oblique justification for such a line of reasoning is provided
by the fact that role orientation is not significantly related to any of the demographic variables often discussed in behavioral research.[24] Socio-economic status,
by almost any index chosen, fails to exhibit such correlation: Legislators with low,
medium or high income fall in all three role-orientation categories with equal
probability.[25] Neither their type of occupation nor their occupational status appears
significantly associated with legislators' role orientation.[26] The urban-or-rural
character of their county-of-residence is likewise unrelated to role orientation,
as is the urban-or-rural character of the places where legislators were brought up.
Nor do the data show a relation between legislators' religious affiliations and their
role orientations toward pressure groups. The one familiar demographic variable
which does emerge significantly related to role orientation is that discussed above —
education. And education, it has already been shown, fails to account for interstate differences.

These findings hardly "prove" the suitability of "political culture" as a
basic concept for the analysis of political systems, let alone prove that role-orientation is determined by such a cultural variable. But they do strongly suggest that,
because the norms and expectations constituting roles in a political system are
by no means wholly or directly dependent on social class, communal type, or
similar supposedly controlling variables, effort should be made to describe any
political system in such a way as to include political culture variables in the basic
structural description.

Interest Inclinations and Role Orientation

Students of the legislative process usually assume there is a relationship
between legislators' personal convictions or group sympathies and their actions
as legislators. In order to inquire into this relationship, legislators were classi-

Table 10   Legislators who are ideologically neutral, where economic interests are
            concerned, are more likely than legislators committed to either business or labor
            to manifest role orientation of Facilitator.

Role	Economic-interest inclination		
	Pro-business (N = 239)	Neutral (N = 130)	Pro-labor (N = 51)
Facilitator	34%	49%	26%
Neutral	36	33	33
Resister	30	18	41
	100%	100%	100%

fied as pro-business, pro-labor or economic neutrals. The process of classification
(too complex to display here fully) involved three main steps: (1) all interest groups
mentioned were classified as economic or other-than-economic, and all economic-
interest groups then classified as either business, labor or agricultural; (2) each
legislator's pattern of reference to each group separately was then classified as
either favorable, neutral or unfavorable;[27] and, finally, (3) each legislator's
interest inclination was determined on the basis of his pattern of favor, disfavor
or neutrality toward the three classes of economic interest.[28]

The question is, how do such interest inclinations affect the role orientations
of legislators toward interest-group activity in general? The most obvious hypothesis is that individuals who are committed to any particular interest (business,
labor, *etc.*) will be less likely than individuals not so committed to look favorably
upon the assertion of demands by other groups or interests, especially if those others are conflicting interests. On the other hand, because the nature of their assertion of their own interests calls attention to the group-basis of those interests, the
more committed legislators will not be likely to be especially resistant to group activity in the abstract. From this we can infer that economic neutrals will tend more
than will pro-business or pro-labor legislators to be Facilitators and tend less to
be Resisters. Table 10 shows this hypothesis is significantly supported.[29]

One other feature of Table 10 deserves comment: Whereas pro-business
legislators tend more to be Neutrals or Facilitators than to be Resisters, pro-
labor legislators tend above all to be Resisters. This suggests but by no means
proves that American pro-labor legislators are more ideologically doctrinaire
and less tolerant of pluralistic diversity than are pro-business legislators. One
possible explanation is that labor-union officials or members, and presumably
other persons who see the world as they do, are likely to see arrayed against them
only one main group antagonist (the employer, or an association of employers), to
be faced with only one, if any, competing labor organization, and, at least until
recently, to feel little need to sell themselves to any consumer interest or organization. The businessman or person viewing the world as he does, on the other
hand, is more likely to be exposed to a multiplicity of groups — not just antagonistic
labor and target consumer groups and interests, but competing groups identical in
kind with his own immediate business organization. It need hardly be emphasized,
of course, that all such reasoning is at this stage highly speculative.

The Political Entailment of
Role Orientation

General role theory holds that roles in any system are to a considerable extent engendered by the very system itself in which the roles occur.[30] Roles, in other words, are functionally specific to the system in which they are played. For example, the role of "buyer" in a market system calls for the complementary role of "seller." On such grounds one can very generally postulate that role orientations toward pressure groups are related to the functions of the political system in general and, more closely, to the functions of the legislative sub-system in particular.

Political scientists distinguish between the different functions of legislature, executive, administration and judiciary *vis-à-vis* pressure groups. As Earl Latham has said,

> The legislature referees the group struggle, ratifies the victories of the successful coalitions, and records the terms of the surrenders, compromises, and conquests in the form of statutes .... The function of the bureaucrat in the group struggle is somewhat different from that of the legislator. Administrative agencies of the regulatory kind are established to carry out the terms of the treaties that the legislators have negotiated and ratified .... The function of the judge is not unlike that of the bureaucrat.[31]

Even those who deny vehemently the adequacy of this view as a *complete* account of the governmental process generally admit that, insofar as *any* agency of government has the legitimate function of basing its decisions to *any* extent upon the expressed demands of organized interest groups, that function belongs more properly to legislative than to executive, administrative or judicial agencies.

If this is so and if, as it is reasonable to assume, commitment to legislative purpose increases with increasing service in the legislature, then legislators with the most tenure should tend more than those with little tenure to be Facilitators. Table 11 shows that, except for Tennessee Resisters, this is indeed the case.[32] By the same reasoning, persons who have been active in legislative office should be more inclined to Facilitative and less to Resistant role orientations than those active in non-legislative offices. This is borne out by Table 12. The table also seems to show that persons who had *no* previous governmental experience are still more likely than are those with legislative experience to be Facilitators. But the differences here, in contrast to the differences between persons with legislative and

Table 11   Legislators with the most legislative service tend most to be Facilitators and least to be Neutrals.

Role Orientation	Median Number Years' Legislative Service Prior to 1957			
	California (N = 99)	New Jersey (N = 79)	Ohio (N = 155)	Tennessee (N = 115)
Facilitators	7. 3	5. 6	6. 2	2. 2
Neutrals	4. 8	2. 5	4. 4	2. 1
Resisters	5. 3	3. 8	4. 6	2. 4

Table 12   Experience in the legislature inclines legislators toward Facilitator role
           orientation and away from Resister role orientation more than does experience
           in executive or administrative office.

Role Orientation	Office held prior to entry to state legislature [a]		
	Executive or Administrative (but not legislative) office (N = 84)	Legislative (but not executive or administrative office (N = 105)	No previous office (N = 202)
Facilitators	24%	36%	41%
Neutrals	39	43	34
Resisters	37	21	25
	100%	100%	100%

[a] At all levels of government — state, federal, local.

persons with executive or administrative experience, are not statistically significant,[33] and this apparent tendency is also counterbalanced by a correspondingly
greater tendency for persons with no previous governmental experience, when
compared with persons having prior legislative experience, to be Resisters.

Role Orientation and The Legislative System

It seems reasonable to suppose that the number and pervasiveness of groups
in American political processes are so great that no legislator can hope to operate
in disregard of them. The individual legislator can work effectively and can feel
he is working effectively as a legislator only if he makes his peace with the world
of pressure groups. In other words, other things being equal, the Facilitator will
probably be a more effective legislator, and will feel himself to be so, than will
the Neutral or the Resister.

A crude measure of legislators' effectiveness is provided by their responses
to the following question:

> We've been told that every legislature has its unofficial rules of the game —
> certain things members must do and things they must not do if they want the respect
> and cooperation of fellow-members. What are some of these things — these rules-
> of-the-game — that a member must observe . . . ?

On the assumption that the more effective legislators are aware of a greater number
and a greater diversity of "rules of the game," one can hypothesize that Facilitators
will outrank Neutrals and Registers in both these respects. In fact, Facilitators
averaged naming 4.13 rules when answering, as compared with 3.88 for Resisters
and 2.53 for Neutrals. That they likewise named rules in greater diversity is
shown in Table 13.[34] It is worth noting that the Neutrals rank lower than either
Facilitators or Resisters in both measures.

It can likewise be shown (see Table 14) that significantly more Facilitators
feel themselves to be effective legislators than do the other two types.[35] But

Table 13   Facilitators name (and presumably, therefore, are aware of) a greater diversity of "rules of the game."

Number of categories [a] in which rules were named	Role orientation		
	Facilitators (N = 162)	Neutrals (N = 160)	Resisters (N = 119)
Two or less	46%	64%	51%
Three or more	54	36	49
	100%	100%	100%

[a] The categories include rules (1) regarding predictability of behavior, (2) regarding restraint or canalization of conflict, (3) expediting legislative business, promoting group cohesion or solidarity, (4) which are tactical, primarily for the benefit of individual members, and (5) which are "personal qualities" rather than rules.

Table 14   Facilitators have highest and Resisters have lowest efficacy sense.

Efficacy sense	Role orientation		
	Facilitators (N = 164)	Neutrals (N = 163)	Resisters (N = 119)
High	43%	31%	29%
Medium	38	46	36
Low	19	23	35
	100%	100%	100%

Table 15   Facilitators are rated higher than Resisters or Neutrals by their colleagues (composite ratings as "friend," respected," and "expert").

Rating	Role orientation		
	Facilitators (N = 163)	Neutrals (N = 164)	Resisters (N = 120)
Top half [a]	53%	40%	47%
Bottom half [a]	47	60	53
	100%	100%	100%

[a] These "halves" are approximate, since tie scores made it impossible to divide some chambers exactly. Standards differed slightly between chambers with the internal distribution, but all in the top half were named by one or more members in each of the three categories, and their mentions in all three categories total six or more. None of those in the bottom half had more than eight mentions in all.

whereas Neutrals rank lowest of the three types in effectiveness, Resisters rank lowest in *sense* of effectiveness.

Another way to look at the problem of legislators' relative effectiveness is to consider other legislators' perceptions and judgments of them. It seems reasonable to assume that those most esteemed by their colleagues will have at least greater potential for influence or effectiveness than their less esteemed colleagues. On this assumption, an index of potential effectiveness was constructed from the replies by respondents in each house to three questions regarding the fellow members they considered to be "personal friends," "experts" in some legislative subject-matter field, and "respected for following the rules of the game." Ranking the members with respect to the number of mentions each received differentiates between those who stand out in the eyes of their fellows and those who are lost in the shuffle or (in a few instances) disliked or distrusted. This ranking of a member, be it noted, is entirely independent of his own responses to the questions, since it is a composite view of the member as seen by his colleagues. Table 15 shows that Facilitators do, in fact, rate higher with their colleagues than do Resisters and Neutrals.[36]

III

Conclusions

Several important, though tentative, conclusions are suggested by the above findings. Perhaps the most important is that the group struggle is mediated in the legislature primarily by the legislators who are relatively *least* committed as advocates or agents to particular conflicting interests and who are rather conciliators among them (see page 271). The emerging picture of the Facilitative legislator who is above or outside of group conflicts even while he more or less consciously defines his official role to include the accommodation of group demands adds a new dimension to the conception of government ordinarily guiding study of pressure groups. At the same time, the detection of Resisters and Neutrals warns against a too simple view of the legislative struggle as a struggle between elementary group demands. There is evidence, if such is required, that a legislature cannot forge public policy out of the raw material of naked group interests alone. Resisters are to be found in all legislatures who do not want to base public policy on such demands; even Facilitators, by standing above most groups, indicate their refusal to recognize the views of any particular groups as specially pregnant with the public interest.

On the other hand, pressure groups occupy too prominent a place in American society to permit a legislator seriously to think of doing his legislative job in complete disregard of them. What is more, the legislative function seems clearly to include the function of harmonizing and integrating group demands, so that incumbency in legislative office itself serves to shape legislators' role orientations so as to promote the group-conciliating function (see page 272), and the effective performance of individual legislators, probably the effective performance of the legislative system itself, depends to some extent upon legislators' acquiring such orientations (see page 273).

The findings also emphasize the "autonomy" of the legislative sub-system and of the larger political system. While the differences among the four states in distribution of legislators' role orientations appear superficially to follow inter-state differences in general educational level, economic status and urban-rural character of the general population, the failure of corresponding demographic characteristics of legislators to correlate with their role orientations (see page 269) warns us against accepting such correlations as "explanations." The fact that the Tennessee legislature is a far more informal and less "professional" legislature than those of California, New Jersey and Ohio is as important as, and is by no means directly the result of, the fact that the Tennessee population is more rural, poorer and less well educated. Whatever the causal mechanism linking such sociological variables to legislative behavior, it seems necessary to visualize a "political culture" intervening between to give to the legislative and political system of each state a characteristic structure which is more immediately significant in determining what gets done there than is the sociological composition of the population or the day-to-day specifics of pressure-group activity.

The most general conclusion, therefore, is that political science can profitably re-direct its attention to basic questions of institutional structure, mechanics and process. These questions can be properly answered by further rigorous attention to the behavior of political actors, the ultimate data for all political investigation.

NOTES

1. Samuel J. Eldersveld, "American Interest Groups: A Survey of Research and Some Implications for Theory and Method," in Henry W. Ehrmann (ed.), *Interest Groups on Four Continents* (Pittsburgh, 1958), pp. 173-196; Oliver Garceau, "Interest Group Theory in Political Research," *Annals of the American Academy of Political and Social Science* 319 (1958), 104-112.

   For discussion of some of the general problems of research, theory and conception, see also Gabriel A. Almond, "A Comparative Study of Interest Groups and the Political Process," *American Political Science Review* 52 (1958), 270-282; Alfred de Grazia, "The Nature and Prospects of Political Interest Groups," *Annals of the American Academy of Political and Social Science* 319 (1958), 113-122; W. J. M. Mackenzie, "Pressure Groups: The 'Conceptual Framework'," *Political Studies* 3 (1955), 247 ff.

2. Henry W. Ehrmann, *op. cit.*, the most extensive work considering pressure groups in a trans-system context, contains a series of studies of particular countries, but not broader comparison or analysis.

   Among the most noteworthy of those few studies which do deal extensively with the behavior of pressured legislators are Oliver Garceau and Corinne Silverman, "A Pressure Group and the Pressured: A Case Report," *American Political Science Review* 48 (1954), 672-691: John Millett, "The Role of an Interest Group Leader in the House of Commons," *Western Political Quarterly* 9 (1956), 915-926; and V. O. Key, "The Veterans and the House of Representatives: A Study of a Pressure Group and Electoral Mortality," *The Journal of Politics* 5 (1943), 27-40.

3. This is one of the main criticisms voiced, for example, by Peter Odegard, "A Group Basis of Politics: A New Name for an Ancient Myth," *Western Political Quarterly* 11 (1958), 689-702. See also Robert M. MacIver's criticism of Bentley in *The Web of Government* (New York, 1947), pp. 220-221. Of course, both those criticized and the critics readily admit, if pointedly asked, that,

> The politician-legislator is not equivalent to the steel ball in a pinball game, bumping passively from post to post down an inclined plane. He is a human being, involved in a variety of relationships with other human beings. In his role as legislator his accessibility to various groups is affected by the whole series of relationships that define him as a person [David B. Truman, *The Government Process* (New York, 1951), pp. 332-333].

The question is not one of recognizing such a basic postulate but of incorporating it in research and explanation.

4. An admirable, research-oriented discussion of role theory, including a review of the relevant literature, which uses "role" and related terms in much the way they are used in this research, can be found in Neal Gross, Ward S. Mason, and Alexander W. MacEachern, *Explorations in Role Analysis* (New York, 1958), pp. 3-75, 244-257, 281-318.

5. The point is forcibly demonstrated by Corinne Silverman, "The Legislator's View of the Legislative Process," *Public Opinion Quarterly* 18 (1954), 180-190.

6. Truman, *op. cit.*, pp. 346-350.

7. Earl Latham, *The Group Basis of Politics* (Ithaca, New York, 1952), pp. 33-40.

8. This proposition is intimated in Truman's discussion of the influence of office and Latham's discussion of officiality. It is more directly suggested in Huitt's discussion of the way in which legislators' differing conceptions of their roles *pro* or *con* interest groups lead them to bring "competing versions of the facts" to their discussions of conflicting group demands [Ralph K. Huitt, "The Congressional Committee: A Case Study," *American Political Science Review* 48 (1954), 350]. It is the basis for empirical research in one very important instance (Garceau and Silverman, *op. cit.*), which differentiates faction-oriented, policy-oriented, program-oriented and non-generalizers' conceptions of the appropriate mode of behavior for legislators, although not formally utilizing role theory or role concepts to do so.

9. Bertram Gross [*The Legislative Struggle* (New York, 1953), pp. 302-303] quotes the following rules set for N. A. M. lobbyists: "Avoid demagoguery before a Committee. It is resented." "Get directly to the facts. Committees are not much interested in long discussions about the trends of the time." "Don't assume a superior attitude." An often-cited rule of lobbying tactics in America, to "build up a bloc of votes in Congress to be backed with appeals from home at the psychological moment" [Stuart Chase, *Democracy Under Pressure* (New York, 1945), pp. 24-26], likewise rests obviously upon assumptions about the motivations and behavior of Congressmen.

10. 94% of the California, 100% of the New Jersey, 94% of the Ohio and 91% of the Tennessee legislature were interviewed, using a fixed schedule of questions. Interviews averaged about an hour and a half in length. For other findings of the study see the authors' "The Political Socialization of American State Legislators," *Midwest Journal of Political Science* 3 (1959), 188-206; "The Role of the Representative: Some Empirical Observations on the Theory of Representation of Edmund Burke," *American Political Science Review* 53 (1959), 742-756; "The Legislator as Specialist," *Western Political Quarterly* 13 (1960), 636-651.

11. The scale was constructed by awarding 4 points for the most friendly answer to a question, 3 points for the next most friendly, 2 points if undecided, 1 point if on the unfriendly side of "undecided" and 0 for the most unfriendly response. Averaging the four question-scores gives a scale-score. The power of each question to discriminate between respondents of high and low tolerance is more than sufficient, as shown by the values of Discriminatory Power obtained when the high and low *thirds* are used (actually, top 32% and bottom 35%) — a much more stringent requirement for a satisfactory scale than the usual one of at least 1.0 D.P. between upper and lower *quartiles*.

	Question Number			
	1	*2*	*3*	*4*
Mean score of upper 1/3	3.5	3.4	3.2	2.6
Mean score of lower 1/3	2.2	1.9	1.2	.7
Discriminatory Power	1.3	1.5	2.0	1.9

12. The exact wording of the question was, "Here are the names of some persons that people have told us are connected with the various interest groups and lobbies. Could you tell me who each of them is or what he does?" A respondent was credited with a "correct" answer if he identified the organizational tie, the general type of interest represented, or some particular legislative measure of concern for each lobbyist listed. Names on the list had been selected to include lobbyists of varying degrees of presumed familiarity. To obtain a more precise measure, scores were weighted to give greater credit for identifying lesser-known than for identifying universally-known lobbyists.

Unlike the tolerance scores, the awareness scores cannot be compared directly across state lines, since there is no way of comparing the recognition-value of lobbyists in different systems. But corresponding quintile groups can be so compared.

Garceau and Silverman *(op. cit.)* measured several other dimensions of awareness — ability to identify selected pressure groups, and ability to recognize more than one issue on which selected groups had been active. Pre-tests indicated that the single measure based on lobbyist-recognition produced awareness scores correlating very closely with those obtained by more complex measures; the simple unidimensional measure was therefore used here.

13. "Accommodation" does not mean "accession," although that is, of course, one form accommodation may take. Accommodation here means conscious consideration. The assumption is that persons voicing demands will far more likely accept decisions as

authoritative, even if their demands are *not* accepted, if they believe the decision-makers have given them explicit consideration than if they have not. This proposition is strongly implied in J. D. Stewart's discussion of "consultation" as the characteristic form of relationship between a group and a governmental organ [*British Pressure Groups* (Oxford, 1958). pp. 3-27].

14. These two dimensions are suggested not only in numerous general social-psychological discussions of role- and self- concepts, but also by two of the very few empirical and analytical studies of group politics. Garceau and Silverman *(op. cit.,* pp. 685ff.) report as the "most striking fact" discovered in their Vermont study "the extremely low level of recognition of interest group activity, " and suggest that differences in legislative behavior toward groups as well as legislators' ideas about appropriate behavior toward them are associated with different levels of information about groups. Samuel H. Beer, in his analysis of operative theories of interest representation in Britain ["The Representation of Interests in British Government: Historical Perspective," *American Political Science Review* 51 (1957), 613-650], suggests a number of respects in which legislators' different conceptions of the appropriate place of interest groups (described as Old Tory, Old Whig, Liberal, Radical and Collectivist theories) imply different conceptions of how legislators should behave toward such groups or their agents. Beer singles out for special attention one facet of the legislator-group role-relationship — that involving the activity of the legislator as agent of a group (the "interested M. P. ").

15. $X^2 = 50.48$, D. F. $= 4$, $p < .001$; the differences are consistent in all four states.

16. Complete data not shown. The differences are statistically significant: $X^2 = 14.9$, D. F. $= 4$, $.01 > p > .001$; the direction of difference is the same in all four states. The question was asked in the following form: "You hear a lot these days about the power of interest groups and lobbies in state politics. What would you say are the most powerful groups of this kind here in [state]?"

17. 62% of the Facilitators named 5 or more groups, compared with 57% of the Resisters and 45% of the Neutrals. If Facilitators are compared with Neutrals and Resisters, $X^2 = 8.91$, D. F. $= 1$, $.01 > p > .001$; the differences are consistently in the same direction in all four states.

18. X^2 for the table $= 15.96$, D. F. $= 6$, $.02 > p > .01$; X^2 for Facilitators compared with Resisters $= 11.86$, D. F. $= 3$, $.01 > p > .001$; X^2 for Facilitators compared with Neutrals and Resisters together $= 14.88$, D. F. $= 3$, $.01 > p > .001$. Again, the differences are consistently in the same direction within each state, except that Tennessee Resisters name somewhat more groups than Tennessee Neutrals (mean of 3.74 as against mean of 3.35). This finding, like the one just preceding, was wholly unanticipated, since interviewers sought to elicit a uniform number of groups from all respondents.

19. $X^2 = 23.40$, D. F. $= 2$, $p < .001$; the differences are consistent within each state.

20. The questions asked were, "[Do you agree to the statements], I get valuable help in drafting bills from interest groups or their agents" (Table 6), and, "Interest groups or their agents give me valuable help in lining up support for my bills" (Table

7). For Table 6, comparing Facilitators with Neutrals-and-Resisters, $X^2 = 4.71$, D. F. = 1, $.05 > p > .02$; for Table 7, $X^2 = 10.03$, D. F. = 2, $.01 > p > .001$. The differences are consistent within all four states, except that, in Table 7, New Jersey Resisters agree in greater proportions than do Facilitators, although New Jersey Neutrals agree much less.

21. $X^2 = 16.64$, D. F. = 2, $p < .001$. Non-college-educated includes some legislators who acquired law-school degrees without attending college beforehand, as well as some who had various non-college postgraduate work after high school (business school, night school,' etc.). There are some intra-state departures from the pattern: California non-college-educated legislators are less likely to be Resisters than are college-educated and are more likely to be Facilitators, and college-educated Tennessee legislators are less likely to be **Facilitators** than to be either Neutrals or Resisters.

22. Inter-state differences are greater than intra-state, inter-level differences when California or Tennessee is compared with either New Jersey or Ohio, but inter-level differences are **slightly** greater than inter-state differences when Ohio or New Jersey is compared with either of the other two states. It must be remembered that the knowledge dimension of role-orientation was normalized in the four states; for this reason the discussion here is directed toward the affective dimension, degree of friendliness (see above, note 12).

23. For discussion of the concept of "political culture" see Gabriel A. Almond, "Comparative Political Systems," *The Journal Of Politics* 18 (1956), 391-409.

24. For a general discussion of these variables see John C. Wahlke and Heinz Eulau (eds.), *Legislative Behavior* (Glencoe, Illinois, 1959), pp. 239-272.

25. Data not shown. Income-level measured by responses to the question, "Now, including your legislative salary, into which of these four income groups would you say your total annual income falls — (1) less than $5000, (2) $5000 to $10000, (3) $10000 to $20000, or (4) over $20000?"

26. Data not shown. Types of occupation include Manufacturing, Construction, Mining, Transportation, Communication, Utilities, Wholesale or Retail Trade, Financial, Real Estate, Law, Other Professions, Religion, Labor, Public Service, Housewives, Miscellaneous. Occupational Statuses include Managers, proprietors and officials; Professional and technical; Clerical; Sales; Craftsmen, foremen and skilled labor; Farmers and farm managers; Housewives.

27. A group or interest could be named in three possible contexts during the interview: (1) *Group power:* Was a group named in response to the question, "What would you say are the most powerful [interest groups or lobbies] here in [state]?" (2) *Worth of group:* Was it named in response to the question, "Would you name some [interest groups or lobbies here in (state)] whose advice ought to be considered, whether or not they are particularly powerful?" (3) *Hostility to group:* Did respondent express hostility toward this same group at any time during the interview? (Interviewers recorded such **volunteered** indications and they were coded for all respondents and

all groups.) Reference to a group in context 2 only or in both 1 and 2 were considered *favorable* references; those in context 1 only, or in both 2 and 3 (an essentially ambivalent response) or in all three contexts (also ambivalent) were considered *neutral*; and references in context 3 only or in both 1 and 3 were considered *unfavorable*.

28. The classification exhausts the logically possible combinations of favorable-neutral-or-unfavorable references to business-labor-or-agricultural interests. "Pro-agricultural" inclinations were combined with "pro-business" while "anti-agricultural" were included with "pro-labor," since neither category contained sufficient cases for analysis, and since it seemed reasonable to assume that most contemporary interest cleavages of the sort relevant to a "conservative-liberal" distinction involve primarily the conflict between business and labor and that in most such conflicts agricultural interests side with business interests.

29. When economic neutrals are compared with pro-business and pro-labor groups combined, $X^2 = 13.13$, D.F. $= 2$, $.01 > p > .001$; the differences in all states are consistent.

30. See especially S. F. Nadel, *The Theory of Social Structure* (Glencoe, Illinois, 1951), pp. 57 *ff.*

31. *Op. cit.*, pp. 35, 38, 39.

32. If the groups are dichotomized into those having less and those having more than the median number of years' legislative tenure in their legislature, then $X^2 = 6.14$, D.F. $= 2$, $.05 > p > .02$.

33. Comparing those with executive-administrative experience and those with legislative experience, and only with respect to the Facilitator and Resister categories, $X^2 = 7.37$, D.F. $= 1$, $.01 > p > .001$. Comparing those with legislative experience (prior to state legislature) and those with no previous experience, $X^2 = 2.39$, D.F. $= 2$, $.50 > p > .30$. Comparing them only with respect to Neutral as against both other categories combined, $X_2 = 1.19$, D.F. $= 1$, $.30 > p > .20$.

34. For Table 13, $X^2 = 11.49$, D.F. $= 2$, $.01 > p > .001$; in both cases the differences are consistent in all four states, except that Tennessee Resisters name slightly more rules than do Tennessee Facilitators. These differences are *not* merely reflections of legislators' differing educational backgrounds. In both cases (number and diversity of rules named), they are significantly greater among Facilitators, Neutrals and Resisters of the same educational level than are the differences between legislators of different educational levels (data not shown).

35. $X^2 = 13.64$, D.F. $= 4$, $.01 > p > .001$. Tennessee Resisters have a higher efficacy sense than do Tennessee Facilitators, but they also outrank the latter in *low* efficacy sense. Efficacy sense was measured by a Guttman-type scale based on the following questions: "[Do you agree or disagree that] (1) There is so little time during a session to study all the bills that sometimes I don't know what I'm voting for or against; (2) Many of the bills are so detailed and technical that I have trouble under-

standing them all; (3) So many groups want so many different things that it is often difficult to know what stand to take; and (4) My district includes so many different kinds of people that I often don't know just what the people there want me to do." The results are not biassed by the inclusion of the item (number 3) dealing specifically with pressure groups.

36. $X^2 = 5.20$, D.F. $= 2$, p = just over .05. The tendency is the same in every chamber in all four states, except the Tennessee House, where Resisters are the top-rated group. If the Tennessee House is eliminated from the table, the percentage of Facilitators in the top half is increased to 55%.

The Role of the Lobbyist: The Case of Oklahoma

Samuel C. Patterson

One of the most crucial relationships in the American political system is that between the lobbyist and the legislator. Our understanding of the political process frequently hinges on description and analysis of the "influences," or "vectors," or "pressures" converging on the legislator from the representatives of public or private interest groups. In recent years a considerable body of empirical findings has been built up concerning interest groups — their programs, organization, internal structure, and tactics.[1] Similarly, we have had in the last decade significant systematic research dealing with the legislator.[2] Strangely, we have no comparable accretion of research dealing with the lobbyist.

The lobbyist is a very significant actor in the legislative system. His role complements that of the legislator. The legislator is indispensable to the lobbyist — his role is inconceivable without the legislator. Although perhaps to a lesser degree, the legislator depends a great deal on the lobbyist. And, while the literature abounds in normative or descriptive distinctions between the "good" and the "bad," or the "old" and "new" lobby, it is now fairly clear that the lobby role is functional for the maintenance of the legislative system. The lobbyist is an important link in the communications process within the legislative system, and he plays an essential representative role.[3]

This being the case, we approach a better comprehension of the legislator-lobbyist interaction insofar as we improve our knowledge of lobbyists — their social and political backgrounds, the types of interests they represent, and the kinds of roles they play. The objective of this paper is to report findings in this connection.

In the summer of 1961, toward the end of the legislative session, the 62 individuals registered to lobby the Oklahoma House of Representatives were mailed brief questionnaires. After a period of three weeks those lobbyists who had not returned questionnaires were sent a second mailing. Forty-three lobbyists (69. 4%) returned questionnaires altogether. The questionnaire sought to get data in connection with 1) the lobbyists' own backgrounds, 2) the extent of their lobbying activity, 3) the kinds of legislation they were most interested in, 4) the extent and nature of their political experiences, 5) their conceptions of their role as lobbyists, and 6) their perceptions of the legislative role.

The sample, reflecting an unusually good return from a mailed questionnaire, appears to be reasonably reliable. Comparisons between respondents who

Reprinted from *Journal of Politics,* Vol. 25 (1963), pp. 72-92 by permission of the publisher.

This research has been made possible by a grant from the Committee on Political Behavior of the Social Science Research Council. Additional assistance was provided by the Research Foundation of Oklahoma State University. This aid is gratefully acknowledged, although the results are the responsibility of the author alone.

returned first and second mailings, and between those who returned questionnaires and those who did not, reveal no distortions in the sample.[4] It cannot, of course, be maintained with absolute certainty that the 62 lobbyists registered with the Clerk of the House of Representatives in 1961 constituted the total population of lobbyists.[5] On the other hand, Oklahoma law requries lobbyists to register in the usual way, and their applications for permission to lobby must, under House Rules, be approved by a majority of the members of the House who are present and voting. What is more, the Rules provide for the exclusion and banishment of any individual who does not comply with the application requirement. When a lobbyist's application is approved by the House he receives an official identification card. Based on the fairly severe sanctions for failure to register, as well as the assurances of several lobbyists who were queried on this point, it seems unlikely that any who persistently lobbied in the Oklahoma House were missed.

This research was admittedly exploratory in character. The general hypothetical propositions which motivated this investigation were 1) that the lobbyist enacts a clearly defined role in the legislative system distinguishable in terms of social and political background characteristics from other political actors; 2) that different kinds of interests who lobby the legislature are likely to be represented by different kinds of lobbyists; and, 3) that the lobby roll is likely to be given different orientations by different individuals. The data are presented in such a way as to probe these hypothesized differences. Further, it seems likely that differences may exist between national and state levels, and between states, in terms of the kinds of individuals who lobby, the types of interests who seek access, and the role orientations of lobbyists. While the opportunity to make inter-level and inter-state comparisons is limited, they will be made wherever possible.

I. THE BACKGROUNDS OF LOBBYISTS

Data relevant to the backgrounds of Oklahoma lobbyists are presented in Table 1. They indicate, to begin with, that the largest proportion of lobbyists in Oklahoma are older men, past middle-age, if we take forty-five as the dividing point. About 58 percent of the lobbyists were over that age, nearly a third were over fifty-five, and only a few of them were under thirty-five. Lobbying is a role played by men of some age and experience, and the number of very young men seems likely to be small.

All of the 1961 Oklahoma lobbyists who were registered were male — not a single woman registered as a lobbyist. And a very large proportion of them were permanent residents of the capital city.[6] If there is abroad a stereotypic picture of the state legislature victimized by professional lobbyists swarming to it from all about the state, it is mistaken. Slightly more than 65 percent of the 1961 lobbyists listed Oklahoma City as their place of residence. The next largest group resided in Tulsa, easily accessible to the capital via turnpikes. Most of the remainder came to the capital from Oklahoma's middlesized cities — El Reno, Enid, Shawnee, Midwest City, Edmond, and Norman.

One of the generalizations about Washington lobbyists which seems fairly secure is that a high proportion of those who lobby the Congress are lawyers. Milbrath's analysis of a sample of 100 Washington lobbyists registered in the first two quarters of 1956 showed that three-fourths were lawyers.[7] At the state level the proportion of lawyer-lobbyists may not be as large.[8] In Oklahoma at least, lawyers are certainly not the dominant occupational group. Only four individuals in the sample of 43 indicated their occupation as lawyer. The largest occupational group by far among Oklahoma lobbyists is the professional association staff (44%) — the executive secretary or legislative director employed by a private association — and only two of these had legal training. If there is a uniform difference between the occupational backgrounds of state and Washington lobbyists, it may perhaps result from the more limited scope of lobbying at the state level. Interests may be more directly represented at the state level by the legislators themselves, many of whom are lawyers.[9] In Oklahoma lobbying has become highly professionalized — performed by the full-time association bureaucrat.

Again, the Oklahoma lobbyist is both fairly well-educated and well-paid for his services. Three-fourths have had some college experience, and very nearly half had a college degree. None of the lobbyists earned a gross income in 1960 of less than $4,000, and almost 46 percent earned more than $10,000.

The profile of the Oklahoma lobbyist that emerges from these findings reveals that he is usually a middle-aged, male, well-trained and well-paid, full-time interest group staff member who resides in the capital city, and who is, at least for part of his time, expected by his principals to lobby the legislature. Now, what about his political activity other than lobbying?

It is not uncommon in impressionistic discussions about lobbyists to find it asserted that many lobbyists are themselves former members of the legislative body. We often say in political science that it is a big advantage in terms of differential access to have a legislator-lobbyist because he knows the "legislative terrain," can go on the house floor during sessions, and so on, and that therefore many lobbyists are former legislators. However, assumptions about the pervasiveness of legislator-lobbyists do not seem to be warranted. Both Zeller and Epstein, for instance, found the incidence of former legislators among lobbyists in New York and Wisconsin relatively small.[10] Similarly, Milbrath found that few Washington lobbyists had served in the Congress.[11] The Oklahoma data support these findings. Only about 12 percent of the 1961 Oklahoma lobbyists had legislative service, and nearly 84 percent had never served in the legislature. That does not mean that it is not an advantage to an interest group to have a legislator-lobbyist in its employ, but it does mean that the pervasiveness of such a phenomenon is fairly limited. Most lobbyists at the state level seem not to have had such experience. But what about the political experience other than service in the legislature?

In state politics at least, Oklahoma is strongly Democratic — and a very large proportion (77%) of the state's lobbyists are Democrats. But the same proportion have never served in any public or party office. In fact, the partisan activity (in terms of holding party office) of Oklahoma lobbyists is very slight. Again, the findings of Milbrath for Washington lobbyists are confirmed by the data for lobbyists in Oklahoma. He found that 77 percent of the national lobbyists he interviewed had never held party office, and 69 percent never held public office. Indeed, strong party attachments, which might be indicated by the holding of party offices or a campaign for public office, "can be impediments to lobbyists who work with people in both parties."[12]

The lobbyist then, tends to limit his political activity to representations with the legislature. His lobbying activities are his most important — and usually

Table 1   Distribution of Oklahoma lobbyists by selected personal and social-political background characteristics.

Characteristic		Number	Percent
Age			
26 – 35		5	11.6
36 – 45		13	30.2
46 – 55		12	27.9
56 – 70		13	30.2
Place of Residence			
Oklahoma City		28	65.2
Tulsa		6	13.9
Other City		9	20.9
Occupation			
Association Staff		19	44.2
Attorney-Insurance		7	16.2
Attorney	4		
Insurance	3		
Professional		10	23.3
Teacher	2		
Pharmacist	2		
Policeman	2		
Fireman	1		
Minister	2		
Editor	1		
Other		6	14.0
Farmer	2		
Electrician	2		
Locomotive Engineer	1		
Gas Plant Employee	1		
No Response		1	2.3
Education			
Grade School		3	7.0
Some High School		3	7.0
High School Diploma		4	9.3
Some College		12	27.9
College Degree		12	27.9
Graduate or Law Degree		9	20.9
Income			
Less than $4,000		0	0.0
$4,000 to $6,000		5	11.6
$6,000 to $8,000		12	27.9
$8,000 to $10,000		6	13.9
$10,000 to $20,000		18	41.9
More than $20,000		2	4.7

Table 1   continued

Characteristic	Number	Percent
Legislative Service		
Served in the Legislature	5	11.6
Did Not Serve in the Legislature	36	83.7
No Response	2	4.7
Political Preference		
Democratic	33	76.8
Republican	4	9.3
Independent	3	6.9
No Response	3	6.9
Non-Legislative Experience		
Held Public Office	5	11.6
Held Party Office	3	6.9
Held Both Party and Public Office	0	0.0
None	33	76.8
No Response	2	4.7
Number of Sessions Registered		
One	20	46.6
Two	4	9.3
Three	7	16.3
Four	6	13.9
Five or More	6	13.9
Time Spent Lobbying During Sessions		
Full-Time	8	18.6
3/4 Time	9	20.9
1/2 Time	9	20.9
Less Than 1/2 Time	17	39.6
Time Spent Lobbying Between Sessions		
Full-Time	1	2.3
3/4 Time	0	0.0
1/2 Time	4	9.3
Less Than 1/2 Time	38	88.4

only — political activities. And, in Oklahoma, even that is fairly limited. A surprisingly large number of Oklahoma lobbyists are "newcomers"; about 47 percent were registered as lobbyists for the first time in 1961. This may have been the consequence of an unusually large turnover in administrative positions in the state's private associations, or it may be, as Zeller suggested, that interest groups tend deliberately to send "novices" to lobby the legislature because of the importance of "new faces" in presenting old arguments. [13]

What is equally significant is that not a very large proportion of Oklahoma lobbyists spent all of their time during sessions in lobbying — less than 20 percent. Over 60 percent of the 1961 lobbyists spend only half of their time or less lobbying during the session. Between sessions (during which time the legislative council holds sessions) the vast majority of Oklahoma lobbyists spend less than half their time engaged in lobbying activities.

II. ANALYSIS BY TYPE OF ASSOCIATION

    In Oklahoma, as in other states, a wide variety of groups and associations seek to be represented before the legislature. The partial list below indicates interest groups for whom lobbyists registered in Oklahoma in 1961:

    Oklahomans for the Right to Work, Inc.
    Oklahoma State Firemen's Association
    Oklahoma State AFL-CIO
    Association of Casualty Companies
    Teamsters Joint Council #92
    Oklahoma Association of Electric Cooperatives
    Oklahoma Graduate Registered Pharmacists Association
    Sooner Alcoholic-Narcotics Education
    Oklahoma State Nursing Home Assn.
    American Mutual Insurance Alliance
    Oklahoma Wheat Growers Association
    Brotherhood of Locomotive Firemen and Enginemen
    Oklahoma State School Boards Association, Inc.
    Oklahoma Farm Bureau
    Oklahoma Farmers' Union
    Oklahoma Medical Association
    Oklahoma Retail Grocers' Association
    Police Pension and Retirement System
    Oklahoma Industrial Petroleum Association
    Oklahoma Police Legislative Committee
    Association of Oklahoma Fire and Casualty Companies
    Kansas-Oklahoma Division, Mid-Continent Oil and Gas Assn.
    Oklahoma Lumbermen's Association
    United Steel Workers of America
    Oklahoma Liquor Wholesalers Association
    Oklahoma Association of Insurance Agents
    Oklahoma Automobile Dealers Association
    Oklahoma Pharmaceutical Association
    Oklahoma Livestock Marketing Assn.
    Association Industries of Oklahoma
    Oklahoma Gasoline Retailers Assn.
    Oklahoma Education Association

Table 2 shows the number of lobbyists in the sample for each major type of association. Business lobbyists constituted the largest proportion (40%) of lobbyists, labor lobbyists, the second most numerous (19%), and farm and governmental group lobbyists, the third (16% each).[14]

    These lobbyists can be differentiated on the basis of their type of employer, as indicated by Table 3. For instance, business and farm group lobbyists tend to

Table 2   Types of associations represented by Oklahoma lobbyists.

Type of Association	Number	Percent
Business	17	39. 6
Farm	7	16. 3
Labor	8	18. 6
Professional	3	6. 9
Governmental	7	16. 3
Other	1	2. 3
Total	43	100. 0

be younger than those of other associations. Well over half of the business and farm lobbyists are under 45 years of age, while more than 70 percent of the labor, professional, and governmental group lobbyists are over 45 years old. Occupationally, a higher proportion of farm lobbyists than others are interest group bureaucrats, and, interestingly enough, all of the attorneys in the sample are lobbyists for business associations.

Business and professional lobbyists are, proportionately, better educated than other lobbyists, but the most striking educational difference among lobbyists involves the labor lobbyists. A much larger proportion of labor lobbyists than others have only a high school education or less, and none of the labor lobbyists in this sample had completed college. Similarly, Oklahoma lobbyists can be differentiated on the basis of income. Business and professional lobbyists are proportionately better paid than other lobbyists. About two-thirds of the business and professional lobbyists earn more than $10,000 per year, whereas 62 percent of the labor lobbyists earn less than that, and 71 percent of the farm and governmental lobbyists earn less.

In terms of lobbying experience and time invested in lobbying activity during the legislative session, there are striking distinctions among the lobbyists for different types of associations. Professional and farm groups in Oklahoma had the most inexperienced lobbyists in 1961, while half the labor lobbyists and 43 percent of the lobbyists for governmental groups had served four sessions or more. Business lobbyists lie between these two combinations. At the same time, lobbying by business, professional, and farm groups in Oklahoma is a part-time activity, and in this connection these groups are clearly distinguished from the labor and governmental ones. The lobbyist for the state labor federation or the education association devotes more of his time to lobbying than do his counterparts representing business associations, farmers, or doctors and pharmacists.

III. LOBBYISTS' ROLE ORIENTATION

The role of the lobbyist, like other political roles,[15] can be expected to be played in somewhat different form by different actors. That is to say, individuals in playing the lobby role give that role various orientations. Three distinctive lobbyist role orientations are suggested by the observations of a student of the Nebraska legislature:

The lobbyists are the visible forces surrounding the legislature and they frequently sit at the rear or alongside of the chamber itself and watch the daily proceedings. They may sit at the rear of rooms used for committee sessions or they may appear at the front also, since they are vocal when their interests are before the legislature especially at the committee stage. Many of them however, on other occasions are not inclined to speak before a committee. Rather they find it more successful to ply their trade in the passageways of the Capitol itself or over lunch, dinner, or a cup of coffee. A chat with a member of the legislature commands personal attention and one need not be adept at public speaking over light refreshments. Many lobbyists are mere watchdogs at best and are intended by those who hire them to send up storm signals when necessary. [16]

These observations suggest the following lobbyist role orientations:

The *Contact Man:* the lobbyist who conceives his job as primarily that of making contacts, personal acquaintanceships and friendships with individual legislators, and of maintaining these contacts. The Contact Man provides a direct communications link between the interest group and the individual member of the legislature. When faced with a legislative problem for his group, the lobbyist with a Contact Man orientation is likely to propose as the solution the personal contacting of as many members of the legislative body as possible, directly presenting the interest group's case to them.

The *Informant:* the lobbyist who sees his lobbying job as primarily that of effectively presenting his client's case by means of prepared information distributed to legislators, or usually by means of a prepared presentation before a legislative committee in the course of hearings. The Informant usually lobbies by testimony, and his lobbying is usually public rather than private.

The *Watchdog:* this is the lobbyist who conceives of his job as simply that of closely scrutinizing the legislative calendars, and carefully watching legislative activity, usually at a distance. His job is to be alert to developments in the legislative system that might affect his client group. Whenever legislation is proposed or introduced which affects his employer, his job is to signal his group so that it can attempt to bring pressure on legislators. His orientation is to alert the membership of his interest group to action when crucial legislative matters arise. In performing this role he may seldom enter the legislative halls or talk to individual members; he may never leave his office downtown in the capital city.

To be sure, many lobbyists at one time or another may do all three things; contact individual legislators, testify before legislative committees, and alert their group to action. However, a fairly successful effort was made with Oklahoma lobbyists to see if they could be distinguished in terms of their *primary,* or most salient role orientation. Oklahoma lobbyists were asked the question: "Would you say that, as a registered lobbyist you spent *most* of your time (1) talking to legislators, (2) appearing before legislative committees, (3) keeping your organization informed about what the legislature is doing, or (4) something else?" Furthermore, for the purpose of clarifying responses or confirming classifications, open-ended responses to two other questionnaire items were very helpful. Lobbyists were asked, "What particular legislation have you been most interested in during the 1961 session of the legislature?" In addition, lobbyists were asked, "In general, what are the most important things a legislative representative should do in order to be *most effective* in his job?" Open-ended items of this kind have limited value

Table 3 Oklahoma lobbyists by type of association and background characteristics.

Characteristic	Type of Association					
	Business (N = 17)	Farm (N = 7)	Labor (N = 8)	Professional (N = 3)	Governmental (N = 7)	Other (N = 1)
Age						
Under 45	10 (59%)	4 (57%)	2 (25%)	0	2 (29%)	0
Over 45	7 (41%)	3 (43%)	6 (75%)	3 (100%)	5 (71%)	1 (100%)
Occupation						
Association Staff	7 (41%)	5 (71%)	4 (50%)	1 (33%)	2 (29%)	0
Attorney-Insurance	7 (41%)	0	0	0	0	0
Professional	2 (12%)	0	0	2 (67%)	5 (71%)	1 (100%)
Other & No Response	1 (6%)	2 (29%)	4 (50%)	0	0	0
Education						
High School or Less	3 (18%)	0	6 (75%)	0	1 (14%)	0
Some College	3 (18%)	4 (57%)	2 (25%)	1 (33%)	2 (29%)	0
College, Graduate of	11 (64%)	3 (43%)	0	2 (67%)	4 (57%)	1 (100%)
Income						
Under $10,000	6 (35%)	5 (71%)	5 (62%)	1 (33%)	5 (71%)	1 (100%)
More than $10,000	11 (65%)	2 (29%)	3 (38%)	2 (67%)	2 (29%)	0
Number of Sessions Registered						
One	8 (47%)	5 (71%)	3 (38%)	2 (67%)	1 (14%)	1 (100%)
2 – 3	4 (24%)	2 (29%)	1 (12%)	1 (33%)	3 (43%)	0
4 or more	5 (29%)	0	4 (50%)	0	3 (43%)	0
Time Spent Lobbying During Session						
More than 1/2 Time	5 (30%)	2 (29%)	5 (63%)	1 (33%)	4 (58%)	0
1/2 Time or less	12 (70%)	5 (71%)	3 (47%)	2 (67%)	3 (42%)	1 (100%)

in a mailed questionnaire; on the other hand, responses to these items taken together made it possible to classify most of the Oklahoma lobbyists reliably into
three role-orientation categories: Contact Man, Informant, and Watchdog.

The proportions of lobbyists with these role orientations are shown in Table
4. More than half (53.3%) of the lobbyists in Oklahoma during the 1961 session of
the legislature were Contact Men, a finding which may temper the generalizations
of some who argue that old-fashioned lobbying at the state level has been eclipsed
by the employment of propaganda and mass communications techniques.[17] Few
Oklahoma lobbyists took the more limited Informant orientation, but more than
one-fourth were Watchdogs.

Table 4   Role orientations of Oklahoma lobbyists.

Role Orientation	*Number*	*Percent*
Contact Man	23	53.5
Informant	5	11.6
Watchdog	11	25.6
Unclassified	4	9.3
Total	43	100.0

Just as the Contact Man, the Informant, and the Watchdog differ in their
orientations to the lobby role, so we might hypothesize other differences between
them — differences in experience, occupation, income, association represented,
and so on. For instance, the data with respect to age suggest a possible age
differential among these role orientations, a higher proportion (48% under 45)
of Contact Men being younger, a larger proportion of older Informants (60% over
45), and an even larger percentage of older Watchdogs (73% over 34). This may
well be a real difference, in that the strenuousness of contact activity (leg work)
may require younger men than the other roles, while the Watchdog may be a rather
sedentary role. The occupational breakdown indicates a higher proportion (48%)
of Contact Men are permanent staff employees of the private associations, while
the largest single occupational category among Informants is the attorney-insurance
category (40%).

The Watchdog orientation contains the highest proportion of lobbyists with
a college, graduate, or law degree (64%). These are the educated observers of the
legislative process who are expected to be articulate about what the legislature is
doing, and frequently to prepare polished newsletters for "the membership" explaining legislative activity.

Informants appear to be paid less for their work, and a higher proportion
have served with only one session of the legislature. This kind of difference could
be the result of the limited demands of the Informant orientation, making for some
rotation in office of relative novices at lobbying activity. Or, it could be that some
newcomers to the lobby role tend to take the more limited Informant orientation
because of inexperience.

With respect to the time spent engaged in lobbying activity during the legislative session, Informants again spend the least time playing the lobby role (all
lobbied less than half the time during the session). A substantially greater pro-

portion (61%) of Contact Men lobby more than half the time during the session, while Watchdogs fall between the two. These data suggest that not only is the Contact Man orientation proportionately taken by a greater number of Oklahoma lobbyists, but also that the Contact Man is on the job a greater portion of the time when the legislature is in session. Clearly then, the most visible lobbying activity is carried on by the Contact Man. He is oriented to regular personal contacts with legislators, and he is on the job more of the time than other lobbyists.

Contact Man and Watchdog orientations are characterized by the spokesmen of different types of associations in roughly the same proportions. While the number of Informants is so small as to make any generalization risky, it is interesting to note that no labor lobbyist took the Informant orientation, nor did any lobbyists for groups related to governmental agencies.

IV. LOBBYISTS' VIEW OF THE LEGISLATIVE ROLE

Just as we can improve our predictability with respect to legislator-lobbyist relationships when we know something about the legislators' role orientations toward lobbyists and pressure groups,[18] so also we better understand these relationships when we can reveal the lobbyists, perceptions and expectations of the legislative role. While the questionnaires mailed to Oklahoma lobbyists required the kind of brevity which limited the data one could gather, inquiry was directed to lobbyists in connection with the representative dimension of the legislative role.

In addition, many of the Oklahoma lobbyists sampled volunteered attitudes about the legislators with whom they dealt. Although on this point there is no systematic data, in general Oklahoma lobbyists expressed very friendly and positive attitudes toward legislators.[19] Lobbyists not only frequently expressed the essentiality of being friendly, honest and honorable in their relations with legislators, but also they clearly believed that legislators behaved that way with respect to them. Among numerous expressions of attitudes of this sort, the following are illustrative:

> In the twenty years of lobbying in the interest of the (name of group) it is my conclusion that the members of the legislature are a hard working group of men dedicated to their jobs that certainly don't receive from the public as a whole credit for the things they are trying to do ... they spend long weary hours that the people back home know nothing about, and for which they receive little credit.

> I am ... of the opinion that the general public is very unfair in some of their criticisms of the Legislature. It has been my experience in dealing with the Legislature that almost without exception, the individual legislator is honest and a man of high integrity, trying to do a good job for the people he represents.

Only one lobbyist expressed hostility toward the legislature or toward individual legislators. General respect for legislators by lobbyists is probably essential for the effective enactment of the lobby role, and it is functional for the resolution of conflict in the legislative system.

As for lobbyists' perceptions and expectations about the representative role of legislators, Oklahoma lobbyists were asked, "As a close observer of the state legislature, whom do you believe legislators actually *best represent,* and whom do you think they ought to represent? 1) the majority of the voters of Oklahoma, 2) the principles of the political party to which they belong, 3) the people of their district, 4) the views of the predominant groups in their counties, or 5) their own idea and judgment of what is best in the long run, even if it is contrary to what others believe." The analysis of responses for this item is shown in Table 5. Lobbyists clearly tend to perceive the legislators' representative role in a particular way — more than 60 percent of the lobbyists perceive legislators as best representing the people of their districts or the dominant groups in their counties. Expectations shift to the more universalistic representative orientations and most notably away from the "views of groups in his county" category.

Table 5   Oklahoma lobbyists' perception of the legislative role.

Legislative Orientations	*Lobbyists Perceive Legislators Do Represent*		*Lobbyists Expect Legislators Ought to Represent*	
	Number	*Percent*	*Number*	*Percent*
Majority of State voters	3	5. 7	17	32. 1
Principles of his party	5	9. 4	1	1. 9
People of his district	21	39. 6	14	26. 4
Views of groups in his county	11	20. 8	3	5. 7
His own ideas, judgment	7	13. 2	14	26. 4
No Response	6	11. 3	4	7. 5
Totals [a]	53	100. 0	53	100. 0

[a] Totals equal more than the sample size (N=43) because some lobbyists chose more than one orientation. The equality of the totals was accidental.

When we examine our three role orientations in relationship to these perspectives on legislative representation, as is shown in Table 6, some differences emerge among lobbyists. A higher proportion of Contact Men perceive the legislator as a delegate from his district — representing the people of his district or the views of the dominant groups in his locality. If we make the assumption that Oklahoma legislators are predominantly district-oriented, [20] then it might be said that the Contact Man makes a more realistic appraisal of the legislators' representative role than other lobbyists. And, the largest proportion of Contact Men (as well as Informants, although the number of non-responses clouds the data) normatively approve the constituency orientation of the legislator. When the Contact Man moves away from district orientation in his normative expectations about the legislative role. Table 6 suggests that he is more willing to rely on the legislators' own judgment, while other lobbyists more likely focus on the more diffuse orientations of the voters of the state as a whole or the principles of the legislators' party. Thus, althouth we have here very limited data, it certainly suggests that the Contact Man is in closer touch with the legislator in terms of their role relationships, and that the Contact Man has a more central place in the legislative system conceived as a system of reciprocally interacting roles.

Table 6 Oklahoma lobbyists' role orientations and perception of the legislative role.

Legislative Orientation	Lobbyists Perceive Legislators Do Represent				Lobbyists Expect Legislators Ought to Represent			
	Contact Man	Informant	Watchdog	Uncl.	Contact Man	Informant	Watchdog	Uncl.
Majority of State voters	0	1 (17%)	1 (7%)	1 (14%)	7 (27%)	3 (43%)	4 (27%)	3 (60%)
Principles of his party	1 (4%)	1 (17%)	2 (13%)	1 (14%)	0	0	1 (7%)	0
People of his district	12 (48%)	1 (17%)	6 (40%)	2 (29%)	9 (35%)	2 (29%)	3 (20%)	0
Views of groups in his county	8 (32%)	1 (17%)	2 (13%)	0	1 (4%)	1 (14%)	1 (7%)	0
His own ideas, judgment	2 (8%)	0	2 (13%)	3 (43%)	9 (35%)	0	3 (20%)	2 (40%)
No Response	2 (8%)	2 (33%)	2 (13%)	0	0	1 (14%)	3 (20%)	0
Total[a]	25 (100%)	6 (101%)	15 (99%)	7 (100%)	26 (101%)	7 (100%)	15 (101%)	5 (100%)

[a]Totals equal more than the same size because some lobbyists chose more than one orientation.

V. CONCLUSIONS

The conclusions stemming from analysis of Oklahoma lobbyists, while tentative and hypothetical, can be classified briefly as follows:

(1) *By the kinds of individuals who play the lobby role:*

(a) The lobby role tends to be played by professional staff employees of private interest groups rather than by individuals in other occupations (i.e., lawyers, insurance agents, teachers, farmers, and the like).

(b) Most lobbyists have not served in the legislature, nor held other party or public offices. Lobbying tends to be a self-contained kind of political activity, recruiting few individuals from other modes of political activity.

(c) Lobbyists are ordinarily engaged in activities other than lobbying. Most lobbyists spend only half their time or less lobbying during the session, and less than half of the time between sessions of the legislature. Also, while most lobbyists have engaged in lobbying for more than one session, a large proportion are newcomers.

(d) In terms of personal characteristics, lobbyists tend to be past middle age, fairly well-educated, relatively well-paid, and residents of the state capital city.

(2) *By the kinds of interest groups for whom lobbyists work:*

(a) A greater proportion of lobbyists are employed by business groups than by other groups, and business and professional lobbyists tend to be both better-educated and better-paid for their services than lobbyists for other groups.

(b) Labor and governmental group lobbyists tend to have more lobbying experience, and tend to devote more of their time to lobbying activity during legislative sessions than other lobbyists.

(c) Farm lobbyists tend to be professional interest group employees more than lobbyists for other kinds of groups, and farm and business group lobbyists tend to be younger than labor, professional, and governmental group lobbyists.

(3) *By the role orientations of lobbyists:*

(a) Lobbyists tend to exhibit differential role orientations, and can be differentiated as either Contact Men, Informants, or Watchdogs. They tend to take the Contact Man role orientation more than that of the Informant or Watchdog.

(b) These distinctive lobby role orientations may, in part, be a function of age; Contact Men tend to be youngest, Informants next in proportion of older individuals, and Watchdogs oldest.

(c) Contact Men tend to spend more time engaged in lobbying activities during the legislative session, Watchdogs less time, and Informants least time. Not only are Informants least involved, but also they tend to be paid less and are more likely to be novices at lobbying than Contact Men or Watchdogs.

(d) More Contact Men represent business and labor groups than Informants or Watchdogs, more Informants speak for farm and professional groups, and Contact Men and Watchdogs represent governmental groups more than Informants.

(e) Lobbyists tend to *perceive* the legislative role in terms of the immediate representation of the legislator's district rather than in broader terms. But their normative expectations tend to go in the broader direction in that more lobbyists expect legislators ought to represent the majority of the voters of the state and his own ideas and judgment on issues.

(f) Contact Men tend to perceive the legislator as a delegate from his district more than Informants and Watchdogs, and both Contact Men and Informants tend normatively to approve the local orientation of the legislator more than Watchdogs.

This analysis clarifies some of our assumptions about lobbyists, and, it is hoped, illuminates some of the influences operating upon the legislative process. It helps us to avoid over-simplified assumptions about relationships between pressure groups and legislators, and to design research so as to capture significant differentials in the legislative role system.

NOTES

1. The literature has become voluminous. The major treatments are: David B. Truman, *The Governmental Process* (New York, 1951), Donald C. Blaisdell, *American Democracy Under Pressure* (New York, 1957); Henry W. Ehrmann (ed.), *Interest Groups on Four Continents* (Pittsburgh, 1960); and Donald C. Blaisdell (ed.), "Unofficial Government: Pressure Groups and Lobbies," *Annals of the American Academy of Political and Social Science,* Vol. 319 (September, 1958), pp. 1-157.

2. See, for instance, John C. Wahlke and Heinz Eulau (eds.), *Legislative Behavior: A Reader in Theory and Research* (Glencoe, 1959); Julius Turner, *Party and Constituency: Pressure on Congress* (Baltimore, 1951); Duncan MacRae, Jr., *Dimensions of Congressional Voting* (Berkeley and Los Angeles, 1958); David B. Truman, *The Congressional Party* (New York, 1959); and Donald R. Matthews, *U. S. Senators and Their World* (Chapel Hill, 1960).

3. See Lester W. Milbrath, "Lobbying as a Communication Process," *Public Opinion Quarterly,* Vol. 24 (Spring, 1960), pp. 32-53. A recent contribution of considerable interest in the systematic study of lobbyists has been made by Walter D. DeVries. See his *The Michigan Lobbyist: A Study in the Bases and Perceptions of Effectiveness* (unpublished Ph. D. dissertation, Michigan State University, 1960).

4. The only variables available for the entire population were age, place of residence, and type of association represented. In each case, there was not a statistically significant difference between respondents sampled and respondents not sampled (using the X^2 model). One registered lobbyist refused to return the questionnaire, but wrote the author protesting that he was not a lobbyist — "the rules of the State Legislature require that I obtain a permit as a lobbyist in order to appear at the capitol to watch any proposed legislation" that might affect his group. The hesitancy of a few registered lobbyists to be identified as such is, presumably, a feedback from widespread public distrust of the lobbying process. Three lobbyists who returned questionnaires indicated they did not think they should be regarded as lobbyists. One wrote a covering letter in which he said "at no time have I felt that I should be considered as a lobbyist. The reason for this is due to the fact that (our association) in these years that I have been associated with them, (has) never instigated legislative pronouncements that would do anything other than (benefit) the general public."

5. The number of registered lobbyists varies a good deal from one state to another, as one might well expect. Some notion of the range is indicated by these figures

for selected states for 1952-53: Idaho, 3; South Carolina, 11; New Hampshire, 61; South Dakota, 64; Kentucky, 69; Vermont, 81; Virginia, 88; Indiana, 94; New York, 113; Maryland, 119; North Dakota, 137; Iowa, 143; North Carolina, 152; Wisconsin, 254; Massachusetts, 295; Florida, 303; Michigan, 310; Maine, 342; Kansas, 365; California, 422. See Belle Zeller, "The State Lobby Laws," *The Book of the States, 1954-1955* (Chicago, 1954), pp. 130-4.

6. Compare Charles D. Hounshell, *The Legislative Process in Virginia* (Charlottesville, 1951), pp. 45-6.

7. Lester W. Milbrath, "The Political Party Activity of Washington Lobbyists," *Journal of Politics*, Vol. 20 (May, 1958), pp. 339-52.

8. Although Hounshell maintained that three-fourths of the Virginia lobbyists in 1948 were lawyers. See Hounshell, *op. cit.*, p. 46.

9. See Wilder Crane, Jr., "A Test of Effectiveness of Interest-Group Pressures on Legislators," *Southwestern Social Science Quarterly*, Vol. 41 (December, 1960), pp. 335-40.

10. Belle Zeller, *Pressure Politics in New York* (New York, 1937), p. 249; and, Leon D. Epstein, *Politics in Wisconsin* (Madison, 1958), pp. 118-9. In Wisconsin a smaller proportion of ex-legislators serve as lobbyists than in Oklahoma. Epstein further found that, of all ex-legislators in Wisconsin from 1919-1953, only 17.5% were ever registered as lobbyists. See also, E. Pendleton Herring, *Group Representation Before Congress* (Baltimore, 1929), pp. 54-7.

11. Milbrath, "The Political Party Activity of Washington Lobbyists," *op. cit.*, p. 346.

12. Milbrath, "The Political Party Activity of Washington Lobbyists," *op. cit.*, p. 346. Milbrath's findings are extremely valuable, and provide a basis for comparative analyses.

13. Belle Zeller found the same to have been true in New York in the late 1930s. See her *Pressure Politics in New York*, pp. 247-9.

14. The predominance of business lobbyists may be fairly general in the state legislative system. See Hounshell, *op. cit.*, p. 45, for pertinent remarks about Virginia lobbyists. More business groups are represented at the Nebraska legislature than any other type — 55% of the associations and groups (not lobbyists) registered in Nebraska in 1955 were business groups. A list of groups registered in 1955 can be found in Adam C. Breckenridge, *One House For Two: Nebraska's Unicameral Legislature* (Washington, D.C., 1957), pp. 92-3.

15. For instance, the roles of state legislators have been differentiated by Heinz Eulau, John C. Wahlke, William Buchanan, and LeRoy C. Ferguson, "The Role of the Representative: Some Empirical Observations on the Theory of Edmund Burke," *American Political Science Review*, Vol. 53 (September, 1959), pp. 742-56.

16. Breckenridge, *op. cit.*, p. 40.

17. Lobbying at the state and national levels may differ in this respect. Milbrath argues that the large number of lobbyists in Washington, and the resultant competition for the time and attention of congressmen, has meant that a large proportion of Washington lobbyists (75%) spend less than 10 percent of their time calling on members of Congress. On the other hand, he found that 65 out of 101 lobbyists "believe that their most effective tactics is the personal presentation of their case to the office-holder." See his "Lobbying as a Communication Process," *op. cit.*, p. 37.

18. See John C. Wahlke, William Buchanan, Heinz Eulau, and LeRoy C. Ferguson, "American State Legislators' Role Orientations Toward Pressure Groups," *Journal of Politics,* Vol. 22 (May, 1960), pp. 203-27. See also Oliver Garceau and Corinne Silverman, "A Pressure Group and the Pressured: A Case Report," *American Political Science Review,* Vol. 48 (September, 1954), pp. 672-01; and, Corinne Silverman, "The Legislators' View of the Legislative Process," *Public Opinion Quarterly,* Vol. 18 (Summer, 1954), pp. 180-90. For a discussion of deviant behavior in a legislative body with respect to lobbyists, see my "The Role of the Deviant in the State Legislative System: The Wisconsin Assembly," *Western Political Quarterly,* Vol. 14 (June, 1961), pp. 463, 465-6.

19. On the other hand, it has been suggested (Hounshell, *op. cit.*, p. 47) that lobbyists tend to take a *negative* position on legislative proposals — that they "most frequently appear to oppose legislation." The data for Oklahoma lobbyists suggest that this is not the case. Lobbyists were asked what particular legislation they had been most interested in during the 1961 session, and further whether they had been concerned with the enactment, defeat, or both, of that legislation. Forty-seven percent responded that they were concerned most with the enactment of legislation, 16 percent with defeat, and 37 percent, with both. In terms of lobbyists' role orientations, to be described forthwith, Informants were most interested in enactment of legislation, and Watchdogs least interested in defeat of proposed legislation.

20. The four-state study of state legislatures as role systems produced the finding that in three of the four states district areal role orientations were the most common. See Heinz Eulau, John C. Wahlke, William Buchanan, and LeRoy C. Ferguson, "The Role of The Representative...," *op. cit.*, p. 753. While we have no systematic data revealing Oklahoma legislative roles, continuous observation of the legislature over a period of several weeks leaves the impression that we are not likely to be off base in making this tentative assumption about Oklahoma lawmakers.

Some Effects of Interest Groups in State Politics

Lewis A. Froman, Jr.

The literature on interest groups is, by and large, either heavily abstract and theoretical or highly concrete and descriptive. There are, on the one hand, several attempts to provide a theoretical framework for the study of interest groups, the major foci being either "the group basis of politics"[1] or "mass society."[2] On the other hand are numerous case-studies which describe in some detail, either for a particular policy[3] or for a particular interest group,[4] relevant political activities which lead to inferred conclusions about the impact that such groups have on the issue or issues. What we lack, and what is needed to raise the study of interest groups to the level of empirically-based generalization, are studies which collect data and generalize about interest groups using multiple units of analysis.

This observation is not meant to depreciate or undervalue the important theoretical and descriptive contributions which have been made in the examination of the role of interest groups in governmental systems. It is simply to state a fact about the literature and to plead for more systematic data collection and empirically-based generalization from which verified propositions about interest groups may emerge.

I think there are two major reasons why the literature on interest groups lacks a comparative base. First, many of the concepts which are employed in theories about interest groups are difficult to operationalize for data collection. Such concepts as "cohesion," "access," "resources," etc., represent complex phenomena and would involve a good deal of effort to apply rigorously and empirically. Take, for example, the interesting proposition that, *ceteris paribus,* "interest groups with high cohesion are more effective than interest groups with low cohesion." Clearly this is an important assertion which attempts to explain why some interest groups may have more influence than others. How such a proposition might be tested is, unfortunately, also clear. Simply take a sample of interest groups, devise measures of group cohesion and political effectiveness, collect the data on both measures, and see whether the proposition is confirmed or invalidated.

Second, it is usually very difficult and expensive to collect data on a wide variety of groups which might then be used for purposes of generalization. Such data are not generally available, and what is available is often imcomplete, inaccurate, or both. Even to collect such relatively simple data as group size often presents serious problems in compiling membership lists, deciding who is a member and who isn't, perhaps identifying those who feel some allegiance to the group but who may participate in the activities of the group only minimally, and other equally

Reprinted from *American Political Science Review,* Vol. 60 (Dec. 1966), pp. 952-962, by permission of the author and the publisher.

I wish to thank Sheen T. Kassouf, Deane E. Neubauer, Jack W. Peltason, and Howard Rosenthal for their comments on an earlier draft of this paper.

knotty problems. To attempt to determine, across groups, what difference a particular independent variable (such as cohesion, group size, leadership ability, etc.)
may have in the distribution of political outcomes raises formidable data problems
indeed.

This paper will suggest how a comparative base for generalization about
the activity of interest groups may be developed. I will attempt to answer the
question: Do political systems that vary in the strength of their interest groups
also vary in a systematic way with regard to certain structural and output variables
within their respective political systems? That is, can we explain certain differences in political systems by knowing something about the strength of interest
groups within the system? The data to be employed will be for forty-eight state
governments within the United States.[5] It is by now comonplace to assert that states
may provide a convenient laboratory to test certain propositions about politics.
The number of states, the fact that they are all part of a larger political system
(and hence share many things in common) while at the same time providing a certain amount of diversity make the states a useful data source in which to generalize
and test political hypotheses.

THE FIRST SET OF DEPENDENT VARIABLES

Political scientists have long been interested in questions regarding constitutions and constitution-making. By and large the focus of attention has been
on national constitutions and more particularly the Constitution of the United States.
It is very difficult, however, to make generalizations about constitutions if the
unit of analysis is a single document.

What will concern us here is how state constitutions differ in certain respects from one another, and how these differences might be explained. There
are, of course, a large number of possible differences in state constitutions.
State constitutions may vary, for example, in the kinds of governments they establish (unicameral vs. bicameral legislatures, a large number of elected executive officials vs. a large number of appointed officials, elected vs. appointed
judiciaries, etc.). State constitutions may also vary in the detail in which they
cover various aspects of government, and in the discretion which they give to
public officials to carry out certain functions. They may also vary in the specific
content which they give to questions of public policy (labor practices, regulation
of utilities, transportation problems, etc.).

The differences among state constitutions which are of most interest to us
here have to do with how specific and comprehensive they are, how easy or difficult they are to amend, how often proposals are made to amend the constitution,
and how often the respective constitutions are in fact changed. More specifically,
there are four dependent variables in which we will be primarily interested.[6]

1. *Length of Constitution.* State constitutions vary greatly in their length.
We are not, however, interested in length of constitutions in and of itself but rather
assume that the longer the constitution the greater the range of activity it attempts
to cover and the more specific and detailed it is in its provisions. Length of constitution, then, will be used as an indirect measure of extent of coverage and
specificity.

2. *Number of Amendments Proposed.* What we are interested in here is the number of official proposals which have been made to amend the respective state constitutions. The measure to be employed will control for age of constitution by taking the number of proposed changes for each state and dividing by the number of years the constitution has been operative.

3. *Number of Amendments Adopted.* This measure is similar to the previous one except that amendments actually adopted rather than simply proposed is the unit employed. Age of constitution is again appropriately controlled.

4. *Percentage of Amendments Adopted.* This is the ratio of amendments adopted to amendments proposed for each state and is expressed in a simple percentage.

Table 1 gives some indication of how the states vary on these four measures.

Table 1   Median and range for states on the four dependent variables.

	Median	Range
Length of Constitution (No. of words)	15,000	4,840–227,000
Number of Amendments Proposed Per Year	1.35	.31–12.63
Number of Amendments Adopted Per Year	.65	.10–9.98
Percentage of Amendments Adopted	58%	23%–94%

Source: *The Book of the States, 1964–1965* (Chicago: The Council of State Governments, 1964), p. 12.

As can be seen from Table 1, there is a wide diversity among states with respect to these four variables. Now, assuming that constitutions are one of the mechanisms through which advantages and disadvantages are distributed in a political system, we would expect that differences in length of constitutions and the frequency with which they are amended would help us to understand, in some measure, how responsive states are to demands made by groups within the political system.

THE INDEPENDENT VARIABLE

The role of interest groups in political systems is an extremely important, and hotly contested, open question. At one level we can talk of the functions which most interest groups, or interest groups collectively, perform in political systems. David Truman, Robert Dahl, William Kornhauser, and V. O. Key, Jr., for example, suggest that, among other functions, interest groups:[7]

1. channel communications to decision-makers,
2. help structure alternative policy choices,
3. act as buffers between the government and the people,
4. help check demands made by others,
5. provide for functional representation,
6. compartmentalize access to decision-makers,
7. lead to a system of minorities rule,
8. provide people with an emotional outlet.

This kind of analysis helps us to understand how interest groups in general fit in with other aspects of a society and policy. What we are interested in here, however, is a somewhat different question. It would be useful to know whether variations in interest group strength make a difference with respect to structural and output variables of political systems. More specifically, do interest groups vary in strength from state to state, and if so, might this variation help to explain why certain other variables also vary?

The major question of this section, then, is how may states be classified according to strength of interest groups? The answer, "obviously," is that some measure of "strength" must be developed by which the states may be ranked. This task would, equally obviously, be an exceedingly difficult, expensive, and time-consuming enterprise.

It is possible, however, to employ a probably less valid and less reliable technique to measure interest group strength. The Committee on American Legislatures of the American Political Science Association sent questionnaires to political scientists located in the various states asking them to judge whether interest groups in their respective states were strong, moderately strong, or weak.[8] On the basis of the responses to this questionnaire the Committee then classified state interest groups into the three categories.

Judgmental measures are not unique with this study. Several psychological measures, for example, rely on this technique (rating scales of various kinds).[9] Seymour Martin Lipset's seminal piece on social requisites of democracy also relies heavily on a judgmental measure of whether countries are democratic and stable.[10] A recent comparative study of polyarchy also employs ratings on several variables.[11]

It is not that, if the authors mentioned above had their "druthers," they would choose this technique rather than another. It is simply that it has advantages in reducing crucial costs of research. The use of this type of measure certainly invites some criticisms, and where it is used it should be viewed as providing only tentative answers to the questions which it attempts to answer. It does, however, provide a useful first step until better resources become available.

On the basis of this classification of state interest group systems into strong, moderate, and weak, Harmon Zeigler, in a very useful study, relates this classification to other variables which help to show why states are likely to vary in strength of interest groups, and how such variation is related to political party structure and legislative cohesion. Zeigler finds that states with stronger interest groups are also more likely to be (1) one-party states, (2) states which have legislative parties with weak cohesion, (3) less urban, (4) less wealthy, and (5) less industrial. Table 2 presents these findings from Zeigler's study.

What we will do now is to employ the Committee's classification of state interest group systems and see whether this classification helps us to explain variations among the states in the four dependent variables previously described.[12]

THEORY, HYPOTHESES, AND FINDINGS

Why would one expect strength of interest groups and certain aspects of state constitutions to be related to one another, and what would be the expected relationships?

Table 2   The strength of pressure groups in varying political and economic situations.

Social Conditions	Types of Pressure System [a]		
	Strong [b]	Moderate [c]	Weak [d]
Party Competition	(24 states)	(14 states)	(7 states)
One–Party	33. 3%	0%	0%
Modified One–Party	37. 5%	42. 8%	0%
Two–Party	29. 1%	57. 1%	100. 0%
Cohesion of Parties in Legislature			
Weak Cohesion	75. 0%	14. 2%	0%
Moderate Cohesion	12. 5%	35. 7%	14. 2%
Strong Cohesion	12. 5%	50. 0%	85. 7%
Socio–Economic Variables			
Urban	58. 6%	65. 1%	73. 3%
Per Capita Income	$1900	$2335	$2450
Industrialization Index	88. 8	92. 8	94. 0

[a] Alaska, Hawaii, Idaho, New Hampshire, and North Dakota are not classified or included.

[b] Alabama, Arizona, Arkansas, California, Florida, Georgia, Iowa, Kentucky, Louisiana, Maine, Michigan, Minnesota, Mississippi, Montana, Nebraska, New Mexico, North Carolina, Oklahoma, Oregon, South Carolina, Tennessee, Texas, Washington, Wisconsin.

[c] Delaware, Illinois, Kansas, Maryland, Massachusetts, Nevada, New York, Ohio, Pennsylvania, South Dakota, Utah, Vermont, Virginia, West Virginia.

[d] Colorado, Connecticut, Indiana, Missouri, New Jersey, Rhode Island, Wyoming.

Source: Harmon Zeigler, "Interest Groups in the States," in Herbert Jacob and Kenneth N. Vines (eds.) *Politics in the American States* (Boston: Little, Brown, 1965), p. 114.

    The answer to the first part of the question, the theory underlying the expected associations, is that where interest groups are stronger one manifestation of this greater strength as compared with weaker interest group systems would be a larger number of requests for, and the actual giving of special privileges and advantages. This distribution of special advantages would be predicted to show up in a political system in a number of ways. For example, we might hypothesize that in states with stronger interest groups the latter would have relatively greater success with state legislatures in receiving legal protection and encouragement for their activities. It would also not be unreasonable to suppose that states with stronger interest groups would differ with respect to the ways in which laws are administered and adjudicated. It would be interesting, for example, to observe if such states also differ in the manner in which administrative personnel are recruited and appointed and, consequently, in the decisions which are reached concerning various regulations and distributions within the political system. An investigation of part of this hypothesis will appear near the end of this paper.

We would also, however, expect there to be a relationship between strength of interest groups and state constitutions. If we assume that constitutions essentially lay out important ground rules by which the game of politics will be played, and that they may place certain restrictions or give certain dispensations to the players involved in the game, then we would expect variations in state constitutions to be intimately related to variations in other aspects of political systems. Generally, we would expect state constitutions in states which have stronger interest groups to reflect, in certain systematic ways, a greater amount of interest group activity than do the constitutions in states with weaker interest groups. More specifically, we would hypothesize the following relationships:

1. The stronger the interest groups, the greater the length of state constitutions.

This hypothesis follows in that states with stronger interest groups would be predicted to make greater efforts to achieve special advantage through constitutional provisions which refer to their activities. These efforts would result in longer and more detailed constitutions than in states with weaker interest groups. Table 3 presents data which test this hypothesis.

As can be seen from Table 3, the twenty-four states which are classified as strong-interest-group states have constitutions which average 33,233 words in length; the fourteen states which are classified as moderate in interest group strength have constitutions which average 17,985 in length; and the seven states which are classified as weak in interest group strength have constitutions which average 14,828 in length.

2. The stronger the interest groups, the greater the number of proposed amendments.

If the theory we have suggested is correct, then we would expect states with strong interest groups to have more proposals for constitutional changes than states with moderately strong interest groups which in turn, would have more proposals for changes than would states with weak interest groups. This hypothesis would reflect a greater number of attempts to gain some special constitutional status.

The data from Table 3 confirm this hypothesis. The average number of proposed amendments per year in states with strong interest groups is 2.97, in states with moderate interest groups 1.14, and in states with weak interest groups .68.

3. The stronger the interest groups, the greater the number of amendments which are adopted.

As with proposed amendments, we would expect stronger interest group states to have a larger number of changes in the constitution than in states with less strong interest groups.

From Table 3 we can see that the data confirm the hypothesis. Strong interest-group states have an average of 1.58 amendments adopted per year, moderate states an average of .76, weak interest-group states an average of .41.

Additional support for this hypothesis, and for the theory being proposed here, is the following. We would also expect states with longer constitutions to have a greater number of changes in their constitutions. This follows if we assume, as we have been doing, that longer constitutions indicate a larger range of activities

Table 3   Relationships between strength of interest groups and three dependent
             variables.

Strength of Interest Groups	Average Length of Constitution	N^a	Average No. of Proposed Amendments per year	N^b	Average No. of Adopted Amendments per year	N^c
Strong	33,233	24	2.97	19	1.58	22
Moderate	17,985	14	1.14	12	.76	14
Weak	14,828	7	.68	5	.41	7

[a] Alaska and Hawaii are excluded from this and the following tables. In addition, Idaho, New Hampshire, and North Dakota were not classified by strength of interest groups.

[b] Arkansas, Colorado, Connecticut, Delaware, Iowa, Michigan, North Carolina, Utah, and Washington are excluded for lack of data.

[c] Michigan and North Carolina are excluded for lack of data.

Sources: *The Book of the States, 1964–1965* (Chicago: The Council of State Governments, 1964), pp. 12–15, and Harmon Zeigler, "Interest Groups in the States," in Herbert Jacob and Kenneth N. Vines, (eds.), *Politics in the American States* (Boston: Little, Brown, 1965), p. 114.

provided for in the constitution, and a greater specificity and detail. The greater constitutional comprehensiveness in states with longer constitutions would also suggest a greater need to revise the constitution as economic, social, and political changes occur. Hence we would predict that the longer the constitution, the greater the number of amendments. Table 4 provides data on this point.

As Table 4 indicates, the average number of amendments adopted per year increases as the average length of the constitution increases.

Since states with stronger interest groups tend to have longer constitutions (Table 3), and since states with longer constitutions tend to have a greater number of amendments (Table 4), hypothesis three, the stronger the interest group, the greater the number of amendments which are adopted, is directly derivable from these other hypotheses. The fact that this three-step chain of hypotheses is true at all three steps lends additional validity to the general theory being proposed here. It is also interesting to note that both strength of interest groups and length of constitution have an independent effect on the number of amendments adopted. When each is held constant, the relationship with the other and number of amendments adopted is attenuated, but still present.

4. States with moderately strong interest groups will have the highest percentage of amendments adopted.

This hypothesis, although not immediately obvious, follows from the following argument. To this point our data indicate a positive relationship between strength of interest groups and both number of amendments proposed and number of amendments adopted. It is clear, however, that it is easier to propose an amendment than to get an amendment adopted. States with strong interest groups, then, would be expected to have a larger number of amendments proposed and a larger number of amendments adopted, but since it is easier to propose amendments

Table 4   Relationship between length of constitution and number of constitutional amendments adopted.

Length of Constitution	Average No. of Adopted Amendments per year	N [a]
Less than 10,000 words	.27	7
10,000–19,999	.67	18
20,000–29,999	.78	12
30,000 & over	3.04	9

[a] Michigan and North Carolina are excluded for lack of data.
Source: *The Book of the States, 1964-1965* (Chicago: The Council of State Governments, 1964), pp. 12-15.

Table 5   Relationship between strength of interest groups and percentage of proposed amendments adopted.

Strength of interest groups	Average % of Amendments Adopted	N [a]
Strong	54.8%	19
Moderate	62.8%	12
Weak	52.6%	5

[a] See footnote 3, Table 3.
Source: See Table 3.

Table 6   Relationship between difficulty in amending the constitution and average number of amendments adopted per year.

Score on Difficulty of Amending Constitution	Average No. of Adopted Amendments per year	N [a]
Less than 3.5	1.29	15
4–5	1.32	16
5.5–9	.66	15

[a] Michigan and North Carolina are excluded for lack of data.
Source: See Table 4.

than to have them ratified, their rate of success would not be expected to be the largest among the states.

Similarly, states with weak interest groups have the fewest number of amendments proposed and the fewest number of amendments adopted. But, again, since it is easier to propose than to adopt, weak interest group states would not have the highest rate of success. This reasoning would predict that states with moderately strong interest groups would have the highest ratio of amendments adopted to amendments proposed. Table 5 provides data on this hypothesis.

As Table 5 indicates, it is the states with moderately strong interest groups that have the highest percentage of amendments which are proposed adopted. States with strong interest groups have a ratio of adopted amendments to proposed amendments of 54.8%, states with moderate interest groups 62.8%, and states with weak interest groups 52.6%. Those states with the weakest interest groups have the lowest rate of success, but those states with the strongest interest groups do not have the highest rate of success. Indeed, their rate of success is much closer to weak interest group states than to moderately strong ones.

A POSSIBLE ALTERNATIVE EXPLANATION

Before accepting the above theory and hypotheses relating strength of interest groups to variations in state constitutions, it might be useful to explore a possible alternative explanation.

States also differ considerably in the extent to which it is easy or difficult to amend their constitutions. Some states, for example, require a two-thirds or three-fifths majority of the legislature and/or passage by two successive legislatures to propose and ratify constitutional amendments. All states but one also require a popular referendum after legislative action, but require differing majorities in the referendum. In addition, states also differ on whether they allow constitutional amendments to be proposed by initiative, and have different ways of calling together and proposing amendments in constitutional conventions. [13]

Given these widely varying practices in states, an index of difficulty of proposing and ratifying constitutional amendments was constructed. This index is derived from the three major ways in which the constitution may be amended and therefore reflects: (1) legislative difficulty, (2) presence or absence of the initiative, and (3) constitutional convention difficulty in proposing and ratifying constitutional amendments. One point was given to each state if a majority greater than a simple majority is required in the legislature, one point if approval by two sessions is needed, and one point if ratification by a majority vote in the election rather than a majority vote on the amendment is required. Additionally, one point is given if there are no initiative procedures in the state. With regard to constitutional conventions, one point is given if greater than a majority in the legislature is required to call a constitutional convention, one point if approval is needed by two sessions of the legislature, one point if a referendum on whether there should be a constitutional convention is necessary, one point if a majority in the election rather than a majority on the proposition is required, one point if after the constitutional convention ratification of the amendment is required (one-half point is given if no provision is in the constitution for a referendum ratifying the amendment but the legislature may determine if a referendum is necessary), and one point if ratification requires a majority in the election rather than a majority on the amendment.

This index of difficulty of amending the constitution, then, can vary from 0 to 10. The median score was 4, the range from 1 to 9. Fifteen states had scores of 3.5 or less, sixteen had scores from 4 to 5, and fifteen had scores from 5.5 to 9.

Given this wide range in difficulty in amending state constitutions, we would expect that such variation might have an impact on the number of amendments which are adopted by the states. More specifically, we would hypothesize that the greater the difficulty in amending the constitution, the fewer the number of amendments which will be adopted. Table 6 provides the data to test this hypothesis.

Table 6 only partially confirms the hypothesis. Those states with the most difficult procedures to amend the constitution do have fewer amendments adopted, but the states with the easiest procedures do not have the greatest number of amendments adopted.

This partial explanation of why states vary in the number of changes in their constitutions may be further explained, however, by variation in states in strength of interest groups. Consistent with our theory, it may be proposed that states would be expected to vary in ease or difficulty in amending their constitutions by strength of interest groups. That is, we would expect the following hypothesis to be true: the stronger the interest groups, the less the difficulty in amending the constitution. Table 7 presents data on this hypothesis.

The data from Table 7 confirm the relationship between strength of interest groups and difficulty of amending the constitution. States with strong interest groups have a difficulty score of 4.21, states with moderately strong interest groups have a score of 5.00, and states with weak interest groups have a difficulty score of 5.65. Hence we may say that even though the number of changes in the constitution is related to difficulty of amending the constitution as well as strength of interest groups, the reason why this additional explanation is at least partially true is because strength of interest groups is also related to difficulty of amending the constitution.

One further piece of data will also help to confirm the theory being proposed here. Since states with strong interest groups have longer constitutions (Table 3), and since strong interest group states also have constitutions which are easier to amend (Table 3), we would also expect there to be a relationship between length of constitution and ease of amendment. More specifically we would

Table 7   Relationship between strength of interest groups and difficulty of amending the constitution.

Strength of Interest Groups	Average Difficulty of Amending the Constitution	N
Strong	4.21	24
Moderate	5.00	14
Weak	5.65	7

Sources: See footnote 3, Table 3.

Table 8   Relationship between length of constitution and difficulty of amending state constitution.

Length of Constitution	Average Difficulty of Amending the Constitution	N^a
Less than 10,000 words	6.29	7
10,000 - 19,999	4.58	18
20,000 - 29,999	4.71	12
30,000 & over	4.11	9

[a] Michigan and North Carolina are excluded for lack of data.
Source: See Table 4.

hypothesize the greater the length of the constitution, the less the difficulty in amending the constitution. Table 8 provides data on this hypothesis.

As can be seen from the Table, this hypothesis is for the most part confirmed. The states with the shortest constitutions have the most difficult amending procedures, and the states with the longest constitutions have the easiest amending procedures, although the two sets of states in the middle do not fall in the predicted order.

Summing up this section, then, there is a partial relationship between the difficulty of amending the constitution and the number of changes made in the constitution. However, this relationship can be accounted for by the fact that there is also a relationship between strength of interest groups and ease of amending the constitution. The alternative explanation, then, may be rejected and the original explanation retained. Strength of interest groups seems to be a major factor in explaining why states vary with regard to certain constitutional practices.

THE SECOND SET OF DEPENDENT VARIABLES

In the previous sections our concern was with the effect of strength of interest groups on some general features of state constitutions. In this section the focus will shift slightly to a combined constitutional-legislative variable, the method of selection of state officials. States differ widely in the number of office-holders who are appointed as opposed to elected to office. We will be concerned, in the following, with an explanation of this variation.

A priori one might predict that states with stronger interest groups would be *either* more likely or less likely to have a larger number of elected as opposed to appointed officials. The major political variable in either prediction is the ability of interest groups to influence the selection of personnel. Those who would predict that interest groups will have more influence if governmental officials are appointed rather than elected would suggest that interest groups would prefer the politics of dealing with the governor and, in some instances, the legislature,

Table 9   Relationship between strength of interest groups and four dependent variables.

Strength of Interest Groups	Average No. of State Elected Officials	Average No. of State Agencies With Elected Officials	% of Elected State Public Utility Com- missions	% of Elected State Courts of Last Resort	N
Strong	19.54	9.17	50%	79%	24
Moderate	14.64	7.14	7%	57%	14
Weak	7.71	5.86	0%	43%	7

Source: *The Book of the States, 1964-1965* (Chicago: The Council of State Governments, 1964).

to the uncertainties of electoral politics. If this hypothesis is combined with the
already-established hypothesis that strength of interest group is related to political outcomes, then one could predict that states with stronger interest groups
would have a greater number of appointed rather than elected officials.

On the other hand one could, with equal logic, agree that interest groups
do want to maintain influence over the selection of governmental personnel but
that such influence can better be established if personnel are elected rather than
appointed. A governor is likely to be responsive to a wide variety of state interests. In some cases he may be a member of a political party which is less responsive to the concerns of certain interest groups. Gubernatorial appointment
combined with legislative confirmation would provide some check on the governor,
but interest groups, on balance, might be better able to influence the selection
of personnel if such persons were elected in what, for minor positions, would
be relatively low turnout elections rather than take a chance with governors. Proponents of this view would deduce an opposite conclusion from that previously
advanced: stronger interest group states would have a larger number of elected
rather than appointed officials.

How does one choose between these competing theories? Since the logic
of each produces contradictory conclusions we might test those conclusions. Although this does not produce a direct test of the competing theories it does provide
an indirect test, since the conclusions drawn from each are clearly contrary to
each other. Evidence on these derivative hypotheses may support one theory as
opposed to the other.

The relationship between interest group strength and selection of governmental officials will be tested in four different ways. First, what is the relationship between interest group strength and the total number of state officials who
are elected? Second, what is the relationship of interest group strength and the
number of state agencies with elected officials? This relationship will give us
some idea of the range of offices which are subject to election.

Each of these variables gives an indication of the overall elective-appointive
system within and among states. But what about specific instances? Third, then,
what is the relationship between strength of interest groups and the selection of
state public utility commissions? Fourth, what is the relationship of strength of
interest groups with the selection of judges on state courts of last resort? Table
9 provides data to test these four relationships.

From Table 9 it is clear, in each instance, that states with strong interest groups rely more heavily on election of state officials than do states with weaker interest groups. The stronger the interest groups the greater the number of elected officials, the greater the number of state agencies with elected officials, the greater the likelihood that public utility commissions will be elected, and the greater the probability that judges on state courts of last resort will be elected.

The data, then, lend support to the second of the alternative theories. States with stronger interest groups are better able to isolate governmental agencies and officials from executive or legislative influence than are states with weaker interest groups, and are more likely to have agencies of government which are independent from the governor and legislature.

One further bit of evidence lends additional support to this conclusion. Given the evidence that elections rather than appointments are related to strong interest groups, it may also be inferred that those states with strong interest groups would have shorter terms of office than those states with weaker interest groups. This would provide additional control by interest groups by making governmental officials run for office more frequently and hence be less independent from outside influence. Table 10 provides data on terms of office of judges of state courts of last resort.

The data in Table 10 confirm this hypothesis. Length of term for judges on state courts of last resort decreases as strength of interest groups increases.

SUMMARY AND CONCLUSIONS

We began our discussion by suggesting that the literature on interest groups, generally speaking, lacks studies which attempt to test generalizations about interest group activity. The emphasis on theory and/or case studies we attributed to two factors: (1) difficulty in operationalizing theoretical concepts, and (2) difficulty and expense in collecting data for many interest groups or on many policies.

This study attempts to test several propositions about the relationship between strength of interest groups and variations among states with regard to structural and output variables centering on the constitution and the election of state officials. A theory was developed which explained why state governments would have such wide variations in their constitutions and the political processes

Table 10   Relationship between strength of interest groups and average length of term of judges on state courts of last resort.

Strength of Interest Groups	Average Length of Term	N
Strong	7. 58	24
Moderate	11. 21	14
Weak	13. 43	7

Source: *The Book of the States, 1964-1965* (Chicago: The Council of State Governments, 1964).

surrounding them. More specifically the following hypotheses about strength of interest groups were tested and confirmed:

1. The stronger the interest groups, the greater the length of the state constitutions.
2. The stronger the interest groups, the greater the number of proposed amendments.
3. The stronger the interest groups, the greater the number of amendments which are adopted.
4. States with moderately strong interest groups will have the highest percentage of amendments adopted.
5. The stronger the interest groups, the less the difficulty in amending the constitution.
6. The stronger the interest groups, the greater the number of state elected officials.
7. The stronger the interest groups, the greater the number of state agencies with elected officials.
8. The stronger the interest groups, the greater the likelihood that state public utility commissions will be elected.
9. The stronger the interest groups, the greater the probability that judges on state courts of last resort will be elected.
10. The stronger the interest groups, the shorter will be the terms of office of judges on state courts of last resort.

In addition, the following subsidiary hypotheses were also tested.

11. The longer the constitution, the greater the number of amendments which are adopted.
12. The longer the constitution, the less the difficulty in amending the constitution.
13. The greater the difficulty in amending the constitution, the fewer the number of amendments which will be adopted (partially confirmed).

All of these hypotheses confirm the theory which has been proposed here. Variation in strength of interest groups does have an impact on political systems. It was expected that states with stronger interest groups would be characterized by attempts by those groups to gain special advantages. Since constitutions are one of the vehicles through which advantages and disadvantages are distributed in political systems, these attempts would have an effect on the length of the constitution, the amending procedures within the states, and the number of changes which are made. Since the selection of governmental personnel is also of primary concern to interest groups, it would be expected that differences in selection procedures would also vary by interest group strength. The data presented in this paper lend credence to these suppositions.

STATISTICAL APPENDIX

A political scientist must, with some data projects, give attention to the possible conflict between data analysis sophistication and general readability. In the text I have attempted to present the findings in the simplest way possible consistent with accuracy and at least minimum precision. However, there are techniques of data analysis which provide more powerful data manipulation. One of these techniques, appropriate for this analysis, is multiple regression analysis. This statistical appendix will present the findings in terms of correlation coefficients, holding some variables constant where appropriate.

Two points, however, should be made immediately. First, the results of the multiple regression analysis are entirely consistent with the findings already reported. The interpretation of the data also remains the same. Second, the entire analysis was performed in two steps, one with all of the states (in most cases this is forty-five states), and the second with the eleven former Confederate states dropped from the analysis. It has been found consistently that in many respects southern states differ from northern states. However, the propositions reported here are true whether one includes or excludes the southern states.

The correlation coefficients for the propositions listed in the summary in the same numerical order, are as follows (correlations in parentheses exclude the southern states):

1. .36 (.34), 2. .40 (.33), 3. .30 (.25), 4. curvilinear, 5. -.30 (-.31), 6. .26 (.27), 7. .52 (.45), 8. .41 (.45), 9. .32 (.31) 10. -.43 (-.42), 11. .53 (.53), 12. -.24 (-.24), 13. -.12 (-.17) (partial relationship reported).

In addition, the relationship between interest group strength and number of constitutional amendments adopted, with length of constitution held constant is .19. Similarly, the relationship between interest group strength and number of constitutional amendments adopted, with difficulty of amending the constitution held constant is .24.

The relationship between strength of interest groups and number of state elected officials is not affected by population size.

NOTES

1. See, for example, David B. Truman, *The Governmental Process* (New York: Knopf, 1951), Chapters 2 and 3; Earl Latham, *The Group Basis of Politics* (Ithaca: Cornell University Press, 1952), Chapter 1; E. E. Schattschneider, *The Semisovereign People* (New York: Holt, Rinehart & Winston, 1960); and Harmon Zeigler, *Interest Groups in American Society* (Englewood Cliffs: Prentice-Hall, 1964), Chapters 1-3. There is also a voluminous journal literature discussing the pros and cons of "the group approach." See, for example, Stanley Rothman, "Systematic Political Theory: Observations on the Group Approach," *American Political Science Review*, 54 (March, 1960), 15-33.

2. See William Kornhauser, *The Politics of Mass Society* (New York: Free Press, 1959).

3. See Raymond A. Bauer, Ithiel de Sola Pool, and Lewis Anthony Dexter, *American Business and Public Policy* (New York: Atherton, 1963) for a policy case study which also develops very interesting and useful theory.

4. See R. Joseph Monsen, Jr, and Mark W. Cannon, *The Makers of Public Policy* (New York: McGraw-Hill, 1965) for a number of discussions of particular interest groups and their activities.

5. Alaska and Hawaii are excluded.

6. Data from *The Book of the States, 1964-1965* (Chicago: The Council of State Governments, 1964), pp. 12-15.

7. David B. Truman, *op. cit.*; Robert A. Dahl, *A Preface to Democratic Theory* (Chicago: University of Chicago Press, 1956); William Kornhauser, *op. cit.*; and V. O. Key, Jr., *Politics, Parties, and Pressure Groups* (New York: Crowell, 1964), 5th ed.

8. Belle Zeller (ed.), *American State Legislatures* (New York: Crowell, 1964), Chapter 12, especially Table 9, pp. 190-191.

9. See, for example, Claire Selltiz, Marie Jahoda, Morton Deutsch, and Stuart W. Cook, *Research Methods in Social Relations* (New York: Holt, Rinehart and Winston, 1961).

10. Seymour Martin Lipset, "Some Social Requisites of Democracy," *American Political Science Review,* 53 (March, 1959), 69-105.

11. Deane E. Neubauer, *On The Theory of Polyarchy: An Empirical Study of Democracy in Ten Countries* (Ph.D. thesis, Yale University, 1966).

12. A note of caution, however, should undoubtedly be entered here. The measurement of "strength" of interest groups being employed may probably best be construed to mean strength of interest groups *vis-a-vis* the state legislature. At least this is the sense in which it appears that the Committee defined strength. It is certainly the case that interest groups could vary in strength in a number of different ways. For example, size of membership, or number of groups may, under certain conditions, be appropriate measures of strength. As strength of interest groups is being used here it will be defined primarily in terms of legislative activity.

    In addition, the results of this study must be interpreted cautiously since the time periods in which the independent and several of the dependent variables were measured are not conterminous. Strength of interest groups was measured by the Zeller Committee in 1954. Length of constitution and difficulty of amending the constitution (a variable to be introduced later in this paper) correspond to this time period, but the three variables having to do with amendments (number proposed, number adopted, and percentage of amendments adopted) are measured to the date when each state's current constitution was adopted. In several cases this reflects many years. It is therefore necessary, in three of the propositions, to make the assumption that strength of interest groups in states is a relatively stable phenomenon. Although there is not much evidence to support or deny the validity of this assumption, it does not appear unduly unrealistic to make it. Changes in governments, barring revolutions, are likely to take place slowly. If this is the case it does offer a certain plausibility to the assumption.

13. For descriptions of the differing state systems see *The Book of the States, op. cit.,* pp. 13-15.

STATE ELECTORAL SYSTEMS

The Two Electorates: Voters and Non-Voters in a Wisconsin Primary

Austin Ranney
Leon D. Epstein

One of the United States' most unique political institutions, the direct primary, has been studied from several different perspectives. Some political scientists have focused upon the role of party organizations in selecting candidates before the primaries and ensuring their nomination.[1] Others have measured the incidence and conditions of competition in primaries.[2] Still others have explored the processes by which primary contestants emerge from the general population.[3]

Only V. O. Key, however, has published a major empirical study of primary *electorates* to see how they resemble and differ from their counterparts in general elections.[4] Most of what theory we have on these questions we owe to Key. But his work, valuable as it is, rests entirely upon aggregate data.[5] Despite the generally acknowledged advantages of sample survey studies for the analysis of mass electorates,[6] and despite the wealth of survey studies of general elections, the present writers have been unable to find any published survey study of voters and non-voters in primary elections.[7]

This is surely a considerable gap in the study of elections and voting behavior. As one contribution toward filling it, this paper reports the principal findings of a survey study of the gubernatorial primary and general elections held in

Reprinted from *Journal of Politics,* Vol. 28 (1966), pp. 598-606 by permission of the authors and the publisher.

We thank the staff of the Wisconsin Survey Research Laboratory, under the direction of Professor Harry Sharp, for collecting our data; the Data Processing Center of the School of Commerce, University of Wisconsin, for the use of its computer facilities; and Mrs. Ada W. Finifter for assistance in analyzing the data.

Wisconsin in September and November, 1964. We are concerned here with two main questions: To what extent do the factors affecting voting and non-voting in general elections influence voting and non-voting in primaries? How representative of the parties' supporters are the persons who vote in their primaries?

Before we present our findings, however, we should briefly describe their setting.

I

In 1903 Wisconsin became the first state to adopt the direct primary for nominating candidates for most statewide offices. Today it is one of the few states using the "open primary"; any registered voter may vote in the primary of either party (but not both) without publicly disclosing his choice. Moreover, Wisconsin's election laws make registering and voting in both primary and general elections easier than in most states: the President's Commission on Registration and Voting Participation in 1963 listed twelve legal features facilitating voting, and Wisconsin has ten — a score excelled by only two states (Idaho and Oregon, each with eleven) and matched by one (Kansas).[8] So the first point to note is that in Wisconsin's primaries voting has fewer legal difficulties than in most other states.

Second, Wisconsin is a highly competitive two-party state for both national and state offices. In 1964, for example, Wisconsin gave Johnson 62. 2 per cent of its popular vote (compared with his national margin of 61. 4 per cent), re-elected a Democratic Senator, sent five Democrats and five Republicans to the House, replaced a Democratic governor with a Republican, replaced a Republican lieutenant-governor and attorney-general with Democrats, and elected a Democratic lower house and a Republican upper house in the legislature — a performance that surely qualifies the state as "two-party competitive"!

Third, Wisconsin's 1964 gubernatorial primaries drew a total of 28. 5 per cent of the estimated adult population — a figure quite close to the 25. 4 per cent average turnout in comparable primaries in two-party states between 1956 and 1960.[9]

Fourth, the two gubernatorial primaries resembled each other in several respects. Each had two candidates. The Democratic contest was between the organization-supported incumbent governor (John Reynolds) and a minor contender (Dominic Frinzi). The Republican primary was contested by an organization-endorsed veteran of state legislative and executive politics (Warren Knowles) and the Goldwaterite Mayor of La Crosse (Milo Knudson). The two primaries had similar results: 343, 236 persons voted in the Democratic primary, and Reynolds won 70. 3 per cent of the vote; 343, 181 voted in the Republican primary, and Knowles won 71. 9 per cent of the vote.

Finally, the Survey Research Laboratory of the University of Wisconsin conducted a clustered area probability sample survey of 702 adult respondents in November and December of 1964. Two hundred and seventy-four (39. 0 per cent) said they had voted in the September gubernatorial primary, compared with the 28. 5 per cent of the estimated adult population who actually voted. This voting over-report of 10. 5 percentage points is larger than we would prefer, but well within the range of overreport experienced and explained by the Survey Research Center of the University of Michigan in their study of the 1956 presidential election.[10] It should also be noted that our interviews were taken two to three months after the primary, during which interval the much more salient presidential election took place. This may have blurred our respondents' recall more than is usual in post-election surveys. However, we believe that, while these facts suggest some caution in interpreting the magnitude of our findings, they do not invalidate our general analysis.

II

For purposes of analyzing voting and non-voting in the primary, it is useful to divide our respondents into three categories: the 274 who reported voting in both the primary and general elections for governor (labeled PG in our tables); the 264 who said they did not vote in the primary but did vote in the general election (NG); and the 119 who reported voting in neither election (NN).[11] How do they compare with each other?

Reasons for Voting and Not Voting in the Primary

Each primary voter was asked, "Why did you vote in the September primary?"; and each primary non-voter was asked, "Why was it that you did not vote in the September primary?" The answers, tabulated in Table 1, are revealing. Of the principal reasons given *for* voting, well over half are of the civic-duty variety, while only just over a quarter bespeak a desire to influence the outcome of the particular primary. Of the principal reasons given for *not* voting, 7 per cent have to do with legal barriers and 24 per cent with personal difficulties; the others suggest an it-wasn't-worth-the-bother attitude. So only 12 per cent of the entire sample perceived the primary as a contest they wanted to help settle — a much smaller proportion than other studies have shown want to influence the outcome of general elections. Part of the difference is explained by our next finding.

Party Identification

The studies of voting behavior in general elections have found that party identification is one of the most powerful psychological forces impelling people to vote. Many persons who are politically aware of little else know that they are Democrats or Republicans, and the desire to support their side and/or keep the other side out is enough to get them to the polls. Moreover, the persons who are most aware of the issues and candidates tend to be the most partisan.[12]

A primary election, however, is not a fight between "my party" and "the other party"; it is a contest *within* "my party," a family fight. Hence it seems reasonable to hypothesize that partisanship is significantly less associated with participation in primaries than in general elections. Table 2 tests this hunch by relat-

Table 1 Reasons for voting and not voting in the primary.

Percent of Voters	Reason for Voting	Percent of Whole Sample
32	Voting is an obligation, a duty, a responsibility	14
7	Voting is a privilege, a right	3
19	Voting is a habit, "I always vote"	8
28	Wanted to support a particular candidate	12
2	Influenced by others, got a ride near there anyway, friends wanted me to	1
5	Other	2
7	Don't know, not ascertained	3
100%		↓

Percent of Non-Voters	Reasons for Not Voting	Percent of Whole Sample
7	Not qualified to vote (not U. S. citizen, hasn't lived in state long enough to qualify)	4
24	Unable to get to polling place, (ill, out of town, no transportation)	14
14	Failed to register (didn't bother, forgot)	8
4	Undecided about candidates (didn't know for whom to vote, confused, disgusted with both candidates)	2
34	Too busy, working, forgot, "just didn't vote"	20
4	Unaware of importance of voting in primary, religion prevents voting in primary	2
2	Other	1
7	Don't know	4
4	Not ascertained	2
100%		100%

ing party identification, as measured by the Survey Research Center's standard questions, to our three levels of participation. The figures in the NN row show the usual relationship between general-election voting and intensity of partisanship in both parties. But while the comparisons between the PG and NG rows show a comparable relationship for the Republicans with a strikingly high primary turnout for Strong Republicans, a slight *inverse* relation appears for the Democrats. This suggests that partisan motivations for voting, which operated more powerfully among the Democrats than the Republicans in the general election, did not have the same effect in the primary. It therefore provides some confirmation for our hypothesis that the party identification factor operates differently in the two kinds of elections.

Table 2 Relation of party identification to differences in participation in primary and
general elections.

	Party Identification						
Participation [a]	Strong Rep.	Rep.	Ind. Rep.	Ind.	Ind. Dem.	Dem.	Strong Dem.
PG	63%	36%	39%	29%	40%	43%	41%
NG	25	38	41	39	37	44	49
NN	12	26	20	32	23	13	10
	100%	100%	100%	100%	100%	100%	100%
Number of cases [b]	75	110	41	66	79	167	119
Primary — General Difference [c]	.716	.486	.487	.426	.519	.494	.455

[a] PG includes all respondents who voted in both the primary and general elections;
NG includes those who did not vote in the primary but did vote in the general election; NN includes those who voted in neither election.

[b] Table 2, as all subsequent tables, omits the 6 respondents who reported voting
in the primary but not the general election, and all respondents whose positions
on either the independent or dependent variable was not ascertained.

[c] This statistic is intended to show the difference between voting in both the primary and general elections and voting in the general election only, while eliminating the influence of general non-voting. It is computed by the formula:

$$\frac{PG}{PG + NG}$$

One possible explanation for the Republican and Democratic differences in
this regard is that the Republican identifiers were more highly educated than the
Democratic (26 per cent had attended college, as compared with 10 per cent of the
Democrats); but when we hold education constant, as in Table 3, we still find substantially higher relative primary participation for Republican identifiers than Independent Republicans in both the college and high school groups, but no such relationship among Democrats in the two higher educational categories.

Our data permit us to go no further in explaining this interparty difference.
But they suggest that, among Wisconsin Democrats at least, the impact of party
identification in primary elections is noticeably different from its effect in general
elections.

Party Activism

Wisconsin is one of the few states in which both major parties have large
extralegal federations of dues-paying amateur party enthusiasts.[15] The Republican

Table 3 Relation of education and party identification to differences in participation in primary and general elections.

| | Education | | | | | |
| | Grade School | | High School | | College | |
Participation	Identi-fiers[a]	Leaners	Identi-fiers	Leaners	Identi-fiers	Leaners
Republicans						
PG	43%	(17%)[b]	40%	27%	54%	(50%)
NG	28	(50)	39	41	36	(36)
NN	29	(33)	21	32	10	(14)
	100%	100%	100%	100%	100%	100%
Number of cases	56	6	81	21	48	14
Primary — General Difference	.606	.254	.506	.397	.600	.581
Democrats						
PG	39%	(20%)	38%	33%	64%	(50%)
NG	44	(40)	52	40	32	(25)
NN	17	(40)	10	27	4	(25)
	100%	100%	100%	100%	100%	100%
Number of cases	94	10	163	53	29	16
Primary — General Difference	.470	.333	.422	.452	.667	.667

[a]"Identifiers" includes Strong Republicans and Republicans, Strong Democrats and Democrats. "Leaners" includes Independent Republicans and Independent Democrats. For those expressing no party preference of any kind, the primary-general differences were: grade school, .327; high school, .358; college, 333.
[b]Percentages in parentheses because of the small number of cases.

activists' state convention publicly endorses particular candidates in advance of the primary, and while their Democratic opposite numbers do not, most of the Democrats' preprimary elimination and encouragement of potential primary contestants takes place in negotiations among Democratic activists. Hence we would expect that, having settled on Reynolds and Knowles as their choices, the activists would go into the primaries to make sure their choices survived the outsiders' challenges.

To identify the activists in our sample, we asked each respondent if he had ever "belonged to an American political party in the sense of paying dues or hav-

Table 4 Relation of party activism to differences in participation in primary and general elections.

Activity

Participation	Belong to Party?		Give Money?		Do Campaign Work?	
	Yes	*No*	*Yes*	*No*	*Yes*	*No*
PG	69%	39%	69%	37%	69%	37%
NG	25	42	22	43	25	43
NN	6	19	9	20	6	20
	100%	100%	100%	100%	100%	100%
Number of cases	52	605	92	565	88	569
Primary—General Difference	.734	.481	.758	.463	.734	.463

ing a membership card, " or "contributed money to a political candidate or party, " or "done any campaign work . . . for any political candidate or party. " There was considerable overlap among the answers, but 160 respondents answered "yes" to at least one of the questions. Table 4 shows that not only did the activists in each category have substantially fewer NN's than the "inactivists, " but they also had much higher relative primary participation. This confirms our expectation that the activists' higher interest in politics which inclines them to become active in the first place, also leads them to participate in the primaries far more than their less interested fellow partisans.

Socioeconomic Characteristics

We found that, with some interesting exceptions, the same socioeconomic characteristics generally found to be associated with high turnout in general elections[14] are also associated with high primary participation. For example, level of formal education is the trait usually found most highly correlated with general-election turnout.

NOTES

1. E.g., Peter H. Rossi and Phillips Cutright, "The Impact of Party Organization in an Industrial Setting, " in Morris Janowitz, (ed), *Community Political Systems* (New York: The Free Press of Glencoe, 1961), pp. 81-116; and Frank J. Sorauf, *Party and Representation* (New York: Atherton Press, 1963), Chs. 3-5.

2. E.g., Julius Turner, "Primary Elections as the Alternative to Party Competition in 'Safe' Districts," *Journal of Politics,* 15 (May, 1953), 197-210; and William H. Standing and James A. Robinson, "Inter-Party Competition and Primary Contesting: The Case of Indiana," *American Political Science Review,* 52 (December, 1958), 1066-1077.

3. E.g., Lester G. Seligman, "Political Recruitment and Party Structure: A Case Study," *American Political Science Review,* 55 (March, 1961), 77-86.

4. *American State Politics: An Introduction* (New York: Alfred A. Knopf, 1956), Ch. 5. For more narrowly focused but useful comparisons of primary- and general-election electorates using aggregate data, see M. Kent Jennings and L. Harmon Zeigler, "Electoral Strategies and Voting Patterns in a Southern Congressional District," in Jennings and Zeigler (eds.), *The Electoral Process* (Englewood Cliffs, N.J.: Prentice-Hall, 1966), pp. 122-138; and Rossi and Cutright, *op. cit.,* pp. 100-109.

5. He drew his conclusions from an ingenious comparison of primary and general election returns in eight northern two-party states.

6. Cf. W. S. Robinson, "Ecological Correlations and the Behavior of Individuals," *American Sociological Review,* 15 (1950), 351-357; and Austin Ranney, "The Utility and Limitations of Aggregate Data in the Study of Electoral Behavior," in Ranney (ed.), *Essays on the Behavioral Study of Politics* (Urbana: University of Illinois Press, 1962), pp. 91-102.

7. Arthur C. Wolfe is presently writing a Ph.D. dissertation at the University of Michigan on "The Direct Primary in American Politics," using both aggregate data and national survey data collected by the Survey Research Center in 1958 and 1964.

8. *Report of the President's Commission on Registration and Voting Participation* (Washington, D.C.: Government Printing Office, 1963), Appendix Two, p. 65.

9. Cf. Herbert Jacob and Kenneth N. Vines (eds.) *Politics in the American States* (Boston: Little, Brown and Company, 1965), p. 75.

10. The SRC's sample overreported voting by 12 per cent. The authors attributed 6 per cent of this to differences between the population sampled and the civilian population of voting age (their sample, like ours, excluded non-citizens, people in institutions, people in transit, etc.), 2 per cent to invalidation of ballots cast, and 1 per cent to the higher reinterview rate among voters; 3 per cent was unexplained: Angus Campbell, Philip E. Converse, Warren E. Miller, and Donald E. Stokes, *The American Voter* (New York: John Wiley & Sons, Inc., 1960), pp. 94-96.

11. Six respondents reported voting in the primary but not in the general election. Since they are too few to analyze as a fourth category, and we do not feel justified in adding them to the PG group, we exclude them from our analysis. The remaining thirty-nine respondents' primary participation was not ascertained.

12. *Cf. The American Voter*, Chs. 5-6.

13. For descriptions, see Leon D. Epstein, *Politics in Wisconsin* (Madison, Wisconsin: University of Wisconsin Press, 1958), Ch. 5; and Frank J. Sorauf, "Extra-Legal Parties in Wisconsin," *American Political Science Review*, 48 (September, 1954), 692-704.

14. For a useful summary of the characteristics, see Lester W. Milbrath, *Political Participation* (Chicago: Rand McNally & Company, 1965), Ch. 5.

Part Three

THE
AUTHORITATIVE
DECISION-
MAKING
AGENCIES OF
STATE POLITICS

All political systems have some individual or institution which transforms the inputs of the system into "public policy." The structure and operation of these agencies may vary, and the form of the policy statement may differ from one system to another, but all political systems have institutions which make authoritative decisions for that system. In the American states these institutions are highly visible offices and individuals who have official titles, a recognized (if little understood) position, and formal-legal status. The governorship, the state legislature, the judicial system, and, to some degree, the state bureaucracy are these institutions.

This section deals with various aspects of these institutions. Although the following articles offer some description of structural arrangements, they seek in the main to determine the effect of variations in these arrangements upon political behavior in the states, to evaluate the importance of interpersonal relations for the functioning of these institutions, and to assess the impact of other features of the political system upon their activities.

THE STATE LEGISLATURE

Patterns of Interpersonal Relations in a State Legislative Group: The Wisconsin Assembly

Samuel C. Patterson

Traditionally, legislative bodies have been studied in terms of the formal structure of the legislative group — the structure of formal leadership or of committee organization, and legislative decision-making typically has been analyzed in terms of "pressures" or "vectors" which influence the decision-making process. The pattern of informal organization of legislative groups based on a variety of interpersonal relationships among legislators has been frequently recognized, but seldom investigated systematically.

The Assembly, the lower house of the Wisconsin State Legislature, consists of one hundred members elected from single-member districts apportioned on the basis of population. Assemblymen are elected in November of even-numbered years, and the Assembly meets in biennial session for about six months in odd-numbered years. The formal organization of the Wisconsin Assembly with respect to the election and powers of elected officers, the organization of committees, and the formal legislative procedure is similar in most respects to the practices in many other states.

During the months of February, March, and April 1958, members of the 1957 session of the Wisconsin Assembly were systematically interviewed by means of a schedule of questions.[1] Seventy per cent of the members were interviewed personally, and an additional 17 per cent were interviewed by mail. Data were therefore available for 87 per cent of the members of the 1957 Assembly.

With respect to the patterns of interpersonal relations in the Assembly,

Reprinted from *Public Opinion Quarterly,* Vol. 23 (Spring 1959), pp. 101-109, by permission of the publisher.

sociometric techniques were employed to determine (1) what the informal pattern of organization was in the 1957 Assembly, and (2) whether, as other social-psychological research has indicated, legislators who have leadership status tend to receive more friendship choices than non-leaders; that is, whether leaders tend to be "overchosen."

The method employed by some social scientists to identify and analyze the interpersonal relations of members of a social group is that of interaction process analysis, a technique which was developed by Bales.[2] Interaction process analysis, is, however, fairly strictly limited in its application to small-group research and certainly would be a monumental, if not an impossible, task for a researcher with limited facilities if it were attempted on a body as large as the Wisconsin Assembly.

The outstanding illustration of an effort to analyze the interpersonal relationships of members of a legislative group in the literature of political science is the classic study of Routt, who counted the number of interactions between members during the first fifteen minutes of each daily session of the 1937 Illinois Senate.[3] Routt's analysis was confined to a sample of eleven senators, and interactions were counted during eighty-six sample periods. This technique is, as Routt himself maintained, limited in its utility to a small group of members who could be observed manageably by the researcher.

Systematic interviewing of members of a legislative body provided an opportunity, however, to analyze the interpersonal relations among members by means of sociometric techniques which have been highly developed by the social psychologists.[4] In the Wisconsin study, members were asked to nominate their closest personal friends within the Assembly — members whom they liked the best and spent the most time with outside the legislative chamber. The analysis of the data was accomplished by the manipulation of a matrix which indicated the friendship choices of members. Members were listed on the top and on the side of the matrix, and friendship choices were then plotted on the matrix. The matrix was squared to reveal mutual choices between members and, finally, cubed to reveal cliques. The procedure is not difficult even with a 100-man legislative group, and is fully and adequately described in Festinger *et al. Social Pressures in Informal Groups.*[5]

The sociometric, or friendship, score for each member was computed simply by totaling the number of sociometric choices for the member. These data were utilized to show a relationship between high friendship scores and leadership status.

THE ROLE OF FRIENDS

Friendship is not a well-defined concept, and for the most part Assemblymen were encouraged to define it for themselves in designating their closest friends in the Assembly. Clearly, friendship among members of any social group can develop in a variety of ways. In the Assembly some friendships develop between members from the same geographical areas in the state who regularly ride together from their homes to the capital. Others are developed between seatmates — members who sit next to each other in the Assembly.[6] The most important friendships for this analysis are those that reflect a community of interests and attitudes among members who share norms.

Legislators have the usual expectations with respect to their friends. They expect them to be honest with them, keep their confidences, and demonstrate compatible psychological characteristics. With respect to the legislative process, by and large Assemblymen expect their friends to support their bills unless there is some compelling reason why they cannot. If a member cannot support a friend's bill, he is expected to tell his friend why he cannot "go along" before he votes against the bill, and to explain why he must vote as he does. Otherwise, his friend will most likely automatically "count" on him, and an unwarned adverse vote may sever the friendship relationship. Since members tend to select persons of like minds as their friends, this problem does not create serious difficulty. A member will be most frequently "forgiven" for voting against his friend if his reason is based on the nature of his district, that, is, if he cannot "go along" because of district pressure.

THE INFORMAL SUBSTRUCTURE OF THE ASSEMBLY

The analysis of perception of friends in the Assembly revealed a total of 81 mutual choices between members, that is, in 81 cases members chose each other reciprocally. In 18 per cent of these cases, the members who chose each other were seatmates, so that it can be hypothesized that friendships in the Assembly are sometimes a function of sitting together in the chamber. In a few other cases friendships can be attributed to the fact that the members often rode back and forth together from Madison to their homes, although these friendship relationships probably did not result in a high frequency of interaction while the members were in Madison. One instance of this kind resulted in a three-way choice, which can be schematically illustrated by means of a simple sociometric diagram (Figure 1).[7] These three members were all from the Green Bay area, one a Democrat and two Republicans.

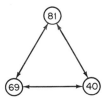

Figure 1 Sociometric diagram of members from Green Bay area.

The most interesting sub-groups, or cliques (which is the term the Assemblyman uses), revealed by an analysis of reciprocal choices are those among Democrats.[8] A third of the members of the 1957 Assembly were Democrats. The Democratic membership of the Assembly was divided into two principal cliques: the Milwaukee County clique and the Dane County clique. The Milwaukee County clique consisted of six Democrats who were referred to by members as the "Unholy Six," and included the Democratic floor leader (Figure 2). The Unholy Six were Democrats who tended to see their role as one of cooperating with the majority party as much as possible in order to get their own legislation passed. Also,

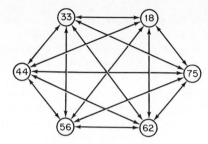

Figure 2 Sociometric diagram of the "Unholy Six."

these members expected the floor leader to play down partisanship and cooperate with the Republican leadership. The Unholy Six were limited partisans. Three other Milwaukee Democrats comprised an additional sub-clique which was often allied with the Unholy Six (Figure 3). In some respects, however, this smaller clique represented a dissident element among Milwaukee Democrats, expressing some dissatisfaction with the party leadership.

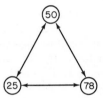

Figure 3 Sociometric diagram of other Milwaukee Democrats.

The Dane County clique was composed of the four Democratic members from the county in which the capital is located, plus their allies (Figure 4). Both the Democratic assistant floor leader and the caucus chairman were members of this clique. These members were more partisan in their role expectations, and tended to see the floor leader as a "party hatchet man." This group was able to defeat Pellant of the Unholy Six, the 1955 session assistant floor leader, for re-election and elect Hardie, one of their allies. The Dane County clique saw Molinaro, the caucus chairman, as the "real" party leader, although he is himself from Kenosha. Molinaro was the Democratic candidate for speaker of the 1957 session, and he lost by a straight party vote to the Republican candidate, Marotz. In addition to the Dane County members, the clique included one Assemblyman from Racine, one from Kenosha, and two from northwestern rural Wisconsin.

An examination of roll-call votes indicates considerable difference in the voting behavior of the Dane County clique and the Unholy Six. The Dane County members were strongly influenced, and to some extent limited, by the editorial policy of one Madison newspaper, *The Capital Times,* and were less likely to vote for legislation introduced by Republican members than were the Unholy Six. The same was true to a lesser extent of the northwestern Wisconsin Democrats in areas where the circulation of that newspaper is considerable.

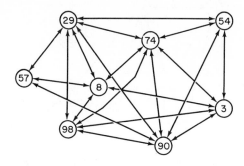

Figure 4 Sociometric diagram of the Dane County clique.

The clique structure of the Democratic contingent in the 1957 Assembly reflects the statewide division between Milwaukee County and the rest of the state in the political behavior of Democratic activists. In this way the state Democratic convention is regularly divided, both in terms of platform policy and, to a greater extent, in the election of officers and the support of candidates.

The friendship clique structure of Republican members was not as spectacular. Interestingly enough, there were no three-way choices among the six members of the Republican steering committee, the group which comprised the primary Republican leadership of the Assembly, although these members met regularly as a group. The best-defined Republican clique had its own name: "Murderers' Row" (Figure 5). This clique was composed of members who sat together in

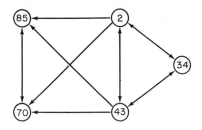

Figure 5 Sociometric diagram of "Murderers' Row."

the Assembly, who voted together most of the time, and who "caucused once in a while" if a member of the clique "got out of line." Three pairs of seatmates made up the clique, plus one other mutual choice and four single choices. Two of these members were chairmen of important committees, and one was Assembly chairman of the powerful joint finance committee.

Another Republican clique consisted of what might be referred to as the younger leadership group, which had as its center the relationship among Grady, the floor leader, Pommerening, Heider, and Bidwell (Figure 6). This clique had friendship ties with other cliques close to the center of leadership in the Assembly.

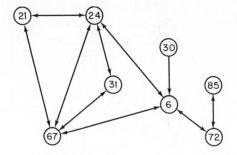

Figure 6 Sociometric diagram of young Republican leader clique.

In terms of friendship expectancies, the clique was related to Rice, the powerful chairman of the agriculture committee, and through him to Stone, chairman of the finance committee and member of Murderers' Row. Heider, one of the members of this clique, sometimes sat in on meetings of the steering committee when one of the regular members was not able to attend. Also, most of the members of this clique had supported Grady for speaker in the initial Republican caucus when Grady lost the speakership election to Marotz. Pommerening was Grady's campaign manager. These members constituted the core of the members who had, during the 1955 session, opposed the dominating tactics of Speaker Catlin, and these members believed at the opening of the 1957 session that the Catlin influence was being continued under the speakership of Marotz, who had been floor leader when Catlin was speaker.

Another clique of young Republican members which can be identified from the friendship patterns in the Assembly is a group, principally of new members, who were not related to the leadership by friendship ties and who were critical of certain aspects of the way the leaders performed (Figure 7). This "new member" clique consisted of Assemblymen who had not been affected by the Catlin leadership in the Assembly, and who thought the legislative process was too cumbersome and inefficient. They believed that it was largely because of the unwillingness of older members that it had not been streamlined and at the end of the 1957 session members of this clique suggested the possibility of new leadership and the necessity for reforms in legislative procedure.

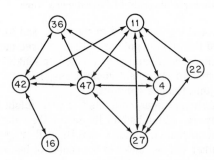

Figure 7 Sociometric diagram of the new member clique.

The remaining Republican clique as determined by friendship patterns illustrates a different kind of relationship among members who mutually perceive
each other in the role of friend. This clique consisted of Rice, former speaker
and chairman of the agriculture committee, and two other southern Wisconsin
farmer-legislators (Figure 8). These two farmer-legislators were new members,
and one had been urged to run for the Assembly by Rice, with whom he was well-
acquainted before he became an Assemblyman. For these two members Rice was,
in effect, a role model. He "took them under his wing" during the session.

Figure 8   Sociometric diagram of the Rice clique.

These patterns of interpersonal relationships in the Assembly in terms of
friendship choices illustrate the structure of the informal organization of the legislative group. But the data with respect to friendship choices can be used not only
to illustrate the patterns of influence and communication in a group, but also to
indicate what kinds of individuals tend to get the most choices.

FRIENDSHIP AND LEADERSHIP

The data on sociometric choices among legislators can be used to test the
hypothesis: If a member has leadership status, then he will tend to be chosen as
a friend by more members than will a non-leader. Leaders in the Assembly tend
to be the prototypes of their group in a variety of ways: they tend to function as
norm models, they tend to be the ideological prototypes of their group, and they
tend to be more loyal to group-defined goals[9]. Since they also occupy positions of
higher status in the legislative group than non-leaders, it should follow that leaders are perceived as friends by more members than are non-leaders.

Such a hypothesis is supported by the data from the Wisconsin Assembly.
There is a clear relationship between the extent of friendship perception and leadership. Among members of both parties, leaders are seen as friends by more
members than are the rank-and-file party members. Table 1 shows that more

Table 1   Relationship between Republican leadership and friendship perception.

Leadership Status	*(N = 67)* 6 or More Friends	Fewer than 6 Friends
Steering committee	5	1
Other Republicans	8	53

$x^2 = 12.9$; $p. < .001$

members selected Republican steering committee members (primary leaders) for the role of friend than other Republican members.

The same relationship is true of the Democratic party members in the Assembly (Table 2). Democratic leaders are seen in friendship roles by more members than rank-and-file Democrats.[10] It appears likely that members identify psychologically with their leaders and thus frequently see them not only as leaders but also as friends.[11]

Table 2   Relationship between Democratic leadership and friendship perception.

Leadership Status	(N = 33) 6 or More Friends	Fewer than 6 Friends
Leaders	3	1
Other Democrats	2	27

$X^2 = 7.9$; p. $< .01$

CONCLUSION

Friendship roles are functional roles in the legislative group. No social group can be maintained if there are not significant and persistent interpersonal relations among members, and large groups like a legislature tend to be broken down into sub-groups on a friendship basis.[12] Friendship roles designated by the reciprocal choices among friends can be used to explore the informal organization of a legislative group. Perception of friendship by members can be related to leadership in the sense that leaders will tend to be perceived as playing friendship roles by more members than non-leaders.

Friendship roles are not only functional for the maintenance of the legislative group but also for the resolution of political conflict. The legislator is not simply the "pawn of contending forces" who seek access to the legislative group in order to get their concepts of the public interest accepted as public policy. The legislator brings to the decision-making process not only his own sociological and psychological make-up and his multiple-group memberships, but also his informal associations within the legislative group. He is part of the informal social structure of the legislative group and is affected by the norms of these informal groups in his own decision-making behavior.[13]

Individuals who assume the legislative role have diverse backgrounds and diverse social, political, and economic experience, and different reference groups are salient for them. The informal friendship structure of the legislature tends to lessen such differences, to militate against the development of potential conflicts, to provide channels of communication and understanding among members who share goals, and to facilitate logrolling.

NOTES

1.   The complete study is reported in Samuel C. Patterson, "Toward a Theory of Legislative Behavior: The Wisconsin State Assemblymen as Actors in a Legislative System," unpublished Ph. D. dissertation, Madison, Wis., University of Wisconsin, 1958.

2. Robert F. Bales, *Interaction Process Analysis: A Method for the Study of Small Groups,* Cambridge, Mass., Addison-Wesley, 1950.

3. Garland C. Routt, "Interpersonal Relationships and the Legislative Process," *The Annals of the American Academy of Political and Social Science,* Vol. 195, 1938, pp. 129-136.

4. Sociogram analysis is, of course, far more refined than the simple application of it here illustrated. The principal reference is J. L. Moreno, *Who Shall Survive?* New York, Beacon House, 1953.

5. Leon Festinger, Stanley Schachter, and Kurt Back, *Social Pressures in Informal Groups: A Study of Human Factors in Housing,* New York, Harper, 1950, pp. 132-150.

6. This analysis of friendship in the legislative group considers primarily the question of who tends to form friendships with whom, and not the process through which these patterns develop. An attempt to study friendship as a process rather than a product is illustrated by the studies of Paul F. Lazarsfeld and Robert K. Merton, "Friendships as Social Process: A Substantive and Methodological Analysis," in Morroe Berger, Theodore Abel, and Charles H. Page, editors, *Freedom and Control in Modern Society,* Princeton, N. J., Van Nostrand, 1954, pp. 18-66.

7. The numbers in the diagrams refer to interview code numbers.

8. A clique is operationally defined as any combination of three or more members who mutually choose each other, plus other related members.

9. These are general characteristics of leadership, but they are borne out in the Wisconsin Assembly. See Patterson, *op. cit.,* Chap. 9, "Leadership Roles in the Assembly."

10. Similar findings with respect to other kinds of social groups can be found in the literature of social psychology. See Henry W. Riecken and George C. Homans, "Psychological Aspects of Social Structure," in Gardner Lindzey, editor, *Handbook of Social Psychology,* Vol. 2, Cambridge, Mass., Addison-Wesley, 1954, pp. 786-832.

11. Routt found that interpersonal contacts "tended to center around individuals who by other indices were shown to play important roles in the process of legislation." See *op. cit.,* p. 132.

12. A variety of related social-psychological research is analyzed in Harold H. Kelley and John W. Thibaut, "Experimental Studies in Group Problem Solving and Process," in Lindzey, *op. cit.,* pp. 761-770.

13. In this connection, see the very valuable recent study of David B. Truman, "The State Delegations and the Structure of Party Voting in the United States House of Representatives," *American Political Science Review,* Vol. 50, No. 4, 1956, pp. 1023-1045.

Metropolitan and Outstate Alignments in Illinois and Missouri Legislative Delegations

David R. Derge

Rural overrepresentation and metropolitan underrepresentation in state legislatures have long been standard targets for the criticisms of students of state and local government. As Murray Stedman, for example, puts it, "Rural minorities control many state legislatures and thereby penalize urban majorities. The virtual serfdom of the urbanite to the rurally controlled state legislatures in many areas is a recurrent plaint in the writings of political scientists. "[2] Commenting on the tendency of state legislators to form blocs reflecting individual localities and their local and regional interests, Alfred DeGrazia concludes that "every American state with any considerable urban population has undergone protracted conflict between rural and urban blocs, often regardless of party lines. "[3] Textbooks on municipal government, and state and local government, universally condemn urban underrepresentation in state legislatures and say, or imply, that the result is consistent defeat or frustration of urban interests in the legislative arena.[4] My purpose here is to introduce a note of factual skepticism into a portion of the discussion.

The literature on "urban-rural" conflict does not proceed from a precise definition of what is "urban. " The census definition, as places of 2,500 or more population, and the fringe in metropolitan areas, has not been adopted; nor does "urban" mean all incorporated places. If either of these definitions were used, many state legislatures now called rural-dominated would have to be classified as urban-dominated on the basis of the percentage of members from districts in which a majority of the population resides in urban places.[5] The "urban-rural" division has instead been characterized usually as a division between the large metropolitan areas and the rest of the state. Thus "urban-rural" conflict is perceived as New York City against upstate New York, Philadelphia and Pittsburgh against outstate Pennsylvania, Chicago against downstate Illinois, St. Louis and Kansas City against outstate Missouri, and Los Angeles and San Francisco against the rest of California.

The argument in the literature on "urban-rural" conflict accordingly may be summarized in the following propositions: (1) there are metropolitan and non-metropolitan interests, distinguishable and incompatible; (2) metropolitan legislators will forward metropolitan interests, non-metropolitan legislators will forward non-metropolitan interests; (3) since non-metropolitan population is overrepresented, non-metropolitan interests will prevail; and (4) if a redress of numerical representation to favor metropolitan areas is brought about, as it should be, then the outcome of this conflict will be reversed and metropolitan interests will prevail.

This study attempts a partial exploration of the alignments within and between metropolitan and non-metropolitan legislative delegations. The voting

Reprinted from *American Political Science Review,* Vol. 52 (1958), pp. 1051-1065, by permission of the author and publisher.

behavior of the metropolitan delegations and other members in the Illinois and Missouri General Assemblies is examined in order to determine the frequency and intensity of conflict between the two groups. Five biennial legislative sessions were chosen for the analysis, from 1949 through 1957. The thesis of this study is that genuine metropolitan against non-metropolitan conflict in the Illinois and Missouri General Assemblies is rare, and that most of the conflict surrounding legislative consideration of metropolitan problems arises from intra-metropolitan party disputes, central city-suburban antagonisms, or factionalism within the metropolitan majority party. So the success or failure of metropolitan delegations in their legislative objectives usually depends on the degree of agreement between metropolitan parties or factions, or between central city and suburban legislators, or both, rather than on the hostility or callous disregard of non-metropolitan legislators toward metropolitan problems.

Illinois is an example of what V. O. Key terms a "unimetropolitan" state,[6] and is frequently selected to demonstrate the frustration of metropolitan interests in a rural-dominated legislature.[7] Cook County comprises most of the Chicago urbanized area and accounts for 52 per cent of the Illinois population, but in the sessions of the Assembly from 1949 through 1955 held only 37 per cent of the House and Senate seats. Legislative reapportionment in 1955 gave Cook County 51 per cent of the House seats, while continuing the control of the Senate in areas outside Cook County. Until 1957, 54 of the 57 Cook County House seats and 18 of the 19 Senate seats were held by legislators whose districts were wholly or substantially within the city of Chicago. Consequently the whole Cook County delegation is treated here as the metropolitan delegation in the analyses of the sessions through 1955. The 1955 reapportionment produced districts either wholly within or wholly without Chicago, and this is reflected in the 1957 analyses by the use of the Chicago delegation as the metropolitan delegation, and the exclusion of the greatly enlarged suburban Cook County delegation. The area wholly outside Cook County, often referred to as "downstate," is treated as the non-metropolitan delegation.

Missouri is a "bimetropolitan" state with two geographically polar but politically similar cities, St. Louis and Kansas City, containing 36 per cent of Missouri's population. Suburban St. Louis County contains another 10 per cent of the population.[8] St. Louis City holds 11 per cent of the House seats and Jackson County, most of which is in Kansas City, holds 8 per cent of them.[9] In this study the three Missouri metropolitan delegations are consequently the St. Louis City delegation, the Jackson County delegation, and the two of these combined. All areas outside of St. Louis City, St. Louis County, and Jackson County are treated as non-metropolitan.

The recorded roll-call vote is used in this analysis to determine the positions taken by legislators, and to uncover group conflict. The organization and conventions of these two legislatures operate to produce a large number of rollcalls each session, and to permit a small minority to force floor action and a roll-call vote on most measures. Observation of the Assemblies and interviews with members have led the writer to conclude that any notable amount of legislative conflict, including that between metropolitan and non-metropolitan legislators, will produce contested roll-calls at some stage of legislative action. Based on their studies of the Illinois and Missouri Assemblies, W. J. Keefe and G. D. Young comment that the roll-call is a proper criterion for measuring attitudes on legislation and that most of the legislation deemed important will receive some sort of floor action. [10] Numerous other studies of legislative behavior in both national and state governments have relied heavily on roll-call analysis.[11]

Roll-calls which occurred during the ten-year period totalled 14, 052 in the Illinois House and Senate and 4, 989 in the Missouri House.[12] Each of these 19, 041 roll-calls was examined for the presence of conflict between metropolitan and non-metropolitan legislators. Most roll-calls were unanimous or nearly so; hence for purposes of analysis a group of roll-calls showing substantial conflict was select-ed. These "contested" roll-calls show at least 15 per cent of the membership on the losing side of the vote in Illinois and 10 per cent in Missouri. This reduced to 3, 662 the number of roll-calls to be analyzed for voting cohesions of party and geographical groups. High speed data-processing equipment facilitated the tabu-lation and correlation of the more than 500, 000 individual legislator votes cast.

Tests of cohesion here are based on the percentage of the full membership of the elected delegation which took the majority position of the delegation on any given roll-call. Except for comparative data this test of "absolute cohesion" is used throughout. For example, if 100 seats are held by Democrats and if 67 Demo-crats vote "yes, " the Democratic cohesion on that vote would be 67 per cent, re-gardless of the number of Democrats who vote "no" or who are absent. This test retains the simplicity of a single, easily understood expression useful in identify-ing groups in conflict, without adding the other dimension of intragroup cohesion which is not the main concern in most of the analyses and which may be handled by manipulations of the absolute cohesion test when necessary.

I. CONFLICT BETWEEN METROPOLITAN AND NON-METROPOLITAN LEGISLATORS

Among the conditions necessary to support the traditional argument are that non-metropolitan legislators in "rural-dominated" legislatures vote together solidly, that they are opposed by a solid metropolitan front, and that in the ensu-ing conflict metropolitan legislators end up on the losing side. In the following sections the voting behavior of Illinois and Missouri legislators will be examined to determine the frequency of these three requisite voting patterns. [13]

1. Non-metropolitan Legislators Seldom Vote Together with High Cohesion Against Metropolitan Legislators

Table 1 contains data showing the degree of non-metropolitan opposition to metropolitan delegations voting with high cohesion in the 1949-1957 sessions.

Over the five-session period in the Illinois House which produced 7, 186 roll-calls no instance of conflict pitted more than 90 per cent of the metropolitan delegation in opposition to more than 90 per cent of the non-metropolitan delega-tion. In the Illinois Senate two instances of conflict in this degree occurred during this period. Fifteen cases of conflict to the extent of 80 per cent on each side were found in the Illinois Senate, but twelve of these took place in the 1955 session when 89 per cent of the metropolitan delegation was Democratic and 94 per cent of the

Table 1 Non-metropolitan opposition to metropolitan delegations voting with a cohesion of 67 per cent or more: 1949-1957 sessions.

| | Illinois | | | | Missouri House | | | |
| | House | | Senate | | St. Louis | | Kansas City | |
	N	%	N	%	N	%	N	%
Non-metropolitan opposition was 67% or more	7	3	28	12	2	—	0	0
Non-metropolitan opposition was less than 67%	239	97	208	88	509	100	561	100
Totals	246	100	236	100	511	100	561	100

non-metropolitan delegation was Republican. If this session is excluded, the other four Illinois Senate sessions and the five Illinois House sessions produced only six instances of metropolitan against non-metropolitan conflict at the 80 per cent degree of cohesion. When the test is lowered to 67 per cent cohesion in conflict between delegations, seven cases are found in the Illinois House and 28 in the Illinois Senate. But 24 of these Senate roll-calls occurred in the 1955 and 1957 sessions when over 80 per cent of the Democrats were metropolitan and over 80 per cent of the Republicans were non-metropolitan. During the five Illinois House sessions, only three instances of conflict involved a combination of more than 67 per cent of both metropolitan Democrats and Republicans in opposition to more than 67 per cent of the non-metropolitan legislators.

The most striking finding for Missouri is that during the five-session period the metropolitan delegations were never opposed by as much as 90 per cent of the non-metropolitan legislators, and that only St. Louis City was met with as much as 67 per cent opposition from the non-metropolitan delegation, This occurred twice over the ten-year period. Neither the Kansas City group nor the combined St. Louis City-Kansas City group was opposed by as much as 67 per cent of the non-metropolitan legislators from 1949 through 1957. Missouri non-metropolitan legislators were practically never united on contested roll-calls. During the five-session period in Missouri, the non-metropolitan legislators voted with a cohesion of 67 per cent or more on 89 (4%) of the 2,047 contested roll-calls, and with a cohesion of more than 80 per cent on only three. At no time did non-metropolitan solidarity reach the 90 per cent degree of cohesion. This is partly due to the close party division within the Missouri non-metropolitan delegations in contrast to Illinois non-metropolitan delegations which were politically more homogeneous. In the Illinois Senate, where most non-metropolitan members were Republicans, the non-metropolitan delegation voted with a cohesion of 67 per cent or more on 34 per cent of all contested roll-calls during the five-session period. The margin of Republican control of the non-metropolitan delegations in the Illinois House was less marked, and these delegations voted with a cohesion of 67 per cent or more on only 10 per cent of all contested roll-calls. Thus it appears that the degree of cohesion in non-metropolitan delegations is mostly governed by the extent of party division within these delegations.

The data also suggest that a further reason for the absence of conflict between metropolitan and non-metropolitan legislators is the unwillingness of non-metropolitan Democrats to vote against metropolitan Democrats. Using roll-call votes on which the metropolitan delegation voted with a cohesion of 67 per cent or more, a support-opposition score was obtained for each Illinois legislator by subtracting the number of times he voted against the delegation from the number of times he voted with it. Practically all legislators in the quartile of the highest opposition to the metropolitan delegation are non-metropolitan Republicans, with non-metropolitan Democrats clustering in the two quartiles of lowest opposition. Support-opposition scores were obtained for the three-member House districts by summing the scores of the three members. Results of the analyses of House and Senate districts using the Spearman rank order correlation significant at the .01 level indicate a positive correlation between: (1) degree of opposition of Senators and of House members of the same party from the same area; (2) opposition to the metropolitan delegation and degree of "Republicanism" of the district as measured by the proclivity of the district to elect Republican legislators. Each non-metropolitan district sent at least one Democrat to the House, and in each case the Democrat had a score showing higher support of the metropolitan delegation than did his Republican colleagues from the same district. Some of the implications of these findings are discussed in later parts of this paper. The support-opposition scores of legislators from Illinois downstate urbanized areas throw interesting light on the hypothesis that the common problems faced by cities throughout the state may lead legislators from these different cities to work together. Although there are wide variations in voting behavior of legislators from urbanized areas outside of Chicago, those legislators are distinguished neither for support of, nor opposition to, the Chicago delegation. Finally, it should be noted that some Republican legislators from Chicago and Cook County are included in the quartile of highest opposition to the Chicago legislators who constituted the cohesive group.

Evidence of the refusal of Missouri non-metropolitan Democrats to vote against their urban colleagues is provided by analysis of their responses on the 166 roll-calls which elicited high cohesion in the combined St. Louis City-Jackson County group in 1957. A majority of the non-metropolitan Democrats voted with the metropolitan Democrats on 149 (90 per cent) of these roll-calls, and against the metropolitan Democrats on only one roll-call. A majority of non-metropolitan Democrats voted against St. Louis City Democrats on only three roll-calls and against Kansas City Democrats on only one roll-call. Thus, when Democrats hold a substantial number of non-metropolitan seats and refuse to vote against their metropolitan colleagues, conflict is avoided.

In summary, these findings show that metropolitan and non-metropolitan delegations in the Illinois and Missouri Assemblies seldom vote solidly against each other, and that metropolitan against non-metropolitan conflict in this sense seldom occurs.

2. The Metropolitan Legislators Usually Do Not Vote Together with High Cohesion

Table 2 contains data on the voting cohesion of metropolitan delegations during the five-session period.

Table 2 Voting cohesion of metropolitan delegations on contested roll-calls: 1949-1957 sessions.

Metropolitan Cohesion %	Illinois				Missouri House			
	House		Senate		St. Louis		Kansas City	
	N	%	N	%	N	%	N	%
91 or more	12	1	20	3	60	3	23	1
67-90	234	24	216	34	451	22	538	26
less than 67	738	75	395	63	1,536	75	1,486	73
Totals	984	100	631	100	2,047	100	2,047	100

In Illinois during the ten-year period studied, metropolitan delegations voted with a cohesion of more than 90 per cent on 32 contested roll-calls (2%), more than 80 per cent on 163 (10%), and 67 per cent or more on 482 (30%). [14] On 70 per cent of all contested roll-calls the metropolitan delegations voted with a cohesion of less than 67 per cent. During this period in Missouri the same pattern is evident, although in 1957 metropolitan cohesion of 67 per cent or more was about five times more frequent than in the other four sessions. During the ten-year period in Missouri the metropolitan delegations voted with a cohesion of 91 per cent or more on less than 3 per cent of all contested roll-calls, and with a cohesion of 67 per cent or more on less than 30 per cent of the roll-calls. It is notable that the two metropolitan delegations, St. Louis City and Kansas City, voted with a combined cohesion of 91 per cent or more on only 4 of the 2,047 contested roll-calls, indicating that wholehearted joint action by these two groups seldom occurred. The metropolitan delegations were not in the habit of voting solidly on issues inciting conflict in the legislature.

Table 3 Frequency of metropolitan delegations voting with prevailing and losing sides of contested roll-calls, when delegation cohesion was 67 per cent or more: 1949-1957 sessions.

	Illinois				Missouri House [a]			
	House		Senate		St. Louis		Kansas City	
	N	%	N	%	N	%	N	%
Prevailing side	222	90	162	69	396	85	474	89
Losing side	24	10	74	31	70	15	56	11
Totals	246	100	236	100	466	100	530	100

[a] Losses in this table have been adjusted to account for later actions of the Assembly which reversed metropolitan losses. In Missouri it is common for several attempts to be made to pass legislation. This pattern of action is not found in Illinois.

3. The Metropolitan Legislators Were
Usually on the Prevailing Side When
They Voted Together with High Cohesion

Table 3 contains data on the positions of metropolitan delegations when they voted with a cohesion of 67 per cent or more.

During the five-session period in Illinois the metropolitan delegations voted with a cohesion of 67 per cent or more on 482 roll-calls and were on the prevailing side of 384 (80%). Three-fourths of the losses occurred in the Senate where party division within the metropolitan delegations confused high Democratic cohesion with high metropolitan cohesion.

Because of the unique system of cumulative voting in the election of each Illinois House district's three-member delegation, House districts, with few exceptions, elect two members of the majority party in the district and one member of the minority party. [15] Thus, although Chicago is a Democratic stronghold, in no session did the Republicans have fewer than 36 per cent of the House metropolitan delegation seats. A roll-call reflecting a cohesion of 67 per cent or more in the metropolitan delegation necessarily included both Democrats and Republicans. This situation makes it possible to examine the success of the metropolitan delegation when it not only voted with a high cohesion (67% or more) but also with substantial support from both parties within the delegation (at least 51% of each party group).

On 168 of the 984 contested roll-calls during the five-session period, the Illinois House metropolitan delegations voted with high cohesion and with intra-delegation bipartisan support. The delegations were on the prevailing side of 153 of these roll-calls (91%). On 10 of the 15 losing roll-calls the metropolitan delegation lost by one vote at a time when 17 members of the delegation were voting against the delegation majority position.

The metropolitan delegation in the Illinois Senate included enough Republicans in 1949, 1951, and 1953 to make feasible an analysis of roll-calls on which the test of cohesion (67% or more) also included the requirement that at least 51 per cent of each party group voted with the delegation position. Under this redefinition the delegations were on the prevailing side of 89 roll-calls (95%) as compared to 71 roll-calls (76%) when the requirement was simply a cohesion of 67 per cent or more.

The total losses under the two definitions of high metropolitan cohesion must be viewed in relationship to the total of 14,052 roll-calls during this ten-year period. The Illinois House and Senate metropolitan delegations lost on 98 (seven-tenths of one per cent) when the test of cohesion was 67 per cent or more of the delegation, and on 71 (five-tenths of one per cent) when the test of cohesion was 67 per cent or more of the delegation including at least 51 per cent of each party group. It is notable that the Illinois metropolitan delegations lost on only three out of 14,052 roll-calls when they voted with a cohesion of more than 90 per cent.

During the five-session period the Missouri metropolitan delegations were on the prevailing side of more than 85 per cent of the roll-calls when they voted with a cohesion of 67 per cent or more. As the cohesion of the delegation increased, the number of losses decreased until at the 90 per cent degree of cohesion St. Louis City was on the losing side of five out of a total of 938 contested roll-calls, Jackson County was on the losing side of four, and the combined St. Louis City-Jackson

County group was on the losing side of only one. Put in another way, the Missouri metropolitan delegations were practically never on the losing side of a roll-call vote when they themselves were highly united. The relatively greater success of the Missouri metropolitan delegations was partly due to the fact that they were primarily Democratic and were operating in a Democrat-controlled chamber, while the Illinois metropolitan delegations were primarily Democratic but were operating in Republican-controlled chambers. The partisan composition of the Illinois metropolitan delegations also influenced the pattern. As demonstrated above, it was possible by controlling the intra-delegation party variable to bring the Illinois patterns more into line with what was found in Missouri.

In sum, metropolitan delegations voting with high cohesion are seldom on the losing side of roll-calls, and as delegation solidarity approaches 100 per cent it is virtually certain that the delegation will be found on the prevailing side of the vote.

II. INTRA-METROPOLITAN POLITICAL DISPUTES AND CONFLICT OVER METROPOLITAN LEGISLATION

If conflict in the legislatures of Illinois and Missouri seldom follows metropolitan against non-metropolitan lines, the frequency of party conflict in these legislatures clearly indicates that party loyalty exerts a much stronger influence than geography on legislative behavior. The ratio of party votes to metropolitan against non-metropolitan votes ranged from 77:0 to 13:1. While party votes accounted for as much as 5 per cent of all roll-calls in Illinois, and 8 per cent of all roll-calls in Missouri, clear-cut metropolitan against non-metropolitan votes never exceeded 0.2 per cent of all roll-calls in either state. How, then, is legislative conflict over metropolitan problems generated?

An examination of the behavior of metropolitan legislative delegations on matters relating to the metropolitan area suggests that most conflict over city legislation comes from the city itself. Political power struggles go on in large cities and legislators reared in these struggles behave in the legislature just as they behave in city politics. Three examples of these struggles were found in Illinois and Missouri: intra-metropolitan party competition; central city-suburban conflict; and factionalism within the metropolitan majority party.

Chicago: Intra-Metropolitan Party Competition

Data on the frequency of votes showing high bipartisan cohesion and partisan conflict within the Illinois House metropolitan delegations of 1955 and 1957 suggest two significant patterns. First, metropolitan Democrats and Republicans were in conflict more often than all Democrats and Republicans in the chamber. Second, metropolitan Democrats and Republicans were more often in disagreement with each other than in agreement. Conflict within the metropolitan delegation was common during the consideration of city legislation. The behavior of the 1957 House Chicago Democrats and Republicans on 32 bills applicable only, or primarily, to the Chicago metropolitan area illustrates the lack of unity on metropolitan legislation. The metropolitan party groups opposed each other on 40 (85%) of the 47 roll-calls taken on these bills, and voted together with a cohesion of 67 per cent or more on only 2 (5%).

The past five sessions of the Illinois Assembly have produced numerous bills introduced by Chicago and Cook County Republicans to embarrass or damage the Democratic-controlled Chicago administration. Conversely, Chicago Democrats have introduced bills to consolidate their political advantages against Republican incursions. The non-metropolitan response to such measures tended to be partisan, producing chamber party votes rather than a division between metropolitan and non-metropolitan legislators. In a number of cases, however, the non-metropolitan legislators adopted a wait-and-see policy, refusing to take sides in an intra-city fight. Several non-metropolitan legislators have said in interviews that they are willing to support Chicago legislation on which both metropolitan parties agree, but are themselves unwilling to settle intra-metropolitan political disputes. It was a rare occasion when legislation supported solidly by both metropolitan parties failed to pass.

S.B. 310 in the 1957 session provides a good example of intra-metropolitan conflict in the Illinois legislature. This Chicago Republican bill proposed to restore a tax rate limit for the City of Chicago after the 1955 session had failed to place limits on how much money the city administration could take from the taxpayers. Such a limit would not only impose an important financial restraint on the Democratic city administration, but would also carry the implication that the incumbents could not be trusted to act according to the best interests of the people of Chicago. The bill passed the Senate on a straight chamber party vote, the Chicago and Cook County Republicans lining up with non-metropolitan Republicans against Chicago and non-metropolitan Democrats. The House Municipalities Committee reported the bill with a "do not pass" recommendation and Chicago House Republicans attempted to revive it by moving to overrule the Committee recommendation. In the ensuing debate the House Majority Whip, a Chicago Republican, accused Chicago Democratic legislators of political treachery in failing to keep 1955 promises to continue the tax limit under which Chicago had been operating until that time. Two bills had been introduced in 1955 by Chicago Democrats to continue this limit, but both bills were allowed by their sponsors to die on the calendar. The Majority Whip charged that without the tax limit "the taxpayers will be at the whim and caprice of the City of Chicago, and the taxpayers of Chicago deserve the protection of a limit." He further argued that

> the people will be at the mercy of a city council controlled by the city administration and that the "home rule" argument that Chicago should not be limited by the legislature is an attempt to take the lid off the property tax, contrary to the historical practice in the state of Illinois.

The House Minority Leader, a Chicago Democrat, countered that "we (sic) of Chicago have treated our taxpayers fairly" and accused the Chicago Republicans of unfair and dilatory action. The debate on the House floor was entirely between Chicago Democrats and Republicans. The vote which defeated the motion to overrule the "do not pass" recommendation illustrates both internecine metropolitan party behavior and the tendency of non-metropolitan legislators to line up along party lines or to ignore intra-metropolitan disputes. Chicago Democrats and Republicans voted solidly against each other, the non-metropolitan Democrats voted with Chicago Democrats and the non-metropolitan Republicans with Chicago Republicans, and a small but decisive number of both non-metropolitan Democrats and Republicans abstained from voting. The silence of 21 non-metropolitan legislators killed Chicago Republican chances to restore the tax limit when the motion fell 18 votes short of the required constitutional majority.

Other 1957 measures sponsored by Chicago and Cook County Republicans to damage or discredit metropolitan Democrats by transferring the quarrel to the state legislative arena included the abolition of the Chicago Department of Public Welfare and removal of its functions to a Cook County agency more amenable to Republican control, the alteration of Chicago aldermanic structures and election procedures to enable increased Republican political opportunities, and a change in the method of filling vacancies in the Cook County Board of Commissioners to protect Republican representation on the Board.

When legislative reapportionment is viewed in terms of this intra-metropolitan political struggle, it becomes doubtful whether correcting urban underrepresentation will necessarily make the city's lot in the state legislature an easier one. The 1955 Reapportionment Act in Illinois produced a new metropolitan power alignment which may not augur well for Chicago. The heaviest gains in seats were made by the suburban Cook County area, a Republican stronghold. Under this new arrangement the net gain in 1957 House seats over 1955 (old apportionment) was 5 per cent for Chicago and Cook County Democrats and 9 per cent for Chicago and Cook County Republicans, and the party division within the Chicago and Cook County delegations remained about the same as in 1955. Chicago and Cook County Republicans enjoyed a 17 per cent gain in Senate seats in 1957 while the Democratic groups suffered a 7 per cent loss. These Republican gains were accounted for largely by the addition of several House and Senate seats in Republican suburbia. The suburban gains are likely to be permanent in both chambers for two reasons: first, further reapportionment of Senate seats can be accomplished only by constitutional amendment; second, the pattern of urban growth suggests that the area of the state most likely to gain in seats as the House is reapportioned decennially will be the Republican suburbs of Cook County. If it is true that the strongest opposition to Democratic Chicago comes from Chicago and Cook County Republicans acting in concert rather than from non-metropolitan legislators, then Chicago may actually be in a weaker legislative position after than before reapportionment. Redress through fundamental changes in political loyalty in Republican suburban Cook County and downstate areas would seem remote.

Furthermore, it is interesting to speculate how far the sharp increase in metropolitan Republican seats may encourage these enemies of the Chicago city administration to appeal many of the intra-city and county power struggles to the state legislative forum. The Chicago and Cook County Republican gain in 1957 House seats was 9 per cent of the total seats, more than offsetting a non-metropolitan Republican loss of 6 per cent, and the Senate gain of the same group was 17 per cent as compared to a non-metropolitan Republican loss of 9 per cent. If Chicago and Cook County Republicans have enjoyed a corresponding increase in power within the Republican legislative parties, it is reasonable to conclude that they will be in a better position than before reapportionment to line up non-metropolitan Republican colleagues in the harassment of Chicago and Cook County Democrats who speak for City Hall.

Finally, political scientists have often proposed "home rule" as a solution to the problems of the big city in the state legislature, although many of them have

thought that unless "fair representation" was first achieved the solution could never
be pushed through. Paradoxically, the reapportionment which many counted on to
make possible subsequent grants of power to Chicago may instead have created a
political situation making the likelihood of such grants even more remote. The Republicans of Chicago and their allies across the city limits in suburban Cook County
may have permanently increased the strength of their opposition to giving their political enemies more autonomy in the operation of Chicago city government. With
their greater legislative power resulting from reapportionment, metropolitan Republicans may effectively veto ambitions for home rule powers. [16]

St. Louis City and St. Louis County: Central City-Suburban Conflict

Although the scarcity of Republicans in the Democratic St. Louis and Jackson County delegations precludes statistical analyses to indicate intra-metropolitan
conflict, evidences of other conflict may be adduced. It is a commonplace in the
Missouri Assembly that the bitter opposition to St. Louis City bills comes from
the suburban St. Louis County delegation, a majority of which is Republican. For
example, it was largely through the efforts of the Republican Minority Leader, a
St. Louis County Republican, that St. Louis City bills were contested in the 1957
session. While this was no doubt partly an attempt to discomfit the St. Louis City
Democratic administration, it was also an expression of grievance against the St.
Louis City earnings tax which requires suburbanites employed in the city to contribute to the city treasury. Any legislation which would cause added expense to
the city was met with opposition from St. Louis County and from whatever non-
metropolitan Republicans the County legislators could enlist. [17]

The penchant of St. Louis County legislators for opposing St. Louis City
in the legislature is further illustrated by their behavior on the 31 contested roll-
calls involving 1957 legislation relating to St. Louis City. More than 67 per cent
of St. Louis County legislators opposed more than 67 per cent of the St. Louis City
legislators on 25 (81%) of these votes, and the two groups were in moderate conflict
on 3 (10%) more. The two groups voted together with a cohesion of 67 per cent or
more on only one roll-call.

Kansas City: Factionalism within the Metropolitan Majority Party

The power relationship between City Hall and the city's legislative delega-
tion has much to do with the delegation's behavior. The Democratic Mayor of
Chicago exercises firm control over the Chicago Democrats in the Illinois Assembly.
As one Chicago House Democrat put it to the writer in 1957: "a telephone call from
Mayor Daley can control 40 of the 42 Chicago Democratic votes in the House." On
the other hand, Kansas City's administration has little, if any, control over the
Kansas City delegation. These legislators emerge from factional battles within the
Jackson County Democratic party, which was largely cut off from Kansas City mu-
nicipal government by reform groups and nonpartisan municipal elections. The
Kansas City delegation is without leadership, and each legislator owes loyalty only
to the faction locally responsible for his election. The leaders of the city administration, a mayor and a city manager, have nothing to do with the nomination and

election of the city's legislative delegation and exercise no control over the delegation's behavior. It is not uncommon to find Kansas City legislators working against legislation urged by the Kansas City administration or sponsoring bills opposed by the administration. For example, of ten bills opposed by the administration in the 1957 session, eight were sponsored by Kansas City Democrats, and several bills urged by the administration found little or no support in the city's legislative delegation.

On a continuum of city administration control over the city's Democratic legislators, Chicago would be placed at the extreme of strong control, Kansas City at the extreme of weak control, and St. Louis somewhere in between. Observations of the behavior of these urban delegations suggests that as city hall control of the legislative delegation becomes stronger, the climate for treatment of city bills in the legislature becomes more favorable. Since both the Illinois and Missouri Assemblies included a substantial number of non-metropolitan Democrats, and since these Democrats demonstrated their willingness to "go along" with metropolitan delegations, the city administration with no control over city legislators was in a weak position to further metropolitan legislative interests. In the case of Kansas City, "nonpartisanship" in city government may nurture a condition in the selection and control of the legislative delegation which operates against city interests in the state capital.

The reaction of non-metropolitan legislators to controversial city legislation in Missouri is much like the reaction found in Illinois: they either vote along party lines, or hold aloof from the conflict. George D. Young reported that "emergency" legislation put before the 1958 Special Session by the Governor at the request of the St. Louis and Kansas City administrations failed because of opposition from metropolitan legislators. For example, the St. Louis administration proposal for an increase in the earnings tax levy was opposed by virtually all of the St. Louis County delegation and many of the St. Louis City legislators. Young concluded that "In the House the difficulty in passing city legislation does not come from rural members but from members of the city's own delegation . . . *it is almost invariably true that if the city's delegation is united upon a measure it will be accepted by the entire General Assembly."* [18]

III. CONCLUSION

This analysis suggests that the traditional belief in bitter conflict between metropolitan and non-metropolitan areas in the state legislature must be rejected for Illinois and Missouri, at least at the roll-call stage. The following findings support such a conclusion:

(1) Non-metropolitan legislators seldom vote together with high cohesion against metropolitan legislators.
(2) Metropolitan legislators usually do not vote together with high cohesion.
(3) Metropolitan legislators are usually on the prevailing side when they do vote together with high cohesion.

A different type of conflict emerges in which political factors within the metropolitan area determine the fate of city legislation. The city's bitterest opponents in the legislature are political enemies from within its own walls, and those camped in the adjoining suburban areas. Non-metropolitan legislators have demonstrated their willingness to cooperate in the solution of metropolitan problems when metropolitan legislators can reach agreement on the solutions, and have demonstrated equally that when metropolitan political groups bring their disputes to the state legislature, non-metropolitan legislators will usually divide along party lines if they are attentive to the dispute at all. If metropolitan areas are to have party systems it is likely that metropolitan legislators will carry their political disputes with them to the state legislature where many metropolitan problems are agitated. Furthermore, it is likely that the city's success in the state legislature will depend on the ability and the inclination of metropolitan parties to resolve differences on policy before putting their case before the state.

NOTES

1. I wish to express appreciation to the Committee on Political Behavior of the Social Science Research Council for a grant-in-aid which made it possible to observe and interview the 1957 sessions and members of the Illinois and Missouri General Assemblies, and the collection of much of the data analyzed in this paper. The Council is not responsible for the findings or conclusions of this paper.

2. Murray S. Stedman, Jr., "American Political Parties as a Conservative Force," *Western Political Quarterly,* Vol. 10 (1957), p. 395.

3. Alfred DeGrazia, "General Theory of Apportionment," *Law and Contemporary Problems,* Vol. 17 (1952), p. 261.

4. For example, see: C. M. Kneier, *City Government in the United States,* rev. ed. (New York, 1947), Ch. 6; S. A. MacCorkle, *American Municipal Government and Administration* (Boston, 1949), pp. 52-54; C. F. Snider, *American State and Local Government* (New York, 1950), pp. 169-172.

5. For example, before the 1955 Reapportionment Act in Illinois, and at a time when the Illinois Legislature was characterized as rural-dominated, 53 per cent of the Senators and Representatives came from districts in which more than half the population resided in a city or cities of 10,000 or more. Fifty-seven per cent represented districts in which more than half the population resided in a city of 5,000 or more.

6. V. O. Key, Jr., *American State Politics* (New York, 1956), p. 234.

7. See Kneier, *op. cit.*; Snider, *op. cit.*; Benjamin Baker, *Urban Government* (Princeton, 1957), pp. 325-328; Gordon E. Baker, *Rural versus Urban Political Power* (Garden City, 1955), pp. 15-19.

8. It should be noted that while Chicago is part of Cook County, St. Louis County and St. Louis City are separate and independent areas and governments. The latter exercises both municipal and county powers. No state legislative district is in both St. Louis City and St. Louis County.

9   In the Missouri House each county has at least one seat, but a multiplier effect in the apportionment formula written into the Constitution gives increased representation to heavily populated counties — not, however, in direct proportion to the population of the county. Thus, St. Louis City has 22 per cent of the population and 11 per cent of the seats, Jackson County 14 per cent of the population and 8 per cent of the seats. The Missouri Senate is reapportioned decennially on the basis of population. At present St. Louis City and Jackson County contain 36 per cent of the population and hold 32 per cent of the Senate seats.

10. W.J. Keefe, *A Study of the Role of Political Parties in the Legislative Process, Illinois General Assembly* (unpublished Ph.D. thesis, Northwestern University, 1951), pp. 73-74. See also Keefe's "Parties, Partisanship, and Public Policy in the Pennsylvania Legislature," *American Political Science Review,* Vol. 48 (1954) p. 450, in which roll-call analyses are used. G. D. Young, *The Role of Political Parties in the Missouri House of Representatives* (unpublished Ph.D. thesis, University of Missouri, 1958), pp. 86-92. Dr. Young (D-Howard County) was a member of the Missouri House in the 1955 and 1957 sessions.

11. M. Jewell, "Party Voting in American State Legislatures. " *American Political Science Review,* Vol. 49 (1955), p. 773: W. Lockard, "Legislative Politics in Connecticut. " *American Political Science Review,* Vol. 48 (1954), p. 166; A. L. Lowell, "The Influence of Party Upon Legislation," *Annual Report of the American Historical Association,* Vol. 1, 1901; D. MacRae, "Relation Between Roll Call Votes and Constituencies in the Massachusetts House of Representatives, " *American Political Science Review,* Vol. 46 (1952), p. 1046; Julius Turner, *Party and Constituency* (Baltimore, 1951).

12. While thousands of roll-calls occurred in the Missouri Senate over the five-session period, few demonstrated enough conflict to be subjected to the analyses made of other roll-calls in this study. The conventions of the Missouri Senate apparently operate to reduce recorded conflict. Committees function more meaningfully in the Missouri Senate than they do in the House, and since roll-calls are more difficult to take than in the House much more of the Senate business is conducted by *viva voce* or show-of-hands votes. Undoubtedly the size of the group (34) facilitates pre-voting compromise and consensus. An examination of the contested roll-calls which did occur in the Senate suggests that there was no more, and possibly less, metropolitan conflict than data included here indicate for the House. This is substantiated by George D. Young in "The 1958 Special Session of the Missouri General Assembly," *Missouri Political Science Association Newsletter,* No. 3 (May, 1958), p. 3.

13. In order to give concrete meaning to "support" or "opposition" in this study, a delegation is considered to have voted with a high cohesion if the absolute test showed a percentage of at least 67 or more. Most of the findings are presented on the basis of this definition, but findings for other degrees of cohesion are included for purposes of comparison. A vote on which less than half of the delegation was in agreement must be eliminated on the basis that a minority expression should not be imputed to the majority. On the other hand, to demand a cohesion of 100 per cent would eliminate all contested roll-calls from the analysis. Interviews with observers of the Assemblies

indicated that, if anything, this 67 per cent level of significance may be too low.

14. The relatively higher incidence of voting cohesion from 67 to 91 per cent in the 1955 and 1957 sessions of the Senate may be accounted for by the fact that Democrats comprised 83 per cent of the Chicago delegation in 1957, and 89 per cent in 1955. In all other House and Senate sessions, some Republican votes were needed to push delegation cohesion above 67 per cent. The 1955 and 1957 Senate data reflected party conflict.

15. For analyses of the cumulative voting system and its political implications see George S. Blair, "Cumulative Voting," *American Political Science Review,* Vol. 52 (1959), p. 123; and Charles S. Hyneman and J. D. Morgan, "Cumulative Voting in Illinois," *Illinois Law Review,* Vol. 32 (1937), p. 12.

16. Edward D. Banfield has pointed out the inherent political difficulties of metropolitan area organization stemming from control of the central city and the suburbs by two different political parties. "The Politics of Metropolitan Area Organization," *Midwest Journal of Political Science,* Vol. 1 (1957), p. 77. He states that "it seems likely that the central cities will become more and more Democratic" and that "the Republican suburban vote has in general suffered little from the increase in population." As a result "these facts suggest that for many years to come it will be difficult or impossible to integrate local governments where the two party system operates" because "in effect, advocates of consolidation schemes are asking the Democrats to give up their control of the central cities or, at least, to place it in jeopardy." It may be that Banfield's argument can be broadened to say that the same forces which bring the central city Republicans and the suburbs into collision with the Democrat central city administration in metropolitan area organization can be expected to appear in legislative consideration of expanded "home rule" powers for the central city.

17. An example of the opposition of St. Louis County to the St. Louis City earnings tax is provided by a series of 18 House votes on H. B. 50 (1951) which authorized extension of the tax. St. Louis City and St. Louis County delegations were in high opposition on 12 roll-calls, in moderate opposition on 3 roll-calls, and in agreement on 3 roll-calls. Ten of the roll-calls were chamber party votes under the definition of 67 per cent of the elected party groups in opposition to each other, and fifteen were chamber party votes under the definition of 80 per cent of the voting members of the party groups in opposition to each other.

18. George D. Young, "The 1958 Special Session of the Missouri General Assembly," *Missouri Political Science Association Newsletter,* No. 3 (1958). My emphasis.

A Comparision of Constituency Influences in the Upper and Lower Chambers of a State Legislature

Thomas R. Dye

It is generally conceded that the voting behavior of legislators is affected by both party and constituency influences. Some legislators identify themselves chiefly with their party, while others perceive their role as one of representing constituency interests.[1] Many inquiries have been made into the relative merits of Burkean representation, accountability to constituency, and party responsibility, but few studies have bothered to investigate the actual extent of insurgency, constituency influences, and party voting in legislative bodies.[2] The only published article to date which has examined the effect of constituency influences on party cohesion in the voting behavior of state legislators, is a study of the Massachusetts House of Representatives by Duncan MacRae, Jr.[3] Working with roll-call votes on legislation which appeared to reflect socio-economic differences, MacRae found that legislators representing districts typical of those which generally elected members of their party on a home-owner occupancy index tended to display greater party loyalty than legislators elected by districts atypical of their party. MacRae also found that representatives whose previous election margins were narrow tended to cross party lines more often than representatives elected by wide margins.

The study summarized by this paper produced similar findings regarding the 1957 session of the Pennsylvania House of Representatives, but, perhaps more significantly, found the patterns which described legislative voting behavior in the lower chambers in both Massachusetts and Pennsylvania to be inappropriate for describing voting behavior in the Pennsylvania State Senate. Variations in the voting behavior of members of the upper and lower chambers of a legislature should not confound readers of the American classics.[4] The *Federalist Papers* discuss the probable behavior of members of the separate chambers and in so doing inadvertently suggest certain hypotheses capable of verification. These hypotheses will be examined later.

ESTABLISHING A TYPOLOGY OF DEMOCRATIC AND REPUBLICAN CONSTITUENCIES IN PENNSYLVANIA

The findings of this study are qualified to the extent that census information on income could not be reassembled by legislative district for 42 of the 154 House districts in Pennsylvania and 6 of the 50 Senate districts. Thus, in effect, the findings are based upon a sample which includes 72.7 per cent of all House districts and 82 per cent of all Senate districts. However, it did not appear that the sample varied

Reprinted by permission of the University of Utah, coypright owners, from *Western Political Quarterly,* Vol. 14 (1964), pp. 473-480.

from the universal in its party composition, rural-urban composition, or even cross-indices of these characteristics.

If Democratic and Republican state legislative districts in Pennsylvania are differentiated by a combination of socio-economic variables, four distinct types of districts emerge, each with a marked political coloration: rural low-income, rural high-income, urban low-income, and urban high-income.[5] Figures 1 and 2 are abstracts of graphs on which Pennsylvania House and Senate districts are appropriately placed on X and Y axes representing available measures of income and ruralism. Republicans predominate in the urban high-income, rural high-income, and rural low-income areas. Democrats control only the urban low-income category. This characterization is equally applicable to both House and Senate districts.

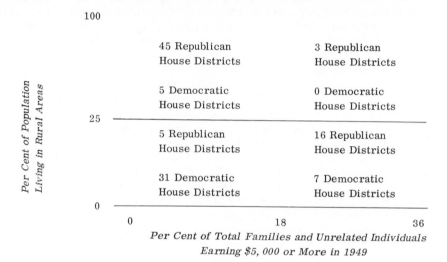

Figure 1 Distribution of Republican and Democratic House districts, 1957 session, by income and ruralism.

In order to confirm this characterization, an investigation was conducted into the locus of political competition for state legislative office in Pennsylvania. The hypothesis was that the areas of greatest political competition would be those districts in which typically Republican socio-economic characteristics balance typically Democratic socio-economic influences. If urban legislative districts are divided into "sure Republican," "sure Democratic," and "close" districts, depending on whether or not the elected representative received as much as 57 per cent of the total votes cast, and then distributed on an income scale, the following pattern is discernible (see Figures 3 and 4). In both the House and the Senate close elections are largely concentrated in the intermediate income intervals. Democrat-safe districts tend to be concentrated in the low-income areas, while Republican safe districts are concentrated in the middle- or upper-income areas.

As interesting as these findings are in themselves to the study of state parties, the degree to which Republican legislators tend to come from one kind of constituency and Democratic legislators from another kind is relevant here only because it permits us to turn to the voting records of legislators representing districts both typical and atypical of their party and to ascertain the effects of constituency characteristics on party cohesion.

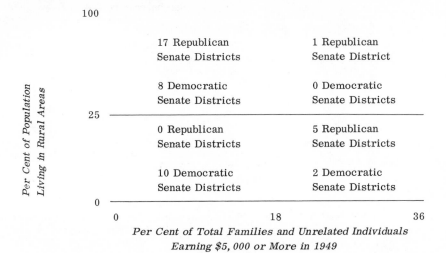

Figure 2 Distribution of Republican and Democratic senatorial districts, 1957 session, by income **and ruralism.**

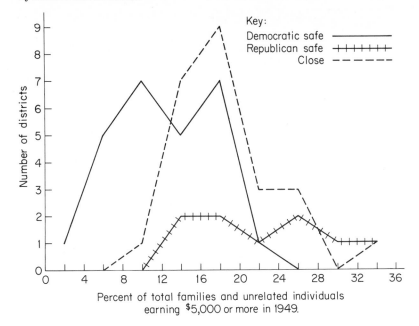

Figure 3 Distribution of Republican and Democratic safe and close urban house districts, 1957 session, by per cent of total families and unrelated individuals earning $5,000 or more in 1949.

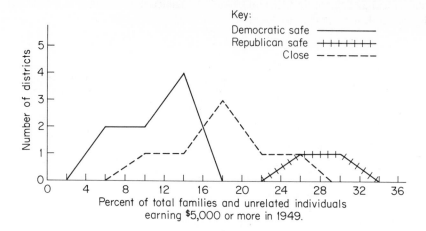

Figure 4 Distribution of Republican and Democratic safe and close urban senatorial districts, 1957 session, by per cent of families and unrelated individuals earning $5,000 or more in 1949.

ESTABLISHING RELATIONSHIPS BETWEEN CONSTITUENCY CHARACTERISTICS AND VOTING BEHAVIOR

One method of measuring the extent of party cohesion displayed by each legislator is the "deviation index." The deviation index is the per cent of the votes on which party majorities were in opposition that the legislator voted with the opposition party's majority and against his own party's majority.[6] A deviation index was computed for each legislator for the entire 1957 session of the Pennsylvania General Assembly.[7]

At this point the study had several measures of degree variables: the deviation index measuring the individual legislator's party loyalty, the margin of electoral victory measuring political competition for state legislative office, and the rural-urban and income indices measuring constituency characteristics. The problem then became one of measuring the proportion of the variation in the dependent variable (in this case the deviation index) which can be attributed to variation in one or another of the independent variables (in this case the electoral margin and the rural-urban and income indices). The coefficient of correlation is such a measure.

Table 1 shows the several correlation coefficients for the relationships between the constituency characteristics measured and the party cohesion displayed by the legislators from these constituencies for both the House and the Senate during the 1957 session. The problem of securing independent measures of selected variables is a difficult one in any science. In this study the problems arose with regard to the fact that the rural districts all tended to be low-income districts. In order to free the coefficients of the relationship between income and deviation from the effects of ruralism, they had to be computed on the basis of urban legislators only.

Table 1 A comparison of correlation coefficients of relationships between constituency characteristics and party cohesion for House and Senate members, 1957 session, Pennsylvania General Assembly.

| | Correlation Coefficient | | | |
| | House | | Senate | |
Relationship	Democrats	Republicans	Democrats	Republicans
Income and Deviation				
Total Urban Legislators .... .45	.45	− .07	.08	− .29
Ruralism and Deviation				
Total Legislators .... .56	.56	− .37	.09	.00+
Electoral Margin and Deviation				
Total Legislators .... − .46	− .46	− .44	− .15	.12

On the other hand, the coefficients of the relationship between ruralism and deviation were computed on the basis of total legislators and consequently not free from the effects of income. However, instead of reinforcing the coefficient, the failure to hold income constant tends to lower the coefficient. Therefore significant correlation between ruralism and deviation based upon total legislators is even more impressive than one based only upon low-income legislators. If one were interested in ascertaining the precise proportion of the total variance in the dependent variable which can be attributed to variation in two or more independent variables, a coefficient of multiple correlation could be computed.[8] The purposes of this study, however, are achieved by simply showing significant relationships between the selected constituency characteristics and deviation.

Determining what constitutes a significant correlation coefficient in the social sciences is no easy task. It is unrealistic to expect to find correlations in the social sciences comparable to those found in the physical sciences, where problems of intruding variables can be more easily controlled. None of the correlation coefficients in Table 1 are particularly high, but a comparison of the several coefficients reveals important variations.

The signs of the coefficients describing relationships between constituency characteristics and party cohesion in the House of Representatives tend to indicate that the hypothesized relationships do exist. As a constituency's income rises, the propensity of its Democratic legislators to cross party lines increases, while the tendency of its Republican legislators to violate party discipline decreases. As the constituencies become more rural (by definition for purposes of this study) in character, their Democratic representatives prove a greater threat to party unity, while their Republican representatives constitute less of a threat to party cohesion. Table 1 also implies that the greater the degree of political competition for House legislative office, the greater the tendency will be for representatives to cross party lines. To summarize these findings in the light of the characterization of House legislative districts mentioned above, it appears that party cohesion is highest among legislators elected by constituencies typical of their party while cohesion tends to break down among legislators elected by constituencies atypical of their party.

A common mistake in the interpretation of correlation coefficients is the belief that a high coefficient can be accounted for by differences in the amounts of the separate variables. For example, one may be tempted to argue that greater deviation among Democrats explains their higher coefficients or that greater cohesion in the Senate explains its lower coefficients. These interpretations are unwarranted, however, since a correlation coefficient measures only the extent to which variation in the dependent variable is associated with variation in the independent variable, and nothing more. In short, amounts are irrelevant and only the degree to which variations are associated can affect the size of the coefficient. Thus, one can safely conclude that the relationships shown in Table 1 possess independent significance and are not merely an artifact of research method.

COMPARING CONSTITUENCY INFLUENCES IN THE UPPER AND LOWER CHAMBERS

The findings above regarding voting behavior in the Pennsylvania House of Representatives agree with those of Turner with regard to Congress and those of MacRae with regard to the Massachusetts House of Representatives. Perhaps of even greater interest, however, is that the relationships between constituency characteristics and voting behavior found to exist in the lower chamber of the Pennsylvania legislature were conspicuously absent in the study of the upper chamber. While there was greater party cohesion displayed in the Senate, there was still sufficient deviation to permit the computation of correlation coefficients between deviation and the several constituency variables. Table 1 shows that the Senate coefficients are uniformly low and that two of their signs contradict the hypothesized relationships. No significant relationship was found to exist between the party cohesion displayed by senators and either their margin of election or the socio-economic composition of their districts. This was so despite the fact that the socioeconomic characterization of constituencies described earlier applies to both the House and the Senate.

These findings may contain important implications regarding the function of the second chamber. The purpose of the second chamber as seen by the founders of the American political structure was stated by James Madison:

> The necessity of a Senate is not the less indicated by the propensity of all single and numerous assemblies to yield to the impulse of sudden and violent passions and to be seduced by factious leaders into intemperate and pernicious resolutions . . . a body which is to avoid this infirmity ought itself to be free from it and consequently less numerous. It ought, moreover, to possess great firmness, and consequently ought to hold its authority by a tenure of considerable duration. [9]

Madison contemplated an indirectly elected chamber, but additional insurance against "faction," or pressures generated by citizens "united and actuated by some common impulse of passion or of interest," was to be achieved by greater selectivity in the recruitment of senators and longer terms. The larger constituencies represented by members of the upper chamber also were thought to be insurance against "faction." In extolling the merits of an extensive republic, Madison wrote:

> The smaller the society the fewer probably will be the distinct parties and interests composing it; the fewer the distinct parties and interests, the more frequently will a majority be found of the same party. . . . Extend the sphere and you take in a greater variety of parties and interests; you make it less probable that a majority of the whole will have a common motive to invade the rights of other citizens; or if such a common motive exists, it will be more difficult for all who feel it to discover their own strength, and to act in unison with each other. [10]

Despite the passage of time and the demise of indirect election, Madison's description of the function of the second chamber is an appropriate summary of the findings of this study. It appears from empirical analysis that the function of the upper chamber in Pennsylvania is to inject into legislative decision-making the influence of a body relatively more free from narrower constituency pressures than the lower chamber. Larger and more heterogeneous constituencies compel senators to align themselves with a wider variety of interests. Not only are senators free to look after more widely shared interests than representatives, but they are probably compelled to do so to please a broader and more heterogeneous constituency. While constituency characteristics had no discernible effect on the decision of senators to adhere to party program, it was nonetheless evident in the study that both parties displayed greater cohesion in the upper chamber. One may conjecture that the moderating of constituency influence via longer terms and larger districts actually clears the way for party affiliation to exert a greater influence on voting patterns. None of the studies of state legislatures cited earlier compared voting behavior in the upper chamber to that of the lower chamber. If anything, the study described here points to the need for a comparative analysis of the role of upper chambers in American state legislatures.

NOTES

1. See Ralph K. Huitt, "The Congressional Committee: A Case Study," *American Political Science Review,* XLVIII (June 1954), 341-65.

2. A notable exception is Julius Turner's *Party and Constituency: Pressures on Congress* (Baltimore: Johns Hopkins University Press, 1951). See also David Truman, *The Congressional Party* (New York: Wiley, 1959); Malcolm E. Jewell, "Party Voting in American State Legislatures," *American Political Science Review,* XLIX (September 1955), 773-91; Heinz Eulau, *et al.,* "The Role of the Representative: Some Empirical Observations on the Theory of Edmund Burke," *American Political Science Review,* LIII (September 1959), 742-56.

3. "The Relation Between Roll-Call Votes and Constituencies in the Massachusetts House of Representatives," *American Political Science Review,* XLVI (December 1952), 1046-55.

4. Charles Hyneman discusses the controversy over whether or not the classics are

"rich with hypotheses ripe for verification" in *The Study of Politics (Urbana:* University of Illinois Press, 1959).

5. These categories were established with data gathered from the 1950 census and reassembled by legislative district. Districts with less than 25 per cent of the population living in rural areas as defined by the Census Bureau, have been designated urban; all other districts are classified as rural. Districts with more than 18 per cent of the total families and unrelated individuals earning $5,000 or more in 1949 are classified as high-income districts; all other districts are designated low income. These are merely operational definitions assigned to quadrants of the scatter-diagram showing the relationship between income and ruralism in legislative districts. See U.S. Bureau of the Census, *1950 Census of the Population,* Vol. 38, *Pennsylvania* (Washington: Government Printing Office, 1950).

6. The deviation index is really the inverse of Julius Turner's "loyalty index." See Julius Turner, *Party and Constituency: Pressures on Congress* (Baltimore: Johns Hopkins University Press, 1951). The lower figures of the deviation index were preferred over the higher figures of the loyalty index to facilitate correlation computations. Party cohesion is comparatively easy to measure; for a discussion of the more complex problems of attitude measurement among legislators see George M. Belknap, "A Method for Analyzing Legislative Behavior," *Midwest Journal of Political Science,* II (November 1958), 377-402.

7. Notice that in this study the deviation index is not based upon an analysis of selected roll calls but upon the total roll-call votes taken during the 1957 session. The possibility of skewing the sample in the selection of roll calls is thereby reduced. This is unlike Duncan MacRae's study of the Massachusetts legislature where he deliberately selects roll calls which appear to reflect socio-economic differences "in an effort to magnify the effect we are concerned with. . . ." The deviation index in this study is based on total roll calls and no attempt has been made to magnify the effect of the independent variables.

8. This particular problem in multiple correlation requires the aid of electronic computers beyond the financial capacity of the researcher.

9. *The Federalist* (New York: Putnam, 1888), No. 62, p. 387.

10. *The Federalist* (Putnam, 1888), No. 10, p. 56.

The Consequences of Malapportionment: A Note of Caution

Herbert Jacob

Legislative malapportionment has become a principal target in the effort to reform state government. It has been demonstrated beyond doubt that state legislative seats are not equally distributed by population. Likewise, few doubt that the states are not as vigorous as they might be in attacking their problems. Many observers attribute much of state governments' weakness to malapportionment. In V.O. Key's words, "it must be assigned a high rank" among the factors which have led to the low stature of state legislatures.[1] Charles Adrian asserts, "Malapportionment, in terms of population, has serious effects upon governmental policies."[2] He goes on to illustrate these effects with examples of harsh treatment of criminals and mental patients in some states, policies which are allegedly imposed by rural legislators upon the states. Malcolm Jewell states, "In a number of states, malapportionment weakens the two-party system. . . . It is most important politically when it produces divided government."[3]

Since the Supreme Court's decision in Baker v. Carr in 1962, legislative malapportionment has won recognition as a national political problem. For the first time in our history, the Court has ordered legislatures to reapportion. As a consequence, efforts to reapportion state legislative seats are under way across the nation. The proponents of reapportionment, reflecting the criticisms of state government, look to their program with great hope. After reapportionment, a new day will dawn for the states; they will be free to assert their rightful place in our governmental system.

The argument that legislative malapportionment is largely responsible for or connected with lack of party competition, divided government, unfair distribution of funds, and unprogressive legislation is based on a series of illustrations. Jewell argues by pointing out Rhode Island and Kentucky where he asserts that malapportionment has made it difficult for the weaker party to win effective power. He uses Louisiana, Florida, and Texas to illustrate the advantage the rural wing of a party may have through its dominant position in the legislature. Adrian cites the case of Alabama where the apportionment system apparently exacerbated rural-urban divisions in the legislature.[4] The arguments would be more convincing, however, if we could measure the effect of malapportionment on all 50 states, for if malapportionment is the villain, those states that are relatively well apportioned would be substantially free from the defects cited while those states which are badly apportioned would suffer from them. In fact it is possible to measure some of these phenomena and test the effect of malapportionment on state politics.

Reprinted from *Social Forces,* Vol. 43, No. 2 (December 1964), pp. 256-261 by permission of the publisher.

I am grateful to my colleagues, Clara Penniman, Lewis A. Froman, Jr., and Robert Alford for their helpful comments on an earlier draft.

MEASURING THE CONSEQUENCES OF MALAPPORTIONMENT

The degree of malapportionment or urban underrepresentation can be measured in a number of ways. We have constructed three indices. [5] The first, an index of equal apportionment, is computed for each state by dividing the most populous district into the least populous one for each house and adding the quotients. The index runs from 0 to 2; the higher the index number, the better apportioned the state. The second index (Index of Rural Dominance) ranks the states according to the proportion of the population that can control the least representative house of the legislature. This measure was chosen because all legislation must win the concurrence of both houses. If one is overwhelmingly dominated by rural elements, that is enough to block consideration of urban problems. However, some might argue that rural domination by itself is not questioned but only the underrepresentation of urban populations in those houses based on population. Therefore, a third index was constructed (Index of Urban Underrepresentation) which ranked the states according to the proportion of the population which can control the least representative house *whose membership is based on population.* [6] As many reapportionment efforts are directed only at the house of the legislature which is based on population, this index may enable us to estimate what changes we might expect from such reapportionment.

The three indices enable us to rank the states in three different ways from best apportioned to worst apportioned. [7] These rankings then can be correlated with rankings of the states according to measures which would indicate some of the alleged effects of malapportionment; we have chosen rankings based on the level of party competition, frequency of divided government, degree of urbanism, level of Old Age Assistance payments, percent of state funds spent on municipal extensions of state roads, [8] and per capita public health expenditures. [9] The correlation coefficents are shown in Table 1.

DISCUSSION

The striking feature of all the correlations is their extremely low value. We would have expected moderate, negative correlations between malapportionment and party competition, for many political scientists have argued that malapportionment suppresses the minority party and leads to weak party competition. Likewise, a rather high correlation between the malapportionment indices and the frequency of divided government was expected, for it is frequently asserted that divided control over the state house with the governorship in the hands of one party and one or both houses of the legislature in the hands of the opposition results from malapportionment. The spectacular examples of Michigan and New Jersey illustrate the argument. Across the nation, however, the relationship between malapportionment as measured by any of the indices and divided government is quite low.

A relatively high negative correlation between malapportionment and urbanism would have been in order, for the urban states allegedly suffer most from this ill. The most urban states are those in which the cities have grown rapidly in

Table 1 Rank order correlation between measures of legislative malapportionment and selected political phenomena for 49 states.[a]

	Index of Equal Apportionment	Index of Rural Dominance	Index of Urban Underrepresentation
Level of Party Competition[b] (Hyp: Mod, pos correl)....	−.05	−.09	.15
Frequency of Divided Government[c] (Hyp: High, pos correl)....	.45	.27	.15
Degree of Urbanism[d] (Hyp: High, neg correl)....	.09	−.12	.04
Level of OAA Payments[e] (Hyp: Mod, pos correl)....	.19	.06	.20
Distribution of State Highway Funds to Municipal Highway Extensions[f] (Hyp: Mod, pos correl)....	−.11	−.04	−.07
Level of Per Capita Public Health Expenditure[g] (Hyp: Mod, pos correl)....	−.11	−.02	−.10

[a] Nebraska is excluded because of its unicameral legislature. Minnesota, Alaska, and Hawaii are omitted from the first correlation (with party competition) because Minnesota's legislature is officially non-partisan and Alaska and Hawaii's recent admission to the Union precluded including them in our measure of party competition; these three states are included in all other correlations. The numbers in the table are Spearman Rank Order Correlation Coefficients. For the definition of the indices, see the text.

[b] The measure used was developed by Richard E. Dawson and James A. Robinson, "Inter-Party Competition, Economic Variables, and Welfare Policies in the American States," *Journal of Politics,* 25 (1963), pp. 270-278. The measure used here takes into account percent of popular vote for governor, percent of seats in Senate held by major party, and percent of seats in House held by major party during the period 1938-1958.

[c] The period 1950-1960 was used.

[d] Used here was the 1960 census data on the 1950 urban definition which underestimates the degree of urbanism. The effect should have been to inflate the correlation coefficient.

[e] The data are for 1954 from Robert S. Babcock, *State and Local Government and Politics* (New York: Random House, 1957), pp. 258-259.

[f] The data are for 1960 from Council of State Governments, *Book of the States 1962-63* (Chicago; Council of State Governments, 1962), pp. 342-343. A control for the degree of urbanism was included: see note 8.

[g] The data are for 1959 from *Statistical Abstract of the United States, 1961* (Washington: Government Printing Office, 1961), pp. 307, 411. A control for the relative wealth of the states was included; see note 9.

the last two decades while legislative redistricting lagged behind. Therefore, the more urban, the worse the apportionment. The data do not support this argument. Degree of urbanism is not related to malapportionment.

Finally, it is frequently asserted that malapportionment has certain policy consequences. It is asserted that cities are maltreated, that rural legislators impose their values and style of life on the urban majority, and that as a consequence the states have not had the vigor necessary to face the problems of the 20th century. Policy outputs are notoriously difficult to measure, but some indicators are available. For instance, the level of Old Age Assistance payments reflects in large part the concern of the state legislature for aiding the needy aged. Rural legislators, it is hypothesized, with their more puritanical outlook on public charity and with the more modest needs of their constituents would tend to suppress the level of such payments (even with the federal grants-in-aid for the program). If this were true, we would expect the worse apportioned the state (and the more dominant the rural legislators), the lower the level of OAA payments. As Table 1 indicates, this relationship does not hold. A second measure of policy outputs is the distribution of highway funds for rural and urban highways. Our data do not reflect all highway expenditures, but we would expect that rural legislators, if they act as described in the texts, would vote proportionately more money for their roads than for highways in the municipalities. Again one is led to expect that the more malapportioned the legislature, the more discriminatory the treatment of cities. Once more, the data do not bear out this hypothesis. The last measure we used was public health expenditures by states. This is a rough check of Adrian's hypothesis that rural dominated legislatures will deal more harshly with (spend less money on) the mentally ill and all indigent ill who might come to state hospitals. The data, however, show that there is no significant relationship on any of our indices.

Table 2 Malapportionment and municipal home rule, right-to-work laws, and perceptions of damage attributable to malapportionment.

	Index of Equal Apportionment		Index of Rural Dominance		Index of Urban Underrepresentation	
	Ten Best	Ten Worst	Ten Best	Ten Worst	Ten Best	Ten Worst
States Having Municipal Home Rule[a]	7	6	6	7	6	7
States Having Right-To-Work Laws[b]	1	5	2	3	1	3
States with Complaints of Damage Attributable to Malapportionment[c]	2	7	1	6	3	6

[a]Russell W. Maddox, Jr., and Robert F. Fuquay, *State and Local Governments* (Princeton: D. Van Nostrand Co., 1962), p. 456.

[b]Council of State Governments, *Book of the States, op. cit.*, p. 493, note 2.

[c]National Municipal League, *Compendium of State Legislative Apportionment* (New York: National Municipal League, 1962).

Another test of the hypothesis that malapportionment has an important and visible impact on state policies is the presence or absence of certain statutes in several states. On the one hand, one might expect to find malapportionment states lacking municipal home rule; on the other hand, one might expect that rural dominated legislatures adopt "right-to-work" laws more frequently than better apportioned legislatures. Table 2 shows how many of the ten best and ten worst apportioned states (as measured by the three indices) possess such laws. While it seems that badly apportioned states are somewhat more receptive to "right-to-work" laws, the relationship is not strong enough to assert that apportionment is the determinative factor in the absence or presence of such legislation. Quite clearly, other factors are more important in determining such matters.

The last item in Table 2 is a curious one. It is based on the National Municipal League's *Compendium on State Legislative Apportionment.* The League asked a political scientist in each state to report claims of actual damage attributable to malapportionment. As the data show, political scientists in those states which are worst apportioned report such claims much more frequently than those in relatively well apportioned states. Here we are dealing not with actual damages (as measured by the indices discussed earlier) but perception of damages. It appears that observers are most sensitive to apparent damage in the worst apportioned states. It is interesting to note, however, that while no state was really well apportioned in 1962, 29 states reported no major complaint of damage attributed to malapportionment.

CONCLUSIONS

We have not argued that malapportionment never has an effect on state policies. However, we have found no measurable effect on the indices which we used. These indices tested the most frequently asserted hypotheses. If malapportionment has a widespread effect on state politics, it is a good deal more subtle than we have hitherto thought. A much more likely conclusion is that malapportionment may have serious consequences only under certain additional conditions. For instance, it can be associated with divided government only where parties effectively compete with each other. In the one party South, malapportionment cannot lead to party divisions of the executive and the legislative.

Perhaps it was naïve to expect visible relationships between malapportionment and various political and policy outcomes, for party conflict is highly discontinuous in most state legislatures. We now know that many issues in state legislatures are neither settled on the basis of urban-rural divisions [10] nor on the basis of party positions. [11] Policies seem rather to be formulated as a result of temporary coalitions constructed by interested pressure groups or molded by a particularly strong governor. Under these circumstances where legislators come from matters less than who they are associated with and to whom they are willing to listen.

It is striking that Jewell and Adrian draw so heavily on southern states for their examples of the alleged impact of malapportionment. This is not because all the southern states were worse apportioned than northern states. Indeed, the median ranking of the 13 southern states on the three indices was 31, 23, and 29 respectively. What attracted Jewell's and Adrian's attention, apparently, was the general conservatism of some of these states and the effervescence of politics in the South.

Our closer analysis indicates that southern states are not very different from their northern neighbors in the degree of malapportionment nor in the impact malapportionment has had on policy outputs.

Our data demonstrate that malapportionment in and of itself is not associated with some of the major ailments of state politics. Consequently, we shall have to moderate our enthusiasm for reapportioning state legislatures. On a moral basis, the proponents of reapportionment have a strong case. The practical impact however, may be quite different than currently expected. Many of the new seats will go to suburban areas which are often more conservative than the rural areas which will lose seats. In the North, the Republican party will not lose nearly as many seats as some Democrats hope, for most of the new suburbs are almost as Republican as the rural areas. [12] Moreover, many of the issues which concern the cores of metropolitan areas divide them from the suburbs. Increasing the voice of suburban voters may not bring additional state aid to the central cities; it is perhaps more likely that a new stalemate will develop on those issues which deeply divide the core cities from suburban areas. Reapportionment may also fail to strengthen state legislatures because of the kind of legislators sent to the capital by metropolitan and suburban areas to replace the rural stalwarts. Legislators from larger cities tend to stay in the legislature for shorter periods; the more ambitious often seek municipal posts which pay higher salaries and impose fewer inconveniences than a legislative seat in a far-off state capital. [13]

Reapportionment of state legislatures will undoubtedly have some impact on politics in the states. We do not know enough to predict exactly what the consequences will be. Our analysis indicates, however, that it is improbable that it will substantially invigorate state governments or dissolve the stalemates which sap public confidence in them.

NOTES

1. V.O. Key, Jr., *American State Politics: An Introduction* (New York: Alfred A Knopf, 1956), p. 76.

2. Charles R. Adrian, *State and Local Governments* (New York: McGraw-Hill Book Co., 1960), pp. 306-307.

3. Malcolm E. Jewell, *The State Legislature, Politics and Practice,* Studies in Political Science No. 37 (New York: Random House, 1962), pp. 30-33.

4. *Ibid.*; Adrian, *op. cit.* See also Gordon E. Baker, *Rural Versus Urban Political Power,* Studies in Political Science No. 20 (New York: Random House, 1955), pp. 19-26.

5. All indices are based on the data reported by National Municipal League, *Compendium on State Legislative Apportionment* (New York: National Municipal League, 1962).

6. For those states which do not use population as the basis of apportionment for either house, the least representative house was used as in the Index of Rural Dominance.

7. The three indices are moderately related to each other as the following Spearman Rank Order Correlation Coefficients show:

	Index of Equal Apportionment	*Index of Rural Dominance*	*Index of Urban Under-representation*
Index of Mal-apportionment	—	.69	.66
Index of Rural Dominance	.69	—	.63
Index of Urban Underrep	.66	.63	—

8. In order to control for the degree to which the several states are urbanized, the index held urbanism constant as follows: percent funds expended on municipal highways minus percent population urban equals index.

9. In order to control for the varying wealth of the several states, per capita income was held constant in constructing this index.

10. David R. Derge, "Metropolitan and Outstate Alignments in Illinois and Missouri Legislative Delegations," *American Political Science Review*, 52 (1958), pp. 1051-65, and Thomas A. Flinn, "The Outline of Ohio Politics," *Western Political Quarterly*, 13 (1960), pp. 716-718.

11. See the summary table showing the proportion of votes with a high degree of party cohesion in Jewell, *op. cit.*, p. 52, as well as the description of educational politics by Nicholas A. Masters, Robert H. Salisbury, and Thomas A. Elliot, *State Politics and the Public Schools* (New York: Alfred A. Knopf, 1964).

12. Bernard Lazerwitz, "Suburban Voting Trends: 1948 to 1950," *Social Forces,* 39 (October 1960) pp. 32-33. Lazerwitz, however, argues that Democratic strength in the suburbs is slowly growing.

13. Systematic data for all the states are not available to substantiate these observations. However, for Wisconsin see Leon D. Epstein, *Politics in Wisconsin* (Madison: University of Wisconsin Press, 1958) pp. 100-111; for Pennsylvania see Frank J. Sorauf, *Party and Representation* (New York: Atherton Press, 1963), pp. 82-84 and 93-94.

THE GOVERNOR

The Office Careers of Governors in the United States

Joseph A. Schlesinger

The means of advancement from office to office is an important characteristic of any political system. In American politics the empirical study of movement
between offices is of special importance, because there is little, if any, prescribed
relation between offices, either in law or in conscious custom. Given an abundance
of elective offices in a constitutional framework of federalism and the separation
of powers, many paths are open to the politically ambitious. However, as is readily
evident, all paths do not lead equally to higher office. No legal prescription keeps
the county clerk from the presidency. Nevertheless, the major national conventions
have yet to nominate a county clerk for the highest national office. Despite a multiplicity of possible career lines in local, state, and national politics, it is certain
that the paths actually followed by successful politicians have not been completely
haphazard.

The object of this study is to determine the offices which have led to a piv-
otal position in American politics, the governorship of the states.[1] In attempting
to describe the governors' office careers, both historical and comparative methods
have been used. From career data on all of the governors elected in the 48 states
from 1870 to 1950,[2] patterns of regularity in the office backgrounds of the governors
have been drawn, with particular reference to their variation from state to state.
At the same time, the eighty-year time span has made possible the observation of
changes in particular career patterns. Thus the study attempts to reveal both the

Reprinted from *How They Became Governor: A Study of Comparative State Politics, 1870-
1950* (East Lansing, Mich.: Governmental Research Bureau, Michigan State University,
1957), pp. 9-21, by permission of the publisher.

historical developments in the office careers of the American governors and the differences among the states in the way they select this particular group of leaders.

There is probably no public office, with the exception of the presidency, which has not at some time been held by a future state governor. However, only a few of these offices have been important numerically as stepping-stones to the governorship. Therefore, in order to gain a faithful picture of gubernatorial career patterns, it is necessary first to reduce the thousands of possible offices to a set of categories which is, at the same time, meaningful and descriptive of the major office career lines. The following, then, are the categories of office careers used in the study.

(1) *State legislative office* is isolated as a typical position which has been of exceptional importance in the careers of governors.

(2) *Statewide elective offices* include such positions as lieutenant-governor, secretary of state, superintendent of public instruction, and the like, wherever they are elective.[3] Excluded from this category are all judicial or legal offices such as attorney general or supreme court justice, despite the fact that in many instances they are elected at large by the state. The latter have been included in the next category.

(3) *Law enforcement offices* cover such positions as attorney and judge at all levels of government. Law enforcement positions such as police commissioner and sheriff have also been included. No distinction is made here between elective and appointive positions. These positions have been singled out and grouped together because they are generally related in the political process, and it was felt therefore, that they should be given a separate category in the promotional scheme.

(4) *Federal elective offices* include all United States representatives, senators, vice presidents, and presidents.

(5) *Administrative offices* are defined here as all appointive positions at all levels of government, with the exception of those appointed in the law enforcement category. However, at the local level of government many positions have been included in the administrative category which may in some instances actually be elected positions. The only local offices classed as local elective for this study are those described below in category six. Such positions as superintendent of schools, county assessor, city clerk, fence viewer, etc., are frequently elective and frequently appointive. The task of dividing them according to mode of selection would be impossible because of the range of varying procedures in an eighty-year period. Furthermore, such executive positions are easily distinguishable from the major local elective, policy directive posts.

(6) *Local elective offices* include the office of mayor, councilman, or alderman, school committeeman, and county commissioner. Again, elective law enforcement positions are not included in this category.

(7) *No office*[4] means no public office experience at all prior to the governorship.

In analyzing office patterns on the basis of the above categories we are concerned with *(a)* the frequency with which an office category appears in the *experience* of governors, and *(b)* the *position* which the office category holds in a career leading to the governorship. The number of governors who have held a particular office indicates the general significance which the office has had in state

Table 1 Pattern of office experience of all elected governors in the United States, 1870-
        1950.

Office Types	No. With This as Experience	No. With This as End Office	No. With This as First Office	No. With This as Only Office	Index of Finality (B/A)	Index of Sequence (D/B)
State Legis- lature........	521	200	312	130	38	65
Law Enforce- ment.........	319	162	200	85	51	52
Administrative...	292	136	167	58	47	43
Local Elective...	197	74	118	35	38	47
Statewide Elective	188	157	21	21	84	13
Federal Elective	138	112	26	25	81	22
No Office........	88	88	88	88		
Other.......		66 [a]	63 [b]			
Total.......		995	995			

a Includes 27 Presidential Electors, 12 members of Constitutional Conventions, 10 Governors' Councilors, and 16 for whom no information was available and one Confederate
official.

b Includes 19 Presidential Electors, 26 members of Constitutional Conventions, 2 Confederate Officials, and 16 for whom no information was available.

politics. Of equal importance is the time placement of the office in the governors'
careers. Many governors may have held a particular office at some point in their
careers, but few may have gone directly to the governorship from it. This office
becomes significant then primarily as a form of *experience*. On the other hand,
those offices which are immediate stepping-stones to the highest office in the state
are specially designated. These we have called *end offices*. In describing the patterns of promotion in the states, the major emphasis has been upon these two measures — experience and end office.

If we assume a national pattern of office recruitment for governors, we see
(Table 1, Column A) that from the point of view of experience the state legislature
has been the most important office. More than half the governors had been in a
state legislature at some time. The next most important group of offices is the law
enforcement category; 32 per cent of the governors from 1870 to 1950 at some
point held such an office. Administrative, local elective, statewide elective, and
federal elective offices were important in the experience of governors in that order.
Only 9 per cent of the governors fell into the no office category. Roughly the same
ordering of offices is found if they are ranked in terms of the office which came
first in the governors' careers (Table 1, Column C). Most governors began their
careers in the state legislature, whereas very few began in either a state-wide or
federal elective position.

Although the order of the office categories according to experience and first office is approximately the same, their ranking according to end office differs (Table 1, Column B). It is true that legislative and law enforcement positions still rank first and second as end offices in governors' careers. But their position of importance has been considerably reduced in comparison with the statewide and federal elective offices. Local elective office, which had ranked fourth according to experience and first office held, drops to last position as an end office. Obviously some offices are more characteristically end offices and others transitional.

Two numerical indices provide a refined measure of the relative positions of the offices in the careers of the governors. The first index is that of *finality*. The index of finality is the percentage of those holding a particular office who held it as an end office (Table 1). It tells us, therefore, the place which an office has had in the governors' careers, whether it has been transitional or an immediate stepping-stone to the governorship. In this respect, the lowest ranking office is the state legislative, because only 38 per cent of the governors with legislative experience held the position as an end office. Local elective follows closely with an index of 39. On the other hand, state-wide and federal elective offices are strong end offices with indices of 84 and 81. They are at the top of the career line, second only to the governorship itself.

The second measure of position indicates which offices leading to the governorship also required prior office experience. This particular measure is called the index of *sequence*. It is the percentage of governors holding a particular office type who held only that office type in their careers prior to the governorship (Table 1, last column). The larger the numerical index for an office, the less the office required some form of prior experience. This index results in a ranking opposed to that found by the index of finality. At the bottom, numerically, as those which required the most previous office experience, are the state-wide and federal elective offices. Of the governors who came directly from state-wide elective office only 13 per cent had no previous office experience. That is, governors who had been lieutenant governors or state treasurers and the like were men who had held other offices as well. On the other hand, 65 percent of the governors coming directly from the legislature had no other office experience. They started in the legislature and went to the governorship directly from that office. Thus promotion from the legislature is a mode of advancement composed of fewer offices than promotion from state-wide elective positions. Law enforcement, administrative, and local elective offices ranked intermediately according to the index of sequence, with about half of their holders having no previous experience.

The analysis of a national pattern of promotion reveals, then, that almost all American governors have had some previous office experience. The most predominant types of experience have been state legislative and law enforcement. These offices, however, tend to be transitional. The offices at the top of the hierarchy, just below the governorship, are the state-wide or federal elective. This ordering of positions gives us a general impression of the relative importance of these offices in the politics of the states.

The national pattern, however, does not focus upon any particular office career, despite differences in positional importance. If we use the end office to designate the pattern, we find that nationally only 20 per cent of the governors held the same end office, the state legislative position. In fact, the distribution of office categories is such that it is impossible to assert that governors' careers are structured nationally, or that one type of career is dominant in the United States. The office of the governor, however, is not a national office. When we examine it within the context of the state, we find that for many of the states the governors' careers do tend to follow similar patterns.

The relative importance of the office types in the governors' careers as they differ by states may be derived from Tables 2 and 3. In Table 2 the states are grouped according to the proportion of their governors who held a particular type of office at any time in their career. The states are thus classified according to the major transitional offices, the state legislative, law enforcement, administrative, and local elective. As is readily apparent, the national figures hide a wealth of variation among the states. In Table 3 are found those states whose governors derive consistently enough from the same type of office to warrant describing their careers as patterned. There are twenty-five states in which 30 per cent or more of the governors came directly from the same office type. These states, therefore, have well-defined paths of recruitment. No state, by this standard, falls into more than one pattern of office recruitment. In Table 3 the states with a tendency (20-29 per cent) to fall into one or another category are also indicated, although none has a sufficient concentration to warrant describing it as patterned.

THE USE OF OFFICE CAREERS BY STATES

State-Wide Elective Office

The most clearly defined path to the governorship is through state-wide elective office. As we have seen, state-wide elective offices are predominantly end offices. Men usually come to these positions with previous office experience and hold them just prior to the governorship. The pattern consists of a minimum of two offices before the governorship: (1) legislative office, and (2) state office (usually the lieutenant governorship). As we shall see later, legislative leadership, i.e., speaker of the house or senate president, is frequently a third stage in the process of advancement. Thus we have here a highly ordered pattern, which enables one to project the future governors of a state over a period of from four to six years and possibly more. Promotion directly from state-wide elective office has occurred often in only a few states. In only four was this the case for more than 30 per cent of the governors; but of these, Massachusetts, Vermont, and Iowa had over 40 per cent of their governors coming from state-wide elective office, evidence of a very strong pattern.

State Legislative Office

To ten states can be ascribed the legislative pattern of promotion. These states satisfy our requirement that at least 30 per cent of all of their governors have come directly from the state legislature. In most instances legislative office was the only one held prior to the governorship. In some states, however, the legislative method of advancement consists of at least two stages, membership in the legislature per se and legislative leadership.

Legislative experience in the careers of governors is distinctly a regional phenomenon. The highest concentration of such experience is found along the eastern

Table 2 The major forms of political office experience — distribution by states.

Per Cent of Governors with Office Experience	Office Types			
	State Legislative	Law Enforcement	Administrative	Local Elective
80–89	Vt.	Mont.		
70–79	Me., Mass., Miss., N.H., R.I.			N. Mex.
60–69	Ala., Conn., Fla., Ga., Ia., Neb., N.J., S.C., N.C.	Ill.		
50–59	Ark., Del., Ida., Kan., Md., Ore., S.D., Tenn., Utah, Va., Wyo.	Ark., Ky., N.C., Tenn., Tex., W. Va.	N. H.	S.D., Wyo.
40–49	Ariz., Cal., Ill., Ind., Mich., Minn., Mont., N.M., N.Y., W. Va.	Ala., Fla., Ga., Mo., N.Y., Ohio, Pa., S.C.	La., Mich., N.J., N.M., Utah, Vt., Wis., W. Va.	Mass., Wash., N.Y., Utah.
30–39	Colo., Ky., La., N.D., Tex., Wis.	Colo., Md., Mich., N.J., Okla., S.D., Vt., Wis.	Cal., Ill., Kans., Me., Md., Wyo., Minn., Neb., Nev., N.Y., S.C.	Idaho., Me., Mich., Neb., N.C., W. Va., Wis.
20–29	Mo., Nev., Wash.	Ariz., Cal., Ind., Ia., Kans., La., Me., Mass., Minn., Miss., N.M., N.D., Va.	Ariz., Ark., Del., Ida., N.C., Ore., R.I., Ind., Miss., Mo., Mont., Okla., Pa., Va.	Cal., Colo., Conn., Fla., Minn., N.H., Ore.
10–19	Ohio, Okla.	Conn., Neb., Nev., N.H., Ore., R.I., Wash., Wyo.	Ala., Colo., Conn., N.D., S.D., Tex., Ga., Ia., Ky., Md., Miss., Mo., Mont., Ohio, Tenn., Wash., Mass.	Ala., Del., Ill., Ind., Kans., Md., Miss., Mo., Mont., N.D., S.C., Tenn., Vt.
0–9	Pa.	Del., Ida., Utah	Fla.	Ariz., Ark., Ga., Ia., Ky., La., Nev., N.J., Ohio, Okla., Pa., R.I., Tex., Va.

Table 3 The major office promotion patterns in the states.

Per cent of Governors	Last Office Held Before Becoming Governor						
	No Office	State Legislature	Law Enforcement	Statewide Elective	Federal Elective	Administrative	Local Elective
50–53			Montana	Mass.			
40–49		Utah	Ark.	Vt., Iowa	Ohio	N. Mex.	
30–39		Ala., Me., Ariz., Miss., Del., Neb., Ga., N.H., Kans.	Mo., Tenn., Tex., W.Va.	La.		Wyo., Utah	Idaho

States with a tendency toward one or another pattern

Per cent of Governors	No Office	State Legislature	Law Enforcement	Statewide Elective	Federal Elective	Administrative	Local Elective
20–29	Colo., Del., Fla., Ind., Ore.	Cal., Conn., Fla., Ida., Ill., Ia., Minn., N.J., N.D., Ore., R.I., Vt., W. Va.	Colo., Fla., Ga., Ill., Ky., La., Md., Minn., N.J., N.C., N.D., Ohio, Pa., S.C., S.D.	Ark., Conn., Ind., Mich., Minn., Mont., N.C., R.I., S.C., S.D.	Ind., Ky., Md., Mass., Minn., Mont., N.Y., Tenn.	Ariz., Del., Ill., Kans., Mich., Neb., Nev., N.J., Okla., Pa., S.D., W.Va.	

seaboard, ranging from New England through the South to Mississippi. A second belt of concentration is found in the midwestern states from Iowa through Nebraska. The concentration is greatest in New England, where 70 per cent of the governors of each state had legislative experience, with the exception of Connecticut (68 per cent). Ohio and Pennsylvania form an area whose governors have had little legislative experience (under 15 per cent each). The career of the governor which includes a stay in the state legislature is thus typical of only some states.

The positional importance of the legislature varies likewise. (Compare Tables 2 and 3). The legislature tends to be important as an end office in those states where it is also important as a form of experience. Yet the relationship between experience and end office is not unitary. The proportion of those with legislative experience who go directly to the governorship differs from state to state. If we look at New England, which had the highest concentration of legislative experience, we find that 72 per cent of Massachusetts' governors had legislative experience, whereas only 3 per cent of the total went straight to the governorship from that office. Thus legislative office appears to be an essential prerequisite for the governorship of Massachusetts, but only as preparation for some other office which is closer to the governorship. On the other hand, Maine drew 37 per cent and New Hampshire 30 per cent of all of their governors directly from the legislature. What in Massachusetts has been an office of transition is an end office in Maine. Legislative office has been even more of an end office in Kansas, where, although only 59 per cent of the governors had legislative experience, 37 per cent of all the governors came directly from the legislature. In the South the legislature is typically an office of transition. Although many southern governors have had legislative experience, only in Mississippi and Georgia has it been significant as an end office. Frequency and position thus vary by state and region.

Law Enforcement Office

The law enforcement category is composed of a number of offices which are related internally to each other in a hierarchy of promotion. At the top of the hierarchy are state judges and attorney generals; at the bottom are state and local attorneys. Typically, then, the pattern consists of at least two law enforcement offices. Other experience, particularly legislative, is frequently a part of the law enforcement career.

The regional character of the third major office pattern is as distinctive as that of the legislative. The two states where this pattern has been most concentrated are Montana and Illinois. Regionally, however, the states bordering the Deep South, Texas, Arkansas, Tennessee, Kentucky, West Virginia, and North Carolina are those with the highest concentrations. Areas where law enforcement offices have been of least importance, on the other hand, are New England (except Vermont) and most of the far western states.

Here again the positional importance of the offices varies. States where law enforcement offices have been clearly transitional are Vermont, New York, Illinois, and Michigan. The number of their governors to come directly from law enforcement office was low in comparison to the number who had had such office experience. On the other hand, law enforcement offices were distinctly end offices in Arkansas, Missouri, Texas, Tennessee, and Montana.

If we compare the geographic incidence of the law enforcement and legislative patterns, we find that the two types of careers are often opposed. In New England this is most clearly seen, since law enforcement offices have been unimportant, even as types of experience, whereas the legislature has been very important. In the South and Border States both types have been important as office experience, but only in West Virginia, Florida, and Alabama did both legislative and law enforcement offices account for as much as 20 per cent each of the end offices of their governors.

Administrative Office

Non-elective public administrative offices have played an important part in governors' careers, primarily as office experience. About 30 per cent of all governors have held such positions, but less than half of these became governor directly from them. The offices within the category of course, vary widely in type and importance.

Regionally, administrative positions have been most important in the West. The three Mountain States, Wyoming, Utah, and New Mexico had over 30 per cent of their governors coming directly from these offices. Adjoining states, Nevada and Arizona, and the tier of states from South Dakota to Oklahoma exhibited tendencies in this direction. Illinois, Michigan, West Virginia, Pennsylvania, New Jersey, and Delaware also had more than 20 per cent of their governors come from administrative office. The South, the Border States, and New England are conspicuously areas in which administrative offices did not lead directly to the governorship. Since these areas exhibited the strongest patterns for the other offices it would be impossible for them to make much direct use of administrative offices in their promotional systems.

As a type of office experience, administrative posts were important (over 30 per cent) in less than half the states. The areas of concentration are much the same for administrative positions as for end offices. In northern New England, in Maine, Vermont, and New Hampshire, however, administrative offices were important as experience, but played no part at all as end offices.

Federal Elective Office

The distinctive character of the federal elective career in state politics is evident in its lack of concentration. Only one state can be said to have a federal pattern, Ohio, which has had 42 per cent of its governors come directly from Congress. States which have used federal offices to some extent as an end office are Maryland (28 per cent of its governors), Kentucky, Minnesota, Tennessee (24 per cent), New York 23 per cent), Massachusetts (22 per cent), and Indiana (21 per cent). Three of these are northern highly populated states. The geographic distribution, however, does not indicate that the more congressmen a state has, the more likely one is to become governor.

Local Elective Office

Quantitatively at least, local elective office is one of the least significant paths to the governorship, there being even more governors with no office experience at all than those coming directly from a local elective post. The distribution of local elective experience among the states shows that in only half did as many as 20 per cent of the governors have this type of experience. In New Mexico, South Dakota, and Wyoming, however, over half of the governors had such experience. In Washington, and Utah in the West, and in New York and Massachusetts in the East, over 40 per cent of the governors in each state had local experience. In all of these states, however, local office was purely transitional; in none of them did even 20 per cent of the governors come directly from such a position. Only in Idaho were there enough governors who came from local office to warrant describing a pattern of local elective office.

No Office

The "no office" category resembles most closely the local elective office in the infrequency of its occurrence and lack of any real concentration in any of the states. The largest single concentration of governors with no previous office experience was in Oregon (29 per cent). Other states with over 20 per cent were Colorado, Delaware, Florida, Indiana, and Texas. There is no regional concentration here, and the percentages do not warrant describing any state as having a pattern of no office experience for its governors.

From this overview of governors' careers we can draw the following conclusions: (1) In no state is there a rigid ladder of promotion followed by all governors; (2) however, in more than one half of the states there is a typical office career followed by about a third or more of the governors; and (3) the typical careers are not distributed among the states haphazardly, but tend to cluster regionally. The latter point gives support to our original assumption that career lines of political leaders are an "expression" or facet of the states' political systems. For the similarity of career lines of governors of states within a region is, in all likelihood, the product of a broader regional similarity in history and political structure.

NOTES

1. The backgrounds of American governors have not been neglected by scholars. A notable series has appeared in the *National Municipal Review*. See A.F. Macdonald, "American Governors, 1900-1910," November, 1927, pp. 715-19; S.R. Solomon, "American Governors Since 1915," March, 1931, pp. 152-58; John A. Perkins, "American Governors — 1930-1940," March, 1940, pp. 178-84; S.R. Solomon, "United States Governors, 1940-1950," April, 1952, pp. 190-97. Some other, more specialized studies, are C.A.M. Ewing, "Southern Governors," *Journal of Politics*, X (1948), 385-409; John K. Gurwell, "The Governors of the States," *State Government*, XIV (1941), 157-58, 172. For the most part these studies have catalogued the general educational and office backgrounds of the governors with no attempt to observe differences among the states. For a general survey of some of the problems and potentialities in the study of the careers of political leaders see Donald R. Matthews, *The Social Background of Political Decision-Makers* (Garden City, N.Y., 1954).

2. In compiling the basic data on individual governor's careers the following sources

were examined for each instance:
Biographical Directory of the American Congress, 1774-1949, Washington, D.C.: 1950.
Johnson, Allen, ed., *Dictionary of American Biography,* 21 vols., New York: 1928-1944.
Lohr, Evelyn, ed., *Current Biography,* 14 vols., New York: 1940-1953.
National Cyclopedia of American Biography, 45 vols., New York: 1898-1952.
Who's Who in America, 27 vols., Chicago: 1899-1953.
Who Was Who in America, 2 vols., Chicago: 1942, 1950.
Not every governor can be found in all five sources, but, wherever there was duplication, the sources were checked against each other.

The most useful over-all source of information was the *National Cyclopedia of American Biography,* which provides the most systematic coverage of state governors. It was used in conjunction with *White's Conspectus of American Biography* (2nd ed., New York, 1937), which lists the governors of the states for the period covered in the study. The list was brought up to date by consulting the Council of State Governments, *The Governors of the States 1900-1950,* (Chicago, 1948). The chief limitation of the *National Cyclopedia* is its tendency to suppress unfavorable information and opinions about its subjects.

The *Dictionary of American Biography* treats its subjects in a scholarly fashion and therefore provided the best single secondary check on the accuracy of the data. Unfortunately, not all governors have been treated in the *Dictionary.* The requirement that an individual have died before being so enshrined, limits the utility of this work largely to the pre-1920 period.

Extremely useful was the *Biographical Directory of the American Congress,* which has been brought up to date, with considerable checking for accuracy, to 1949. This volume gives brief career data on all persons who have ever been members of Congress. Since a large percentage of our governors have at some time, either before or after the governorship, held this position, the *Biographical Directory* proved to be an excellent source.

For recent governors the most complete source of information is *Current Biography.* It presents a brief sketch of the individual, based upon newspaper and magazine sources. Again, for our purposes, its major defect was the lack of systematic coverage of all governors.

Who's Who, along with *Who Was Who,* does attempt to cover systematically all governors, and these volumes were examined in each instance. Their limitations, however, are those of any self portrait. For this reason, they were relied upon only when there was no other source for a desired piece of information.

The sources described were the ones which were examined in a systematic manner for information on all the governors. In addition to these, current magazines, the obituary columns of the *New York Times,* and full scale biographies were used occasionally, wherever they contributed to the completeness of the information desired.

3. The men who have been included in this study are all those who were elected governor in their respective states in the period from 1870 to 1950. There were many who served as governor, although not elected to the office, as in the case of lieutenant governors, secretaries of state, senate presidents, etc., who succeeded to the position

upon the death or resignation of the governor. Such men have been included only if subsequently they were elected. No individual has been counted more than once, the first time he was elected governor being considered the central point in his career from which his pre-gubernatorial career extends in one direction and his later career in the other. Where a man has been elected again, with a hiatus between terms, the second term is considered a post-gubernatorial office. In a very few instances where the governor served a term, with a hiatus, before 1870, the first term he served after 1870 has been taken as the base point.

4. There are a number of offices which do not fall into any of the above categories. These are presidential elector, representative at a constitutional convention, and the position of governor's councilor in a number of the New England States. These have been recorded and where relevant presented in this study, but for the most part they are relegated to a residual or *other* category. There are a few instances in which an individual held office in one state and then migrated to another state and eventually became governor of the latter state. On the presupposition that such outside political experience may have been personally relevant, but not relevant as a prerequisite of office within a state, it was not considered as office experience.

The Governor and His Legislative Party

Sarah P. McCally

When the dust settles following the reapportionment upheavals, the traditional problems of legislative policy-making will remain. This process is divided
between the governor and (with due respect to Nebraska) the two legislative houses,
with the governor generally taking the lead. A governor represents the totality of
interests within his party. No single legislator or faction represents as wide a
variety of interests as the governor. The governor proposes and vetoes and normally plays an even greater legislative role in state government than the President
in the national government because of the infrequent sessions, low seniority, lack
of state-wide influence or prestige and inadequate staff of the legislators. The governor's legislation is geared to please his state-wide constituency and, depending
largely upon his degree of control over his party, is passed, modified or rejected.

What affects the ability of the governor to control his legislative party is a
question seldom asked and rarely investigated except by the harassed occupant of
the executive mansion. This is surprising, since the definition of party responsibility is closely related to executive control. By common agreement, a definition
of party responsibility would include the ability of the party to control nominations,
to present a united front in the election and thereafter to discipline the legislators
to uphold the program of the executive in order to make a good record for the next
election.[1]

Those who investigate the behavior of legislative parties in the interest of
party responsibility equate the latter phenomenon with party voting loyalty. The
loyalty rate of legislators on party votes is not the same animal as their degree
of support of administration bills. Executive request legislation has received little
attention from scholars. We will set this distinction aside for the moment in order
to examine the factors which have been claimed to cause party responsibility or
voting loyalty, as it has been defined for research purposes. The two characteristics of inter-party conflict and intra-party cohesion in legislative situations are
the major conditions for party responsibility as recently restated by Thomas A.
Flinn.[2]

If inter-party conflict means that the governor's party has a reasonable
chance of obtaining a working majority of the legislature, this variable has

Reprinted from *American Political Science Review,* Vol. 60 (Dec. 1966), pp. 923-942,
by permission of the author .

This paper is a revision of two chapters in my *The Effects of Competition Upon the Structure and Function of State Political Parties* (Ph. D. Dissertation, Department of Political
Science, Yale University, 1964). I am indebted to a Danforth Fellowship from Wellesley
College for 1960-1961 and to the Yale Computer Center where the calculations presented
here were performed. I wish to thank Hayward R. Alker, Jr. for his helpful suggestions
on section IV.

immediate surface appeal as a condition for gubernatorial control. With the resources at his disposal, a governor can forge party agreement on legislation which is vital to his program. He will be disadvantaged if his party has a permanent minority position in the legislature, for he will have to use his resources to bargain with the opposition. If he has an overwhelming percentage of seats in the legislature he may be unable to control rival factions. It is the expressed hope of proponents of reapportionment that governors with new majority parties will bring about promised reforms; but it is doubtful that the possession of a majority in a competitive legislature guarantees that the governor's program will be passed. Enough exceptions come to mind to cast suspicion on this as a controlling variable. His success in state-wide competition for the governorship may play a part in his influence over his legislative party.

Intra-party cohesion indicates unity which can be forged either by power resources or by ideological agreement. Students of legislative voting loyalty commonly assume that cohesion results from similarity of districts within a party's legislative contingent. If legislators from similar districts vote alike because they have the same interests to defend, then the most unified party would be the one in which the districts were most similar. From the governor's point of view, the most loyal legislators would come from districts which reflect the characteristics of his state-wide constituency. Yet one need not dig too far into the study of power structures to discover that they are not necessarily fed by ideological agreement. Organizational rivalries, personal ambitions or side payments need not follow demographic differences. Reapportionment will bring about increased suburban representation within both parties, but new demands, rather than increased cohesion, may result from suburban factions with increased legislative voting strength to use at the bargaining table.

The discussion to this point has been intended to show that satisfactory operational definitions of competition and cohesion must be formulated before these concepts can be used to test the governor's control over his legislative party. A review of the research related to these concepts may aid the quest for accuracy of definition.

COMPETITION AND COHESION: PREVIOUS RESEARCH

There have been several probes in the areas of party competition and cohesion and their effect on legislative voting behavior. Malcolm Jewell compared several competitive states with respect to the degree of voting loyalty to the parties, using all the roll call votes in a session.[3] His findings do not confirm the hypothesis that party competition for control of the legislature can of itself explain party voting loyalty. Furthermore, since party voting loyalty did not vary with the degree of state-wide competition for governor, this variable was also rejected as a meaningful explanation. Since neither state-wide competition nor legislative competition could explain the voting behavior he witnessed, Jewell turned to intra-party cohesion for an explanation. He advanced the proposition that there is more ideological cohesion within the parties of urban states because he discovered a higher degree of party loyalty in urban than in rural states. Jewell did not consider the strength of the state party organization as a factor in legislative voting loyalty.

It was Duane Lockard's major thesis that close party competition at the state level produces party voting loyalty in the legislature. However, the connecting link in this causal chain is party organizational strength.[4] Lockard comes closer than Jewell to affirming the party-responsibility school's two major conditions of party competition and party cohesion. Jewell and Lockard agree on the measurement of party competition either as a state-wide vote for governor or President or as competition for a legislative majority but disagree over its effect on legislative voting loyalty. Lockard claims that competition produces cohesion which in turn produces voting loyalty. Jewell finds no direct correlation between competition and loyalty although he states that a certain type of competition — urban-rural competition — produces ideological cohesion followed by voting loyalty within the parties. The two writers disagree on the measurement of cohesion, one defining it as party organizational strength, the other as ideological agreement, but both claim it influences voting loyalty.

A different research approach, which tends to reaffirm the importance of electoral competition and organizational cohesion, is that of Wahlke and his associates, who interviewed legislators in four states in an attempt to determine the influence of many outside variables affecting their roles.[5] They found that political career patterns and orientations are likely to be shaped by the degree of competition in a given system. Also, the varying degrees of a particular party's organizational strength and morale may be an important factor affecting the legislators' career patterns and orientations. The authors state that party organizational strength is probably related to degree of competition between the parties, but, as the case of California Democrats in one direction and Ohio Democrats in another direction indicated, it may also operate independently of it. Another major determinant of legislative behavior was the relative strength of the majority and minority within the legislature.

Another area of research assumes that legislative voting behavior is a result of ideological cohesion brought about by the economic composition of the districts represented by the individual legislators. The more alike the districts are within each party, the more ideological cohesion and therefore voting agreement exists. On the other hand, the theory goes, the more diverse the districts within the party, the more disunity, because of lack of ideological agreement.[6] Thomas Flinn tested this theory of party unity based on similarity of district in the Ohio Assembly of 1949 and 1959. He concluded that differing constituencies do not give rise to intra-party voting disagreement and that policy differences between the parties are not due to differences in the composition of the legislative parties in terms of constituencies represented.[7]

This theory of constituency influence has been used with more success in explaining the deviant members of the legislative party. It cannot account for average party loyalty, but it can account for a few of the deviant cases. Duncan MacRae attempted to measure the comparative effectiveness of party power and constituency interest over the roll call voting of the individual legislator on issues chosen to reflect class differences.[8] Both Thomas R. Dye and Thomas A. Flinn give some support to the theory that constituency economic pressures affect the extremes in party loyalty.[9]

The degree of competition in a constituency measured singly or in combination with economic characteristics has been offered as an additional variable affecting the extremes in legislative voting loyalty. It is assumed that members with comfortable margins are a more loyal group than those from competitive districts because they are freed from constituency pressures and hence can vote the party line without fear of voter retribution. On the other hand, the legislators with close races will reflect the interests of their constituencies — be they for or against the party line. Thus the most deviant legislators are to be found from competitive atypical districts. The findings are not conclusive and differences exist with respect to these variables between parties, between legislative bodies and between sessions.[10]

The study of the deviant members of a state legislative party suffers from lack of justification. No one in the party-responsibility school would require a "party line" vote on all issues on which the majority of both parties are opposed. Taking all votes on which there is substantial disagreement may not be a true test of party responsibility. It does not separate the votes which the administration wants passed from those on which the administration has taken a hands-off policy. The leadership of each party tolerates deviations in party voting as long as the necessary vote is achieved.

The studies reviewed so far confirm the warning that the evidence sifted governs the results achieved. Three definitions of competition have been used: state, legislative and constituency, with conflicting results. Three definitions of intra-party cohesion have been used: structural, state-wide ideological and similar-constituency. The roll calls chosen to test the theories have ranged from the total number to those which represent party conflict to those which are of economic importance. The reason for this may be that there has not been an operational definition of party responsibility upon which researchers can agree. With respect to legislative policy-making, party responsibility can be defined as the ability of the governor to command enough votes in the legislature to pass his legislation. The major question to be asked is: What affects the ability of the governor to get his legislation passed?

THE USE OF VETO VOTES TO MEASURE GUBERNATORIAL INFLUENCE

Because we are interested in measuring the influence of the governor in the legislative process, two traditional methods of identifying significant partisan roll calls are not appropriate. Neither Lowell's party vote nor Rice's index of likeness[11] takes into consideration the raw number of votes necessary to pass legislation. Both indices assume that partisan activity can be identified by comparing the percentage of members of each party (or group) who agree or disagree. But the passing of legislation is not purely mechanical. The proponents do not have unlimited favors to pass out to supporters. Because of this they make marginal calculations, procuring enough votes to pass their measure, but no unnecessary surplus. Most bills require for passage a majority of those voting. If the party of the sponsors of legislation has an overwhelming percentage of the legislature (80% for example), the bill needs the affirmative vote of only 63% of their party members in order to pass. If the other party is unanimous in opposition, the index of likeness would approximate 40%. This is far from complete disagreement, and those looking for roll calls which exhibit partisanship might disregard it entirely. However, a great deal of partisanship was present. Does a party which needs only 63% of its members to pass legislation and gets it show any less partisan activity than a party which needs and gets 100%?

William H. Riker developed an index of significance which *does* take into consideration the minimum votes necessary for victory on a roll call, [12] but it gives less indication of partisan activity than the previous two indices, and in fact completely obscures party. A vote of 50-50 could mean two highly disciplined parties, two widely split parties or one split majority party and a cohesive minority party.

The above three measures will have to be discarded as not appropriate for our use. They are not valid indicators of party activity except in legislatures where the party split is approximately 50-50; and they cannot distinguish between trivial and important legislation except in a mechanistic way.

We want to test the governor's influence over his party on measures which are important to him. The most satisfactory way would be to test the influence of the governor on administration bills — those bills which the governor wants passed. This would provide the best test of the party in power — the ability to get its program passed. The governor's position is clear. If the administration bills could be identified, the roll call votes on this legislation would provide a clear indication of the behavior of the parties on issues of major importance. David Truman used this type of legislation for the 81st Congress. He automatically included votes on sustaining Presidential vetoes, votes on Presidential reorganization plans, and (in the Senate) votes on the confirmation of Presidential nominations and the ratification of treaties. Other votes were included if the public record revealed an express Presidential preference concerning the precise content at stake in the vote. [13]

The identification of governor's program bills for the seven legislative sessions for each state during the period (1946-1960) proved to be too difficult. In the attempt, the Legislative Reference Bureaus of thirty-five northern states were contacted and asked to send lists of administration bills for each session. With the exception of Pennsylvania, Nevada, Wisconsin and Oregon, for which lists of administration bills for some sessions were sent, the only help came in the form of suggested procedures to be used in identifying the administration bills. In all of the states, the governor presents a program message to the legislature in which he outlines the substance of the program he wants passed for the session. This is usually translated into administration bills which are often introduced by the governor's party leaders in the house or senate or by legislators whom the governor may specify. In the states in which this is an iron-clad custom, the name of the party floor leader attached to a bill may identify it as an administration bill. This is the case in Connecticut, Illinois, Indiana, Massachusetts, New York and West Virginia. For the bulk of the states, however, no fool-proof procedures exist for the identification of program bills. [14]

As a substitute for votes on administration bills, votes on vetoes were used because, as with administration bills, (1) the position of the governor is clearly stated and (2) the governor's party leaders would exert maximum influence to see that the veto was sustained. The veto calls for a vote of confidence in the governor. In most cases he uses it sparingly, more as a threat than an actuality, so that when a veto does come before the legislature, the greatest amount of party activity attends it.

One might question why a governor who had considerable influence in his legislative majority would ever allow unapproved legislation to slip through. In this regard, it must be remembered that the governor recommends for passage only a small amount of the total legislative product. If offensive legislation is called to his attention, he may threaten to veto it if passed and must do so enough to give credibility to his threats. Cases have arisen in which the governor vetoed a bill in his program because it was altered substantially in the legislative process. Furthermore, it is possible for the minority party to gain enough support to pass a bill on which the governor has taken no stand, whereupon the governor might send it back with a veto message if it is not in his conception of the "public interest."[15]

Table 1 gives the number and substance of vetoes used in the fifty-eight house sessions on which this research rests.[16] These sessions are broken down by percent of seats of the governor's party. The Democratic sessions follow a pattern we would expect. There are more vetoes when a party has a hopeless minority position than when it has 40%-70% of the legislature. There are also more vetoes when the party has an overwhelming percent of the legislature, and therefore may have less control over its own members. The Republicans, however, show the reverse of the expected. We cannot say, therefore, that the number or substance of the vetoes are related in any significant degree to the party balance in the legislature. It is interesting to note that the largest number of vetoes on taxation come from Democratic governors whose legislative parties are hopeless minorities.

After choosing veto votes as the most efficient indicators of the influence of the governor, we need a measure which will indicate the degree to which his party supported him on these issues. Rice's index of cohesion is not suitable because it is not directional.[17] It does not indicate whether the majority supported or opposed the governor. It may be that the party was more cohesive in opposition to the governor than in support. In this case the index would be misleading. For instance, in the Arizona House session of 1949, the majority Democrats voted 39-8 to override the governor's veto on H.B. No. 71, which would have removed the supervision of real estate from the state.[18] The percent of cohesion is 83. (If this is converted to a scale of 0-100, the index of cohesion becomes 66.)

Index of Administration Support

What we need for our purposes is an *index of administration support* which measures the degree to which the governor's party members support him. For a single roll call, the index is obtained by dividing the number of votes cast by the party members who voted for the governor by the total number of party members who voted. When several vetoes were used, the average index was the arithmetic mean of the indices derived for the various roll calls in the session. David Truman used this type of measure for the 81st Congress.[19] Using the example from Arizona mentioned above, the index of administration support would be 17.

Index of Administration Success

Neither the index of cohesion nor the index of administration support indicates whether the governor was successful in obtaining enough votes from his party to win. If he has an overwhelming percentage of the legislature, the number

Table 1 Number and substance of vetoes according to percent of seats of the governor's party in fifty-eight house sessions.[a]

Percent of Seats	Class I Party Interest[b]	Class II Substantive	Class III Taxation	Class IV Procedural	Total	No. of Sessions	Average Per Session
			Democratic				
0–39.9	3	22	11	25	61	14	4.4
40–54.9	1	7	2	0	10	5	2.0
55–69.9	1	3	0	8	12	7	1.7
70–	2	3	1	0	6	2	3.0
Totals	7	35	14	33	89	28	
			Republican				
0–39.9	2	1	1	3	7	4	1.8
40–54.9	2	5	1	6	14	4	3.5
55–69.9	0	14	5	14	33	9	3.7
70–	1	25	1	10	37	13	2.8
Totals	5	45	8	33	91	30	

[a]The states and number of sessions are: Arizona (2), Calif. (1), Colorado (1), Conn. (1), Delaware (1), Idaho (2), Illinois (1), Indiana (3), Iowa (2), Kansas (3), Maine (3), Maryland (2), Mass. (6), Mich. (5), Montana (1), Nevada (1), N.H. (2), N.Y. (1), N.D. (1), Ohio (6), Oregon (2), R.I. (2), S.D. (1), Utah (1), Wisc. (6), Wyo. (1).

[b]The four categories of vetoes involved the following issues:

Class I	Party Interest
	Elections and Reapportionment
	Appointments
	Legislative Procedure and Organization
Class II	Substantive
	Fish and Game Laws (Conservation)
	Labor
	Appropriations for other than those listed
	Veterans Affairs
	Welfare, Health, Education
	Business Regulation
Class III	Taxation
Class IV	Procedural
	Civil Service
	State Administration
	Local Administration
	Judicial and Legal

of votes necessary to win does not form a large percent of his party. An index of cohesion or administration support takes no account of the percentage of the governor's party which must support him in order to pass his legislation. For instance, in the Iowa House session of 1953, the majority Republicans had an index of cohesion of .59 and an index of administration support of .41 on a veto. [20] Neither figure would make one suspect that the governor was in good shape, but the governor needed only 36% of his party to uphold his veto, and thus was comfortably over his margin. The *index of success* is obtained by dividing the percent of those who voted in favor of the governor by the percent of his party votes he needed in order to uphold his legislation. One-third-plus-one of those elected is the usual requirement for upholding the veto. The index of success is a ratio of percents instead of votes because when the governor's party had fewer than 34% of the seats in the legislature, it was assigned 100 as the required percentage of votes. It should be recognized that this imposes an almost hopeless requirement on the minority party. One maverick makes it impossible for the governor to make his quota. The arithmetic mean of the individual indices for success was used in order to obtain an average index for a session.

I substituted the veto votes for votes on administration bills to make it possible to use many more sessions in my analysis. I assumed that the governor would receive the same support on vetoes that he would receive on administration bills. Table 2 compares the index of support for veto votes with the same index applied to votes on administration bills for seven state sessions for which lists of program bills had been supplied by the governors or methods of identification of program bills had been related. In all cases except two, the program bills received a higher index of support than the veto bills. The two sets of support indices have a correlation of .71. The first guess might be that passing program legislation is more important to a governor than having his vetoes upheld. The second guess might be that the animosities which develop over program legislation might be ironed out by the time the vote reaches the floor, whereas a veto comes to the house directly in the form of a message from the governor, and the anger of those who voted for the measure may not have been assuaged.

If our assumption is correct that a governor does not use his limited supply of favors to obtain more votes than he needs, it is logical for him to receive a different degree of support for roll calls on vetoes for which he needs only 34% of the house than for program legislation for which he needs 50% of the house. On this basis, we would expect the index of success to be about the same for the governor for both sets of votes. The index of success was previously defined as the ratio of the percent he needed to pass (or uphold) his bills (or vetoes) to the percent he received. If the governor has the influence and resources to obtain what he needs, and if he calculates at the margins, he should be equally successful with program bills as with veto votes. Comparing the two indices of success state by state, we note that the governor was more successful with the veto than with program legislation in four sessions. In only two sessions, however, did he receive over 100% on one success index and under 100% on the other. In both cases his success was well over 90% on the other index. The index of success on vetoes can be fairly confidently used to indicate the governor's success on program legislation. The correlation between the two indices is .63. The index of success has the disadvantage of requiring 100% of any legislative party which does not have the required minimum number of seats for victory. This imposes a hard task on a hopeless minority party.

Table 2 Comparison of roll call votes on program bills and vetoes with respect to indices of administration support and success for seven house sessions. [a]

State, Session (Party, % Seats)	Mean Index of Support	Percent of Party Needed [b]	Mean Index of Success	Mean Index of Cohesion [c]	No. of Roll Calls
Connecticut, 1955					
Democratic, 33%					
Program	94.6	100	94.6	94.6	2
Vetoes	89.4	100	89.4	89.4	2
Wisconsin, 1957					
Republican, 67%					
Program	80.5	75.9	106	83.7	8
Vetoes	68.4	50.8	135	73.1	12
Oregon, 1959					
Republican, 45%					
Program	72.2	100	72.2	80.4	18
Vetoes	74.2	100	97.5	83.2	6
Nevada, 1953					
Republican, 38%					
Program	68.7	100	68.7	81.2	7
Vetoes	55.6	97.7	56.9	69.8	3
Wisconsin, 1951					
Republican, 76%					
Program	65.6	67.5	97.2	97.2	6
Vetoes	52.3	46.2	113	52.3	1
Massachusetts, 1959					
Democratic, 60%					
Program	75.7	82.5	91.8	84.0	8
Vetoes	40.2	54.1	74.0	62.7	12
Massachusetts, 1957					
Democratic, 55%					
Program	84.9	91.0	93.3	84.9	10
Vetoes	89.7	58.7	153	89.7	1

[a] Program bills were "screened" in the same way as vetoes.

[b] States differ with respect to the percentage of votes needed to uphold vetoes. In some states, the one-third required is based on total membership; in others, on those present. In Connecticut, a majority present could uphold the veto. (As of 1965, one-third of the members are needed to uphold.)

[c] This is the percent of those voting who took the majority position on roll calls. It is not converted to a scale of 0–100.

Seldom is even the most cohesive party unanimous. One or two mavericks carry more negative weight in a minority or bare majority party than in a party which has votes to spare. Although the index of success would seem to be a better measure of gubernatorial influence than the index of support, it does not do as reliable job of predicting the comparative influence of the governor on program bills and vetoes on a session-by-session basis. This may be due to the inaccuracy of measurement just mentioned.

The index of cohesion was given for comparative purposes only. Note that in Nevada 1953, in Wisconsin 1951 and in Massachusetts 1959, the party was more cohesive in opposition to the governor than in support. When the states are compared, as they will be in the rest of this study, it is more important to know that the governor was 135% successful on a veto than that he received 68.4% of his party. In Wisconsin in 1957, the 68.4% meant that the governor was 135% successful, whereas in Nevada in 1953, the governor received 68.7% of his party on program legislation and was only 68.7% successful.

Some Correlates Of
Gubernatorial Influence

Because there is so little agreement as to the appropriate measures to be used for electoral competition or intra-party cohesion, several indicators of each concept were used in the initial analysis.[21] This procedure has been suggested recently by Richard F. Curtis and Elton F. Jackson.[22] The use of multiple indicators is called for when the researcher has definite theoretical concepts which he wishes to relate but for which he is unable to obtain or defend "single, unambiguous, direct, operational definitions."[23] Examining the effects of several indicators on gubernatorial influence will postpone the choices among them until the individual associations have been observed.

A survey was made of the vetoes in the entire universe of 476 legislative sessions held in thirty-four states outside the South during the period 1946-1960;[24] all the senate and house sessions (76 house sessions; 64 senate sessions) in which there were one or more veto roll calls were used in the research. The vetoes were, of course, subject to the screening procedure described in footnote 16. Altogether, 525 votes were used.[25]

Table 3 gives the results for fifty-eight house sessions which followed a gubernatorial election. It seemed reasonable to assume that a governor might have more control over legislators elected concurrently, rather than in midterm, or on staggered terms as in many senates. The results of the product-moment correlations between the variables of competition, party structure and legislative behavior run contrary to the expectations of previous hypotheses and offer the following findings of speculative interest.

(1) State-wide electoral competition does not appear to be a major explanatory factor of legislative discipline. In only three cases do we get a correlation higher than .30 between electoral competition and legislative behavior, and two of these correlations are not in the anticipated direction. If competition produces disciplined parties, as the party-responsibility theorists suggest, we should expect a negative correlation between percent of the electoral vote and amount of support and success. The mean percent of the electoral vote over the past seven elections

Table 3 Product-moment correlations between certain variables of party competition and structure and legislative behavior variables of support, success and cohesion within the governor's legislative party in fifty-eight house sessions.[a]

Measures of Party Competition and Structure	Index of Support		Index of Success		Index of Cohesion	
Electoral Vote						
Mean percent of Gubernatorial vote — 7 elections	−.38[b]		.15[b]		−.23[b]	
Percent of elections won by Governor's party	−.28		.26		−.25	
Percent of Alternation	−.02		−.22		−.05	
Percent of Pre-session vote	−.05		−.25		−.02	
	Gov. [c]	Party [c]	Gov. [c]	Party [c]	Gov. [c]	Party [c]
	Gov. [c]	Party [c]	Gov. [c]	Party [c]	Gov. [c]	Party [c]
Percent of Post-session vote	.27	.06	.22	.29	.18	−.05
Over 50%	*.32	−.11	*.36	.20	.23	−.28
Under 50%	−.19	.03	−.02	.14	−.09	−.03
Primary Vote						
Before: Governor's % of total	.26		.02		.15	
Winning % of highest two	.25		.02		.16	
% of highest two	.25		.01		.17	
Incumbent	.39		−.03		.32	
Non-incumbent	.16		.13		.07	
After: Governor's % of total	.60		.49		.17	
Winning % of highest two	.46		.37		.21	
% of highest two	.61		.49		.18	
After: Candidate's % of total[c]	.54		.15		.36	
Winning % of highest two	.52		.27		.37	
% of highest two	.50		.13		.32	
Legislative Seats						
% of seats — Governor's party	−.60		.20		−.49	
Over 50%	−.45		−.05		−.36	
Under 50%	.09		.46		.10	
Absolute number of seats	−.12		.31		−.15	
Average percent six sessions	−.55		.22		−.45	

[a] These sessions are the same as those in Table 1.

[b] For all correlations higher than .30, $p \leq .05$ for a two-tailed test except for those correlations asterisked. For those, $p \leq .10$ for a two-tailed test. Correlations above .40 in magnitude are underlined for convenience.

[c] The vote for the post-session is the vote for the governor or for his replacement.

is more highly correlated with the degree of support and success of the governor than are the other measures of competition, and in the anticipated direction. A plausible explanation is that the correlation is caused by the lack of discipline of traditional majority parties over the previous 14-28 years. This modest negative correlation may indicate that, over a long period, lack of competition will produce lack of cohesion. Competition in any single election does not appear to produce cohesion. The gubernatorial election success of the governor following the legislative session is positively correlated with his support and success in the legislature. This may be an indication of a major effort on the part of the governor to consolidate his party for a decisive win. In the fourteen-year period within which the legislative sessions fall, the gubernatorial elections became more competitive. During that period in 24 of the 32 states outside the South the election results were within 45%-55%. The eroding of the traditional majority party and the close competition which followed may have brought about the positive correlation between the legislative support and the electoral record of the governor, both indicative of his personal efforts. These correlations are not high, and do not support the theory that electoral competition produces legislative support or success due to the efforts of the governor to make a vote-getting record for the next election.

(2) Intra-party cohesion on the state level has a high positive correlation with the support and success of the governor in the legislature. The highest correlations are obtained between the governor's primary percentage after the legislative session and the degree of loyalty he receives from his legislators during the session. The high correlation between outside party cohesion and legislative loyalty would seem to support the theory that the outside party organization generates discipline in the legislative party. The *direction* of this influence needs to be explained, since the legislative discipline predates the organizational cohesion. One would expect that the primary of an *incumbent* governor held before an election in which both he and the legislature ran concurrently would correlate as highly with legislative loyalty as his primary after the session was over. This expectation is based on the assumption that the strength of the governor's faction as measured by his ability to make a strong primary showing is reflected in his ability to induce his legislative party to back him. Surprisingly, this is not true. As Table 3 shows, even with incumbents it is the post-session primary which correlates most highly with support and success.

Correlation does not indicate causation, and we ponder whether it is the legislative success which affects primary results, or whether both indicators are part of a general control exercised by the governor. The latter hypothesis makes more intuitive sense. In that case the progression of events would start with the efforts of a governor to build support within his party, both electoral as well as legislative, to help him win the next primary and election. With his supply of rewards and punishments and his own ability and effort, he forges a coalition to stand by him at primary time. The degree of his success is measured both within the legislature and by the primary results. Additional evidence can be garnered to support this interpretation of the results. The correlations between party structure and primary voting for the three remaining categories of legislative sessions included in the study are presented in Table 4. They are even higher than those previously reported for the fifty-eight house sessions. Of particular interest is the fact that the governor's success with his party increases as the election approaches. The senates and houses elected mid-way through the term of a four-year governor produce extremely high indices of success. The assumption that the governor wields his maximum influence over legislators elected concurrently with him appears to be in error. His influence grows as the time for election approaches. His strategy is oriented toward the next election, and the strength of the coalition he builds is measured both in legislative and primary support.

The governor's success in receiving the necessary votes to pass his legislation is a more personal matter than his degree of support. While the index of support has a correlation of well over .40 in most cases with the primary fortunes of the party's next candidate, the index of success was not correlated highly with the primary success of the party's candidate. Success is correlated with the strength of the individual governor, and not with the strength of the leadership faction of the party. It would appear that the strength of the leadership faction within the party has a definite relationship to legislative support, but that the personal efforts of an incumbent governor who plans to run again make the difference between support and success.

Comparison between the index of cohesion and those of support and success shows that cohesion is not as highly related to the governor's primary and election as the other variables. This is to be expected, since a party which was completely opposed to the governor would be assigned an index of 100%, as would a party which completely supported him. Cohesion does not measure the direction of loyalty within a party, but only the extent of agreement among its members.

Common sense also suggests that the percentage of seats a governor's party holds in the legislature would affect his support and success. Assuming that governors calculate at the margins and do not expend more rewards or punishments than necessary to gain support for their projects, we would expect a high negative correlation between the percentage of seats a governor has and the percentage of his party which supports him. This is confirmed by the statistics in Table 3. Fifty percent of the seats was used as a break-point to investigate this relationship further. Again the results show that the size of the governor's majority affects his support. If he has under 50% of the seats, there is little relationship — presumably the governor works to rally all of his party members behind him, or the deviations which do occur do not show any consistent pattern. If he has over 50%, he does not work for as many votes and the correlation is negative. This finding is important to bear in mind when comparing different parties with respect to indices of cohesion or loyalty. Legislative voting is not a "rally-'round-the-flag-boys" type of support, but a carefully calculated operation in which energy is not expended unnecessarily to force conformity among party members whose votes are not needed to pass. Part of this strategy may be a planned pattern of deviations, in which those whose constituencies or philosophies make it uncomfortable for them to support certain measures are allowed independence. As the majority hovers close to the 50% level, however, deviations are not tolerated because every vote counts.

Before we assume that this strategy is crowned with accomplishment it is necessary to consider the factor of success. Success is the ratio of the percent of the party the governor received to what he needed. We would think that the more seats the governor had to spare, the more successful he would be. This is not the case. There is a low negative relationship between the number of seats over a majority and success. Apparently an excess of seats is not in the governor's favor. A more logical break-point might fall somewhere about 55%, with extra seats an advantage until then. Thereafter, the surplus may generate rivalries within the house that the governor cannot control. This finding may modify the total strategy assumption related above. The governor may be able to handle a modest majority, but when his party has an overwhelming majority coalitions form against him which he cannot undermine by his traditional stock of rewards and punishments.

The absolute number of seats was correlated with the indices of support and success as a control over the assertion that it is the percentage of seats rather

Table 4 Product-moment correlations between gubernatorial primary results and support, success and cohesion within the governor's legislative party for designated sessions.

Primary Vote	Index of Support [a]	Index of Success [a]	Index of Cohesion [a]
Forty-two Senates Elected Concurrently with the Governor [b]			
Before Session:			
Governor's % of total	.23	.08	.08
Winning % of highest two	.24	.08	.12
% of highest two	.24	.08	.13
After Session:			
Governor's % of total	.71	.48	.48
Winning % of highest two	.63	.48	.55
% of highest two	.67	.45	.46
After Session:			
Candidate's % of total [e]	.40	.03	.26
Winning % of highest two	.40	.03	.28
% of highest two	.30	−.04	.19
Eighteen Houses Elected Mid-term [c]			
Before Session:			
Governor's % of total	.21	−.12	.12
Winning % of highest two	.21	−.12	.12
% of highest two	.19	−.15	.11
After Session:			
Governor's % of total	.63*	.82	.69
Winning % of highest two	.32	.70	.42
% of highest two	.64*	.71	.67
After Session:			
Candidate's % of total [e]	.39	.15	−.03
Winning % of highest two	.28	.16	.04
% of highest two	.36	.20	.05

Table 4   continued.

Primary Vote	Index of Support	Index of Success	Index of Cohesion
	Twenty-two Senates Elected Mid-term [d]		
Before Session:			
Governor's % of total	.08	−.20	−.13
Winning % of highest two	.24	.07	.12
% of highest two	.03	−.23	−.20
After Session:			
Governor's % of total	.69	.89	.47*
Winning % of highest two	.56*	.86	.47*
% of highest two	.72	.85	.42*
After Session:			
Candidate's % of total [e]	.51	.40	.19
Winning % of highest two	.47	.44	.17
% of highest two	.48	.41	.14

[a] Correlations above .40 in magnitude are underlined for convenience.

[b] For all correlations higher than .30, $p \leq .05$ for a two-tailed test.

[c] For all correlations higher than .50, $p \leq .05$ for a two-tailed test, except for those correlations asterisked. For those, $p \leq .10$ for a two-tailed test.

[d] For all correlations higher than .50, $p \leq .05$ for a two-tailed test except those asterisked. For those, $p \leq .10$ for a two-tailed test. All correlations between .40 and .50 have $p \leq .10$ for a two-tailed test except those asterisked. For those, $p \leq .20$ for a two-tailed test.

[e] This is the party candidate, who may be either the governor or his replacement.

than the raw number of seats which affects the governor's support and success. The control proves this assertion to be true. The *success* of the governor is advantaged slightly by a larger numerical contingent in the legislature (the difference between .31 and .20). For instance, a governor with 36% of a 100-member legislature may have a harder time in obtaining the necessary one-third vote than a governor who has 36% of a 200-member legislature. The first governor can tolerate two defectors and the second four defectors. This advantage is not large, however, and percentage of seats remains a good indicator.

So far the legislative behavior of both parties has been grouped together. Table 5 affords a comparison between the two parties. The major reason for the differences can be laid to the larger majorities which the Republicans traditionally hold in these legislatures.[26] The mean scores for the three types of legislative competition for the 58 sessions are:

	Republicans	Democrats
Percent of seats of governor's party	67	46
Absolute number of seats	83	58
Average percent for six sessions	64	39

Table 5 Product-moment correlations between variables of party competition and structure and legislative behavior variables of support, success and cohesion within the governor's legislative party in fifty-eight house sessions by political party.[a]

Measures of Party Competition and Structure	Index of Support		Index of Success		Index of Cohesion	
	Republicans (M=62. 4)	Democrats (M=80. 5)	Republicans (M=113. 9)	Democrats (M=100. 2)	Republicans (M=77. 3)	Democrats (M=88. 0)
Electoral Vote						
Mean percent of gubernatorial vote — 7 elections	−.03[b]	−.55[b]	.33[b]	−.12[b]	−.18[b]	−.18
Percent of the Elections won by Governor's party	.06	−.42	.41	−.05	−.19	−.15
Percent of Alternation	−.28	.11	−.45	.11	.06	−.20
Percent of the Pre-session vote	−.24	.11	.21	.27	−.24	.23
Percent of the Post-session vote — Governor	.31	.24	.30	.21	−.08	.24
Percent of the Post-session vote —Party [c]	−.06	−.08	.37	−.06	−.30	−.06
Primary Vote						
Before: Governor's % of total	.29	.14	.14	−.08	.26	−.11
Winning % of highest two	.34	.08	.17	−.12	.27	−.11
% of highest two	.36	.06	.16	−.13	.29	−.13
After: Governor's % of total	.59	.55	.74	.28	−.05	.13
Winning % of highest two	.51	.04	.68	−.10	−.03	.05
% of highest two	.58	.54	.68	.28	−.08	.12
After: Party candidate [c]						
Percent of total	.47	.59	.06	*.39	.35	.34
Winning % of highest two	.51	.48	.14	*.34	.28	.28
% of highest two	.50	.46	.12	*.33	.28	.26
Legislative Seats						
Percent of Governor's party	−.59	−.50	.22	.05	−.49	−.16
Absolute number of seats	.09	−.10	.37	.23	.09	−.16
Average percent 6 sessions	−.40	−.56	.33	−.03	−.40	−.18

[a] These sessions are the same as those in Table 1. There are 30 Republican sessions and 28 Democratic sessions.

[b] For all correlations higher than .35, p≤.05 for a two-tailed test except for those correlations asterisked. For those, p≤.10 for a two-tailed test. Correlations above .40 in magnitude are underlined for convenience.

[c] The party vote for the post-session is the vote for the governor or his replacement.

This explains why the mean index of support for the Republican Party is lower. The Republicans do not need as many votes to pass legislation. It was necessary for the Democrats to mobilize all of their party members to sustain a veto 40% of the time while the Republicans needed unanimity only 14% of the time. Thus there was no spread over 100% success to distinguish one particularly successful Democratic governor from another. The measure of success makes the Democratic party appear less loyal than the Republican, but this is an accidental and misleading byproduct of the method. We proceed with the assumption that the Democratic party would behave the same as the Republican with respect to success *given the same opportunities.*

A MODEL OF GUBERNATORIAL INFLUENCE

The Linear Regression Model

So far we cannot assess the relative weights to give to the independent variables of party structure and competition in explaining their effect on gubernatorial influence. If we assume a linear model for explaining a single dependent variable such as gubernatorial legislative success as the sum of separate effects from several independent variables such as primary support and percentage of seats in the legislature, multiple regression analysis helps us to estimate the size of such effects. For each individual session, the residual difference between the actual and predicted value of success can be calculated and subjected to further analysis; for the group of sessions, the squared multiple correlation coefficient indicates the percentage of gubernatorial success which can be explained by the model.[27] Coefficients in such regression models may be interpreted in either of two ways. The b-coefficient before each independent variable in a regression equation indicates the direction and amount of change in gubernatorial success associated with a unit change in only that one variable. When each of the variables has been standardized, different versions of the b-coefficients called beta-weights are appropriate. These beta-weights tell how much each independent variable contributes toward explaining success when its potential contribution has been equalized and when all the other independent variables have been held constant. Beta-weights are comparable; b-coefficients, on the other hand, have the advantage of concreteness. They are more likely to remain stable in different samples having unequal variances than the beta-weights.

From an analysis of the inter-correlations between independent variables correlating most highly with the dependent variables of support and success, several were chosen for the regression subject to the restriction that they not be intercorrelated at higher than .50 level themselves.[28] One exception was made in the case of the majority factor, which has a correlation of .84 with the percentage of seats a governor's party controls. This variable has potential importance because of the many advantages which accrue to a governor who has a majority. The speaker is from his party as well as the chairmen and majorities of committees. The speaker controls the membership of committees and the assignment of bills. This gives the governor, through the speaker, a control over legislation which he does not have with a minority, in which the leadership positions are in the hands of the opposite party. In order to check the supposition that the majority variable has an independent contribution to make in explaining support and success, I did not include this variable in the initial regression.

Since it is the primary record of a governor who runs again which has the highest correlation with support and success, thirty-four house sessions preceding an incumbent's election campaign were used to provide the data.[29] The regression estimates for support and success are as follows:[30]

Index of Support for the governor's party ($R = .66$ with the majority variable; $R = .66$ without the majority variable)

$$\hat{S}up._i = 58.6 - .13 \text{ G.E.}_i + .66 \text{ Prim.}_i - .71 \text{ Seats}_i + 1.9 \text{ Maj.}_i \quad \text{With the majority}$$
$$\quad\quad (0) \quad (.03) \quad\quad (.36) \quad\quad\quad (.50) \quad\quad (.04) \quad\quad \text{variable}$$
$$\hat{S}up._i = 57.4 - .12 \text{ G.E.}_i + .65 \text{ Prim.}_i - .67 \text{ Seats}_i \quad \text{Without the majority variable}$$
$$\quad\quad (0) \quad (.03) \quad\quad (.35) \quad\quad\quad (.47)$$

Index of Success for the governor's party ($R = .55$ with the majority variable; $R = .47$ without the majority variable)

$$\hat{S}uc._i = 1.2 - .57 \text{ G.E.}_i + 1.4 \text{ Prim.}_i - .38 \text{ Seats}_i + 38.2 \text{ Maj.}_i \quad \text{With the majority}$$
$$\quad\quad (0) \ (.09) \quad\quad (.54) \quad\quad\quad (.19) \quad\quad (.38) \quad\quad \text{variable}$$
$$\hat{S}uc._i = 23.3 - .37 \text{ G.E.}_i + 1.4 \text{ Prim.}_i + .44 \text{ Seats}_i \quad \text{Without the majority variable}$$
$$\quad\quad (0) \quad (.06) \quad\quad (.53) \quad\quad\quad (.22)$$

The coefficients and the multiple correlation coefficients serve to test succinctly a number of hypotheses and answer a number of questions about the relative contribution of electoral competition and party structure to gubernatorial support and success. We will first interpret the unstandardized b-coefficients in the explanatory models. The addition of the majority variable to the other independent variables makes an appreciable change in the value of R in the equation for success, but no change in the value of R in the equation for support. Apparently, holding a majority of seats in the house and the ability to organize its procedures barely affects the negative relationship which exists between the percentage of seats and the support of the governor. The results in Table 3 indicate that this negative relationship can be interpreted in either of two ways: (1) Legislative support is a matter of gubernatorial strategy. The governor makes marginal calculations concerning the votes needed to pass his legislation and does not try to marshal excess votes. Therefore as the proportion of seats held by the party goes up, the proportion of party votes needed to pass legislation goes down. (2) Excess seats are a liability to a governor. As the proportion of his party seats in the house rises, rivalries are generated which a governor cannot control. Therefore gubernatorial support falls as the percentage of seats rises.

Nor does the possession of a majority change the positive relationship which exists between the governor's primary showing and his support. With or without a majority of the legislature, a stronger governor gets higher support on upholding his vetoes; the weaker governor less support. This indicates that a strong governor can make use of the advantages which come to him as a result of majority control while a weak governor cannot. It may indicate that a strong governor calculates at the margins, but can counteract rivalries which develop with a large majority. The success equation clarifies many of these queries and will be considered next. The index of success controls for the "strategy" interpretation since, by definition, it is the percentage of party votes received out of the party votes needed.

The addition of the majority variable to the regression equation for success makes a noteworthy increase in the value of R. It changes the independent influence on the equation of the percentage of seats from positive to negative. Without the addition of the majority variable, it appears that the higher the percentage of seats, the more the governor is advantaged. The addition of the majority variable indicates that when the governor has a majority of the seats, however, extra seats over this majority become a disadvantage. Before the addition of the majority variable, the b-coefficient for seats indicated that the governor needs excess party seats to be successful. His success in getting the percentage of his party he needs is aided by increasing the number of seats in his party up to a certain limit. Probably a few seats over a majority are to his benefit. This explains the positive relationship which existed before the addition of the majority variable. With the addition of this variable the independent effect of the percentage of seats changed. The negative influence of seats over a majority indicates the attrition which excess seats brings to even the strongest governor. Thus the "rivalry" explanation for the negative relationship between seats and party support must account for the negative relationship between excess seats and success, since we have controlled for the "strategy" interpretation in our measure of success.

The equation for support which includes the majority factor tells us that a one percent increase in the post-primary support of the governor causes a .66% increase in his index of support. On the other hand, a one percent increase in the governor's legislative party contingent causes a .71% loss of support by the governor.

The equation for success which includes the majority factor indicates that receiving 80% in a primary vote is worth three times the advantage of having a majority in the legislature in terms of the ability to get the necessary votes to sustain a veto. In other words, possessing a majority of the legislature is not an automatic guarantee that vetoes will be upheld. It is the impact of a popular governor which contributes much more to the equation for success. A one percent increase in the general election support leads us to expect a little over one-half of one percent decrease in legislative success. While this looks like an influential variable, it must be remembered that the election returns rarely swing outside of the 45%-55% range, so the actual effect of this variable is minimized.

The preceding examination of the unstandardized b-coefficients in the explanatory models confirms the hypothesis that there is an appreciable difference between the effects of the same independent variables on gubernatorial support and their effects on success. In the equations for support, defined as the percentage of the governor's party which voted to support him, the influence of his strength in the outside party amounted to only half as much as it did in the equation for success, the measure of his ability to get the votes he needed. On the other hand, the influence of the percentage of seats in the legislature was twice as much in the first support equation as in the first success equation. This indicates that most governors make marginal calculations based on the votes needed to pass, but that the governors who are successful in achieving what they need are those who are also in control of the outside party.

The comparison between the variables would be on a more equitable basis if we used the beta weights. The use of beta-weights corrects for the fact that there are differences in range and variability involved in measuring the independent variables. We measure changes in the dependent variable in terms of standard deviation units for each of the other variables, a method which assures us of the same variability in each of these variables. These beta-weights can be presented by means of a bar graph. The direction in which a bar extends from the midline indicates the direction of the variable on support and success. If it extends to the left, it is exerting a negative force on the dependent variable; if it extends to the right, it is exerting a positive influence on the dependent variable. The length of the bar indicates the magnitude of a variable's force on support and success.

These beta weights are compared in Figure 1, which gives the direction and degree of change in both support and success brought about by the standardized variables. From the comparison one can see that the gubernatorial election does not affect the support or success of the governor to a very great degree. The primary accounts for more positive change in the success index than any other variable and affects support to a very large degree. Success, which indicates whether or not the governor received the deciding number of votes to uphold his veto, is more closely allied with the governor's post-session primary vote than is support, which is simply his percentage of support by his own party, unrelated to whether or not he got what he needed. A comparison of the relative contribution of the percentage of seats and majority factors confirms the previous findings. The fact that a governor has a majority has very little to do with his support, which is affected

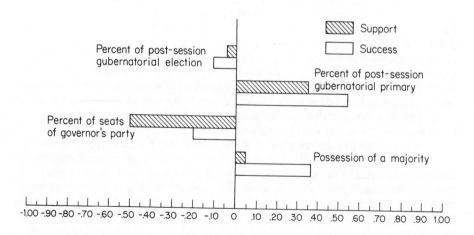

Figure 1 Effect of four variables of party competition and structure on gubernatorial support and success in the legislature. (Beta weights)

in the high negative by the percentage of seats. Success, however, is much more affected by the possession of a majority than by the percentage of seats. This may indicate the contribution of such organizational factors as the speakership and control over committees, or it may indicate, more simply, that the governor has sufficient votes to uphold his veto if he works on it.

R and the Residuals

The multiple correlation (R) is given with each regression equation for support and success. The non-squared multiple correlation coefficient associated with the support equation is .66, which is higher than any of the single correlations between an independent variable and the dependent one. Squaring this correlation shows that about 44% of the governor's support can be explained by a linear model using the independent variables we have chosen. A multiple correlation of .55 is also "respectable" as an indication of the correlation between the actual and predicted values of success. That these multiple correlations are fairly high even when the indices we have used are rather crude is quite encouraging. As indicators of legislative support and party structure the veto votes and post-session primary results are at best approximate.

An analysis of the residual differences between actual and predicted values for the sessions reveals several reasons why the R's were not even higher. Table 6 gives the residuals for the thirty-four house session. The model for support was close to being correct in 24 out of the 34 sessions. The model for success is not quite as accurate, predicting within 30% of the actual success in 21 out of 34 sessions. The over-or under-predicted sessions serve to lower the correlations between the actual and predicted values.[31] There are several possible explanations for the deviant sessions. Local factors not amenable to interstate comparisons may account for some of the cases. The effects of constituency interests upon the behavior of the individual legislator have not been considered in this paper. The role perceptions of the legislator may account for deviations. Further research on the deviant cases is clearly indicated.

Strengths and Limitations of the Linear Regression Model

The linear equations which were presented represent an attempt at both economy and accuracy of prediction. They have the advantage of indicating when certain variables are only spuriously correlated with the dependent variables, although the "independent-dependent" interpretation of the regression model ignores the more complicated interdependent and nonadditive causal interrelations of the variables involved.[32] For instance, we know that the degree of success in the primary after the session has a high positive correlation with gubernatorial success in the legislature. It can hardly cause this because it comes later in point of time. We used the post-session primary to indicate the cohesion of the party structure outside the legislature. Like malaria's high positive correlation with marshes via the mosquito, there is undoubtedly a causal connection between legislative discipline and primary success. We have assumed throughout this paper that the governor provides this causal connection through his efforts to consolidate his party to win in the primary and in the election.

A Suggested Causal Model

Based on the findings we have just presented, a model of gubernatorial influence would give the most weight to the ability of the governor to form winning coalitions both within and outside the legislature. There may not be a time lag here. The two processes probably occur simultaneously. Instead of the legislative party being an independent entity, it is subject to the direction and influence of the governor's coalition within the electoral organization. The fact that the two variables of legislative party support of the governor and primary cohesion are so highly correlated indicates that the governor provides the connecting link. Correlations between legislative performance and primary results of the party candidate were not as high. Also, it was the primary *following* a session which correlated

Table 6 Actual and predicted values for support and success for the thirty-four house sessions.

State	Session	Governor's Party	Support Actual Percent	Predicted[a] Percent	Percent-age[c] error	Success Actual Percent	Predicted[b] Percent	Percent-age[c] error
			Governor's Party with Less than 50% of the House Seats					
Rhode Island	1959	R	100	90.0	+11	100	90.8	+10
Maryland	1951	R	65	91.0	−29	65	90.2	−28
Ohio	1951	D	54	97.7	−45*	54	103.0	−48*
Maine	1955	D	97	100.0	−04	97	102.8	−06
Ohio	1953	D	79	99.8	−21	79	104.9	−25
Idaho	1959	R	93	81.3	+15	110	80.6	+36*
Connecticut	1955	D	89	84.4	+05	89	78.3	+14
Iowa	1957	D	87	94.2	−08	87	101.9	−15
Kansas	1957	D	98	93.1	+05	98	99.8	−02
Michigan	1949	D	95	90.4	+05	103	102.0	+01
Michigan	1951	D	98	94.0	+04	98	103.7	−05
Michigan	1953	D	100	93.2	+05	100	100.5	+00
New York	1955	D	100	81.7	+22	118	85.7	+27
Michigan	1957	D	100	76.5	+31*	112	77.6	+44*
Kansas	1959	D	100	86.9	+15	116	103.0	+13
Oregon	1959	R	78	73.7	+06	100	70.5	+42*

a For each session the equation for support including the majority variable was applied.
b For each session the equation for success including the majority variable was applied.
c The formula for the percentage error is:

$$\frac{\text{actual value-predicted value}}{\text{predicted value}} \times 100.$$

*The sessions under-or over-predicted by over 30% are asterisked.

Table 6, continued

State	Session	Governor's Party	Support Actual Percent	Predicted[a] Percent	Percent-age[c] error	Success Actual Percent	Predicted[b] Percent	Percent-age[c] error

Governor's Party with More than 50% of the House Seats

State	Session	Party	Actual Percent	Predicted Percent	error	Actual Percent	Predicted Percent	error
Illinois	1957	R	42	56.0	−03	55	40.0	+30
Nevada	1947	D	95	61.6	+54*	143	92.4	+35*
Ohio	1949	D	41	73.6	−44*	44	112.0	−61*
California	1959	D	87	73.8	+18	118	122.2	−03
Colorado	1957	D	38	77.0	−51*	62	126.5	−50*
Massachusetts	1949	D	96	82.9	+16	144	126.5	−14
Massachusetts	1957	D	90	80.1	+12	153	130.0	+18
New Hampshire	1949	R	95	59.2	+60*	166	93.7	+77*
Massachusetts	1947	R	96	78.6	+22	175	137.2	+27
Montana	1949	D	98	77.5	+26	182	131.5	+38*
Wisconsin	1957	R	68	72.9	−07	135	131.3	+03
Rhode Island	1947	D	100	60.2	+66*	142	102.9	+38*
Kansas	1955	R	18	41.5	−57*	38	68.2	−44*
Ohio	1957	R	29	47.4	−39*	45	80.3	−44*
Wisconsin	1953	R	66	66.5	−01	143	125.3	+14
Wisconsin	1951	R	52	65.0	−20	113	122.0	−07
Ohio	1947	R	36	53.0	−31*	67	113.4	−41*
Michigan	1947	R	40	53.0	−25	103	120.8	−15

a For each session the equation for support including the majority variable was applied.
b For each session the equation for success including the majority variable was applied.
c The formula for the percentage error is:

$$\frac{\text{actual value-predicted value}}{\text{predicted value}} \times 100.$$

*The sessions under-or over-predicted by over 30% are asterisked.

most highly with the legislative success of the governor, indicating that influence builds upon a future reward, rather than a past success.

Within most states outside the South, enough competition exists for either party to consider winning the election a possibility. In Figure 2 the broken line indicates the influence of the variable of state-wide competition upon the governor because this variable is potentially strong, but cannot be used as an effective predictor of the cohesion of most of the states in the North whose election competition is within the 40%-60% range. Because either party can win, competition for the party nomination is keen. Active and potential factions exist within both parties. The governor must compete for the nomination and, in order to do so, he starts building a coalition within the party which will be large enough to assure him of an uncontested primary nomination, or at least guarantee victory in the primary election.

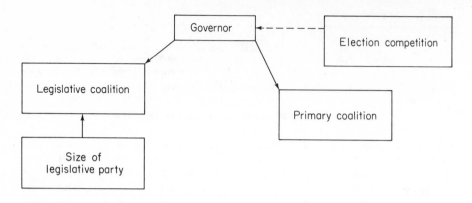

Figure 2 Causal relationships in the model of gubernatorial influence.

This faction, we hypothesize, includes members of the legislature who come from areas where the governor has organization support. With his supply of resources the governor can "pay" other legislators to back him. The model does not separate the legislative from the electoral party, but considers it to be a partner in the forming of party coalitions which later battle in the primary.

Within the legislature itself, a variable which has a great deal of weight upon the success of the governor in building his faction is the size of the legislative party. If the governor has an overwhelming majority, he has trouble building a coalition large enough to pass his legislation. The excess may fall prey to rival factions who can gain a strong enough foothold to entice a deciding number of potential supporters from the governor's coalition. Insofar as reapportionment is able to make it possible for either party to gain control of the legislature in a state in which the electorate is fairly evenly divided between the parties, the handicap of excess seats will be diminished. The governor will find his legislative party more manageable with his supply of limited resources.

CONCLUSIONS

There are several avenues of future research which lead from these findings. The only factors which have been considered are state-level factors which bear an influence on the governor's support. At best we were able to explain only 44% of the support with these factors, and the predictive value of the equation cannot be improved unless we know more about the following components of gubernatorial influence:

1. The amount and availability of economic resources such as jobs and contracts and their effect on the ability of the governor to form coalitions;
2. The personal basis of gubernatorial coalitions as a possible reason for the lack of permanence of controlling coalitions within the party;
3. The bases for permanent coalitions within a political party which can outlive any one governor; and
4. The economic and social components of a coalition and the effect on coalition building brought about by a diversity of economic interests within

a party;

a. The relationship of constituency economic interests upon the success of the governor. (Flinn discovered that members from constituencies more typical of the party supported the party position more often. [33]); and

b. The relationship of constituency economic interests upon the failure of the governor to pass his legislation. (There is more agreement among researchers that variance in party loyalty can be related to constituency characteristics.)

The ability of the electoral party organization to influence the voting loyalty of the legislators is unquestionable. Further test borings into the resources which feed successful gubernatorial coalitions should be of interest to those who claim that a party should be able to pass its program.

NOTES

1. Committee on Political Parties, American Political Science Associations, "Toward a More Responsible Two-Party System," [American Political Science Review,]44 (September, 1950), Supplement.

2. Thomas A. Flinn, "Party Responsibility in the States: Some Causal Factors," American Political Science Review, 58 (March, 1964), 60.

3. Malcolm E. Jewell, "Party Voting in American State Legislatures," American Political Science Review, 49 (September, 1955), 773-791. Jewell chose eight competitive states and limited his research to sessions in which the party balance in the legislature was reasonably close, for he assumed that there would be less party voting even in strong two-party states during the years of one-sided legislative control. He discovered, however, that the three states with the highest levels of party loyalty had long records of Republican legislative control, with only a few Democratic years, while the Democrats frequently held large legislative minorities and (except in Pennsylvania) won control of the governorship. In the states with a closer balance between the parties in the legislature, a lower level of party unity was found. He used all the roll call votes in a session and paid no attention to their sponsorship.

4. W. Duane Lockard, New England State Politics (Princeton: Princeton University Press, 1959). In the then essentially non-competitive states of New Hampshire, Maine and Vermont, policy-making was primarily a function of the dominant party in the legislature. The factions within this party, both inside and outside the legislature, determined the fate of legislation. In the competitive states of Massachusetts, Connecticut and Rhode Island, Lockard discovered considerable discipline in both legislative parties. He used votes on which there was disagreement between the parties.

5. John C. Wahlke et al., The Legislative System (New York: John Wiley and Sons, Inc., 1962).

6. David R. Derge, "Metropolitan and Outstate Alignments in Illinois and Missouri Legislative Delegations," American Political Science Review, 52 (December, 1958),

1051-1065. Since this study, it has been acknowledged that party is a more important determinant than rural-urban conflict, and the subsequent studies have dealt with the presumed relationship between similarity of district and degree of ideological cohesion within the party contingent.

7.   Flinn, *op. cit.,* p. 63.

8.   Duncan MacRae, "The Relationship Between Roll Call Votes and Constituencies in Massachusetts," *American Political Science Review,* 46 (December, 1952), 1046-1055. MacRae maintained that those legislators who come from districts which are most typical of their parties tend to show highest party loyalty on roll calls. Those who come from districts atypical of their party tend to cross party lines more often. We do not know whether the roll calls selected by MacRae were administration-supported measures or whether deviations were sizable enough to prevent passage.

9.   Thomas R. Dye, "A Comparison of Constituency Influences in the Upper and Lower Chambers of a State Legislature," *Western Political Quarterly,* 14 (June, 1961), 473-481; Flinn, *op. cit.,* pp. 64-69. Both writers used all party opposition votes whether or not the issues were economic. Dye measured voting deviation and Flinn measured voting support.

10.   MacRae, *op. cit.* Dye, *op. cit.,* p. 477; and Samuel C. Patterson, "The Role of the Deviant in the State Legislative System: The Wisconsin Assembly," *The Western Political Quarterly,* 14 (June, 1961), 460-472.

11.   A. Lawrence Lowell, "The Influence of Party Upon Legislation in England and America," *Annual Report of The American Historical Association for 1901,* Vol. I (Washington: American Historical Association, 1902), p. 323; and Stuart Rice, *Quantitative Methods in Politics* (New York: Alfred A. Knopf, 1928), pp. 209-211.

12.   William H. Riker, "A Method for Determining the Significance of Roll Calls in Voting Bodies," *Legislative Behavior,* John C. Wahlke and Heinz Eulau (eds.), (Glencoe, Illinois: Free Press, 1959), pp. 377-384. He defined the most significant roll call as one in which (1) all members vote, and (2) the difference between the minority and the majority is the minimum possible under the voting rules.

13.   David B. Truman, *The Congressional Party* (New York: John Wiley and Sons, 1959), p. 327.

14.   As a second try, all the governors from 1946-1960 were contacted and asked for lists of program bills from their personal files. In all, 101 governors were contacted and replies were received from 72. Only one governor had such a list: Governor Williams of Michigan sent his worksheet "Priority Points of Democratic Legislators and Governor Williams" for 1960. A considerable amount of strategy was admitted by some governors. Some declared the necessity of including certain items in a message as an aid to secure the enactment of legislation more seriously sought. Capital newspapers could provide the type of information needed. Usually capitol reporters either know specifically what measures are aimed at enacting part of the Governor's program or make their own evaluations in covering the legislative session.

15. The substantive importance of these vetoes varies. It must be remembered that the governor vetoes frivolous as well as major substantive legislation. For instance, the one veto of the late Governor Stevenson which was put to a roll call vote in the Illinois Senate in 1949 was S.B. No. 93, an act to provide protection to insectivorous birds by restraining cats. (Illinois, *Journal of the Senate*, 1949, p. 541). In the following session of 1951, on the other hand, the one veto roll call was on S.B. No. 102, an act to protect against subversive activities. (Illinois, *Journal of the Senate*, 1951, pp. 1946-50). Regardless of the substance of the veto, the roll call vote puts on record the degree of party support the governor can muster. Not all veto votes are taken by roll call, but the assumption is that most votes of real controversy are recorded in this way.

16. As an additional test of the ability of a governor to have his veto upheld against opposition, the following screening procedure was used: (1) 80% or more of the legislature must vote on the veto; and (2) there must be 10% or more of those voting in disagreement. We hoped in this way to reject low-interest, low-tension vetoes. A large percentage of these are technical vetoes. In California, for instance, this method cut 185 out of 189 roll call votes in the seven sessions studied. It seems logical that in a state where so little party voting exists, a governor's veto may be the only check on hasty and ill-advised legislation.

17. Rice, *op. cit.*, pp. 208-209.

18. Arizona, *Journal of the House of Representatives*, 1949, p. 638.

19. Truman, *op. cit.*, p. 60. Truman used the arithmetical mean of the legislators' *individual* administration support indices as the average index for the session.

20. Iowa, *Journal of the House of Representatives*, 1953, p. 1234. (H.B. 123, relating to exemptions for debts).

21. With respect to measuring inter-party competition see: Robert I. Golembiewski, "A Taxonomic Approach to State Political Party Strength, I" *Western Political Quarterly,* 11 (September, 1958), 499; V.O. Key, *American State Politics: An Introduction* (New York: Alfred A. Knopf, 1956), p. 98; Austin Ranney and Willmoore Kendall, "The American Party Systems," *American Political Science Review,* 48 (June, 1954), 477-485; Coleman B. Ransone, *The Office of Governor in the United States* (University, Alabama: University of Alabama Press, 1956), pp. 12-94; Joseph A. Schlesinger, "The Structure of Competition For Office in the American States," *Behavioral Science,* 5 (July, 1960), 197-210, and William H. Standing and James A. Robinson, "Inter-Party Competition and Primary Contesting: The Case of Indiana," *American Political Review.* 52 (December, 1958), 1066-1077. For measures of party cohesion based on primary voting see: V.O. Key, op. cit., pp. 109-118; and Joseph A. Schlesinger, *How They Became Governor* (East Lansing: Governmental Research Bureau, Michigan State University, 1957), p. 27.

22. Richard F. Curtis and Elton F. Jackson, "Multiple Indicators in Survey Research," *American Journal of Sociology,* 68 (September, 1962), 195-204.

23. *Ibid.*, p. 195.

24. The eleven southern states were not included because they did not offer sufficient two-party competition to be directly comparable with the northern states. Nebraska and Minnesota were excluded because their legislatures are elected on a non-partisan basis. New Mexico did not publish a record of the legislative proceedings during this period.

25. The following information was collected for the 140 legislative sessions and processed on an IBM 709 Computer.
    I. Independent Variables
        A. Electoral Competition
            1. The mean percent of the vote for the seven elections preceding the session won by the Governor's party.
            2. The percent of the preceding seven elections won by the Governor's party.
            3. The percent of alternation of control of office between the parties for the preceding seven elections.
            4. The Governor's percent of the pre-session vote.
            5. The Governor's percent of the post-session vote.
        B. Party Structure
            1. The Governor's percent of the total primary vote both pre-session and post-session.
            2. The Governor's "winning percentage" of the highest two primary candidates both pre-session and post-session (as in Joseph A. Schlesinger, *loc. cit.*).
            3. The Governor's percent of the highest two primary candidates both pre-session and post-session.
        C. Control of the Legislature
            1. Percent of seats held by the Governor's party.
            2. Absolute number of seats held by the Governor's party.
            3. Average percent of the seats held by the Governor's party over the previous six sessions.
    II. Dependent Variables.
        A. Index of support
        B. Index of success
        C. Index of cohesion (This is based on a scale of 50–100. It is not converted to a scale of 0–100.)

26. An additional reason for the high negative correlations between the first two electoral variables and support for the Democrats is that there are high positive correlations between the electoral and house seat measures for the Democrats but not for the Republicans. Thus the variables for elections may be measuring the same phenomena as seats.

27. A good explanation of the technique appears in Hubert M. Blalock, *Social Statistics* (New York: McGraw Hill Book Company, Inc., 1960), Chapters 17–19. For two applications see Donald E. Stokes, Angus Campbell and Warren E. Miller, "Components of Electoral Decision," *American Political Science Review*, 52 (June, 1958), 367–387; and Hayward R. Alker, Jr., "Dimensions of Conflict in the General Assembly," *American Political Science Review*, 58 (September, 1964), 642–657.

28. The regression equation for explaining a governor's index of support (Sup.) was:
$\hat{Sup.}_i = K + b_1 \, G.E._i + b_2 \, Prim._i + b_3 \, Seats_i + b_4 \, Maj._i$. In this equation the i subscript may indicate any of the 34 sessions being analyzed. K is an appropriate constant; $G.E._i$ equals the governor's percent of the post-session election; $Prim._i$ equals the governor's percent of the post-session primary vote; $Seats_i$ equals the percent of seats the governor's party has for the session; $Maj._i$ equals one if the governor's party has 50% or more of the House, zero if it does not. K equals zero when the explanatory variables are standardized. A similar equation was used for explaining a governor's index of success (Suc.).

29. The states and number of sessions used are: Republican: R.I. (1), Maryland (1), Idaho (1), Oregon (1), Illinois (1), N.H. (1), Mass. (1), Wisconsin (3), Kansas (1), Ohio (2), and Michigan (1). Democratic: Maine (1), Ohio (3), Conn. (1), Iowa (1), Kansas (2), Michigan (4), N.Y. (1), Nevada (1), California (1), Colorado (1), Mass. (2), Montana (1) and R.I. (1). There were 16 sessions in which the governor had a minority of the legislature: (4 Republican: 12 Democratic). There were 18 sessions in which he had a majority: (10 Republican: 8 Democratic).

30. In these equations b-coefficients are given with the independent variables; beta weights are given below them in parentheses. Beta weights are obtained by multiplying a concrete b-coefficient times the standard deviation of its independent variable and dividing by the standard deviation of the dependent variable.

31. Multiple correlation represents the zero-order correlation between the actual values obtained for the dependent variable and those values predicted from the equation. If all of the points are on a least-squares line in a scattergram, which is a geometrical interpretation of the equation, the actual and predicted values will coincide and the multiple correlation will be unity. The greater the scatter about the line, the lower the correlation between the actual and predicted values.

32. A way of deciding between alternative models of the causal interrelationships among variables has been elaborated by Hubert M. Blalock, "Correlation and Causality: The Multivariate Case," *Social Forces,* 39 (March, 1961), 246-251. It was used by Warren E. Miller and Donald E. Stokes, "Constituency Influence in Congress," *American Political Science Review,* 57 (March, 1963), 45-56.

33. Flinn, *op. cit.,* pp. 61-66.

STATE COURT SYSTEMS

The Effect of Institutional Differences in the Recruitment Process: The Case of State Judges

I. INTRODUCTION

In recent years political research has focused its attention on the socio-economic correlates of political behavior. In a revolt against a formalistic tradition, many political scientists discounted institutions because their effect could usually not be measured and because formal structure so often seemed to be a facade behind which reality was hiding. Economic determinism conditioned observers to go beyond this facade; the empirical revolution of the last two decades encouraged the measurement of noninstitutional factors.

Institutions themselves have been subjected to critical, microscopic analyses as social groups. Yet only on occasion have political scientists explicitly studied the impact of formal institutions on behavior. Members of the Survey Research Center recently concluded that the form of the ballot significantly affects split-ticket voting.[1] Whereas most students of the legislative process seek to examine it in terms of role behavior or socio-economic influences on legislators, a few have examined the impact of committee structures on the flow of legislation.[2] In the field of political recruitment, few have followed V. O. Key's pioneering examination of electoral institutions in the states;[3] instead almost all recent work has

Reprinted from *Journal of Public Law,* Vol. 13 (1964), pp. 104-119, by permission of the author and publisher.

Assistant Professor of Political Science, University of Wisconsin. The author is grateful for research assistance from his students and for comments on an earlier draft by Lewis A. Froman, Jr. and Kenneth N. Vines. The research was conducted under a grant from the University of Wisconsin Graduate School Research Committee.

sought to relate socio-economic variables with the recruitment of political leaders. The institutions which constitute the formal selection process have not been considered as independent variables by which part of the outcome could be explained.

Yet it seems likely that formal selection procedures are more than a facade. The process — whether it be an election, appointment, or some other procedure — may often be a formality which rarely trips the nominee; nevertheless, the formal procedures are likely to affect the nominating process by establishing certain informal qualifications, by giving access to particular categorical groups, or by placing some individuals at an advantage and others at a disadvantage for particular offices. If this is true, when formal procedures vary, the recruitment process will select different categories of individuals. Regardless of other variables, each formal selection procedure will be associated with a typical outcome which can be described in terms of the backgrounds of the men who win office.

This view of the recruitment process is little more than an explicit statement of the working assumptions of the Jacksonians and of more recent critics of judicial selection procedures. The Jacksonians successfully substituted popular election for gubernatorial appointment or legislative selection because they felt that judges (and other officials) should be close to the people and reflect popular attitudes. They intended that their changes would elevate a different group of individuals to office. More recently, the bar has lobbied for reforms in the manner of selecting judges so that "better qualified" men would win judgeships and so that the bar itself would obtain a more influential role in selecting them.

In the following pages the impact of two institutional characteristics on the outcome of the judicial recruitment process will be analyzed. First, the relationship between formal selection procedures and the characteristics of trial judges will be described to see whether different procedures produce judges with different backgrounds. Second, the relationship between the level of office and judges' characteristics will be examined to discover whether the level of the office attracts judges with different traits.

The judiciary affords a particularly good opportunity to test the impact of formal institutions on the recruitment process, because the states employ five distinct selection procedures to recruit judges for trial and appellate positions. The most common procedures are partisan (20 states) and non-partisan (17 states) elections.[4] Such elections are similar to those for other kinds of governmental office. They differ only in that candidates must restrict themselves to quite nominal campaigns according to their bar association code of judicial ethics; in addition, the governor has the right to fill vacancies by appointment in thirty-two states. When judges are not elected, they are either appointed by the governor (7 states), selected by the legislature (5 states), or selected through a variant of the Missouri plan (4 states).[5]

In order to assess the effect of the several selection procedures on the recruitment of trial and appellate judges, we examined the social and professional backgrounds of judges in twelve states. The states were selected to represent every selection system, all sections of the country, and all degrees of partisan competition. The states picked were California, Connecticut, Illinois, Maine, Massachusetts, Missouri, New Jersey, Pennsylvania, South Carolina, Vermont, Washington, and Wisconsin. The selection of these states left only one omission — southern states which elect their judges on partisan ballots.[6]

In each of the states all judges of the major trial court[7] and all justices of the supreme court were included in the study. The background data were collected for all judges sitting in 1955 as reported by the *Directory of American Judges*[8] or by the state's blue book. Thus, 850 trial judges and seventy-three supreme court justices were included. In addition to personal background data for judges, the degree of party competition in the judicial district was determined by examining the composition of the legislative delegation from the district in 1955; population data for the judicial district were added from the 1950 census.

II. THE EFFECT OF SELECTION SYSTEMS ON THE CHARACTERISTICS OF JUDGES

It seems likely that different selection systems establish varying of informal requirements for office, give access to different groups, and grant special advantages to some aspirants. A partial test of these hypotheses consists of examining: whether judges selected under one system more often grew up in the locale which they served than those selected by another system; whether judges recruited by one system have a better education than those recruited by another; whether judges had more or different political experience under one system than another; and whether more Republicans, Democrats, or nonaffiliators held office as a consequence of one recruitment procedure or another. If there are marked differences between judges which cannot be accounted for otherwise when they are grouped according to the procedures by which they reached office, it can be concluded that formal procedures make a noticeable difference.

Informal Qualifications

Localism   A variety of informal qualifications for office often develop in the course of an institution's history. Presidents must be men, and supreme court justices must be lawyers, although the Constitution is silent on both points. Elections were established not only to make officials responsive but also to require that candidates be well known in their locale before winning office. Thus, it would not be unreasonable to expect that where judicial offices are filled by elections, most judges were born in the district in which they serve and received their professional education in their home state. The same is likely to be true with legislative selection, for state legislatures are notoriously parochial-minded. On the other hand, both gubernatorial appointment and the Missouri plan are likely to place less weight on local ties as a prerequisite for office. Where the governor appoints, he may well select from his own circle of political friends who, because they are concerned with statewide affairs, are likely to include a substantial number having no deep roots in any particular locale. Likewise, the Missouri plan with its emphasis on merit seems to place no premium on local ties.

As Table 1 indicates, the selection systems do indeed place a varying emphasis on local birth place and local professional education, but the variations are

Table 1 Localism and education of trial judges according to selection system.

	Appt [a] % (N = 148)	Leg [a] % (N = 41)	Mo [a][d] % (N = 12)	Part-el [a] % (N = 321)	NP-el [a] % (N = 329)
Localism					
Born in district	37.2	22.0	33.3	53.6	9.4
Law school in state	33.1	48.8	91.7	62.9	54.7
Localism index [b]	70.3	70.8	125.0	116.5	64.1
	Low	Low	High	High	Low
Education					
Prior college degree	32.4	68.3	50.0	45.2	53.2
Law school honors	9.5	4.9	16.7	7.2	7.3
Attended substandard law school	28.4	2.4	33.3	19.6	1.5
Education index [c]	13.5	70.8	33.4	32.8	59.0
	Low	High	Med	Med	High

[a] The states represented in each of these columns are as follows:
Gubernatorial Appointment — Massachusetts, Maine, New Jersey.
Legislative Selection — Connecticut, South Carolina, Vermont.
Missouri Plan — Missouri (St. Louis and Kansas City).
Partisan Election — Missouri (remainder of state), Pennsylvania, Illinois.
Non-Partisan Election — California, Wisconsin, Washington.

[b] Localism index = sum of percentages.

[c] Education index = (prior college degree + law school honors — attended substandard law school).

[d] The small number of Missouri-plan judges, although constituting all those in office in 1955, makes our conclusions regarding the effect of the plan highly tentative.

not quite in the expected directions. Only *partisan* elections gave preference to locally born men; nonpartisan elections distinctly favored those not born in their district. A local legal education was more common than local birth but also was emphasized to varying degrees by the several selection systems. It was almost universal among Missouri-plan judges, but only one-third of the gubernatorially appointed judges went to a local law school. When we combine both measures of localism in an index, we find that the Missouri plan and partisan elections placed most emphasis on local ties (index = 125 and 116.5 respectively) while the other systems placed much less weight on this factor (index = 70.8 for legislative selection, 70.3 for gubernatorial appointments, and 64.1 for nonpartisan elections).

Such variations are probably associated with the political requirements each system imposes on the candidates for judicial office. Partisan elections require local connections in order for the candidate to win a place on the ballot. For instance, Sayre and Kaufman report that in New York City judicial nominations are often the reward for long, local political service.[9] Our evidence suggests that in other states where partisan elections are used similar considerations are important, for newcomers to the community seldom win judicial office. Nonpartisan elections, on the other hand, afford greater opportunity for a newcomer to become a judge. These elections are influenced more by members of the business community,[10] itself an increasingly transient group in many areas. It is quite natural that businessmen and their lawyers pay less attention to ascribed characteristics such as place of birth and more to attained traits such as expertise in the law and association with particular groups. The Missouri plan's emphasis on local ties is most pronounced in its heavy preference for judges who went to a local law school. This preference underscores the influence of the bar under the plan, for bar association politics quite likely revolve around the school tie more than partisan politics.

Education   Most states require that judges be lawyers, but the quality of their legal education is not specified. Popular prejudice assumes that elections produce poorly educated judges, whereas appointments lead to better selections; therefore, the American Bar Association plan provides for initial appointment of judges.

Our data show that almost all judges attended law school; in this regard, one selection system is as good as another. This discovery simply reflects the fact that most lawyers are now graduates of a law school. Probing more deeply, however, it is found that there are distinct differences in the extent and quality of education received by judges. Those selected by legislatures were most likely to have finished college and to have received a bachelor's degree; those selected by governors were least likely. Here there is no difference between those elected by partisan or nonpartisan ballots and those chosen through the Missouri plan. Another measure of education is the type of law school which judges attended. It is generally agreed that night classes and proprietary schools provide a poorer legal education than most full-time schools accredited by the American Bar Association or the American Association of Law Schools. Most judges, indeed, avoided poor quality law schools, but there are significant differences between the results of selection systems. Almost no judges elected on a nonpartisan ballot or selected by a legislature attended a proprietary or night law school,[11] 28 per cent of the gubernatorially appointed judges and 33 per cent of the Missouri-plan judges received such substandard legal education.

The surprisingly high proportion of Missouri-plan judges attending substandard law schools may be due to the fact that the Missouri-plan judges studied were entirely an urban group, for in 1955 there were no rural trial judges selected by this system. From other studies[12] it is known that urban lawyers are more likely to have attended night or proprietary law schools than rural attorneys; moreover, urban judges selected by the other systems were also more likely to be graduates of such schools (see Appendix A). Consequently, the high percentage of poorly educated judges recruited by the Missouri plan is probably a result of the urban locale in which these judges were selected. The same, however, cannot be said of the gubernatorially selected judges. They served in both urban and rural areas. Rather, one may conclude that gubernatorial selection places less emphasis on formal education than other selection systems do.

Finally, the degree to which judges excelled during their legal education was measured by whether they served on their school's law journal or were elected to the legal honor society. The level of such excellence is low for all systems, but the Missouri plan clearly recruited a larger proportion of honor graduates for the bench than the other systems.

In summary, the data show that the popular prejudice against election as a system producing poorly trained officials is unfounded. Although legislative selection produced the best trained judges, nonpartisan elections did not trail far behind. Gubernatorial appointment produced the least well-trained judges. Although not all the differences found were in the expected direction, the evidence gives clear support to the notion that the several selection systems impose quite different informal prerequisites for judicial office. As the data show, some place a high premium on local ties; others place a high premium on a good legal education.

Differential Access: Political and Judicial Experience   Another important question is whether the several selection systems give access to different groups of aspirants. To discover whether or not this is true, the degree and type of prior political and judicial experience of judges was measured.

Table 2 Political and judicial experience of trial judges according to selection system.

	Appt % (N = 148)	Leg % (N = 41)	Mo % (N = 12)	Part-el % (N = 321)	Part-el % (N = 329)
Political experience					
Held prior public office	56.8	95.1	16.7	53.6	30.4
Elected law enforcement[a]	39.1	19.2	100.0	78.6	71.7
Legislature[a]	66.2	80.7	——	24.5	22.1
Actual procedure					
Appointed to vacancy by governor				19.6	35.9
Judicial experience					
Held prior judgeship	3.4	—	8.3	2.5	1.8

[a] Percentages computed on basis of number who held public office. Total may be more than 100 as some judges held both law enforcement and legislative offices.

The data as shown in Table 2 indicate that selection systems do indeed weigh prior political experience quite differently. As might be expected, few Missouri plan or nonpartisan judges held prior office; almost all legislatively selected judges, and most partisan-elected and gubernatorially appointed ones held prior political office.

Even more important than the quantity of experience is its character. As the data show, judges acquired their political experience in quite different places according to the selection system in effect. Where the governor or legislature chose them, judges most frequently had served in the legislature rather than elsewhere. Where judges were elected (be it on a partisan or nonpartisan ballot) or chosen by the Missouri plan, they usually had law enforcement experience, primarily as district attorney. Here, as with the other characteristics, we see the differential impact of institutions. Every selection system demands that candidates for a position make themselves known to the proper authorities. When judges are selected at the state capital, the legislature is the best place to become known and to be perceived as judicial timber. When local elections or local nominating commissions select the judge, law enforcement offices provide the best avenue to the bench.

Moreover, where the selection system provides options, such as whether in an elective system the governor appoints to vacancies or they are filled by election, the formal systems again produce variant results. In each of the election states studied, the governor had the power to fill vacancies. In general, appointment did not replace election as the normal mode of selection, as has been previously asserted by Wood.[13] However, appointment was much more frequent with nonpartisan elections than with partisan ones.[14]

In summary, almost half of all judges held prior public office, but those selected by legislatures had such experience almost without exception, while Missouri-plan judges seldom held prior office. Gubernatorially appointed and legislatively selected judges usually came from the legislature; elected and Missouri-plan judges usually had law enforcement experience. Finally, nonpartisan elections provided more frequent opportunities for gubernatorial appointment to vacancies than did partisan elections, although in neither case was appointment the normal method of selection.

Just as some selection systems give preferential access to those with political experience, so it might be expected that prior judicial experience would be advantageous in some situations and not in others. Specifically, it might be expected that the Missouri plan most frequently chooses men with judicial experience for seats on major trial courts.

The data in Table 2 show that this is the case; however, so few trial judges selected by any system had prior experience that the variance is too small to be statistically significant. Judicial experience in minor courts is apparently considered irrelevant under all selection systems; the structure of the judiciary prevents the adoption of any selection procedure for the choosing of experienced jurists, for few states have minor trial courts which would give judicial candidates significant experience.

Group Advantage: Partisan Affiliation   Finally, the several recruitment systems give an advantage to different group-affiliated aspirants. It is expected from experience with other kinds of nonpartisan elections that more Republicans would win judgeships in nonpartisan than in partisan elections. It might be expected that the same result would obtain under the Missouri plan, for that procedure gives the organized bar an influential role, and in many locales, the bar is decidedly Republican.

The data in Table 3, however, indicate that Republicans held most judgeships in non-Southern states in 1955 regardless of selection system. Contrary to our expectations, Democrats did not do appreciably better in partisan elections than in nonpartisan ones. They seem to have done best where the legislature

Table 3 Party affiliation of trial judges according to selection system and compared to legislators in same states.

	Appt % (N = 148)	Leg % (N = 41)	Mo % (N = 12)	Part-el % (N = 321)	NP-el % (N = 329)
Party affiliation					
Republican judges	50.0	48.8	—	44.2	36.2
Democratic judges	20.3	43.9	16.7	24.3	13.4
No party identification	29.7	7.3	83.3	31.5	50.4
Democratic Legislators	48.7	41.1	*	51.6	41.8

*Not computed as Missouri plan is not used throughout the state.

selected judges, but this is a result of South Carolina's inclusion in the sample. Excluding South Carolina where *only* Democrats were chosen, the results are not different than with other systems. Nor is the Republican advantage a result of low-level party competition, for as the table shows, Democrats held a far larger proportion of legislative seats than judgeships in these states.

Accounting for the signal failure of Democrats to win trial judgeships is not easy. Three explanations come to mind. First, it is plausible that more lawyers are Republican than Democrat, for legal practice tends to bring lawyers into close association with the business community which is undoubtedly Republican everywhere except in the deep South. Second, it is possible that Republicans have much more influence in the bar association than Democrats, because, at least at the national level, the American Bar Association's policy pronouncements have a decidedly Republican tinge to them. This Republican influence in the bar then makes its weight felt in the judicial selection process. Third, the image of the conservative Republican and that of the judge coincide in a striking fashion; both are thought to be moderate, cautious, and respectable. All three factors probably combine to give Republicans their striking advantage in judicial positions.

It should also be noted that the Republican advantage remained constant from system to system with only two exceptions. The deviant behavior of legislative selection has already been explained by South Carolina's inclusion. The number of judges chosen by the Missouri plan who identified with either party was exceptionally low; indeed, the number of judges who identified their party affiliation varies markedly from system to system. In the Missouri plan, 83.3 per cent of all judges refused to indicate their party affiliation; likewise, more than half the nonpartisan-elected judges refused to use a party label. The other systems, all of which are openly partisan, did not encourage such nonidentification. Thus, Missouri-plan judges do not show the Republican predominance shown elsewhere because most Missouri judges refused to reveal their party. Whereas selection systems do not markedly differ in the advantage granted one party, they do differ in the degree to which party affiliation is discouraged. Formally eliminating party from the selection processes reduces overt identification with political parties. from the selection processes reduces overt identification with political parties.

Summary   The data indicate that judicial selection procedures recruit judges with some different background characteristics. They impose somewhat different informal prerequisites for office. Some require local birth, some require local professional education, while others require neither. The selection systems also give access to judgeships to different categories of candidates. Legislative selection favors those who have been previously active in politics; nonpartisan elections apparently bar those with prior public experience. Partisan elections and the Missouri plan give access to judgeships to those who previously served as district attorney; legislative selection and gubernatorial appointment give preference to former legislators. Finally, most selection systems favor Republicans. However, nonpartisan plans give some preference to nonidentifiers, whereas the other systems give an advantage to those who state a party affiliation.

Is it possible that the differences that have been associated with selection procedures are really the result of other variables such as the peculiarities of the states examined or the degree of urbanism or party competition? This seems unlikely. There appears to be no evidence from other studies that partisan or nonpartisan ballots are associated with particular socio-economic variables. The adoption of these ballots (and of other procedures) by various states was the result of popular reform movements at various stages of history. In some states one movement was successful; in others a different movement left its imprint. The selection systems (with the exception of the Missouri plan) are a vestige of the past; they are constants within which social and political conflicts are resolved. The history of their adoption makes clear that they are not associated with any socio-economic variable that currently characterizes politics in these states. The data used in this study substantiate this view. When the judges were compared state by state, small differences between states were found where judges were selected by the same system and large differences between states where judges were selected by different systems.[15]

However, it is not my contention that the characteristics of judges are not in any way associated with socio-economic variables. The data (see Appendices A and B) demonstrate that urban and rural judges are quite different on a number of points, but these differences do not lessen the differences associated with selection systems, nor would they be expected to. Likewise, the degree of partisan competition in the states where judges were elected made a slight difference in the characteristics of the jurists chosen. Whatever the effect of other variables, the impact of the formal selection system is such as to produce quite distinct characteristics among trial judges.

III. THE EFFECT OF THE LEVEL OF OFFICE ON THE CHARACTERISTICS OF JUDGES

Another institutional characteristic which might affect recruitment is the stature of the office and the degree to which it is regarded as one with high power potential. Clearly some offices have great prestige and potential for making important decisions; others have little substance. Are different individuals recruited for such different offices? Data current in the literature suggest that such differences exist.[16] If this be true, it should be expected that such differences would also appear in state judicial systems where both trial and appellate positions must be filled.

If the level of office makes a difference, it would be expected that trial and appellate judges would differ on each of the characteristics previously examined. As appellate judgeships require a higher degree of legal expertise, it would be expected that supreme court justices would be better educated than trial judges. Since appellate positions have a greater potential for making important policy decisions, it might be expected that supreme court justices more frequently possess political experience and that that experience be more varied than with trial judges. It might also be expected that more appellate judges possess prior judicial experience.

Each of these questions can be examined by comparing the supreme court justices with trial judges for the twelve states. Except in Missouri and California the same selection system was used for trial and appellate judges. Thus no significantly extraneous institutional factors are present which might promote spurious relationships.

Table 4 Characteristics of trial judges and supreme court justices.

	Trial Judges % (N = 851)	SC Justices % (N = 73)
Education		
Prior college degree	47.2	57.5
Substandard law school	13.5	6.8
Law school honors	7.6	27.4
Political experience		
Prior public office	47.1	64.4
Elected law enforcement*	65.9	53.6
Legislature*	34.0	51.2
Judicial experience		
Prior judgeship	2.4	50.7
Party affiliation & competition		
Republican	41.7	39.7
Democratic	20.2	26.0
If elected, opposition first election	71.0	23.5

*Percentages computed on basis of number who held public office. Total may be more than 100 as some judges held both law enforcement and legislative offices.

Education   As expected, the education of higher court judges is better than that of trial judges, though not on all counts. Only an insignificantly larger number of supreme court justices held baccalaureate degrees and went on to accredited law schools. However, a significantly larger number of justices won law school honors.

The level of position, then, is somewhat related to the quality of education of the men who win office in the judiciary.

Prior Political Experience   Supreme court justices also had experience in other public offices more frequently than trial judges did. Novices in public life were not usually chosen for these highly valued positions. The previous experience of the two groups of jurists was generally similar. Both legislative and law enforcement offices led to a supreme court position, although legislative experience was more frequent among supreme court justices than among trial judges. The larger proportion of ex-legislators on supreme courts is an apparent recognition of the fact that supreme courts are sometimes engaged in policy formulation and that legislative experience is particularly appropriate for a would-be justice.

Prior Judgeships   In the same way as the recruitment system discriminated in terms of prior political experience, it also preferred men who had previously held a judgeship. However, while the difference between trial and supreme court judges is great in the proportion having previous judicial experience, one should note that barely half the supreme court justices held a previous judgeship. The system, while sensitive to the institutional differences between a trial and appellate court, does not exclude outsiders from high judicial office. While judges had an advantage in seeking supreme court posts, they did not have a corner on the market.

Party Affiliation and Electoral Experience   Republicans predominate in state supreme courts in non-Southern states just as they do in trial courts.[17] Democrats, however, won a slightly larger proportion of supreme court positions than trial judgeships.

   The higher prestige of supreme courts had another consequence. Where justices of the supreme court won office through election, competition occurred much less frequently than for trial judgeships. This appears to run contrary to the common observation that as the office becomes more important, competition for it becomes a little more likely. In the case of the state judiciary, competition decreases with the importance of the post. The prestige of appellate courts may be responsible for this tendency. The aura of a supreme court is great enough to fend off competition even during a justice's first election. Indeed, competition for supreme court posts is so rare that the justice who is confronted by an opponent may cry "foul" as Justice Fournier of Louisiana recently did when forced to campaign for re-election.

Summary   As was found with the selection procedures, institutional differences in the form of level of office affect the outcome of the recruitment process. Different kinds of men are chosen for appellate positions than for trial judgeships. Supreme court justices are more likely to be well educated, more likely to have prior public and judicial experience, and when elected, less likely to face opposition. As with trial courts, more Republicans than Democrats held appellate judgeships.

   These data do not, of course, indicate what it is about supreme court positions that attracts this different breed of men — whether it is the higher prestige, longer tenure, higher pay, more interesting work, or some other characteristic. What is happening, however, is that the institutional characteristics mold the perceptions and actions of those who participate in the recruitment process so that different men are recruited for the two offices.

IV. CONCLUSIONS

Many variables affect the recruitment process. Earlier studies emphasized psychological and sociological characteristics of office-holders; the institutional variables were taken for granted or ignored because it seemed impossible to measure their impact. Where it is possible to control institutional variables, as in the case of state judges, one can see in striking fashion the impact of two kinds of institutional factors. On the one hand, the formal characteristics of the selection process clearly affect the kind of men who become judges. On the other hand, the characteristics of the judgeship also affect the quality of those winning a seat on the bench.

As formal institutions prescribe the last step in the recruitment process, they apparently influence the informal procedures which precede nomination. The formal characteristics of the recruitment process specify some of the contacts which a candidate for office must have. In addition, they designate which points of access shall be useful for winning a given post. Thus local birth is useful in partisan elections, while a legislative post is useful in gubernatorial selection. Previous judicial experience is irrelevant for those seeking trial judgeships; it helps considerably when seeking a supreme court position.

Insofar as the judicial process is concerned, the data mark the bare beginning for a deeper understanding of the recruitment of judges and its effect on the decision-making process. In this paper, it has been assumed that the formal characteristics of the selection process defined a uniform set of variables. For the purpose of this study that was sufficient. However, in order to assess who is influential in the selection of judges, it will be necessary to go beyond the formal characteristics of the selection systems. In the case of federal judges, the influence of senators and of the American Bar Association, which operates behind the President's formal power of appointment, is already known.[18] Likewise, the influence of local bar associations,[19] local political leaders,[20] and governors under the several selection systems needs to be assessed if one is to know who counts in the selection of judges.

Moreover, for those with an interest in judicial decision making, it is necessary to go beyond our data in another direction. Having found that the several selection systems produce different sorts of judges, it must be determined whether they decide cases in a systematically different pattern. If those who reach the judgeship from the district attorney's office decide in the same way as those who were legislators, it might be concluded that the selection system ultimately makes no difference.[21]

The agenda for research has, therefore not been decreased by these findings. The context in which this research has taken place, however, can be enriched by paying close attention to the differences that have been found to be related to the institutions which characterize the judicial selection process.

Appendix A Background characteristics of trial judges holding degree of urbanism constant.

	Rural [a]	Urban [a]	High Urban [a]	Rural [a]	Urban [a]	High Urban [a]
	% Judges Born in District			% Judges Educated in State		
Appt.	29.6(27)	43.9(57)	34.4(64)	18.5(27)	31.6(57)	40.6(64)
Part. elec.	51.4(103)	60.6(94)	50.0(124)	56.3(103)	58.5(94)	71.8(124)
N-Part. elec.	16.0(94)	12.0(83)	3.9(152)	53.2(94)	61.4(83)	52.0(152)
	% Prior College Degree			% Substandard Law School		
Appt.	25.9	36.9	31.3	18.5	19.3	40.6
Part. elec.	52.4	50.0	35.5	7.8	12.8	34.7
N-Part. elec.	48.9	54.2	55.3	—	—	3.3
	% Prior Public Office			% Democratic		
Appt.	40.7	61.4	64.4	3.7	15.8	31.3
Part.elec.	59.2	62.8	41.9	25.2	20.2	26.6
N-Part. elec.	37.2	43.4	19.1	14.9	10.8	13.8
	% Prior Law Enforcement			% Prior Legislature		
Appt.	66.6	42.8	22.6	44.4	64.3	77.2
Part. elec.	88.6	80.0	66.1	14.5	25.4	37.0
N-Part. elec.	74.4	76.3	65.3	16.2	21.0	28.3
	% Appointed to Vacancy by Gov.			% Opposed First Election		
Part. elec.	22.3	14.9	21.0	29.1	34.0	34.7
N-Part. elec.	30.9	28.9	42.8	13.8	9.6	2.0

[a] The categories are defined as follows:

      rural   = 0-49.9% urban by 1950 census.
      urban   = 50-79.9% urban by 1950 census.
      high urban = 80-100 % urban by 1950 census.

[Note: Totals are given in parentheses. Legislative and Missouri plan selection are omitted as the number of judges was too small to permit meaningful cross tabulation.]

Appendix B Background characteristics of trial judges selected by partisan and non-partisan elections holding degree of party competition constant. [a]

	Democratic	Competitive	Republican	Democratic	Competitive	Republican
	% Born in District			% Educated in State		
Part. elec.	68. 9(74)	59. 3(91)	56. 5(115)	68. 9(74)	73. 6(91)	72. 2(115)
N–Part. elec.	26. 1(23)	50. 0(24)	26. 3(38)	65. 2(23)	66. 6(24)	76. 3(38)
	% Prior College Degree			% Substandard Law School		
Part. elec.	46. 0	46. 1	59. 0	24. 3	33. 0	12. 9
N–Part. elec.	56. 5	58. 4	63. 1	4. 4	—	—
	% Prior Public Office			% Democratic		
Part. elec.	44. 6	73. 6	59. 1	43. 2	38. 5	9. 6
N–Part. elec.	21. 7	33. 3	52. 6	39. 1	8. 3	2. 6
	% Appointed to Vacancy by Gov.			% Opposed First Election		
Part. elec.	13. 5	27. 5	12. 1	28. 4	59. 3	25. 2
N–Part. elec.	21. 8	33. 3	23. 6	8. 7	12. 5	50. 0

[a] Categories defined in terms of proportion of legislative seats held by each party in 1955:

Democratic = 70% + seats held by Democrats
Competitive = 30. 1-69. 9% seats held by Democrats
Republican = 0-30% of seats held by Democrats
[Note: Totals are given in parenthesis.]

NOTES

1. Campbell, Converse, Miller, and Stokes, *The American Voter,* pp. 265-76 (1960).

2. See, *e.g.,* Robinson, "Role of the Rules Committee in Arranging the Program of the U.S. House of Representatives, " *Western Political Quarterly,* Vol. 12, (1959), p. 653.

3. Key, *American State Politics: An Introduction* (1956).

4. The number of states in each category is for the year 1960, according to Council of State Governments, *State Court Systems* (1960). Since then, Iowa and Nebraska have adopted variant of the Missouri plan and Illinois has modified its use of partisan elections.

5. The total is fifty-three as several states use one system to select some judges and a different one to choose others.

6. Several recent studies of partisan election of judges in southern states indicate that on some points results differ from those described below. See Bashful, "The Florida

Supreme Court: a Study in Judicial Selection, 1955 (unpublished dissertation in University of Illinois Library);Vines, "The Selection of Judges in Louisiana," *Tulane Studies in Political Science,* Vol. 8 (1962), p. 99; Henderson and Sinclair, "The Impact of the Selection Process Upon the Role of the Judge," May 1963 (paper read at the Midwest Conference of Political Scientists).

7. The following trial courts were included: Superior Court in California, Connecticut, Illinois, Maine, Massachusetts, New Jersey, and Washington; Circuit Court in Missouri, South Carolina, and Wisconsin; Court of County Pleas in Pennsylvania; and County Court in Vermont.

8. *Directory of American Judges* (Liebman, ed., 1955). Unfortunately, no more recent data are available. Little has occurred, however, in the intervening years to suggest that judges possess markedly different characteristics now than then.

9. Sayre and Kaufman, *Governing New York City,* pp. 522-54 (1960).

10. For the influence of businessmen on nonpartisan elections, see Lee, *The Politics of Nonpartisanship* (1960).

11. Proprietary and night law schools were identified by the listing in Reed, *Training for the Public Profession of the Law,* pp. 435-41 (1921). Those schools requiring no undergraduate training for admission and those offering only afternoon and evening classes were categorized as substandard.

12. Carlin, *Lawyers on Their Own,* pp. 3-40 (1962).

13. Wood, "State Judicial Selection: Realities vs. Legalities," *State Government,* Vol. 31 (1958), p. 17, concludes that elections are a sham; appointment by the governor is the more frequent mode of selection in states which purportedly elect their judges. Wood cites no data to substantiate his claim; our data clearly contradict his conclusions.

14. James Herndon comes to the same conclusion regarding supreme court justices in "Appointment as a Means of Initial Accession to State Courts of Last Resort," *North Dakota Law Review,* Vol. 38 (1962), p. 60.

15. The only exception was, as noted above, that South Carolina judges were all Democrats whereas other judges selected by legislative appointment were predominantly Republicans.

16. See, *e.g.,* Matthews, *The Social Backgrounds of Political Decision-Makers,* pp. 20-33 (1954).

17. Stuart Nagel draws the same conclusion in "Unequal Party Representation on the State Supreme Courts, "*Journal of the American Judicial Society,*Vol. 45 (1961), p. 62.

18. Harris, *The Advice and Consent of the Senate* (1953); Grossman, "The Role of the

American Bar Association in the Selection of Judges, " 1963 (unpublished dissertation in the State University of Iowa Library).

19. A notable beginning was made in Martin, *The Role of the Bar in Electing the Bench in Chicago* (1936).

20. See Sayre and Kaufman, *op. cit.* note 9.

21. See Nagel, "Political Party Affiliation and Judges' Decisions, " *American Political Science Review,* Vol. 55 (1961), p. 843, for an interesting attempt to relate state supreme court decisions with the background characteristics of judges who made the decisions.

Southern State Supreme Courts and Race Relations

Kenneth N. Vines

A leading characteristic of the American political process is the frequent participation of courts in policy-making. The dramatic decisions of the Supreme Court are familiar landmarks in the literature of political history, but much less familiar are the decisions made by lower federal courts and by the state and local courts. While we have a good estimate of the impact of Supreme Court decisions in the political process, the political significance of the cases decided in other courts is largely unknown.

Each year thousands of cases are decided in the lower federal courts and in the hundreds of state and local courts. Undoubtedly a major portion of these decisions, like the majority of the bills passed in Congress and in the state legislatures, has little political importance. But lack of knowledge of decision-making in the lower federal and the state and local courts makes difficult any assessment of the roles of these courts in their respective political systems.

We cannot generalize our knowledge concerning the Supreme Court, necessarily, to the operation of other courts. Judges in lower courts may not follow the same patterns of behavior; lower courts may not make decisions according to similar judicial procedures nor fulfill the same functions in the political system. While other courts may be subject to some of the same legal influences that affect the Supreme Court, they clearly are involved with political factors in their peculiar environments. Neither can we generalize our knowledge of other political institutions such as the legislature to the operation of courts. Such factors as training in legal values, the distinctive methods of recruitment of officials to the courts, and the varied degrees of insulation of the courts from the political system emphasize that we must accumulate concepts and knowledge appropriate to courts and court officials to increase our knowledge of the judiciary.

Although the literature of political science has described mainly the role of national courts (especially the Supreme Court), state and local courts undoubtedly also make decisions of political import; for they all have much the same potential for affecting policy outcomes. Not only can they exercise judicial review and extensively interpret statutes and constitutions, but they are easily accessible for lobbying by litigation. State courts in the state political process, like courts on the national level, provide points of access at which opinions and pressures may be presented, and at which societal values may be maintained and social changes resisted or facilitated. Furthermore, interest stymied elsewhere in the political process may turn to the state courts.

The literature of political science offers only scattered descriptions of the political activities of state courts. The function of judicial review has been partially described [1] and a few other aspects of state judicial politics have been exam-

Reprinted by permission of the University of Utah, copyright owners, from *Western Political Quarterly*, Vol. 18, No. 1 (March 1965), pp. 5-18.

ined.[2] For the most part attention has been focused on the state supreme courts and only the non-unanimous opinions have been examined, a limitation that severely circumscribes the character of the studies.

This paper investigates the role of state courts through a study of their decisions. Our primary data consist of a subset of state supreme court decisions, namely all race relations cases involving Negroes decided by the supreme courts of the eleven states of the traditional South in the period from May 1954 (the date of the Supreme Court school desegregation decision) through December 1963.[3] Race relations decisions were selected for two reasons. First, they constitute a sensitive area of much political concern in the South. Second, they permit the performance of state courts to be compared conveniently with those of other political agencies in the South concerned with the issue.

Analysis of the data in these state court decisions facilitates the examination of several questions about the political functions of state courts. For example, what groups are represented in state courts and who are the original plaintiffs who bring the cases to court? Do state courts, like their federal counterparts, lend support to Negro interests? In what manner do state courts decide cases involving Negroes and what symbols and references do they use? And how does the record of state judges compare with that of other Southern officials who make decisions on civil rights?

ACCESS TO STATE COURTS

Civil rights politics in the South virtually always concerns the position of Negroes, seldom any other groups. And as expected, Negroes are involved in all civil rights cases here, as defendants or plaintiffs. Table 1 indicates the identity of plaintiffs before the state courts and offers a general description of the groups with cases there during the period under study. Of all civil rights cases, some 60 per cent were originally brought by Negroes. This would seem to indicate that state courts — like federal district courts where Negroes initiated over 90 per cent of all civil rights cases[4] — have been an important instrument in the handling of Negro grievances in the South.

Table 1 Interested parties before the state courts: identity of original plaintiffs in civil rights cases before southern state supreme courts, 1954-63.

Parties	All Cases	All Cases Except Trial Procedure Cases
Negroes	61.6	33.0
State and Local Governments	26.3	44.7
Whites	12.1	22.3
Total	100.0 (N = 198)	100.0 (N = 103)

But further analysis, according to type of cases, presents a different picture. Nearly half of the civil rights cases involved trial procedure issues. (In contrast, civil rights cases in the federal district courts for the same states in a similar period involved trial procedure cases in only 3.3 per cent of all instances.) Trial procedure cases are concerned mainly with the appeals of individuals convicted of felonies; the grounds of appeal alleged some defect in the procedure of conviction such as discrimination against Negroes in the selection of the jury, failure to provide proper counsel, or some evidence of prejudice in the conduct of the trial. The importance of trial procedure cases should not be minimized since they involve a continuous testing and representation of Negro interests in the administration of justice and on occasion involve important policy matters. However, the immediate, important political conflicts in race relations are located in other areas. Moreover, when we filter out trial procedure cases from the remainder we find that while Negroes initiated almost two-thirds of all cases, they initiated only about one-third of all non-trial procedure cases. The really important issues in state courts were thus brought there not by Negroes but by state and local governments and white plaintiffs.

Considering the amount and intensity of political conflict in the South in race relations, the amount of civil rights litigation handled by the southern supreme courts has been slight. During a period of almost ten years, the eleven courts handled only 103 cases among them that did not invove trial procedure issues; in comparison, during the same period of time, the federal district courts handled 282 such cases; southern state legislatures passed over 500 acts during a similar period of time dealing with civil rights.[5]

There are several factors affecting the amount and nature of civil rights litigation. For example, the frequency with which any group goes to the courts depends in part on its perceptions of chances for success and for favorable representation before the courts. Decision-making authority in the American political system is diffused among different institutions of government. In many instances groups may go to the legislature or the executive or the judiciary, seeking favorable public decisions upon a given issue. The choice of institutions is made partly on estimate as to how the institution will behave in particular political situations.

It is well known that Negroes ordinarily would prefer to litigate issues before the federal courts than before the state courts in the South. On occasion Negroes have formally pleaded before the southern federal courts that civil rights issues should not be heard in the state courts because of the lack of favorable representation there. In one case before the federal courts they asserted that "remedy in the state courts is not merely inadequate, it is nonexistent," and argued further that state courts were inappropriate vehicles for the decision of civil rights issues because state courts were committed to a policy of maintaining segregation at all costs.[6] In a study of Negro attitudes toward government institutions in a southern state, Negro leaders ranked state courts low as places in the political structure where Negroes might receive fair representation.[7]

The amount of litigation initiated by groups hostile to civil rights indicates that these groups made frequent use of the courts in an attempt to resist change in the status of race relations. This suggests that such groups anticipated a more friendly reception in the courts than did Negroes. As Murphy has pointed out, the combined activities resisting civil rights amounted to a counterattack leveled against the proposed innovations.[8] By legislation, by executive action, and, as our data indicate, by activities in the courts this counterattack was pursued in the state political structure.

But certain rules of the legal process tended to force Negroes into the state courts when perhaps they would have preferred litigation in the federal courts. As a beginning, entrance into the federal courts required either federal jurisdiction or a constitutional issue in the case. While federal entrance was not difficult, it was not always immediately possible in cases involving local situations. One rule operating to push Negroes into the state courts was the requirement that state remedies must be exhausted before appeals could be taken to the national Supreme Court.[9] Negroes were usually seeking, in civil rights cases, to secure rights attained in the federal courts or statutes. Although state courts have concurrent jurisdiction in protecting these rights, Negroes did not normally seek relief there. Federal courts have voluntarily restricted the exercise of their jurisdiction in some civil rights areas, forcing Negroes to resort to the state courts more often than they would desire. Moreover, the "exhaustion of remedies" rule often required Negroes to go through the state courts, no matter how clear the constitutional question, before an appeal could be taken to the U.S. Supreme Court from some state action.

DISPOSITION OF CASES

Certain characteristics of state courts might lead judges to join in policies of resistance to civil rights. In particular, except in Virginia and South Carolina where judges are chosen by the legislature, the supreme court is elected on partisan ballots[10] in southern states and subject, therefore, to the usual symbols and statements about the racial status quo in the campaigns of those officials who run for election in the South. Furthermore, state judges ascend to the judiciary by careers which generally include the tenure of other state and local offices.[11] This means that in electoral campaigns and in service in state and local political positions, judges had both the opportunity and the motivation to be involved in civil rights politics. State judges thus come to the supreme court with experiences in political situations where resistance to civil rights policies is an important element.

Table 2 indicates the disposition of cases by the eleven supreme courts.[12] Overall, decisions were rendered in favor of Negroes in about one out of three instances; but in non-trial procedure cases Negroes fared somewhat better than in trial procedure cases. Negroes fared a little better in the more important policy cases such as those dealing with education and sit-in demonstrations.

A comment is in order about the kinds of cases decided in favor of Negro litigants. It is remarkable, in some sense, that any cases could be decided favorably for Negroes in the South of the immediate post-school-desegregation-decision period. In the two most politically sensitive areas of race relations, the question of sit-in demonstrations and state actions against the organization and legal activities of the NAACP, less than 20 per cent of the cases were decided favorably for Negro litigants. In the areas of desegregation of schools and universities, the desegregation of government facilities, and registration and voting, state supreme courts decided much more frequently, at around the 40 per cent level, for Negro

Table 2 Disposition of cases by Southern supreme courts, 1954–63.

	Per Cent Favorable to Negroes	Per Cent Unfavorable to Negroes	Total Per Cent
All Cases	29.2	70.8	100.0 (N = 198)
Trial Procedure Cases	21.3	78.7	100.0 (N = 92)
Non-Trial Procedure Cases	35.8	64.2	100.0 (N = 106)

plaintiffs. Sometimes cases favoring Negroes involved unimportant issues. For example, the court of Mississippi compiled its score of cases decided for Negroes in the areas of miscegenation and trial procedures. It is significant, however, that while racial demagoguery was rife in the Mississippi legislature and in state elections, the Supreme Court of Mississippi was holding that racial demagoguery would not be allowed in the courts, that a conviction of a Negro where the district attorney used appeals to racial prejudice should be reversed.

State supreme courts' decisions on civil rights may be compared with decisions made by other political agencies. Southern federal district courts decided slightly more than half (51.3 per cent) of similar civil rights cases on the side of Negroes during roughly the same period of time.[13] This confirms the Negroes' perception that they have a better chance for favorable decisions in the federal courts than in the state courts. However, the difference is not one of very great magnitude. Federal courts decided civil rights cases about 60 per cent more frequently in favor of Negroes. And if we consider only the more important non-trial procedure cases the two levels of courts are even closer together.

Civil rights decisions in southern state legislatures present quite a different picture. Out of over 500 legislative acts passed between 1954 and 1963, not one may be characterized as directly favorable to Negroes.[14] Practically all are part of the counterattack by southern state and local governments against the changing civil rights situation. We do not know how many acts were not passed by the southern legislatures, attacking Negroes' interests in civil rights situations, and so our index of comparison is an incomplete one. However, we do not observe evidence of restraint in the legislatures, reported in descriptions of their activities.

The record of southern supreme courts is not one of uniform reaction against Negroes. Considering all cases, Negroes won about one of three conflicts. While this record is less favorable than the record in the federal district courts, in some states Negroes fared better in the state court than in the federal courts. Given the favorable reputation of the federal courts for civil rights and the relation of the state courts to the local political structure, Negroes did better than many persons might have predicted.

The records of individual southern states are compared in Table 3. While in the South as a whole Negroes won one case out of every three, there is considerable variation in the record among the individual states, ranging from a low of 7.7 per cent cases won in Alabama to a high of 54.5 per cent cases won in Georgia. In general, Negroes fared slightly better in the peripheral southern states than in the states of the Deep South. The peripheral or marginal states have better records of school desegregation, contain more important "moderate" political officials,

Table 3 Disposition of cases by Southern supreme courts, by states, 1954-63.

States	Per Cent of Cases Favorable to Negroes
Alabama	7.7
Arkansas	33.3
Georgia	54.5
Louisiana	29.1
Mississippi	23.8
South Carolina	28.6
Average of Deep South States	29.3 (N = 126)
Florida	9.5
North Carolina	46.6
Tennessee	40.0
Texas	40.0
Virginia	50.0
Average of Peripheral Southern States	37.2 (N = 72)

and have a smaller Negro population in the states as a whole. Consequently, we might have expected the difference between the records of the two groups of states to be more pronounced than it actually is. Reference to the two groups of states indicates that several atypical performances tend to pull the records of the two groups of states closer together. Among the peripheral states the extremely low score of the Florida Supreme Court reduces the average of the remainder of the states, all of which have records of 40 per cent or above in deciding cases for Negro litigants. In the cases of the Deep South states, Georgia and South Carolina raise the average of the group.

A systematic examination of the factors associated with different state records cannot be undertaken here. A brief examination of some features in the deviant states, however, may prove suggestive. In only two states, Virginia and South Carolina, are judges of the highest court not chosen by popular election. In both states they are chosen by the legislature and for relatively long terms of ten years. Since both states rank high in deciding cases for Negroes in civil rights conflicts, we may speculate that the greater independence from popular control makes possible a more independent response on civil rights cases. While Virginia and South Carolina judges must undergo legislative elections every ten years, they can avoid the partisan election which is so often the occasion for racial demagoguery and the inspection of records of office-holders for evidence of deviation from the principle of white supremacy. The extreme differences in the disposition of cases of Georgia (54.5 per cent) and Florida (9.5 per cent) call for careful investigation. The method of judicial selection does not help since both states choose their judges in partisan elections and for relatively brief terms of six years. Yet, the Georgia Supreme Court has decided race relations in favor of Negroes over half of the time while Florida has so decided in only one case out of every ten. Undoubtedly, an examination of the recruitment of the judges, their backgrounds and experiences, and their role in state partisan politics would yield better understanding of the differences.

These considerations lead us to ask, what general factors are involved in the political behavior of state judges? First, although state courts are more closely linked to the political structure than are federal courts, they do possess a measure of insulation from the state political process. Although generally elected, southern judges have longer terms (6-14 years) than most other public officials in the South.[15] In contrast, legislators are elected for terms no longer than six years and a great many of them must seek office every two years. Furthermore, there is evidence that tradition in judicial elections tends to reduce the amount of competition judges face and to facilitate automatic return of the incumbent to office.[16] This tradition combined with the longer terms affords the supreme court judges some security of office and less frequent contact with the state partisan system involved in campaigning for office. Supreme court judges, we would conclude, are better protected from the effects of public opinion and partisan political activities which would dictate more active participation in the counterattack against civil rights for Negroes.

Finally, the style, language, and form of judicial decisions tend to hide them from public view. Cast in the traditional rhetoric of the law, court decisions are more recondite than legislative decisions and less amenable to treatment by the mass media. A court may reverse the conviction of Negroes convicted of sit-in demonstrations by finding simply that the conviction is not consistent with longstanding state precedents. Several southern supreme courts reversed the convictions of Negroes arrested in sit-in demonstrations and for trespassing on state public facilities on the grounds that the warrants of arrest were defective. In such instances the courts said little about the main policy issues involved in the case and voided the arrest of the Negro plaintiffs on these narrow technical grounds. Such legalistic findings are important civil rights policies but the rhetoric and symbols of law keep them from sounding like favorable civil rights decisions.

A clue to the role of the state supreme courts in southern politics may be found in Table 4, showing the rate of dissent in cases for and against civil rights positions. In general southern courts dissented infrequently and there was little difference between the types of cases. Dissents occurred slightly but not significantly more often in cases decided in favor of Negroes. A survey of dissenting patterns indicates that a low rate of dissent exists on most state courts. While the national Supreme Court dissents usually in more than 50 per cent of all cases, only five state courts dissented, according to one study, in as many as 15 per cent of all cases. On the average, state supreme courts dissented in less than 5 per cent of all cases.[17]

From observation of southern politics, we know that opinion in the South is far from monolithic in the field of race relations and we might expect, therefore, members of southern courts to differ among themselves. Doubtless southern judges did disagree but they, like other state judges, rarely expressed such disagreements in formal dissents. The dissent seems to play a different role in state than in national courts, with different expectations and assumptions. While in national courts dissenting judges can expect to have their views made the basis of a minority viewpoint or possibly transformed later into a majority opinion, state judges, it appears, can seldom entertain these expectations. The differences seem

Table 4 Rate of dissent in race relations cases in Southern state supreme courts, 1954–63.

	Per Cent Cases with Dissents
Cases Decided in Favor of Negroes	11. 3 (7 of 62)
Cases Decided Against Negroes	8. 1 (11 of 136)
All Cases	9. 1 (18 of 198)

to be due partly to the high visibility of national court opinions and the relatively low visibility of state court opinions.

NATIONAL-STATE COURT RELATION-SHIPS

The foregoing raise interesting questions concerning the role of the state judges in the judicial process and particularly about the linkages of state judges to the norms of the Constitution and the federal courts. Some recent off-the-bench events suggest that the state judges sometimes view federal judicial norms with hostility.[18] The formal relationship of state judges to the national judicial norms is outlined in the Constitution in Article VI: "This Constitution . . . shall be the supreme law of the land; and the judges in every state shall be bound thereby, anything in the Constitution or laws of any state to the contrary notwithstanding."

The Constitution thus suggests that state judges be linked to the national judiciary. But the immediate functional linkages of state judges are with the state political system. Through the requirements of survival in the state electoral system and service in the partisan system of the state, it is likely that state judges are much more sensitive to the values of state politics than to the national political system, despite the formal requirements stated by the Constitution. There are, however, various ways in which state judges may be sensitized to national norms. Legal training, in particular, strongly emphasizes hierarchical procedure in the judicial process and this includes the observance of precedents from higher courts, defined in the United States as the federal courts. And in the law journals and other legal literature, in bar association meetings, and in the distribution of decisions from the federal courts, state judges have an opportunity for contact with federal authorities and with the content of the federal judicial process.

State judges may thus respond to a variety of factors in their particular political situations, some of which would make for relative insulation from the political, some of which would relate the judge closely to the state partisan and electoral structure. The effects of those factors on the voting behavior of the judge could be studied by relating judicial careers to patterns of alignment on the courts. We note here that state judges respond in much more varied fashion to the civil rights issues in the states than do the state legislators.

While Article VI of the Constitution declares that state judges are to be bound by the values of the Constitution where there is a conflict with local conditions, the clause does not provide for procedures to insure this, nor spell out any method of enforcement. Two comcepts in the judicial process, however, provide reasons for state courts to comply with Article VI. First, the widely accepted practice of judicial review means that the Supreme Court interpretations of the Constitution are ultimate and binding on all levels of courts, and an accepted notion of the judicial process is that lower courts should accept the authority of higher courts and should reach decisions by referring to the judgments previously made by the relevant higher courts. Clearly, all things considered, the federal system does, in one sense, set up a kind of hierarchy of lower and higher courts, with the Supreme Court of the United States at the apex and state courts further down in the scale.

One formal method the judicial process provides for the enforcement of national authority over state courts is the remand order by which state courts may be formally ordered by the Supreme Court to rehear a case and decide it in a manner consistent with the higher court decision. Several factors make the remand procedure ineffective as a means of securing Supreme Court authority over state courts. Only a small group of cases, given the limitations of the Supreme Court's total case load of a maximum of 200 cases a year, can be reviewed by the high Court. The expenses of appeal, lethargy of the plaintiffs, and inadequate legal skills also act to reduce the number of state cases that go to the top of the legal hierarchy. Finally, remand orders are not always obeyed by state courts. A determined state court may ignore the remand order, may "distinguish" away the substance of the order or may give priority to state judicial procedures over the remand order.

In making decisions on race relations cases state judges may base their judgments on a variety of political and social materials: (a) they may take their cues from higher federal courts and from Supreme Court interpretations of the national Constitution, thus accepting the prescription of national-state court relationships posited by Article VI; (b) they may emphasize local needs and problems of race relations and stress the primacy of state law and judicial processes in dealing with these situations; (c) or state judges may vacillate between (a) and (b), sometimes reluctantly accepting the authority of the national courts and at other times referring to local judicial processes and state problems as the basis for making decisions.

The reaction of state courts to the problem of national-state court relationships may be described by positing three positions roughly corresponding to roles equivalent to (a), (b), and (c) above: The Federals correspond to (a) and tend to accept the authority of the decisions of the U.S. Supreme Court in race relations cases. The Compromisers correspond to position (c) and often accept the authority of the Supreme Court, but with reluctance and with frequent reference to the priority of local authorities. The States Righters correspond to position (b) and usually appeal to the primacy of local conditions and the legality of state judicial processes.

The Supreme Courts of Tennessee, Texas, and North Carolina may be classified as Federals. These courts have frankly acknowledged the authority of decisions of the Supreme Court in race relations and in doing so have openly referred to the obligations of state courts under Article VI. For example, the Texas Supreme Court declared in a school desegregation case:

> . . . we are met with the argument that since the constitution and statutory provisions requiring segregation in Texas were not before the Supreme Court in the Brown case they were not condemned and we should hold them valid and enforce-

able. That proposition is so utterly without merit that we overrule it without further discussion except to say that Section 2 of Article VII [sic] of the Constitution of the United States declares. . . . [19]

The Tennessee Supreme Court has held that in the wake of express holdings of the national Supreme Court the "force and effect" of the state's segregation laws are discontinued [20] while the North Carolina court declared that "in the interpretation of the Constitution of the United States the Supreme Court is final arbiter" and that anything to the contrary in the constitution or statutes of North Carolina "must be deemed invalid." [21]

An example of the attitude of the Compromiser court may be seen in a decision of the Virginia court:

> Having reached the conclusion that certain provisions of the act with which we are concerned violate the provisions of the constitution of Virginia. . . it is not necessary that we consider the question whether these acts likewise violate the provisions of the Fourteenth Amendment to the Federal Constitution. . . . There is no occasion for us to discuss these decisions other than to say that we deplore the lack of judicial restraint evinced by that court in trespassing on the sovereign rights of this Commonwealth. . . . [22]

While statements such as the above were perhaps typical of the Virginia and Arkansas courts, other courts obeying remands with reluctance or referring to Supreme Court precedence frequently expressed their lack of sympathy with national decisions in the process of obeying them.

State courts we classify as States Righter courts sometimes defended the conditions of segregation in the South and espoused theories of race relations. A striking example may be found in a decision of the Florida Supreme Court in commenting on the segregated system of education in the southern states:

> To replace it with antithetical doctrine will take years of skillful nurture in a soil that must be made congenial to the change. The ratio of Negro to White population makes the way to change difficult. . . . To homogenize Topsy, Little Red Riding Hood and Mary who carried her little lamb to school will be difficult. [23]

At other times States Righters deliberately deferred to their own judicial process and its results in preference to national Supreme Court decisions as in an Alabama decision refusing to honor a remand to abandon a state attack on the NAACP.

> While the Supreme Court of the United States, in its opinion supra, seems to recognize its lack of jurisdiction over matters of state (non-federal) procedure, it nevertheless assumed jurisdiction. . . and this upon the premise that the interpretation of this court of its own procedure rules was erroneous. [24]

As participants in southern state politics, judges probably reacted negatively to national civil rights symbols. We might expect, therefore, that state judges will tend to use state court precedents and local law and will avoid use of the federal court precedents and civil rights provisions of the Constitution. Avoidance of national civil rights citations could afford them some protection in those cases where the courts decide in favor of Negroes.

An analysis of the content of cases decided in favor of Negroes was undertaken and these cases were checked for references to the national Constitution and for citations of federal civil rights cases. The results are presented in Table 5,

Table 5 References to national Constitution and to federal civil rights precedents in cases decided in favor of Negroes.

Reference	Per Cent of Cases (N = 62)
National Constitution	41.9
Federal Civil Rights Precedents	48.4
When Federal Civil Rights Precedents Were Half or More of All Cases Cited.	42.9

which indicates that in well over half of the pro-civil rights decisions no mention was made of the provisions of the national Constitution, normally associated with the guarantee of civil rights in the United States. In about half of the cases the decisions cited no precedents from federal courts bearing on civil rights. When the courts did mention federal precedents, these references constituted a majority of all case citations (in individual cases) less than half the time (42.9 per cent). Favorable civil rights decisions are thus often barren of any reference to the symbols of national civil rights, either the Constitution or the guiding precedents of federal courts. Such decisions in southern supreme courts are justified in terms of local bills of rights or by precedents cited from the state and local courts.

RELATION TO LOWER STATE COURTS

Most of the business of state supreme courts involves the review of cases brought up by appeal from lower courts. By looking at the number and character of the cases affirmed and reversed from lower courts, we can obtain additional information on the role of the supreme courts in the state judicial processes.

Table 6 indicates that supreme court reversals of lower courts in over 90 per cent of the cases favored Negro litigants in race relations cases. The limited success that Negroes have had in litigating civil rights issues in the state courts is largely due to the supreme court reversals of unfavorable court decisions elsewhere in the lower courts.[25] While the amount of litigation Negroes have won in the state supreme courts has not been large, the supreme courts have performed an important function in reversing lower court decisions.[26]

The role of the southern state supreme court has paralleled that of the national Supreme Court. In both cases the higher court has tended to protect minority groups by reversing decisions made against them in lower courts. The cases won in state supreme courts have been neither numerous nor of great political importance; yet, the high courts are one of the few places in southern state political systems where Negroes might expect any favorable actions.

We may speculate about the reasons: Supreme Court judges often serve longer terms than lower court judges and they tend to face less competition in electoral races; they are also elected from larger electoral districts or from the state as a whole and hence may be less identified with local influences than lower court judges. Thus a supreme court judge in Louisiana may serve 35 years on the court and not have to stand election more than two or three times while district judges have to stand for re-election some six or seven times. District judges

Table 6 Reversals of lower court decisions in Southern supreme courts, 1954-63.

	Per Cent of Cases
All Cases Reversed	22.7 (N = 45)
Of Those Reversed:	
Cases Favoring Negroes	93.8
Cases Against Negroes	6.2

have a constituency of one to four parishes for their election and as sources of litigation while supreme court judges serve several times that many parishes. Possibly, supreme court judges are less identified with local districts than other state judges and do not have to follow rigidly the values of the local political system.

CONCLUSIONS

By requiring that state judges adhere to its norms the Constitution supposes that the judges become part of the national political process, supporting national norms and giving effect to the decisions of the national courts in the state political system. The state political system, on the other hand, by requiring that judges be elected and be recruited from lawyers with predominantly state political experience, links judges to the state political system and to the political norms of state politics. Of these linkages, the relationship of the state judge to state politics seems to include a greater share of the political activities and needs of the judge, especially the activities needed to get elected and the experiences involved in recruitment for political office.

Civil rights cases must also be understood in terms of the parties interested in litigating in the state courts. In the crucial period of southern politics from 1954 to 1963, Negroes have not often sought favorable political decisions on civil rights in the state courts. Litigation has more often been instituted by white groups and state and local governments interested in resisting change. The decision record of state courts justifies the unfavorable perceptions which led Negroes in large part to avoid them.

As our data indicate, the amount and character of litigation in a given policy area in the courts depends upon the perceptions the possible litigants have and their desire to exploit or avoid decisions taken in the courts. And yet, closely as southern judges are related to the local political structure, their record is more favorable to Negro claimants than is any other part of the state political system. Since these judges do not hold office for life and are vulnerable to public opinion in electoral campaigns, their record of decisions in favor of Negroes suggests that other factors may be involved in their ability to record decisions in favor of civil rights. We have suggested that the recondite character of language involved in court decisions may enable southern judges to make favorable civil rights decisions and escape general notice. Thus a southern judge may rule an arrest of sit-in demonstrators illegal not on the basis of the Fourteenth Amend-

ment or of national civil rights decisions but on the basis of local decisions phrased
in terms of what seems to the general public "legal technicalities." This is particularly true if the legal concepts used are those of more local law rather than
the better known precedents of the national courts.

The questions, so important in the analysis of judicial behavior, whether
judges are moved by the legal concepts and the content of the law, may be approached by regarding the symbols and the content of the law as functional to
different political situations and the judges' roles. Judges, in different political
situations, for example those with life tenure, those appointed by the legislature,
or those elected frequently for short terms, may require different symbolic supports for their decision-making; they may find national law more useful than state
law in one situation, in another, local law more useful than national law. The
use of law in judicial decision-making would be related, therefore, to the political needs of the judges, political and psychological, at different times.

NOTES

1. Oliver Field, *Judicial Review in Ten Selected States* (Bloomington: Indiana U. Press,
   1943); Margaret Nelson, *A Study of Judicial Review in Virginia* (New York: Columbia
   U. Press, 1947).

2. Herbert Jacob and Kenneth Vines, "The Role of the Judiciary in American State Politics," *Judicial Decision Making,* ed. Schubert (Glencoe: Free Press, 1963), pp. 245-
   57; Stuart S. Nagel, "Political Party Affiliation and Judges' Decisions," *APSR,* 55
   (1961), 843-51; "Ethnic Affiliations and Judicial Propensities," *Journal of Politics,*
   24 (1962), 92-111, Glendon Schubert, *Quantitative Analysis of Judicial Behavior*
   (Glencoe: Free Press, 1959), pp. 129-43; S. Sydney Ulmer, "Leadership in the
   Michigan Supreme Court," *Judicial Decision Making,* ed. Schubert (Glencoe: Free
   Press, 1963), pp. 13-29, and "The Political Party Variable in the Michigan Supreme
   Court," *Journal of Public Law,* 11 (1962), 352-62; and Kenneth Vines, "Political
   Functions of a State Supreme Court," *Tulane Studies in Political Science* (New Or-
   leans, 1963), VIII, 51-75.

3. The gathering of data was facilitated by the collection and identification of the cases
   in the volumes of the *Race Relations Law Reporter.* The definition of the *Reporter*
   of race relations cases was accepted for the purposes of this study.

4. Here and elsewhere, data on the civil rights decisions in the federal district courts
   are derived from my "Federal District Judges and Race Relations Cases in the South,"
   South," *Journal of Politics,* 26 (1964), 337-57.

5. The collection of southern legislative acts is found in the *Race Relations Law Reporter,* vols. 1 through 9.

6. *NAACP v. Gallion,* 290 F.2d 337.

7. Dianne Jennings, "Access to Governmental Machinery as it is Perceived by Negro
   Leaders" (unpublished paper, Tulane University).

8. Walter Murphy, "The South Counterattacks: The Anti-NAACP Laws," *Western Political Quarterly,* 12 (June 1959), 371-90.

9. For an excellent exposition of the rules, cases, and implications of this point see: "Exhaustion of State Judicial Remedies," *Race Relations Law Reporter,* 2 (1957), 1215-37.

10. *State Court Systems,* Council of State Governments, unpaged statistical summary prepared for the Conference of Chief Justices, Chicago, 1962.

11. Herbert Jacob, "The Effect of Institutional Differences in the Recruitment Process: The Case of State Judges," *Journal of Public Law,* 12 (1963), 7-8; Kenneth Vines, "The Selection of Judges in Louisiana," *Tulane Studies in Political Science* (New Orleans, 1963), VIII, 99-119.

12. In cases where the courts decided partly in favor of Negroes and partly against, the cases were counted as half a decision in favor of Negroes. This was done in order to pick up all possible favorable reactions toward Negro litigants. (There were eight such cases.) It is possible that one of the "permissable" ways of deciding for Negroes is in cases where a balanced decision can occur — that is, a case in which Negroes win in one aspect of the case and lose in the other. For example, Negroes may be convicted of trespass in a sit-in case but exonerated of resisting arrest charges.

13. See note 4 *supra.*

14. See note 5 *supra.* While Negroes benefit from some of the general acts passed, I found no act designed to help Negroes as a group.

15. *State Court Systems, op. cit.*

16. John W. Wood, "Judicial Selection: Realities v. Legalities," *State Government,* January 1958, pp. 17-19; *Selection of Judges,* Publication No. 211 (1956), Kansas Legislative Council; Vines, "The Selection of Judges in Louisiana."

17. *Workload of State Courts of Last Resort,* Council of State Government. Unpaged summary prepared for the Conference of Chief Justices, Chicago, 1962.

18. For example, the criticisms of the Conference of Chief Justices against the Supreme Court of the United States.

19. *McKinney v. Blankenship,* 282 S.W. 2d 691 (1955).

20. *Roy v. Brittain,* 297 S.W. 2d 72 (1956).

21. *Constantian v. Anson Co.,* 938 S.E. 2d 163 (1955).

22. *Harrison v. Day,* 106 S.E. 2d 639 (1957).

23. *Manatu v. Florida Board of Public Instruction,* 75 So. 2d 691 (1954).

24. *Ex parte* NAACP 109 So. 2d 138 (1957).

25. An analysis of a selection of lower court decisions taken from the *Race Relations Law Reporter,* volumes I-IX, indicates that lower courts in the southern states decided in favor of Negroes 18. 1 per cent of the time in civil rights cases.

26. For a somewhat different view see Robert Dahl, "Decision Making in a Democracy: The Supreme Court as a National Policy Maker," *Journal of Public Law,* 6 (1959), 279-95.

Political Party Affiliation and Judges' Decisions

Stuart S. Nagel

Several scholars within the public law field of political science have compiled data on differences in the backgrounds of American judges, but without attempting to correlate these characteristics with differences in the decisions of the judges.[1] Other scholars have compiled data on the different decisional tendencies of American judges, but again without correlating these tendencies with differences in the backgrounds of the judiciary.[2]

The first purpose of this paper is to explore the empirical relationships between one background characteristic and fifteen areas of judicial decision-making. Political party affiliation was chosen as the one background characteristic because it is of particular interest to political scientists, and is an especially useful indicator for predicting how judges on bipartisan appellate courts will divide when they do not agree. The second purpose is to explore empirically the effectiveness of three judicial reforms (judicial appointment, non-partisan ballot, and long term of office) which are frequently advocated as means of decreasing partisan influences in judicial decisions.

I. THE RESEARCH DESIGN [3]

The judges covered in this study consist of the 313 state and federal supreme court[4] judges listed in the 1955 *Directory of American Judges*[5] except for 15 of them who left the court before the end of the year — a net total of 298. Their party affiliation was determined by consulting the *Directory, Who's Who in America*,[6] and the governmental directories published by many of the states. Those supreme court judges who gave no party affiliation in any of the sources consulted probably do not closely identify themselves with any political party.[7]

The cases analyzed consist of the full-court cases in the 15 fields listed in Table 1 which these 298 judges heard in 1955.[8] "Full-court" cases mean those on which all the judges in the sample sat who were on the court involved. The table excludes courts that were solidly Democratic or solidly Republican, since in these situations intra-court comparisons between judges from the two parties cannot be made. The table also excludes cases decided unanimously, because

Reprinted from *American Political Science Review,* Vol. 55 (1961), pp. 843-850, by permission of the author and publisher.

The writer gratefully thanks the Political Theory and Legal Philosophy Committee of the Social Science Research Council for providing the funds for his study of the influence of judicial backgrounds and attitudes on judicial decision-making, of which this paper is a part. Thanks are also due Professors Rosenblum, Guetzkow, Snyder, and Milbrath of Northwestern for their suggestions relevant to the completion of the larger study.

these shed no light on differences in the behavior of individual judges. The 15 categories of cases present typical issues drawn from the major fields of law which are covered in the courts on both the trial and appellate levels. These fields are not mutually exclusive, and thus a case may fall into more than one category.

Each judge was given a "decision score" for each field of law. These scores represent the proportion of times the judge voted for the party listed in the left-hand column of Table 1, out of the total number of times he voted in the type of case involved. Thus in the 21 Pennsylvania criminal cases,[9] Justice Arnold voted three times for the defense, giving him a decision score of .14. Sometimes a judge did not vote clearly for the prosecution or the defense, particularly if he concurred in part and dissented in part. In one of the 21 Pennsylvania criminal cases,[10] Justice Musmanno cast such a half-way vote, giving him a decision score of 11.5 out of 21, or .55.

The data were analyzed to determine what party affiliation, if any, went consistently with a decision score above the average of each court in each type of case. For example, the question was asked whether being a Democratic rather than a Republican judge tends to go with being above the average decision score for each court in criminal cases. The answer to this and similar questions for the data used are given in Table 1.

The probability at the right of each row represents the likelihood of finding the observed difference purely by chance, given the number of judges involved in each group.[11] If the probability is less than .05 (i.e., less than 5 out of 100), then it is conventional to call the observed difference statistically significant.

II. RELATIONSHIPS BETWEEN PARTY AFFILIATION AND DECISIONAL PROPENSITIES

Table 1 shows that in all 15 types of cases the Democratic judges were above the average decision score of their respective courts (in what might be considered the liberal direction) to a greater extent than the Republican judges. Democratic judges sitting on the same supreme courts with Republican judges were more prone to favor (1) the defense in criminal cases, (2) the administrative agency in business regulation cases, (3) the private party in regulation of non-business entities, (4) the claimant in unemployment compensation cases, (5) the broadening position in free speech cases, (6) the finding of a constitutional violation in criminal-constitutional cases, (7) the government in tax cases, (8) the divorce seeker in divorce cases, (9) the wife in divorce settlement cases, (10) the tenant in landlord-tenant cases, (11) the labor union in labor-management cases, (12) the debtor in creditor-debtor cases, (13) the consumer in sales-of-goods cases, (14) the injured party in motor vehicle accident cases, and (15) the employee in employee injury cases, than were the Republican judges.

Nine of these 15 differences are statistically significant below the 5 out of 100 degree of chance probability (groups 1, 2, 4, 6, 7, 10, 13, 14, and 15). Three of these are statistically significant below .01, namely those relating to administrative regulation of business, unemployment compensation cases, and employee injury cases. These three relationships are worth illustrating in detail.

Table 1 Differences in decisions of Republican and Democratic judges, by types of issues (using the divided decisions of state and federal supreme courts of 1955 on which both political parties were represented.

Type of issue	Number of Judges Involved Rep.	Number of Judges Involved Dem.	Republican judges above their court average %	Democratic judges above their court average %	Difference (in % pts.)	Probability of the difference being due to Chance
Public Law						
Criminal Law						
For the defense in criminal cases	45	40	31	55	+24	.01 to .02½
Administrative Law						
For the administrative agency in business regulation cases	35	25	23	68	+45	less than .01
For the private party in regulation of non-business entities	11	13	55	77	+22	.10 to .15
For the claimant in unemployment compensation cases	15	7	0	57	+57	less than .01
Civil Liberties Law						
For broadening free speech	5	7	40	71	+31	.15 to .20
For finding a constitutional violation in criminal cases	27	24	26	54	+28	.01 to .02½
Tax Law						
For the government in tax cases	22	19	41	68	+27	.02½ to .05
Private Law						
Family Law						
For the divorce seeker in divorce cases	6	4	17	75	+58	.05 to .10
For the wife in divorce settlement cases	10	13	30	54	+24	.10 to .15
Business Relations Law						
For the tenant in landlord-tenant cases	13	11	38	73	+35	.02½ to .05
For the labor union in labor-management cases	19	14	26	50	+24	.05 to .10
For the debtor in creditor-debtor cases	14	7	43	71	+28	.10 to .15
For the consumer in sales-of-goods cases	20	10	25	60	+35	.02½ to .05
Personal Injury Law						
For the injured in motor vehicle accident cases	41	33	36	61	+25	.01 to .02½
For the employee in employee injury cases	34	28	35	68	+33	less than .01

In 1955 ten full-bench bipartisan state supreme courts heard administrative regulation of business cases which they decided by split votes. The cases included questions of zoning regulation, price regulation, franchise grants and product regulation. As shown in the second row of Table 1 the ten courts comprised 60 judges who gave a political party affiliation in the sources consulted. Two-thirds of the 25 Democrats were above the average of their respective courts on the decision score, whereas less than a quarter of the 35 Republicans were above the average of their respective courts. As a specific example, the seven judges of the Ohio Supreme Court sitting together heard and divided their votes on three business regulation cases.[12] There were four Republicans and three Democrats on the court. In the first case, the court held for the administrative agency in a matter involving the regulation of an independent telephone company. The only dissent in favor of the telephone company came from one of the four Republicans. In the second case involving the zoning of power company facilities, the court in a 4-to-3 decision held for the zoning board, but three of the four Republicans dissented in favor of the utility. The third case involved the zoning of a gas station and the majority of the court decided in favor of the gas station. The dissenters in this case, unlike the previous two, included both Republicans and Democrats. Overall, the Democrats averaged a decision score in the three cases of 78 per cent for the administrative agency position, whereas the Republicans averaged only 50 per cent. Other supreme courts on which the Democrats had a higher average decision score for the administrative agency than the Republicans included those of Illinois, Michigan, New York, Oregon, Pennsylvania, and Utah. Of the ten courts involved only the California and Idaho supreme courts went contrary to this pattern. On the New Jersey Supreme Court, the known Democrats and the known Republicans both had the same average decision score.

Four bipartisan state supreme courts in 1955 heard unemployment compensation cases and divided their votes on them, with all their listed judges present. As shown in the fourth row of Table 1, these courts comprised 22 judges who acknowledged a party affiliation. Four of the seven Democrats were above the average of their respective courts on the decision score, whereas none of the fifteen Republicans were. The Michigan Supreme Court illustrates the general finding. Sitting as a full court it heard and divided on two unemployment compensation cases.[13] In both, the only dissenter for the claimant was Justice Smith, one of the two Democrats on the court. On all of the other three supreme courts involved — Idaho, Minnesota and New Jersey — the Democratic judges had a considerably higher average decision score for the claimant than the Republican judges.

Eleven bipartisan full-bench state and federal supreme courts in 1955 heard and divided their votes on employee injury cases. The issues were raised under workmen's compensation statutes and in common-law suits by employees against employers. As shown in the last row of Table 1, 62 judges participated, for whom a party affiliation was available. Two-thirds of the 28 Democrats were above the average of their respective courts on the decision score, whereas only a dozen of the 34 Republicans were above the average of their respective courts. The New Jersey Supreme Court is a good example of the relationship in employee injury cases. Of its seven judges, Brennan, Heher, and Wachenfeld indicated they were Democrats; and Oliphant and Vanderbilt, Republicans. Burling gave no party affiliation in the post-1950 sources consulted, but he was listed as a Republican member of the New Jersey Senate in the Legislative Manual of 1937. He may have dropped or changed his party identification since then, and therefore was not classified as a partisan in the analysis. Jacobs also listed no party affiliation. It was common knowledge too that Chief Justice Vanderbilt sought to promote a non-partisan atmosphere in the court. When the court divided in employee injury cases, however, it clearly divided along party lines. In 1955 the court decided seven such cases.[14] Republican Vanderbilt voted for the employee in only one of these, as did Republican Oliphant; and putative Republican Burling voted for the employee in only two of them. On the other hand Democrats Brennan and Heher voted for the employee in six of the seven; and Democrat Wachenfeld voted for the employee in three of the cases. The known Republicans thus had an average decision score of only 14 per cent for the employee, against 72 per cent for the known Democrats.

Split votes in employee injury cases in general seem to correlate especially well with divisions along party lines on bipartisan courts. On the United States Supreme Court in 1955 Republican Warren and Democrat Reed frequently voted with members of the other party when splits occurred, thereby disrupting party-correlated divisions somewhat. In the divided votes on four employee-injury certiorari petitions which were filed with the Court,[15] however, the Democrats[16] had an average decision score of 55 per cent for the employee, in comparison with only 17 per cent for the Republicans, in spite of the voting records of both Warren and Reed. Other supreme courts on which the Democrats had a higher average decision score for the employee than the Republicans include those of California, Idaho, Illinois, Montana, New York, Minnesota, and Michigan. Of the eleven supreme courts involved, only those of Missouri and Ohio failed to follow this pattern.

III. EXPLAINING THE RELATIONSHIPS

All of the relationships found can be attributed in some degree to chance. But where that degree is less than 5 per cent it is reasonable to look to other factors for explanation. The propensities observed in each of the nine statistically significant relations all appear to be a part of a general affinity for the "liberal" as contrasted to the "conservative" position. In this context the term "liberal" labels the viewpoint associated with the interests of the lower or less privileged economic or social groups in one's society and (to a lesser extent) with acceptance of long-run social change; and the term "conservative" refers to the viewpoint associated with the interests of the upper or dominant groups and with resistance to long-run social change.[17]

Through a detailed analysis of congressional roll-call votes in three sessions of Congress over a 23-year period, Turner found that Democratic congressmen favored the interests of labor and the needy more than Republican congressmen did, to a statistically significant extent.[18] He also found that in the regulation of business and finance, Republican congressmen regularly favored the business position more often than Democratic congressmen did.[19] Through a nationwide opinion survey in 1952, Campbell, Gurin, and Miller found that those who preferred the Democratic candidate for President also favored governmental social welfare activity and opposed the Taft-Hartley Act more, to a statistically significant degree, than did those who preferred the Republican candidate for President.[20] Thus the differences found between the decisions of Democratic and Republican judges are consistent with differences in partisan attitudes expressed elsewhere.[21]

The relationships between political party affiliation and judicial decision-making that have been shown in Table 1 are not meant to imply that some judges consciously vote for or against a party line. It is more likely that in some cases judges rely on their personal standards of value in reaching a decision, and these same personal standards also frequently account for their party affiliation. That is to say that party affiliation and decisional propensity for the liberal or conservative position correlate with each other because they are frequently effects of the same cause.[22] Indirectly, party affiliation may be responsible for some decisional propensity by virtue of the fact that a judge's party affiliation may have a feedback reinforcement on his value system which in turn determines his decisional propensities.

Although definite correlations are shown in Table 1, several factors tend to make them imperfect. First, judges on the same court may have similar value systems, although they are members of different political parties; and conversely, judges on the same court may have different value systems although they are members of the same political party. The attitudes of a judge on social issues, that is, may be an important factor, but not always the sole or determining one in his choice of party affiliation. Like other people, a judge may join one party rather than another — or stay with it — in spite of its stands on issues, either because it is the dominant party in his area, because his parents were members of it, or for ethnic or other reasons, not necessarily involving a congruence between his values and the general values of the party. Chief Justice Warren may be a Republican not because he shared the views characteristic of the Republican Party nationally, but rather because the Republican Party was dominant in California when he was an aspiring young politician; and the same for Justice Reed as a Democrat.

Another factor making for imperfect correlations between party affiliation and decisional propensity is the influence of particular personal experiences in the backgrounds of the judges. Attitudes on social issues that are commonly found associated in a syndrome of "liberalism" or "conservatism" are not invariably so linked together; and deviations from them may govern votes in particular legal areas. One judge, for instance, who in general has strong liberal sympathies, may have been a prosecuting attorney before becoming a judge, and as a result his liberal sympathies may not extend to criminal cases. Another may once have been an insurance company lawyer, and as a result his liberal sympathies may not extend to personal injury cases; and so on.

A third factor disrupting perfect correlations relates to technical difficulties in the measurement of the variables. When a judge's political party affiliation is not publicly disclosed, some arbitrariness in determining the sources to consult is inevitable. The content analysis of decisions and dissents also may not always yield unambiguous results. But the principal difficulty lies in the vagaries of the sample of cases—the highly accidental nature of the arrival of particular law suits before particular appellate courts in a particular year. The number of cases in a given field before a given court is small enough so that a few shifts in timing, or out-of-court settlements, for instance, may materially affect computations for that court and that field. So variations in correlations between fields are not surprising.

A final disruptive factor in the correlations is attributable to differences among judges in the intensity of their feelings even when they share the same general outlook or belong to the same party. This may result in one judge dissenting frequently without being joined by his less vigorous associate of the same party. Nevertheless, despite these several factors, most of the propensities shown in Table 1 are statistically significant; they are logically consistent with each other; and they are consistent also with studies of differences between Democrats and Republicans who are not judges.

IV. DECREASING THE RELATIONSHIPS

Judicial appointment, a non-partisan ballot, and long terms of office have been proposed or defended as devices for decreasing the role of partisan influences on judicial decisions. Judges selected or holding office where these devices are operative possibly have a greater tendency to vote contrary to their party pattern than other judges. To test these hypotheses, a measure of "voting contrary to one's party pattern" is needed.

I have attempted such a test, using three types of cases, namely administrative regulation of business, unemployment compensation, and employee injury cases. These were selected because in the decision on them one can most confidently say that political party patterns emerged. Some of the judges did not hear all three types of cases. For purposes of this study, however, a judge was considered to have voted contrary to the pattern of his party if he was a Republican who was above (or a Democrat who was below) the average of his court on the decision score on all three or two out of three or — if he did not vote on all three — then on both of the two, or on the one, of the types of cases he heard. A judge was considered to have voted in accordance with the pattern of his party, conversely, if he was a Republican who was below (or a Democrat who was above) the average of his court on the decision score in all three, two out of three, two out of two, or the one of these types of cases he voted on. Judges who fell between these limits, i. e., whose decision scores departed from their court averages in one of two of the case types, were not counted either way. Using these definitions, 65 judges serving through 1955 on bipartisan state and federal supreme courts were counted as having voted either contrary to or in accordance with the pattern set by their respective parties.

Table 2 shows the relationships between being a judge who operated under each of the various arrangements listed and being a judge who voted contrary to his party pattern. It includes all those judges who could be assigned a voting position contrary to or in accordance with their party pattern. According to row one of Table 2, seven of the 18 appointed judges voted contrary to their party patterns, whereas only seven of the 47 elected judges did so.[23] This was the most striking of the several differences that emerged, and it was statistically significant slightly below the .05 level of chance probability.[24] The non-partisan versus partisan ballot comparison showed an insignificant negative relation between being a judge elected by a non-partisan ballot and being a judge who voted contrary to his party pattern.[25] As for length of term, eight years was the median term in 1955 for supreme court judges.[26] A greater proportion of the judges with terms longer than this median voted contrary to their party pattern than of the judges with shorter terms. This difference, however, disappears when long-term judges are compared with short-term judges while the method of selection is held constant as is shown on the fourth

Table 2 Judicial tenure, methods of selection and conformity to party voting patterns, 1955.

Group 1	Group 2	Number of judges in each group		% in Group 1 who voted contrary to their party pattern	% in Group 2 who voted contrary to their party pattern	Probability of the positive difference being due to chance
		(1)	(2)			
Appointed judges	Elected judges	18	47	39	15	.02½ to .05
Judges elected by a non-partisan ballot	Judges elected by a partisan ballot	29	18	14	17	a
Judges with terms longer than 8 years	Judges with terms of 8 or less years	37	28	27	14	.15 to .20
Elected judges with terms longer than 8 years	Elected judges with terms of 8 or less years	20	27	15.0	14.8	a
Appointed judges with terms longer than 8 years	Elected judges with terms longer than 8 years	17	20	41	15	.02½ to .05

a Negative or negligible difference.

row of Table 2. On the other hand, if length of term is held constant, as in the fifth row, the difference between appointed and elected judges still remains strong. Thus the method of selection can account for the difference between the long- and short-term groups, but the length of term cannot account for the difference between the appointed and elected groups.

What is there about appointed judges, in contrast to elected judges, which might account for the significantly higher percentage of them who voted contrary to their party patterns? Appointed judges probably reflect their personal values in their decisions just as much as elected judges.[27] The difference may lie in the possibility that the values of appointed judges are less clearly correlated with their party affiliation than the values of elected judges. In other words, appointed judges who are Democrats possibly tend to be non-typical Democrats in their values, and appointed judges who are Republicans likewise possibly non-typical Republicans — at least more so than elected judges. In terms of liberalism and conservatism, appointed judges serving on bipartisan courts are possibly more likely to be conservative Democrats or liberal Republicans. Two considerations support this hypothesis.

First, appointive systems for choosing state supreme court judges generally provide for a non-partisan or bipartisan body which nominates or approves the executive appointments to the court. In Missouri and California, for example, there is a special nominating commission composed of distinguished members of the bar, the judiciary, and the lay public. Such a nominating commission is less likely to consider party consistency in picking judges than the nominators for an elected court at a party caucus, convention or primary. It is somewhat more debatable whether a prospective judge on the federal or the New Jersey supreme court is helped toward a bipartisan senate confirmation if he is not too closely identified with a political party; but evidently that might handicap him in a partisan election system.

Second, appointive systems for choosing supreme court justices may provide by tradition or law that the executive should occasionally appoint judges not of his own party to the court. The appointed courts covered in Table 2 were the supreme courts of California, Missouri, New Jersey, and the United States. From 1910 to 1960 nine of the 33 judges appointed to the United States Supreme Court were not of the president's party.[28] In a survey of state supreme courts conducted by the Council of State Governments the question was asked as to what attempts, if any, were made by each state to obtain supreme courts of a bipartisan composition.[29] The responses and subsequent checking indicated that the appointive court systems of California, Missouri, New Jersey, Delaware, and New Hampshire made such attempts by tradition or law, whereas no elective court system did so. If a Democratic governor or president appoints a Republican, he is likely to appoint a Republican with values closer to the relatively liberal wing than to the relatively conservative wing of that party. Likewise, a Republican governor or president who appoints a Democrat will probably choose one with values closer to the relatively conservative wing than to the relatively liberal wing of the Democratic Party. Electorates, on the other hand, are never required to choose judges of the party opposite to their own.[30]

The reason for the near-zero correlation with regard to the non-partisan ballot hypothesis is probably the near-meaninglessness of non-partisan ballots where there are organized and competing political parties running the elections behind the scenes. Three states — Michigan, Tennessee, and Arizona — have non-partisan ballots for supreme court elections, but openly recognize the role of political parties by providing partisan primaries or party conventions to pick the judges who run on the non-partisan ballot.[31] Even non-partisan elections preceded by non-partisan primaries may have partisan influences behind the formalities of the election and nomination procedure. If party affiliation does make a difference in judicial behavior, as the data from Table 1 tend to show, then non-partisan ballots only deprive the voter of information useful to him in intelligently voting for judges, assuming he does not learn their party affiliation by some other means.

The reason for the zero correlation with regard to the length-of-term hypothesis is probably that a long term does not cause a judge's value system and his party affiliation to become inconsistent if they were formerly consistent. A long term of office may well make a judge more independent of a party boss. Judges on state supreme courts, however, as previously stated, probably vote in accordance with their party pattern because their value system determines both their voting behavior in certain cases and their party affiliation, not because some party boss asked them to do so.

Regardless of judicial tenure and modes of selection, there probably will always be a residue of party-correlated judicial subjectivity so long as political parties are at least partly value-oriented and so long as court cases involve value-oriented controversies. Ultimately the problem becomes not how to remove this irreducible residue of judicial subjectivity, but rather what direction it should take. If judges should have value positions that are representative of the public at large, then it seems arguable that judges (at least on the higher court levels) should be elected, since presumably a judge elected at large will tend to have more representative values than a judge chosen in any other manner.

NOTES

1. John Schmidhauser, "The Justices of the Supreme Court: A Collective Portrait," *Midwest Journal of Political Science,* Vol. 3 (1958), pp. 1-57; Cortez M. Ewing, *The Judges of the Supreme Court,* 1789-1937 (Minneapolis: U. of Minnesota Press, 1938); Rodney Mott, "Judicial Personnel," *Annals of the American Academy of Political and Social Science,* Vol. 167 (1933), pp. 143-155.

2. Glendon Schubert, *Quantitative Analysis of Judicial Behavior* (Glencoe, 1959); C. Herman Pritchett, *The Roosevelt Court: A Study in Judicial Politics and Values, 1937-1947* (New York, 1948); S. Sydney Ulmer, "The Analysis of Behavior Patterns on the United States Supreme Court," *Journal of Politics,* Vol. 22 (November, 1960), pp. 629-653.

3. For a more detailed analysis and defense of the research design than can be given here see S. Nagel, "Testing Relations between Judicial Characteristics and Judicial Decision-Making" (mimeographed, presented at the 1961 Midwest Conference of Political Scientists). Copies available on request from the writer.

4. The term is used here as a synonym for "highest court" or "court of last resort."

5. Charles Liebman, ed., Chicago, American Directories; sometimes referred to below as the Directory.

6. Wheeler Sammons, ed., Chicago, Marquis, 1954, 1956, 1958.

7. For an analysis of the distribution of political party affiliation among the judges, see S. Nagel, "Unequal Party Representation on the State Supreme Court," *Journal of the American Judicature Society,* Vol. 45 (August, 1961), pp. 62-65. Only 11 per cent of 313 judges gave no party affiliation.

8. For a more exact description of each field of law included, see S. Nagel, *Judicial Characteristics and Judicial Decision-Making,* Ph. D. dissertation, Northwestern University, Evanston, 1961.

9. Commonwealth v. Burdell, 380 Pa. 43 (1955); Commonwealth v. Edwards, 380 Pa. 52 (1955); Commonwealth v. Mackley, 380 Pa. 70 (1955); Commonwealth v. Grays, 380 Pa. 77 (1955); Commonwealth ex rel. Dunn v. Ruch, 380 Pa. 152 (1955); Commonwealth ex rel. Lane v. Baldi, 380 Pa. 201 (1955); Commonwealth v. Chaitt, 380 Pa. 352 (1955); Commonwealth v. LaRue, 381 Pa. 113 (1955); Commonwealth v. Lane, 381 Pa. 293 (1955); Commonwealth v. Thompson, 381 Pa. 299 (1955); Commonwealth v. Mason, 381 Pa. 309 (1955); Commonwealth v. Cisneros, 381

Pa. 447 (1955); Commonwealth v. Bolish, 381 Pa. 500 (1955); Commonwealth ex rel. Matthews v. Day, 381 Pa. 617 (1955); Commonwealth v. Farrow, 382 Pa. 61 (1955); Commonwealth v. Capps, 382 Pa. 72 (1955); Commonwealth v. Wable, 382 Pa. 80 (1955); Commonwealth ex rel. Taylor v. Superintendent of the County Prison, 382 Pa. 181 (1955); Commonwealth ex rel. Bishop v. Marnoey, 382 Pa. 324 (1955); Commonwealth v. Thomas, 382 Pa. 639 (1955); Commonwealth v. Moon, 383 Pa. 18 (1955).

10.   Commonwealth v. Edwards, 380 Pa. 52 (1955).

11.   Harold Yuker, *A Guide to Statistical Calculations* (New York, 1958), pp. 64-66; and Sidney Siegel, *Non-Parametric Statistics for the Behavioral Sciences* (New York, 1956), pp. 13-14.

12.   Chillicothe Telephone Co. v. Public Utilities Commission of Ohio, 163 Ohio 398 (1955); State ex rel. Kearns v. Ohio Power Co., 163 Ohio 451 (1955); State ex rel. Selected Properties v. Gottfried, 163 Ohio 469 (1955).

13.   Cassar v. Appeal Board of the Michigan Employment Security Commission, 343 Mich. 380 (1955); Pazan v. Michigan Unemployment Compensation Commission, 343 Mich. 587 (1955).

14.   Piantanida v. Bennett, 17 N.J. 2d 291 (1955); Morris v. Hermann Forwarding Co., 18 N.J. 2d 195 (1955); DeMonaco v. Renton, 18 N.J. 2d 352 (1955); Lester v. Elliot Bros. Trucking Co., 18 N.J. 2d 434 (1955); Green v. DeFuria, 19 N.J. 2d 290 (1955); Secor v. Penn Service Garage, 19 N.J. 2d 315 (1955); Buccheri v. Montgomery Ward and Co., 19 N.J. 2d 594 (1955).

15.   Schwartz v. Kansas City Southern R. Co., 349 U.S. 931 (1955); Anderson v. Atlantic Coast Line R. Co., 350 U.S. 807 (1955); Zientek v. Reading Co., 350 U.S. 346 (1955); Cahill v. New York, New Haven, and Hartford R. Co., 350 U.S. 898 (1955).

16.   Frankfurter was classified as an independent; he gives no party affiliation in any recent biographical directory.

17.   Robert MacIver, *The Web of Government* (New York, 1951), pp. 215-19.

18.   Julius Turner, ***Party and Constituency: Pressures on Congress*** (Baltimore, John Hopkins Press, 1951), p. 60.

19.   *Ibid.*, p. 66.

20.   Angus Campbell, Gerald Gurin, and Warren Miller, *The Voter Decides* (Evanston, 1954), pp. 118-19.

21.   The 313 judges studied in this paper were mailed attitudinal questionnaires based on the "liberalism" test of Hans Eysenck's *The Psychology of Politics* (London: Routledge and Kegan Paul, 1954), pp. 122-24. The data compiled for the 119 judges who responded tended to show that on bipartisan courts having both high-scoring (liberal) judges and low-scoring (conservative) judges, there is a positive correla-

tion between (1) being a Democratic judge as contrasted to being a Republican judge, and (2) being a high scoring judge.

22. The mailed questionnaire survey just mentioned tends to show that the difference between the decisional propensities of Democrats and Republicans decreases when liberalism is held constant. Thus when only liberal Democrats and liberal Republicans were matched, there was virtually no correlation between (1) being a Democrat as contrasted to being a Republican and (2) being above rather than below the average decision score of one's bipartisan court in criminal cases. Likewise when only conservative Democrats and conservative Republicans were compared, there was also virtually no correlation between (1) being a Democrat and (2) being above the average decision score of one's bipartisan court in criminal cases. The sample sizes involved in these analyses were, however, exceedingly small.

23. Elected and appointed judges were sorted out from the entries and the designation table in the Directory.

24. These probabilities were calculated by using a chi-square formula with a Yates correction in view of the skew toward voting in accordance with party patterns. See J. P. Guilford, *Fundamental Statistics in Psychology and Education* (New York, 1956), pp. 207-208, 228-239.

25. Judges elected on a non-partisan ballot were identified by first determining, through the *Directory* entries, in what year the most recent term (prior to 1955) of each judge began and then checking the judicial election law for his state in that year in the *Book of the States* (Chicago: Council of State Governments, 1938-1955).

26. The terms of office were traced through the same sources as the methods of selection.

27. This hypothesis was partially tested by using the attitudinal data mentioned in note 21 to see if any correlation existed between (1) being an appointed rather than an elected judge and (2) voting contrary to rather than in accordance with one's value position in criminal cases. The correlation, as hypothesized, was practically zero with a sample of 65 judges.

28. Glendon Schubert, *Constitutional Politics: The Political Behavior of Supreme Court Justices and the Constitutional Policies that They Make* (New York, 1960), pp. 37, 711-712.

29. *Courts of Last Resort of the Forty-Eight States* (Chicago: Council of State Governments, 1955), Table 4.

30. The mailed questionnaire survey mentioned in note 21 showed no positive correlation between (1) being an appointed judge rather than an elected judge on a bipartisan court and (2) being a conservative Democrat or a liberal Republican rather than a liberal Democrat or a conservative Republican. The slightly negative correlation, however, was only a -.04 phi coefficient and was only based on 25 judges.

31. *Courts of Last Resort of the Forty-Eight States, op. cit. supra,* note 29.

Part Four

OUTPUTS OF
STATE POLITICAL
SYSTEMS

Public policy is the response of the political system to the demands made on it. In one sense it is the "terminal point in an intricate process through which demands and supports are converted into decisions and actions."[1] That is, it is the "product" of "the joint operation of external forcings and system properties."[2] At the same time, outputs are "transactions" between the political system and the environment. They are "part of a continuous chain of activities . . . in which inputs and outputs each directly and indirectly affect each other and together, the rest of the political system and its environment."[3]

The articles in this section illustrate some of the factors which affect the nature of the outputs of the American states. These articles attempt to account for variations in commitment to certain kinds of policy by looking at the nature of the states' environments, their "political" characteristics, and the perceptions of certain people who make decisions within the system. They do not, obviously, focus on every aspect of public policy at the state level. However, the factors that are examined for their implications for these three areas of state policy may also be assumed to have an effect on other areas of policy-making, even though different policy variables may be related differently to various "independent" variables.

1.   David Easton, *A Systems Analysis of Political Life* (New York: John Wiley, 1965) p. 344.

2.   Herbert M. Blalock, Jr., *Causal Inferences in Nonexperimental Research* (Chapel Hill: University of North Carolina Press, 1965), p. 8.

3.   Easton, *op. cit.*, p. 345.

WELFARE POLICY

Inter-Party Competition, Economic Variables, and Welfare Policies in the American States

Richard E. Dawson
James A. Robinson

I. INTRODUCTION

The object of this paper is to discover the relationship among the extent of inter-party competition, the presence of certain economic factors, and the extent of nine public welfare policies, using the American states as the units for investigation. The fifty states share similar institutions and a similar cultural history, but they differ with respect to economic and social structure, political activity, and public policy. Therefore, they provide a large number of political and social units in which some important variables can be held constant while others are varied.

Our primary concern is to investigate the relation between political processes and the policies adopted by political systems. In this study, public policies, or more particularly, social welfare policies of the various state political systems, are the dependent variables. Public policy, its formulation, implementation and effects, is one of the major interests of students of politics. Political science is concerned with ways in which formal and informal institutions, economic, social, philosophical and geographic conditions influence the adoption and implementation of policy.[1] For purposes of clarity it seems useful to place the problem of the relationship between party competition and welfare policies within a larger context of orienting political studies.[2]

Reprinted from *The Journal of Politics,* Vol. 25 (1963), pp. 265-289, by permission of the authors and publisher.

This is a revision of a paper prepared for the 20th annual meeting of the Midwest Conference of Political Scientists, South Bend, Indiana, April 26-28, 1962.

We begin with the assumption that public policy is the major dependent variable that political science seeks to explain. The task of political science, then is to find and explain the independent and intervening variables that account for policy differences. The major categories of political theory might be portrayed in this manner:

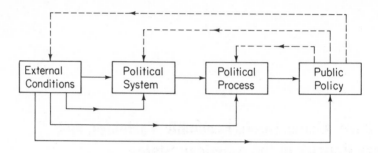

Moving from left to right, this diagram assumes that a variety of external conditions (external, that is, to boundaries of the political system) influence the development of different types of political systems. Process, as activity and interaction between the variables and parts of that system, in turn gives rise to the formulation and implementation of public policies. Policy in this context is the outcome of activity or interaction among external conditions, political system, and political process. As the outer solid arrows indicate, external variables and system variables might also affect policy directly, without being mediated by process variables. Likewise external variables may directly influence process without being specifically influenced by system variables. We assume that the most likely mechanism of development is that in which external conditions and system are mediated by process, and that external conditions are mediated by both system and process, and that external conditions are mediated by both system and process as they influence policy outcomes. As the broken lines suggest, policy outcomes also may influence the other variables. One would expect policy outcomes to affect the external conditions of one point in time, which would then act on future policy outcomes.[3]

Because the terms political system, political process, and public policy have been used in different ways, it might be useful to designate more specifically what we mean by them in this context, although this is obviously not the occasion for resolving the argument about what uses are universally appropriate. The term system refers to an integrated group of interacting elements designed jointly to perform a given function.[4] *Political system* refers to that group of related variables whose task is the authoritative allocation of values for a given society; the search for typologies of political systems is a continuing occupation of political science.[5] *Process* refers to the activity within the system, the inter-action of the system's sub-variables and sub-components, throughout a period of time, types of policy processes include bargaining, hierarchy, polyarchy, and the price system.[6] *Policy* consists of the *goals* (objectives of or commitments made by the political system), the *means* by which they may be implemented and the *consequences* of those means.[7] As such, public policies are the chief output of the political system and constitute the allocation of values for the society.

When our study is put in this context, it will be clear that we are primarily concerned with whether differences in policy are related to differences in process, holding system variables constant. More specifically, we want to discover whether differences in social welfare policies are related to a particular political process within these systems, namely the degree of inter-party competition.

By using the American states we are able to hold many of the most important system characteristics constant. It would obviously be erroneous to say that the states are exactly alike in all respects but in fundamental formal structure the forty-six states that we consider are very similar.[8] They have written constitutions, with authority divided among legislative and judicial branches. They have bicameral legislatures, and, except in North Carolina, the governor participates in the legislative process through the potential use of the veto. The state constitutions contain a bill of rights similar to the first ten amendments to the United States Constitution, and the highest court has the right of judicial review. Although other details of political organization, structure and process within the systems vary from state to state, the basic institutions are remarkably similar. Thus, by using the American states as units of analysis we can hold the basic system variables constant, concentrating attention on the relation between process and policy.

However, the external socio-economic conditions within which these state systems operate vary markedly. Wealth, the per cent of population living in urban areas, and the per cent of residents engaged in industrial, professional and commercial occupations, as well as the complex of social, economic and ideological factors that surround these conditions, are not the same in all of the states. For example, the per capita income of Connecticut ($2,817) is nearly three times that of Mississippi ($1,053). To further illustrate, the per cent of residents living in urban areas ranges from 86.6 in New Jersey to 26.6 in North Dakota.[9] The relation betwen various socio-economic conditions and political systems, process and public policy has long been of concern to the student of politics.[10] Golembiewski, in a recent study of the relation between a group of "sociological factors" and state political party strength, reports significant statistical relationships between variables such as per cent of population urban, population density, per cent of Negroes in the population, median income and industrialization on the one hand and classifications of party competition on the other.[11]

Although the concept process has long been widely used in the study of politics, relatively little research on the relations between process variables and types of public policy has been undertaken. In recent years interest has increased in ways in which processes within organizations affect policy.[12] Two studies have formulated hypotheses regarding the influence of process upon policy in the relationship between inter- or intra- party competition and the adoption of welfare policies. Key offered several hypotheses concerning the differences in public welfare policies in states with loose multifactional one-party systems and states with two cohesive factions competing in a one-party system.[13] He found that the southern states with loose multi-factional systems, in which the coherence and continuity of competition is less, tend to pursue more conservative policies, i.e., policies favorable to the interest of the upper socio-economic groups or the "haves." In states with competition between two cohesive and enduring factions, more liberal policies are adopted, i.e., policies more responsive to the interests, needs and/or desires of the "have nots." Lockard expanded on the work of Key and asked "How much difference does it make in the long run whether a state has a set of competitive parties or whether one-party dominance prevails?"[14] He divided the six New England states into one-party (Maine, New Hampshire and Vermont) and two-party states (Massachusetts, Rhode Island and Connecticut) and found that the two-party states receive a larger portion of their revenue from business and death taxes; spend more money for services such as aid to the blind, old-age assistance, and aid to dependent children; and are less likely to have legislative apportionment schemes that favor small minorities, especially certain economic interest groups.[15]

Our study expands on the hypotheses of Key and Lockard concerning party competition and welfare policies, testing them with a larger number of states and policies and applying slightly more rigorous statistical techniques. Our initial hypothesis can be briefly stated: *The greater the degree of inter-party competition within a political system, the more liberal the social welfare measures that system will adopt.* After testing this hypothesis, we shall consider whether a state's economic condition is more closely related to its liberalism than is inter-party competition.

II. INTER-PARTY COMPETITION

The traditional classification of party systems into one-, two-, and multi-party types is inadequate for American state parties.[16] As Ranney and Kendall point out, this simple three-category scheme classifies Mississippi and the Soviet Union as one-party systems. But the party systems of these two political units differ in certain vital respects. "Opposition candidates can (and sometimes do) oppose candidates of the dominant party in Mississippi. They can not (and do not) in the Soviet Union. So the question arises whether any useful purpose can be served by continuing to call them both 'one-party systems.'"[17] Even if totalitarian one-party systems were excluded, difficulties would remain in using this classification scheme. Because of Republican dominance in Vermont and New Hampshire and Democratic dominance in Mississippi and South Carolina, all four of these political party systems are often lumped together as one-party systems. This classification, however, overlooks significant differences between the inter-party competition found in South Carolina and that in New Hampshire. Although the Republicans nearly always win the major offices in New Hampshire, the opposition almost always runs a candidate who polls from 30 to 49 per cent of the vote. In South Carolina, on the contrary, the minority party seldom runs a candidate, and when it does, he ordinarily polls a mere 5 to 20 per cent of the vote. Lumping the states together encourages a disregard for certain important differences between these states.

To meet these problems, Ranney and Kendall, Key, and Golembiewski devised other classifications. Ranney and Kendall divide American systems into the multi-party, two-party, and modified one-party, the one-party and the totalitarian one-party types.[18] Key classifies the states as Strong Republican, Less-Strong Republican, Competitive, Leaning Democratic, and Strong Democratic.[19] Golembiewski revives a three-fold scheme, but one more applicable to the American state parties: one-party states, weak minority-party states, and two-party states.[20]

The basis for dividing the state party systems in each of these schemes is the level of competitiveness between the two major political parties within each state.[21] At least three factors must be considered in designing a tool for measuring inter-party competition: (1) time period; (2) offices; and (3) which of several ways of looking at competitiveness, within the context of the two preceding factors, most accurately measures competition?

Competition must be measured for a period of time, but how long a period should be considered in formulating an adequate measure? Students of inter-party competition vary in the time periods they select. Ranney and Kendall, for example, use election results since 1914.[22] Schlesinger bases his study on election results since the 1870's.[23] Golembiewski considers three separate years — 1937, 1941 and 1951.[24] Zeller uses a base period of only six years.[25] Although it is useful to consider long periods of time, like those used by Ranney and Kendall and Schlesinger, long base periods may obscure one or more shifts in voting and party identification.[26] On the other hand, short time periods may measure only deviations from normal patterns of voting, owing to special economic conditions, particular personalities, and specific short-term issues. For instance, if one were to measure competition for the presidency using only the 1950's as a base period, he would get a distorted picture of the competitiveness of the presidency both in regard to the direction and degree of competition. To avoid the dangers in both extremes, and to take advantage of the ready availability of certain election data, it seemed most useful to adopt the twenty-one period from 1938 to 1958 as a base. This period appears long enough to lessen the influence of short-term deviating factors and short enough to avoid the impact of basic shifts in party identification such as occurred in the 1860-1864 and the 1932-1936 elections.[27] Likewise it eliminates the extremely one-sided election results of the early New Deal when many states deviated from previous and subsequent patterns of voting.

The next step in designing a measure of inter-party competition is the selection of offices. The units adopted by other researchers vary. Key used only the office of governor.[28] Ranney and Kendall included electoral results for president, governor and United States senator.[29] Golembiewski used only state offices, the governor, and the legislature.[30] In his 1955 study, Schlesinger used the offices of governor and president.[31] In his 1960 study he considered the governor, senators, congressmen and six state-wide elective offices.[32]

The decision about which offices to consider is partly arbitrary and partly dependent upon the problem. If, for instance, one wants to describe the competitiveness of a state party system as part of the national party system, it is relevant to consider national offices as well as state offices. Our study, however, is concerned with the relationship between inter-party competition and the types of welfare policies adopted *within* state political systems. It is necessary, therefore, to take into account those offices that play the most important role in the recommendation and prescription of public policies within the state political systems, and little reason can be found to include the competitiveness of national offices. The consideration of competition for state offices as divorced from national offices also is defensible in light of the basic decentralization or independence of American state party systems from the national parties.[33] For this study the office of governor and each branch of the state legislature are used. These are the state institutions most directly involved in identifying problems of public policy, and recommending and selecting alternatives to meet them.

After the base time period has been selected and the choice of offices has been made, it is necessary to decide how to measure the degree of competition for the selected offices for the chosen time period. The degree of inter-party competition refers primarily to the extent to which both parties possess the opportunity of gaining control of the various offices around which the competition takes place. In a competitive situation the "out-party" must have the possibility to become the "in-party," and the position of the in-party must be threatened by the possibility that the out-party could gain control. The assumption is that the possibility of gaining control of the decision-making machinery influences the behavior of the out-party and the constant threat of being put out of office influences the behavior of the in-party.[34]

At least three dimensions of inter-party competition form the competitive process: (1) the margin of comparative popular support, including the relative strength of the two parties in the electorate and/or the relative number of seats they hold in the legislature;[35] (2) the relative percentage of time that the parties have controlled the offices or institutions under consideration;[36] and (3) the percentage of time that control of the offices has been divided between the parties, one party controlling one office and the other party the other offices at the same time.[37] Although these three dimensions are related, it is possible to obtain different results from them. For example, New Hampshire, when measured according to the percentage of times the governorship and both houses of the state legislature have been controlled by the predominant party, would be ranked with Georgia, Mississippi and other Southern states. However, when competition is measured according to the percentage of popular vote the predominant party has received in the race for governor and the percentage of seats it has held in the legislature over the twenty-one years period, New Hampshire appears much more competitive than any of the Southern states. Although the Republicans have controlled the governorship in New Hampshire and the Democrats in Mississippi during the entire twenty-one year period, the Republican party in New Hampshire received 55.5 per cent of the two-party vote for governor, while the Democrats received 100 per cent of the popular vote for the same office in Mississippi.

We measured each of these dimensions of inter-party competition. In measuring the first dimension we ranked each state according to the total percentage of the two-party popular vote the predominant party received in the elections for governor from 1938 to 1958; according to the percentage of seats the predominant party has held in the state senate over the same period of time; and according to the percentage of seats held by the predominant party in the "lower" house of the state legislature. This was done by averaging the per cent of major party vote the parties received in each gubernatorial election and the per cent of seats the parties have held in each house during each term of the state legislature of the twenty-one year period. The states were ranked on a continuum from those closest to fifty per cent to those most distant from fifty per cent. Competition along this dimension was first considered separately for each of the three institutions, then the three measurements were combined into one by averaging the three percentages. According to these measurements the states are ranked as shown. In some instances, *e.g.,* California and Connecticut, great differences occur in the rankings of a state for the different political units. In spite of several cases like this, however, the correlations between these rankings are quite high, as indicated in Table 1. Because each of these three institutions — the governorship, the senate and the house of representatives — plays a key role in the determination of state policy, the average of the percentages of popular vote for governor, the per cent of seats held in the senate, and the per cent of seats held in the house is the best over-all measure of inter-party competition along this dimension.

State	Rank: Per Cent of Popular Vote for Governor	Rank: Per cent of Seats in Senate Held by Major Party	Rank: Per cent of Seats in House Held by Major Party	Rank: Average of the three Percentages
1. Ala.	41	43.5	41.5	41
2. Ariz.	30	36	32	33
3. Ark.	40	43.5	40	40
4. Calif.	34	9	5	11
5. Colo.	1	4.5	11	15
6. Conn.	7.5	2	22.5	9.5
7. Del.	2.5	1	3	1
8. Fla.	39	40	39	39
9. Ga.	45	39	41.5	43
10. Idaho	15	4.5	9	6
11. Ill.	4.5	10	4	4
12. Ind.	9	16	15	13.5
13. Iowa	23	31	31	29
14. Kans.	20.5	32	27.5	23
15. Ky.	25	25.5	26	24
16. La.	43	43.5	45	44
17. Me.	28	33	29	30
18. Md.	16	19	27.5	25
19. Mass.	10	7	2	3
20. Mich.	4.5	22	18	17
21. Miss.	45	43.5	45	46
22. Mo.	17	11.5	6	22
23. Mont.	11	3	1	2
24. Nev.	24	15	16.5	16
25. N.H.	26	23	16.5	19
26. N.J.	6	24	19	20
27. N.Mex.	12	28	25	26
28. N.Y.	18.5	11.5	14	12
29. N.C.	36	38	37	37
30. N. Dak.	27	34	36	35
31. Ohio	2.5	18	20	17
32. Okla.	32.5	35	34	34
33. Ore.	32.5	25.5	24	27
34. Pa.	14	14	7	7
35. R.I.	20.5	6	13	8
36. S.C.	45	43.5	45	45
37. S. Dak.	31	29	33	31
38. Tenn.	38	21	30	32
39. Tex.	42	43.5	43	42
40. Utah	7.5	8	8	5
41. Vt.	35	30	35	36
42. Va.	37	37	38	38
43. Wash.	18.5	13	10	9.5
44. W.Va.	22	20	21	21
45. Wis.	29	27	22.5	28
46. Wyo.	13	17	12	13.5

Table 1 Rank order correlations between four measures of inter-party competition.

	Popular Vote for Governor	Membership in Senate	Membership in House	Average
Per cent Popular vote for Governor		.80	.80	.85
Per cent Members of Major Party in Senate	.80		.93	.95
Per cent Members of Major Party in House	.80	.93		.95
Average of above Three Percentages	.85	.95	.95	

In measuring the second dimension, the relative per cent of time during the twenty-one year period that the major party has controlled the offices under consideration, the rank order of the states is determined by taking the number of terms of the Senate, the number of terms of the house of representatives, and the number of terms for governor and finding the per cent of terms that the major party has been in control. Thus, if there were eleven terms of the state senate, eleven terms of the house of representatives and five terms of governor, and the major party controlled five terms of the senate, seven terms of the house of representatives, and three terms as governor, the major party would have controlled the offices about 56 per cent of the time. The states are then ranked on a continuum with the states closest to 50 per cent considered the most competitive and those most distant from 50 per cent the least competitive. Separate rankings can be made for each office by considering the per cent of time the major party has controlled that particular institution. Again, because policies are made by the three institutions and because the parties compete for control of each of them, the measure considering the three jointly is appropriate to measure the competitiveness between the parties for control of the formal policy-making machinery of government. It must be pointed out that there were no changes in control of any of these offices in 14 of the 46 states. Thus, there are fourteen ties in the ranking of the states on this dimension.

The final dimension of competition is the percentage of times that control of the government, in this case the governorship, the senate, and the house, has been divided between the two parties during the twenty-one year period. This measure is computed by counting the number of times, at two year intervals, that one party has held one of three institutions and the other party has controlled the other two and then computing what percentage this is of the total number of two year periods. The states are then ranked according to these percentages, 100 per cent being the most competitive and 0 per cent being the least competitive. Once more there are a substantial number of ties, fifteen.

These three operations are our measures of inter-party competition. We have said that these three dimensions are related but that there can be significant differences between them in particular states. Nonetheless, the high coefficients obtained from correlating the ranks of the states along these dimensions suggest that they are measuring either the same phenomena or at least very closely related phenomena. The correlations between these measures are given in Table 2.

Table 2 Rank order correlations between three dimensions of inter-party competition.

	Margin of Control	Extent of Control	Divided Control
Margin of Control		.86	.84
Extent of Control	.86		.90
Divided Control	.84	.90	

III. WELFARE POLICIES

Welfare policies are those programs that directly or indirectly redistribute wealth, *i.e.*, whose purpose is to benefit the lower socio-economic groups at the expense of the upper income groups. The extent of welfare policies is assumed to be related in part to the ability of the lower-bracket groups to find political channels for the expression of their viewpoints and to exert influence upon the decision-makers.[38] Welfare measures include a wide range of public policies, some of which, like gift and death taxes, are specifically designed to redistribute wealth, and others, like educational expenditures, which are designed for other purposes but whose latent effect is redistribution of wealth and other values by providing equal educational opportunities for all in spite of wide discrepancies in private income.

The basic means by which governments affect the distribution of values include the collection of money through tax or revenue policies and the expenditure of money through a variety of programs. We use nine state policies or programs as indices of welfare measures. Four of these are revenue policies and five are expenditure policies. The selection of policies has been arbitrary, based to a great extent on the ready availability and comparability of data, as well as on an attempt to cover a wide range of substantive policies, and to include policies not affected by federal programs as well as those that are encouraged by federal action. As with the previous variables, the states are comparatively ranked. In all of the policies except the per cent of revenue coming from the federal government, the higher the tax rate or the higher the expenditures, the more extensive are the state's welfare programs. In regard to the per cent of revenue coming from the federal government, the higher the percentage, the lower the willingness of the state to support its own social welfare programs. To compare their welfare policies, we have ranked the forty-six states according to: (1) The per cent of the state's revenue derived from death and gift taxes. (2) The per cent of the state's revenue from the federal government. (3) The per capita amount of all general revenue. (4) State and local tax revenue according to personal income. (5) The average per pupil expenditure for education. (6) The average payment per recipient of aid to the blind. (7) The average payment per family for aid to dependent children. (8) The average payment per recipient in old-age assistance. (9) The average weekly benefit for total unemployment compensation in the state's unemployment insurance program.[39]

IV. EXTERNAL CONDITIONS: ECONOMIC FACTORS

Theories of political science contain a great deal of both speculative and empirically-founded suggestions on the influence of external socio-economic-physical and psychological factors on the development of political systems, the processes that take place within them, and, the policies that systems and processes produce. A large number of external conditions can be hypothetically related to these political variables. The factors most commonly related to political systems and processes have been economic ones. Aristotle, DeTocqueville, Hegel, Marx, Beard, Dahl and Lindblom, Golembiewski, and Lipset discuss, with varying degrees of empirical verification, the relationship between economic factors and processes within the political systems. Lipset, in his study of the relations between economic development and stable democratic governments in Western Europe, the English speaking democracies and Latin America, uses four major indices of economic development: (1) wealth, (2) industrialization, (3) urbanization, and (4) education. [40]

As indicators of external conditions, the forty-six states will be ranked according to per capita income; the percentage of inhabitants engaged in occupations other than agriculture, forestry, and fishing; and the percentage of the state's population residing in urban areas.[41] Inasmuch as different levels of wealth, urbanization and industrialization represent modes of life, values, or attitudes, each of these indices probably measures a complex of factors. For instance, living in urban areas generally means greater interdependence, greater access to cultural and educational facilities, and greater exposure to a wider range of religious and ideological positions, than does living in rural areas. Thus, when one measures the degree of urbanization, he measures much more than the fact of living in an

Table 3 Rank order correlations between three measures of external conditions.

	Per capita Income	Industrialization	Urbanization
Per capita income		.74	.82
Industrialization	.74		.81
Urbanization	.82	.81	

urban area. He also measures the complex of patterns that accompany urban life. The same can be said for wealth and industrialization. Because it is presumed that these indices are measuring economic factors, one would expect to find a fairly close relationship between these three factors, expecially between industrialization and urbanization. The rank order correlations between these three variables among forty-six states are reported in Table 3. We shall now investigate the relation between these three external factors and both the process and policy variables. We shall then look at the relation between process and policy variables, controlling for the influence of these external conditions.

V. REPORT AND ANALYSIS OF RE-SULTS

To investigate the hypothesis that the greater the degree of inter-party competition in a political system, the more extensive or "liberal" the social welfare policies a political system will adopt, rank order correlations were tabulated between the three major indices of competition and the nine social welfare policies. The rank order correlation coefficients between these two sets of variables are in Table 4. The correlation coefficients between the competitive measures and the per cent of revenue from death/gift taxes and the per cent of revenue from the federal government are somewhat lower than those for other policies. The correlations between tax revenue based on personal income and the competitive measures are slightly negative. With these exceptions, the data confirm a relationship between the degree of inter-party competition and the extent to which the states have adopted social welfare measures. If the indices are measuring what we presume they are, the hypothesis that more liberal social welfare measures are adopted by more competitive party systems holds for the forty-six states. This is consistent with the reports made by Key and Lockard.[42]

If these findings are valid, the more competitive a party system, the more responsive it is to the interests and desires of the lower economic groups or the "have nots." Conversely, the less competitive a party system, the less responsive it is to the lower bracket economic groups and the more responsive it is to the interests of the "haves" and to powerful special economic interests. Lockard offers the following propositions to explain this relationship:

> (Proposition 1) "In the two-party states the anxiety over the next election pushes political leaders into serving the interests of the have-less elements of society, thereby putting the party into the counter-vailing power operation."[43]
>
> (Proposition 2) ". . . in the one-party states it is easier for a few powerful interests to manage the government of the state without party interference since the parties are not representative of the particular elements that might pose opposition to the dominant interest groups."[44]

Similarly, writing about southern politics, Key suggests that

> (Proposition 3) ". . . over the long run the have-nots lose in a disorganized politics. They have no mechanism through which to act and their wishes find expression in fitful rebellions led by transient demagogues who gain their confidence but often have neither the technical competence nor the necessary stable base of political power to effectuate a program."[45]
>
> (Proposition 4) "A loose factional system lacks the power to carry out sustained

Table 4 Rank order correlations between public policies and inter-party competition.

Policies	Party Competition Measures		
	Average Per cent of popular support for Governor, Senate, and House	Per cent of time the predominant party has controlled units of government	Per cent of times control has been divided between parties
Per cent of revenue from death/gift taxes	.44	.37	.25
Per cent of revenue from federal government	.32	.27	.41
Per capita amount of state revenue	.55	.50	.47
Tax revenue in relation to personal income	-.23	-.08	-.21
Per pupil expenditure	.64	.65	.71
Aid to blind	.58	.57	.55
Aid to dependent children	.63	.59	.52
Unemployment insurance	.63	.69	.63
Old age assistance	.53	.55	.53

programs of action, which almost always are thought by the better elements to be contrary to its immediate interests. This negative weakness thus resounds to the benefit of the upper brackets. "[46]

These hypotheses suggest that the process of competition between two organized and enduring political parties, or as is the case in the South, two stable factions within a one-party arrangement, lead to more liberal social welfare policies because competition forces the candidates and/or parties to appeal to the have-not groups for support. At the same time, the competitive process inhibits the influence of special economic interests by its development of countervailing forces. In regard to the relationship between party competition and the importance of pressure politics, Golembiewski offers and tests the following proposition:

(Proposition 5) "Weak party cohesion is generally associated with strong pressure politics, and strong party cohesion with weak pressure politics. And party cohesion is a direct function of the degree of competition between political parties, that is, the more marked is interparty competition the more pronounced is party cohesion." [47]

Using his own classification of party systems and Zeller's measures of pressure politics and party cohesion, Golembiewski confirmed this position.

A correlational analysis suggests a common variance between two or more variables. A correlation indicates the extent to which one variable changes when another is changed; it alone cannot prove causal relations between variables. The high correlations between competition and policy suggest only that the welfare policies vary in direction and extent as variations occur in inter-party competition. They do not reveal whether the adoption of welfare measures is an effect of party competition or vice-versa. This co-variance may result from the fact that one of the two variables influences the other or from the fact that both are related to a third variable or set of variables.

There has been a competing hypothesis throughout this investigation that both inter-party competition and welfare policies might not be related to various external socio-economic factors. In regard to the relationship between external conditions and the level of inter-party competition, Lockard suggests that:

(Proposition 6) "The diversity or lack of diversity of economic interests in a state tends to be reflected in the prevailing party system and the mode of its operations." [48]

(Proposition 7) "In the first place, of course, it is the diversity in part that creates the atmosphere for two-party competition and the absence of diversity facilitates one-partyism." [49]

We now report our findings on the relation of economic factors to inter-party competition and welfare policies. The rank order correlations between the three socio-economic variables and the three major measures of inter-party competition are summarized in Table 5.

Table 5 Rank order correlations between external conditions and inter-party competition.

	Party Competition Measures		
External Conditions	Average Per cent of popular support for Governor, Senate and House	Per cent of times the predominant party has controlled units of government	Per cent of times control has been divided between parties
Per Capita Income	.71	.65	.73
Urbanization	.58	.54	.56
Industrialization	.59	.48	.57

These correlations confirm a relationship between these external conditions and the level of inter-party competition. Note that the relationship between per capita income and the competitive measures is consistently higher than that with the other socio-economic measures. Golembiewski found statistically significant relations between a group of "sociological" factors and categories of party competition. His findings support the following propositions: [50]

> (Proposition 8) Where the per cent of urban population is high the political party system is likely to be competitive or two-party.
>
> (Proposition 9) Where the population density is high the party system is likely to be competitive or two-party.
>
> (Proposition 10) Where the Negro percentage of the population is low the system is likely to be competitive or two-party.
>
> (Proposition 11) Where the total median income is high the party system is likely to be competitive or two-party.

Finally, the relation between the external socio-economic conditions and public welfare policies must be considered. One might hypothesize important relations between socio-economic conditions and public policies for at least two reasons. First the wealth of a state might condition the ability of a state to pay for welfare policies.

> (Proposition 12) The wealthier the state, the greater its ability to afford extensive social welfare policies.

Second, different types of societies presumably desire and/or require varying degrees of policies or programs that might fall under the heading of welfare legislation. In a more industrialized and urbanized state more social welfare legislation, such as unemployment insurance and aid to dependent children, presumably would be needed or desired than in a less urbanized or industrialized state.

> (Proposition 13) The more urbanized and industrialized a state, the greater the desire and/or need of its inhabitants for social welfare legislation.
>
> (Proposition 14) The more urbanized and industrialized a state, the greater the degree of interdependence between its population; and the greater the level of interdependence, the greater the tendence of the people to look toward the government or the political system to handle basic socio-economic problems, or to adopt social welfare policies.

The rank order correlation coefficients tabulated between the socio-economic variables and the policy variables are presented in Table 6.

These correlations signify rather strong relations between the three socio-economic factors and public welfare policies. As with the party competition variables, the socio-economic variables are negatively correlated with the amount of tax revenue in relation to the level of personal income variable. The highest correlations are between per capita income and policy. As was found in the correlations between the socio-economic factors and party competition, the per capita income coefficients are consistently higher than those with the other two socio-economic variables. Note also that the correlations between per capita income and policy are higher than any of those found between measures of inter-party competition and the welfare policies.

Thus far we have found that the policy variables are related to competition variables, competition variables are related to socio-economic factors, and the policies are also correlated with the socio-economic factors. These conform to hypothesized relations. With system variables held constant, the socio-economic

Table 6   Rank order correlations between public policies and external conditions.

Policies	Socio-economic variables		
	Per capita Income	Urbanization	Industrialization
Per cent of revenue from death/gift taxes	.54	.46	.41
Per cent of revenue from federal government	.62	.65	.69
Per capita amount of state revenue	.55	.33	.24
Tax revenue in relation to personal income	-.03	-.41	-.44
Per pupil expenditures	.88	.67	.63
Aid to blind	.74	.63	.47
Aid to dependent children	.64	.56	.47
Unemployment insurance	.73	.64	.56
Old age assistance	.69	.61	.47

factors influence the political process, both directly and through their influence on system, and process variables influence the adoption of public policies and socio-economic factors also affect policy outcomes, hypothetically mediated by process.

The policy variables correlated highly with both inter-party competition (process) and the socio-economic factors; and process variables, in turn, are associated with socio-economic conditions. The finding of associations among these variables still leaves unanswered the question of the effect inter-party competition has upon the adoption of public social welfare measures. It is not known from these statistics whether inter-party competition has any independent influence upon the level of social welfare or whether the high positive correlations between policies and competition stem from the dual relationship between socio-economic factors and policy and between socio-economic factors and competition. Conversely, the meaning of the relationship between socio-economic factors and policy is unclear because both are so highly correlated with competition. To what extent, for example, are the high correlations found between inter-party competition and policies independent of the relationship between both of these variables and per capita income? The correlations computed thus far suggest that the wealthier states have more competitive party processes and more "liberal" social welfare measures. Do they have the more liberal welfare measures because they are wealthier, or does the process of competition between the parties intervene to influence the extent of welfare policies?

In order to sift out the relative influence of these factors, it is necessary to measure the relation between party competition and public policies while holding wealth constant. This has been done by dividing the states into three groups according to their per capita income. Because there are forty-six states, the first fifteen on the per capita income continuum were placed in one group, the wealthiest one-third; the next sixteen into a second group, the middle one-third; and the remaining fifteen into a third group, the poorest one-third. Then rank order correlations were computed between inter-party competition and policies within each of the three groups. The rank order correlations are shown in Table 7.

Table 7 Rank order correlations between per capita income and three welfare policies, holding inter-party competition constant.

	Per Capita Income			
Policies	Upper 1/3	Middle 1/3	Lower 1/3	46 States
Per pupil expenditures	.75	.70	.81	.88
Unemployment compensation	.37	.60	.41	.73
Old age assistance	.47	.46	.70	.69

They suggest that the correlations not controlling for wealth were more a reflection of per capita income and its relationship with inter-party competition than they were of inter-party competition.

In order to further isolate the influence of inter-party competition and wealth upon welfare policies, correlations were computed between per capita income and the same three policy measures, controlling for inter-party competition. The states were divided into three groups according to competition as measured by the average per cent of popular support for governor, the senate and the house of representatives. The results are displayed in Table 8.

Table 8 Rank order correlations between inter-party competition (average popular support measure) and three welfare policies, holding wealth (per capita income) constant.

	Average Popular Support for Governor, Senate, and House			
Policies	Upper 1/3	Middle 1/3	Lower 1/3	46 States
Per pupil expenditures	.13	.34	.37	.64
Unemployment insurance	-.13	-.22	.41	.63
Old age assistance	.07	.24	.21	.53

With inter-party competition controlled for, a somewhat different situation is found than that resulting from controlling wealth and correlating competition and policies. Although most of the correlations are lower for the three controlled groups than they were for the forty-six states, they are not as low as those between competition and policies when wealth was controlled. In fact, one of the correlations is even slightly higher in the controlled group, and each is higher than all but one of the correlations when wealth is controlled.

These last two sets of correlations indicate that wealth influences, or at least is related to the extent of welfare policies, independent of the influence of party competition. On the other hand, inter-party competition is related to the extent of public social welfare policies through their joint relationship with per capita income. If the data reported and operations used have measured what we have presumed them to measure, inter-party competition does not play as influential a role in determining the scope of welfare policies as earlier studies suggested. The level of public social welfare programs in the American states is more an effect of socio-economic factors, especially per capita income. High levels of inter-party competition are highly related both to socio-economic factors and to social welfare legislation, but the degree of inter-party competition does not seem to possess the important intervening influence between socio-economic factors and liberal welfare programs that our original hypothesis predicted. In short, the evidence points to the relatively greater influence of certain external conditions over one aspect of the political process in the formulation of welfare policies.

NOTES

1. For discussions of the use of the concept policy as a focus for research in political science, see: David Easton, *The Political System* (New York: Alfred A. Knopf, 1953), esp. pp. 125-148; Charles S. Hyneman, *The Study of Politics* (Urbana: University of Illinois Press, 1959), esp. pp. 101-108 and 165-173; Harold D. Lasswell, "The Policy Orientation," in *The Policy Sciences* (eds.) Daniel Lerner and Harold Lasswell, (Stanford, California: Stanford University Press, 1951), pp. 3-15; and James A. Robinson, "The Major Problems of Political Science," in *Politics and Public Affairs,* (ed.) L.K. Caldwell, (Bloomington, Indiana: Institute of Training for Public Service, Indiana University, 1962), pp. 161-188.

2. Robinson, *loc. cit.*

3. Harry Eckstein, *Pressure Group Politics: The Case of the British Medical Association* (London: Allen and Unwin, 1960), p.8.

4. Easton, *op. cit.,* p. 129.

5. See James S. Coleman, "The Political Systems of the Developing Areas," in Gabriel Almond and James S. Coleman, *The Politics of the Developing Areas* (Princeton: Princeton University Press, 1960), pp. 532-576.

6. Robert A. Dahl and Charles E. Lindblom, *Politics, Economics and Welfare* (New York: Harper & Brothers, 1953).

7. Robinson, *loc. cit.,* p. 169.

476   *WELFARE POLICY*

8.   Forty-six of the fifty states are used. Alaska and Hawaii are omitted because they were states for only part of the twenty year period considered. Nebraska is left out for two reasons: it does not have a bicameral legislature, and its legislature is elected on a non-partisan basis. Minnesota is also excluded because its legislature is non-partisan.

9.   United States Department of Commerce, Bureau of the Census, *Statistical Abstract of the United States: 1960* (Washington: U.S Government Printing Office, 1960), p. 312. United States Department of Commerce, Bureau of the Census, *Census of Population: 1950,* Vol. I, (Washington: U.S. Government Printing Office, 1952), Part I, pp. 18-23.

10.   See, for instance: Aristotle, *Politics,* translated by Benjamin Jowett, (New York: Random House, Inc. 1943), esp. Books IV and V; Dahl and Lindblom, *op. cit.,* and Seymour Martin Lipset, *Political Man* (Garden City, New York: Doubleday & Company, 1960), esp. Chapter II, "Economic Development and Democracy."

11.   Robert T. Golembiewski, "A Taxonomic Approach to State Political Party Strength," *The Western Political Quarterly,* XI (1958), pp. 494-513.

12.   *E.g.,* James A. Robinson, *Congress and Foreign Policy-Making* (Homewood, Illinois: The Dorsey Press, 1962), pp. 168-190; Robinson, *The House Rules Committee* (Indianapolis: Bobbs-Merrill Co., 1963), Chapters IV-V.

13.   V.O. Key, Jr., *Southern Politics in State and Nation* (New York: Alfred A. Knopf, 1951), esp. pp. 298-314.

14.   Duane Lockard, *New England State Politics* (Princeton, New Jersey: The Princeton University Press, 1959), pp. 320-340.

15.   *Ibid.,* pp. 326-337.

16.   V.O. Key, *op. cit.;* Duncan MacRae, Jr., "The Relation between Roll Call Votes and Constituencies in the Massachusetts House of Representatives," *American Political Science Review,* XLVI (1952), pp. 1046-1055; Julius Turner, "Primary Elections as the Alternative to Party Competition in 'Safe Districts'," *Journal of Politics,* XX (1953), pp. 197-210; William J. Keefe, "Parties, Partisanship and Public Policy in the Pennsylvania Legislature," *American Political Science Review,* XLVII (1953), pp. 450-464; V.O. Key, Jr., *American State Politics* (New York: Alfred A. Knopf, 1956), Chapter 8; Austin Ranney and Willmoore Kendall, "The American Party System," *American Political Science Review,* XLVIII (1954), pp. 477-485; Joseph A. Schlesinger, "A Two-Dimensional Scheme for Classifying the States According to Degree of Interparty Competition," *American Political Science Review,* LIX (1955), pp. 1120-1128; Robert Golembiewski, *loc. cit.,* pp. 494-513; Lockard, *op. cit.,* Chapter 12; Joseph A. Schlesinger, "The Structure of Competition for Office in the American States," *Behavioral Science,* V (1960), pp. 197-210; William H. Standing and James A. Robinson, "Inter-Party Competition and Primary Contesting: The Case of Indiana," *American Political Science Review,* LII (1958), pp. 1066-1077.

17. Ranney and Kendall, *loc. cit.*, p. 478.

18. *Ibid.*, pp. 480-481.

19. Key (1956), *op. cit.*, p. 99.

20. Golembiewski, *loc. cit.*, p. 501.

21. We also consider competition only between the two major national political parties. Thus, the measure of competition does not account either for intra-party competition or the impact of minor third parties.

22. Ranney and Kendall, *loc. cit.*

23. Schlesinger, *loc. cit.*, (1955), pp. 1120-1123.

24. Golembiewski, *loc. cit.*, pp. 498-499.

25. Belle Zeller, *American State Legislatures* (New York: Thomas Y. Crowell, 1954), pp. 200-205.

26. See Golembiewski, *loc. cit.*, p. 298.

27. For a discussion of the stability and changes in American party identification see Angus Campbell, *et. al.*, *The American Voter* (New York: John Wiley & Sons, Inc., 1960), esp. pp. 149-167. Also see V.O. Key, Jr., "A Theory of Critical Elections," *Journal of Politics,* XVIII (1955), pp. 3-18, and Duncan MacRae, Jr., and James A. Meldrum, "Critical Elections in Illinois: 1885-1958," *American Political Science Review,* LIV (1960), pp. 669-683.

28. Key (1956), *op. cit.*, p. 99.

29. Ranney and Kendall, *op. cit.*, pp. 482-484.

30. Golembiewski, *loc. cit.*, pp. 499-500.

31. Schlesinger (1955), *loc. cit.*, pp. 1120-1128.

32. Schlesinger (1960), *loc. cit.*, p. 199.

33. See for example, E.E. Schattschneider, *Party Government* (New York: Farrar & Rinehart, 1942), Chapter 6.

34. These assumptions are based primarily on two-party systems. The mechanisms would be somewhat different for the various parties in a multi-party system.

35. The closeness of the vote was used in the measures of competition employed by Ranney and Kendall and Key. The percentage of the seats of the state legislature controlled by the minority was used by Golembiewski.

36.   Golembiewski and Schlesinger consider this dimension as part of their measurement devices.

37.   Golembiewski and Schlesinger also consider this dimension.

38.   See Key (1951), *op. cit.*, p. 309 and Lockard, *op. cit.*, pp. 326-327.

39.   The data upon which these rankings are based are taken from the Council of State Governments, *The Book of the States, 1960-1961,* Vol. XIII (1960), (Chicago: The Council of State Governments).

40.   Lipset, *op. cit.*, pp. 54-60.

41.   Data for these socio-economic measures were taken from Bureau of the Census, *Statistical Abstract of the United States: 1960* (Washington: U.S. Government Printing Office, 1960) and Bureau of the Census, *Census of Population: 1950, Vol I* (Washington: U.S. Government Printing Office, 1952).

42.   Key (1951), *op. cit.*, pp. 298-314, and Lockard, *op. cit.*, esp. pp. 320-340.

43.   *Ibid.,* p. 337.

44.   *Ibid.*

45.   Key, *op. cit.*, p. 307.

46.   *Ibid.*, p. 308.

47.   Golembiewski, *loc. cit.*, pp. 510-512.

48.   Lockard, *op. cit.*, p. 337.

49.   *Ibid.,* p. 9.

50.   Golembiewski, *loc. cit.*, p. 511.

EDUCATION POLICY

How State Legislators View the Problem of School Needs

LeRoy C. Ferguson

SOLUTIONS AND ACTIONS

Concern for the Problem

The introductory question in the education series (Table 3) was intended to produce a raw measure of the legislator's degree of affect or involvement with the school needs issue. The replies did not give us a very satisfactory measure for discriminating among the respondents, since more than three-fourths of them indicated that the matter of school needs was of "great concern" to them personally. We did, however, get some verification for our original assumption that this problem would be regarded as of major importance in each of the states in the study.

Although the great majority of the legislators in every state showed "great concern" for education, Table 3 shows that there were some interstate differences in the degree of concern expressed, and that California legislators were considerably more likely than those in Ohio to express "great concern". We shall see later that the legislators in these two states were also considerably different in their other attitudes toward educational problems. Table 3 also shows that the educational experts were more likely than other members to indicate that they felt "great concern" with regard to the school needs issue.

Reprinted from How *State Legislators View the Problem of School Needs* (Report to the United States Office of Education, Dept. of Health, Education and Welfare, 1960), pp. 5-17, 53-61; by permission of the author.

This article appears in abridged form; several tables are omitted.

Table 3   Degree of concern with school needs.

(Q. 30)   "Now I'd like to ask you some questions about the work of this session of the legislature. The issue of *school needs* is one almost every legislative session faces. Would you say that this particular matter is of great concern to you person- ally, of some concern, of little concern, or of no concern?"

	Great concern	Some concern	Little concern	No concern	Don't know can't say	Total
State						
California (N = 82) M	86%	11	3	—	—	100%
New Jersey (N = 64)	75%	22	3	—	—	100%
Ohio (N = 154)	73%	21	3	2	1	100%
Tennessee (N = 114)	80%	17	1	—	2	100%
Total (N = 414)	78%	18	2	1	1	100%
Educational Experts						
Self named educational experts (N = 81)	89%	8	1	1	1	100%
Educational experts named by 5% of chamber (N = 21)	90%	—	5	—	5	100%
Other legislators (N = 333)	75%	21	2	1	1	100%

Character of Perception of Problem

The next question in the education series was a wide open one where the legislators were asked to describe their own personal solutions for the general problem of school needs. In Table 4 we have presented a broad delineation of the ways in which they perceived the character of the problem. Since we knew that educational budgets were a major concern of all four of the state legislatures, we were not surprised to find that most of the legislators viewed the problem primar- ily in terms of finance. More than one-half of them mentioned *only* finances in explaining their personal solutions to the problem, but about one-third suggested

Table 4   Character of perception of school problem.

(Q. 31),   "Can you tell me what solution you would personally favor for this general problem?" (Or, if matter settled: "Can you tell me what solution you would personally have favored for this general problem?")

	California (N = 79)	New Jersey (N = 71)	Ohio (N = 155)	Tennessee (N = 113)	Total (N = 418)
Financial problem	94% [a]	85%	74%	82%	82%
Administrative problem	14	34	41	29	32
Curriculum problem	5	8	12	12	10
Other perception of school problem	1	8	6	4	5
Unable to analyze school problem	3	3	8	7	6

[a] Totals are more than 100% since some legislators characterized the problem in more than one way. The proportion of those interviewed who mentioned *only* a financial problem were: California, 84%; New Jersey, 51%; Ohio, 42%; and Tennessee, 55%; for all states combined, 55%.

administrative solutions, and a few (10%) were concerned with curriculum problems.

Included under the general category "financial" in Table 4 were all mentions of both sources (taxes, state and federal aid), and allocation of funds (teacher salaries, school construction), as well as general discussion of budgetary economy or expansion.

Under the category "administrative" were included solutions dealing with consolidation or reorganization, standardization of construction, teacher training, use of facilities, and control of educational programs. Most of those in the category "curriculum" advocated either retrenchment (more 3 R's; teach only fundamentals; less auto-driver training), or expansion (broaden curriculum, vocational guidance, special education). Proposals for consolidation, reorganization, expansion or retrenchment, were, of course, frequently discussed in terms of finance, in which case they were coded in both categories.

There were, of course, a few legislators who were unable to analyze the school problem, or who discussed the school problem but suggested no solution. There were also widely scattered, more or less exotic or esoteric solutions suggested, one of the more intriguing being that of the legislator who advocated "some type of birth control to cut down on the number of pupils". Another legislator proposed as a solution the abolition of the State Education Association and the State Board of Education.

While the most important thing to be noticed in Table 4 is the large proportion of legislators in *all four* states who were concerned with school finance, there were some important differences *among* the states in the manner in which legisla-

Table 5   Experts' perception of character of school problem.

	Self named educational experts (N = 79)	Educational experts named by 5% of the chamber (N = 20)	Other legislators (N = 339)
Financial problem	91%	95%	80%
Administrative problem	38	40	30
Curriculum problem	18	15	8
Other perception of school problem	3	—	6
Unable to analyze school problem	—	—	7
Characterized problem in more than one way	42	45	26

tors characterized the school needs problem. California legislators were more likely to mention finances than those in other states, and they (Californians) were also less likely than legislators in the other states to discuss the school problem in administrative terms. On the other hand a relatively large proportion of Ohio legislators mentioned administrative problems. One possible explanation for the fact that the Ohio legislators were somewhat more likely to mention administrative solutions and somewhat less likely to mention financial solutions was the fact that just prior to the 1957 session of the legislature a new program of state aid had gone into effect in that state.

The educational experts in the legislatures were similar to other members in the pattern of their perception of the school needs problem, in that they were primarily concerned with financial solutions. It can be seen in Table 5, however, that the experts were much more likely than other members to give a broad characterization to the problem. That is, the experts were likely to mention both financial *and* administrative, or financial *and* curriculum solutions, or a combination of all three.

Table 6 presents a more detailed picture of the various sources of school finance that were mentioned by the legislators who discussed the educational problem in those terms. In every state except Tennessee there were more who *advocated* new taxes (or tax increases) than there were who said that they *opposed* new taxes.

The state of New Jersey was the only one of the four states in the study that had neither a sales tax nor an income tax (California had both), and this probably helps explain why a considerably higher proportion of New Jersey legislators were willing to propose new taxes than in any of the other states.

State aid was much more likely to be mentioned in California than in the other states. This was apparently related to the fact that there was a surplus source

Table 6 Suggested solution: Source of finances.

	California (N = 79)	New Jersey (N = 71)	Ohio (N = 155)	Tennessee (N = 113)	Total (N = 418)
New taxes	13%	37%	18%	6%	17%
No new taxes	11	4	6	8	7
State aid (general reserve fund, surplus sources, etc.)	62	21	11	26	26
Federal aid	1	7	3	4	4
No federal aid	3	11	5	4	5
More local financial effort; local districts should help themselves, less state aid	6	14	16	18	14
Other sources	1	13	1	13	6

of money available at the time the interviews were being conducted. The Revenue Deficiency Fund ("rainy day fund") was the last of the money put aside for postwar contingencies by Governor Earl Warren during the war years when the state regularly had surplusses.

Even though the Tennessee legislators were less likely than those in any other state to suggest new taxes, they were second only to California in the likelihood of suggesting state aid as a source of school finance.

Out of the total group of legislators interviewed only nine per cent mentioned federal aid to education, and these were about equally divided for and against such action. A few said that they favored federal aid for school construction, but not for general operating purposes.

The California legislature had the smallest proportion of those who advocated less state aid or more local financial effort. This appears to be consistent with the California emphasis on state aid as a source of educational finance.

Among the other possible sources of income for schools mentioned by the legislators were state lotteries, racing, and other forms of legalized gambling. A few Tennesseans also favored state-owned liquor stores with the profits going for education.

The legislators' suggestions for the allocation of educational funds are shown in Table 7. More than one-fourth of the lawmakers advocated providing more money for teachers' salaries and 14% of them mentioned the need for more money for school construction.

The data suggest that Ohioans were less likely than those in other states to want more money allocated to either salaries or construction. The most striking interstate difference shown in Table 7, however, is the much higher proportion of Tennessee legislators who advocated more money for teachers' salaries. This is

Table 7   Suggested solution: Allocation of funds.

	California (N = 79)	New Jersey (N = 71)	Ohio (N = 155)	Tennessee (N = 113)	Total (N = 418)
More money for construction, capital outlays	18%	18%	10%	15%	14%
More money for teachers' salaries	18	23	14	51	26
More money for student scholarships	—	5	5	—	3

understandable in view of the fact that teacher salary scales are considerably lower in Tennessee than in the other three states, but it is not very consistent with the previous indication (Table 6) that very few Tennessee legislators proposed new taxes.

A few legislators in both New Jersey and Ohio suggested allocation of more money for student scholarships, and among the other allocation suggestions made in the various states were funds for parochial schools, paying teachers for summer work, and increased retirement benefits.

As has already been noted above (Table 4) relatively few of the legislators mentioned administrative or curriculum solutions to the school needs problem, however, those who did characterize the problem in this way covered a rather wide range of suggested solutions, most of which are shown in Table 8. The most frequently mentioned solution in this general area was administrative economy. Included in this category were such suggestions as "keep expenses in line with revenue", "cut out frills", use of larger classes, and elimination of free textbooks. Ohio legislators were more likely than those in other states to mention the administrative economy category, and they also were more likely to mention the desirability of school district consolidation.

A need for standardization and economy in school construction received some attention, particularly in New Jersey, and there were also suggestions for more efficient use of existing facilities, such as more hours of classes per day and summer sessions. A few of the legislators thought that colleges were doing an inadequate job of training teachers, and there were some feelings that tenure systems made it difficult to reward good teachers and get rid of unsatisfactory ones. In this general area of personnel there were also suggestions for the elimination of "unnecessary" supervisors.

Five per cent of the law-makers interviewed emphasized that they wanted to maintain local control of the schools, and a similar number gave some attention to curriculum expansion or retrenchment. Among the suggestions for retrenchment were "more 3 R's", "teach only fundamentals", and "less auto driver training". Those who wanted to broaden the curriculum mentioned such things as student counseling, vocational guidance, and various types of special education.

In both New Jersey and Ohio there were a few legislators who spoke of the need for developing the state institutions of higher learning. The need for further

Table 8   Suggested solutions: Administrative and curriculum.

	California (N = 79)	New Jersey (N = 71)	Ohio (N = 155)	Tennessee (N = 113)	Total (N = 418)
Administrative economy; cut out frills, no free texts, etc.	6%	10%	23%	4%	13%
Consolidation of school districts	4	—	17	3	8
Standardization of construction	1	14	3	—	4
More efficient use of existing facilities	—	4	5	6	4
Better teacher training	1	1	2	8	3
Relaxing of certification and tenure requirements for teachers	3	—	—	7	2
Streamline personnel, cut out unnecessary supervisors	—	1	6	—	2
Maintain local control	4	10	3	5	5
Curriculum retrenchment	1	3	3	5	3
Curriculum expansion	1	3	2	2	2
Develop and expand colleges and universities	—	6	7	1	4
Solution depends on further study	20	1	4	6	7

study of the problem of school needs was mentioned in every state, but Californians were considerably more likely than other legislators to say that a solution depended on such study.

Tables 4 through 8 have shown the substance of the various suggestions made by the legislators for solving the problem of school needs, classified according to subject matter covered in the replies to question 31 in the interview schedule. These same data are shown in Table 9 classified according to the general attitude toward education demonstrated in the legislators' replies to the question.

Table 9   Responses used to measure attitude toward education.

Favorable	Per cent giving response	Unfavorable	Per cent giving response
New taxes: sales tax; industrial property tax; real estate tax; severance tax; bond issue; etc.	17%	No new taxes	7%
		No further state aid, less state aid	2
State aid from surplus source: general revenue fund; rainy-day fund	11	No federal aid	5
State aid (particular source not specified)	15	More local financial effort; state aid only if local districts help themselves	6
Federal aid	4	Local districts should help themselves	6
More money for construction, capital outlays	14	More efficient use of existing facilities: summer sessions; more hours per day; etc.	4
More money for teachers' salaries	26		
More money for student scholarships	3	Streamlining top personnel: appointive boards; cut out unnecessary supervisory personnel; etc.	2
Consolidation of school districts: for greater efficiency; wider tax base; etc.	8		
		More economy: administrative economy; equitable distribution of available funds; keep expenses in line with revenue; cut out frills; cut down huge school districts; no free texts; larger classes; etc.	13
Better teaching training	3		
Curriculum expansion (broaden curriculum; vocational guidance; slow-learner groups; special training for crippled children; etc.)	2		
		Relaxation of certification and tenure requirements for teachers	2
Colleges: develop and expand state university system	2		
		Curriculum: retrenchment (more 3 R's; less auto driver training; teach only fundamentals)	3
Colleges: develop and expand junior or community colleges	2		

Since most of the subsequent questions in the interview schedule were stated in the context of the legislators' personal perceptions of a solution to the problem, we thought that a general measure of each legislator's attitude toward education would make the analysis of these other questions more meaningful.

Accordingly, the replies to question 31 were classified into three groups; (1) those favorable to education; (2) those unfavorable; and (3) those not indicating an attitudinal dimension. Classified as favorable were all references to the need for more taxes, state or federal aid, more money for construction and salaries, consolidation of school districts, and curriculum expansion. Among the replies classified as unfavorable were those opposing new taxes and state or federal aid, as well as proposals for administrative economy and curriculum retrenchment. A complete listing of the replies used in this classification is shown in Table 9.

Using this classification the legislators were then separated into four groups: (1) those who made only favorable remarks in reply to question 31; (2) those who made *both* favorable and unfavorable remarks (ambivalents); and (3) those who made *only* unfavorable remarks; and (4) those whose remarks had no attitudinal dimension (neutrals).

This is, of course, a rather crude measure of legislative attitudes toward education, which is limited by the open-ended nature of the question. The obvious fact that the legislators varied considerably in both articulateness and information on educational problems may have affected the classification. For example, the legislators who gave lengthy replies to the question were probably more likely to fall into the ambivalent category, and those who were less verbose may have been more likely to be classified as neutrals.

Similarly, since most of the legislators answered the open-ended question in terms of finance, most of the responses shown in Table 9, particularly those most frequently mentioned, refer to either sources or allocation of funds. In interpreting the use of this attitude measure in subsequent tables the reader should bear in mind that, for the most part, legislators classified as "favorable" to education were those who wanted to spend more money on schools, while those classified as "unfavorable" were, for the most part, advocates of economy.

It is possible that some educators or legislators might disagree with our subjective judgement as to which replies were "favorable" and which "unfavorable" to education. Several dimensions have been combined, and several not completely compatible objectives have been lumped together. Bearing in mind these limitations, we still think it reasonable to at least dichotomize between those legislators who advocated *expansion,* (more money for teacher salaries, school construction, colleges, specialized programs, etc.) and those who were for the *status quo,* (economy, no new taxes, and retrenchment — including those who, justifiably or not, insisted on more efficiency and self-help). We feel that the general measure of attitude toward education based on such a dichotomy provided a useful variable which helped us to interpret replies to other questions in the interview schedule.

It might have been preferable to have used a set of scale items or some other type of "forced answer" question to measure the legislators' general attitude toward education, but, as has been indicated before, at the time the questionnaire was designed we did not anticipate the use of the educational material in the manner that it is presented in this report.

The distribution of the legislators according to this measure of general attitude toward education is shown in Table 10. Of the entire group of legislators who were asked to give their personal solution to the problem of school needs, almost one-half gave replies that were entirely favorable to education, and the remainder were divided into three groups (ambivalent, unfavorable, and neutral) of approximately equal size. This distribution is consistent with the general impression from

Table 10 Attitude toward education by state, expertise, and degree of concern.

| | Attitude Toward Education | | | | |
	Favorable	Ambivalent	Unfavorable	Neutral	Total
State					
California (N = 79)	66%	11	13	10	100%
New Jersey (N = 71)	54%	21	8	17	100%
Ohio (N = 155)	30%	21	24	25	100%
Tennessee (N = 113)	44%	20	21	15	100%
Total (N = 418)	44%	19	19	18	100%
Experts					
Self named educational experts (N = 79)	51%	25	13	11	100%
Educational experts named by 5% of chamber (N = 20)	50%	25	15	10	100%
Other legislators (N = 339)	43%	17	20	20	100%
Degree of Concern for School Needs					
Great concern (N = 324)	48%	19	17	16	100%
Some concern (N = 74)	32%	22	23	23	100%

the interviewing experience that most state legislators have a favorable attitude toward education. We note in Table 10, however, that there were rather marked attitudinal differences among the four states in the study.

Less than one-third of the Ohio legislators expressed only favorable attitudes toward education, and they differed markedly in this regard from the legislators in each of the other three states. In California, on the other hand, almost two-thirds of those interviewed made only favorable remarks, considerably more than in any of the other three states.

In the unfavorable category, Ohio had a considerably higher proportion than either California or New Jersey, and there was also an important difference in this regard between these two states and Tennessee.

Some of the reasons for and possible implications of these interstate differences will be presented in the analysis that follows. We would be led to believe from these data that there might be some similarity between New Jersey and California in their approach to educational problems, and that these two states would differ considerably in this regard from both Ohio and Tennessee. We might also expect that in some cases there might be differences between Tennessee and Ohio. Table 10 also shows the relation of attitude toward education to degree of concern for the problem of school needs expressed in reply to question 30 (Table 3). Those legislators who said that they had "great" concern for the problem were considerably more likely to be favorable, and less likely to be unfavorable or neutral than those who indicated only "some" concern for the issue.

There were also differences in attitude toward education between the legislative educational experts and other members. It can be seen in Table 10 that the experts were more likely than other legislators to be favorable or ambivalent, and less likely to be unfavorable or neutral.

Action in Support of Proposed Solution

After the legislators had described their solutions to the school needs problem, they were asked what they had done, or expected to do to promote the solution that they favored. The types of action most frequently mentioned are shown in Table 11. More than 70% of those interviewed reported at least one action, over one-half of them mentioned more than one action, and one-third mentioned three or more.

It can be seen in Table 11 that the Tennessee legislators were considerably more likely than those in New Jersey and Ohio to report at least some activity. This appears to be a reflection of the fact that the major battle during the 1957 legislative session in Tennessee concerned the General Education Bill, and centered almost entirely on the issue of teacher salary increases.

The relatively large proportion (38%) of Ohio legislators who reported no action may possibly be due to the larger size of that legislature, and it may also have been related to the fact that there were no major educational matters before the 1957 session of that legislature. The fact that over one-third of the New Jersey members also reported no individual activity is probably a reflection of the power of the majority caucuses which controlled all activity in the New Jersey Legislature and left relatively little room for meaningful activity on the part of individual members.

With regard to the specific activities reported, the New Jersey legislators were considerably more likely than California and Tennessee members, and somewhat more likely than Ohioans, to say that they had authored or sponsored a particular bill. The proportions in each legislature who reported that they had worked for their solutions in committee gave an accurate reflection of the relative impor-

Table 11   Type of action on school needs by state.

(Q. 32a) "Just what have you done, or what do you still expect to do, to promote the solution you favor in this school needs matter?"

	California (N = 79)	New Jersey (N = 66)	Ohio (N = 154)	Tennessee (N = 113)	Total (N = 412)
No action	23%	35%	38%	16%	29%
Author/sponsor particular bill	15	35	25	20	26
Work for solution in committee	46	14	42	30	35
Speak for solution on floor	39	12	30	31	35
Offer amendments favoring solution	13	—	18	26	16
Try to convince other members in private	61	26	45	73	53
Seek support for solution outside legislature	39	35	32	48	39
More than one action	60	36	50	65	54

tance of the committee systems in the four legislatures. California and Ohio legislators were much more likely than those in Tennessee and New Jersey to report committee activity, and there was also considerable difference in this regard between the latter two states, with New Jersey members reporting the least amount of committee activity.

The previously mentioned power of the majority caucus in New Jersey also appears to be reflected in the fact that legislators there were less likely than those in other states to report that they had spoken for their solution on the floor or offered amendments. New Jersey legislators were much less likely than those in the other three states to say that they had tried to convince other members in private, and in this regard there was also considerable difference among the other three states with the largest amount of "private convincing" reported in Tennessee. The importance of the education issue in the 1957 session is further indicated by the fact that Tennesseans were also more likely than those in the other states to report that they had worked for their solutions outside the legislature.

Table 12 Type of action on school needs by attitude and expertise.

(Q. 32a.) "Just what have you done, or what do you still expect to do, to promote the solution you favor in this school needs matter?"

| | Attitude Toward Education | | | | Experts | | |
	Favorable (N = 185)	Ambivalent (N = 77)	Unfavorable (N = 76)	Neutral (N = 68)	Self-named educational experts (N = 78)	Educational experts named by 5% of chamber (N = 21)	Other legislators (N = 334)
No action	21%	23%	32%	51%	12%	5%	33%
Author/sponsor particular bill	28	23	17	19	46	48	18
Work for solution in committee	39	42	32	16	68	62	27
Speak for solution on floor	36	31	24	18	49	67	25
Offer amendments favoring solution	16	19	18	9	24	14	14
Try to convince other members in private	58	57	55	32	73	76	48
Seek support for solution outside legislature	44	43	42	21	46	38	37
More than one action	60	57	55	32	83	81	47

The relation of attitude toward education to activities reported is shown in Table 12. We are not surprised to note in this table that those legislators who were neutral in attitude toward education were much less likely than those in other attitudinal categories to report any activity in support of their solutions. There was little difference in the pattern of activities reported by those in the favorable and ambivalent categories, but both of these categories were likely to report more activity than those who were classified as unfavorable to education. As might have been expected, Table 12 also shows that the educational experts reported much more activity than other members, and the leadership position of the experts named by other members is demonstrated by the fact that over two-thirds of this category reported that they had spoken for their solution on the floor. . . .

CORRELATES OF ATTITUDE TOWARD EDUCATION

The purpose of this section of the report is to discuss some of the correlates of the measure of attitude toward education which was first presented in Part I and used as interpretive variable throughout the report. In spite of the fact that this was a very crude attitudinal measure, it proved to be of considerable value in analyzing the legislators, replies to several of the questions on the school needs issue, and we have also shown in Part IV that there was some relation between the attitudes indicated by this measure and the votes of the legislators as recorded in the legislative journals.

This led us to believe that it would be desirable to try to determine some of the independent variables that were related to educational attitude. This was made possible by the fact that we had already assembled a considerable amount of data on the personal, social, economic, and ideological characteristics of each individual legislator in the study.

Age

In Tables 37 through 43, we have shown some of these independent variables that appeared to have some relation to the attitude expressed toward education in the legislators' replies to question 31. The first of these that was considered was age. We had no very strong expectation that this variable would be related to educational attitude, but it did appear plausible to expect that younger legislators, who might be more likely to have children in school, would be favorable to educational expansion. This expectation was borne out, however, in only one of the states, New Jersey, where legislators over 45 were rather clearly *less* likely than younger members to be favorable. In Ohio and Tennessee, however, Table 37 shows that the legislators who were over 45 were *more* likely to be found in the favorable category. There were equal proportions of older and younger members in the favorable category in California, but the younger Californians had a higher percentage in the unfavorable category. We are at a loss to explain these interstate differences, or, for that matter, the fact that there should be *any* relation between age and attitude toward education, except, as is indicated below that legislative tenure and experience did have some relation to attitude.

Table 37   Relation of age to legislators' attitude toward education.

| Age | Attitude Toward Education | | | | |
	Favorable	Ambivalent	Unfavorable	Neutral	Total
Four state total					
40 and under (N = 128)	37%	23	20	20	100%
41–55 (N = 181)	47%	20	18	15	100%
Over 55 (N = 108)	49%	12	19	20	100%
California					
45 and under (N = 30)	66%	10	17	7	100%
Over 45 (N = 49)	66%	12	10	12	100%
New Jersey					
45 and under (N = 35)	63%	20	6	11	100%
Over 45 (N = 36)	45%	22	11	22	100%
Ohio					
45 and under (N = 68)	24%	29	21	26	100%
Over 45 (N = 87)	34%	14	28	24	100%
Tennessee					
45 and under (N = 60)	33%	22	27	18	100%
Over 45 (N = 52)	56%	17	15	12	100%

Education

The legislators in our study were a quite highly educated group compared to the total population, and since most of them had had at least some college training, the only very meaningful way of classifying them according to education was by dividing them into those who were college graduates and those whose education had not reached that level. We had expected that the college graduates would be more aware of the advantages of education and thus more likely to be favorable on the school needs issue. The data shown in Table 38, however, indicate that in Ohio and Tennessee the college graduates were considerably less likely than those with less education to be found in the favorable category. The relation between amount of education and attitude on the school needs issue is less apparent in California and New Jersey, but it appears that in the former state the college graduates were more likely to be ambivalent, and in the latter state they were more likely to be either ambivalent or unfavorable and less likely to be neutral. These data force us to revise our original hypothesis and come to the tentative conclusion that legislators who have had less educational opportunity are more likely than those who were college graduates to be favorable in their attitudes on the issue of school needs. Although the proportion of legislators who had not been to college at all was too small to make possible a very conclusive analysis, the data suggested that this group was even more likely to have a favorable attitude on school needs than those who had been to college but had not graduated.

Table 38   Relation of amount of education to legislators' attitude toward education.

Amount of Education	Attitude Toward Education				
	Favorable	Ambivalent	Unfavorable	Neutral	Total
Four state total					
Less than completed college (N = 171)	50%	16	16	18	100%
College graduate (N = 247)	41%	20	21	18	100%
California					
Less than completed college (N = 31)	68%	6	16	10	100%
College graduate (N = 48)	65%	15	10	10	100%
New Jersey					
Less than completed college (N = 19)	53%	16	5	26	100%
College graduate (N = 52)	54%	23	10	13	100%
Ohio					
Less than completed college (N = 63)	36%	19	21	24	100%
College graduate (N = 92)	25%	22	27	26	100%
Tennessee					
Less than completed college (N = 58)	53%	19	14	14	100%
College graduate (N = 55)	35%	20	29	16	100%

Occupation

There were not enough legislators in any single occupation except law to make a meaningful analysis within each individual state on any other basis except a comparison of law and all other occupations. We had expected that, because of the rigorous educational requirements of their profession, lawyers might be more likely to be favorable to education than other occupations, but this proved to be the case only in New Jersey. Lawyer-legislators in California were only slightly more likely than other California lawmakers to take a favorable position, and in both Ohio and Tennessee the lawyers were definitely less likely than other occupa-

tional groups to be found in the favorable category. We have presented the attitude data for each state in Table 39 for law, business, and other occupations, but
we are not encouraged to do very much in the way of generalizing about the difference in educational attitude between law and business when we note in the four
state total that there were quite wide differences among the various specific business occupations in their attitudes on the school needs issue. These four state
totals show that legislators in the transportation and communication industry were
much more likely to be favorable to education than those who were in banking, insurance, and real estate.

Table 39   Relation of occupation to legislators' attitude toward education.

	Attitude Toward Education				
Occupation	*Favorable*	*Ambivalent*	*Unfavorable*	*Neutral*	*Total*
Four state total					
Agriculture (N = 49)	47%	14	20	19	100%
Wholesale & retail trade (N = 46)	54%	20	13	13	100%
Banking, insurance, real estate (N = 40)	40%	15	25	20	100%
Transportation & com- munication (N = 21)	57%	19	14	10	100%
Other business occupa- tions (N = 47)	38%	17	19	26	100%
Law (N = 158)	41%	20	19	20	100%
Other professions (N = 30)	54%	23	20	3	100%
All other occupations (N = 27)	44%	19	15	22	100%
California					
Business (N = 27)	59%	—	30	11	100%
Law (N = 25)	68%	20	4	8	100%
Other occupations (N = 27)	70%	15	4	11	100%
New Jersey					
Business (N = 17)	41%	29	12	18	100%
Law (N = 39)	61%	18	8	13	100%
Other occupations (N = 15)	47%	20	6	27	100%
Ohio					
Business (N = 61)	39%	18	15	28	100%
Law (N = 57)	25%	30	25	20	100%
Other occupations (N = 37)	22%	24	41	13	100%
Tennessee					
Business (N = 49)	49%	22	18	11	100%
Law (N = 37)	24%	22	32	22	100%
Other occupations (N = 27)	63%	11	11	15	100%

Although there were not enough agricultural legislators in any single state to make a very meaningful analysis of their educational attitudes, the data suggested that this occupational group was more likely to be favorable than unfavorable to education in California and Tennessee, but that the reverse held true in Ohio. In short, we are forced to conclude that, if there is any relation between occupation and legislative attitude on the issue of school needs, this relation is likely to vary considerably with the individual state situation.

Table 40   Relation of place of residence to attitude toward education.

Urban–Rural Nature of County of Residence	Attitude Toward Education				
	Favorable	*Ambivalent*	*Unfavorable*	*Neutral*	*Total*
Four state total (N = 418)					
Metropolitan areas (N = 207)	44%	16	18	22	100%
Non-metropolitan areas					
Less than 30% rural-farm (N = 110)	53%	20	12	15	100%
30% to 49% rural-farm (N = 44)	23%	25	38	14	100%
50% or more rural-farm (N = 57)	46%	20	20	14	100%
California					
Metropolitan areas (N = 49)	63%	10	19	8	100%
Non-metropolitan areas (N = 30)	70%	13	4	13	100%
New Jersey					
Metropolitan areas (N = 57)	53%	19	9	19	100%
Non-metropolitan areas (N = 14)	57%	29	7	7	100%
Ohio					
Metropolitan areas (N = 75)	27%	19	23	31	100%
Non-metropolitan areas					
Less than 30% rural-farm (N = 51)	41%	19	18	22	100%
30% or more rural-farm (N = 29)	17%	28	38	17	100%
Tennessee					
Metropolitan areas (N = 26)	42%	12	19	27	100%
Non-metropolitan areas					
Less than 50% rural-farm (N = 43)	33%	25	33	9	100%
50% or more rural-farm (N = 44)	57%	18	11	14	100%

Urban-Rural Nature of Home County

Table 40 shows the relation of the nature of the county in which the legislators resided to attitudes on the school needs issue. In this case we had expected that legislators who lived in counties located in metropolitan areas might be less sensitive to the problem because of the fact that the issue of school needs appears to be somewhat less critical in large urban centers than in rural sections of the country. This tentative hypothesis was given some support by the data shown in Table 40, for it can be seen that in each of the four states the legislators who lived in metropolitan areas were somewhat less likely to have a favorable attitude to education than those who lived elsewhere.

There were not enough legislators who lived outside metropolitan areas in California and New Jersey to do a further analysis in those states, but when we divided the non-metropolitan Tennessee and Ohio legislators according to the percentage of rural-farm population in their home counties the results, as shown in Table 40, were quite different. In Tennessee the legislators who came from non-metropolitan areas with less than 50% rural-farm population were even less likely to be favorable (and more likely to be unfavorable) than those who resided in metropolitan areas. The legislators from the "most rural" (50% or more rural-farm) areas of Tennessee, however, were much more likely than other members to take a favorable position on the school needs issue.

Since Ohio was relatively "less rural" than Tennessee, it was necessary to

Table 41   Relation of ideology to legislators' attitude toward education.

Ideology	Attitude Toward Education				
	Favorable	Ambivalent	Unfavorable	Neutral	Total
Four state total					
Liberals (N = 248)	50%	18	14	18	100%
Conservatives (N = 166)	35%	20	27	18	100%
California					
Liberals (N = 58)	67%	14	9	10	100%
Conservatives (N = 20)	60%	5	25	10	100%
New Jersey					
Liberals (N = 44)	59%	16	9	16	100%
Conservatives (N = 27)	44%	30	7	19	100%
Ohio					
Liberals (N = 78)	38%	20	16	26	100%
Conservatives (N = 76)	20%	22	33	25	100%
Tennessee					
Liberals (N = 68)	44%	20	18	18	100%
Conservatives (N = 43)	44%	19	28	9	100%

use a different breaking point for analysis purposes in that state, but the data rather clearly show that, in contrast to Tennessee, the Ohio lawmakers from the "most rural" counties (30% or more rural-farm) were considerably *less* likely to be favorable (and more likely to be unfavorable) than other members. This difference between Tennessee and Ohio is consistent with the previously noted tendency for agricultural legislators to be more favorable in the former state and less so in the latter.

Ideology

On the basis of their responses to a three item "ideology scale" it was possible to divide the legislators into two categories that we labeled "Liberals" and

Table 42   Relation of party to legislators' attitude toward education.

Party	Attitude Toward Education				
	Favorable	*Ambivalent*	*Unfavorable*	*Neutral*	*Total*
Four state total					
Democrats (N = 203)	50%	18	18	14	100%
Republicans (N = 215)	40%	19	19	22	100%
California					
Democrats (N = 38)	76%	16	5	3	100%
Republicans (N = 41)	56%	7	20	17	100%
New Jersey					
Democrats (N = 25)	56%	16	8	20	100%
Republicans (N = 46)	52%	24	9	15	100%
Ohio					
Democrats (N = 49)	43%	20	20	17	100%
Republicans (N = 106)	24%	21	26	29	100%
Tennessee					
Democrats (N = 91)	41%	18	25	16	100%
Republicans (N = 22)	59%	27	5	9	100%
Party Orientation					
Democrats					
Weak (N = 69)	48%	13	23	16	100%
Moderate (N = 53)	51%	21	15	13	100%
Regular (N = 71)	52%	21	14	13	100%
Republicans					
Weak (N = 51)	53%	21	10	16	100%
Moderate (N = 48)	39%	19	21	21	100%
Regular (N = 114)	33%	19	22	26	100%

"Conservatives". Our measure was a rather crude one, and there is a serious possibility of terminological confusion in trying to interpret it, but for whatever they may be worth we have presented the data in Table 41 which show that in three of the four states in the study the "Liberal" legislators were more likely than the "Conservatives" to take a favorable position. In Tennessee the Liberal and Conservative groups contained equal proportions of legislators favorable to education, but the Conservatives were more likely to be unfavorable, while the Liberals were more likely to be ambivalent or neutral.

Party

It will be recalled from the discussion of Table 24 that most of the legislators did not perceive any differences between legislative members of the two major political parties on the school needs issue. Our analysis indicates, however, that there were differences between Republicans and Democrats in the attitudes they expressed in discussing this issue. Table 42 shows that Democrats were slightly more likely to be favorable to education in New Jersey, and much more likely to express a favorable attitude in the states of California and Ohio. In Tennessee, on the other hand, it appears that the Republicans were more likely than the Democrats to take a favorable position on the school needs issue.

Table 42 also gives an indication of the relation of the legislators' party orientations to their educational attitudes. It will be recalled that party orientation was previously discussed in connection with Table 20. In this case the data indicate that the "Regular" Democrats were more likely than Democrats with a "Weak" party orientation to take a favorable position. In the Republican Party, however, it was the Weak Party Men who were more likely to be favorable, while the Regular Republicans were more likely to take an unfavorable position on the school needs issue. This appears to substantiate the finding that educational attitude is related to ideology, ranging the members from conservative to liberal.

Legislative Experience

There was considerable variation in the tenure and turnover of the four legislatures in our study, and for this reason we have shown the data on legislative experience in Table 43 with the legislators in each state divided into those with more and those with less than the median number of years of legislative experience. In the case of Tennessee there was such a high proportion of new members in the legislature, that the only meaningful way of dividing them was into those who had any prior service and those who were serving their first terms.

We had expected that the members with longer experience in trying to deal with the problem might be more likely than those with less experience to take a favorable position on the school needs issue. While the differences are not large, this is shown to be the case in all four of the states. It should be pointed out, however, that in most cases the legislators with less experience were more likely to be ambivalent or neutral rather than unfavorably inclined on the school needs issue.

Unrelated Variables

In concluding this section it seems appropriate to mention some of the variables that were shown not to be related to attitude on the school needs issue, ac-

Table 43 Relation of legislative experience to legislators' attitude toward education.

Experience in the Legislature	Attitude Toward Education				
	Favorable	Ambivalent	Unfavorable	Neutral	Total
California					
Five years or less (N = 42)	62%	17	12	9	100%
Over five years (N = 37)	70%	5	14	11	100%
New Jersey					
Three years or less (N = 38)	50%	24	8	18	100%
Over three years (N = 33)	58%	18	9	15	100%
Ohio					
Four years or less (N = 82)	26%	21	26	27	100%
Over four years (N = 73)	35%	19	23	23	100%
Tennessee					
No previous experience (N = 50)	42%	24	16	18	100%
Two or more years (N = 63)	46%	16	25	13	100%

cording to our analysis. Among the variables tested and found to have no such relation were income, previous governmental experience, and place of upbringing. Educational attitudes were also found to be unrelated to representational roles, interest group roles, and state-district orientation. There was a suggestion in the data that Catholic legislators in New Jersey might be less likely than other members to be favorable, and more likely to be neutral, on the school needs issue, but there was definitely no relation between religion and educational attitude in Ohio, and in California out of nine Catholic legislators interviewed, eight expressed entirely favorable attitudes and one was ambivalent. . . .

FISCAL POLICY

Interstate Variation in State and Local Government Expenditures

Glenn W. Fisher

There are wide variations in the level of expenditure of state and local governments in the United States. These variations are the result of various political decisions — current decisions and decisions of the past which have become embodied in constitutions, charters, statutes, ordinances, and, more informally, in customary practices and procedures.

A number of the factors which create demand for and resistance to governmental expenditure can be quantified in such a way as to make possible a study of the association which exists between a given factor and the level of expenditure for a particular purpose. Solomon Fabricant used multiple correlation analysis to study the relationship between three of these factors — per capita income, population density, and per cent of population living in urban places — and interstate variations in the level of 1942 operating expenditure of state and local governments.[1] These three variables explained 72 per cent of the interstate variation in per capita operating expenditures and from 29 to 85 per cent of the variation in expenditure for the various functions analyzed.[2]

This writer used the same variables to study 1957 expenditures, including capital outlay. The results were generally similar to those of Fabricant except that the percentage of variation explained was somewhat lower.[3]

Using a somewhat different functional classification of expenditures, Seymour Sacks and his associates analyzed 1960 expenditure data utilizing the same three variables plus per capita state aid and per capita federal aid.[4] The addition of of these two variables increased the percentage of variation explained, especially in the case of highway and welfare expenditure where the coefficients of multiple

Reprinted from *National Tax Journal,* Vol 17 (March, 1964), pp. 57-74 by permission of the publisher.

Table 1   Variation in per capita state and local government expenditure, 1960.

Expenditure Category	Range High	Low	Median	Mean $\bar{x}$	Standard Deviation s	Coefficient of Variation $\frac{s}{\bar{x}}(100)$
Total general expenditure	$454.22	$183.11	$288.42	$289.34	$59.22	20.5
Total general expenditure less federal grants	347.22	145.19	239.56	239.14	50.36	21.1
Education	171.99	70.00	104.32	106.32	24.96	23.5
Local schools	134.04	53.30	83.53	84.24	18.72	22.2
Institutions of higher education	37.71	5.84	18.56	19.62	7.97	40.6
Highways	140.06	32.46	55.05	60.42	21.20	35.1
Public welfare	55.17	8.57	22.35	23.71	9.11	38.4
Health and hospitals	36.11	10.77	18.00	18.95	5.81	30.7
Police	16.63	4.53	8.16	8.76	3.10	35.4
Local fire protection	11.59	1.74	3.77	4.60	2.21	48.0
Sewers, sewage disposal and other sanitation	16.66	2.57	8.24	8.34	3.24	38.8
General control	25.35	6.40	11.48	11.82	3.67	31.0
Interest on general debt and all other expenditure	121.03	22.06	40.64	46.42	20.07	43.2

Source: Per capita expenditure data from U.S. Census Bureau, *Governmental Finances in 1960* (Washington, D.C., September 19, 1961).

Table 2   Simple correlation coefficients, per capita state and local government expenditure categories.

	Local Schools	Higher Education	Highways	Public Welfare	Health and Hospitals	Police	Fire	Sewerage and Sanitation	General Control	Interest and Other
Local schools	. . .	.662 [a]	.322 [a]	.080	.397 [a]	.450 [a]	.165	.388 [a]	.681 [a]	.542 [a]
Higher Education	.662 [a]	. . . .	.488 [a]	.186	-.012	-.051	-.228	-.038	.424 [a]	.158
Highways	.322 [a]	.488 [a]	. . .	-.032	.010	-.220	-.225	.049	.274	.021
Public welfare	.080	.186	-.032	. . .	-.020	.014	.104	-.110	.055	-.013
Health and hospitals	.397 [a]	-.012	.010	-.020	. . .	.753 [a]	.617 [a]	.496 [a]	.601 [a]	.649 [a]
Police	.450 [a]	-.051	-.220	.014	.753 [a]	. . .	.801 [a]	.513 [a]	.673 [a]	.735 [a]
Fire	.165	-.228	-.225	.104	.617 [a]	.801 [a]	. . .	.429 [a]	.461 [a]	.527 [a]
Sewerage and sanitation	.388 [a]	-.038	.049	-.110	.496 [a]	.513 [a]	.429 [a]	. . .	.307 [a]	.392 [a]
General control	.681 [a]	.424 [a]	.274	.055	.601 [a]	.673 [a]	.461 [a]	.307 [a]	. . .	.825 [a]
Interest and other	.542 [a]	.158	.021	-.013	.649 [a]	.735 [a]	.527 [a]	.392 [a]	.825 [a]	. . .

[a] Significant at .05 level.

determination increased several fold, but the statistical procedures used over-state the importance of federal aid as a cause of variation in expenditure.

This article is a report on an attempt to explain a greater percentage of 1960 variation by expanding the number of variables and to indicate the relative importance of the variables used. Multiple-partial coefficients are computed to indicate the relative importance of certain variables considered as a group.

"Level of expenditure" in a given state is defined to be the per capita state and local government general expenditure in that state as reported by the U.S. Census Bureau. This figure, of course, represents an "average" which is determined by the expenditures of hundreds of local governments in each state as well as by the expenditures of the state government itself. Expenditure for several functional categories as well as total general expenditure have been analyzed.

It is important to note that multiple correlation shows the degree of association. It does not, in itself, prove that variation in the independent variables causes variation in the dependent variable (expenditure). There are undoubtedly complicated interactions among the independent variables and there may well be significant "feedback" effects whereby variations in expenditure affect the independent variables. Nevertheless, this type of analysis can be very useful if care is taken to exclude variables which are likely to be strongly affected by the level of expenditure.

EXTENT OF VARIATION

Table 1 summarizes the variation in per capita state and local expenditure that existed in 1960. The categories of expenditure are those of the U.S. Census Bureau except that some of the categories have been combined. Specifically, sewerage and sewerage disposal has been combined with other sanitation while interest on general debt has been combined with all other expenditure. The second expenditure category, total general expenditure less federal grants, provides a close approximation of the sums spent by state and local governments from revenue raised from state and local government sources.

The range of expenditure for thirteen expenditure categories is indicated by the high and low expenditure figure. Two measures of central tendency, the mean and the median, are provided. Further indications of the amount of state-to-state variation are provided by the standard deviation and the coefficient of variation. The latter measure is useful because it makes it possible to compare the amount of variation in the different expenditure categories even though the magnitudes involved are different.

All of the functional categories of expenditure show greater coefficients of variation than does general expenditure. The greatest variation is in expenditure for local fire protection. The catch-all category, interest on general debt and all other general expenditure, shows the second greatest variation. Other categories for which variation are great include higher education, public welfare and sewerage disposal and sanitation. The functional category with the smallest variation is local schools.

Table 2 shows the correlation which exists between expenditures for each pair of functional categories. These data indicate the extent to which per capita expenditures for the various functional categories vary in a similar fashion from state to state.[5] Examination reveals that some functions show almost no correlation with other functions. For example, expenditure for public welfare is not significantly correlated with expenditure for any other function.[6] Local schools expenditure, on the other hand, is significantly correlated with expenditures for all the other categories except public welfare and fire protection.

It is also worthy of note that expenditures for the following categories are significantly correlated with each other:

> Health and hospitals
> Police
> Local fire protection
> Sewerage and sanitation
> General control
> Interest and others

The first four of these are of a kind that are sometimes designated as "municipal-type" functions. It would be reasonable to expect that expenditures for these functions are similarly correlated with economic and demographic factors.

Although several pairs of expenditure categories are shown in Table 2 to be significantly correlated, the correlation coefficients are low enough to suggest that the factors which affect the level of expenditure for various purposes operate rather differently. In other words, to explain satisfactorily the differences in the level of expenditures in the states it will be necessary to examine each functional category separately.

INDEPENDENT VARIABLES

Twelve independent variables were used in the preliminary stages of the analysis. Each was selected because it had been shown to be of some significance in previous studies or because, in the judgment of the writer, there was logical reason for expecting it to be related to expenditure in some way. The variables were all "general" in the sense that no variables were used which would logically be related to expenditures for one or two functions but not to any others.

The original list of 12 variables included several which overlapped other variables in the sense that each was highly correlated and appears to measure much the same thing. In the preliminary analysis five of the overlapping variables were dropped.[7] No hard and fast statistical test for determining which variables to drop was used, although both the size of the beta coefficients and the extent to which dropping a variable reduced the coefficient of multiple correlation were important considerations. Other considerations included a preference for fewer variables. Thus, if one variable yielded a coefficient of correlation which was almost as high as that yielded when two variables were substituted, the single variable was retained.[8]

The independent variables were grouped into three divisions. These are designated as economic, demographic and socio-political. The designations indicate not only the nature of the data but also indicate something about the presumed effect of the variables. Grouping the variables in this way represents somewhat of an oversimplification, but, at the same time, provides some useful insights.

Economic Variables

Five variables which might be classified as economic were utilized in the preliminary analysis. They were:

(1) Per capita personal income, 1959.
(2) Median income of families, 1959.
(3) Per cent of families with income under $2,000, 1959.
(4) Per capita yield of representative property tax, 1960, as per cent of U.S. average.
(5) Per capita yield of representative tax system, 1960, as per cent of U.S. average.

It has long been recognized that governmental expenditure is closely related to the income level of the state. In fact, Fabricant's study, apparently the first to use multiple-correlation analysis to study state-to-state variation in the level of governmental expenditure, revealed that income was far more important than urbanization and density of population in accounting for 1942 interstate differences.[9] Presumably the relationship between the level of income and the level of governmental expenditure comes about primarily because income represents taxpaying ability. It would be expected that persons with higher incomes would desire that the governmental units serving them provide a higher level of services. Economic factors may, however, affect governmental expenditure in other ways. High income may be associated with less need for certain types of services and thus depress expenditure for these purposes. Also, the level and distribution of income may, in the long run, affect attitudes toward government and governmental expenditure.

Median income of families, obtained from 1960 population census is probably a better indicator of the economic well-being of the typical resident of a state than is per capita income. The existence of a few very high income persons in a state would substantially raise the per capita income figure but would have little effect upon the median income. These high incomes, of course, represent taxpaying ability and, to the extent that the tax system of the state is able to tap that income, may affect the level of government expenditure. There is a rather high (.93) correlation between these measures of "average" income.

The third economic variable, per cent of families with income under $2,000, has not commonly been used in comparative expenditure analysis. It was added to the list of economic variables in the belief that the existence of a large number of low income persons would generally exert downward pressure on government expenditure, but, at the same time would result in greater "need" for certain specific expenditures such as public welfare. This measure is negatively correlated with per capita income (-.85) and with median income (-.93).

The fourth and fifth variables are taken from a recent report of the Advisory Commission on Intergovernmental Relations.[10] Per capita yield of a representative property tax is an estimate of the amount of revenue which would be produced if each state levied a "representative" tax upon property assessed at a uniform percentage of true value. This measure produces results which differ considerably from those obtained from more commonly used measures of tax capacity. In particular, the yield of the representative property tax is relatively a great deal higher in several western agricultural states than is the yield of income or sales-oriented taxes. Yield of representative property tax is not highly correlated with either per capita income (.41) or median income (.40).

The final economic variable to be considered was the Advisory Commission's index of the yield of a representative tax system. In computing this index the Advisory Commission developed a hypothetical tax system which was intended to be representative of tax practice now prevailing in the majority of states. Any tax which is employed by states containing more than half the nation's population or containing more than one-half of the potential tax base of a given tax was included in the system. The relationships between yield of a representative tax system and the other economic variables is indicated by the following coefficients of correlation:

Per capita personal income, 1959	.58
Median income of families, 1959	.53
Per cent of families with less than $2,000 income, 1959	-.60
Yield of representative property tax, 1960, as per cent of U.S. average	.96

The high correlation between the yield of the representative tax system and yield of the representative property tax results, in part, from the fact that the yield of the representative property tax makes up 43.6 per cent of the yield of the representative tax system.

After running correlation with several combinations of the economic variables it was decided to drop all economic variables except per cent of families with less than $2,000 income and yield of a representative tax system. Multiple correlation coefficients with all twelve variables and with the three economic variables excluded were:

	Included	Excluded
Total expenditure	.84	.82
Total expenditure — less federal	.84	.83
Education	.86	.81
Local schools	.85	.82
Higher education	.85	.78
Highways	.90	.88
Welfare	.64	.49
Health and hospitals	.72	.65
Police	.91	.90
Local fire	.88	.87
Sewerage and sanitation	.70	.67
General control	.79	.79
Interest and other	.74	.73

In the case of most functions, the two remaining economic variables result in correlation coefficients almost as high as do the five. In addition the two remaining variables overlap to a limited extent so that logical analysis of the reasons for the observed correlations is facilitated.

Demographic Variables

It is widely assumed that density of population, the distribution of population and changes in population influence the level of government spending. Presumably, the need for certain types of governmental services is increased when population is concentrated while sparsity of population increases the cost of certain other governmental services.

No single statistical series can adequately describe the spacial distribution of population in a given state. As a result, five variables relating to demographic factors were utilized in the preliminary analysis. They were:

(6) Population per square mile, 1960.

(7) Per cent of population living in urban places outside Standard Metropolitan Statistical Areas, 1960.

(8) Per cent of population in Standard Metropolitan Statistical Areas, 1960.

(9) Per cent of population in urban places, 1960.

(10) Per cent increase in population, 1950-1960.

Preliminary analysis indicated that separating the per cent of urban population into those living in metropolitan areas and those living outside metropolitan areas added little to the level of correlation obtained. As a result, variables 7 and 8 were dropped and variable 9, previously widely used in comparative tax and expenditure studies, was retained.

Socio-Political Variables

Few attempts have been made to quantify social or political factors as they affect the level of governmental expenditure. A recent exception is an attempt made by Professor John Fenton to determine whether or not the degree of competition between the major political parties has a significant effect on governmental spending. In a paper read at the annual meeting of the American Political Science Association in 1962, Professor Fenton reported on an attempt to test the hypothesis that two-party competition leads to governmental action addressed to the needs of the less well-to-do of the society. Specifically, he constructed an index of two-party competition which, along with per capita income and urbanization, were correlated with the following dependent variables:

(1) Per capita welfare expenditure, less federal grants.

(2) Per recipient aid to dependent children payments.

(3) Per pupil expenditure for education.

(4) Per capita general expenditure less federal grants.

Professor Fenton concludes that the data tend to support the hypothesis but that the degree of correspondence is not as great as might be expected and that the two-party competition has little or no significance with respect to overall expenditure. Professor Fenton's index is included among the variables used in this project to see whether or not two-party competition is important in explaining per capita expenditures for various functions when the number of economic and demographic variables is expanded from the two used by Professor Fenton.[11]

"Percent of population over 25 with less than 5 years schooling" was used in an earlier study of welfare expenditure conducted by the writer in the expectation that there would be a relationship between the high levels of illiteracy and the number of recipients of public assistance. Instead, it was found that there is a high negative correlation between this variable and the average payment to welfare recipients, even when such economic variables as per cent of families with less than $2,000 income have been taken into account.[12] This rather surprising result led to curiosity as to the relationship which might exist between this variable and other measures of governmental expenditure and accounts for its inclusion in the list of variables used here.

DETAILED ANALYSIS

The seven independent variables which were used in the detailed analysis were:

Economic variables

(1) Per cent of families with less than $2,000 income, 1959.

Table 3   Statistical relationships between levels of expenditure and independent variables.

	Mean	Seven Variables			Three Variables
		Standard Error	Coefficient of Multiple Correlation R	Coefficient of Multiple Determination R^2	Coefficient of Multiple Determination R^2
Total general expenditure	$289.34	$34.82	.809	.654	.497
Total general expenditure less federal grants	239.14	29.14	.816	.666	.569
Education	106.32	14.64	.810	.656	.542
Local schools	84.24	10.87	.814	.663	.617
Higher education	19.62	5.10	.769	.591	.424
Highways	60.42	10.48	.869	.755	.187
Public welfare	23.71	8.18	.440	.194	.091
Health and hospitals	18.95	4.49	.663	.440	.436
Police	8.76	1.39	.892	.796	.767
Fire	4.60	1.10	.866	.750	.728
Sewerage and sanitation	8.34	2.43	.660	.436	.303
General control	11.82	2.29	.781	.610	.475
Interest and other	46.42	14.32	.701	.491	.359

(2) Yield of representative tax system, 1960, as per cent of U.S. average.
Demographic variables
   (3) Population per square mile, 1960.
   (4) Per cent of population in urban places, 1960.
   (5) Per cent increase in population, 1950-1960.
Socio-political variables
   (6) Index of two-party competition.
   (7) Per cent of population over 25 with less than 5 years schooling, 1960.

The extent to which the seven independent variables explain the variation in the level of expenditure is indicated in Table 3. The first data column of this table shows the arithmetic mean (average) expenditure for the fifty states. These data, also shown in Table 1, are repeated here to permit easy comparison with the standard error shown in the following column. The third column contains the coefficients of multiple correlation. The fourth column contains the coefficient of multiple determination which is the square of the coefficient of correlation. Although less widely used than the coefficient of correlation, the coefficient of determination may be more meaningful since it can be interpreted as being the proportion of variation in the dependent variable which is explained by the independent variables.

If we assume that the 50 states represent a sample drawn from a normal universe and apply a standard *(F)* test of significance we find that all the coefficients of correlation are significant at the .001 level except for welfare which is not significant even at the .10 level. It is possible to consider the 50 states as the "universe" and to argue that tests of significance are not needed, but, in any case, it is clear that little of the state-to-state variations in public welfare expenditures is associated with the independent variables and that the regression coefficients which show the relation between welfare expenditure and each of the independent variables are not very reliable.[13]

For several functions the seven independent variables explain a substantially higher percentage of variation than do the three variables used in the 1942 and 1957 studies. The coefficient of multiple determination obtained from the three variables, per capita income, per cent of urban population, and population per square mile, are shown in the last column of Table 3. It will be noted that the largest increases in percentage of variation explained is for highway expenditure while there is very little increase for municipal-type expenditures such as fire, police, and health and hospitals.

Importance of Independent Variables

The degree of association between each of the seven independent variables and the level of expenditure can be measured in several ways. The regression coefficients, shown in Table 4 constitute one such measure.

From this table it can be seen that a state with a given per cent of its families having an income of less than $2,000 would be expected to spend $5.54 less than a state having one percentage point fewer of its families in that category — assuming that the other independent variables are identical for the two states. Unfortunately, it is not easy to assess the relative importance of the several independent variables by this method. The variables are measured in different units of measurement and exhibit differing amounts of variation so that examination of the regression coefficients themselves is of little value. It is possible, however, to eliminate these problems by standardizing the regression coefficients. This is done by stating both the dependent and independent variables in units of its own standard deviation. The resulting "beta" coefficient can be regarded as a measure of the relative importance of the independent variables.[14] Thus, it can be said that per cent of families with less than $2,000 income is the most important variable in explaining total general expenditure since the beta coefficient of .693 is higher than any other in the first line of Table 5. The negative sign attached to this coefficient in the table indicates that the relationship is inverse, that is, that a higher percentage of low income families is associated with low government expenditure.

Perhaps the most significant thing revealed by Table 5 is the great importance of the variable per cent of families with less than $2,000 income which has the highest beta coefficient for nine out of the 13 expenditure categories. In 11 out of the 13 cases, the beta coefficient is more than 1.5 times as large as the standard error of the beta coefficient. The two cases for which the beta coefficient is not significant by this rule-of-thumb test are public welfare and higher education. They are also the only two functions for which the coefficients have a positive sign. Most studies of the relationship between government expenditure or the level of taxation and economic factors have stressed the relationship between expenditure and the ability (or capacity) of governmental units.[15] Usually, ability has been measured in terms of such factors as per capita income or per capita assessed value. The high negative association between per cent of families with less than $2,000 income and per capita expenditure found in this study suggest that much more attention should be given to the way that ability is distributed among families. In view of the importance of this variable, an analysis of the effect of substituting several related measures for per cent of families with incomes under $2,000 was

Table 4 Regression coefficients: Per capita state and local government expenditure, 50 states, 1960 fiscal year.

Expenditure Category	Constant Term	Per Cent of Families With less Than $2,000 Income	Yield of Representative tax System	Population per Square Mile	Per Cent of Population in Urban Places	Increase in Population 1950–1960	Two-Party Competition	Per Cent of Population over 25 with less Than 5 years Schooling
Total general expenditure	$249.19	-5.540 [a] (1.732)	1.558 [a] (.398)	-.052 (.040)	-.844 (.619)	.289 (.340)	-.087 (.358)	3.151 (2.383)
Total general expenditure—less federal grants	166.54	-3.540 [a] (1.450)	1.057 [a] (.333) [a]	-.031 (.034)	.531 (.518)	.004 (.284)	-.205 (.299)	.548 (1.994)
Education	74.78	-1.278 [a] (.728)	.489 [a] (.167)	-.045 [a] (.017)	-.236 (.260)	.306 [a] (.142)	.153 (.150)	.772 (1.001)
Local schools	60.42	-1.155 [a] (.541)	.365 [a] (.124)	-.021 [a] (.013)	-.183 (.193)	.263 [a] (.106)	.110 (.112)	.771 (.744)
Higher education	7.53	.047 (.254)	.129 [a] (.058)	-.024 [a] (.006)	-.017 (.091)	.049 (.050)	.048 (.052)	-.137 (.349)
Highways	79.01	-.845 [a] (.521)	.810 [a] (.120)	.005 (.012)	-.869 [a] (.186)	-.231 [a] (.102)	-.319 [a] (.108)	-.849 (.717)
Public welfare	-1.28	.549 (.407)	-.041 (.093)	-.017 [a] (.009)	.414 [a] (.145)	-.112 (.080)	.040 (.084)	-.308 (.560)
Health and hospitals	12.12	-.438 [a] (.224)	.080 [a] (.051)	.001 (.005)	.060 (.079)	.021 (.044)	-.031 (.046)	.367 (.307)
Police	1.11	-.169 [a] (.069)	.018 (.016)	.002 (.002)	.074 [a] (.025)	.039 [a] (.014)	.014 (.014)	.213 [a] (.095)
Fire	4.59	-.133 [a] (.055)	-.014 (.013)	.004 [a] (.001)	.053 [a] (.020)	.001 (.011)	-.007 (.011)	-.013 (.076)
Sewerage and sanitation	10.27	-.431 [a] (.121)	.030 (.028)	.000 (.003)	-.005 (.043)	-.024 (.024)	-.008 (.025)	.318 [a] (.167)
General control	9.88	-.273 [a] (.114)	.061 [a] (.026)	.000 (.003)	-.060 (.041)	.060 [a] (.022)	.016 (.024)	.163 (.157)
Interest and other	58.30	-2.516 [a] (.712)	.125 (.164)	-.002 (.017)	-.273 (.255)	.231 [a] (.140)	.056 (.147)	2.495 [a] (.980)

Standard errors of regression coefficients appear in parenthesis below each coefficient.
[a] Indicates that coefficient is at least 1.5 times its standard error.

Table 5   Beta coefficients: Per capita state and local government expenditure, 50 states, 1960 fiscal year.

Expenditure Category	Per Cent of Families with less Than $2,000 Income	Yield of Representative Tax System	Population per Square Mile	Per Cent of Population in Urban Places	Increase in Population 1950-1960	Two-Party Competition	Per Cent of Population over 25 with less Than 5 years Schooling
Total general expenditure	-.693 [a] (.217)	.555 [a] (.142)	-.167 (.129)	-.215 (.158)	.097 (.114)	-.043 (.176)	.273 (.206)
Total general expenditure — less federal grants	-.520 [a] (.213)	.443 [a] (.139)	-.118 (.127)	.159 (.155)	.002 (.112)	-.118 (.174)	.056 (.203)
Education	-.379 [a] (.216)	.413 [a] (.141)	-.345 [a] (.129)	-.143 (.157)	.244 [a] (.112)	.179 (.176)	.159 (.206)
Local schools	-.457 [a] (.214)	.411 [a] (.140)	-.217 [a] (.128)	-.148 (.156)	.279 [a] (.113)	.172 (.174)	.211 (.204)
Higher education	.044 (.236)	.341 [a] (.154)	-.570 [a] (.141)	-.032 (.172)	.121 (.124)	.175 (.192)	-.088 (.225)
Highways	-.295 [a] (.182)	.806 [a] (.119)	.041 (.109)	-.618 [a] (.133)	-.217 [a] (.096)	-.440 [a] (.148)	-.206 (.174)
Public welfare	.446 (.331)	-.095 (.216)	-.355 [a] (.198)	.686 [a] (.241)	-.246 (.174)	.127 (.269)	-.173 (.315)
Health and hospitals	-.558 [a] (.285)	.289 [a] (.186)	.049 (.170)	.155 (.208)	.073 (.150)	-.158 (.232)	.324 (.272)
Police	-.405 [a] (.166)	.122 (.108)	.136 (.099)	.358 [a] (.121)	.251 [a] (.087)	.136 (.135)	.353 [a] (.158)
Fire	-.446 [a] (.184)	.134 (.120)	.345 [a] (.110)	.365 [a] (.134)	.008 (.097)	-.087 (.150)	-.030 (.175)
Sewerage and sanitation	-.985 [a] (.277)	.193 (.181)	-.017 (.165)	-.022 (.201)	-.145 (.146)	-.068 (.225)	-.504 [a] (.264)
General control	-.552 [a] (.230)	.352 [a] (.150)	-.015 (.137)	-.247 (.167)	.324 [a] (.121)	.129 (.187)	.228 (.219)
Interest and other	-.928 [a] (.263)	.131 (.172)	-.015 (.157)	-.205 (.191)	.229 [a] (.138)	.081 (.214)	.638 [a] (.250)

Standard errors of beta coefficients appear in parenthesis below each coefficient.
[a] Indicates that the coefficient is at least 1.5 times its standard error.

made. The effect of such substitution upon the coeffecient of determination (R^2) is shown in Table 6. It appears from this table that it makes little difference which of the four measures is used. Although R^2 is larger for more functions when per cent of families with less than $3,000 income is used, the differences are generally quite small. Examination of the effect of substituting "less than $3,000" for "less than $2,000" upon the beta coefficients also indicates that the changes are very slight.

Because of the similarity of results obtained from the use of these alternate measures, it is important that little significance be attached to the particular income figure used. It would be a mistake, therefore, to attempt to explain the importance of this variable by studying the political behavior of the "under $2,000" income group. Pending further analysis of this factor, it is more appropriate to think of this variable in more indefinite terms such as "per cent of low income families."

Table 6   Coefficients of multiple determination alternate measures of percentage of low income families.

	Per Cent of Families with Income:			
	Less Than $2,000	*Less Than* $3,000	*Less Than* $5,000	$2,000–$5,000
Total general expenditure	.654	.666	.654	.596
Total general expenditure — less federal grants	.666	.671	.664	.632
Education	.656	.670	.691	.679
Local schools	.663	.679	.711	.694
Higher education	.591	.591	.594	.601
Highways	.755	.753	.741	.750
Public welfare	.194	.205	.189	.166
Health and hospitals	.440	.412	.432	.394
Police	.796	.805	.814	.796
Fire	.750	.760	.767	.743
Sewerage and sanitation	.436	.446	.428	.312
General control	.610	.612	.593	.561
Interest and other	.491	.514	.480	.378

The data presented here do not reveal how the existence of a larger number of low income families operates to depress the level of governmental expenditure. One possibility that comes to mind is that low income persons feel tax pressures more keenly and thus resist increases in governmental expenditure more strongly than do persons with larger incomes. The generally regressive nature of state and local tax systems would, of course, reinforce any such tendency if it exists.

Yield of representative tax system also shows a high degree of positive correlation with expenditure for most functions. The beta coefficient exceeds 1.5 times the standard error of estimate for eight of the thirteen expenditure categories and is larger than any other coefficient in the case of highway and education expenditure.[16] In general, yield of representative tax system is less important in the case of the municipal type functions than in the case of educational and highway expenditure.[17]

Population per square mile is generally inversely correlated with level of expenditure. Although the coefficient is more than 1.5 times its standard error for five expenditure categories, it is the most important variable only in the case of higher education. The inverse correlation generally found between population per square mile and expenditure can probably be attributed to the greater cost of providing services in thinly populated states. The case of higher education, however, illustrates the problems involved in making cause-effect generalizations on the basis of correlations. Of the 15 states which spend the most per capita on higher education all except one (Michigan) are west of the Mississippi, and several of them are very thinly populated. In these states a very high proportion of the college student population attend public institutions. The problem involved in trying to determine the "cause" of the relationship between expenditure for higher education and sparsity of population is that we do not know how much weight to assign to such historical factors as the earlier settlement of the eastern part of the country and the influence of the land grant act upon public higher education.

Per cent of population in urban places is significant for four expenditure categories. In the case of highways, this variable is the second most important factor and the relationship is inverse. This undoubtedly reflects, at least in part, the fact that urban streets and highways are cheaper, per unit of vehicle travel, than are rural roads.[18] Expenditures for the other three functions increase as urbanization increases. These functions are public welfare, police, and local fire protection. This relationship undoubtedly results from the greater need for these services in urban places.

Percentage increase in population from 1950 to 1960 is significantly associated with expenditure for six expenditure categories. In five of the six cases the correlation is positive but in the case of highways there is an inverse relationship. In no case does increase in population rank more than third among the independent variables in importance.

The beta coefficient for two-party competition is more than 1.5 times its standard error only in the case of highway expenditure. The relationship is negative, indicating that the more intensive the party competition the less is spent for highway purposes. Because of the strong influence which federal grants have upon highway expenditure and the degree to which the federal grants are affected by geographic factors,[19] further analysis is needed before any firm conclusions are drawn from this relationship. Nevertheless, it does suggest some interesting hypotheses concerning the popularity of highway expenditure and the role of earmarked funds and pressure groups in determining the level of highway expenditure.

Per cent of population over 25 with less than five years schooling shows its greatest association with police, sewerage and sanitation, and interest and other expenditure. The association is positive in all of these cases. All of these functions are negatively associated with per cent of families with less than $2,000 income.

FISCAL POLICY

Because of the positive association between poverty and illiteracy the fact that these variables have opposite effects on expenditure would be obscured by simple correlation analysis.

MULTIPLE-PARTIAL CORRELATION

The coefficients of multiple-partial determination shown in Table 7 make it possible to determine the relative importance of groups of variables. These coefficients indicate the proportion of variation, unexplained when the specified group of variables is excluded, that is explained when the group of variables is added to the analysis. [20]

Examination of these data reveals that demographic factors are much more important in explaining variations in the level of expenditure than might be assumed from examination of beta coefficients alone. Demographic variables, as a group, are more important than economic variables for the following expenditure categories:

> Education
>> Local schools
>> Higher education
> Public welfare
> Police
> Fire
> General control

For all other expenditure categories economic variables are the most important. The socio-political variables are not the most important group for any expenditure category but do rank as second most important in three cases:

> Sewerage and sanitation
> Health and hospitals
> Interest and other

In addition, the socio-political variables are of some importance in the case of highway expenditure, where they explain 17 per cent of the variation not explained by the other five independent variables.

THE ROLE OF FEDERAL AID

No attempt to determine the effect which federal grants have upon the level of expenditure has been made in this study except for the inclusion of "total general expenditure — less federal aid" as one of the dependent variables. Unfortunately, this tells little about the importance of federal aid as a determinant of the level of expenditure in a state, although the results do show that the same factors which influence spending from state and local funds generally have a similar influence on total spending.

The study by Sacks, Harris and Carroll,[21] published after the research for this paper had largely been completed, raises some important questions about the role of both federal and state aid as determinants of the level of state and local government expenditure. Sacks and his associates used the three independent vari-

Table 7   Multiple-partial coefficients of determination, per capita state and local government expenditure, 50 states, 1960 fiscal year.

	Economic Variables	Demographic Variables	Socio-Political Variables
Total general expenditure	.364	.176	.057
Total general expenditure — less federal grants	.265	.032	.020
Education	.208	.368	.027
Local schools	.228	.298	.033
Higher education	.107	.410	.036
Highways	.529	.442	.174
Public welfare	.044	.177	.021
Health and hospitals	.123	.030	.070
Police	.141	.384	.106
Fire	.151	.492	.008
Sewerage and sanitation	.241	.025	.109
General control	.202	.214	.027
Interest and other	.233	.105	.144

ables which were used in the 1942 and 1957 studies and then, in stepwise fashion, added state aid per capita and federal aid per capita as additional independent variables. The resulting coefficients of multiple determination (based on 48 states) were: [22]

Expenditure Category	Three Basic Variables	State Aid Added	Federal Aid Added	Federal and State Aid Added
Total general	.532	.667	.813	.869
Highways	.370	.374	.834	.856
Public welfare	.114	.181	.830	.858
Local schools	.604	.721	N.C.	N.C.
Health and hospitals	.435	.547	.472	.557
Not specifically aided and all other	.577	.602	.627	.645

It will be noted that, because of limitations on the availability of federal aid data, expenditures were divided into fewer categories than in the present study.

The large increase in the coefficients of multiple determination which results from the addition of per capita federal aid, emphasizes the importance of federal aid in connection with expenditures for these purposes, but the results must be interpreted with great caution in view of the nature of the relationship between the amount which a state spends for a function and the amount of federal aid which it receives. The nature of this relationship can be illustrated by assuming a federal aid program which provides dollar for dollar matching with no limit and no ceiling. In such a case, the amount of federal aid would always be 50 per cent of the state expenditure and the correlation would be perfect (1.0). In this case it would obviously be unrealistic to assume that the amount of federal aid is independent of the amount of expenditure or that federal aid explains the interstate variations in expenditure.

The formulas actually used for determining the amount of federal aid do not tie the amount of aid as closely to expenditure as assumed in the example, but the relationship is close enough to raise serious doubts about the validity of including federal aid as an independent variable in a multiple correlation analysis.[23] The highway aid programs are on a percentage matching basis, although the percentage is higher for a few "public land" states; furthermore, it varies from program to program, and the programs do contain ceilings beyond which further expenditures are not matched. The public assistance program is on a matching basis. Here the percentage paid by the federal government is graduated on a per case basis. There are "per case" ceilings but no ceilings on the number of cases.

Unfortunately, there seems to be no easy way to handle properly the influence of federal aid in a multiple correlation analysis of interstate differences in state and local expenditures. One possibility which might be worth exploring would be to develop an index of the amount of grants which would be made to each state under a "representative expenditure program." Similar in concept to the index of yield of a representative tax system developed by the Advisory Commission on Intergovernmental Relations, such an index would be based upon a calculation of the amount of federal aid each state would receive if its programs in federally aided fields were "representative." Such an index would be used as a measure of financial resources in much the same way that yield of representative tax system is used in this study.

The criticism of the use of federal aid as an independent variable in correlation analysis does not apply to a similar use of state aid, when the state is the unit of analysis. Sacks and his associates have uncovered enough evidence of the importance of this variable that it should be included in future studies of this type.

CONCLUSIONS

Levels of expenditure, as measured by per capita expenditure, for 12 of the 13 categories are very significantly correlated with the seven independent variables. Only in the case of public welfare is the correlation so low as to be of little significance. More detailed analysis of public welfare expenditure, not reported here, suggests that the weak correlation for this category results from the fact that the factors associated with high welfare recipient rates are also associated with low payments to recipients. For a few functions, notably health and hospitals, police, and fire, the level of correlation was little higher than when only three variables — per capita income, population per square mile, and per cent urban — are used. On the other hand, there is a very large increase in the level of correlation for highway expenditure and moderate increases for several other functions.

Perhaps the most important finding of the analysis is the high degree of negative association between levels of expenditure and per cent of low income families in the state. This suggests the hypothesis that political resistance to increased governmental expenditure and the accompanying higher taxes may be greater among low income persons. A second important finding is that the use of multiple-partial coefficients shows the demographic factor to be more important than would be suspected by looking at beta coefficients alone. It appears that when a factor such as the population factor cannot be adequately described by one or two statistical series there is danger of overlooking the importance of the factor when only coefficients of multiple correlation are computed. The use of multiple-partial analysis permits us to represent the effect of such a factor by several series and then to "sum" the effect into multiple-partial coefficients.

The index, yield of a representative tax system, computed by the Advisory Commission on Intergovernmental Relations proved to be a useful measure of state fiscal capacity which generally yielded higher coefficients of multiple correlation than did per capita personal income.

The two socio-political variables contributed less to the levels of correlation obtained than did the economic and demographic factors, but are of some importance in the case of highways, sewerage and sanitation, health and hospitals, and interest and other.

Although the results of standard tests of statistical significance have been reported, it is important to realize that there are problems involved in considering the fifty states as a sample from a normal universe. It is doubtful that the results can be extended through space to explain governmental expenditure patterns in other parts of the world or to explain expenditure patterns of local government within a state, if only because the institutional setting is different. It would not be surprising, of course, to find that some of the factors which have been found to be important here are also important in other settings.

It appears more reasonable to expect that a repetition of this analysis in future years will yield similar results, just as a repetition of Fabricant's 1942 analysis yields results which are generally similar to his findings.[24]

NOTES

1. Solomon Fabricant, *The Trend of Government Activity in the United States Since 1900* (New York: National Bureau of Economic Research, Inc., 1952), pp. 112-39.

2. Variation $= \Sigma(Y - \overline{Y})^2$.

3. Glenn W. Fisher, "Determinants of State and Local Government Expenditures: A Preliminary Analysis," *National Tax Journal,* December, 1961, pp. 349-355. It has been suggested that the inclusion of capital outlay in the 1957 analysis is responsible for the lower coefficients of correlation. A complete analysis of this possibility has not been made but an analysis of 1960 expenditure for local schools and health and hospitals, two functions which seem likely to be affected the most, indicates that very little difference in the coefficients result from excluding capital outlay.

4. Seymour Sacks, Robert Harris and John J. Carroll, *The State and Local Government, . . . The Role of State Aid,* Comptroller's Studies in Local Finance, No. 3 (New York State Department of Audit and Control, 1963), pp. 107-142.

5. General expenditure, general expenditure less federal grants and educational expenditure are omitted since they are made up of, or include, the functional categories.

6. At the .05 level of significance. It should be noted that standard statistical tests are developed upon the assumption of random sampling from a normal universe. Since the "sample" dealt with here includes all fifty states, such tests have meaning only if the fifty states are considered to be a random sample of a universe extended through time to other years or through space to other governmental units. In Table 2 all coefficients are reported whether "significant" or not but those which are above the .05 level are marked with an asterisk.

7. In order to have a valid statistical test of a hypothesis, the variables should be selected in advance. The procedure used here is acceptable if it is understood that the results are merely a measure of association among the variables in this particular instance and not a measure of association in the "universe."

8. The decision to use the same independent variables for every functional category in the final analysis resulted in somewhat lower coefficients of multiple correlation for some expenditure categories. However, using different independent variables for each category would have complicated the presentation and reduced the generality of the conclusions.

9. Fabricant, *op. cit.*, p. 127.

10. Advisory Commission on Intergovernmental Relations, *Measures of State and Local Fiscal Capacity and Tax Effort* (Washington, D.C., 1962).

11. Index values taken from a mimeographed copy of Professor Fenton's paper distributed at the meeting. Since values were computed for only 46 states the mean value of the index was used for Nebraska, Minnesota, Alaska and Hawaii. This procedure tends to result in an understatement of the importance of the variable.

12. Glenn W. Fisher, "Public Assistance Expenditure," *Report of the Commission on Revenue of the State of Illinois* (Springfield, Ill., 1963).

13. A more detailed analysis of welfare expenditure indicates that the factors which are positively correlated with the number of recipients are often negatively correlated with the average payment per recipient. This suggests that "need" factors and "ability" factors tend to offset each other and may explain why there is little correlation between welfare expenditure and the independent variables considered here. Glenn W. Fisher, *ibid.*

14. The partial coefficient of correlation which is the square root of the proportion of variation unexplained by the other variables which is explained when the given variable is added, can be used for the same purpose. Ranking the independent variables by the size of the coefficient of partial correlation produces somewhat different results than does ranking them on the basis of the beta coefficients shown in Table 6. Only rarely, however, does a variable move more than one place in rank.

15. In some cases this relationship has been demonstrated by correlation analysis or by simply ranking or grouping the states. In a greater number of studies, however, it

has been assumed that there is, or should be, a relationship between a state's capacity or ability and expenditure. Hence, the frequent use of such measures as "taxes as a per cent of personal income" or "expenditure as a per cent of personal incomes."

16. If coefficients of partial correlation, rather than beta coefficients, are used to rank the variables, yield of representative tax system has the highest coefficient for five of the 13 expenditure categories while per cent of families with less than $2,000 income is high for only three. Thus it is probably not justifiable, on the basis of existing evidence, to rank either of the economic variables as "most important."

17. Because of the wide use which has been made of per capita income in earlier studies of governmental expenditure and because yield of representative tax system is available only for one year, a supplemental analysis was made to determine the effect of substituting per capita income for yield of the representative tax system. This substitution reduced the coefficient of multiple correlation for all expenditure categories except four — health and hospitals, police, fire, and interest and other. In none of the four cases are the differences large. The most striking change produced by this substitution is that per capita income becomes the most important variable associated with expenditure for local fire protection, sewerage and sanitation, general control, and interest and other, while percentage of families with less than $2,000 income drops sharply in importance for these four variables.

18. The attention which has been focused upon the "urban transportation problem" for the past several years has tended to obscure the probability that transportation is more costly in rural areas. Data developed in the Highway Cost Allocation Study indicate that rural roads are more expensive, per vehicle mile of travel, than are urban roads. *Final Report of the Highway Cost Allocation Study,* House Document No. 54, 87th Congress, 1st Session, pp. 126-27. Unfortunately, the Highway Cost Allocation Study was concerned almost entirely with allocation costs to various vehicle classes and the data developed were not used to allocate costs on a geographic basis.

19. Regular federal grants are increased to those states which have large areas of federally-owned land. Grants for the Interstate Highway System are proportioned to the estimated cost of completing the portion of the interstate system in each state.

20. This measure is directly analogous to the coefficient of partial determination.

21. Sacks, et al., *op. cit.,* pp. 107-142.

22. *Ibid.,* p. 131.

23. It was pointed out earlier that the independent variables used in this study may not be completely independent of the level of expenditure, but it seems clear that the feedback effect of the level of state and government expenditure upon such variables as population density of income distribution is of a much smaller order of magnitude than that which exists in the case of federal aid.

24. Seymour Sacks, et al., *op. cit.,* pp. 120-126.

Conclusion

The concluding section of this book contains one article which attempts to tie together, in explicit fashion, the various elements of state political systems.

The article illustrates the usefulness of a technique which allows us to measure, in empirical fashion, policy outputs which cannot be expressed in monetary terms. It goes on to show how much of the variation in this output is explained by various elements of the system and to show the relationship of these elements to each other. It is, I believe, a major development in our attempt to understand politics as a system of activities.

On Measuring Public Policy

Donald J. McCrone
Charles F. Cnudde

Systems analysis as a paradigm for the study of politics is increasingly structuring empirical inquiry among political scientists.[1] A key element in the concept of the political system is that of outputs. This concept refers to the policies or actions performed by the political system in processing the demands which arise both from the environment and from within the political system itself.[2] Empirical systems analysis of politics, therefore, requires the identification and measurement of relevant policy dimensions.

Recent empirical research on public policy has focused on output dimensions which can be measured in terms of dollar and cents since these dimensions are most susceptible to quantitative analysis. For example, welfare and education policies have been measured by per recipient dollar benefits and per pupil expenditures, respectively.[3]

Many significant policy dimensions, however, are not susceptible to measurement in terms of expenditures. The enactment of civil rihgts legislation in the American states is one such significant dimension. Anti-discrimination legislation in education, employment, public accommodations, and housing can not be

The research reported here was supported by funds granted to the Institute for Research on Poverty at the University of Wisconsin by the Office of Economic Opportunity pursuant to the provisions of the Economic Opportunity Act of 1964. The conclusions are the sole responsibility of the authors. The authors wish to gratefully acknowledge the assistance of Mr. Martin Abrauanel.

measured normally by the amount of money expended. Instead, these policies are, by their very nature, qualitative. Nevertheless, we do have the notion that some of the American states are more oriented toward preventing discrimination than others.

This brief essay proposes a method for measuring civil rights policies in state political systems. The proposed measure enables us to place the American states along a cumulative scale of civil rights orientation.

I

The idea of a cumulative scale of individuals' attitudes and behavior is well known. We have attitude scales of civil rights orientation, for example, which measure an individual's degree of support for civil rights by his responses to a series of agree-disagree statements. We also have behavioral scales of civil rights orientation which measure a congressman's degree of support for civil rights legislation by his roll call votes on a series of legislative proposals.[4] These studies clearly indicate that civil rights orientation is a single dimension for individuals.

Guttman scaling is a widely used cumulative scaling procedure.[5] This scaling procedure enables us to empirically infer several important properties about the dimension being studied. First, it enables us to infer that the attitudes or behavior being measured are unidimensional. In our case, we can determine whether the various forms of anti-discrimination legislation found in the American states constitute a unidimensional policy domain or whether other policy domains intrude. Second, Guttman scaling enables us to determine the relative degree of "difficulty" for each attitude or behavior studied. Through the use of this procedure, then, we can determine the rank order of difficulty in the enactment of anti-discrimination legislation. And third, it enables us to determine the scale position and score for each individual. Therefore, we can determine the degree of support for civil rights of each of the state political systems by reference to its score on the cumulative scale of anti-discrimination legislation.

II

Table 1 demonstrates clearly that anti-discrimination legislation in the American states in 1961 constituted a cumulative Guttman scale. The coefficient of reproducibility (.985) is well within the suggested required limits for acceptance as a cumulative scale (.900).[6] The more stringent test, the coefficient of scalability (.954), is remarkably higher than suggested limits for acceptance (.600-.650).[7] These high scale coefficients are the result of surprisingly few "errors". Only three states have non-scalar responses or laws. Two states, Delaware and Missouri, had legislation prohibiting discrimination in employment, but did not have a public accommodations law. Illinois, on the other hand, lacked an employment law even though the state had prohibitions against discrimination in public accommodations and education. Civil rights legislation in the American states is an unidimensional public policy domain.

The most difficult form of anti-discrimination legislation among the four areas included in the scale is in the area of private housing. Only seven states had

Table 1   A scale of anti-discrimination legislation in the American states.

State	Public Accomodations	Employment	Education	Private Housing	Score
Colorado	+	+	+	+	4
Connecticut	+	+	+	+	4
Massachusetts	+	+	+	+	4
Minnesota	+	+	+	+	4
New York	+	+	+	+	4
Oregon	+	+	+	+	4
Pennsylvania	+	+	+	+	4
Idaho	+	+	+	−	3
Illinois (error)	+	−	+	−	3
Indiana	+	+	+	−	3
Michigan	+	+	+	−	3
New Jersey	+	+	+	−	3
Rhode Island	+	+	+	−	3
Washington	+	+	+	−	3
Wisconsin	+	+	+	−	3
Alaska	+	+	−	−	2
California	+	+	−	−	2
Delaware (error)	−	+	−	−	2
Kansas	+	+	−	−	2
Missouri (error)	−	+	−	−	2
New Mexico	+	+	−	−	2
Ohio	+	+	−	−	2
Iowa	+	−	−	−	1
Maine	+	−	−	−	1
Montana	+	−	−	−	1
Nebraska	+	−	−	−	1
New Hampshire	+	−	−	−	1
North Dakota	+	−	−	−	1
Vermont	+	−	−	−	1
Wyoming	+	−	−	−	1
Alabama	−	−	−	−	0
Arizona	−	−	−	−	0
Arkansas	−	−	−	−	0
Florida	−	−	−	−	0
Georgia	−	−	−	−	0
Hawaii	−	−	−	−	0
Kentucky	−	−	−	−	0

(continued)

Louisiana	-	-	-	-	0
Maryland	-	-	-	-	0
Mississippi	-	-	-	-	0
Nevada	-	-	-	-	0
North Carolina	-	-	-	-	0
Oklahoma	-	-	-	-	0
South Carolina	-	-	-	-	0
South Dakota	-	-	-	-	0
Tennessee	-	-	-	-	0
Texas	-	-	-	-	0
Utah	-	-	-	-	0
Virginia	-	-	-	-	0
West Virginia	-	-	-	-	0
Total	28	21	15	7	

Scale Distribution				
Score	Frequency	Percentage		
4	7	14%	Coefficient of	
3	8	16	Reproducibility	= .985
2	77	14		
1	8	16	Coefficient of	
0	20	40	Scalability	= .954
	50	100%		

Source: United States Commission on Civil Rights, *1961 Report,* Vol. I, "Voting" (Washington, 1961), pp. 208-210.

such anti-discrimination legislation in 1961. Apparently, political decision-makers in state political systems are reluctant to intrude on the home in the quest for civil rights. Prohibition of discrimination in education (fifteen states) and employment (twenty-one states) were somewhat more frequent. State political systems enacted legislation against discrimination in public accommodations with the greatest frequency (twenty-eight states). No less than twenty states were not motivated sufficiently to enact even one piece of anti-discrimination legislation.

The degree of civil rights orientation on the part of each state political system can be determined by reference to its scale score. New York has a score of four, Michigan a score of three, Ohio a score of two, Iowa a score of one, and Alabama and Maryland a score of zero. Civil rights orientation, therefore, can be treated as a quantified dependent variable susceptible to empirical analysis.

III

Before examining the utility of this scale, a fundamental limitation should be noted. This scale measures the absence or presence of state anti-discrimination legislation. It does not measure the enforcement and the success of each type of legislation. Nevertheless, as in studies of attitudes and roll call behavior, the identification and measurement of the presence of such a dimension is a crucial phase in political analysis. The enforcement and success of such legislation presumes the presence of the law. Moreover, the relative infrequency of such legislation attests to the difficulty of obtaining "authoritative allocation of values" in this area. The centrality of the values involved in this issue domain make even symbolic legislation difficult. Finally, even if the law is purely symbolic, it indicates the necessity and/or willingness to make difficult symbolic acts.

The validity of the scale itself seems fairly certain. First, since civil rights constitutes a single dimension for individuals' attitudes and behavior, it is not surprising to find that civil rights constitutes a single dimension for political systems. Second, the rank order of the anti-discrimination items makes intuitive sense. People are more reluctant to support legislation in the area of private housing than public accommodations. Third, the clustering of southern and border states at the lower end of the scale and the northern industrial states at the other also squares with our expectations. Finally, the scale correlates with numerous factors such as percent Negro in the direction earlier research would predict. For these reasons, we feel that this is a valid cumulative scale of anti-discrimination policies in the American states.

IV

The utility of such a scale is obvious. First, the unidimensionality of the civil rights dimension implies an historical sequence. Anti-discrimination laws should be adopted in accordance with their rank order of difficulty. Preliminary indications are that this is in fact the case, for private housing laws are adopted last and public accommodations laws first. Second, the roles performed by public opinion and legislative elites in the enactment of such legislation can also be examined. For example, is public opinion in high scoring states really more supportive of civil rights legislation than in low scoring states? Are legislative elites more cohesive in pro-civil rights states than in anti-civil rights states? Third, the social, economic, and political correlates of civil rights policies in the American states can be identified. For example, percent Negro has a negative correlation (-.44) and party competition a positive correlation (.63) with the anti-discrimination scale.[8]

Fourth, and most important, the concept of the political system directs us to an attempt to construct empirical causal models based on the interaction of environmental and political factors as influences on public policy. Presuming percent Negro to be an independent variable, Figure 1 notes three logically alternative causal relationships between percent Negro, party competition, and the anti-discrimination scale. Model 1a predicts that the relationship between party competition and anti-discrimination is spurious due to their common causation by percent Negro. Model 1b, on the other hand, predicts that the original relationship between percent Negro and party competition is interpreted through the scale. Model 1c, as the third possible alternative, predicts that the developmental sequence from percent Negro through party competition to anti-discrimination interprets the original relationship between percent Negro and the scale.

The prediction equations for 1a, 1b, and 1c in Table 2 show the Simon-

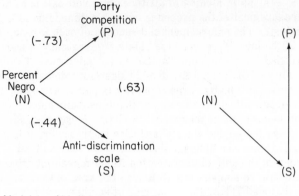

Model 1a. No direct casual link   Model 1b. Developmental sequence
        between P and S.   from N to S to P.

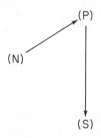

Model 1c. Developmental sequence
        from N to P to S.

Blalock causal model test of each of these alternative models.[9] Clearly, the excellence of the test results for Model 1c, as opposed to the results for 1a and 1b, provides a basis for inferring that the direction of causation is indeed from percent Negro to party competition to anti-discrimination legislation. In other words, percent Negro is important in determining the degree of state support for civil rights through the enactment of anti-discrimination by its inhibiting effects on the level of party competition. The direct effect on this dimension, therefore, is the level of party competition in the state. A political factor interprets the effect of a social variable on policy formation in state political systems. Our model, then, constitutes an empirical systems analysis of some of the relationships between environmental, political, and output variables in state political systems.

Table 2 Simon-Blalock prediction equations and degree of fit for three alternative models.

	Predictions		*Degree of Fit*	
Models		*Predicted*	*Actual*	*Difference*
1a. rNPrNS = rPS		(-.73)(-.44) = .32	.63	.31
1b. rNSrSP = rNP		(-.44)(.63) = -.28	-.73	.45
1c. rNPrPS = rNS		(-.73)(.63) = -.46	-.44	.02

V

The most important conclusion of this brief essay on measuring qualitative policy outputs of the political system is that the behavior of political systems, like the attitudes and behavior of individuals, is subject to empirical analysis. The actions of political systems are not random, but are in fact quite consistent, at least on the civil rights dimension. Moreover, we have briefly illustrated how causal model analysis can be usefully integrated into the paradigm provided by the concept of the political system.

NOTES

1. A measure of the impact of the concept of the political system on political science as a discipline is provided by the fact that at least one introductory text, Marian D. Irish and James W. Prothro, *The Politics of American Democracy* (Englewood Cliffs, New Jersey: Prentice-Hall, 1965) is based explicitly on this approach.

2. For the basic statement of the concepts underlying systems analysis of politics see David Easton, "An Approach to the Analysis of Political Systems," *World Politics,* Vol. 9 (1957), pp. 383-400. Also see Easton's subsequent explications of this concept in *A Framework for Political Analysis* (Englewood Cliffs, New Jersey: Prentice-Hall, 1964) and *A Systems Analysis of Political Life* (New York: John Wiley and Sons, 1965).

3. Two notable examples are Ricard E. Dawson and James A. Robinson, "Inter-Party Competition, Economic Variables, and Welfare Policies in the American States," *Journal of Politics,* Vol. 25 (1963), pp. 265-289 and Thomas R. Dye, "Malapportionment and Public Policy in the States," *Journal of Politics,* Vol. 27 (1965), pp. 586-601.

4. Many studies have ordered either individual attitudes or legislative behavior in the civil rights area through scaling techniques. For an ingenious interrelation of these two types of data see Warren E. Miller and Donald E. Stokes, "Constituency Influence in Congress," *American Political Science Review,* Vol. 57 (1963), pp. 441-456.

5. For an excellent discussion of this technique see Samuel A. Stouffer, *et al., Measurement and Prediction* (Princeton: Princeton University Press, 1950), especially chapters 1 and 3.

6. *Ibid.*

7. See Herbert Menzel, "A New Coefficient for Scalogram Analysis," *Public Opinion Quarterly,* Vol. 17 (Summer, 1953), pp. 268-280.

8. Our measure of party competition is drawn from Austin Ranney, "Political Parties," in Herbert Jacob and Kenneth Vines, (eds.), *Politics in the American States: A Comparative Analysis* (Boston: Little, Brown and Company, 1965), pp. 64-65, which

combines competition for governor, the lower house, the upper house, and percent of divided executive-legislative control into one overall index of party competition.

9.   For the most complete statement of this technique see Hubert M. Blalock, Jr., *Causal Inferences in Nonexperimental Research* (Chapel Hill: University of North Carolina Press, 1964). For political science applications see Miller and Stokes, *op. cit.*; Thad L. Beyle, "Contested Elections and Voter Turnout in a Local Community: A Problem in Spurious Correlation," *American Political Science Review,* Vol. 59 (March, 1965), 111-116; Charles F. Cnudde and Donald J. McCrone, "The Linkage between Constituency Attitudes and Congressional Voting Behavior: A Causal Model," *American Political Science Review,* Vol. 60 (March, 1966), pp. 68-72; Hayward R. Alker, Jr., "Causal Inferences and Political Analysis," in Joseph Bernd, (ed.), *Mathematical Applications in Political Science* (Dallas: Southern Methodist University Press, 1966); and Donald J. McCrone and Charles F. Cnudde, "Toward a Communications Theory of Democratic Political Development: A Causal Model, "*American Political Science Review,* Vol. 61 (March, 1967), 72-79.